Contributions to Management Science

For further volumes:
http://www.springer.com/series/1505

Nils Kemme

Design and Operation of Automated Container Storage Systems

Physica-Verlag
A Springer Company

Nils Kemme
University of Hamburg
Hamburg
Germany

ISSN 1431-1941
ISBN 978-3-7908-2884-9 ISBN 978-3-7908-2885-6 (eBook)
DOI 10.1007/978-3-7908-2885-6
Springer Heidelberg New York Dordrecht London

Library of Congress Control Number: 2012951403

Printed on acid-free paper

Physica-Verlag is a brand of Springer
Springer is part of Springer Science+Business Media (www.springer.com)

Foreword

The container box is sometimes hailed as one of the ten greatest inventions of the last century and has certainly transformed the way cargo moves around the world. This is due to the fact that different goods—which would otherwise require individual loading procedures using specialised machinery along their shipment routes—can be packed into such containers of various sizes and thus become standardised transportation objects. This makes them amenable to handling in seaports and other hubs by readily available equipment such as quay cranes, straddle carriers and gantry cranes. The latter are often used to store, retrieve and shuffle containers in a container-storage yard. Such yards are typically divided into several blocks. Depending on the overall design of the storage yard, the cranes can either be rather flexibly driven around the entire yard (so-called Rubber-Tyred Gantry Cranes, RTGC) or are installed on rail tracks along each block (Rail-Mounted Gantry Cranes, RMGC); these cranes are hence mainly dedicated to a particular block. In contrast to an RTGC which always requires a driver for each crane, RMGC systems can be largely automated and are hence very efficient which becomes increasingly more important—in particular, in high labour-cost countries. Of course, the potential savings in salaries of such a highly automated system incur a comparably higher up-front investment for equipment that cannot easily be used in different blocks of the yard. An efficient planning and operation of such a yard block is therefore highly relevant for achieving a sufficient utilisation of the block in order to tip the cost balance in favour of such a system.

Nils Kemme surmounts this particularly important and at the same time difficult problem that many people—even in container logistics—are not even aware of and which has, as a consequence, often been solved by gut instincts. Looking at the problem at different levels, there are a lot of fascinating aspects and details to be discovered. On the surface level, at least four different crane systems can be found which are specified by the number of cranes and whether the cranes (if there is more than one) can pass one another. Of course, a sensible number of cranes will then depend on the overall layout, i.e. on the dimensions of the yard block. But it is analytically impossible and even by simulation experiments by far not straightforward to determine the optimal design of an RMGC system from these parameters alone. On a detailed level, various operational decisions (such as how to stack containers in the yard as well as sequencing and routing strategies for the cranes) need to be taken into account. Many of these decisions can be made by solving corresponding optimisation problems, and Nils Kemme discusses and develops quite a good number of such problems just along the way to his main goal of carrying out the extensive simulation experiments for different layouts and RMGC systems. It constitutes a remarkable achievement that, for some of these problems, not only a theoretical analysis is provided and solution approaches are suggested and implemented but also new research threads are identified in their own right besides the main agenda of this book.

The numerical results alone which are carefully documented are already noteworthy as a seaport-design manager may look up the yard layout of interest and find the corresponding performance figures for the different RMGC systems under standard conditions. For practitioners consulting different seaport-design projects the underlying simulation tool might be even more helpful as it can be easily adapted to yield these results for the real framework at hand. From a methodological point of view, the researcher may find the—often only theoretically discussed—interconnections of strategic optimisation, simulation and operational optimisation on at least three levels (with the arising subproblems) most interesting. Additionally, Nils Kemme points out a number of very promising open questions which will be a helpful guidance for future research in this area. Summarising, different audiences will find the book useful and fascinating. As it is an important contribution to this field, I anticipate a wide dissemination and a very good reception in the scientific community.

Hamburg, Germany Wolfgang Brüggemann
June 2012

Preface

The research presented in this doctoral dissertation has been carried out over a period of almost 4 years at the Institute for Operations Research at the University of Hamburg under the supervision of Professor Dr. Wolfgang Brüggemann. Although a dissertation is an individual work, many people have contributed to its realisation and completion—by motivating and encouraging me, giving me helpful advice and tolerating the leisure time spent on research. Here, I would like to thank some people who have been particularly important to me and my research.

First of all, there is my doctoral supervisor Prof. Dr. Wolfgang Brüggemann. He created a warm-hearted and friendly working environment at the institute, which made me enjoy coming to work every day and kept me motivated throughout my research project. Without his trust in me, his ongoing support and his advice, this thesis would probably never have been started and would certainly not have come to a successful end. In addition, I would like to thank Prof. Dr. Stefan Voß for taking on the chair of the dissertation committee and Prof. Dr. Knut Haase for reviewing my work as a co-supervisor.

Without all my wonderful colleagues the time at the world's best institute would certainly not have been the same. They completed the wonderful working atmosphere created by Wolfgang and made me feel at home immediately. I would like to thank all of them for extended coffee breaks and talking about everything under the sun. Particular thanks go to Mareike and Dennis for showing me how it is done in every sense, Hanne and Inga for making this work readable and Henrik for knowing it all. I loved working with you and will always look back at that time as one of the best in my life.

Above and beyond the university environment, many thanks go to my friends for tolerating the time spent on this work and being interested in my research and the progress I made—although I was a little annoyed by the question of completion in the end. Many thanks go to my long-standing friends Malte, Jens and Jörn for taking over the proofreading without hesitation. The greatest thanks are due to Vera. Without her tolerance, patience and endless support, the dissertation would never have been completed. Your share in this work cannot be expressed in words.

Last but not least, I want to thank my mother and my father, who supported me all my life with huge energy and all available means. Without their backing this book as well as much else in my life would not have been possible. Therefore, I dedicate this thesis to my parents, to whom I owe everything.

Hamburg, Germany
June 2012

Nils Kemme

Contents

List of Symbols and Abbreviations

α	significance level
β_0	regression parameter
β_1	regression parameter
β_2	regression parameter
β_3	regression parameter
Γ	number of planning periods (bay-movement time units)
γ	period index
$\Delta_{jg}^{\text{pp}+}$	planned lateness of crane g at the origin of job j
$\Delta_{jg}^{\text{pp}-}$	planned earliness of crane g at the origin of job j
$\overline{\delta}$	mean container-dwell time
$\overline{\delta}^{\text{ts}}$	mean dwell time of transshipment containers
$\overline{\delta}^{\text{ie}}$	mean dwell time of import/export containers
δ_c	dwell time of container c
ϵ	error term of regression model
η	period index
θ^{x}	end of the portal-driving range
θ^{y}	end of the trolley-driving range
θ^{z}	end of the spreader-driving range
$\kappa_{\text{gam}}^{\text{al}}$	aspiration level
$\kappa_{\text{gam}}^{\max\Upsilon}$	maximum allowed size of the population
$\kappa_{\text{gam}}^{\text{itinit}}$	maximum number of initially generated solutions s
$\kappa_{\text{gam}}^{\text{maxit}}$	maximum allowed repititions of the inheritance process
$\kappa_{\text{gam}}^{\text{mut}}$	mutation probability
$\kappa_{\text{gam}}^{\text{noinit}}$	maximum number of initially generated solutions s that are included in Υ
$\kappa_{\text{hhs}}^{\text{al}}$	acceptance level of possible cost improvement for deserving relocation
$\kappa_{\text{hhs}}^{\text{mci}}$	minimum realisable cost improvement for initiating relocation
$\kappa_{\text{sfe}}^{\text{jobs}}$	maximum number of plannable jobs by the SFE method

κ_{zb}^{ls}	zone border defining the beginning of the landside zone
κ_{zb}^{ws}	zone border defining the end of the waterside zone
$\lambda_{\tau(j)}^{cat}$	weighting factor for the category-based shuffle-move costs
$\lambda_{\tau(j)}^{dist}$	weighting factor for the workload-smoothing costs
$\lambda_{\tau(j),g}^{dd}$	weighting factor for the due-date assignment criterion
$\lambda_{\tau(j),g}^{early}$	weighting factor for the crane-earliness assignment criterion
$\lambda_{\tau(j),g}^{empty}$	weighting factor for the empty-movement-time assignment criterion
$\lambda_{\tau(j),g}^{late}$	weighting factor for the crane-lateness assignment criterion
$\lambda_{\tau(j)}^{gs}$	weighting factor for the ground-position costs
$\lambda_{\tau(j)}^{mod}$	weighting factor for the modality-intermingling costs
$\lambda_{\tau(j)}^{rts}$	weighting factor for the retrieval time-based shuffle-move costs
λ^{area}	weighting factor for the utility contribution of the area performance
λ^{cost}	weighting factor for the utility contribution of the cost performance
λ^{opnl}	weighting factor for the utility contribution of the operational performance
μ^{rtls}	average vehicle-residence time in the landside handover area after un-/loading
μ^{rtws}	average vehicle-residence time in the waterside handover area after un-/loading
$\pi^{fillavg}$	average filling rate of the yard block
$\pi^{fillmax}$	maximum allowed filling rate of the yard block
π^{peak}	peak factor of the required storage capacity
π^{sc}	capacity of the container-storage yard (TEU)
π^{scmin}	minimum storage capacity required to handle the throughput (TEU)
π^{teu}	TEU-factor, average container length (TEU)
$\pi^{through}$	annual terminal throughput (containers)
π^{ts}	transshipment factor
ρ_j	direct predecessor of job j
$\tau(j)$	type of job j
Υ	set of all generated solutions
υ	solution index
Φ	set of all piles in the yard block
$\Phi_c^{allowed}$	set of technically allowed piles for container c in the yard block
ϕ_c^{xy}	potential stacking position (pile) for container c in the yard block
$\phi_c^{xy,cu}$	current stacking position of container c
$\overline{\psi}$	mean number of shuffle moves per retrieval job of a single simulation run
$\overline{\overline{\psi}}$	mean number of shuffle moves per retrieval job of a simulation experiment

$\omega^{\text{hr}+}_{jg}$	realised vehicle-waiting time in the handover area for job j
$\overline{\omega}^{\text{hr}+}_{\text{total}}$	mean vehicle-waiting time per job of a single simulation run
$\overline{\overline{\omega}}^{\text{hr}+}_{\text{total}}$	mean vehicle-waiting time per job of a simulation experiment
$\overline{\omega}^{\text{hr}+}_{\text{ls}}$	mean XT-waiting time per job of a single simulation run
$\overline{\overline{\omega}}^{\text{hr}+}_{\text{ls}}$	mean XT-waiting time per job of a simulation experiment
$\overline{\omega}^{\text{hr}+}_{\text{ws}}$	mean AGV/SC-waiting time per job of a single simulation run
$\overline{\overline{\omega}}^{\text{hr}+}_{\text{ws}}$	mean AGV/SC-waiting time per job of a simulation experiment
$\overline{\omega}^{\text{hr}+}_{\text{wsout}}$	mean AGV/SC-waiting time per waterside retrieval job of a single simulation run
$\overline{\overline{\omega}}^{\text{hr}+}_{\text{total}}$	mean AGV/SC-waiting time per waterside retrieval job of a simulation experiment
$\omega^{\text{hr}-}_{jg}$	realised crane-waiting time in the handover area for job j
$\overline{\omega}^{\text{hr}-}_{\text{total}}$	mean crane-waiting time per job of a single simulation run
$\overline{\overline{\omega}}^{\text{hr}-}_{\text{total}}$	mean crane-waiting time per job of a simulation experiment
a^{xe}_g	portal acceleration of crane g when unladen
a^{xf}_g	portal acceleration of crane g when laden
a^{ye}_g	trolley acceleration of crane g when unladen
a^{yf}_g	trolley acceleration of crane g when laden
a^{ze}_g	spreader acceleration of crane g when unladen
a^{zf}_g	spreader acceleration of crane g when laden
b^{xe}_g	portal deceleration of crane g when unladen
b^{xf}_g	portal deceleration of crane g when laden
b^{ye}_g	trolley deceleration of crane g when unladen
b^{yf}_g	trolley deceleration of crane g when laden
b^{ze}_g	spreader deceleration of crane g when unladen
b^{zf}_g	spreader deceleration of crane g when laden
C	set of container
c	container index
C^{deep}	set of containers that are planned to depart by deep-sea vessel
C^{feeder}	set of containers that are planned to depart by feeder vessel
C^{relocate}	set of containers that are candidates for relocations
C^{top}	set of containers that are located on top of a pile
C^{xt}	set of containers that are planned to depart by XT
d^{x}_j	destination of transport job j along the x-axis of the yard block
d^{y}_j	destination of transport job j along the y-axis of the yard block
d^{z}_j	destination of transport job j along the z-axis of the yard block
e^{cat}_c	stacking category of container c
e^{outmode}_c	mode of transportation container c is planned to depart from the terminal
e^{size}_c	length of container c
$f^{\text{ac}}(j)$	costs of assigning job j to crane g
$f^{\text{ccfs}}(c, \phi^{\text{xy}}_c)$	costs of stacking container c in pile ϕ^{xy}_c

$f^{\mathrm{ac}}(s_\upsilon)$	costs of scheduling solution s_υ
G	set of gantry cranes
g	gantry-crane index
h^{b}	expected final-handover time in the yard block
h^{ls}	expected final-handover time in the landside handover area
h^{ws}	expected final-handover time in the waterside handover area
h_{jg}	expected container-handover time for job j by crane g
i	crane-transport-job index
J	set of crane transport jobs
j	crane-transport-job index
J_t^{p}	set of plannable jobs at time t with $J_t^{\mathrm{p}} \subset J$
J_{tg}^{p}	set of plannable jobs for crane g at time t with $\bigcup_g J_{tg}^{\mathrm{p}} = J_t^{\mathrm{p}}$
$J_t^{\mathrm{p}'}$	set of scheduled jobs at time t with with $J_t^{\mathrm{p}'} \subseteq J_t^{\mathrm{p}}$
J_t^{pe}	extended set of plannable jobs at time t
$J_t^{\mathrm{pe}'}$	extended set of scheduled jobs at time t with $J_t^{\mathrm{pe}'} \subseteq J_t^{\mathrm{pe}}$
K	set of separator tasks
k	separator task
l_{ij}^{x}	empty-portal-driving distance between destination of job i and origin of job j
l_{ij}^{y}	empty-trolley-driving distance between destination of job i and origin of job j
l_j^{x}	laden-portal-driving distance between origin and destination of job j
l_j^{y}	laden-trolley-driving distance between origin and destination of job j
l_j^{zd}	spreader-hoisting distance at destination of job j
l_j^{zo}	spreader-hoisting distance at origin of job j
$l_{\mathrm{in}}^{\mathrm{x}}\left(\phi_c^{\mathrm{xy}}\right)$	portal-driving distance between the current position of container c and pile ϕ_c^{xy}
$l_{\mathrm{out}}^{\mathrm{x}}\left(\phi_c^{\mathrm{xy}}\right)$	portal-driving distance between pile ϕ_c^{xy} and the handover area container c is planned to be collected
M	big positive number
m_j^{cit}	duration of crane-interference time during the execution of job j
$\overline{m}_{\mathrm{total}}^{\mathrm{cit}}$	mean crane-interference time per job of a single simulation run
$\overline{\overline{m}}_{\mathrm{total}}^{\mathrm{cit}}$	mean crane-interference time per job of a simulation experiment
m_{jg}^{xye}	duration for empty movement of portal and trolley of crane g to origin of job j
$\overline{m}_{\mathrm{total}}^{\mathrm{xye}}$	mean crane-empty-movement time per job of a single simulation run
$\overline{\overline{m}}_{\mathrm{total}}^{\mathrm{xye}}$	mean crane-empty-movement time per job of a simulation experiment
m_{jg}^{xyf}	duration for laden movement of portal and trolley of crane g from origin to destination of job j

m^{zd}_{jg}	duration for container-drop-off operation of crane g at the destination of job j
m^{zo}_{jg}	duration for container-pick-up operation of crane g at the origin of job j
m^{lat}_{j}	look-ahead time of job j
n^{b}	number of yard blocks in the container-storage yard
n^{J}	number of jobs to be scheduled
n^{run}	number of stochastically independent simulation runs for a simulation experiment
n^{x}	length of the yard block (bays of TEU)
n^{y}	width of the yard block (rows of TEU)
n^{z}	height of the yard block (tiers of TEU)
n^{zo}	number of yard zones, with $n^{\mathrm{zo}} = n^{\mathrm{x}} + 2$
o^{x}_{j}	origin of transport job j along the x-axis of the yard block
o^{y}_{j}	origin of transport job j along the y-axis of the yard block
o^{z}_{j}	origin of transport job j along the z-axis of the yard block
p^{b}_{c}	yard block container c is stored in
p^{cross}_{g}	position the trolley of the outer large crane has to be located in for crane-crossing manoeuvres
p^{drive}_{g}	position the spreader of crane g has to be located in during portal and trolley movements
p^{x}_{c}	bay (of TEU) container c is positioned in the yard block
p^{y}_{c}	row (of TEU) container c is positioned in the yard block
p^{z}_{c}	tier (of TEU) container c is positioned in the yard block
q	bay index
r	bay index
R^2	coefficient of determination
S	solution space of the crane-scheduling problem
s	solution of the crane-scheduling problem
$s^{*\mathrm{init}}$	initially best solution
t	point in time during considered time frame of storage yard operations
T	considered time frame of storage yard operations, simulation length
T^{warm}	length of the warm-up period for simulation runs
t^{in}_{c}	point in time at which container c arrives by vehicle in the handover area
t^{out}_{c}	point in time at which vehicle arrives in the handover area to collect container c
t^{a}_{j}	announcement time of job j, with $t^{\mathrm{a}}_{j} = t^{\mathrm{hd}}_{j} - m^{\mathrm{lat}}_{j}$
t^{finish}_{j}	finishing time of crane transport job j
t^{hr}_{jg}	realised arrival time of crane g in the relevant handover area of job j
t^{pp}_{jg}	planned arrival time of crane g at the origin of job j

t_j^{hd}	handover-area due date of job j
t_j^{pd}	pick-up due date of job j
t_j^{start}	starting time of crane-transport job j
u	utility function
u^{area}	utility contribution of the area performance
u^{cost}	utility contribution of the cost performance
u^{opnl}	utility contribution of the operational performance
U^{late}	upper bound on vehicle-waiting time
v_g^{xe}	maximum portal velocity of crane g when unladen
v_g^{xf}	maximum portal velocity of crane g when laden
v_g^{ye}	maximum trolley velocity of crane g when unladen
v_g^{yf}	maximum trolley velocity of crane g when laden
v_g^{ze}	maximum spreader velocity of crane g when unladen
v_g^{zf}	maximum spreader velocity of crane g when laden
W	makespan of a crane-job schedule
$w_{c,c'}^{\text{cat}}$	binary variable modelling the category of containers c and c'
$w_{\phi_c^{\text{xy}}}^{\text{gs}}$	binary variable modelling the ground position of ϕ_c^{xy}
$w_{c,c'}^{\text{mod}}$	binary variable modelling the departing modality of containers c and c'
x_{ijg}	binary variable modelling the job sequence of crane g
$y_{r\gamma g}$	binary variable modelling the bay crane g is positioned in period γ
$z_{j\gamma g}^{\text{drop}}$	binary variable modelling the completion of drop-off for job j
$z_{j\gamma g}^{\text{pick}}$	binary variable modelling the completion of pick-up for job j
3D-BPP	three-dimensional bin-packing problem
AGV	automated-guided vehicle
ALV	automated lifting vehicle
AS/RS	automated storage and retrieval system
ASC	automated stacking crane
B&B	branch and bound
BLUE	best linear unbiased estimators
BS	beam search
CaS	category stacking
CCFS	combined-cost-function stacking (name of container-stacking strategy)
CCP	crane-crossing process
CFS	container-freight station
CI	confidence interval
CTA	Container Terminal Altenwerder
CTB	Container Terminal Burchardkai
CTT	Container Terminal Tollerort
DP	dynamic programming
DRMGC	double rail-mounted gantry crane
EDD	earliest due date

EDT	empty-driving time
ETD	estimated time of departure
FIFO	first-in-first-out
FLP	facility-layout problem
FrS	free stacking
GA	genetic algorithm
GAM	GA-based method (name of crane-scheduling strategy)
GCR	gross crane rate
HAC	handover-area access control
heu	problem-specific heuristic
HHS	heuristical housekeeping stacking (name of container stacking strategy)
IMO	international maritime organization
IP	integer programming
ISO	international organization for standardisation
JIT	just in time
KPI	key performance indicator
LeS	levelling stacking
M&R	maintenance and repair
MBPP	master bay-plan problem
MTS	multi-trailer system
MTSP	multiple traveling-salesman problem
NN	nearest neighbour
NP	non-deterministic polynomial-time
OOG	out of gauge
OR	operations research
PoD	port of destination
PoS	positional stacking
PRIO1	multi-objective priority rule 1 (name of crane-scheduling strategy)
PRIO2	multi-objective priority rule 2 (name of crane-scheduling strategy)
prio	priority rule
QC	quay crane
RaS	random stacking
ReS	remarshalling stacking
RMGC	rail-mounted gantry crane
RTGC	rubber-tyred gantry crane
RTS	retrieval-time stacking
RvS	reservation stacking
SC	straddle carrier
ScS	scattered stacking
SFE	subset full enumeration (name of crane-scheduling strategy)
SRMGC	single rail-mounted gantry crane
TEU	twenty-foot equivalent unit
TOS	terminal-operating system
TriRMGC	triple rail-mounted gantry crane

TRMGC	twin rail-mounted gantry crane
TSP	travelling-salesman problem
TS	tabu search
TTU	truck-trailer unit
VCP	vessel-call pattern
VDI	Verein Deutscher Ingenieure—association of german engineers
VRP	vehicle-routing problem
XT	external truck

Chapter 1
Introduction

The sea traffic and trade has always been of great importance for both the business success of individual companies as well as the welfare of nations. Long before economic trends like globalisation and containerisation were known, the importance of the sea trade has already been identified by Smith (1776), who states in his principal work:

> Were there no other communication between those two places, therefore, but by land-carriage, as no goods could be transported from the one to the other, except such whose price was very considerable in proportion to their weight, they could carry on but a small part of that commerce which at present subsists between them, and consequently could give but a small part of that encouragement which they at present mutually afford to each other's industry. There could be little or no commerce of any kind between the distant parts of the world. What goods could bear the expense of land-carriage between London and Calcutta? Or if there were any so precious as to be able to support this expense, with what safety could they be transported through the territories of so many barbarous nations? Those two cities, however, at present carry on a very considerable commerce with each other, and by mutually affording a market, give a good deal of encouragement to each other's industry (Smith 1776, p. 23).

Today, in the middle of a globalised and containerised world, this statement appears to be even more relevant than at that time. Since 1970, the world seaborne trade has increased by a factor of 3 to 8,022 million tons in 2007 (UNCTAD 2008, pp. 5–6). At present, more than 60% of the value of the world's general cargo trade and over 70% of the world's international seaborne trade is transported in containers (UNCTAD 2007, pp. 19–21). In 2007, global container trade was estimated at 143 million TEUs (twenty-foot equivalent unit), which is five times more than in 1990. For 2016 and 2020 forecasts are even expecting yearly container turnovers of 287 and 371 million TEUs, respectively (UNCTAD 2008, p. 22).

N. Kemme, *Design and Operation of Automated Container Storage Systems*, Contributions to Management Science, DOI 10.1007/978-3-7908-2885-6_1,

1.1 Definition of the Subject Area

Along with the growth in worldwide container transportation, the world container fleet, the global seaport container terminals as well as the intermodal hinterland connections have changed radically over the last decades. In this work, it is focused on seaport container terminals, which are important links in the intercontinental trade flows. Seaport container terminals are areas in the port where containers are transshipped from deep-sea vessels to feeders, trucks, trains and barges and vice versa. In addition, a location is provided where containers, full and empty, can be stored until they are transshipped to the next mode of transportation (Saanen 2004, p. 1). Parallel to the increase of container trade volumes, the number and size of container terminals as well as the competition among them have increased (Sciomachen and Tanfani 2007). While in 2005 only five seaport container terminals had a yearly turnover of ten million TEUs or higher, in 2008 already ten terminals were exceeding this number (see Table 1.1). Overall, the world container-terminal turnover increased from 76 million TEUs in 1988 to 520 million TEUs in 2008, which is equivalent to a compound annual growth rate above 10% (see Fig. 1.1).

Over the last decade, there have been several global changes and trends in the international supply chains that greatly affect both the working environment and the demands seaport container terminals are faced with. Today, increasing container volumes and vessel sizes have to be served in reliably short periods of time. Increasing container volumes and limited resources of land for port operations require dense stacking operations. Increasing scarcity and cost of labour require personnel reductions, and environmental regulations on noise and air pollution require low-emission terminal equipment (Rijsenbrij and Wieschemann 2011). These demands together with improved abilities in the fields of automated terminal equipment as well as in information and communication technology lead the terminal operators to reconsider traditional terminal operations and to increasingly adopt automated handling concepts for parts of seaport container terminals (Saanen 2004, pp. 6–8). As confirmed by several comparisons between manual and automated terminal concepts, remarkable cost reductions of up to 25% (including labour, operation and capital costs) may be realised by terminal automation if the labour cost make up for a sufficiently high fraction of total terminal costs (Saanen 2006, 2007, 2008).

Most automated seaport container terminals make use of automated terminal equipment for the transport operations between the QCs (quay crane) and the container-storage yard as well as for the storage-yard operations themselves (Wiese et al. 2009a). The container-storage yard is of special importance for container terminals, as it is the terminal's central part from both the geographical and the processual point of view. The storage yard is not just the area where containers are temporarily stored, moreover it is the interface between seaborne and continental transport chains. Most of the terminal operations either originate from or cease at the container-storage yard, such that most terminal operations are directly or indirectly affected by the storage-yard operations. As a consequence, the operational performance of seaport container terminals as a whole—which is often measured in

Table 1.1 The largest container ports of the world (Port of Hamburg 2011a)

Port	TEU 2005	TEU 2006	TEU 2007	TEU 2008
Singapore (Singapore)	23,192,000	24,792,400	27,932,000	29,918,200
Shanghai (China)	18,084,000	21,710,000	26,168,000	27,980,000
Hong Kong (China)	22,602,000	23,538,580	23,881,000	24,248,000
Shenzhen (China)	16,197,173	18,468,900	21,099,000	21,413,888
Busan (South Korea)	11,843,151	12,038,786	13,270,000	13,425,000
Dubai (United Arab Emirates)	7,619,222	8,923,465	10,653,026	11,827,299
Ningbo (China)	5,191,000	7,068,000	9,349,000	11,226,000
Guangzhou (China)	4,684,000	6,600,000	9,200,000	11,001,300
Rotterdam (Netherlands)	9,286,757	9,654,508	10,790,604	10,783,825
Quingdao (China)	6,310,000	7,702,000	9,462,000	10,320,000
Hamburg (Germany)	8,087,545	8,861,804	9,889,792	9,737,110

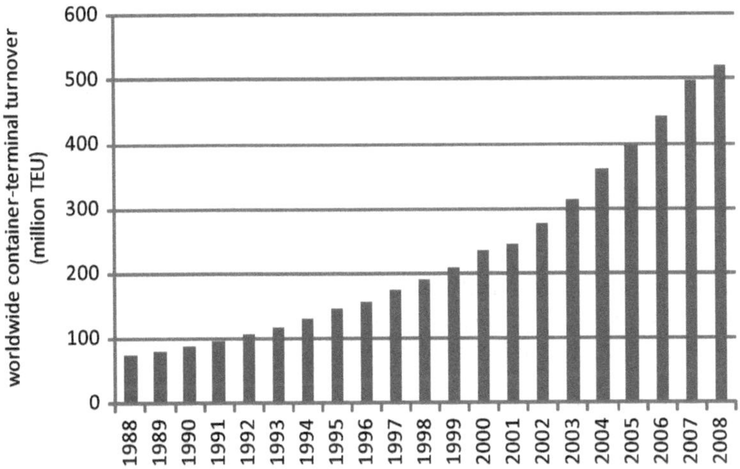

Fig. 1.1 Development of world container-terminal turnover (Port of Hamburg 2011a)

terms of quay-crane productivities and vessel-turn-around times—is greatly affected by the operations of the container-storage yard (Petering 2009).

At present, the storage-yard operations can either be automated by means of ALVs (automated lifting vehicle) or RMGCs (rail-mounted gantry crane). While an ALV system is employed only by a small-sized terminal in Brisbane (Australia) so far, where it has been introduced in 2005 (Vis and Harika 2004), up to now eight automated RMGC systems have been put into operation at medium- to large-sized terminals since the early 1990s (Wiese et al. 2009a). Therefore, automated RMGC systems can be regarded as proven technology. RMGCs are gantry cranes that traverse on rail tracks alongside the length of yard blocks that are several TEUs long, wide and high (see Fig. 1.2). These yard blocks can either be laid out perpendicular or parallel to the quay wall and the handover to other modes of transportation can either take place only at the front ends of the blocks or in

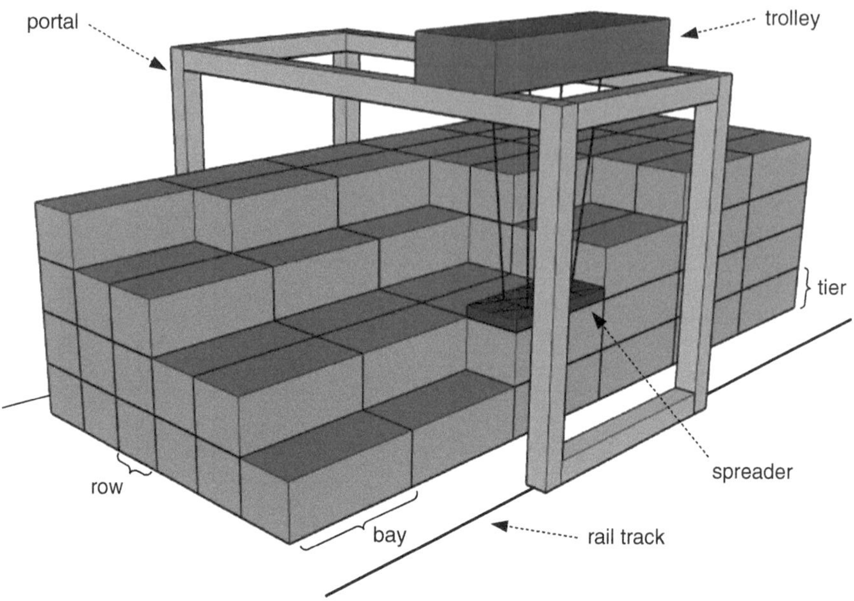

Fig. 1.2 Schematic RMGC yard block

parallel to the blocks, respectively. In this work, it is focused on automated RMGC systems with yard blocks perpendicular to the quay wall, like they are in operation in Hamburg (Germany) and Rotterdam (Netherlands).

1.2 Problem Description and Research Objectives

Although all seaport container terminals with automated RMGC systems are conceptually comparable, major differences in the design of these systems can be observed by having a closer look at the operating systems around the world. While at the ECT Delta Terminal in Rotterdam (Netherlands), for instance, only one RMGC is deployed for yard blocks that are 28 bays (of TEU) long, 6 rows wide and 2 tiers high, two RMGCs of different sizes are deployed at the CTA (Container Terminal Altenwerder) in Hamburg (Germany) for yard blocks with 37 bays, 10 rows and 4 tiers (Saanen and Valkengoed 2005). At the CTB (Container Terminal Burchardkai) in Hamburg (Germany), even three RMGCs are deployed for yard blocks with 42 bays, 10 rows and 5 tiers (HHLA 2009). Overall, the design of automated RMGC storage yards can be distinguished according to the operating type of RMGC system and the layout of the individual yard blocks. While different types of RMGC systems are characterised by the number of cranes per yard block and their crossing abilities, different yard-block layouts are defined by their lengths, widths and heights in terms of the numbers of bays, rows and tiers, respectively.

So far, four relevant types of RMGC systems have been developed—the single, twin, double and triple-crane system. Each of these types of RMGC systems can be combined with hundreds of different yard-block layouts, that result from different combinations of reasonable numbers of bays, rows and tiers. Typically, the order of magnitude for automated RMGC yard blocks is 28–48 bays long, 6–12 rows wide and 2–6 tiers high. Altogether, the number of possible designs for automated RMGC systems is huge, which makes the selection of the most suited RMGC design a complicated task.

Although the business success as well as the operational performance of seaport container terminals are greatly affected by the strategical decisions on the RMGC design, by now only little attention is given to this problem. So far, most studies only compare different types of RMGC systems for a given yard-block layout (e.g., Valkengoed 2004; Saanen and Valkengoed 2005; Saanen 2007). Whereas the effects of different yard-block layouts are hardly investigated, and, to the author's knowledge, no insights into the dynamic performance interactions between decisions on the operating type of RMGC system and the yard-block layout are available at all. In this work, it is among other aspects investigated

- Which effects for the operational performance of RMGC systems are induced by increases of the number of bays, rows and tiers,
- Whether it is preferable to stack longer, wider or higher in order to increase the yard-block capacity,
- At what block dimensions additional cranes per yard block really pay off in comparison to fewer cranes and
- To what extent the operational performance ranking of the types of RMGC systems is affected by the yard-block layout.

In general, the performance of complicated systems—like that of automated RMGC storage yards—is not only affected by strategical design decisions. Moreover, the performance of such systems is usually influenced by several parameters describing the framework conditions and the operational processes of the considered system, which in turn may induce changes for the optimal design of these systems. This is also the case for the design of RMGC systems at seaport container terminals, which are expected to be influenced by parameters defining the terminal-framework conditions, the design and the operation of connected terminal subsystems and the operational processes of the RMGC system itself. While some design-influencing parameters of automated RMGC systems have already been identified (e.g., the transshipment factor; Saanen 2007), the design influence of several other parameters has not been identified and/or quantified by now (e.g., crane kinematics, vessel-call pattern). In the context of design-influencing parameters of RMGC systems, it is analysed throughout this work

- To which extent the operational performance of RMGC systems is affected by certain parameters and
- In how far decisions on the RMGC design are sensitive to changes of these parameters.

A special group of design-influencing parameters characterises which solution approaches are applied to the operational planning problems of automated RMGC systems. As it is shown by several studies on these planning problems, the operational performance of automated RMGC systems is greatly influenced by the selection and parametrisation of the corresponding solution approach. In particular, several solution approaches are reported for the container-stacking and crane-scheduling problems, which are often regarded as the most important operational planning problems for RMGC systems (e.g., Dekker et al. 2006; Park et al. 2010). While the determination of stacking positions for individual containers in the yard block is addressed by the container-stacking problem, crane assignment and sequencing of transport jobs for the RMGCs are dealt with by the crane-scheduling problem.

In contrast to other design-influencing parameters, which can often be expressed by a simple value, these operational solution approaches are very complicated parameters that require more comprehensive analyses in order to allow for a profound evaluation of their design influences. In doing so, some observations can be made that raise questions on the container-stacking and crane-scheduling problems. Until now, the RMGC-scheduling problem has not been appropriately formulated as a linear optimisation model. Instead, most solution approaches are based on elaborated (meta) heuristics in order to schedule as many transport jobs as possible in real-time. However, frequent replanning of the crane-scheduling problem is usually required, due to the fact that the planning situation at seaport container terminals is continuously changing. In addition, several rule-based container-stacking strategies are available, but no systematic stacking approach has been presented so far that is able to determine container-stacking positions as a weighted trade-off between the rational stacking objectives of these rules. Here, it is investigated with regard to the operational planning problems of automated RMGC systems

- Whether it is possible and practically useful to model the crane-scheduling problem as a linear optimisation programme,
- To what extent comparably simple crane-scheduling strategies are outperformed by more elaborated (meta-) heuristics as well as
- Whether and in how far container stacking can be improved by well-balanced combinations of different stacking rules.

Altogether, both the design and the operation of automated RMGC systems at seaport container terminals are addressed here. The primary focus is on the design of RMGC systems and its influencing parameters, among which the solution approaches for the operational planning problems of RMGC systems are ranked. Here, in the first place, the operational planning approaches are only regarded in order to support the design investigations. In this sense, the development and evaluation of alternative planning approaches can be regarded as a spin-off of the design investigations. Hence, the primary objectives are concerned with the RMGC-design planning, while the secondary objectives deal with its operational planning problems. More explicitly, the primary objectives are

- The quantification and explanation of mutual operational-performance effects of decisions on the operating type of RMGC system and the yard-block layout as well as
- The identification and evaluation of parameters that influence decisions on the operating type of RMGC system and the yard-block layout.

Whereas the secondary objectives are

- The development and evaluation of alternative container-stacking, crane-scheduling and crane-routing approaches and,
- In particular, the formulation and evaluation of an IP (integer programming) model for the combined solution of RMGC-scheduling and routing problems.

1.3 Outline of the Thesis

After this short introduction, Chap. 2 is dedicated to the description of the container-terminal logistics. There, the basic terms, facts and problems of seaport container terminals are introduced in order to lay the foundation for all following analyses. Firstly, the container logistics sector is introduced. Thereafter, the container terminal along with its functions, related subsystems and equipment is presented, which is followed by definitions of several design and performance indicators for container terminals. Finally, an overview on planning problems is provided that arise at seaport container terminals.

Based on the definitions and introductions of Chap. 2, the container-storage yard in general and the automated RMGC system in particular are addressed in Chap. 3. There, the container-storage yard is firstly characterised and thereafter its performance measures and their importance for the performance of seaport container terminals as a whole are discussed. Then, different types of storage-yard systems are compared and—to motivate the further investigation—the automated RMGC system is found to be of great relevance for the performance of modern container terminals. As a consequence, this comparison is followed by a detailed description of the RMGC system and its variants. In particular, the relevant strategical and operational planning problems of RMGC systems—which are in detail addressed in Chaps. 4 and 5, respectively—are shortly introduced in this context.

The discussion on the strategical design-planning problems of automated RMGC systems in Chap. 4 starts with a detailed problem description, including a classification of decisions to be made, a discussion on objectives to be aimed at and an overview on parameters to be considered. In this context, the connection between the operational and the strategical planning problems of RMGC systems is clarified, as the operational planning strategies are discussed to be influencing parameters for the design-planning decisions. Thereafter, in Sect. 4.2, relevant literature on design planning of container-storage yards is presented and discussed. Based on the literature overview as well as the following comparison of different types of research approaches, it is concluded that simulation is most suited to investigate the design of automated RMGC systems.

In Chap. 5, the operational planning strategies for automated RMGC systems are addressed in depth. Firstly, the container-stacking problem is discussed and different types of stacking strategies are classified on basis of a preceding literature survey. A new stacking approach is presented which allows for a weighted combination of the previously introduced stacking strategies. Secondly, the crane-scheduling problem is addressed. After this problem is discussed and an overview on known solution approaches is given, some new scheduling strategies are presented which are based on priority rules, IP, enumeration and GA (genetic algorithm). Finally, the problem of routing RMGCs is introduced, relevant literature for that problem is discussed and different claiming-based routing strategies are presented.

The use of simulation as decision-support approach with respect to terminal-planning problems is the subject of Chap. 6. The chapter starts with a discourse of simulation approaches and its requirements. Thereafter, the use of simulation within the field of container terminals is reviewed. Based on the shortcomings of other terminal simulations, a new simulation model of RMGC systems is developed for the special purpose of this study, which is introduced at the end of that chapter.

Numerous computational experiments are carried out with this new simulation approach and their results are shown in Chap. 7. Before the results are regarded in detail, the experimental design is briefly introduced. Thereafter, the results on the operational-performance effects of decisions on the operating type of RMGC system and the yard-block layout are shown and analysed using several descriptive and inferential statistical methods. Then, the results of several sensitivity analyses on the preceding findings are presented and analysed in order to evaluate the design influence of selected parameters. In particular, the operational-performance effects of some newly developed operational planning strategies are studied in this context.

The work is closed with a concluding summary and an outlook on further research topics in Chap. 8.

Chapter 2
Container-Terminal Logistics

Within this chapter, the container terminal, as the major interface between the waterside and landside container-logistics sector, is introduced. At first, in Sect. 2.1, the container-logistics sector—including its development, its transport objects and its modes of transportation—is described. Afterwards, in Sect. 2.2, the container terminal along with its functions, related subsystems and equipment is presented. Thirdly, the assessment of container terminals by means of design and performance figures is explained in Sect. 2.3. In Sect. 2.4, an overview is given on planning problems that arise at seaport container terminals. Finally, some concluding remarks about this chapter are made.

2.1 Introduction to Container Logistics

According to the definitions of logistics and containers (Krieger 2005a,c), container logistics can be defined as the integrated planning, coordination, execution and control of all flows of standardised ISO (international organization for standardisation) 668 steel boxes and of the related information from the origin to the final destination. In comparison to conventional bulk transportation, the usage of containers has the advantages of less packaging, less damaging and being more productive (Hecht and Pawlik 2007, pp. 13–14). Nowadays, the oversea transport of finished consumer goods is almost always carried out in these standardised steel boxes—the so-called containers—on deep-sea container vessels. In addition, the fraction of liquids as well as piece and bulk goods shipped in specialised containers is also increasing (UNCTAD 2008, pp. 22–25). But the container logistics comprises more than just the oversea transport that is carried out by container vessels. Moreover, also stripping, stuffing, storing and handling containers as well as its hinterland transportation is included in the container logistics.

Examples of the intercontinental container-transport chain are given by Saanen (2004, pp. 1–2) as well as Hecht and Pawlik (2007, p. 89). In Fig. 2.1, a generalised

N. Kemme, *Design and Operation of Automated Container Storage Systems*, Contributions to Management Science, DOI 10.1007/978-3-7908-2885-6_2,

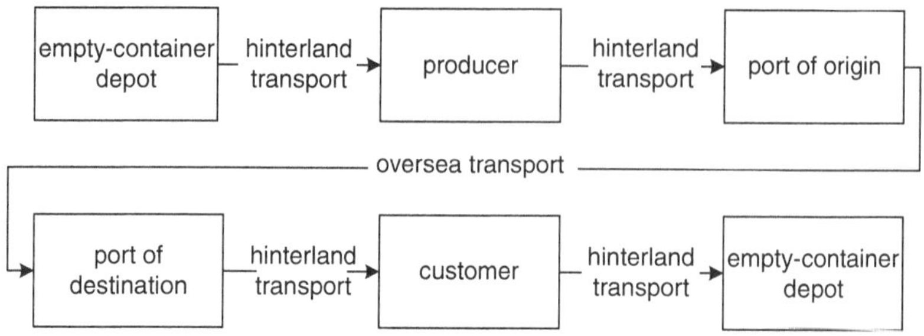

Fig. 2.1 Schematic container-transport chain (based on Hecht and Pawlik 2007, p. 89)

flow of containers within the framework of container logistics is illustrated. Usually, the flow of an unladen container starts at a special depot where only empty containers of certain carriers are stacked. From the empty depot, a container is transported by truck to the point where it is stuffed with cargo—which may be the producer of a certain good. Afterwards, the laden container is transported by hinterland modes of transportation to the next seaport container terminal from where it is shipped overseas to another container terminal. The hinterland transport is not necessarily executed by only one mode of transportation. Moreover, several modes can be involved, as the container may firstly be transported by truck to an inland container terminal from where it is transported by train to the seaport container terminal. Also the oversea transport may consist of several vessel journeys. Firstly, the container may be transported by a smaller vessel to a bigger port, from where it is shipped by means of a larger vessel to another port. From the port of destination, the container is then moved by hinterland modes of transportation to the customer, where it is stripped. Finally, the empty container is transported to the next empty depot of the corresponding carrier.

Altogether, container logistics play a major role in the supply chain of most producing companies. Subsequently, the history of the container logistics is described and its importance for the global economy is explained. Thereafter, different existing types and sizes of the standardised container are presented. Finally, all modes of transportation that may be involved in the container-transport chain are presented.

2.1.1 Development and Importance of Container Logistics

The triumphal procession of the civil container logistics began with a fleet of old oil tankers, which were bought in 1956 by the carrier Malcolm McLean. His shipping company—which is named Sea-Land—began to change the world of shipping and logistics immediately. On the 26th of April, 1956 McLean's modified tanker 'Ideal-X' left the port of Newark (New Jersey) in direction of Houston (Texas) with 56 containers on board. Subsequently, he established the first shipping services between the US-American East and West Coast. The great success induced the installation of international shipping services in the 1960s. Until the end of that decade, the first original container vessels had carrying capacities up to 700 containers. The success of the container logistics continued due to the standardisation of the container sizes by the ISO, which enables a simplified transshipment between international container-shipping lines and other modes of transportation (see Sect. 2.1.2). In the forthcoming years, special facilities with specialised equipment for container handling were built in the ports around the world—so-called container terminals (Hecht and Pawlik 2007, pp. 13–15).

During the last decades, the container volume handled world wide has continuously increased as a result of globalisation, economical growth and geographical distribution of activities. Before the economic crisis in the years 2008 and 2009, it has even been expected that this growth will continue for the next decades with annual rates of 5–8% (Saanen 2004, p. 8). However, first studies (Min et al. 2009) and current figures (Port of Hamburg 2011b) indicate that the path of growth will be continued in the future.

A lot of maritime transportation results from missing resources in the country of destination, while other cargo flows are induced by cheaper production costs in the country of origin than in the country of destination. Nowadays, the international trade is based on low transport costs, so that the difference in production costs between country of origin and destination do not need to be that big (Hecht and Pawlik 2007, pp. 16–17). During the last decades, the oversea transport costs of containers have been substantially decreased due to economies of scale which have been facilitated by continuously increasing vessel sizes (Scholtens et al. 1999, p. 7). While container vessels of the first generation (until 1970) had carrying capacities up to 1,000 containers, the vessels of the fourth generation (early 1990s) already had capacities of about 4,000 containers. Today, vessels with carrying capacities of more than 8,000 containers are increasingly common. However, the correct answer to the question of the world's largest container vessel has a rather short lifetime. In 2006, Maersk Line presented its 'Emma Maersk' with an officially announced capacity of 11,000 containers, but experts expect actually larger capacities of up to 14,300 containers (Hecht and Pawlik 2007, p. 47).

Along with the growth of vessel sizes, the requirements for the ports and the container terminals that handle these larger vessels are growing as well. Especially, the draught of the ports and the lifting height and outreach of the QCs have to be increased. But also the other terminal equipment has to be adjusted in order to handle and store more containers within similar periods of time. Therefore, huge investments are involved with the handling of the biggest container vessels, which cannot be afforded by every terminal. Thus, the hub and spoke concept has evolved (see Sect. 2.1.3), in which only some terminals—the hubs—handle the big vessels and other terminals—the spokes—only handle smaller vessels (Saanen 2004, pp. 8–16).

Altogether, container shipping and globalisation depend on each other. Without the success of the container logistics far less international trade could be expected, but at the same time the growth of the world trade with its division of labour induces the demand for container-shipping services and container-terminal capacities (Hecht and Pawlik 2007, p. 17).

2.1.2 Container Size and Type

In spite of its standardisation, several different sizes and types of containers have to be distinguished. However, all these different freight containers that are handled around the world are standardised according to the ISO 668 standard. The size of a container refers to its metrics in terms of length, width and height, which are usually expressed in feet and inches. The length of a freight container is either 20′, 40′ or 45′ and commonly used container heights are 0′, 8′, 8′6″ and 9′6″. A standardised ISO-container is always 8′ wide. A 9′6″ high container is usually called high-cube, whereas the 0′ high container is referred to platform containers, which only have foldable walls or even no walls (Nazari 2005, p. 5). Sizes and capacities of vessels and container terminals are generally measured in terms of TEU, which refers to the length of a 20′ container. Consequently, a 40′ container accounts for two TEUs. The tare weight of a 20′ container is around 2,250 kg and its maximum payload is 22,750 kg (Hecht and Pawlik 2007, p. 73).

Besides its size, a container can be classified according to several other characteristics. On the basis of its cargo, a container can be classified into the main types dry container, tank container, open container and reefer (Nazari 2005, p. 5). A dry container is a closed standard container with two doors which is used for carrying solid cargo without any special requirements. A tank container is used for carrying liquids or gases. It consists of a tank surrounded by a metal frame that enables stacking like for dry containers. An open container does not have a roof and some walls may be missing too. It is designed for carrying OOG (out of gauge) cargo which is slightly higher or wider than will fit standard dry containers. Some commonly used open containers are open top (i.e., having no roof), open side (i.e., having no side walls), flat racks (i.e., having only foldable end walls) and platforms (i.e., having no walls). A reefer is a dry container which is designed for carrying cargo that needs to be refrigerated. Two types of reefer can be distinguished: conair-container and integral reefer. While integral reefers have an incorporated electric cooling unit, conair-containers need a special clip-on cooling unit in case the container is used for cargo that requires refrigeration (Hecht and Pawlik 2007, pp. 76–79). Nowadays, the oversea transport of finished consumer goods is almost always carried out in dry containers. The other types only make up for a fraction of about 15% of the turnover of a container terminal (Petering et al. 2009).

In addition, a container may be classified according to its load or IMO status (international maritime organization). The load status of a container, which is either full or empty, is required for the stacking operations, as container weight matters and empty containers are often stored in special empty-container blocks. The IMO status of a container indicates which kind of special handling and storage is required, in case dangerous goods are loaded (Nazari 2005, p. 5). Subsequently, the term container is mostly used as synonym for the standard dry container with lengths of 20′ and 40′.

2.1.3 Types of Container-Transport Modes

The container transport is realised by several different modes of transportation. The waterside transport is carried out by vessels (see Fig. 2.2) and the landside transport is executed by XTs (external truck) and trains. Depending on its routes, carrying capacities and other characteristics, the following types of transport modes can be distinguished (Nazari 2005, p. 6):

Deep-sea vessels travel the long oversea distances between different continents and larger areas. Usually, deep-sea vessels have huge carrying capacities of several 1,000 TEUs and they are mainly used for interlinking Europe, North America, South America, the Far East and the Middle East. Lengthwise, the carrying capacity of deep-sea vessels is subdivided into several holds which consist of several bays with the length of 20′ or 40′ containers. Containers may be stacked on deck or below deck. For a detailed description of deep-sea vessels it is referred to Hecht and Pawlik (2007, pp. 25–38). Today, a deep-sea vessel usually calls at several ports on a cyclic route and in each port containers are discharged and loaded. The containers that are loaded onto the vessel are destined for subsequent ports on its route (Meersmans and Dekker 2001).

Short-sea vessels travel shorter distances across the small seas, mostly between countries of the same continent. Usually, the carrying capacities of short-sea vessels are a lot less than for deep-sea vessels, often only several 100 TEUs.

Feeder vessels travel comparable distances and have similar-sized carrying capacities like short-sea vessels. But in contrast to short-sea vessels, they carry containers that come mainly from or are destined for deep-sea vessels.

Barges are small vessels that do not usually travel overseas, instead, they mainly serve the hinterland of a seaport via rivers and channels. They only have carrying capacities of several dozen TEUs.

XTs also serve the hinterland of seaport container terminals. They transport containers overland by usage of roads and usually have carrying capacities of only 2 TEUs. However, depending on the legal regulations, longer XTs with bigger capacities are possible.

Trains transport containers overland to hinterland destinations of seaport container terminals. Its carrying capacity depends on the number of deployed rail cars and may be up to 90 TEUs (Boysen and Fliedner 2010).

Altogether, a seaport is connected to other oversea ports by deep-sea, short-sea and feeder vessels and it is connected to the hinterland by XTs, trains and barges. Depending on the flow direction of a container, it is either imported, exported or transshipped at a seaport container terminal. The corresponding container flows are summarised in Table 2.1. An import container arrives by vessel and leaves the terminal by XT, train or barge, while an export container is delivered by XT, train or barge and departs via vessel. Transshipment containers both arrive and depart by vessel.

Fig. 2.2 Example illustration of deep-sea vessel (*left*) and feeder/short-sea vessel (*right*)

Table 2.1 Classification of container flows at seaport container terminals

		Leave terminal via	
		Deep-sea Short-sea Feeder	Rail Road Barge
Arrive at terminal via	Deep-sea Short-sea Feeder	Transshipment	Import
	Rail Road Barge	Export	Land-land

The feeder and deep-sea vessels are part of the concept of hub and spoke container terminals which has emerged due to orientation towards economies of scale. While the transshipment from deep-sea to feeder vessels and vice versa takes usually place at large hub container terminals, the spoke terminals are generally smaller terminals which only serve smaller feeder and short-sea vessels (Nazari 2005, pp. 14–15). Most arriving containers at typical hub terminals are transshipped, whereas containers at spoke terminals are mostly imported or exported. The largest port in the world—Singapore—is a typical hub, as 80% of the handled containers are transshipment. A terminal with such a container flow is also called transshipment terminal. In contrast, the largest European port (see Table 1.1)—Rotterdam (Netherlands)—is not a transshipment port, as most containers (70–80%) are either imported or exported. Therefore, a container terminal with such a container flow is called import-export terminal (Saanen 2004, p. 11).

2.2 Introduction to Container-Terminal Systems

In general, a seaport container terminal is an open system of material flow with two external interfaces. At the waterside interface—which is the quay wall—vessels and barges are loaded and discharged, while at the landside interface trains and XTs are served. The storage area for containers facilitates as decoupling point of waterside and landside operations (Steenken et al. 2004). Furthermore, a container terminal can be considered as a rather sophisticated system of which the main attributes are its functions, its main operations and its resources (Saanen 2004, pp. 27–33). In the following subsections, these attributes are explained and discussed in detail. Firstly, the functions of the whole terminal system are explained. Thereafter, the subsystems of a container terminal and the relevant operations are described. Finally, different types of terminal equipment are presented.

2.2.1 Container-Terminal Functions

In Fig. 2.1, it is shown that the seaport container terminal plays a major role within the container logistics, as it is the interface between the oversea and hinterland transport. The primary functions of a container terminal are shown in Fig. 2.3, which illustrates the role of the container terminal in more detail. In particular, these are the transshipment from one mode of transportation to another as well as the temporary storage of containers. In addition, some secondary functions are fulfilled by the container terminal which may be summarised as added services (Saanen 2004, pp. 27–29; Nazari 2005, pp. 17–19).

The transshipment function—which should not be confused with the transshipment container (see Sect. 2.1.3)—refers to discharging and loading vessels, barges, XTs and trains. The added value of theses processes is provided by the speed at which vessels are handled and the decoupling of oversea transport and hinterland transport. However, direct transshipment from one mode of transportation to another is nearly impossible. Therefore, the storage function of a container terminal is of particular importance for the performance of the container terminal (Saanen 2004, p. 28). Some reasons for the essential importance of the storage function are provided by Zijderveld (1995, pp. 2–3):

- The terminal process would become too complicated in case of direct transshipment, since all individual XTs would have to be controlled in such a way that they arrive in the right sequence, at the right time and at the right place in order to process the relevant transshipment operation without any delays.
- For terminals with more than two different modes of transportation, direct transshipment would require a sophisticated terminal design. All handled modes of transportation have to be located very close to each other, which would cause serious problems for terminals with deep-sea vessels, barges, trucks and trains.
- Both individual means of transportation between which containers are transshipped have to be simultaneously present if containers are transshipped directly. Especially for transshipment between two vessels as well as between trains and vessels it is virtually impossible, as vessels and trains may be very long and sequence relations for loading and unloading of vessels and trains would have to be simultaneously respected.

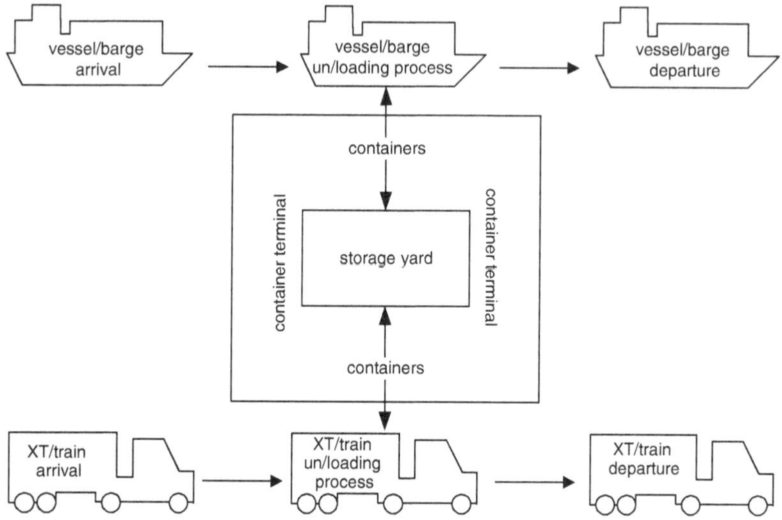

Fig. 2.3 Schematic processes of container terminals (based on Saanen 2004, p. 28)

- The receivers of a container do not always need their cargo very fast. Thus, they are not always interested in direct transshipment, in contrast, they may be interested in inexpensive storage possibilities. In addition, containers have to be stored on the terminal due to customs demands and financial requirements. Some containers stay even longer than 6 months on the terminal (Saanen 2004, p. 29).

Usually, container terminals provide sufficient area for the storage functionality. This storage area is often subdivided into smaller areas for the storage of special container types like reefer, empty container and IMO container. The total size of a storage yard is determined by the terminal-specific throughput and the average container-dwell time. Most container terminals are interested in a high throughput and short container-dwell times, since their original business model is usually based on the transshipment of containers and not their storage. Therefore, the storage function of container terminals cannot be compared with that of a typical warehouse. Moreover, it is like a buffer in order to facilitate the transshipment function. Reasonable container-dwell times in the sense of the buffer function are normally 3–8 days (Nazari 2005, p. 18). Altogether, the storage yard at seaport container terminals provides relatively inexpensive, secure and easily accessible buffer storage locations, from which JIT (just in time) deliveries of containers can take place (Saanen 2004, p. 28).

Container terminals may offer several added services, which can be qualified as inessential secondary terminal functions. Some of these functions are stripping and stuffing of containers in a CFS (container-freight station), container repair and washing as well as equipment maintenance. Furthermore, some terminals may offer a depot function for empty containers and shipping-line-owned road chassis (Saanen 2004, p. 29; Nazari 2005, p. 19).

2.2.2 *Container-Terminal Subsystems and Related Operations*

The container terminal is a rather complicated system with several interrelated types of operations, numerous controllable objects (equipment) and thousands of plannable items (jobs, containers). Thus, the terminal is often subdivided into several subsystems according to the related operations and the equipment involved (Steenken et al. 2004). Here, the whole terminal system is viewed to consist of the ship-to-shore subsystem, the waterside horizontal-transport subsystem, the storage subsystem and the hinterland-connection subsystem.

Despite this division into several subsystems, the handling capacity and the performance of the whole terminal system is determined by all of the subsystems, which means that the subsystem with the smallest handling capacity determines—as the bottleneck—the handling capacity of the container terminal as a whole (Nazari 2005, pp. 9–10). Since the different subsystems are linked with one another, each subsystem should be designed and managed in such a way that the connected subsystem(s) may be operated most efficiently. Subsequently, the general layout of a container terminal along with the positioning of the subsystems is introduced. Thereafter, each of the subsystems is described in detail.

2.2.2.1 Container-Terminal Layout

Hundreds of container terminals with different layouts, different container-handling concepts and different types of equipment exist around the world. Nevertheless, most terminals have a comparable arrangement of their subsystems and facilities, which is schematically shown in Fig. 2.4.

Of course, the ship-to-shore subsystem is located at the waterside edge of the terminal where quay cranes are used to load and discharge vessels and barges. In general, the ship-to-shore subsystem is followed by the horizontal-transport subsystem, which is responsible for the transport of full and empty containers between the quay cranes and the storage subsystem. Usually, this horizontal transport is executed by different types of transport vehicles.

The storage subsystem is the place on the terminal where containers are temporarily stored. Besides the regular storage area, most container terminals exhibit a special empty depot where empty containers are stored according to the needs of the shipping lines (Steenken et al. 2004). In addition, most facilities for the added services that are offered by container terminals may be assigned to the storage subsystem. Here, a CFS and facilities for maintenance and repair of containers are linked with the storage subsystem. Due to its decoupling function between waterside and landside terminal operations, the storage subsystem is located in the centre of the terminal. According to its main function, the regular storage area takes up most of the space of the storage subsystem.

On the landside, the storage subsystem is followed by the hinterland-connection subsystem, which fulfils the function of an interface between the terminal and

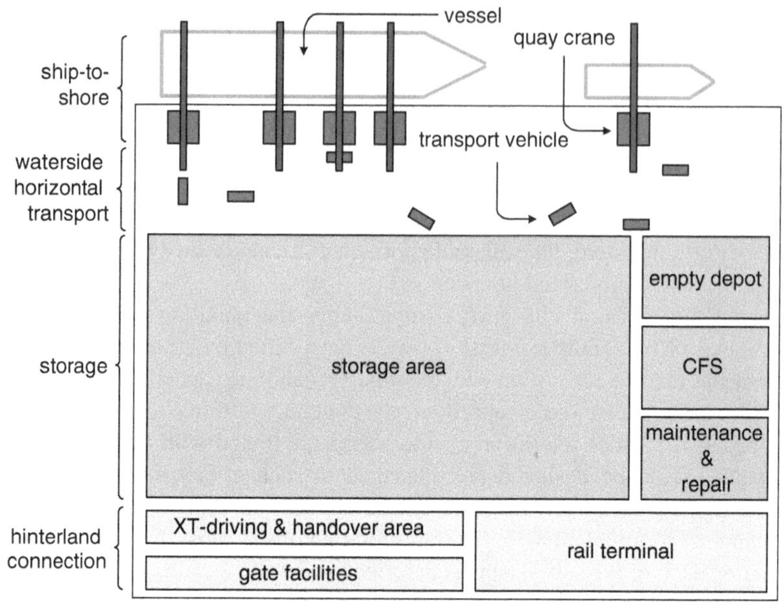

Fig. 2.4 Schematic terminal layout

its hinterland. As both XTs and trains act as landside connecting modes of transportation of seaport container terminals, the hinterland-connection subsystem may comprise facilities for both modes. Trains are loaded and discharged at the rail station of the terminal by special equipment—usually gantry cranes (Meersmans 2002, pp. 8–10). XTs enter the terminal at the gate facilities, where they are checked and administrative tasks are fulfilled. Next, the XTs drive on dedicated streets or driving areas to a handover area where the relevant container is loaded onto or discharged from the XT by special terminal equipment.

2.2.2.2 Ship-to-Shore Subsystem

The ship-to-shore subsystem is designated to the loading and discharging operations of vessels. As it is the direct interface to one of the terminals most important group of stakeholders—the shipping lines—the ship-to-shore subsystem is often regarded as the key subsystem of seaport container terminals (Nazari 2005, pp. 10–11). Several operational planning problems of container terminals are related to the ship-to-shore system. These problems are the stowage planning for deep-sea vessels as well as berth and QC allocation for arriving vessels. An introduction to these planning problems along with a brief overview on the relevant literature is provided in Sect. 2.4.

Before the loading and discharging process of containers begins, the relevant vessel has to moor at the quay of the terminal. As illustrated in Fig. 2.4, several berthing places are available at most container terminals (Meersmans and Dekker 2001; Vis and de Koster 2003). Usually, a vessel is assigned to a berthing place prior to its arrival. In case the arriving vessel is part of a liner service, normally the same berthing place is assigned to each arriving vessel of that service. Nowadays, most arrivals of deep-sea vessels follow a periodically repeated vessel-call pattern, which usually consists of weekly or 2-weekly arrivals for each calling liner service. Besides berthing places, also specific QCs have to be assigned to the loading and discharging processes of calling vessels prior to their actual arrival. While feeder vessels are usually served by one or two QCs, deep-sea vessels—depending on their size—may be served by four to six QCs (Steenken et al. 2004).

After a vessel has moored at the assigned berthing place, the discharging process begins. The containers which have to be discharged and loaded at the terminal are in practice usually only known shortly before the arrival of the vessel. While an unloading plan contains information on the containers that have to be unloaded and in which bay of the vessel they are located, the loading or stowage plan indicates which containers have to be loaded onto the vessel, in which sequence and in which bay they should be stacked. The number of all containers that have to be discharged from and loaded onto an individual vessel at the terminal is usually called moves per call and determines the workload for the QCs. Firstly, the containers that are listed in the unloading plan are successively discharged by the assigned QCs. Usually, the crane driver is free to determine the sequence in which containers are discharged within a specific hold. Since the discharging time for an individual container depends on its position on the vessel and the skills of the crane driver, a large variance in the discharging times is observed. After a QC has finished its discharging operations, it starts loading the containers that have to be stowed in holds to which the relevant QC is assigned. As the workload may be imbalanced between different cranes and due to the variance in the discharging times, it may occur that some cranes already start the loading operations while other QCs are still discharging. As container size and weight as well as the sequence in which the ports are visited by the relevant vessel have to be respected during the loading process, there is hardly any flexibility in the loading operations (Shields 1984); the crane drivers have to follow the stowage plan for the vessel accurately. After all QCs have finished the loading operations for a specific vessel, it unmoors and continues its tour to the next port (Vis and de Koster 2003).

The major objective of the ship-to-shore subsystem is the minimisation of the turn-around times (i.e., the berthing times) of vessels (Steenken et al. 2004). Hence, along with the steadily growing vessel sizes, the requirements for the ship-to-shore subsystem have increased as well. The terminals are faced with an increasing pressure on the ship-to-shore subsystem in terms of size and productivity of the QCs. Ever-increasing moves per call have to be handled during nearly unchanged berthing times—a typical deep-sea vessel should be turned in approximately 24 h (Rijsenbrij and Wieschemann 2011). As a consequence, high investments into new crane equipment are made (see Sect. 2.2.3) and much effort is spent on the development of elaborated planning methods (see Sect. 2.4).

2.2.2.3 Waterside Horizontal-Transport Subsystem

The waterside horizontal-transport subsystem acts as the interface between the ship-to-shore subsystem and the storage subsystem. Containers that are discharged by QCs are transported by horizontal-transport vehicles from the QC to the storage yard, and before containers can be loaded onto a vessel, they have to be transferred from the storage yard to the QCs. The general objectives of this subsystem are efficient, smooth and fast transfer of containers between the QCs and the storage yard (Nazari 2005, pp. 11–12). In order to achieve these aims, the right decisions on type and number of applied transport machines as well as on scheduling and routing of the machines have to be made (Vis and de Koster 2003).

The container transfer between QCs and storage yard may be executed by different types of transport vehicles, which differ in carrying capacity, flexibility, velocity, degree of automation and other characteristics. However, the horizontal-transport processes are most of all affected by the container-lifting capabilities of the transport vehicles (see Sect. 2.2.3.2). In case the vehicles have no lifting capability, they have to be loaded and discharged at the QCs and storage yard, which means that some additional stacking equipment is needed in the yard area. Hence, a smooth and timely coordinated transfer between QCs and stacking equipment is of major importance for the productivity of the whole terminal system, as otherwise some of the involved equipment has to wait for each other and valuable equipment resources are wasted. However, if the transfer vehicles are equipped with a container-lifting device, they are able to load and discharge containers themselves. Consequently, horizontal-transport vehicles with lifting capability do not depend on the lifting capabilities of the QCs and stacking equipment. Thus, the interdependency of the ship-to-shore, horizontal-transport and storage subsystem is reduced—these subsystems are slightly decoupled from each other (Meersmans and Dekker 2001; Steenken et al. 2004; Saanen 2007).

Different transport cycles and QC-allocation schemes have to be distinguished for the horizontal-transport vehicles. The vehicles can either be exclusively assigned to one QC (dedicated allocation scheme) or several different QCs (pooled allocation scheme). In addition, the vehicles can either be operated in the single-cycle or dual-cycle mode. Within the single-cycle mode, the vehicle either transports containers only from the storage yard to the QCs or vice versa, while in the dual-cycle mode the vehicles transfer containers in both directions. In general, the single-cycle mode is connected with the dedicated allocation scheme, whereas the dual-cycle mode requires the pooled allocation scheme (Steenken et al. 2004).

Furthermore, there are differences in the transfer direction of containers. For container transfers from the QCs to the storage yard, no sequences have to be respected, which means that the containers do not need to arrive at the storage yard according to a certain schedule, whereas for the vessel-loading process the containers have to arrive at the QCs according to the scheduled stowage plan. Therefore, the transfer to the QCs has to be planned in such a way that different transportation times and the stowage plans are respected. Otherwise, the horizontal container transport would be connected with congestions at the QCs and stacking equipment as well as unproductive idle times for QCs, stacking equipment and transport vehicles (Meersmans and Dekker 2001; Steenken et al. 2004).

2.2.2.4 Storage Subsystem

The storage subsystem is probably the most important subsystem as it is the actual decoupling point between the waterside and landside container-transportation chain (Nazari 2005, p. 12). Since steadily increasing container volumes have to be stored in the storage yards and at the same time space is an increasingly scarce resource, the importance of the storage subsystem has continuously grown over the last years along with the increasing traffic volume (Steenken et al. 2004; Rijsenbrij and Wieschemann 2011). In this subsection, only a short introduction into the field of container storage is given, since it is the major research object of this work and detailed descriptions on the underlying operations and the applied equipment are provided in Chap. 3.

Superficially, two ways of storing containers at seaport container terminals can be distinguished. Firstly, containers may be stored on chassis, which enables direct access to each individual container. Secondly, containers may be stacked on the ground and piled up. Hence, not every single container is directly accessible. In order to get access to containers that are stored below others, the upper ones have to be shuffled, which means that they have to be repositioned to other storage locations (Meersmans and Dekker 2001). Nowadays, due to limited storage space, storing containers on the ground is most common, while storage on chassis is only partly used in North America (Vis and de Koster 2003; Kalmar 2011a).

Storage yards in which containers are stacked on the ground are usually separated into several blocks that consist of several bays, rows and tiers. The maximum stacking height (i.e., the maximum number of tiers) depends on the used stacking equipment. Most container terminals form separated blocks according to the attributes of the containers. There are different yard blocks for containers that are planned for vessel loading and that are planned for hinterland departure. In addition, there may be special storage areas for empty, IMO and damaged containers as well as for reefer. The storage yard of large European container terminals is on average filled with about 15,000–20,000 containers.

When an XT or an internal transport vehicle without lifting capabilities arrives laden at the interfaces of the storage yard, the container is discharged by some kind of stacking equipment. The container is then transferred by the stacking equipment to the dedicated stacking position in the yard block. If an XT or internal transport vehicle arrives empty at a yard block, the stacking equipment picks up the demanded container in the block and positions it on the corresponding vehicle. However, in case the internal vehicles are equipped with lifting devices, no additional stacking equipment may be required. Depending on the storage-yard system, the vehicles may drive into the block and pick up or position containers in the block themselves (Meersmans and Dekker 2001). In addition, there may be internal transfers between the different storage areas that are depicted in Fig. 2.4. While full containers in the main storage area may be transported to the CFS for stripping, empty containers may firstly be transported to the CFS for stuffing and afterwards moved to the main storage area for further transshipment. Furthermore, due to imbalances in the distribution of empty containers, they may be needed for transfer by vessel, truck or train and thus they have to be moved to the respective yard or transition area. Other reasons for internal transports are named by Steenken et al. (2004).

As most of the terminal operations either originate or terminate at the yard block, efficient stacking is of crucial importance for the effective execution of the remaining terminal operations. The efficiency of the stacking operations is determined by strategical decisions on the stacking equipment and the yard-block layout as well as by operational decisions about container stacking and about the scheduling and routing of the stacking equipment (Meersmans and Dekker 2001; Vis and de Koster 2003). These decisions usually have to be made with respect to the available space, the planned container throughput, the expected container-dwell time, the planned yard utilisation as well as external regulations concerning customs control, environmental protection and occupational safety (Nazari 2005, p. 12).

2.2.2.5 Hinterland-Connection Subsystem

The hinterland connections are of great importance for the competitiveness of container terminals. Without a fast, highly available, reliable and regular connection between the terminal and its hinterland, the flow of import and export containers would be impaired, which would harm the terminal performance as a whole. According to the modes of transportation, that are named in Sect. 2.1.3, connections by street, rail and waterways have to be distinguished (Nazari 2005, pp. 12–13).

XTs arrive by street at the gate of the terminal either laden or empty. While the containers of laden XTs are checked at the gate along with the corresponding data, the retrieval of certain containers is declared by empty arriving XTs at the gate. Afterwards, the XTs drive to dedicated handover areas, where they are either discharged or loaded by internal stacking equipment. In container-storage yards that are operated by yard cranes, the handover areas are usually located directly adjacent to the yard blocks and the XTs are served by the cranes. Whereas the XTs may also be served by internal transport vehicles with lifting capabilities if this technology is applied in the storage yard. Depending on the modal split, large European container terminals handle several thousand XTs per day (Steenken et al. 2004).

Most European seaport container terminals are connected with the public railway network. As a consequence, these terminals have their own rail stations where containers are loaded and discharged for ongoing transportation to hinterland and oversea destinations, respectively. Terminal machines are needed for loading and discharging of rail containers as well as for transfer of these containers between rail station and container-storage yard. The rail station is connected with the storage yard by internal transport vehicles with lifting capabilities or by internal trucks and trailers. If trucks and trailers are used, the containers are directly buffered on trailers alongside the rails, whereas two possibilities exist in case internal transport vehicles with lifting capabilities are deployed. Firstly, the containers may be buffered in container stacks alongside the rail. Secondly, the containers may be directly loaded on and discharged from the train by the internal transport vehicle which is able to drive over the waggons to pick up and drop off the containers. In case containers are buffered alongside the rails, the loading and discharging operations of freight trains are executed by special gantry cranes, which is the most common handling equipment for rail terminals (Steenken et al. 2004).

Freight trains may be up to 700 m long and carry up to 90 TEUs (Boysen and Fliedner 2010). The requirements of the loading and discharging operations of these trains are quite similar to those of deep-sea vessels. For each container that has to be loaded onto a certain train, the specific position on the waggons of the train are given by the relevant loading plan. This position is determined by type, weight and destination of that container as well as by the maximum load of the waggon and its position in the sequence of the train. A loading plan is either produced by the train operator or the container terminal. While the former one is interested in the minimisation of shunting moves during further train transport, the terminal is primarily interested in the minimisation of required shuffle moves in the storage yard (Steenken et al. 2004).

2.2.3 *Container-Terminal Equipment*

After having described the processes of the different subsystems of seaport container terminals in the previous subsection, this subsection is devoted to the equipment that is involved in the relevant operations. Equipment issues are of great importance for container terminals, as decisions on type and number of terminal equipment greatly influence the terminal design and operations (Saanen 2004, p. 31). Here, different types of equipment along with the corresponding attributes, facts, figures and operational restrictions are presented in order to facilitate a substantiated understanding and evaluation of explanations and assumptions that are made within the later chapters. According to the division into subsystems, the equipment overview is subdivided into quay cranes, horizontal-transport machines and storage equipment.

2.2.3.1 Quay Cranes

QCs—which are sometimes also called ship-to-shore cranes or simply gantry cranes—are used for loading and discharging vessels at container terminals (Nazari 2005, p. 6). At international seaport container terminals numerous types of QCs are in operation, which differ in size, handling capacity, logistical concept and other attributes.

First of all, there are two main types of QCs, which are mobile harbour cranes and rail-mounted gantry cranes. The former one is rubber-tyred and therefore it is more

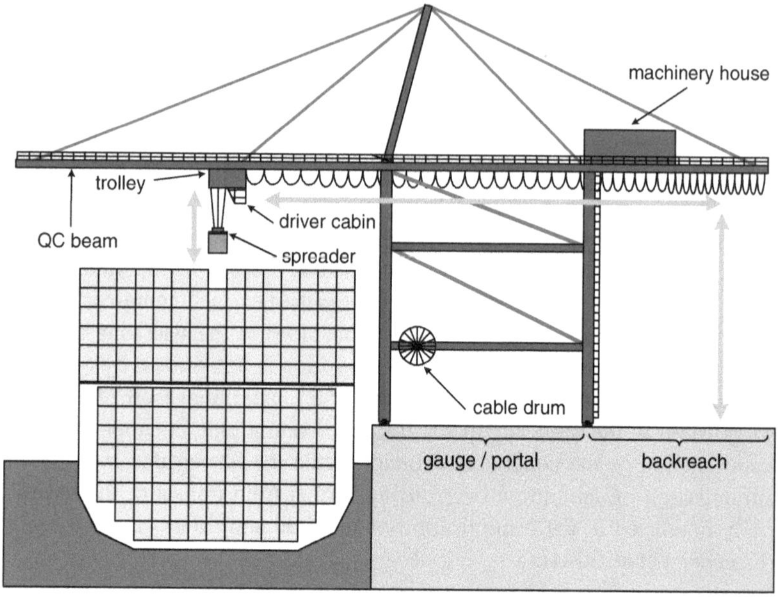

Fig. 2.5 Schematic illustration of QC

flexible than its rail-mounted opponent, which has only limited moving abilities. However, nowadays, modern container terminals mostly deploy rail-mounted gantry QCs, as they offer higher productivities, which means that they handle containers at higher speeds, and they are better suited to cope with the steadily increasing vessel sizes. While in practice mobile harbour cranes are used to handle vessels up to 13 containers wide on deck, the latest rail-mounted gantry QCs can handle vessels up to 26 containers wide on deck (Saanen 2004, pp. 31–32; ZPMC 2009). For that reasons, only the rail-mounted gantry crane is considered in this work and subsequently the term QC is used as synonym for this type of crane.

The three-dimensional movements which are required for loading and discharging of vessels are performed by three moving components of a QC: portal, trolley and spreader. In order to be able to load and discharge containers to/from different bays or even vessels, the portal (i.e., the whole QC) can move on rails alongside the quay wall. Due to being fixed to rails, QCs cannot pass each other, which means that their positions in the quay wall order cannot be changed. A schematic illustration of a commonly used QC is provided in Fig. 2.5, where typical QC movements for loading and unloading of containers are indicated by yellow arrows. It is shown that QCs are equipped with trolleys that are connected with spreaders by means of cable winches. The trolley can drive along the quay-crane beam and it is responsible for the transfer of containers between ship and shore. Onshore containers may be picked up or dropped off by the QC in two different zones, which considerably differ in the required driving distances for the trolley. Depending on the equipment type used for the horizontal transport, the organisational worklflows and the positioning of the hatch covers of the vessels, containers may either be handled in the backreach or in the portal/gauge of the QC. The spreader is a special device to pick up containers (Vis and de Koster 2003). It is equipped with pins that exactly fit into the openings which are located at each corner of a container. By turning the pins, the container is closely linked with the spreader, which enables loading and discharging of the container onto/from vessels. By means of the cable winches the spreader can be lowered or hoisted to the level a container has to be dropped off or picked up (Hecht and Pawlik 2007, p. 102). Common QCs are completely man-driven, which means that all movements of portal, trolley and spreader are controlled by the crane driver who is located in a cabin that is connected with the trolley (Steenken et al. 2004). A clear description of the crane-driver job is provided, for example, by Hecht and Pawlik (2007, p. 106).

The competitiveness of large container terminals greatly depends on the technical specifications of the deployed QCs. The trend towards larger vessels requires larger and faster QCs. In order to load and discharge containers properly, in particular onto/from the largest vessels, the clearance and the outreach of the QCs have to be increased. As a consequence, the handling times for container-loading and discharging operations increase as well due to longer driving distances for trolley and spreader (Saanen 2004, p. 32). Therefore, container terminals and crane manufacturers are continuously striving for increases in the QC productivities, in terms of the number of loaded and discharged containers per QC-working hour (see Sect. 2.3). The productivity may be increased by shortening the required time for QC moves and/or by handling more containers per QC move. While the former one is facilitated by shortening the horizontal driving distances for the trolleys as well as by increasing the maximum velocities and accelerations of trolleys and spreaders, the development of new spreader technologies allows for handling more than one container per QC move. A detailed table on the ranges of velocities and accelerations of different QC types is provided by Stahlbock and Voß (2008) along with other technical QC figures.

While conventional telescopic spreaders can either handle a single 20′, a single 40′ or even two 20′ containers simultaneously, the latest spreader technology—which is called tandem or twin 40′—allows for handling up to two 40′ or even four 20′ containers simultaneously. This is facilitated by attaching two standard telescopic spreaders with independent hoisting systems to each other. However, the tandem spreader technology puts increasing pressure on the crane-driver abilities, the stowage planning and the horizontal-transport processes, as all containers have to be simultaneously and accurately picked up and dropped off on land and on vessel (Johansen 2006; Kalmar 2011a).

The double-trolley QC is a rather new development that is designed to reduce the horizontal driving distances for the trolleys (Steenken et al. 2004). While single-trolley QCs require the only trolley to drive the whole horizontal distance between ship and shore, for double-trolley QCs this driving distance is shared between the man-driven main trolley and the preferably automated portal trolley, which allows for more container movements in the same period of time. The main trolley moves containers between the vessel and the lashing platform, that is located in the lower seaside part of the portal. The container movements between the lashing platform and the horizontal-transport system on shore is then performed by the portal trolley, which can drive along a portal beam between the lashing platform and the backreach of the QC (Steenken et al. 2004; Kalmar 2011a). The lashing platform is required as a container buffer and—due to occupational safety—as decoupling point between the manually controlled main trolley and the automated portal trolley. Double-trolley cranes are in operation, for example, at the CTA in Hamburg (Germany) (Stahlbock and Voß 2008).

Altogether, the handling speed of QCs and their maximum performance depends on the crane type. Today, modern QCs can technically perform around 50 loading and discharging moves per hour, while in operation usually only 22–30 moves per hour are realised (Steenken et al. 2004; Saanen 2004, p. 46). Considering the latest spreader technologies, even 80–100 40′ containers may technically be handled per QC working hour (Stahlbock and Voß 2008). Depending on size and other technological specifications, the prices for the latest QCs are in the range from 6,000,000 € to 9,000,000 € (ZPMC 2009).

2.2.3.2 Horizontal-Transport Machines

The vehicles that are used for the horizontal transport between the quay cranes and the storage area vary considerably at international container terminals. However, four vehicle types may be identified that are used with different characteristics at almost all terminals: SCs (straddle carriers), AGVs (automated-guided vehicles), TTUs (truck-trailer units) and MTSs (multi-trailer systems) (Vis and de Koster 2003; Steenken et al. 2004). These four vehicle types are schematically illustrated in Fig. 2.6.

Horizontal-transport vehicles can be classified into two different classes: passive and active vehicles. While passive vehicles are not able to lift containers by themselves, active vehicles are equipped with a container-lifting device that enables to load and to discharge containers by themselves. Passive vehicles require the assistance of other terminal equipment with container-lifting capabilities for loading and discharging containers. At the waterside interfaces of the horizontal-transport system, these loading and unloading operations of passive vehicles are carried out by QCs, while different possibilities exist at the landside (see Sect. 2.2.3.3). In contrast to AGVs, TTUs and MTSs which belong to the class of passive vehicles, SCs are classified as active vehicles (Steenken et al. 2004).

MTSs consist of a tractor that pulls several trailers, each with a carrying capacity of two TEUs. In Fig. 2.6d, such an MTS with three trailers is depicted, but even longer MTSs with four or five trailers are possible. On its journey across the container terminal, several destinations are visited by an MTS where some containers may be discharged, some new containers may be loaded and some containers stay on the MTS for further transfer to upcoming destinations (Kalmar 2011a).

TTUs are technically quite similar to MTSs, as they also consist of tractors and trailers. But here only a single trailer with a carrying capacity of two TEUs is pulled

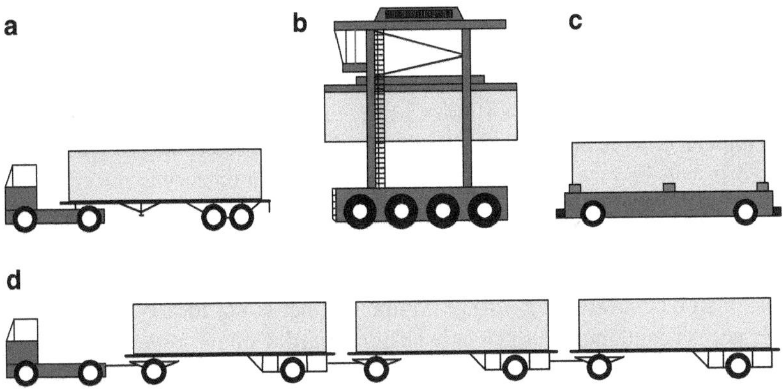

Fig. 2.6 Schematic illustration of horizontal-transport vehicles. (**a**) Truck-trailer unit (TTU). (**b**) Straddle carrier (SC). (**c**) Automated-guided vehicle (AGV). (**d**) Multi-trailer system (MTS)

by each truck (see Fig. 2.6a). Thus, on the one hand, the total carrying capacity of a TTU is far below that of an MTS, while on the other hand TTUs are more flexible and logistically simpler than MTSs, as not the whole journey with several pick-up and drop-off locations has to be planned. Instead, only one transfer job from a pick-up to a drop-off location is usually performed simultaneously by a TTU. The investment costs for a typical TTU add up to about 90,000€ (Saanen 2006).

AGVs (see Fig. 2.6c) are unmanned robotic transport vehicles that drive along predefined paths. The road network for AGVs is defined by electric wires or transponders in the ground, which enable accurate positioning of these vehicles (Steenken et al. 2004). This vehicle type has been widely used for many years in indoor warehouses and production facilities (Egbelu and Tanchoco 1984), before it is introduced for large-scale outdoor operations at seaport container terminals in the 1990s (Saanen 2008). Within the maritime working environment, AGVs are capable of carrying either one 40′/45′ container or two 20′ containers and the maximum load capacity is up to 60 t. In order to detect obstacles and to avoid collisions, the front and the back of AGVs are equipped with infrared sensors. However, if an obstacle is hit by an AGV, its engine is immediately switched off by dead man's switches at the front and the back of the AGV. In addition, the AGV-road network is subdivided into several segments in order to avoid deadlock situations and collisions. Before a certain segment of the road network is entered by an AGV, the relevant segment has to be claimed exclusively for that AGV and consequently no other AGV will be allowed to access the claimed segment (Steenken et al. 2004). Since high investment costs of about 350,000€ per piece (Saanen 2004, p. 49) are involved with AGV systems, they are more practical for high-labour-cost countries, whereas manned vehicles are preferable in countries with low labour costs. Nowadays, AGV systems are in operation, for example, at the CTA in Hamburg (Germany) and at the ECT Delta Terminal in Rotterdam (Netherlands) (Vis and de Koster 2003; Steenken et al. 2004).

The SC—also called van carrier—is a very popular active transport vehicle that is usually man-driven. It consists of a metal frame, usually eight wheels, a driver cabin, a telescopic spreader, a cable winch and an engine (see Fig. 2.6b). Due to the profile of the metal frame—that looks like a turned 'U'—the SC is able to drive across one-TEU-wide container rows. By means of the telescopic spreader, that is mounted in between the frame and is connected with a cable winch on top of the frame, the SC can lift containers that are stacked on container piles, trucks and even trains (Bruns et al. 2007). They are able to transport either one 20′ container, one 40′ container or even two 20′ containers simultaneously. Due to their stacking abilities, SCs can also be classified as storage equipment that is not locally bound and may flexibly access containers in the whole terminal yard. Commonly used SCs are able to stack containers up to three or four tiers high, which means that they can move laden over two or three containers, respectively (Steenken et al. 2004). Typically, costs of around 650,000 € are involved with each additional SC (Saanen 2006).

Within the last years, some enhancements and modifications of the common SC variants have been introduced: Firstly, in 2005 an automated SC system was put into operation at the Patrick Terminal in Brisbane (Australia) (Grunow et al. 2006). These automated SCs—which are often called ALVs—stack four tiers high and are used for horizontal transport and all stacking operations (Stahlbock and Voß 2008). Secondly, some small SC variants have been introduced that only stack 1-over-1. These SCs are called shuttle carriers or sprinter carriers and may be operated man-driven or automated (Noell 2011; Kalmar 2011b). In contrast to SCs of normal height, they are not designed for stacking, but for horizontal transport only. Nevertheless, their container-lifting capabilities allow for partly decoupling of the horizontal transport from the crane operations at the quay and in the storage yard (Pirhonen 2011). In addition, due to their limited height, shuttle carriers can drive faster than SCs of normal height—in particular in curves, as they are less vulnerable to falling over (Noell 2011).

2.2.3.3 Storage Equipment

International container terminals that store containers in stacks—not on chassis—make use of different types of stacking equipment to store containers in the stacks, to move containers within the storage yard and to get them out of the stacks. The most common types of storage equipment are reachstackers, forklifts, SCs and different variants of yard cranes (Vis and de Koster 2003; Saanen 2004, p. 33). While the SC is illustrated and explained in the previous subsection, the three other types of storage equipment are schematically illustrated in Fig. 2.7.

Reachstackers (see Fig. 2.7a) and forklifts (see Fig. 2.7b) are quite similar in their appearances and their capabilities. Both are rubber-tyred vehicles that are usually powered by diesel engines and that are equipped with a driver cabin in the rear of the vehicle (Kalmar 2011a). Forklifts and reachstackers are mainly deployed in local ports that do not have larger machines like yard cranes in operation. Both vehicle types are very flexible, as they can be moved between different stacks and

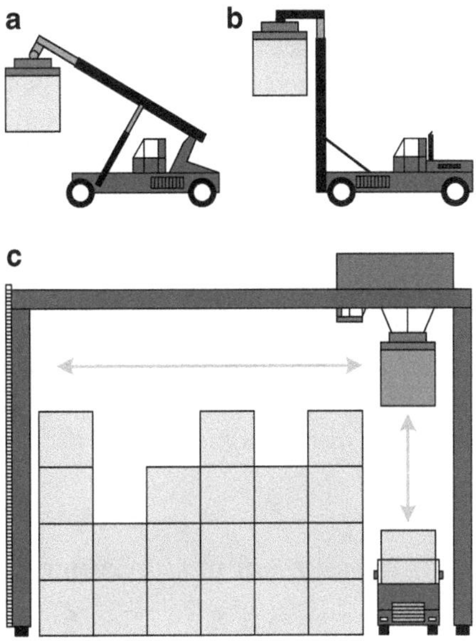

Fig. 2.7 Schematic illustration of storage equipment. (**a**) Reachstacker. (**b**) Forklift. (**c**) Yard crane

storage areas and because they can be used for both stacking and horizontal transfer of containers (Alvarez 2006; Brinkmann 2011). While investment costs of around 325,000€ may be involved with each reachstacker, the purchasing costs of a typical forklift add up to 250,000€ (Saanen 2004, p. 49).

For several reasons, forklifts are nowadays continuously replaced by modern reachstackers at stevedoring facilities and local seaport container terminals. Firstly, the spreader of reachstackers is fixed at the end of a sloped beam that is comparable to those of telescopic cranes, while the spreader of forklifts is mounted on a lifting frame. Therefore, reachstackers are able to lift containers over the outer piles of a stack and to store or retrieve them onto/from inner piles, so that even storage positions in the inside of a stack—which require a lot of shuffle moves for forklifts—may be directly accessible for reachstackers. While a reachstacker may have a dead weight of up to 100 metric tons, its lifting capacity—which may be up to 50 metric tons—depends on the outlay of the telescopic beam. Secondly, more freedom of manoeuvring with laden containers is provided by reachstackers, which allows for a more accurate container positioning. Thirdly, due to the absence of a mast, reachstackers have a better forward visibility for the driver than forklifts. Fourthly, due to the absence of a mast and the low vehicle height, reachstackers can drive into warehouses more easily (Mizunuma et al. 2005; Mietschnig 2005; Brinkmann 2011).

The most common storage equipment for larger seaport container terminals is shown in Fig. 2.7c—the yard crane. This type of storage equipment is on the one hand involved with high investments, but on the other hand high-density storage along with good productivities are provided by it. Comparable to QCs, yard cranes mainly consist of portal, trolley and spreader, which allow for easy access to each pile of a yard block (Vis and de Koster 2003). Rail cranes that are deployed for loading and discharging of trains at the rail station of a terminal are very similar. The main difference is that no yard block is located within the portal, but rail tracks (Boysen and Fliedner 2010). Several variants of yard cranes—that differ in technical and logistical attributes—are in operation at international container terminals: The portal of a yard crane can either move on rubber tyres or on rails over an entire yard block and horizontal-transport vehicles are either loaded and discharged in parallel to the yard block or at its fronts. In addition, the degree of automation, the yard-block dimensions and the number of deployed yard cranes per yard block may vary considerably. Depending on the technical specifications of a yard crane, the investment costs may be up to 2,000,000€ per crane (Saanen 2006). In Chap. 3, the logistical operations and the technical attributes of these yard-crane variants are explained, discussed and assessed in detail.

2.3 Assessment of Container Terminals

Several hundreds of seaport container terminals are in operation around the world, which differ greatly in framework conditions, appearance and performance (Watanabe 2001; Saanen 2004, pp. 34–36). Therefore, in order to allow for a substantiated and objectifiable evaluation and comparison of container terminals, dozens of indices and ratios are developed to classify and to evaluate the design and the performance of different container terminals. In this section, the most frequently used indices and ratios for the categorisation and evaluation of seaport container terminals are introduced. Firstly, the most common design indicators for classifying different types of seaport container terminals are presented. Thereafter, commonly used performance indicators for evaluating the service level and the efficiency of different container terminals are introduced.

2.3.1 Design Indicators

Container terminals can be classified by two closely linked types of indicators. Firstly, design-influencing factors greatly affect the resulting design of a container terminal in terms of equipment choice and capacities. Secondly, resulting design indicators give useful information on the main design characteristics of a container terminal and mainly depend on the design-influencing factors. The size of the QCs—as a resulting design indicator—is for example determined by the size of the calling vessels, which belongs to design-influencing factors.

The three main design indicators of container terminals are the annual terminal throughput π^{through}, the annual container-handling capacity and the storage capacity π^{sc}. The annual terminal throughput π^{through} is expressed as the number of containers that are loaded and discharged to/from sea-going vessels per year. This number is mainly determined by the location of the terminal and local economic conditions. In contrast to the terminal throughput, the annual container-handling capacity does not only take into account the realised QC moves, but also the theoretical container-handling capacity, which is expressed as TEUs per year, of the container terminal as a whole is indicated by this number. It is determined by the limiting factor of quay length, waterside-handling capacity, storage capacity, landside-handling capacity, hinterland-connection capacity and available handling equipment. Another important design indicator is the storage capacity π^{sc} of a terminal which is usually measured in TEUs and computed as the product of the number of TEU groundslots and the number of container-stacking tiers in the storage yard (Saanen 2004, pp. 36–40).

Design-influencing factors are the transshipment factor, the mean container-dwell time, the TEU-factor and various others. The transshipment factor π^{ts} gives the fraction of the annual terminal throughput $\pi^{through}$ that is induced by containers that both arrive and depart by sea-going vessels. As explained in Sect. 2.1.3, different types of container terminals can be distinguished on basis of the transshipment factor. While terminals with very high transshipment factors are simply called transshipment terminals, facilities with rather small fractions of transshipment containers are termed import-export terminals. For the performance of transshipment terminals, the waterside operations, including the ship-to-shore subsystem and the waterside horizontal-transport subsystem, are of major importance, whereas the hinterland-connection subsystem with its truck and train-handling facilities is more important for import-export terminals. The storage subsystem is of great importance for both terminal types, but the waterside interface of the storage subsystem is more important for transshipment terminals, as the imbalance between waterside and landside usage of storage equipment is continuously increasing with the transshipment factor. As a rule of thumb, terminals with values of $\pi^{ts} \geq 66\%$ are mostly termed as transshipment terminals, while terminals with smaller fractions of transshipment containers are usually classified as import-export terminals (Watanabe 2001; Saanen 2004, pp. 38–39).

The mean container-dwell time $\overline{\delta}$, which is discussed along with the storage function of the terminal in Sect. 2.2.1, is measured as the number of days that containers stay on average in the container-storage yard of the terminal. Usually, most containers stay a rather short period of time on the terminal—often only 1 or 2 days—while much fewer containers stay notably longer, sometimes even up to several weeks. Average dwell-time figures of container terminals usually depend on their transshipment factors. While the average dwell time of transshipment terminals is around 3–5 days, the average dwell time for import-export terminals may vary between 5–15 days (Saanen 2004, pp. 42–43). The relation between 20′ and 40′ containers is specified by the TEU-factor π^{teu}, which is usually given as the fraction of 40′ containers plus one. For example, a typical value of $\pi^{teu} = 1.5$ indicates that an average container is of the size of one and a half TEU, which means that half of the handled containers are 20′ and the other half 40′ long.

Further site-specific design-influencing factors of container terminals are draught restrictions, soil conditions, the shape of the land (width and depth) and the user-type of the terminal (dedicated or multi-user) (Saanen 2004, pp. 34–40). Firstly, the maximum vessel size in terms of loaded draft that can be served at a terminal is limited by the available draught in the port and in the access course. Secondly, the load-bearing capacity of a terminal area and along with it the stacking height and the applicable equipment types and dimensions are greatly affected by the soil conditions of the terminal. Thirdly, the used stacking and horizontal-transport equipment as well as the yard layout in terms of width, length and height are to a large extent defined by the given shape of the terminal area. Finally, several design-influencing factors like the size of the calling vessels and the transshipment factor might be influenced by the user-type of the terminal (Saanen 2004, pp. 18–21). While dedicated terminals often are subsidiaries of shipping lines and are mainly used by these shipping lines and their allied partners, multi-user terminals are usually called by vessels of several different shipping lines and/or alliances (i.e., they have multiple users) (Biebig et al. 2008, p. 228).

The storage capacity π^{scmin} that is required in order to comply with the annual terminal throughput greatly depends on the aforementioned design-influencing factors. It may be computed by

$$\pi^{\text{scmin}} = \pi^{\text{through}} \times \left(1 - \frac{\pi^{\text{ts}}}{2}\right) \times \pi^{\text{teu}} \times \frac{\bar{\delta}}{365} \times \pi^{\text{peak}}, \tag{2.1}$$

which is the product of the average storage-capacity requirements and the storage-peak factor π^{peak} (Saanen 2004, pp. 36–37). Multiplying the throughput with the mathematical term in the brackets yields the number of total stack visits per year in terms of containers. This value is usually smaller than the throughput, as each transshipment container leads to only one stack visit but two QC moves. For reasons of simplification, only import, export and transshipment container flows are considered in (2.1), whereas land-land container flows are neglected, due to being of minor importance (see Sect. 2.1.3). Multiplication with the TEU-factor yields the number of stack visits per year in terms of TEU. This number is then multiplied with the fraction of a year that containers stay on average in the yard, which yields the average storage-capacity requirements. However, for several reasons the occupancy rate of the storage capacities is not a constant value. Moreover, it is subject to terminal-dependent variations, which have to be taken into account for the storage-yard design as otherwise bottlenecks of the storage capacity will be the result from time to time. Therefore, the storage-yard design should be based on the maximum storage-capacity requirements and not the average requirements. Hence, the average storage-capacity requirements have to be multiplied by the storage-peak factor π^{peak}. First of all, hourly variations of the occupancy rate occur because usually the vessel-loading operations do not start before the discharging operations have (nearly) been finished. In addition, daily variations may be induced by the vessel-call pattern of the terminal and seasonal variations are dependent on the transshipped goods. Altogether, the greater the variations of the occupancy rate of the storage yard, the more storage capacities have to be available in order to cope with the annual terminal throughput.

2.3.2 *Performance Indicators*

Seaport container terminals are simultaneously faced with several restrictions and demands of their different stakeholders: Workers want security of employment, residents demand low noise and exhaust emissions, authorities require the compliance with laws, truckers are interested in short processing times and shipping lines require short, flexible and reliable turn-around times for vessels as well as low rates for loading, discharging and storage of containers. But, the final decision makers are the owners (shareholders) which are generally interested in a high shareholder value (Copeland et al. 2003, pp. 20–21). As a consequence, there are many different types of indicators for measuring the performance of seaport container terminals, of which the most common are subsequently presented. Firstly, several service-level indicators are introduced, which are related to the demands of the customers of container terminals. Thereafter, terminal and equipment-efficiency indicators are presented, which can be used to evaluate the efficiency of the whole terminal facility and the efficiencies of different types of terminal equipment. Finally, cost-efficiency indicators are discussed, which allow for cost-based comparisons of different container terminals.

2.3.2.1 Service-Level Indicators

Service-level indicators provide figures about the demands of terminal customers and the degree of fulfilment of these demands. Therefore, these indicators are of great importance for the terminal customers which include shipping lines, truckers and rail operators. Six different service-level indicators are mentioned by Saanen (2004, pp. 40–41): the maximum vessel size, the vessel-berthing time, the landside-service time, the degree of flexibility, the handling charge and the storage charge.

Along with the steadily increasing vessel size, the draught, width and height of the vessels are increasing as well. Therefore, the maximum vessel size that can call at a terminal is defined by the available draught at the quay wall and on the waterway to the terminal as well as by the size and outreach of the used QCs (see Sect. 2.1.1). For shipping lines, the capability to handle a vessel is an essential foundation for calling a certain terminal on their routes.

The time vessels stay in port is of great importance for shipping lines—in particular for deep-sea vessels—since these high investments only earn money when shipping containers at sea. Therefore, shipping lines prefer rather short vessel-berthing times, which are usually contractually defined in terms of guaranteed time windows for vessel service upon arrival (e.g., 24 h). An excess of the defined time window may result in a costly disturbance of the sail scheme of the vessel, which is usually the basis for the contractually defined time window. Altogether, the vessel-berthing times are often regarded as the most important service-level indicators of container terminals (e.g., Ng 2005; Sciomachen and Tanfani 2007; Böse 2011).

As for the shipping lines the vessel-berthing time is of great importance, the landside customers greatly focus on the service times of their equipment. The truckers and rail operators desire short service times for delivery and pick-up of containers in order to perform more transport jobs within the same period of time. In addition, the rail transport may be dependent on certain time windows for some rail routes. Thus, late train departures from the rail station of the terminal may induce even further delays for the trains due to blocking of certain rail routes. However, terminal operators usually regard shipping lines to be the more important group of customers than landside customers (Nazari 2005, p. 25).

The shipping lines are forced to demand more and more flexibility from the container terminals due to the ever-increasing trend towards JIT processes on the part of its customers (Siepermann and Krieger 2005). In this context, flexibility means that the shipping lines want to be allowed to make changes in the load plans of the vessels as late as possible and that even containers that arrive on the landside after loading has started are processed. Although more flexibility may be involved with longer vessel-berthing times or reduced equipment efficiency, the importance of flexibility is continuously increasing (Steenken et al. 2004).

Usually, container terminals yield most revenue by the handling charge that is raised from the shipping lines for each container handled by the QCs. Therefore, the handling charge is of major importance for both the business success of the terminal and its attractiveness for shipping lines. Due to different cost structures and different degrees of competition, the handling charges may vary widely between different regions. In addition, the handling charges may even vary considerably between different shipping lines, as they are based on individual contracts.

Besides the handling charge that is raised for the transshipment function of a terminal, an additional charge is usually raised per storage day of a container for its storage function. These storage-day charges and the underlying pricing system differ considerably among international container terminals because of regional differences in scarcity of land and terminal competition. For example, some terminals raise constant charges for all storage days, while the first couple of days may be free of charge at other terminals. However, the less yard space is available, the more terminal operators tend to increase the storage-day charges in order to keep the container-dwell times low.

2.3.2.2 Terminal-Efficiency Indicators

As a container terminal is a rather complex system (see Sect. 2.2.2), it is hardly possible to evaluate the performance and the efficiency of a whole container-terminal facility by a single figure. Referring to Saanen (2004, pp. 42–48), five different terminal-efficiency indicators can be distinguished: the standardised quay-wall-handling capacity, the standardised storage-handling capacity, the storage-yard fraction, the yard density and the accessibility of containers. While the first two indicators may be used to assess the transshipment function of terminals, the latter three indicators may be involved with the evaluation of its storage function.

The standardised quay-wall-handling capacity gives the theoretical annual handling capacity of a container terminal (see Sect. 2.3.1) for a standardised length of the quay wall. It is measured as annual TEU per quay wall metre and calculated by dividing the annual handling capacity of a terminal by the length of its quay wall. But the required length of the quay wall can usually not be influenced by terminal operations, moreover it is just determined by the size of the calling vessels and the vessel-call pattern of the terminal. Hence, typical figures of the standardised quay-wall-handling capacity vary greatly between 150 and 2,000 yearly TEUs/m. While high values may be the result of a balanced quay-wall occupation, an uneven distribution of vessel arrivals yields lower values of the standardised quay-wall-handling capacity.

The standardised storage-handling capacity is comparable to the former indicator, as it gives again the theoretical annual handling capacity of a container terminal, but here for a standardised area of the terminal. It is measured as annual TEU per hectare and yielded by dividing the annual handling capacity of a terminal by the total terminal area. Due to shorter dwell times and lower storage-area requirements of transshipment containers (see Sect. 2.3.1), it may be expected that higher values of the standardised storage-handling capacity are realised by transshipment terminals. As a rule of thumb, the values do not exceed 23,000 and 50,000 yearly TEUs/ha for import-export and transshipment terminals, respectively (Watanabe 2001).

The share of the total terminal area that is used for storage of containers is given by the storage-yard fraction. Terminals are normally seeking to increase this value as far as possible without worsening other indicators in order to increase the storage capacity of the terminal, which may enable higher annual terminal throughputs. For example, the horizontal-transport area may be reduced, but possibly negative consequences for terminal operations due to traffic congestions have to be considered. Typical values of the storage-yard fraction are in the range from 0.5–0.7 to 0.6–0.8 for terminals with and without a CFS, respectively (Watanabe 2001).

The quality of the stacking operations and storage-area utilisation is indicated by the yard density, which gives the number of TEU per hectare of the container-storage yard. It is computed by dividing the on average used storage capacity π^{sc} (see Sect. 2.3.1) by the number of hectares that are used for storage of containers. In practice, the values differ greatly for different storage equipment, which is illustrated in Fig. 2.8. While storing containers on chassis yields only 250 TEUs per hectare, a storage density of up to 1,100 TEUs per hectare may be realised by usage of yard cranes (Kalmar 2011a).

Finally, the accessibility of containers in the storage yard is defined by the average number of shuffle moves required to make a certain container available to take it out of the stack to the the horizontal transport. This indicator is of great importance for the annual handling capacity of a container terminal, because a better accessibility and fewer shuffle moves are involved with a higher productivity of the terminal equipment (see Sect. 2.3.2.3). Storing containers on chassis or stacking just one tier high yield the best possible accessibility, as each container is directly retrievable. In contrast, a rather bad accessibility is usually yielded by

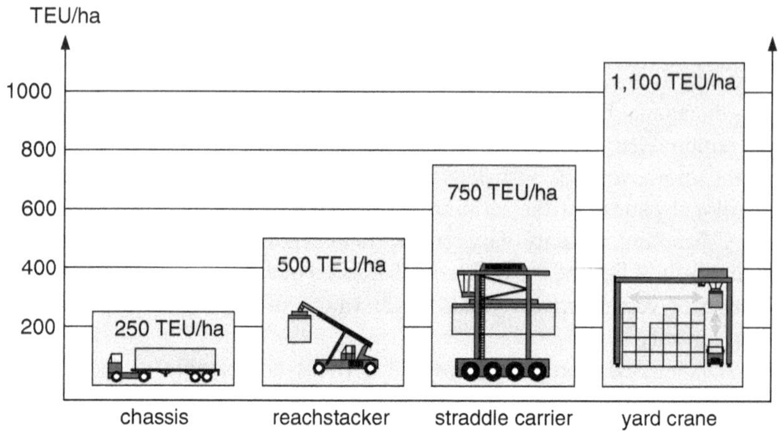

Fig. 2.8 Storage-equipment-dependent yard density (based on Kalmar 2011a)

stacking several TEU high, as not each container might be directly accessible. The accessibility is determined by the stacking height in the storage yard and the knowledge of the sequence in which containers are retrieved from the stacks. On the one hand, a reduction of the stacking height would improve the accessibility, while on the other hand the yard density would decrease, which means, there is a trade-off between both indicators (De Castilho and Daganzo 1993; Kim et al. 2008). Knowledge about the container-retrieval sequence at the waterside interface of the container-storage yard depends on the quality of the available information about the stowage plans. In case the stowage plans are timely available and reliable, the containers may be stacked in the order they are needed at the QCs such that shuffle moves are reduced. However, in real life this assumption will often not hold, as shipping lines demand more flexibility of the terminals concerning the stowage plans (see Sect. 2.3.2.1).

2.3.2.3 Equipment-Efficiency Indicators

The efficient usage of all kinds of terminal equipment is indicated by the corresponding equipment productivity, which is usually given as the number of containers that are handled by the relevant equipment per hour. The equipment productivity can be measured for each type of terminal equipment, like QCs, SCs, TTUs, AGVs, reachstackers, yard cranes and rail cranes. In practice, typical productivity figures vary greatly with the regarded type of terminal equipment as well as with the specific kind of productivity measure. In fact, the following four different kinds of equipment-productivity measures can be distinguished: technical productivity, operational productivity, net productivity and gross productivity (Saanen 2004, pp. 44–47).

The technical equipment productivity is defined as the theoretically maximum possible number of handled containers per hour. All kind of disturbances like interferences with other equipment, stochastics of manual operations and further external influences are neglected. Moreover, the technical productivity is only based on 100% reliable technical figures like driving distances, accelerations and velocities. In contrast, the operational and net productivities of terminal equipment take into account delays due to drivers and other external influences (e.g., weather conditions). But while the operational productivity assumes at least ideal circumstances for all other terminal equipment, such that no delays due to interferences or waiting times with other equipment occur, these disturbances are explicitly considered by the net productivity. Finally, the gross productivity is measured over longer periods of time (e.g., day, vessel-operation time).Therefore, additional disturbances of the equipment operations like meal breaks, shift changes and machine breakdowns are grasped as well. These disturbances, which are not inherent to regular operations, are not observed by the former three productivity measures. Altogether, the relation between these four productivity measures is described by:

$$\text{technical} > \text{operational} > \text{net} > \text{gross}. \tag{2.2}$$

In practice, terminal operators are mostly seeking for improvements of net or gross productivities, as the operational reality is best represented by these figures. Vessel-berthing times and decisions on the number of required equipment are determined by these productivities and changes in technical as well as operational productivities will be reflected by the net and gross productivities as well. As a consequence, most productivities are given as net or gross values.

The probably most popular equipment productivity measure is the GCR (gross crane rate), which gives the gross productivity of QCs (Petering et al. 2009; Goussiatiner 2009). It is defined as the average number of containers that are loaded and discharged by a single crane per allocated crane hour, which is consistent with the general definition of gross productivities, as not any kind of disturbances during QC operations is excluded from the allocated crane time (Goussiatiner 2009). The GCR is often regarded as the most important performance indicator of seaport container terminals for both the shipping lines and the terminal operators themselves (Goussiatiner 2009). Firstly, due to its inverse relation with the vessel-berthing time, the GCR directly affects the turn-around times of vessels, which is of particular importance for shipping lines (see Sect. 2.3.2.1). Secondly, terminal operators may use the GCR as a benchmark on the efficiency of the overall terminal operations, since most terminal operation either originate from or terminate at the QCs. Therefore, the GCR is either directly or indirectly affected by efficiency changes of other terminal equipment (e.g., yard cranes or AGVs). As a consequence, the GCR depends on numerous factors, like for example crane speed, lifting capacity, spreader type, wind conditions, driver skills, delays in horizontal transport, delays in storage-yard operations and various others. A detailed discussion of these factors influencing the GCR is given by Goussiatiner (2009).

Two less popular efficiency indicators for QCs are the QC-throughput index and the QC-density index. Usually, the QC-throughput index is used as a rule-of-thumb-based indicator on the appropriateness of the number of deployed QCs in relation to the throughput of the terminal. It is computed by dividing the annual terminal throughput π^{through} by the number of deployed QCs. Nowadays, the latest QC technologies allow for reasonable values of the QC-throughput index in the region of 100,000 containers per QC. However, substantially lower values may indicate rather inefficient terminal operations, whereas higher values may indicate the possibility to increase the annual terminal throughput by deploying additional QCs (Saanen 2004, p. 45).

The average length of a QC operation zone is represented by the QC-density index, which is computed by dividing the length of the quay wall that is equipped with rails by the number of QCs. Typical values of this index are greater than 100 m per QC, only some Asian terminals have smaller QC densities. Furthermore, usually higher values are observed for import-export terminals than for transshipment terminals. Comparatively high values of this index may indicate (cost-) inefficient operations due to an oversized quay wall and longer driving times of horizontal-transport machines. Whereas comparatively low values may indicate inefficient operations due to heavy congestions of horizontal-transport machines at the QCs (Saanen 2004, p. 47).

2.3.2.4 Cost-Efficiency Indicators

Finally, terminal operators do not seek for improvements of terminal and equipment efficiency for reasons of self purpose. Moreover, at least privately owned container terminals are generally striving for high long term profits, since, like for most companies, the overall business objective is the maximisation of the shareholder value. Therefore, terminal operators strive for increases of the annual terminal throughput and the profit margin per handled container. While the profit margin is directly determined by the expenses of the terminal, also the terminal throughput is indirectly affected by the terminal costs, since the possibility for handling-charge reductions in order to attract additional throughput without worsening the profit margin is greatly dependent on the cost situation of a terminal. As a consequence, the costs of seaport container terminals are of major importance for their competitiveness and the resulting shareholder value (Copeland et al. 2003, pp. 22–23).

Cost-efficiency indicators allow a comparison and assessment of the cost situation of a terminal. The most familiar indicator is the container-cost index, which indicates the average costs that are involved with the handling of a single container. It is computed by dividing the total costs of a terminal per year by its annual throughput π^{through}. However, different cost categories can be distinguished. Thus, different variants of the container-cost index exist as well. First of all, it can be distinguished between the yearly operating and the initial investment costs. The investment costs mainly consist of investments in facilities (e.g., quay walls, pavings, buildings) as well as purchasing costs for terminal equipment (e.g., QCs, SCs, AGVs) and required software products (e.g., TOS—terminal-operating system). Depending on the dimensions and the technical equipment of a container terminal, the investment costs may sum up to several 100 million Euros (Saanen 2004, pp. 48–50).

In form of capital costs for both debt capital and equity, these investment costs may be implicitly taken into account within the operating costs as interest payments and opportunity costs. In addition, the operating costs consist of labour costs, material costs (e.g., spare parts, fuel, energy), service costs (e.g., lashing, maintenance, administration) and lease costs (e.g., land, quay walls). Thereof, the labour costs make up for the biggest part. Of course, due to local wage rates, union power and other historical factors, labour costs vary notably between different ports and countries. Depending on the location of a terminal, the fraction of the labour costs may vary between 35% (East Asia) towards 50% (Northwest Europe) and 65% (US West coast). The labour costs for a Northwest European container terminal vary in the range from 30 to 38 Euro per TEU. As a consequence, a reduction of workforce by automated terminal equipment may offer remarkable savings of labour costs. However, the comparatively high investment costs of these equipment types only pay off for terminals with rather high fractions of labour costs, as otherwise the cost savings are outbalanced by additional capital costs (Saanen 2004, pp. 49–50).

2.4 Classification of Terminal-Planning Problems

In the 1990s, only little attention was given to the area of container logistics by the OR (operations research) community, but due to its societal importance it has gained a lot of attention in the last years (Meersmans 2002, p. 27). Several hundreds of OR articles and other scientific sources are available today that deal with problems of the container logistics sector—in particular with planning problems of seaport container terminals. The most recent comprehensive literature survey on container-terminal logistics is presented by Stahlbock and Voß (2008). Further overviews are provided by Meersmans and Dekker (2001), Vis and de Koster (2003), Steenken et al. (2004), and Günther (2005).

In this section, the most popular terminal-planning problems are introduced and an overview on selected OR models and methods is given in order to clarify the application of OR methodologies in this area. Firstly, a classification of planning and decision problems that arise in the context of seaport container terminals is provided. Secondly, problems and selected methods concerning terminal-design planning are roughly dealt with. Thereafter, the most important operational planning problems are discussed in detail.

2.4.1 Classification of Decision Problems

Numerous planning and decision problems arise in the context of seaport container terminals that differ with respect to the hierarchical level involved and the terminal subsystem affected. Therefore, decision problems are often classified into several groups of planning problems. In Meersmans and Dekker (2001), decisions are classified according to the hierarchical level involved only. It is distinguished between the strategical, tactical, operational and real-time decision level. Decisions on the strategical level deal with the design of container terminals in terms of layout and equipment types. The tactical level concerns decisions on terminal structures that can be implemented within several weeks or months (e.g., numbers of equipment and employees). On the operational level, the daily and hourly available capacities in terms of workforce and equipment are allocated to the actual work. Finally, decisions on the real-time level deal with quite short-termed problems, which have to be decided within a few seconds or minutes (e.g., routing of vehicles).

Another classification scheme for terminal decision problems is proposed by Günther and Kim (2006). In addition to Meersmans and Dekker (2001), the decision problems are not only categorised according to the hierarchical level involved, moreover, the concerned planning object (e.g., AGVs, storage yard, QCs) is also used as a classification criterion. Contrary to Meersmans and Dekker (2001), Günther and Kim (2006) distinguish only three decision levels: the terminal-design level, the operational planning level and the real-time control level. The design level comprises all former strategical decisions as well as parts of the former tactical decisions (e.g., numbers of equipment), while the operative level consists of most of the former tactical decisions. Finally, the real-time level of Günther and Kim (2006) combines the operational and the real-time level of Meersmans and Dekker (2001).

Here, a modified classification scheme is introduced which—comparable to that of Günther and Kim (2006)—categorises decision problems according to the involved hierarchical level as well as the related subsystem of the terminal. The detailed classification scheme is shown in Fig. 2.9. Different from Meersmans and Dekker (2001) and Günther and Kim (2006), only the terminal-design level and the operational planning level are distinguished here for the categorisation according to the hierarchical level of a decision problem. While the terminal-design level is identical to that of Günther and Kim (2006), the operational planning level combines both the former operative and real-time levels. Altogether, each decision problem that is associated with one of the four terminal subsystems (see Sect. 2.2.2) is either categorised to be a terminal-design or operational planning problem.

2.4.2 *Terminal-Design-Planning Problems*

In general, the terminal-design level comprises all kinds of decisions on the layout and the choice of equipment of seaport container terminals (see Fig. 2.9). These decisions are usually made by terminal planners during the initial planning phase of a completely new terminal facility, an expansion of an existing terminal or a conversion of an existing terminal (Böse 2011). Usually, the decisions are made with respect to technical feasibility, economic profitability and operational performance (Günther and Kim 2006). The decisions on type and number of terminal equipment as well as terminal layout usually involve investments of several million Euros, which cannot be changed easily within short time horizons of only several months.

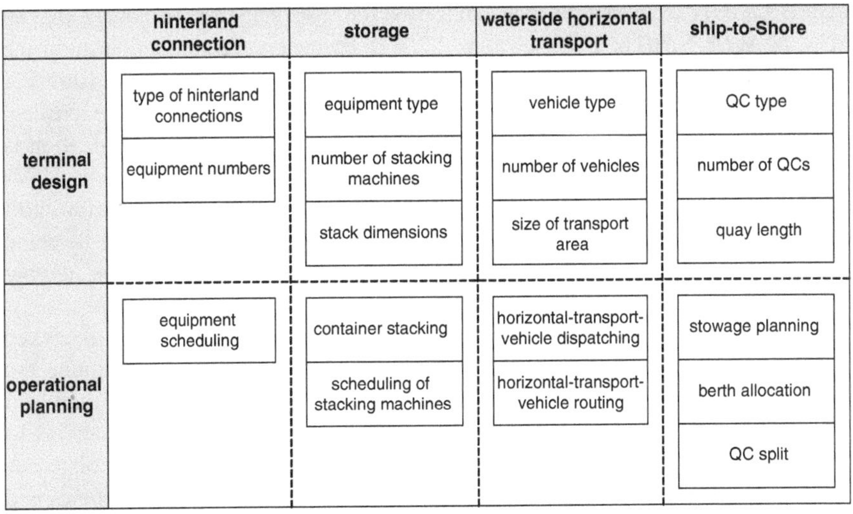

Fig. 2.9 Classification of decision problems

In general, building up new terminals (including civil and structural engineering) may take some years and only pays off after 10–15 years of operating time. Once the civil engineering of a terminal is completed, decisions on both the equipment types and the logistical terminal operations are usually more or less fixed for the next decades. Due to long-winded delivery times, even the numbers of certain terminal equipment cannot be changed within a few months. Altogether, the effects of the decisions that belong to the design level are characterised by rather long-ranging validity and huge investments.

For the ship-to-shore subsystem, mainly three decisions have to be made on the terminal-design level: the QC type, the number of required QCs and the length of the quay wall have to be determined (Böse 2011). The decision on the QC type consists of some detailed questions concerning the outreach and the clearance of the planned QCs as well as their trolley (i.e., single or double) and spreader technologies (i.e., single, twin or tandem) (see Sect. 2.2.3.1). In order to save costs, terminal operators initially try to minimise the length of the quay wall and the number of QCs in such a way that the planned annual terminal throughput or certain performance indicators (see Sect. 2.3.2) can just be met with respect to some external input (e.g., vessel-call pattern). For that purpose, a mathematical optimisation model is proposed by Meisel and Bierwirth (2011) to determine the optimal number of QCs with respect to cost and performance aspects for a terminal with given length of the quay wall, while Hartmann et al. (2011) present a simulation model to verify both the planned length of the quay wall and the planned number of QCs.

For the waterside horizontal-transport subsystem, the design level comprises decisions on the vehicle type that should be used for horizontal transport, the required number of these vehicles and the dimension of the corresponding driving area (Böse 2011). The vehicle type that is used for horizontal transport may either be AGV, ALV, MTS, SC or TTU (see Sect. 2.2.3.2). By means of a simulation study, the usage of AGVs, TTUs and ALVs is evaluated by Duinkerken et al. (2006) in terms of cost and performance indicators for a realistic scenario of the Maasvlakte terminal in Rotterdam (Netherlands). Another simulation-based performance evaluation is presented by Yang et al. (2004), who compare the alternative deployment of AGVs and ALVs. One interesting finding is that savings in the number of required transport vehicles can be realised by the usage of ALVs instead of AGVs. Due to being interested in cost savings, terminal operators usually try to minimise the number of transport vehicles with respect to the desired annual container-handling capacity. While a system to determine the necessary number of SCs is provided by Steenken (1992), Vis et al. (2001) present a polynomial-time algorithm to determine the number of AGVs required at a semi-automated container terminal. Finally, in order to optimise the storage-yard fraction, terminal operators are often seeking to minimise the dimensions of the driving area with respect to certain safety distances between passing vehicles and required manoeuvring space at the quay cranes and in the storage yard. In order to do so, Ranau (2011) presents a planning approach for the optimal dimensioning of the driving area for automated horizontal-transport systems and compares the space requirements of AGVs and ALVs.

Comparable to the horizontal-transport subsystem, the following decisions have to be made on the design level of the storage subsystem: the equipment type that should be used in the storage yard, the required number of these machines and the layout of the storage yard (Böse 2011). Mainly four types of storage equipment can be distinguished, namely SCs, yard cranes, forklifts and reachstackers (see Sect. 2.2.3.3), whereof only the first two types are commonly used at bigger seaport container terminals. In addition, several technically and logistically different variants of yard cranes are available that are explained in detail in Chap. 3. Both the decisions about the required number of storage machines as well as the decision about the layout of the storage yard heavily depend on the selected equipment type. However, in order to yield good results in terms of cost and performance indicators, terminal planners usually try to minimise the number of storage machines and the storage area with respect to the storage capacity π^{scmin} that is required to achieve the intended container-handling capacity. The decision on the layout of the storage yard does not only concern its space requirements, moreover also the arrangement of yard blocks as well as the length, width and stacking height of these blocks have to be determined.

Numerous authors have investigated the design-planning problem of the storage subsystem at seaport container terminals—in particular for different kinds of yard-crane systems. A comprehensive overview on this literature is provided in Chap. 4 of this work, where the selection of stacking equipment and the layout planning of the container-storage yard are addressed in great detail for a special type of gantry-crane system: the RMGC system.

Finally, on the design level of the hinterland-connection subsystem it has to be decided on the required types of hinterland connections and the equipment of the corresponding facilities (Böse 2011). While no hinterland connection is required for pure transshipment terminals, for all other terminals a hinterland connection for XTs, trains and/or barges has to be implemented. For all types of hinterland connections, it has to be decided on the type and number of equipment that should be used for loading and discharging of the corresponding modes of transportation. In addition, the gate capacities have to be defined for the hinterland connection by XT and the number and length of rail tracks on the rail station need to be defined for the hinterland connection by train.

2.4.3 Operational Terminal-Planning Problems

In this subsection, an overview on some of the most popular operational planning problems of seaport container terminals is given. Decisions on the sequences in which transport tasks are executed by the horizontal-transport equipment may, for instance, lead to an improvement of the gross productivity of these machines (see Sect. 2.3.2.3), which then allows for reduction of the number of transport vehicles needed and, along with it, a reduction of the container-cost index (see Sect. 2.3.2.4). Therefore, the performance of seaport container terminals and several decisions on the terminal-design level are greatly influenced by these operational planning decisions.

Because of its relevance to most operational terminal-planning problems, there is a need to discuss the special planning situation of online optimisation which is characterised by uncertain and incomplete planning information. This is carried out in the first subsection. Thereafter, the problems as well as related models and methods are presented for decisions on stowage planning, berth allocation, QC split, horizontal-transport-vehicle dispatching, horizontal-transport-vehicle routing, container stacking and scheduling of stacking machines.

2.4.3.1 Online Optimisation

In classical optimisation, which is here referred to as offline optimisation, it is assumed that all input data of an instance is known before the application of solution methods. But since in many applications decisions have to be made based on incomplete or uncertain information, this assumption is not realistic. In fact, it may be necessary to decide on a part of the total problem while new data of the problem still arrive. Such planning situations are termed online. An algorithm runs online if decisions are made whenever a new piece of data demands an action (Ascheuer et al. 1998). In addition, real-world applications often require decisions to be made within very tight time frames, which means that the problems have to be solved in real-time. Introductions and overviews to the field of online optimisation are given, for instance, by Ascheuer et al. (1998), Fiat and Woeginger (1998) as well as Grötschel et al. (2001).

Obviously, the solution quality of online algorithms cannot be expected to be as good as that of omniscient offline algorithms. Since the online algorithm has to compute the pieces of solutions before the complete problem set is known, some pieces of the solution computed will turn out to be suboptimal after the complete set of data is available. Applying an offline algorithm to the same data set after all information is available, will therefore lead to an optimal decision which cannot be worse than the online solution. But since this is not possible for online situations, special online algorithms have to be applied. Independently of the precise planning problem, the following concepts can be distinguished for the general design of online algorithms (Grötschel et al. 2001):

FIFO: The FIFO (first-in-first-out) strategy strictly serves requests in order of appearance. Efficiency issues are not regarded.

Greedy: A greedy algorithm serves that request next which leads to least cost with respect to the current system state and the corresponding objective (i.e., the algorithm acts greedily).

Replan: A replan algorithm computes an (near) optimal solution at a specific point in time. Every time some new piece of data is available, a new optimal solution is computed. All schedules made beforehand are replanned.

Ignore: An ignore algorithm computes (near) optimal solutions at a specific point in time, but the schedule made is executed and not replanned. When the current schedule is finished a new one is computed for the new requests which have become available in the meantime.

The concept of online optimisation is of great relevance to the field of container terminals, since most operational planning problems have to be regarded as online situations (Stahlbock and Voß 2010). To a large extent, the daily terminal operations are dependent on external processes like the arrival of ships, trucks and trains. None of them is very predictable. While the planned arrival times of vessels may not be met due to bad weather or delayed departure in the previous port, the arrival times of XTs are even more—almost completely—unpredictable. Besides these external processes, also the internal operations give raise to some degree of uncertainty. While the driving times and, along with them, the performance of QCs, SCs and other manual terminal equipment are somehow uncertain due to the drivers' skills, the operations of automated equipment may be disturbed by machine breakdowns. Furthermore, some dynamic events like queues at the QCs or yard cranes as well as traffic jams of the horizontal-transport machines cannot be completely predicted, as container terminals are complex facilities with several types and numbers of equipment in several dozens of possible states that can be located in a large number of yard locations (Saanen 2011). Altogether, decisions made far in advance of the actual operation may turn out to be sub-optimal by the time that decision is realised, because the planning situations of most operative problems are continuously changing due to imperfect and uncertain data. Therefore, most operational terminal-planning problems are amenable to online optimisation methods.

2.4.3.2 Stowage Planning

In former times, stowage plans (see Sect. 2.2.2.2) were created by the captain of the relevant vessel (Sciomachen and Tanfani 2007), but nowadays the creation of stowage plans is a two-step process. Firstly, a rough stowage plan is created by the shipping line that considers stowage positions on the vessel for all containers that are loaded and discharged during the journey of a vessel. But the containers that are planned at this process step are no precisely specified containers that can be identified by an ID. Moreover, containers are only assigned to positions according to their attributes in terms of type (e.g., standard dry, reefer), size (20′, 40′), weight and PoD (port of destination). Thus, containers having exactly the same attributes (i.e., they belong to the same category) are still exchangeable in the stowage plan at this process step. Usually, the stowage plans of shipping lines are created with the objectives to minimise the number of required QC-shuffle moves in the ports along the route of a vessel and to maximise the utilisation of the vessels, with respect to some constraints on the stability of the vessel (Steenken et al. 2004).

Secondly, based on the rough stowage plan of the shipping line, that only assigns container categories to stowage positions on the vessel, the ship planners of the container terminal create a more precise stowage plan with specific containers that can be identified by unique IDs. All attributes of a container that has to be loaded onto the vessel have to match exactly the category of the assigned stowage position on the vessel. Usually, the objective of the ship planners is the minimisation of the number of required shuffle moves in the container-storage yard, that is induced by the stowage plan due to planning a container to be loaded onto the vessel prior to another container that is stored on top of the firstly needed container (Steenken et al. 2004).

Although stowage plans are usually created offline by the ship planners (i.e., before the actual loading process of a relevant vessel has started), the underlying planning situation of vessel-loading operations is best suited for online optimisation due to several reasons (Steenken et al. 2004). However, if online stowage planning is applied by the ship planners, no specific container will be assigned to a position on the vessel in advance of the loading process. Instead, a container in the storage yard is selected that matches the required attributes and that seems to be most appropriate in terms of required shuffle moves and estimated arrival time at the relevant QC only shortly before a container of a certain category has to be loaded onto the vessel. As a consequence, a precise stowage plan is created successively and simultaneously with the actual vessel-loading process (Dekker et al. 2006).

The stowage-planning problem has been widely studied in the OR literature. Wilson and Roach (1999) as well as Wilson et al. (2001) split up a special type of the stowage-planning problem that is denoted as MBPP (master bay-plan problem) into a strategical and a tactical level. They apply local-search algorithms and techniques based on combinatorial optimisation. A similar three-phase algorithm is presented by Ambrosino et al. (2006). Sciomachen and Tanfani (2003) as well as Sciomachen and Tanfani (2007) utilise the relation between the 3D-BPP (three-dimensional bin-packing problem) and the MBPP. While Sciomachen and Tanfani (2003) aim at the minimisation of the vessel-loading time, Sciomachen and Tanfani (2007) try to maximise the net productivity of the QCs by means of a heuristic.

2.4.3.3 Berth Allocation

At large international container terminals several dozens of vessels arrive per week that all have to moor at the quay wall of the terminal. The berthing capacity is limited by the length of the quay wall. The berth-allocation problem is to assign all vessels to certain sections of the quay wall taking into account the corresponding vessel lengths and service times such that there is no overlap in the assigned sections at any point in time. The berth-allocation problem can either be treated as a discrete or continuous case. In the discrete case, only a finite number of berthing places is available (e.g., berth 1: 0–250 m; berth 2: 250–550 m, ...), whereas, in the continuous case, a vessel can berth anywhere along the quay (e.g., between 200 and 450 m). While the arrivals of deep-sea vessels are usually known several months in advance, which allows for a far-sighted planning of the berth allocation, the arrivals of feeder vessels are only known shortly before the actual arrival at the quay (Steenken et al. 2004).

In general, the decisions on the berth allocation are mainly made with the objectives to minimise the anchoring time of the vessels before berthing at the quay is possible and to maximise the equipment productivity of the terminal. It is often tried to facilitate the latter objective by assigning berthing places relatively close to the yard area where most containers are stacked that are planned for loading onto the relevant vessel. Thus, driving times for the horizontal-transport equipment are reduced, equipment productivity is improved and the vessel-berthing time may be reduced as well (Meersmans and Dekker 2001). But decisions on the berth allocation have to take into account the technical requirements of vessels and the technical restrictions of the berthing places. Usually, not all vessels can be served at each berthing place due to limited outreach or clearance of the corresponding QCs or insufficient draught at the berthing place (Steenken et al. 2004). In addition, the number of available QCs for the berthing places should be considered for the decisions about the berth allocation, as the vessel-berthing time—and along with it the time the berth becomes available for the next vessel—is directly affected by the number of deployed QCs.

Many authors have studied the berth-allocation problem. Wang and Lim (2007) transform the berth-allocation problem into a multiple-stage decision-making procedure that is solved by means of a stochastic beam-search algorithm. A performance comparison with an approach from Dai et al. (2008) shows that the proposed algorithm is more accurate and efficient than both the state-of-the-art meta-heuristic and the traditional deterministic beam search. A TS (tabu search) algorithm for the berth-allocation problem with the objective to minimise the vessel-berthing time is presented by Cordeau et al. (2005). Furthermore, a simulation model for evaluating different berth-allocation policies is presented by Henesey et al. (2004).

2.4.3.4 Quay-Crane Split

Subsequent to the berth allocation of arriving vessels, the decisions have to be made which QCs should be used for loading and discharging these individual vessels. But this decision problem, that is termed QC-split problem, does not only comprise the allocation of QCs to vessels, moreover the QCs have to be assigned to individual bays of the vessel (Vis and de Koster 2003). In general, the number of cranes that can be deployed for a certain vessel is restricted by two factors. Firstly, not every crane can be driven to each berthing place, due to being fixed to rails. Secondly, usually terminals are historically grown facilities with QCs of different sizes, of which not all are operable for the largest vessels.

In contrast to other operational planning problems, there is no universal objective for the QC-split problem. Moreover, several situation and terminal-dependent objectives exist, like balancing the QC utilisation, minimising the sum off all delays in relation to the contractually agreed vessel-berthing times for all vessels or minimising the vessel-berthing time for an individual vessel (Steenken et al. 2004). For example, Kim and Park (2004) propose a B&B (branch-and-bound) algorithm and a greedy randomised adaptive-search procedure for the QC-split problem with the objective to minimise the weighted sum of the makespan of a vessel and the total completion time of all QCs. Whereas an early work of Daganzo (1989) provides an MIP model with the objective to minimise the sum of all delays. The assumptions are rather unrealistic (e.g., unlimited length of the quay wall), but the model can be solved exactly for small instances. In addition, Lee et al. (2008) present an MIP model with the objective of minimising the makespan for a single vessel. They propose a GA that produces near optimal solutions of the MIP model.

In addition to the berth allocation and QC split, it has to be decided on the QC mode that defines the sequence in which containers are loaded and discharged by a QC. Mainly four different modes have to be distinguished, as bays can be loaded either horizontally or vertically and it can be started either from the quay or the waterside. Altogether, the exact loading sequence of each individual QC is defined by the decisions on the relevant stowage plan, on the QC split and on the QC mode (Steenken et al. 2004).

2.4.3.5 Horizontal-Transport-Vehicle Dispatching

At international seaport container terminals, several QCs simultaneously load and discharge different vessels with a gross productivity in the range of 22–30 containers per hour (see Sect. 2.2.3.1). As a consequence, some hundreds of containers have to be transported per operating hour by the horizontal-transport vehicles between the quay and the container-storage yard. During the discharging operation of a vessel, the relevant containers have to be transferred from the quay to the storage area and vice versa for the loading operations. The corresponding transport jobs are termed import and export jobs, respectively. Each of these transport jobs has to be performed by one of several dozens horizontal-transport vehicles that are usually in operation at large container terminals. Therefore, decisions have to be made about the vehicle assignment and the sequencing of transport jobs (i.e., which vehicle performs which transport jobs in which sequence). This so-called vehicle-dispatching problem is more or less a combinatorial assignment problem. But in practice not hundreds of jobs have to be allocated simultaneously, moreover, because of the online character of container terminals (see Sect. 2.4.3.1), only some transport jobs that occur in the next few minutes are usually classified as plannable. In fact, changes in the stowage plans and inaccurate estimates of vehicle-driving times lead to frequent changes in the planning data and to a rather short planning horizon that requires frequent replanning (Steenken et al. 2004).

Like for most operational planning problems, the superior objectives of the vehicle-dispatching problem are the minimisation of the vessel-berthing time and the maximisation of the GCR with a given number of terminal equipment. But these objectives cannot be used directly as an objective function for the vehicle-dispatching problem. In fact, different operative objectives may be formulated to achieve the superior goals, such as minimisation of the QC-waiting time due to late arrivals of transport vehicles, minimisation of vehicle-waiting time at the QCs and yard blocks due to early arrivals, minimisation of total empty-driving times of vehicles and minimisation of vehicle congestion due to uneven vehicle distributions among QCs and yard blocks (Briskorn et al. 2006). Of course, the superior objectives may also be facilitated by terminal-design decisions on enhancing the number and the velocities of the vehicles. But as additional costs and congestions are provoked by such measures, operational planning decisions should usually be the first choice of the terminal operators for reaching the superior objectives.

However, the exact configuration of an objective function depends on several factors, like the lifting capability of the selected equipment type, the applied QC-allocation scheme and the deployed transport cycle mode (see Sect. 2.2.2.3). For instance, by using SCs instead of TTUs or AGVs, the horizontal transport may be partly decoupled from the QC and storage operations, which may lead to a higher importance of EDT (empty-driving time) compared to late and early vehicle arrivals. In addition, only little potential for optimisation is available when applying the dedicated allocation scheme and vehicles are operated in the single-cycle mode. The highest potential for optimisation occurs for multi-load vehicles that are operated in a pooled allocation scheme (Steenken et al. 2004).

Numerous authors have investigated the vehicle-dispatching problem—mainly for either SCs or AGVs. Kozan and Preston (1999) as well as Böse et al. (2000) look at the problem of optimising container transfers with SCs by means of GAs. While Böse et al. (2000) aim at minimising late arrivals of SCs at the QCs, the objective of Kozan and Preston (1999) is the minimisation of the vessel-berthing time. In addition, Das and Spasovic (2003) present an assignment algorithm for SCs that is shown to be superior over two alternative methods by means of a simulation study. An extensive overview on research in the design and control of AGV systems, comprising OR methods such as mathematical programming, queueing theory, network models and heuristics, is provided by Vis (2006b). Briskorn et al. (2006) propose an AGV-assignment algorithm that is based on a rough analogy to inventory management. It is shown by means of a simulation study that this formulation is superior to standard earliness-tardiness formulations. Dispatching of multi-load AGVs by means of MIP models and priority rules is dealt with by Grunow et al. (2004a,b). It is shown that performance improvements are yielded by using the multi-load mode.

2.4.3.6 Horizontal-Transport-Vehicle Routing

On a more detailed level, decisions about the exact driving behaviour have to be made for the horizontal-transport vehicles. In detail, for each drive of a horizontal-transport vehicle, a certain path has to be selected towards its destination. In addition, interferences of different transport vehicles should be solved in such a way that collisions and deadlocks are avoided. For instance, at crossings, one vehicle has to be granted the right of way, while the other vehicle has to wait. Further decisions on the driving behaviour concern the locations for space extensive turns and the shunting positions, where vehicles can wait for new transport jobs. Altogether, these decisions may be subsumed under the heading of the horizontal-transport-vehicle-routing problem. However, for manned vehicles like TTUs and SCs, all these decisions are made by the driver on a real-time level. Therefore, no control systems or algorithms are required for these vehicle types. But for automated vehicles like AGVs and ALVs, decision rules and algorithms have to be implemented, which allow for short and collision-free driving times between different locations (Meersmans and Dekker 2001).

Until today, only few authors have published works that are directly devoted to the transport-vehicle-routing problem at container terminals. In contrast to the central AGV control system that is deployed at the ECT Delta Terminal in Rotterdam (Netherlands), Evers and Koppers (1996) propose a distributed control system using a hierarchical system of semaphores, which offers more flexibility and requires less communication to control the AGVs than centralised systems. Stenzel (2008) models the AGV-routing problem as time-expanded graphs and presents different algorithms to solve this problem formulation. Further simulation studies that investigate the routing of horizontal-transport vehicles are conducted by Duinkerken and Ottjes (2000).

2.4.3.7 Container Stacking

Usually, each container that is handled at a seaport container terminal is temporarily stored in the storage yard of the terminal. The container-stacking problem deals with the question where to place containers in the storage yard that arrive at the interfaces of the storage yard or need to be relocated inside the storage yard. As a storage yard is usually subdivided into several blocks, for each container, the stacking problem consists of the choice of the yard block as well as positioning that container within the chosen yard block. A decision about the prospective position of a container in the storage yard is then addressed by the numbers of the block, the bay, the row and the tier (Steenken et al. 2004). The quality of the stacking decisions is in most cases measured in terms of the accessibility of containers in the storage yard (see Sect. 2.3.2). But due to growing container volumes and scarce land resources, it is often decided on the terminal-design level to improve the yard density by increasing the stacking height of the yard blocks, which normally leads to additional shuffle moves. However, the trade-off between the conflicting objectives of maximising the yard density and minimising the number of shuffle moves may be mitigated by stacking approaches which make use of the available information on the future container-retrieval sequence. Altogether, the minimisation of the average number of required shuffle moves for a given yard layout is often regarded as the main objective for the container-stacking problem (Dekker et al. 2006; Kang et al. 2006a,b).

In addition, there does not exist a basic stacking problem, moreover the structure of the container-stacking problem depends on several terminal-specific factors, which are mostly decided on the terminal-design level. Firstly, the stacking problem differs depending on the flow direction of the container, since usually more information on the expected retrieval times are available for containers that are planned to depart by deep-sea vessel than for containers departing by feeder vessel or XT. Secondly, different stacking problems result from different approaches of organising the yard area. While some terminals firstly stack containers in a rough pile and reposition them later to a marshalling area according to the sequence in which they are needed, other terminals stack the containers in different yard zones, that may be reserved for certain vessels or berthing places, without repositioning them later. Thirdly, the stacking problem may also differ depending on the deployed stacking equipment (Steenken et al. 2004).

Numerous authors have investigated different types of the container-stacking problem—mostly for container yards with gantry-crane systems. A comprehensive overview on this literature is for instance provided by Caserta et al. (2011). In Sect. 5.2 of this work, the container-stacking problem for container-storage yards with RMGC systems is addressed in great detail and the literature relevant to that operational terminal-planning problem is summarised.

2.4.3.8 Storage-Machine Scheduling

After the stacking problem has been solved and a storage position has been chosen for a container, it has to be decided which storage machine transports the container to its designated pile and at what time this transport job takes place. These two decisions, which are the machine-assignment and transport-job-sequencing decisions, respectively, are combined to the storage-machine-scheduling problem. Comparable to the stacking problem, a much more detailed description of the scheduling problem for container-storage yards with RMGC systems together with a comprehensive review of the relevant literature are provided in Sect. 5.3, while the scheduling problem for storage machines in general is only briefly introduced in this subsection.

All types of transport jobs have an origin and a destination, which are positions where the corresponding container is picked up and where it is placed by the used storage machine, respectively. Mainly three types of jobs have to be scheduled: storage jobs, retrieval jobs and repositioning jobs. While the origin of a storage job is usually a designated handover area, where containers are forwarded from horizontal-transport equipment to the storage machines, its destination is a position in a yard block that has been determined by solving the stacking problem. Vice versa, the origin of a retrieval job is located in a yard block and its destination is located in a handover area. For repositioning jobs, both origin and destination are located in a yard block.

In a mid-sized container terminal, hundreds of transport jobs have to be scheduled for the storage machines per operating hour. However, comparable to the vehicle-dispatching problem (see Sect. 2.4.3.5) only some transport jobs that occur in the next few minutes are usually classified as plannable, due to the underlying online character of this planning problem. In addition, the scheduling problem may be further reduced by regarding the transport jobs of each yard block as a distinct planning problem. The exact structure of the storage-machine-scheduling problem depends on the deployed type of storage equipment, due to determining where the handover between the storage and horizontal-transport machines takes place. In case SCs are used for the waterside horizontal transport, a handover to other storage machines may not even be necessary, as these are active horizontal-transport machines which can also stack the containers in the yard blocks by themselves (see Sects. 2.2.3.2 and 2.4.3.5).

In the fashion of the vehicle-dispatching problem, the superior objective of the storage-machine-scheduling problem is the minimisation of the vessel-berthing time. However, this objective cannot be directly applied and therefore several objectives are reported for this problem: maximising the equipment productivity, minimising empty-driving and waiting times of the equipment, minimising the makespan and synchronisation with the horizontal-transport system. An extensive overview on these scheduling objectives and a discussion on how they foster the superior terminal objectives is given in Sect. 3.2.

2.5 Concluding Remarks

Container terminals are very special from a material-handling point of view. For several reasons—mainly because of the particular attributes of containers and the applied handling equipment—they cannot be treated as large, open-air variants of classical warehouses (Meersmans and Dekker 2001). In this chapter, an introduction into the field of container logistics is given, in particular, the container terminal and the related planning problems are presented. OR can provide valuable contributions for the solution of these problems. Therefore, the number of OR publications has remarkably increased over the last two decades along with the growing economic importance of the container-logistics sector. Nowadays, several hundred OR papers on container-terminal-related planning problems are available, but still not all planning problems are treated satisfyingly. In addition, new handling equipment and improving information systems continuously lead to modified or even completely new planning problems for seaport container terminals.

By introducing the terminal functions, subsystems and planning problems, it is already indicated in this chapter that the storage yard is of utmost importance for the functionality and the performance of a seaport container terminal as a whole. In the next chapter, the storage yard of seaport container terminals is regarded in more detail—different storage-yard systems are compared and the related processes and performance figures are discussed. Thereby special attention is given to some of the latest developments within the field of storage equipment—namely automated RMGC systems—whose planning problems are not yet completely treated in the OR literature.

Chapter 3
Container-Storage Yard

Within this chapter, one of the subsystems of seaport container terminals is regarded in detail, which is found to be of crucial importance for the functionality of the overall terminal system in the preceding chapter: the container-storage yard. While general storage-yard operations and basic types of storage equipment at seaport container terminals are already briefly introduced in Chap. 2, different types of storage equipment and the resulting yard operations are addressed in great detail in this chapter. In particular, special attention is given to automated RMGC systems, which are one of the latest and most promising trends in the field of storage equipment for seaport container terminals.

In Sect. 3.1, the container-storage yard at seaport container terminals is classified and characterised with respect to its functions and processes. Thereafter, in Sect. 3.2, the relation between the performance of the whole terminal and that of the storage subsystem are discussed in depth. After introducing and comparing different types of commonly used container-storage systems at seaport container terminals in Sect. 3.3, the automated RMGC-based storage system and its variants, processes and planning problems are regarded in somewhat more detail in Sect. 3.4. Finally, some concluding remarks for this chapter are given in Sect. 3.5.

3.1 Classification of the Container-Storage Yard

The container-storage yard is a place in the container-transport chain where containers are temporarily stored. Therefore, the container-storage yard might be regarded as a typical store. However, it is not that obvious what can be termed a typical store, since a store can fulfil several functions and may comprise several different processes, thus defining dozens of different store types. In this section, the store in general along with its functions, types and processes is explained and the container-storage yard is classified and characterised according to these general store definitions.

N. Kemme, *Design and Operation of Automated Container Storage Systems*,
Contributions to Management Science, DOI 10.1007/978-3-7908-2885-6_3,

3.1.1 Storage Functions

In general, the storage of goods can be regarded as planned interruption of the material flow. It is needed where in- and outgoing material flows are not synchronised with regard to time (Schneider 2008). The area and/or room where the storage of goods takes place is the store. It is defined as a node in the logistical system where goods are temporarily stored and where in addition often picking and packing takes place (Krieger 2005b). The storage process comprises the initiation and the execution of a sequence of transport and storage operations with the aim of planned changes of the stored goods in terms of time, quantity and assortment. Based on these definitions, five functions of the storage process are identified by Schneider (2008):

Bridging: All kinds of stores are designed to bridge planned temporal or spatial asynchronicities of certain goods. As a consequence, this task is termed bridging function.

Security: Besides planned asynchronicities also unknown or stochastic asynchronicities can occur, which have to be bridged by the store. This security function is usually fulfilled by certain safety stocks or minimum inventories.

Transformation: The transformation function is concerned with sorting, picking and packing of incoming goods in order to create consumer-specific consignments.

Provisioning: The provisioning function is concerned with providing the good that is demanded by the customer in the right quantity, at the right time, at the right place.

Control: The control of up- and downstream processes in the supply chain of certain goods by the store itself is termed the control function of the storage process.

These functions are more or less performed by each store, in particular the bridging and security functions are crucial for most stores (Schneider 2008). For container-storage yards at seaport container terminals, most of all the bridging and provisioning functions are relevant, while the remaining functions are only of minor importance. The probably most important storage function is the bridging function, which is extensively stressed in the container-terminal literature (Zijderveld 1995, pp. 163–170; Saanen 2004, pp. 27–29) as the direct handover between different means of transportation that arrive at container terminals is almost impossible (see Sect. 2.2.1). Furthermore, the stored goods have to be timely provided for further transportation by XTs and internal horizontal-transport machines, which means that the containers have to be retrieved from the yard block and to be transferred to the relevant handover areas by the used storage equipment. Timely container retrievals are of great importance for the performance of the total terminal system (see Sect. 3.2), therefore the provision function can be regarded as greatly relevant for the container-storage yard. Whereas the control function is only partly fulfilled by the container-storage yard, as up- and downstream processes (e.g., the horizontal transport) may be influenced in their performances (e.g., waiting times for horizontal-transport equipment), but decisions for these processes are usually not directly determined by the container-storage yard.

Similarly, the original security function is also usually not performed by the typical container-storage yard. Of course, stochastic asynchronicities in terms of late XT and vessel arrivals may be buffered by the container-storage yard by means of prolonged dwell times of the relevant containers. In contrast, demand asynchronicities cannot be buffered by safety stocks, as full containers are usually individual objects that cannot be substituted by other ones. The individuality of the storage units is probably one of the most important differences of the container-storage yard to many other stores, where several identical units of each object are stored that can be used equivalently. However, in contrast to typical storage yards for full containers, the security function may be more relevant for empty-container depots, where containers of the same size and type are usually regarded as replaceable. Therefore, safety stocks can be applied to fulfil the security function within empty-container depots. Finally, the transformation function is also not performed by the container-storage yard, as usually no sorting, picking and packing takes place in the regular storage area. These activities may take place in a CFS as a part of the terminal's added services (see Sect. 2.2.1) or somewhere in the hinterland of the terminal.

3.1.2 Types of Stores

Several thousand stores exist around the world. Most of them differ from each other—at least in certain aspects. As a consequence, stores can be classified into many categories on the basis of several aspects. In total, eight aspects are identified by Schneider (2008) that facilitate the classification of different types of stores:

- Position of the store in the logistical system (e.g., procurement store),
- Status of the stored goods in terms of the manufacturing process (e.g., raw material store),
- Material of the stored goods (e.g., steel store, oil store),
- Type of the stored goods (e.g., piece goods store, dry bulk store),
- Degree of centralisation (e.g., central store, decentralised store),
- Construction type (e.g., open store, roofed store, closed store),
- Construction height (e.g., flat store, high rack store) and
- Organisational and technical requirements (e.g., quarantine store, consignation store).

In contrast to Schneider (2008), only three main types of stores are distinguished by Krieger (2005b) on the basis of the storage purpose: the procurement store, the transshipment store and the distribution store. The procurement store is closely connected with the production. Its main function is to provide sufficient storage space for incoming goods that are needed for the production process. In a transshipment store, incoming goods are just stored for a short time until they are needed for ongoing transportation. Thus, the transshipment store fulfils a buffer function for the transshipment of goods between two modes of transportation. Finally, the distribution store serves as connection to the customers, where different goods are collected and compounded to customer-specific consignments.

According to the store categorisation of Krieger (2005b), the container-storage yard at seaport container terminals has to be classified as typical transshipment store, since containers are just temporarily stored in the yard until they are needed for ongoing waterside or landside transportation. This is in line with the main function of the whole container terminal—the transshipment function (see Sect. 2.2.1). From the aspect of the store position in the logistical system, according to the multi-dimensional store categorisation of Schneider (2008), the container-storage yard is also classified as a transshipment yard.

Type, status and material of the stored goods are manifold in container-storage yards, as nowadays almost all kinds of products and materials are transferred in containers. In addition, type, status and material of the stored goods are usually completely unknown to the terminal operator. In spite of the differing contents, most standard dry containers are treated as homogeneous storage units that can mainly be distinguished on the basis of their sizes, types and load status. Only for special types of containers like reefers or hazardous-goods-carrying containers additional information of the stored goods may be available. However, all containers are stored in the container-storage yard—even specials, which may be stored in suitable zones of the yard according to technical and organisational requirements. Therefore, the aspects of type, status and material of the stored goods, as suggested by Schneider (2008), can hardly be used to classify the store type of the container-storage yard in more detail.

Considering the construction aspect (Schneider 2008), the container-storage yard can be classified as an open store, as no roof or similar constructions are installed. The construction height, as a further classification aspect for stores (Schneider 2008), may be measured in terms of the stacking height for container-storage yards, which may be determined by the available space as well as by the applied storage equipment. Therefore, the construction height of container-storage yards at seaport container terminals differs greatly per terminal and this aspect cannot be used to define the general container-storage yard. However, the stacking height is commonly used to classify different design variants of container-storage yards (e.g., 3-high, 4-high).

3.1.3 Storage Processes

Depending on the type of store, several different processes are connected with the storage of goods. Based on the guideline VDI 3629 (VDI 2005) (association of German engineers), eight main processes are listed by Schneider (2008). In sequential order these processes are:

Goods Input: The goods input comprises several technical and organisational tasks that have to take place prior to admission into the store. Arriving deliveries of goods are discharged, unpacked, checked, sorted and bundled to storage units.

Storage-Area Distribution: As stores usually consist of several storage areas that are designed for different types of goods or types of storage units, it has to be decided in which precise area a bundled storage unit should be stored. This decision as well as the transport to the selected storage area belong to the storage-area-distribution process.

Admission into Store: Within this process, the storage units are transferred to the final destination of the selected storage area. Besides the transfer itself, this process also comprises decisions about the final destination, about the transferring storage machine as well as about the routing of the selected storage machine.

Store Management: The store management comprises monitoring and administration of storage data, including information on the status of the store (e.g., filling rate, full and free storage positions) and the stored goods (e.g., unique ID, size, weight).

Relocation: For some reasons, it may be required (e.g., to get access to other storage units) or desired (e.g., to improve the storage productivity) to relocate certain storage units to other destinations within the store. All the decisions on the storage unit that needs to be relocated and its new destination as well as control and execution of the planned relocation are included in the relocation process.

Retrieval: The retrieval process is the counterpart of the admission into store. Within this process, the storage units are transferred from the corresponding storage position to the control point of the corresponding storage area. Like the admission process, the retrieval comprises the transfer itself as well as decisions about the transferring storage machine and about the routing of the selected storage machine. Finally, the retrieved storage units are identified at the control points and their retrievals are confirmed.

Outbound-Zone Distribution: At the end of the storage process, a storage unit is usually handed over to a certain transport mode, which transfers this unit to its next destination. Depending on the type of storage unit that is retrieved (e.g., pallet, container) and the next mode in the transport chain (e.g., truck, train, ship), not each handover can take place in the same outbound zone. Therefore, retrieved goods have to be distributed to different outbound zones.

Goods Output: After an outbound zone is selected, the storage units are prepared for the handover to the customer, which includes several technical and organisational tasks, like damage checking, bundling and repacking of storage units to shipping units as well as preparation of shipping documents. Finally, the shipping unit is handed over to the customer.

All these processes take place in more or less comparable kinds at seaport container terminals. Firstly, the goods input takes place at the waterside and landside interfaces of the terminal, which are the quay and the gate area, respectively. There, technical and administrative tasks like damage checks, registration, twist look handling, etc. are performed for the arriving containers. Secondly, the arrived containers are distributed over different storage areas, which exist for example for import and export containers, for different berthing places and for different types of containers. It is determined on the basis of the applied stacking strategy (see Sect. 2.4.3.7) in which storage area a container should be stored, and the containers are transported to the selected storage area. While containers that arrive via hinterland road connection at the terminal may be transported to the selected storage area by the corresponding XT itself, the transport of waterside-arriving containers to the selected storage area always needs to be performed by the horizontal-transport machines of the terminal.

Thirdly, the admission into the store is performed by the storage equipment. Prior to the physical execution of this process, the exact storage position of the container in the selected storage area and the executive storage machine along with the planned execution time have to be determined, which are the container-stacking (see Sect. 2.4.3.7) and storage-machine-scheduling problems (see Sect. 2.4.3.8), respectively. Fourthly, all information on the status of the store itself—in terms of filling rate and slot occupancy—as well as information on the stored containers and the status of the storage equipment are controlled in real-time by the store-management process. The available information is usually needed for decision-making on the afore-mentioned operational storage-planning problems. Fifthly, the relocation process within container-storage yards is concerned with determining new positions for containers in the store and performing the transfer to the selected position. In container-storage yards, a relocation may occur for two reasons: On the one hand, a shuffle move may be necessary to get access to another container, while on the other hand containers may also be relocated in order to optimise their positions according to certain objectives. However, both types of relocation processes are once again involved with the container-stacking and storage-machine-scheduling problems.

Finally, the processes retrieval, outbound-zone distribution and goods output are the outgoing counterparts of the ingoing processes admission into store, storage-area distribution and goods input, respectively. Like the admission into the store the retrieval process is performed by the storage equipment. The process is connected with the storage-machine scheduling problem but not with the container-stacking problem, as the containers are simply transferred from the stack to the control points—which are the handover areas—of the respective storage area. The outbound-zone distribution is concerned with the transfer of the retrieved container from the container-storage yard to the corresponding outbound zone of that container, which can either be, depending on the planned destination of the container, one of the QCs, the XT-handover area or the rail station of the terminal. The goods output along with its technical and organisational tasks takes place at the quayside and landside interfaces of the terminals.

Altogether, it is shown that not all processes that are typically involved with stores take place in the storage subsystem of seaport container terminals. Moreover, only the processes admission into store, store management, relocation and retrieval are directly performed within the container-storage yard, while the remaining four store processes take place in the other subsystems, namely ship-to-shore, waterside horizontal transport and hinterland connection (see Sect. 2.2.2). Hence, from a procedural point of view, not only the storage subsystem of the terminal is the store, but the whole container terminal may be regarded as a store whose central part is the container-storage yard. However, in this work it is focused on the container-storage yard and its related processes. In particular, the efficient execution of the processes admission into store, relocation and retrieval are regarded in more detail within the next chapters.

3.1.4 Summarising Definition of the Container-Storage Yard

Altogether, the whole seaport container terminal can be defined as an open transshipment store, where standardised ISO containers are temporarily stored and transshipped from one mode of transportation to another. The container-storage yard is the place at seaport container terminals where the containers are actually stored. It is the most important part and/or subsystem of the terminal as most storage functions are provided by the storage yard and most storage processes take place in the storage yard. In particular, the most crucial functions of seaport container terminals, which are the bridging and the provisioning functions (see Sect. 3.1.1), are directly performed by the container-storage yard itself. The core storage processes—which are the admission into store, the store management, the relocation and the retrieval—all take place within the storage yard (see Sect. 3.1.3). Goods of almost all types, materials and status may be stored in the storage yard. The stored units are measured as TEU and they are classified according to the container attributes like size, weight and destination.

3.2 Performance Interrelation of Container Terminals and Container-Storage Yards

In the foregone sections and chapters, it is argued that the container-storage yard is the central part and the most important subsystem of seaport container terminals, not only with regard to the terminal area occupied for container storage, but also with regard to the investment volume and the total terminal operations. Thus, the performance of seaport container terminals as a whole may greatly be determined by the performance of the corresponding container-storage yards. As a consequence thereof, container-storage yards should be designed and managed in such a way that the realisation of the superior terminal objectives is facilitated. But as the design and operation of seaport container terminals are multi-objective planning problems (see Sect. 2.3.2), it is not that obvious which superior terminal objectives should be supported by the container-storage yard. Some common terminal objectives are the maximisation of the annual terminal throughput, the minimisation of the vessel-berthing time and the maximisation of the equipment productivity. In addition, several different planning objectives of the container-storage yard are pursued in the logistics and OR literature, which comprise, among others, the maximisation of the storage-equipment productivity, the maximisation of the yard density and the maximisation of the container accessibility in the yard.

Considering the great variety of different planning objectives for both the container-storage yard and the whole terminal system, it needs to be discussed, in order to come to target-oriented planning decisions for the design and the operation of container-storage yards at seaport container terminals, which are the main planning objectives of seaport container terminals as a whole and in which way the design and the operation of container-storage yards can contribute to achieve these superior terminal objectives. Subsequently, both questions are addressed. Firstly, based on the development of a system of objectives for seaport container terminals, three superior terminal objectives are derived and three corresponding KPIs (key performance indicator) are defined for measuring the performance of seaport container terminals as a whole. Thereafter, by evaluating different planning objectives of container-storage yards with respect to their causal effects for these KPIs, three planning objectives of container-storage yards are identified to be of crucial importance for the performance of the whole terminal system.

3.2.1 Performance Definition of Seaport Container Terminals

Seaport container terminals are simultaneously faced with the objectives and demands of several stakeholders. Important stakeholders are the staff, the residents, the authorities, the truckers, the shipping lines and the owners (Rijsenbrij and Wieschemann 2011). In most privately owned corporations, the final decision makers are the owners which are usually seeking for increases of their shareholder value (Copeland et al. 2003, p. 20, 21). Therefore, the maximisation of the shareholder value, which can be measured in terms of the expected profits in the long run and/or the value of the terminal, might be regarded as the superior objective of all terminal-planning problems. However, this objective can hardly be operationalised directly for any terminal-planning problem. Instead, the objective of maximising the shareholder value needs to be broken down into certain subgoals which are more operationable for decisions on the design and the operation of seaport container terminals.

In general, the shareholder value of a company is improved by increasing the revenues and the unit contribution margins (Copeland et al. 2003, p. 22, 23). Thus, with regard to seaport container terminals, the maximisation of the shareholder value requires the annual terminal throughput to be increased (see Sect. 2.3.1) and/or the gross margins per handled container to be increased. Assuming that the handling charge raised from the shipping lines is externally defined by market prices and/or previously agreed contracts, the unit contribution margins of the handled containers can only be increased by decreasing the terminal-investment and operating costs per handled container (see Sect. 2.3.2.4). In order to increase the throughput of a seaport container terminal, the container-handling capacity of that terminal needs to be increased and the demand for that capacity has to be increased as well by improving the attractiveness of the terminal for its potential customers. Assuming that the available terminal area is a given planning parameter for all planning problems of seaport container terminals, which is a reasonable assumption due to the scarcity of land area in most ports (Steenken et al. 2004; Rijsenbrij and Wieschemann 2011), increases of the container-handling capacity require the available land-area and quay-wall resources to be used as efficiently as possible. Owing to the assumption of fixed container-handling charges, the attractiveness of seaport container terminals for shipping lines is only influenced by the vessel-berthing times that can be guaranteed by the terminal. Similarly, from the perspective of truck and rail companies, a terminal is more attractive the shorter the landside-service times (see Sect. 2.3.2.1).

The analysis of the objectives of seaport container terminals can be summarised into the system of objectives that is shown in Fig. 3.1. There, it is also illustrated that the planning objectives derived for the whole terminal system can be classified into three main classes of performance objectives for seaport container terminals—objectives that aim at improving the cost performance, the operational performance and the area performance (Rijsenbrij and Wieschemann 2011). In order to reduce the difficulty of terminal-planning problems, that arise from the variety of different terminal objectives and possible trade-offs and/or interrelations among them, it might be reasonable to focus only on the optimisation of a single KPI for each class of terminal-performance objectives that is of crucial importance for the relevant class. Taking into account that the shipping lines are of much greater importance for the business success of container terminals than truck and rail companies, since the earnings of a container terminal are most of all dependent on the handling charge that is raised from the shipping lines, it is reasonable to focus primarily on the interests of the shipping lines for evaluating the operational performance of seaport container terminals. In fact, the minimisation of the vessel-berthing times at the terminals is frequently regarded as the superior objective for all decisions on the design and operation of seaport container terminals in the relevant literature (e.g., Ng 2005; Ambrosino et al. 2006). Furthermore, the available land area is usually considered to be a more scarce resource at seaport container terminals than the available length of the quay wall (e.g., Steenken et al. 2004; Rijsenbrij and Wieschemann 2011), thus making it reasonable to focus primarily on the land-use efficiency for evaluating the area performance. In summary, the performance of seaport container terminals as a whole in terms of cost performance, operational performance and area performance is improved by mainly aiming at minimising the investment and operating costs per handled container, minimising the vessel-berthing times and maximising the land-use efficiency, respectively.

While cost and area performance of seaport container terminals can directly be evaluated on the basis of the previously introduced container-cost index (see Sect. 2.3.2.4) and the standardised storage-handling capacity (see Sect. 2.3.2.2),

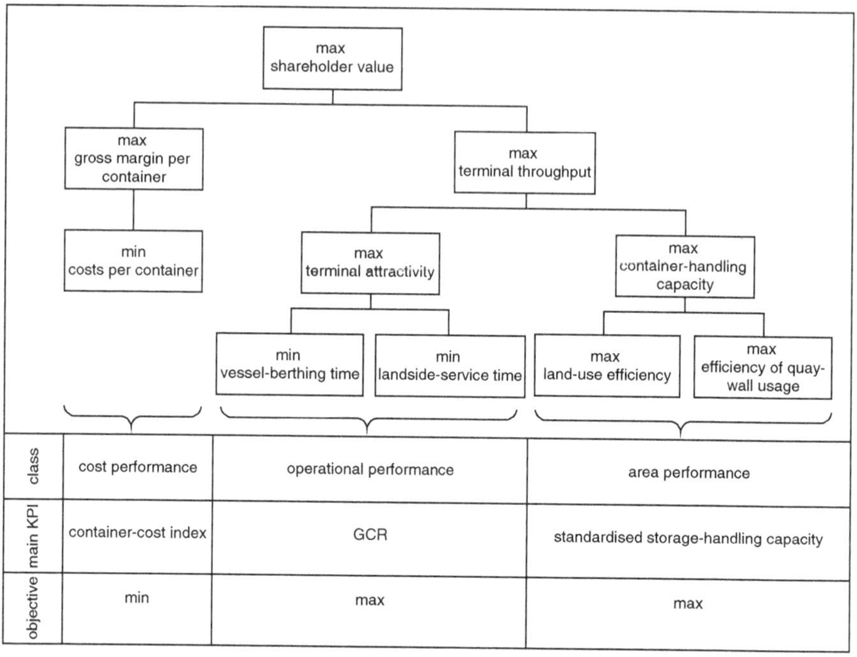

Fig. 3.1 Overview on planning objectives of seaport container terminals as a whole

respectively, the operational terminal performance cannot only be evaluated by the resulting vessel-berthing times but alternatively also by a more common KPI—the GCR (see Sect. 2.3.2.3). In fact, cost-efficient decreases of the vessel-berthing times at seaport container terminals require the QCs to discharge and load unchanged amounts of containers in shorter periods of time, which is equivalent to increasing the GCR. Considering the simple and quick comparability of different GCR figures, the maximisation of the GCR is frequently used as superior planning objective for all kinds of terminal-planning problems, instead of minimising the inversely related vessel-berthing times, in the logistics and OR literature (e.g., Petering et al. 2009; Petering and Murty 2009). In addition, maximising the GCR also has positive side effects on the costs per handled container as less QC costs account for each handled container when handling more containers within the same operating QC hours. More generally, the improvement of most common performance indicators of seaport container terminals (see Sect. 2.3.2) is directly supported by and/or at least implicitly facilitated by increases of the GCR. Another incentive for the seaport container terminals, in order to maximise the GCR, is the additional prestige and reputation that comes along with it.

At first glance, the GCR is only a measure for the productivity of the QCs. But, the GCR is also a measure for the operational performance of the whole terminal system, since the QCs are just one end of the transport chain of the terminal that affects the GCR as a whole. In fact, the QC performance is considerably affected by the horizontal-transport and storage-yard processes. The QCs can only load and discharge containers when the inflow and outflow of containers is properly processed by the horizontal-transport machines, which means, the QC operations should not be disturbed due to late arrivals of AGVs, SCs or TTUs. The horizontal-transport operations are then again affected by the operations in the container-storage yard, as they can only work properly if they need not wait at the interfaces of the storage yard. Export containers as well as outgoing transshipment containers have to be accurately retrieved by the storage machines, since otherwise the horizontal-transport machines have to wait. The situation for import boxes and ingoing transshipment containers needs to be distinguished between active and passive transport machines (see Sect. 2.2.3.2). Active transport machines that are laden with import or transshipment boxes need not wait for late storage machines, while import operations of passive transport machines may be disturbed by delays of the storage equipment. The great impact of the yard operations for the operational performance of the terminal system as a whole, in terms of the GCR, is for instance postulated by Goussiatiner (2009) and confirmed by a simulation study of Petering et al. (2009). Thus, the GCR is a useful indicator to evaluate the quality of the synchronisation of ship-to-shore operations, horizontal-transport operations and container-storage-yard operations.

In summary, the GCR is of great importance for several commonly used terminal performance indicators, well suited to evaluate the degree of synchronisation between the terminal subsystems and frequently used in the relevant literature to evaluate the performance of the terminal system as a whole. In view of these aspects, the operational performance of seaport container terminals can best be subsumed in terms of a single performance indicator by the GCR. Thus, altogether the performance of seaport container terminals as a whole is assumed to be jointly defined in this work by the resulting values of the three KPIs container-cost index, GCR and standardised storage-handling capacity, which should be optimised by planning decisions on the terminal-design and operation.

3.2.2 *Performance Definition of Container-Storage Yards*

As long as the design and the operation of the ship-to-shore, waterside horizontal-transport and storage subsystems are not planned integratedly—which is usually regarded as far too complicated—the superior terminal objectives of minimising the container-cost index, maximising the GCR and maximising the standardised storage-handling capacity can usually not be operationalised directly for the planning problems of the horizontal-transport and storage subsystems (Briskorn et al. 2006). Hence, planning objectives have to be defined for the terminal subsystems that can positively contribute to the optimisation of these superior terminal-planning objectives. In fact, several different objectives and performance indicators for the container-storage subsystem are introduced in the logistics and OR literature:

- Minimisation of waiting times for horizontal-transport machines at the interfaces of the container-storage yard (e.g., Stahlbock and Voß 2010),
- Minimisation of unit cost of container-storage and retrieval operations (e.g., Saanen 2006),
- Maximisation of storage-equipment productivity (e.g., Dorndorf and Schneider 2010),
- Minimisation of unproductive shuffle moves (e.g., Dekker et al. 2006) and
- Maximisation of yard density (e.g., Steenken et al. 2004).

The waiting times of horizontal-transport machines at the interfaces of the container-storage yard are of great importance for the operations and the performance of the connected subsystems. While vehicle-waiting times at the waterside interface have negative effects on the operations of the waterside horizontal-transport machines, waiting times at the landside interfaces have negative effects on the vehicles operating in the hinterland-connection subsystem. In the previous subsection, it is argued that the GCR is greatly dependent on a timely accurate flow of containers to and from the QCs, which require no or only short waiting times of the waterside horizontal-transport machines at the interfaces of the container-storage yard. In practice, the waterside horizontal-transport machines should not stay longer than several seconds or very few minutes in the waterside handover area, as longer waiting times of several minutes can be expected to have greatly harmful effects on the vessel-loading and unloading operations. In fact, the vehicle-waiting times at the waterside interfaces of the container-storage yard are found to be very strongly negatively correlated with the GCR by Petering et al. (2009). Thus, they conclude that the primary objective for the design and the operation of container-storage yards at seaport container terminals should be the minimisation of the vehicle-waiting times for the waterside horizontal-transport machines at the storage-yard interfaces. The vehicle-waiting times at the landside interfaces of the container-storage yard have no effects on the GCR and the vessel-berthing times, but for the service times of landside-arriving XTs and trains. But because truck and train operators are usually considered to be far less important for the business success of seaport container terminals than shipping lines, the minimisation of the vehicle-waiting times at the landside storage-yard interfaces is often regarded as a matter of minor importance compared to the minimisation of the waterside vehicle-waiting times (Nazari 2005, p. 25).

The unit cost of container-storage and retrieval operations, which are computed by dividing the yearly investment and operating costs of the container-storage yard by the number of container-storage and retrieval operations in that period of time, can be regarded as a kind of storage-yard-related container-cost index. Hence, decreasing the costs per storage and retrieval operation, ceteris paribus directly leads to reductions of the container-cost index for the whole terminal system. Therefore, aiming at minimising the costs per storage and retrieval operation in the container-storage yard, when deciding on design and operation of that terminal subsystem, can be expected to contribute positively to the superior terminal objective of minimising the container-cost index.

The objective of maximising the storage-equipment productivity is closely related to the objective of minimising the unit cost of container-storage and retrieval operations, as fewer costs account for each storage and retrieval operation when performing more operations within unchanged operating hours of the storage equipment and/or performing the same number of operations with fewer operating hours. But different from the expectations of several terminal operators, who often overemphasise the importance of the storage-equipment productivity (Dorndorf and Schneider 2010), its maximisation does not always contribute positively to the superior terminal objective of maximising the GCR. In fact, a high storage-equipment productivity is not necessarily equivalent to well synchronised operations between the waterside horizontal-transport and container-storage-yard subsystems, since horizontal-transport machines may suffer from storage equipment being late, in spite of high productivities. Actually, the storage-equipment productivity is maximised by minimising the execution times on the storage machines per storage and retrieval operation, without considering the resulting waiting times of horizontal-transport machines at the storage-yard interfaces. Thus, some operations may be performed late compared to the arrival time of the corresponding horizontal-transport machines in order to realise short execution times for the operations of the storage equipment. As a consequence, the affected vehicles may need to wait for the storage equipment at the interfaces of the container-storage yard, thus leading to unsynchronised terminal operations and adverse effects for the GCR.

The number of unproductive shuffle moves that need to be performed by the storage equipment is expected to be of great importance for both its productivity and the resulting vehicle-waiting times at the waterside and landside interfaces of the container-storage yard. The more containers need to be shuffled in a certain period of time, the more storage-equipment resources are tied up for these shuffle operations and the fewer resources are available for container-storage and retrieval operations, thus decreasing the storage-equipment productivity and increasing the risk for and the extent of vehicle-waiting times at the interfaces of the container-storage yard. Therefore, minimising the number of shuffle moves can be regarded as a sub-goal that has to be implicitly aimed at in order to achieve the minimisation of the vehicle-waiting time at the interfaces of the storage yard and/or the maximisation of the storage-equipment productivity.

By increasing the yard density of a seaport container terminal, a greater number of containers can be stored in the storage area of that terminal, thus increasing its storage capacity. Provided that the storage capacity is the critical factor for the container-handling capacity, which usually is the case for terminals that are located in grown industrial port areas, both the handling capacity in absolute terms and the standardised storage-handling capacity of that terminal are increased as well. Hence, aiming at increasing the land-use efficiency of the storage yard by maximising the yard density when deciding on its design and operation can greatly contribute to the superior terminal objective of maximising the land-use efficiency of the whole terminal in terms of the standardised storage-handling capacity.

Altogether, several objectives can be applied for planning the design and the operation of container-storage yards at seaport container terminals, which all can more or less contribute to achieve certain superior planning objectives of the terminal system as a whole. But, in view of the preceding analysis, it is reasonable to expect the pursuit of the storage-yard objectives of minimising the unit cost of container-storage and retrieval operations, minimising the vehicle-waiting times at the interfaces of the container-storage yard and maximising the yard density to contribute most positively to the superior terminal-planning objectives of minimising the container-cost index, maximising the GCR and maximising the standardised container-handling capacity, respectively. Therefore, these three storage-yard objectives are considered to be the primary objectives for all decisions on the design and the operation of container-storage yards throughout this work.

3.3 Comparison of Different Types of Container-Storage-Yard Systems

In Sect. 2.2.3.3, different types of storage equipment for seaport container terminals are briefly introduced: straddle carriers, gantry cranes, forklifts and reachstackers. While the latter two types of storage equipment are mostly applied for rather small container terminals that require very flexible machines, SCs and gantry cranes are the most common types of storage equipment for medium- to large-sized terminals (Brinkmann 2011). According to a survey on container-terminal characteristics and equipment types by Wiese et al. (2009a), SCs or gantry cranes are employed as storage equipment by 110 of 114 terminals of relevant size all around the world.

As noted in Sect. 2.2.3.3, different variants of gantry-crane systems have to be distinguished that differ in technical and logistical aspects. The two main variants are the RMGC system and the RTGC system (rubber-tyred gantry crane). In spite of the general validity of the storage operations that are described in Sect. 2.2.2.4, notable differences in terms of terminal layout and storage processes are involved with these different types of storage equipment. In this section, these differences are regarded in detail for the most common types of storage equipment for terminals of relevant size (i.e., for SCs, RTGCs and RMGCs). It is focused on the terminal layouts, the storage operations as well as the comparative advantages and disadvantages of the three storage and/or terminal systems that result from applying these types of storage equipment. Firstly, the storage systems are separately described and, finally, they are compared on the basis of several technical and logistical criteria.

3.3.1 *Straddle-Carrier System*

SCs can be used for all container-handling functions on seaport container terminals except loading and discharging of vessels. In case SCs are deployed as storage equipment, they are usually also used for horizontal transport between the quay and the storage yard as well as for loading and unloading of XTs. Thus, no additional equipment and no handover between storage and horizontal transport is required. The stacking height of SC-operated storage yards is usually two or three layers high, which leads to yard densities of about 500–750 TEUs per hectare (Kalmar 2011a). SCs are usually powered by diesel engines and are man-driven but they can also be automated. In addition, SCs have the features of moving with relatively high speeds and being very flexible, as they can easily be assigned to different handling functions on the terminal based on operational requirements (Kalmar 2011a). Pure SC systems are mainly used in medium and large-sized terminals and are in operation, for example, at the Hanjin and Maersk terminals in Kaohsiung (Taiwan) as well as at the CTT (Container Terminal Tollerort) in Hamburg (Germany) (Chu and Huang 2005; HHLA 2009).

A typical SC-operated storage yard—like it is schematically depicted in Fig. 3.2—consists of several blocks and driving lanes as well as one handover area for loading and discharging XTs. Each block contains long rows with the containers placed end to end. The rows have to be separated from each other by a distance such that an SC can move along the row, straddling the containers to reach the required storage position. Considering the internal span of an SC, spaces for wheel travelling and some safety distance, there has to be a clearance of 1.5–2 m between two rows of a block. Nevertheless, passing of SCs in adjacent rows of a block is usually not possible. The rows can either be arranged parallel or perpendicular to the quay wall, but most common are parallel layouts (Chu and Huang 2005). The number of rows per block and the length of the rows are influenced by several factors and vary notably between different terminals. However, short blocks of 10–15 TEUs length are commonly used, as longer blocks increase the risk of damages and reduce accessibility (Atkins 1983; UNCTAD 1985, pp. 144–146).

The yard blocks are separated and surrounded by parallel and perpendicular driving lanes that are used by the SCs to move between the quay, the yard blocks and the XT-handover area. The width of the driving lanes should be dimensioned such that an SC, that usually has a turning radius of about 9.4 m, is able to manoeuvre in and out of the rows and to travel between blocks (Chu and Huang 2005). A width of about 20 m is for example suggested by UNCTAD (1985, pp. 144–146). In Fig. 3.2, four blocks as well as three parallel and three perpendicular driving lanes are shown.

For reasons of occupational safety, XT and SC-driving areas are usually clearly separated from each other. The only interfaces are the handover lanes in the XT-handover area, where SCs are allowed to straddle XTs in order to load or discharge them. The handover area for XTs is usually located at the landside of the terminal, near the gate facilities, in order to avoid long XT movements across the terminal. The number of handover lanes greatly depends on the throughput of the terminal. In Fig. 3.2, the handover area is located in the bottom left corner and contains 14 handover lanes for XTs. The separation of the driving areas for XTs and SCs is indicated by the dotted line. The dimensions of the handover area in terms of width and length are determined by the number of lanes as well as by the required parking, moving and manoeuvring space for the XTs (Chu and Huang 2005).

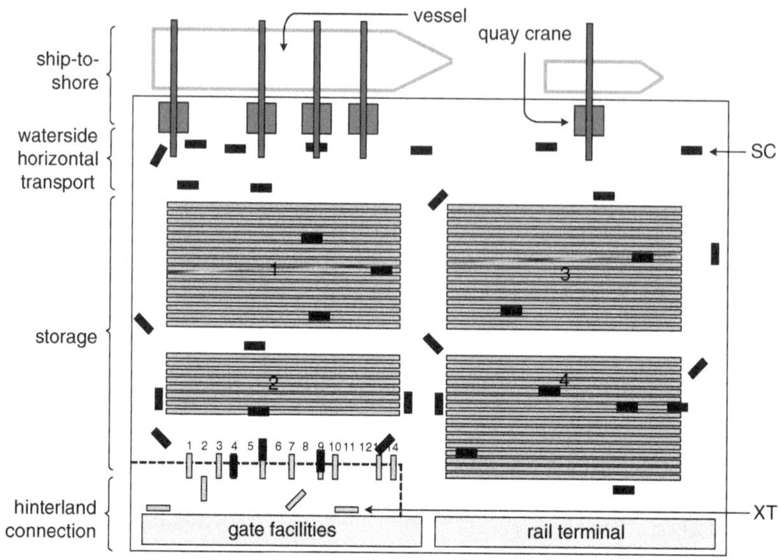

Fig. 3.2 Schematic terminal layout using SCs as storage equipment

3.3.2 Rubber-Tyred-Gantry-Crane System

An RTGC is a gantry-crane type (see Sect. 2.2.3.3) that is typically used at seaport container terminals for storage purposes only. Hence, it has to be combined with equipment for the performance of the horizontal transport between the quay and the storage yard. Typically, RTGCs are combined with TTUs, but MTSs are also possible (Kalmar 2011a). While RTGCs with electric engines are theoretically available, cranes that are powered by diesel engines are still far more common than electric systems, which may be considered to be more eco-friendly. RTGCs are typically manned with a crane driver and there is hardly any potential for automation, due to the needs of occupational safety and the heavy interaction with unautomated TTUs and XTs. The stacking height of RTGC-operated storage yards varies greatly. Most common are RTGC cranes that facilitate stacking heights of 1-over-4 and 1-over-5 (Chu and Huang 2005), but 1-over-7 cranes are also available, leading to yard densities of up to 1,000 TEUs per hectare. Therefore, RTGC-operated storage yards are typically found at large and very large terminals that require dense stacking operations (Brinkmann 2011). Examples of the RTGC system are in operation in the ports of Hong Kong (China) and Kaohsiung (Taiwan) (Wiese et al. 2009a).

An RTGC-operated storage yard is usually subdivided into several yard blocks and driving lanes. The yard blocks, which are laid out parallel to the quay wall, consist of several rows, in which the containers are stacked end to end, as well as an additional handover lane, which is reserved for TTUs and XTs that interact

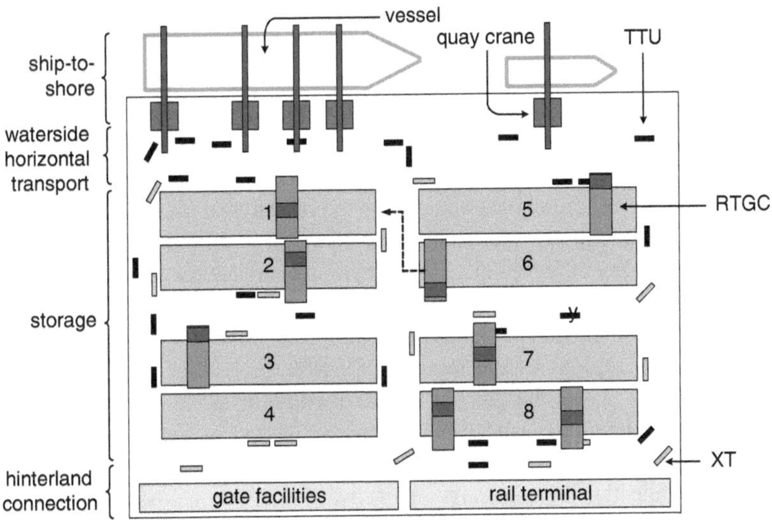

Fig. 3.3 Schematic terminal layout using RTGCs as storage equipment

with the RTGCs (Petering et al. 2009). In contrast to SC blocks, additional wheel spaces are not needed between the rows. Only 30–40 cm space are required in order to ensure safe crane operations (Chu and Huang 2005). All yard blocks that are arranged in an alignment form a yard zone. In Fig. 3.3, the general layout of an RTGC-operated container terminal with eight yard blocks and four yard zones is schematically illustrated from a bird's eye view. Blocks 1 and 5 are in zone 1, blocks 2 and 6 are in zone 2, and so on. Length, width and quantity of the yard blocks vary notably between international container terminals and depend on several factors. Block lengths in the range from 18 to 90 bays are reported by Petering and Murty (2009) for RTGC systems. Typically, containers are stacked 6 rows wide in RTGC-operated yard blocks, which means, the blocks are 6 + 1 rows wide due to the additional handover lane. Yard blocks up to 8 + 1 rows wide are reported by Chu and Huang (2005).

The RTGCs are dimensioned such that the whole yard blocks, including the handover lanes, are spanned by their portals (see Fig. 2.7c). RTGCs easily traverse bay-wise along an entire yard block and from block to block within the same yard zone—such movements are called linear-gantrying. In addition, as the cranes are able to turn the wheels by 90°, they can also move to blocks of adjacent yard zones by using the driving lanes perpendicular to the quay wall. Such a crane movement is a rather time-consuming manoeuvre (about 15 min) that is called cross-gantrying (Petering et al. 2009). In Fig. 3.3, this manoeuvre is illustrated by the dotted line, indicating a cross-gantrying movement of a crane from block 6 to 1. As a consequence, multiple cranes can simultaneously work in one yard block and RTGC systems can flexibly react on workload imbalances between different yard blocks. However, due to technical restrictions, RTGCs generally do not traverse bay-wise when laden with containers. They only move containers within the rows of the same bay by trolley movements (Pirhonen 2011). Therefore, TTUs and XTs have to drive to the bay where the relevant containers have to be stored or retrieved by an RTGC. Likewise, containers can also only be shuffled within the same bay. After finishing work within one bay, the RTGC can traverse unladen to the next bay and/or block. Owing to the heavy weight of this storage equipment, RTGC systems require costly groundworks with concrete piles underneath the runways of the crane legs.

XT and TTU operations are usually intermingled at RTGC-operated container yards, since XTs are not served at a special handover area at the edge of the terminal but in handover lanes that are spread across the storage yard and simultaneously used by the TTUs. The driving lanes are required by both TTUs and XTs to move between different regions of the terminal. Once a truck reaches the relevant bay of a yard block, it leaves the driving lane and waits for loading or discharging by the RTGC in the handover lane. Like for the SC layout in Fig. 3.2, three parallel and three perpendicular driving lanes are depicted in the RTGC terminal layout in Fig. 3.3. While the driving lanes at the waterside and landside border of the storage yard can only be used to enter the handover lane of just one yard block, the horizontal driving lane in the middle of the yard can be used to access the handover lanes of blocks 2 and 3 as well as 6 and 7. However, more space-intensive layouts that require driving lanes between all yard blocks are also reported (Petering et al. 2009).

3.3.3 *Rail-Mounted-Gantry-Crane System*

Superficially, RMGCs are quite similar to RTGCs—both are gantry-crane types that are used at seaport container terminals for storage purposes only. From a technical perspective, the most obvious difference is that an RMGC moves on rail tracks while an RTGC is rubber-tyred. But contrary to an RTGC-operated storage yard, two alternative yard-block arrangements are reported for the RMGC system that are involved with two different yard-operation schemes. The yard blocks are either laid out parallel or perpendicular to the quay wall. According to Table 3.1, 11 RMGC systems are currently in operation around the world, whereof five systems are laid out parallel to the quay wall and six systems perpendicular. The parallel RMGC layout is very similar to the RTGC system—apart from having no cross gantrying possibility—and the horizontal-transport equipment is only served alongside the yard blocks. In contrast, the operations for the perpendicular RMGC layout differ a lot from the RTGC system, as horizontal-transport machines are loaded and discharged at the front ends of the blocks. As a consequence, the parallel and perpendicular RMGC systems are also referred to as sideway-loading and front-end-loading systems, respectively (Saanen 2006). The following analysis will only be focused on the perpendicular and/or front-end-loading type of the RMGC system. For a description of the parallel RMGC system it is referred to Chu and Huang (2005).

Table 3.1 Container terminals using RMGC systems (Based on Wiese et al. 2009a)

Terminal name	Region	Layout	Operation
Busan New Port East CT	Asia	Parallel	Automated
Busan New Port North CT	Asia	Parallel	Manual
Taichung CT	Asia	Parallel	Manual
Antwerp Gateway	Europe	Perpendicular	Automated
ECT Delta Terminal	Europe	Perpendicular	Automated
ECT Euromax	Europe	Perpendicular	Automated
HHLA CTB (Burchardkai)	Europe	Perpendicular	Automated
HHLA CTA (Altenwerder)	Europe	perpendicular	Automated
La Spezia CT	Europe	Parallel	Manual
London Thamesport	Europe	Parallel	Automated
APM Terminals Virginia	North America	Perpendicular	Automated

RMGC systems are connected with high capital costs, as not just the crane itself, but also costly ground works for concrete piles and rails are needed. Similar to QCs, RMGCs are usually supplied with electric power by cable connection, which leads to locally reduced exhaust emissions (Kalmar 2011a). Most common are RMGCs that facilitate stacking heights of 1-over-4 (Chu and Huang 2005), but 1-over-6 cranes are also available, leading to high yard densities exceeding 1,200 TEUs per hectare (Saanen and Valkengoed 2005; Saanen 2006). Therefore, front-end-loading RMGC storage yards are mostly applied at large and very large terminals that require dense stacking operations (Kalmar 2011a). Such systems have been put into operation, for example, at the ECT Delta Terminal in Rotterdam (Netherlands) and at the CTA in Hamburg (Germany) (Dekker et al. 2006). The perpendicular RMGC system can be combined with both active and passive horizontal-transport equipment, but most popular are combinations with passive AGVs.

A typical front-end-loading RMGC system—as it is schematically shown in Fig. 3.4 from a bird's eye view—consists of yard blocks, corresponding waterside and landside handover areas and service lanes in between the yard blocks. Apart from their arrangements, the yard blocks are very similar to RTGC-operated yard blocks, as containers are stacked end to end in several rows that are separated by only 30–40 cm clearance. Since the handover takes place at the front ends of the block, no handover lane is required inside the crane portal. The dimensions of yard blocks differ between terminals, but typically the order of magnitude for perpendicular RMGC yard blocks is 28–48 bays long and 6–10 rows wide. The yard blocks at the CTA in Hamburg (Germany) are for instance 37 bays long, 10 rows wide and the containers are stacked 1-over-4 (Saanen and Valkengoed 2005).

The service lanes in between the yard blocks are used by workshop cars for M&R (maintenance and repair) purposes only, but usually not by horizontal-transport equipment. Thus, waterside horizontal-transport equipment and landside-operating XTs are clearly separated from each other (see Fig. 3.4). The handover to both waterside and landside horizontal-transport equipment takes only place in the corresponding handover areas at the front ends of the blocks. The size of these

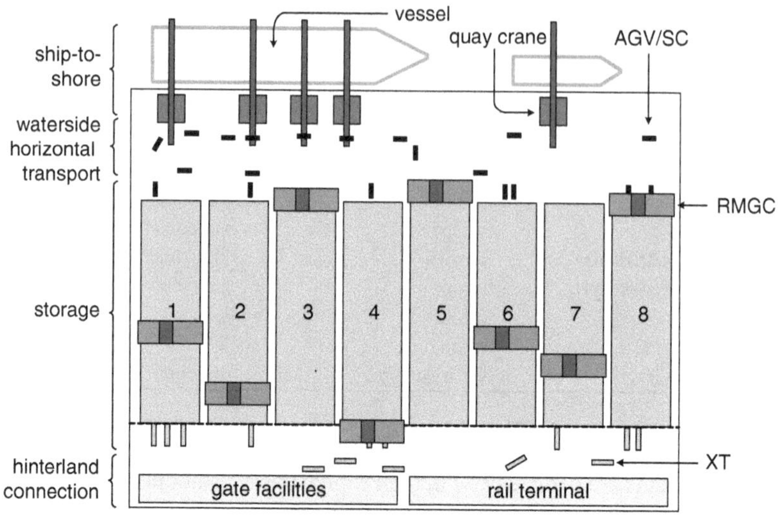

Fig. 3.4 Schematic terminal layout using RMGCs as storage equipment

handover areas mainly depends on the width of the corresponding yard blocks. Usually, the handover areas on both sides are divided into several lanes, where individual vehicles are waiting to be loaded or discharged and/or where containers are picked up or dropped off. While passive vehicles like XTs and AGVs have to wait for the RMGC to be loaded or discharged, active vehicles like SCs simply pick up or drop off containers in the handover area. The transfer between the handover areas and the storage positions in the block is performed by the RMGCs by means of bay and row-wise portal and trolley movements, respectively. Thus, different to RTGCs, long laden crane movements alongside the yard block are an inherent part of front-end-loading RMGC systems.

Each yard block of the example storage yard, that is depicted in Fig. 3.4, is equipped with only one RMGC, which is not able to move to another block, as it is fixed to rails. Hence, RMGCs cannot flexibly react on workload imbalances between different blocks. As a consequence, RMGC systems with two or even more cranes per yard block are deployed to allow for the absorption of peak situations. In addition, RMGC systems are available that allow for more intra-block flexibility of multiple cranes, as the cranes are able to cross each other within the same yard block. All these variations of the front-end-loading RMGC system are in detail presented in the next section.

From Table 3.1 it can be seen that 8 of 11 worldwide used RMGC systems are already automated and six of them are laid out perpendicular to the quay wall. Automated RMGCs are sometimes also referred to as ASCs (automated stacking cranes). The wide-spread automation of RMGC systems can mainly be explained by two reasons: Firstly, due to being fixed to rails, the crane operations are comparably simple and the RMGCs are rather stable, which allows fast and laden linear-gantrying. Secondly, for reasons of occupational safety, automated and manual operations usually have to be strictly separated from each other. Therefore, the handover between the yard crane and manually driven horizontal-transport equipment cannot be computer-controlled. But for front-end-loading RMGCs the clear separation of waterside and landside horizontal-transport equipment facilitates the usage of automated equipment at the waterside, which then again allows for an automated handover between the RMGCs and this equipment type. The handover to XTs at the landside front ends of the blocks is usually manually controlled by remote operators. An extensive statement of reasons for automating container-terminal operations in general is given by Saanen and Rijsenbrij (2007).

3.3.4 Concluding Comparison

The three most common storage-yard systems—SCs, RTGCs and RMGCs—are presented in detail in the preceding subsections. But it remains unclear, which system is the best one and/or which one is preferable for certain terminals. In order to facilitate profound evaluations of existing terminals as well as equipment decisions for container-storage yards to be built, the main differences of the three yard systems along with their advantages and disadvantages are shortly compared in this subsection. In Table 3.2, SC, RTGC and RMGC systems are compared on the basis of some key facts and several selection criteria. It turns out that no generally dominating yard system is available, moreover each system is best for certain selection criteria. Thus, each of the systems may be most suitable for certain seaport container terminals—depending on the underlying planning objectives and framework conditions.

The SC system is on the one hand connected with high inter-terminal flexibility and minimal infrastructure requirements (e.g., ground works, power supply, TOS), but on the other hand it performs rather poorly in terms of yard density and cost aspects. Therefore, the SC system may be most appropriate for medium- to large-sized terminals that have sufficient storage area available (Brinkmann 2011). Indeed, nowadays SCs are deployed at 26 seaport container terminals of relevant size all around the world (Wiese et al. 2009a).

In contrast, high equipment productivities and yard densities as well as low investment and operating costs (e.g., maintenance, energy) are offered by the RTGC system. Hence, it is most appropriate for large- to very large-sized terminals with scarce area resources. In addition, since the RTGC system performs rather poorly in terms of labour costs and environmental friendliness, it is more appropriate for developing countries, where the labour force is not as costly and environmental aspects are not considered to be that critical (Brinkmann 2011). Nowadays, RTGC systems can be found at 77 container terminals of relevant size all around the world, but in particular in Asian countries, it seems to be the dominating yard system (Wiese et al. 2009a).

Table 3.2 Comparison of different storage-yard systems (Based on Sects. 3.3.1–3.3.3; Saanen 2006; Kalmar 2011a; Brinkmann 2011)

	SC	RTGC	RMGC
Preferred terminal layout:	None	Rectangular	Rectangular
Typical block layout:	(Parallel)	Parallel	(Perpendicular)
Horizontal transport:	SC	TTU, MTU	AGV, SC, TTU
Engine:	Diesel	Diesel/electric	Electric
Max. stacking height:	1-over-3	1-over-7	1-over-6
Infrastructure requirements:	+	O	–
Inter-terminal flexibility:	+	O	–
Intra-block flexibility	–	–	O
Automation potential:	O	–	+
Productivity:	O	+	O
Yard density:	–	O/+	+
Investment costs:	O	+	–
Operating costs:	–	+	O
Labour cost:	–	–	+
Eco-friendliness:	–	–	+

Finally, likewise RMGC systems are connected with high yard densities. Therefore, they are also mostly applicable for terminals with scarce area resources. But due to their high potential for automation, they are also involved with rather low labour costs, environmental friendliness and high investment costs. As a consequence, the RMGC system is most appropriate in regions, where labour costs make up for a comparable big fraction of the total terminal costs and where environmental aspects are rather important (Brinkmann 2011). Nowadays, RMGC systems are mostly in operation in industrial countries in Europe, North-America and parts of Asia (Wiese et al. 2009a). Altogether, the RMGC already is a relevant storage equipment for seaport container terminals and its importance may still increase along with the growing international trade and an increasing cost competition among seaport container terminals that in turn leads to a growing pressure on the labour costs of the terminal.

3.4 Automated RMGC Systems

In the previous section, the RMGC system is compared with other popular storage-yard systems at seaport container terminals. It is found that the RMGC systems are of great relevance for seaport container terminals, in particular for those terminals that are located in high-labour-cost countries. In this section, the RMGC system—as it is described in Sect. 3.3.3—is regarded in more detail. Firstly, different types of RMGC systems are presented. Secondly, some additional technical data on the RMGCs are provided. Thirdly, the operations and processes of RMGCs are described and classified. Fourthly, planning problems on both the strategical and the operational level that are connected with RMGC systems are shortly introduced. Finally, similarities to other logistical systems with related planning problems are pointed out.

3.4.1 *RMGC Types*

To this date, four different main types of automated RMGC systems have been put into operation at seaport container terminals around the world. These types of RMGC systems—which are called single (SRMGC), twin (TRMGC), double (DRMGC) and triple (TriRMGC)—mainly differ in the number of cranes that are deployed per yard block and their crossing ability. Subsequently, these types of RMGC systems are introduced along with their characteristics and their comparative advantages and disadvantages.

3.4.1.1 Single-Crane System

The single-crane system is the oldest RMGC system. It was introduced in 1993 at the ECT Delta Terminal in Rotterdam (Netherlands) (Saanen 2008). There, each yard block is operated by only one automated RMGC, which serves both the landside and waterside handover areas. The major advantage of the single system is its comparably simple behaviour, as no complicating interferences with other cranes have to be regarded for the crane-scheduling problem. But the handling capacity of just one crane is rather small. Therefore, it may be expected that SRMGCs are only suitable for small-sized yard blocks, as otherwise long waiting times for horizontal-transport machines and disturbed QC-job sequences may be the result. At the ECT Delta Terminal, the original yard blocks are only 28 bays long, 6 rows wide and containers are stacked 2 tiers high. In Fig. 3.5, an example yard block is depicted that is operated by a single RMGC. The SRMGC system is shown from the landside interface and consists of 12 bays, 8 rows, and 4 tiers. A complete terminal layout with an SRMGC system is schematically illustrated from a bird's eye view in Fig. 3.4.

3.4.1.2 Twin-Crane System

A consequent derivative of the single-crane system is the twin system which uses two identical cranes per block. The cranes have the same size and share the same pair of rail tracks. Thus, crossing of the cranes within the same block is impossible. As a consequence, the crane that is located closer to the waterside can only serve the waterside handover area and never the landside interface. For the crane that is located closer to the landside this relation is reversed. However, a crane may still support operations at the opposite side of the block by pre or post-positioning

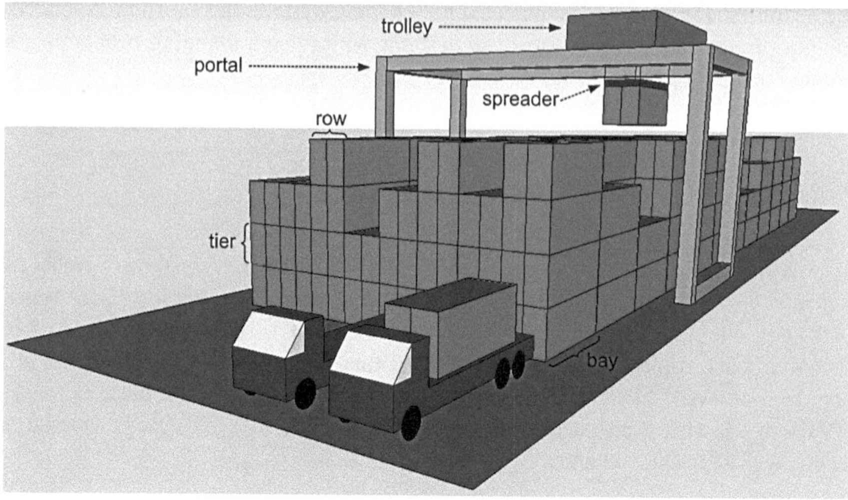

Fig. 3.5 Schematic illustration of an example SRMGC system

containers. On the one hand, it is beneficial that the system offers more handling capacity than the single system does, but on the other hand, it is more complicated to operate, since crane interferences have to be regarded. A crane interference may for instance occur when both cranes have target positions that are located behind the other crane. In such a situation, it has to be decided which crane is granted the right of way and which one has to be moved to a shunting position in order to avoid crane collisions or deadlocks. In addition, the system is very vulnerable to machine breakdowns, since crossing of the cranes is not possible and thus, a defective crane would jam the whole yard block. In Fig. 3.6, a twin-crane system is exemplified for the same yard block that is shown in Fig. 3.5 with a single crane.

TRMGCs are in operation, for example, at the APM Virginia Terminal in Portsmouth (US) (Edmonson 2007) and at the ECT Euromax Terminal in Rotterdam (Netherlands) (Saanen and Valkengoed 2005). The RMGCs at the Euromax Terminal facilitate a stacking height of 1-over-5 for yard blocks of up to 10 rows width. The space requirements for a TRMGC system are the same as for SRMGC systems, since the second crane is of identical size and uses the same pair of rail tracks. As a consequence, the terminal layout of a TRMGC system—which is shown in Fig. 3.7 from a bird's eye view—remains unchanged in comparison to the SRMGC layout (see Fig. 3.4), which means, the same number of same-sized yard blocks can be installed on a given yard area.

3.4.1.3 Double-Crane System

The double-crane system also deploys two cranes per yard block. But in contrast to the twin-crane system, the two cranes of a DRMGC yard block are of different

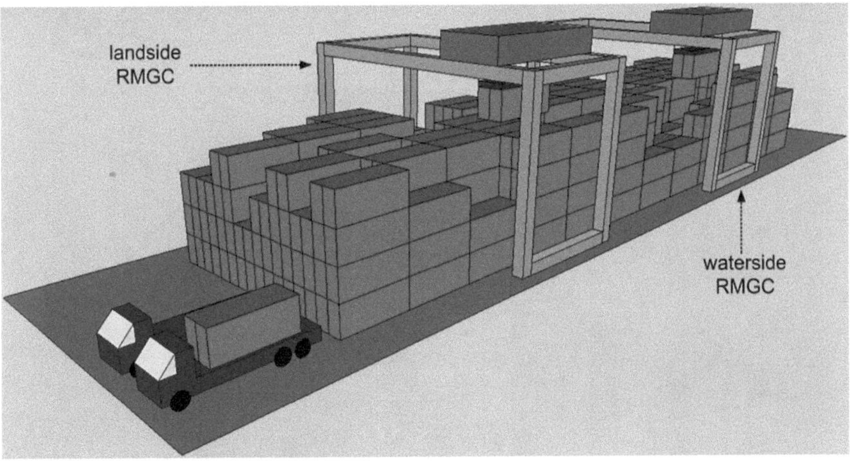

Fig. 3.6 Schematic illustration of an example TRMGC system

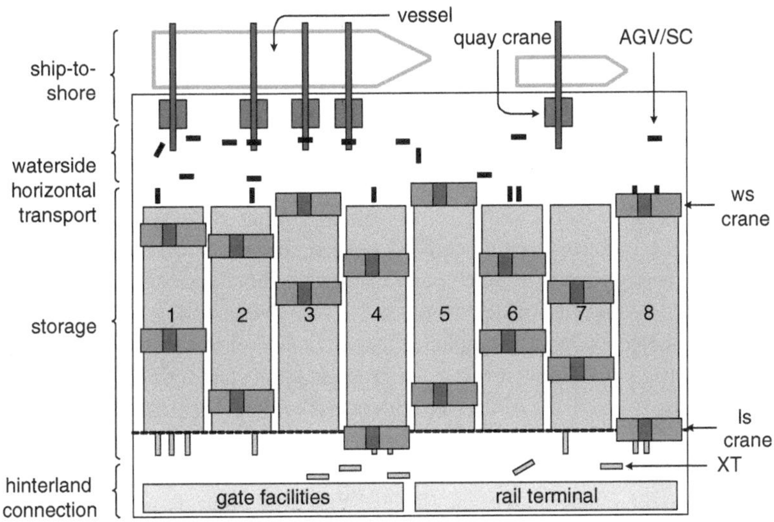

Fig. 3.7 Schematic terminal layout with TRMGCs

sizes and do not share the same pair of rail tracks, but have their own pair of rails each. As a consequence, the cranes are able to cross each other, which allows both cranes to serve the handover areas at both front ends of the block. Usually, crossing is only possible if the trolley of the outer large crane is moved to a special crossing lane which is located at the side of the large crane, beyond the profile of the inner small crane. This crossing lane, which is illustrated in Fig. 3.8 for the same yard block as shown for the SRMGC and TRMGC systems, is also used by workshop cars for M&R purposes. Such a double-crane system is in operation at the CTA in

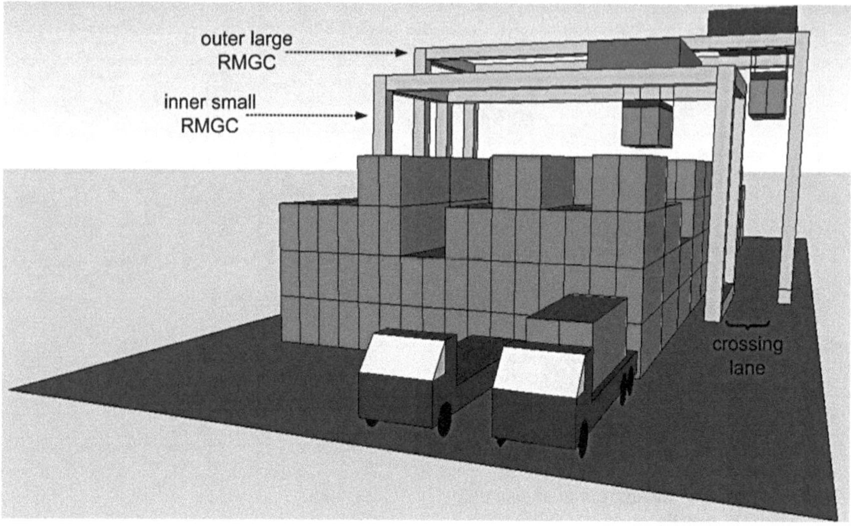

Fig. 3.8 Schematic illustration of an example DRMGC system

Hamburg (Germany), where the yard blocks are 37 bays long, 10 rows wide and the containers are stacked 1-over-4 high (Koch 2004).

In total, a comparable handling capacity as for the twin-crane system along with a higher degree of flexibility can be reached by the double-crane system. The benefits of the crossing possibility are reduced (but nevertheless existing) crane interferences and reduced consequences of machine breakdowns. Here, crane interferences occur as both cranes cannot be located in the same bay if the trolley of the outer large crane is not located in the crossing lane. The downside of this possibility is that due to the second track per block, more space is needed that cannot be used for container stacking. Thus, with DRMGCs fewer and/or less wide blocks can be installed in a given yard area and the yard density is ceteris paribus reduced in comparison to TRMGC and SRMGC systems. In fact, at the CTA the outer large crane is about 9 m wider than the inner small crane (Koch 2004). But, contrary to the SRMGC and TRMGC systems no special service lanes are needed in between all yard blocks for workshop cars, as the crossing lanes can be used for that purpose in the DRMGC system. Therefore, considering a width of approximately 2 m for each service lane between the yard blocks of the SRMGC and TRMGC systems, the DRMGC system needs 7 m more space width than the SRMGC and TRMGC systems for a same-sized yard block (Saanen 2007). Thus, with the DRMGC system, five yard blocks that are 10 TEUs wide require roughly the same space width ($(2.8\,\text{m} \times 10 + 12\,\text{m}) \times 5 = 200\,\text{m}$) as six same-sized yard blocks with the SRMGC or TRMGC systems do ($(2.8\,\text{m} \times 10 + 5\,\text{m}) \times 6 = 198\,\text{m}$). In Fig. 3.9, it is illustrated that the same number of, but smaller (as compared to the layouts in Figs. 3.4 and 3.7) yard blocks can be installed on a given terminal area with DRMGCs.

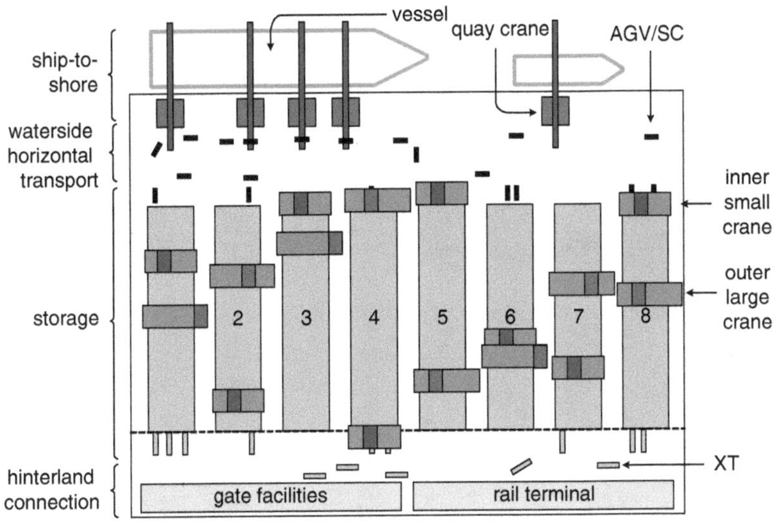

Fig. 3.9 Schematic terminal layout with DRMGCs

3.4.1.4 Triple-Crane System

The latest development of automated RMGC systems is the triple-crane system. It has recently been put into operation for the first time at the CTB in Hamburg (Germany) as a part of a terminal-redesign project with the goal to double the annual container-handling capacity of the terminal (Dorndorf and Schneider 2010). Three cranes will be used per block: Two small identical cranes sharing the same pair of rail tracks and one outer large crane with its own rails. The triple-crane system contains parts of both DRMGC and TRMGC systems: Firstly, comparable to the twin system, the two small identical cranes cannot cross each other and both cranes only access the handover area on their side of the block. Secondly, comparable to a double system, the outer large crane can cross both inner small ones when its trolley is located in the crossing lane. The benefit of the triple-crane systems is an increased handling capacity compared to the other systems, which allows for high productivities and acceptable waiting times even for large yard blocks. At the CTB, the yard blocks are 42 bays long, 10 rows wide and containers are stacked 1-over-5 high (HHLA 2009).

The downside of the triple-crane system is that additional crane interferences have to be considered, which makes the crane-scheduling problem even more complicated and which further reduces the crane productivities in comparison to TRMGC and DRMGC systems. In addition, due to the second pair of rail tracks, the TriRMGC system is as space-consuming as the DRMGC system. The triple-crane system is shown by similar figures as for the other systems: In Fig. 3.10, a single TriRMGC yard block is illustrated in three dimensions from the side, while

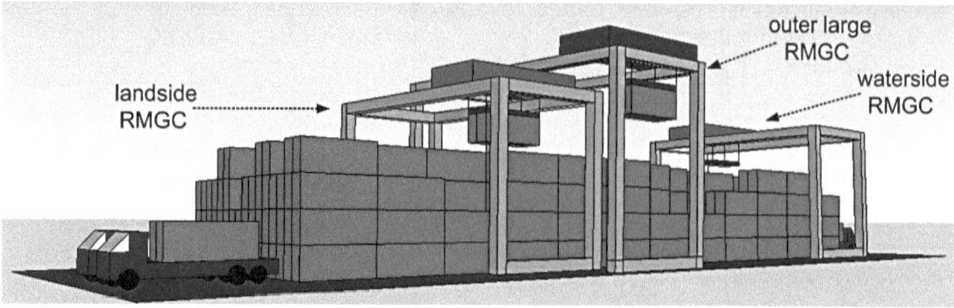

Fig. 3.10 Schematic illustration of an example TriRMGC system

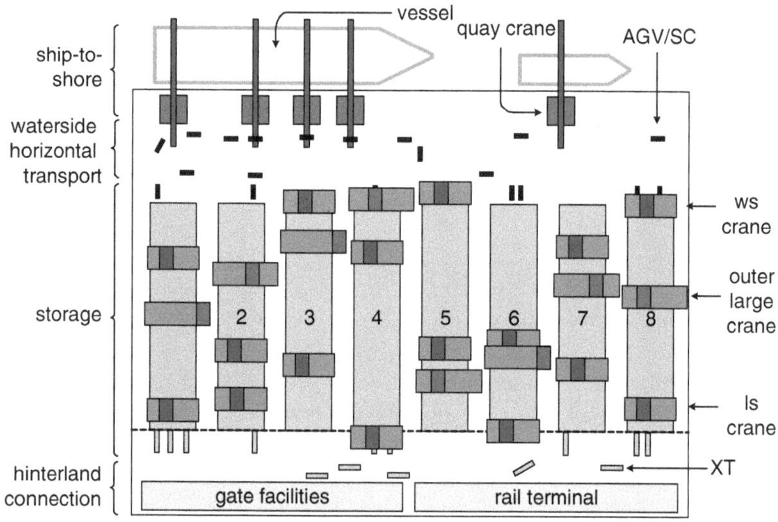

Fig. 3.11 Schematic terminal layout with TriRMGCs

in Fig. 3.11, a complete terminal layout with TriRMGCs is schematically shown from a bird's eye view. Prospectively, even larger RMGC systems with four or more cranes per yard block are conceivable.

3.4.2 Technical Specification

The main technical data of RMGCs—which are their dimensions, weight, velocity, acceleration and maximum lifting capacity—depend on several factors. These factors are the yard-block dimensions, the load status and the abilities of the corresponding crane producer.

Firstly, the technical specification of RMGCs greatly depends on the dimensions of the underlying yard blocks. The more rows and the higher the stacking height,

Table 3.3 Technical specification of an RMGC (Saanen and Valkengoed 2005; Koch 2004; Stahlbock and Voß 2008; Konecranes 2011)

Maximum span	20–50 m
Maximum lifting height	12–22 m
Maximum payload	40–50 t
Gantry velocity	3.0–4.0 m/s
Gantry acceleration/deceleration	0.3–1.0 m/s^2
Trolley velocity	0.8–1.1 m/s
Trolley acceleration/deceleration	0.3–0.5 m/s^2
Hoisting velocity	0.5–1.5 m/s
Hoisting acceleration/deceleration	0.3–0.5 m/s^2
Positioning time on an XT	~30 s
Positioning time on an AGV/on ground	~10 s

the wider and higher, respectively, is the portal of the RMGC. While for instance the yard blocks at the ECT Delta Terminal in Rotterdam (Netherlands) are 6 TEUs wide and the deployed RMGC is only 23.7 m wide (Saanen and Valkengoed 2005), at the CTA in Hamburg (Germany) the yard blocks are 10 TEUs wide and the inner small and the outer large RMGC are 31 and 40 m wide, respectively (Koch 2004). Along with an increasing width and height of the RMGC, its weight increases as well. For instance, at the CTA the inner small crane—which is 22 m high and 15 m long—has a deadweight of about 250 t, while the outer large crane—which is 27 m high and 15 m long—has a deadweight of about 310 t (Koch 2004). In addition, the kinematics of the RMGCs are also affected by their dimensions. The velocity and the acceleration of the RMGCs decrease with increasing crane size due to the additional weight. The small crane at the CTA is for instance capable of a gantry velocity of 3.5 m/s, while its bigger counterpart only travels at 3.0 m/s maximum velocity (Saanen and Valkengoed 2005).

Secondly, the kinematics of an RMGC also depend on its load status. In particular the hoisting velocity is greatly influenced by the payload underneath the spreader, while the velocities of gantry and trolley are not negatively affected by heavy load. The hoisting speed for RMGCs at the CTA varies load-dependent between 1.0 and 1.5 m/s. In addition, the maximum possible dimensions of RMGCs as well as their kinematics vary between the crane producers. Well-known RMGC producers are, among others, Kalmar Heavy Industries, Konecranes and Terex Cranes. A summarising overview on the ranges of the most important technical specifications of RMGCs is given in Table 3.3.

Several hightech positioning systems are required by RMGCs in order to store or retrieve containers automatically. These systems—which make for instance use of technologies like photoelectric barriers and laser scanners—are needed for rough and fine positioning of gantry, trolley and spreader as well as for collision avoidance between multiple RMGCs. In order to position gantry and trolley roughly above the target pile in the block, their positions are ascertained by means of rotating wheels and photoelectric barriers. Once the RMGC has roughly reached its target position, firstly the target piles and its neighbours are measured by means of laser scanners and thereafter the crane position is appropriately adjusted. The hoisting movements of the spreader are continuously observed by a laser-scanner-based load-positioning system, which is also able to detect load swinging that are immediately counter-balanced by special spreader technologies. The crane-positioning process in the waterside handover areas is expected to be faster than in the landside handover areas, as containers are usually either automatically placed on the ground or on well positioned AGVs, while at the landside containers have to be placed on less-good positioned XTs by remote controllers. In total, the RMGC fine positioning takes about 30 s in the landside handover area and about 10 s in the waterside handover area as well as inside the yard block (Koch 2004).

3.4.3 Processes

Each ingoing and outgoing box at a container terminal induces at least one transport job for the automated RMGCs. Besides the pure yard-crane transport of the container from its start position to its place of destination, several other crane movements are involved with a transport job. Certain sequences of these crane movements form different yard-crane processes. Depending on the start position of a transport job, its place of destination as well as its purpose, the following six types of yard-crane processes can be distinguished:

Waterside Storage: The crane performs an empty movement to the waterside handover area, picks up the container, performs a laden movement to the dedicated stacking position in the block and drops off the container.

Landside Storage: The crane performs an empty movement to the landside handover area, picks up the container from an XT, performs a laden movement to the dedicated stacking position in the block and drops off the container.

Waterside Retrieval: A container stored in the block has to be loaded onto a vessel. The crane performs an empty movement to the current stacking position of the container, picks up the container, performs a laden movement to the waterside handover area and drops off the container.

Landside Retrieval: A container stored in the block is called by an XT. The crane performs an empty movement to the current stacking position of the container, picks up the container, performs a laden movement to the landside handover area and places the container onto the XT.

Shuffle: If a container is stacked on top of a container that is to be retrieved, a shuffle move is required. All containers stacked upon the needed one have to be moved to other slots before the needed container can be retrieved. The crane performs an empty movement to the current stacking position of the container, picks up the container, performs a laden movement to the new stacking position and drops off the container. Usually the new stacking position is located close to the original pile, often within the same bay. In general, shuffle processes should be avoided if possible because they are unproductive (i.e., they absorb valuable crane resources as they are not directly related to storage or retrieval requests).

Housekeeping: These yard-crane processes are similar to shuffle jobs, as they also only take place inside the yard block, while both handover areas are not involved. However, in contrast to shuffle jobs, housekeeping jobs are not necessarily required, moreover this type of process is optional, as it is done to improve the storage location of containers in the block with respect to certain stacking objectives.

Waterside and landside storage and retrieval processes can be regarded as the main processes of automated RMGCs, as they are directly requested by up- and downstream transportation to and from the yard block, respectively. In contrast, shuffle and housekeeping jobs may be called auxiliary processes, as they are not directly requested by connected means of transportation, but are only indirectly requested (shuffle) or even optionally performed by an idle RMGC (housekeeping) (Park et al. 2010).

3.4.4 *Planning and Decision Problems*

Several planning and decision problems are involved with automated RMGC systems, both on the strategical design level and on the operational level. The design level mainly concerns greenfield projects for terminal new buildings as well as terminal-extension and conversion projects. A general introduction to the field of terminal-design problems is given in Sect. 2.4.2. In case automated RMGCs are selected as storage equipment—which is considered here—mainly two decisions have to be made on the terminal-design level: the operating type of RMGC system and the dimensions of the yard blocks have to be selected. The system decision concerns the question whether a single, twin, double or even triple-crane system should be deployed, while the decision on the block layout comprises the definition of the block length, width and height. In Chap. 4, the design-planning problem for container-storage yards with automated RMGC systems is addressed in great detail.

On the operational level of RMGC systems, three relevant planning problems have to be regarded: the container-stacking problem (see Sect. 2.4.3.7), the crane-scheduling problem (see Sect. 2.4.3.8) and the crane-routing problem. The container-stacking problem deals with the selection of stacking positions for newly arriving and to-be-relocated containers inside the RMGC blocks of the container-storage yard, with respect to certain stacking objectives. Usually, the quality of the stacking operations is evaluated on the basis of the resulting container accessibility (see Sect. 2.3.2.2). Typical objectives, to be considered restrictions and different solution approaches for the container-stacking problem of automated RMGC systems are extensively addressed in Sect. 5.2.

The crane-scheduling problem deals with the crane assignment and sequencing of all main and auxiliary transport jobs that occur within a yard block. For a single-crane system, it only needs to be decided about the execution sequence of all known transport jobs with respect to certain scheduling objectives, while for multi-crane systems additionally the executing crane of each transport job has to be decided. For multi-crane systems, it has to be taken into account that not all jobs are equally well suited for all cranes of a block. In particular, for the identical cranes within the TRMGC and TriRMGC system, the waterside storage and retrieval jobs are only executable for the crane that is located closer to the waterside handover area, while landside storage and retrieval jobs are only executable for the landside crane. Shuffle jobs and housekeeping jobs may usually be performed by all cranes of a block. Typically the quality of the crane-scheduling approach is assessed on the basis of the resulting crane productivities and vehicle-waiting times in the handover areas of the yard block. In Sect. 5.3, planning objectives, problem setting and solution approaches for the crane-scheduling problem of automated RMGC systems are addressed in great detail.

The question, in which way the gantry cranes of a yard block should be moved between origins and destinations of crane-transport jobs, is addressed by the crane-routing problem. At first glance, there might be hardly any room for decision-making, as portal and trolley can be moved simultaneously in the direction of the next target position, thus yielding the shortest possible driving distance between two different coordinates in the block. However, for multi-crane systems like TRMGC, DRMGC and TriRMGC systems, conflicts between the movements of the cranes have to be regarded. In order to avoid collisions or deadlocks between the cranes of a yard block, it needs to be decided, which crane is given the right of way in conflicting situations and which crane has to wait and/or evade. The quality of the crane-routing approach is often measured against the resulting interference time of the cranes, which is the time the crane movements are prolonged due to waiting and/or evading compared to the shortest possible direct connection between two points without any waiting and/or evading involved. In Sect. 5.4, the crane-routing problem along with its objectives, restrictions and solution approaches is addressed.

3.4.5 Similar Problems and Comparable Logistic Systems

Automated RMGC yard blocks at seaport container terminals are comparably new, highly specialised logistical systems that are only studied by a small group. However, logistically similar systems exist and many of the problems in container terminal logistics can be closely related to some general classes of transportation and network-routing problems that are comprehensively discussed in the literature (Steenken et al. 2004). Subsequently, general classes of logistic systems and planning problems are introduced, whose solution methods may be applicable for the RMGC system and its problems.

In fact, an automated RMGC yard block can be regarded as a special type of the general logistic concept of automated storage and retrieval systems (AS/RS). This concept refers to relatively complex computer-controlled storage systems, which are integrated into manufacturing or warehousing processes. AS/RS have been operating successfully in hundreds of manufacturing and distribution centres since the early 1960s; well known examples are automated high-rise storage racks. As a consequence, strategical and operational planning problems of AS/RS are comparable to those of RMGC systems and it is therefore worth examining AS/RS-related literature. Several overviews on AS/RS planning problems are available (Sarker and Babu 1995; Rouwenhorst et al. 2000). There is a broad range of AS/RS in terms of input-output-positions, capacity and number of order-pickers, which refers to the handover areas, the yard-block capacity and the number of RMGCs, respectively, in the context of container-storage yards. Randhawa et al. (1991) as well as Bozer and White (1990) consider AS/RS with two input-output-positions at the ends of the aisles. For scheduling, the FIFO and NN (nearest neighbour) priority rules are applied. Performance advantages of the NN rule compared to FIFO are reported by Eben-Chaime (1992).

Vis (2002) studies the problem of scheduling AS/RS in general and for the special application of automated storage yards at container terminals. Known methods are reviewed and a new scheduling policy for a unit load AS/RS is presented and tested for container yards. She distinguishes between block and dynamic scheduling concepts, which are comparable to the online concepts ignore and replan, respectively (see Sect. 2.4.3.1). Her review of existing AS/RS scheduling methods reveals that the block-scheduling problem is mostly treated as an assignment problem with the objective of minimising empty-travel times, whereas the dynamic sequencing problem is mostly solved with priority rules. Vis (2002) develops an algorithm that solves the travel-time-minimisation problem for a unit load AS/RS system with multiple aisles and handover positions at both ends of the aisles to optimality. This algorithm is applied in a simulation study to scheduling an SRMGC system.

The crane-scheduling problem differs a lot between the different types of RMGC systems. For SRMGCs, only the order in which the pick-up and drop-off positions of the plannable jobs are visited have to be scheduled. Thus, for SRMGC systems it is equivalent to the travelling-salesman problem (TSP) (Bohrer 2010, pp. 13–17), which asks for the shortest closed path or tour through a set of cities that visits every city exactly once. In Lawler et al. (1985), the TSP is well explained, while more recent information is provided by Gutin and Punnen (2002).

For multi-crane systems, not just job sequences have to be built, but also the jobs have to be assigned to the different cranes. Therefore, the crane-scheduling problem of twin, double and triple-crane systems is not a typical TSP. Moreover, these problems may be regarded as variants of the multiple travelling-salesman problem (MTSP) (Carlo and Vis 2008), the vehicle-routing problem (VRP) (Park et al. 2010) and/or the general machine-scheduling problem. For the MTSP, each crane has to be treated as a salesperson with its own Hamiltonian cycle that will be followed in order to serve the requests. Detailed information on the MTSP and its relation to the TSP are provided in Bellmore and Hong (1974). The main difference between the crane-scheduling problem and the MTSP is that the crane-deployment problem aims at minimising the waiting times for connected means of transportation, as opposed to the traditional objective of minimising the total travel time. A recent survey on the VRP is given by Toth and Vigo (2002).

For the application of methods from the general machine-scheduling problem, the RMGCs have to be seen as parallel machines. For instance, the scheduling problem for the DRMGC system can more generally be regarded as scheduling two identical machines with arbitrary processing times, release times (defined by the due date) and setting-up times (represents empty-movement times). Even without the complicating job characteristics of release and setting-up times, these scheduling problems have been identified as NP-hard (MacCarthy and Liu 1993). Several introductions and literature overviews on scheduling research in general are available (MacCarthy and Liu 1993). In addition, Cheng and Sin (1990) provide a special survey of major research results in parallel-machine-scheduling theory. It turns out that until today, hardly any source is directly related to the scheduling problems addressed here. However, there is an important difference between all these classical OR problems and the crane-deployment problems: Neither the MTSP, nor the VRP, nor the machine-scheduling problem consider mutual interferences of the salespeople, vehicles and/or machines, while, in contrast, they play a major role for the performance of the RMGC systems. Therefore, the solution methods of these classical OR problems cannot be applied directly to the crane-deployment problems, moreover there is a need for revised and/or new planning approaches.

3.5 Concluding Remarks

In this chapter, the container-storage yard as a subsystem of seaport container terminals is regarded in detail. Firstly, the general functions, processes and objectives of the container-storage yard are discussed. Thereafter, different types of storage yards are described and compared. It is found that an RMGC system is already a relevant storage type for seaport container terminals, which additionally has promising future prospects due to its high potential for automation. Therefore, this system is specified in detail: different types of RMGC systems, its processes and its planning problems are introduced.

Among all types of storage systems for seaport container terminals, the strategical design-planning problem is probably most important for the automated RMGC system. In comparison to other types of storage systems, the decisions on the design of an automated RMGC storage yard are mostly irreversible and involved with the highest investment costs. Once implemented, huge financial and organisational efforts would be induced by any change of the yard-block layout and/or the operating type of RMGC system. An increase of the stacking height would at least require that all RMGCs are replaced by new cranes with an appropriate height. In addition, it may be required to renew the ground works in order to cope with the additional weight of the containers and cranes. Similarly, changes of the block width require the cranes to be replaced by appropriate ones and due to the need of the RMGCs for rail tracks and concrete piles the ground works have to be revised as well. Even alterations of the type of RMGC system (e.g., TRMGC to TriRMGC) may be involved with complete revisions of the ground work, as additional rail tracks and/or more stable concrete piles may be needed.

In total, taking into account the costs of cranes, groundworks, rail tracks and handover areas, the investment costs of an automated RMGC storage yard for a medium-sized seaport container terminal may easily exceed 100 million Euros, which is a substantial fraction of the total terminal investment. Hence, decisions on the design of the RMGC storage yard have great financial impact and notable effects on the profitability of seaport container terminals. Further considering the crucial importance of the container-storage yard for the operational performance and the area performance of seaport container terminals as a whole, it is worth examining the strategical design-planning problem of automated RMGC storage yards at seaport container terminals in more detail in the following chapter.

Chapter 4
RMGC-Design-Planning Problem

Within this chapter, a central planning problem of the probably most important terminal subsystem is regarded in detail—the design-planning problem of the container-storage yard. While the design-planning problem of seaport container terminals is briefly introduced in Sect. 2.4, the importance of the storage subsystem for the performance of the whole terminal system is explained in Sect. 3.2. Here, it is in particular dealt with the design of automated RMGC systems, which are comprehensively described in the previous chapter.

In Sect. 4.1, the problem of designing RMGC systems at seaport container terminals is introduced in detail along with all individual decisions to be made, all relevant objectives, possible restrictions and parameters to be considered. Thereafter, in Sect. 4.2, an extensive review of the literature relevant to the problem of designing container-storage yards at seaport container terminals is provided. In particular, it is focused on the research approach used and the most important findings of the papers discussed. Based on the findings of the literature review, different types of general research approaches are introduced and discussed with respect to their applicability for the RMGC-design-planning problem, in Sect. 4.3. The chapter is closed with some concluding remarks in Sect. 4.4.

4.1 Problem Description

Basically, the design-planning problem for the container-storage yard comprises all decisions on the type and numbers of stacking equipment as well as all decisions about the layout of the container-storage yard. Such decisions are usually characterised by long-ranging validity and huge investments. In this section, the design-planning problem of container-storage yards with automated RMGC systems is introduced in detail. It is started with an introduction of all relevant subproblems and decisions to be made within the framework of RMGC-design planning. Thereafter, the objectives of the RMGC-design-planning problem are defined and

N. Kemme, *Design and Operation of Automated Container Storage Systems*, Contributions to Management Science, DOI 10.1007/978-3-7908-2885-6_4,

their interrelationship is discussed. Finally, a wide range of parameters of the RMGC-design-planning problem is introduced and discussed with respect to their effects on the objectives of that problem and the resulting decisions.

4.1.1 Decisions

Considering that this work is devoted to the design of automated RMGC systems with yard blocks that are laid out perpendicular to the quay wall (see Sect. 3.5), two important decisions about the design of the storage yard are already made: The equipment type—automated RMGC—is selected and a basic yard layout—perpendicular, front-end-loading yard blocks—is defined. Therefore, the RMGC-design-planning problem, that is addressed in this chapter, may be regarded as a subproblem of the more general problem of designing a container-storage yard in all its aspects. Basically, the design of an RMGC-operated container-storage yard is defined by the specific type of RMGC system (i.e., SRMGC, TRMGC, DRMGC or TriRMGC), the layout of the yard blocks (i.e., length, width and height) and the number of these yard blocks. In addition, next to these three main decisions about the design of RMGC systems, several auxiliary decisions have to be made to specify the design of an automated RMGC system in detail.

The main RMGC-design-planning problem on the choice of the operating type of RMGC system for the container-storage yard, which is shortly called the system-choice problem hereinafter, deals with the detailed equipment selection for the container-storage yard. Either the single, twin, double or triple-crane system can be selected as operating type of RMGC system. For container terminals with no typically rectangular-shaped storage-yard area, even mixed systems are theoretically conceivable, as it may be advisable to use more cranes per block for longer yard blocks than for shorter ones. The two other main RMGC-design-planning problems, which are shortly called the block-layout problem and the block-number problem, are concerned with the detailed layout of the container-storage yard. In detail, the length, width and height of the yard block in terms of bay, lanes and tiers of TEU have to be decided, which are denoted by n^{x}, n^{y} and n^{z}, respectively. Additionally, the number n^{b} of yard blocks in the container-storage yard needs to be determined. However, these two decisions are greatly interrelated, since the total storage capacity $\left(\pi^{\mathrm{sc}} = n^{\mathrm{b}} \times n^{\mathrm{x}} \times n^{\mathrm{y}} \times n^{\mathrm{z}}\right)$ and the dimensions of the storage area are defined by both the block dimensions $(n^{\mathrm{x}} \times n^{\mathrm{y}} \times n^{\mathrm{z}})$ and the number of yard blocks $\left(n^{\mathrm{b}}\right)$. Thus, taking into account that the area for container storage is usually limited and a minimum storage capacity $\left(\pi^{\mathrm{scmin}}\right)$ is required in order to comply with the annual terminal throughput π^{through} (see Sect. 2.3.1), a decision on the block dimensions will implicitly also define the number of blocks allowed by the available storage area and/or required to comply with the annual terminal throughput. As a consequence, it may be possible to only focus on the block-layout problem during the design process, as the block-number problem will be implicitly solved. However, the reversed relation does not apply, as deciding the block-number problem does not completely solve the block-layout problem. Moreover, only the width and/or the needed capacity of the yard blocks may be determined by fixing the number of yard blocks. Thus, there is still freedom of decision with respect to the length and height of the yard block. In total, it appears to be reasonable to only focus on the system-choice and block-layout problem as the main RMGC-design-planning problems.

The auxiliary decisions about the design of RMGC systems can be classified into decisions of civil engineering, equipment configuration as well as IT and process design. Subsequently, these classes of auxiliary design-planning problems are explained on the basis of some selected decision problems for each class.

Decisions on the civil engineering probably exhibit the longest-ranging validity. For the design of RMGC systems, several auxiliary decisions fall into the class of civil engineering: Firstly, it has to be decided about the foundation for the cranes and the container-storage area. In particular, the type of foundation for the rail tracks has to be determined, which can either be realised as raft or deep foundation. The realisation of the foundation of the rail tracks depends on the size of the selected cranes and the state of the soil. Secondly, it has to be decided about the structure of the drainage system in the yard. In particular, the slope of the yard area and the positioning of drainage gutters have to be specified, which cannot be done without prior to defining the yard-block layout. Thirdly, the structure of the power supply lines and data cables has to be planned. Fourthly, the constructional layout of the waterside and landside handover areas has to be specified, which means that the number of handover lanes and their dimensioning has to be planned. As the handover areas are the interfaces to the waterside horizontal-transport and hinterland-connection subsystems, the specification of the handover areas needs to be synchronised with the decisions for these systems. For the waterside handover area, the specification greatly depends on the used horizontal-transport equipment. While AGVs are usually loaded and/or unloaded in several parallel handover lanes which are clearly separated from each other, SCs may stack the containers in several parallel rows that are several containers long and high (Ranau 2011). On the landside ends of the yard blocks, the handover lanes for the XTs need to be separated by crash barriers and certain communication devices have to be installed between the handover lanes in order to allow the truckers to initiate automated loading or unloading of the XTs by the RMGCs. Therefore, the civil engineers require the dimensions and the number of handover lanes per yard block, which is more or less implicitly determined by the width of the yard block. Depending on the terminal-specific conditions, several other decisions about the civil engineering of the container-storage yard may be required.

A further important class of auxiliary decisions on the design of RMGC systems is the equipment configuration. In detail, the crane dimensions, the crane manufacturer and many technical details have to be specified. Of course, the crane dimensions, in terms of span and clearance, are greatly determined by the width and height of the planned yard-block layout. The crane manufacturer has to be carefully selected, as several technical details—which may be important for the logistical concept and the (operational) performance of the RMGC system—may be implicitly defined by the selection of a certain manufacturer. Such technical details are for instance the crane kinematics (i.e., velocities, accelerations and decelerations), the spreader system (i.e., single-lift or twin-lift) and/or the anti-sway system, which is needed to counterbalance the crosswind sensitivity during hoisting operations. Considering that the waiting times of horizontal-transport vehicles in the handover areas may, among others, be determined by the movement times of the cranes, the times for container fine positioning and the number of simultaneously moved containers, the (operational) performance of RMGC systems is expected to be influenced by the technical specifications of the crane kinematics, the anti-sway-system and the spreader system, respectively. Thus, decisions specifying these technical details are greatly interrelated with the main design-planning problems of the block layout and the system choice.

Finally, several decisions about the IT system and the storage processes need to be made within the framework of the RMGC-design-planning problem. Although most storage processes are implicitly defined by selecting an automated RMGC system (see Sect. 3.4.3), on a more detailed level, several logistical sub-processes and/or process steps need to be defined more precisely. Usually, the IT and software infrastructure is mostly affected by such processual decisions, but also the civil engineering or the equipment configuration may be influenced by these logistical process definitions. Of great importance is, for example, the organisation of the handover processes, which requires decisions on the entry permission for cranes and horizontal-transport equipment (for reasons of occupational safety) as well as decisions on the triggering of landside storage or retrieval jobs by the truckers (e.g., by means of communication pillars). In addition, for the landside handover to XTs, the interface processes between the automated cranes and the remote operators (see Sect. 3.3.3) as well as the assisting devices for the remote operators (e.g., video cameras, laser sensors) have to be specified. Furthermore, it has to be decided if the cranes should make use of the twin-lift possibility (see Sect. 2.2.3.1), which has great influence on the stacking module of the TOS. In case of making use of the twin-lift option, the containers should be stacked in such a way that two adjacent containers can be retrieved at the same time. In general, unlike other storage-yard systems like SCs or RTGCs, automated RMGCs strongly require carefully designed and implemented yard processes, as usually no manual intervention is provided by the system to overcome certain conflicts or unexpected events. In detail, besides the typical TOS modules for the yard administration as well as the planning of stacking positions and the deployment of the storage equipment, automated RMGCs additionally require TOS modules for the automated execution of all crane movements, including mechanisms for the collision and deadlock avoidance as well as control of crane-crossing manoeuvres.

In summary, auxiliary decisions about the design of RMGC systems are to a great extent interrelated with and/or predetermined by the decisions on the main design-planning problems of the system choice and the block layout. In addition, these auxiliary decisions are affected by terminal-specific conditions, which can hardly be used to derive universally valid recommendations for the design of RMGC systems. Thus, it is reasonable to focus on the main decisions of the system choice and the block layout for the investigation of the RMGC-design-planning problem.

Therefore, the type of RMGC system and the yard-block layout are considered to be the only decision variables of the RMGC-design-planning problem here.

4.1.2 *Objectives and Restrictions*

In order to support the performance of seaport container terminals as a whole by the design of RMGC systems, all decisions on the design of these systems have to be made with respect to the main planning objectives of container-storage yards, that are identified in Sect. 3.2 to contribute most to the area performance, the operational performance and the cost performance of the whole terminal system. Hence, the RMGC system should be designed in such a way that the yard density is maximised and both the average waiting times of horizontal-transport vehicles in the handover areas of the yard blocks as well as the unit cost of container-storage and retrieval operations are minimised. Thus, decisions on the design of RMGC systems at seaport container terminals belong to the discipline of multi-criteria decision-making (Ballestero and Romero 1998, pp. 5–8).

In order to increase the yard density by decisions about the design of RMGC systems, it is, on the one hand, required to increase the stacking height of the yard blocks, but, on the other hand, this can be expected to induce a greater number of shuffle moves and/or to require larger-sized and more expensive cranes, thus being harmful for the resulting vehicle-waiting times in the handover areas and/or the unit cost of container-storage and retrieval operations. In contrast, the vehicle-waiting times in the handover areas can be reduced by designing RMGC systems with low stacking heights and several cranes per yard block, which, in turn, can be expected to decrease the yard densities and to increase the costs per storage and retrieval operation, respectively. Finally, the unit cost of container-storage and retrieval operations can be minimised by decreasing both investment and operating costs of the RMGC system, which may be realised by reducing the number of cranes per yard block and decreasing the stacking height of the yard block in order to avoid the operation costs for unproductive shuffle moves. However, at the same time reducing the number of cranes per yard block can be expected to increase the vehicle-waiting times in the handover areas, while decreases of the stacking height would lead to diminishing yard densities. In view of this qualitative analysis of the mutual effects of minimising the vehicle-waiting times, minimising the unit cost of container-storage and retrieval operations and maximising the yard density, it can be seen that each objective of the RMGC-design-planning problem can only be optimised at the cost of the other two objectives. Hence, the optimal RMGC design has to be determined as a trade-off between these conflicting objectives. This interrelationship between the objectives of the RMGC-design-planning problem is also illustrated by the 'magic triangle' that is shown in Fig. 4.1. There, the complete fulfilment of each objective is represented by one of the corner points, thus indicating that none of the objectives can be fully realised without accepting comparably worse realisations with regard to the other objectives.

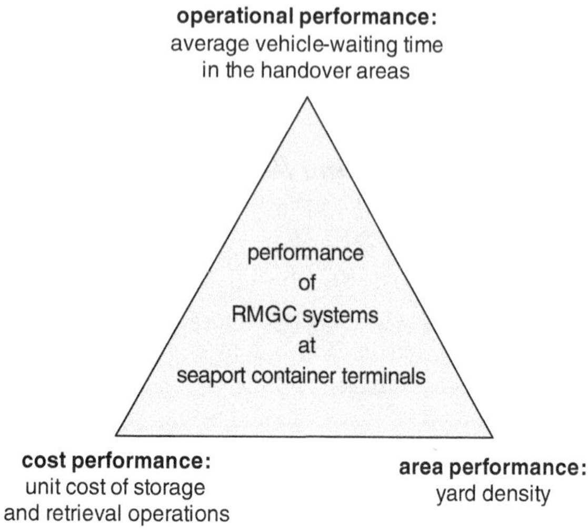

Fig. 4.1 'Magic triangle' of RMGC-design-planning objectives

The trade-off between the objectives of the RMGC-design-planning problem can be formalised by evaluating alternative RMGC designs with respect to a multi-attribute utility function $u(n^{\mathrm{x}}, n^{\mathrm{y}}, n^{\mathrm{z}}, \mathrm{RMGCtype})$ that is composed of the utility contributions of the vehicle-waiting times in the handover areas $\left(u^{\mathrm{opnl}}\right)$, the yard densities (u^{area}) and the unit costs of container-storage and retrieval operations (u^{cost}) of an RMGC design (Ballestero and Romero 1998, pp. 51–55). Taking into account the individual objectives of the utility-contribution-defining KPIs, u^{area} is assumed to increase with increasing yard density, while u^{opnl} and u^{cost} are assumed to decrease with increasing vehicle-waiting time and unit cost, respectively. Altogether, in order to optimise the design of RMGC systems at seaport container terminals, decisions about the operating type of RMGC system and the yard-block layout should aim at

$$
\begin{aligned}
\max\ u(n^{\mathrm{x}}, n^{\mathrm{y}}, n^{\mathrm{z}}, \mathrm{RMGC\,type}) = {} & \lambda^{\mathrm{area}} u^{\mathrm{area}} \left(n^{\mathrm{x}}, n^{\mathrm{y}}, n^{\mathrm{z}}, \mathrm{RMGC\,type}\right) \\
& + \lambda^{\mathrm{opnl}} u^{\mathrm{opnl}} \left(n^{\mathrm{x}}, n^{\mathrm{y}}, n^{\mathrm{z}}, \mathrm{RMGC\,type}\right) \\
& + \lambda^{\mathrm{cost}} u^{\mathrm{cost}} \left(n^{\mathrm{x}}, n^{\mathrm{y}}, n^{\mathrm{z}}, \mathrm{RMGC\,type}\right) \qquad (4.1)
\end{aligned}
$$

$$\text{subject to RMGC type} \in \{\mathrm{SRMGC}, \mathrm{TRMGC}, \mathrm{DRMGC}, \mathrm{TriRMGC}\} \qquad (4.2)$$

$$n^{\mathrm{x}}, n^{\mathrm{y}}, n^{\mathrm{z}} > 0 \qquad (4.3)$$

where λ^{area}, λ^{opnl} and λ^{cost} are the weighting factors for the utility contribution of the area-performance, the operational-performance and the cost-performance effects of a certain RMGC design, respectively.

Apart from the objectives of the RMGC-design-planning problem, it may be necessary to observe some planning restrictions for the design of RMGC systems. Depending on terminal-specific framework conditions, it may be required to design the RMGC system with respect to the available land-area dimensions, the required storage capacity π^{scmin}, the available budget, the maximum acceptable vehicle-waiting time and various other constraints. Additionally, considering that the utility functions u^{area}, u^{opnl} and u^{cost} as well as the corresponding weighting factors λ^{area}, λ^{opnl} and λ^{cost} usually vary between different seaport container terminals, depending on the importance of the corresponding planning objective, which is determined by terminal-specific framework conditions and individual requirements of the relevant decision makers, it is straight-forward to expect the optimal RMGC design to differ as well between seaport container terminals. Hence, it is impossible to determine the one and only optimal RMGC design for all container terminals. Instead, the effects of the RMGC design on the operational performance, the area performance and the cost performance of the container-storage yard can be analysed, thus providing helpful recommendations and guidelines for the design of RMGC systems.

Among all three performance dimensions of the container-storage yard, the operational performance of RMGC designs is probably most difficult to evaluate, as the resulting waiting times for horizontal-transport vehicles in the handover areas of the yard blocks cannot be determined analytically (see Sect. 4.3). In contrast, based on the costs for equipment, land area and ground work as well as the space requirements of containers and types of RMGC systems, the unit cost of container-storage and retrieval operations and the yard density of different RMGC designs can be computed analytically, which yields a comparably easy evaluation of the area and cost-performance effects of RMGC designs (Wiese et al. 2011). In view of this analysis, it is focused here on quantifying and examining the effects of the RMGC design on the operational performance of the container-storage yard at seaport container terminals in terms of vehicle-waiting times in the handover areas of the yard blocks. Area and cost-performance effects are only evaluated qualitatively en passant.

4.1.3 Parameters

Taking into account that container-storage yards at seaport container terminals are complex, highly dynamic, stochastic systems that are greatly interrelated with up- and downstream processes of other terminal subsystems (see Sect. 2.2.2), the performance of RMGC systems is not only determined by the operating type of RMGC system and the layout of the yard block, but also by several other parameters on terminal-specific framework conditions and configurations. While the area performance of RMGC systems is mainly influenced by parameters that define the space requirements for container slots and crane systems, the cost performance is primarily affected by cost-defining parameters like the local wage level, the electricity price, the purchase prices of RMGCs and the civil-engineering costs per metre rail track and per square metre storage area. Owing to the crucial importance of container-storage yards for the operations and the performance of the whole terminal system (see Sect. 3.2), it can be expected that the operational performance of RMGC systems is not just sensitive to changes of parameters that specify the detailed technical and processual implementations of the RMGC system itself, but also to parameter changes of the terminal-framework conditions and the configuration of the up- and downstream subsystems. Since decisions on the design of RMGC systems are determined by the performance effects of alternative designs, it is reasonable to expect the RMGC design to depend on all these performance-influencing parameters of container-storage yards.

In this section, a great number of parameters, that specify the framework conditions and the configuration of container-storage yards, is discussed with respect to their influence on the operational performance of RMGC systems. Basically, the risk for and the extent of vehicle-waiting times in the handover areas of RMGC systems increase with the number of transport jobs which need to be performed by the cranes of these systems and/or decrease with the crane resources that are available to handle these requests. Therefore, it can be expected that the operational performance of RMGC systems is mainly determined by the crane workload a system is faced with and the crane resources available to handle that workload. Apart from the performance effects, also the controllability of these performance-influencing parameters is of importance for the performance and/or the design of seaport container terminals as a whole. Performance-influencing parameters that are mainly controllable by the terminal operators themselves allow coordinated decisions between the RMGC design and these parameters, thus possibly improving the performance of the whole terminal system, whereas parameters that are mostly externally defined (e.g., by shipping lines, technical restrictions, legislation as well as local and global economic trends) do not allow such coordinated decisions about the design of RMGC systems.

Altogether, apart from the decision variables of the RMGC-design-planning problem, 15 parameters are identified here on the basis of qualitative analyses, which affect the operational performance of RMGC systems at seaport container terminals, whereof six influence the performance by changes of the workload situation and nine by changes of the available crane resources. Eight of these performance-influencing parameters are mainly controllable by the terminals themselves and seven are mainly externally given. Subsequently, these performance-influencing parameters of RMGC systems are introduced and discussed with respect to their operational-performance effects and their controllability. It is started with crane-workload-defining parameters and thereafter crane-resource-defining parameters are addressed.

4.1.3.1 Crane-Workload-Defining Parameters

The average and the maximum allowed filling rate of the yard blocks, the transshipment factor, the TEU-factor, the mean container-dwell time and the distribution of container arrival and collection times are identified here to affect the operational performance of RMGC systems by changes of the workload the cranes are faced with.

The average filling rate of the yard block π^{fillavg} is implicitly defined by the annual terminal throughput π^{through} and the storage capacity π^{sc}. The higher the throughput for a given storage capacity, the higher will be the average filling rate of the yard blocks. For a pure import-export terminal with a mean dwell time of $\bar{\delta} = 4$ days, a TEU-factor of $\pi^{\text{TEU}} = 1.6$ and a storage capacity of $\pi^{\text{sc}} = 28,000$ TEUs, an annual terminal throughput of $\pi^{\text{through}} = 1,250,000$ containers leads to an average filling rate of

$$\pi^{\text{fillavg}} = \frac{\pi^{\text{through}} \times \pi^{\text{TEU}} \times \bar{\delta}}{\pi^{\text{sc}} \times 365} = \frac{1,250,000 \times 1.6 \times 4}{28,000 \times 365} \approx 78.3\%, \tag{4.4}$$

whereas an annual terminal throughput of $\pi^{\text{through}} = 1,375,000$ containers will be connected with an increase of the average filling rate to $\pi^{\text{fillavg}} = 86.1\%$. As discussed in Sect. 3.2, the annual terminal throughput cannot be directly decided upon by the terminal operator. Moreover, it is usually determined by the container-handling capacity and the attractiveness of a seaport container terminal. Because the container-handling capacity of a terminal is defined by the dimensions of all terminal subsystems, which are defined by the terminal operator, and the attractiveness of seaport container terminals is greatly affected by its operational performance and the raised handling charges, which can both be controlled and/or influenced by the terminal operator, the annual terminal throughput π^{through} and as a consequence also the average filling rate π^{fillavg} may be regarded as mainly terminal-controlled.

An upper limit for the filling rate of the yard block during daily yard operations is defined by the maximum allowed filling rate of the yard block π^{fillmax}. Such an upper limit is usually defined by the terminal operator in order to preserve some flexibility in the yard-block operations—even in peak situations with high filling rates. In order to enable the execution of all required shuffle moves within the same bay, which is often desired, a minimum number of $n^{z} - 1$ slots has to be kept free in each bay in all situations. For instance, at least three slots have to be kept free in the bay of a yard block with $n^{y} = 8$ rows and $n^{z} = 4$ tiers, resulting in a maximum allowed filling rate of

$$\pi^{\text{fillmax}} = 1 - \frac{n^{z} - 1}{n^{y} \times n^{z}} = 1 - \frac{3}{4 \times 8} \approx 90.6\%. \tag{4.5}$$

Both the average filling rate as well as the maximum allowed filling rate of the yard blocks affect the operational performance of an RMGC system by influencing its workload situation. The higher the average filling rate, the greater is, ceteris paribus, the total crane workload, as more containers need to be stored, retrieved and shuffled in a certain period of time by the same amount of crane resources, thus increasing the risk for and the extent of vehicle-waiting times in the handover areas. In particular, the number of shuffle moves can be expected to increase with the filling rate, as the containers usually need to be stacked higher in order to increase the average filling rate. For a yard block with four tiers, an increase of the average filling rate from $\pi^{\text{fillavg}} = 78.3\%$ to $\pi^{\text{fillavg}} = 86.1\%$ is for instance connected with an increase of the average stacking height from 3.132 to 3.444 tiers, thus increasing the risk for shuffle moves (Duinkerken et al. 2001). In contrast, the maximum allowed filling rate of the yard blocks has no effects on the total workload the cranes are faced with, but on the risk for and the extent of peaks in the distribution of the total crane workload over time. While comparably uniform filling rates of the yard blocks would lead to an evenly distributed workload for the cranes, very imbalanced filling rates over time for one and the same average filling rate would result in many and/or heavy peak workloads for the cranes. In the case of rather even distributions of the filling rate, the risk for and the extent of vehicle-waiting times in the handover areas of the yard blocks is usually expected to be comparably low, since a constant supply of crane resources is faced with a rather constant demand for these resources. Whereas comparably uneven filling-rate distributions are usually connected with some situations of oversupply of crane resources and other situations with a lack of crane resources. As a consequence, some jobs may be performed timely by the crane without any waiting times for the horizontal-transport vehicles involved, while other jobs may be performed (much) too late. In particular during situations of high peak workloads, several jobs are simultaneously waiting for execution, so that a vast amount of total crane lateness will be accumulated within short periods of time. Thus, an uneven workload distribution over time can be expected to induce more vehicle-waiting times in the handover areas than evenly distributed crane workloads. By defining the maximum allowed filling rate of the yard blocks in relation to the average filling rates, the terminal operator can greatly determine the risk for and the extent of peaks in the distribution of the crane workload.

Another parameter, that can be expected to affect the risk for and the extent of peak workloads for one and the same total crane workload, is the distribution of container arrivals and collections at the yard blocks. Similar to the maximum allowed filling rate of the yard blocks, a balanced distribution of container arrivals and collections over time is expected to lead to evenly distributed workloads for the RMGCs, whereas rather imbalanced container arrivals and collections can be expected to induce a greater number of and/or more pronounced peak workloads for the cranes, thus increasing the risk for and the extent of vehicle-waiting times compared to evenly distributed vehicle arrivals at the yard blocks.

Concerning the controllability of the timely distribution of container arrivals and collections at the yard blocks, it has to be distinguished between the waterside and landside interfaces of the block. For the distribution of container arrivals and collections at the landside, it has again to be distinguished between arrivals and collections by XT and by train. As explained in Sect. 2.4.3.1, the arrival times of individual XTs at the terminal are usually completely unknown for the terminal operator. But, certain seasonal, weekly and/or daily arrival patterns are usually observed for landside XT arrivals, which allow predictions of the landside workload distribution. These arrival patterns may among other things be determined by legal requirements (e.g., night and/or weekend driving ban), the hours of operation on the terminal (e.g., 24/7 or closed at night/weekend), the vessel-call pattern for deep-sea vessels, the transport distances of XTs (i.e., short vs. long), the quality of the local road network and the risk for traffic congestions. By introducing a truck-appointment system, which requires that the truckers book certain timeslots with limited capacities in advance to their actual arrival and commit themselves to arrive in these timeslots, the terminal can try to smooth the distribution of XT arrivals. The distribution of landside train arrivals over time is mostly determined by factors like the timetables of the railway, the availability of hinterland railway routes, the availability of shunting capacities in the local port area and the handling capacity of the rail station on the terminal. Usually, only the last factor can be directly managed by the terminal operator, whereas the others are outside the terminal manager's sphere of influence. In total, both arrivals of XTs and trains have to be regarded as mainly externally controlled influence factors.

For the distribution of container arrivals and collections at the waterside interface of the yard blocks, it has to be distinguished between arrivals and collections by deep-sea vessel and by feeder vessel (see Sect. 2.1.3). While the distribution of container arrivals and collections by deep-sea vessel is usually based on a vessel-call pattern (see Sect. 2.2.2.2), that is jointly agreed upon by the terminal and the shipping lines, the distribution of container arrivals and collections by feeder vessel may be based on several factors, that often lead to randomly appearing arrival distributions. Due to their function within the hub and spoke system (see Sect. 2.1.3), it is often observed that many feeder vessels arrive in close time proximity to the deep-sea vessel to/from which most containers are transshipped. Hence, the vessel-call pattern is also an important factor of influence for the arrival distribution of feeder vessels. Thus, terminal operators are even more striving to influence the vessel-call pattern towards a more balanced arrival-time distribution of the deep-sea vessels. But due to the competitive situation with other terminals, the terminal operators are usually constrained to accept the arrival-time targets of the shipping lines in so far as there still is sufficient handling capacity (i.e., QCs and/or berthing places) available for the demanded berthing times. By deciding on the design of the ship-to-shore subsystem (see Sect. 2.2.2.2), the terminal operator may at least be able to control the upper limit for the peak waterside workloads. Nevertheless, all in all the distribution of container arrivals and collections at the waterside ends of the RMGC blocks can be regarded as mostly externally determined.

Similarly, also the transshipment factor, the mean container-dwell time and the TEU-factor can hardly be controlled by the terminal operators themselves. Basically, these parameters are determined by global and local economical circumstances and developments, which are beyond the sphere of influence of the terminal. The transshipment factor usually is a result of decisions of shipping lines and the demands of their customers. If a shipping line decides to transship more containers from vessel to vessel at a certain terminal, the transshipment factor of that terminal will increase. Similarly, if more customers are demanding container transports to/from the hinterland of a certain terminal, the transshipment factor will decrease. Both decisions and/or demands can hardly be directly influenced by the terminals, except if it is a so-called dedicated terminal instead of a traditional multi-user terminal (see Sect. 2.3.1). Then, the shipping line decisions and, along with it, the transshipment factor of the terminal might, to some extent, be mutually agreed by the same decision makers. In contrast, the demand for container transports to/from the hinterland of the terminal can more or less not be influenced by the terminal. It is mainly determined by quantity and quality of the available hinterland connections and the Loco-ratio of the port (e.g., Hamburg 30%, Rotterdam 17%, Bremerhaven 10%), which gives the share of goods that are produced, reprocessed and/or extensively handled in the nearby region of the terminal (Brandt and Jung 2007, pp. 25–26). The TEU-factor (see Sect. 2.3.1) is mainly determined by the demands of producing and transporting companies for certain container sizes. Over the last decades, a general trend towards larger containers can be observed, leading to a monotonously increasing TEU-factor. The mean container-dwell time is by definition determined by the container-arrival and collection times which mainly depend on the needs of the shipping lines and their customers. However, through changes of the storage-day charges for containers, the terminal operator is theoretically able to influence the container-dwell times to some degree. By raising the storage-day charges, the terminal operator can try to set incentives for his customers to reduce dwell times (see Sect. 2.3.2.1). But in order to avoid competitive disadvantages in comparison to other ports, the charges can only be raised to some extent. In view of this analysis, the transshipment factor, the mean container-dwell time and the TEU-factor have to be seen as mainly externally defined parameters of the RMGC-design-planning problem.

Referring to (2.1) (see Sect. 2.3.1), the TEU-factor and the mean container-dwell time have similar effects on the total crane workload of RMGC systems. Considering that by definition a fewer number of containers is stored in a container-storage yard with on average longer containers than in another identically sized and filled container-storage yard, increases of the TEU-factor are, ceteris paribus, expected to reduce the number of storage and retrieval operations that need to be performed by the cranes in a certain period of time. In a similar way, increases of the mean container-dwell time directly lead to later retrieval operations for each stored container and to longer blocked storage slots for the storage of other containers. As a consequence thereof, fewer numbers of containers are, ceteris paribus, stored and retrieved within a certain period of time, thus reducing the total crane workload.

Finally, the transshipment factor of a seaport container terminal has no effects on the total crane workload of an RMGC system, but for its spatial distribution between the waterside and landside handover areas. By definition, increases of the transshipment factor induce a greater fraction of the annual terminal throughput that is transferred from vessel to vessel (see Sect. 2.3.1). As a consequence thereof, a greater number of storage and retrieval operations need to be performed by cranes at the waterside ends of the yard blocks, but at the same time fewer storage and retrieval operations occur in the landside handover areas, thus increasing the workload imbalance between the waterside and landside handover areas and amplifying the peak workloads in the waterside handover areas.

4.1.3.2 Crane-Resource-Defining Parameters

In addition to the operational-performance effects of the crane workload, the crane kinematics, the required time for final container handovers, the type, the number and the control of the used equipment for the waterside horizontal transport, the used stacking strategy, the used crane-scheduling strategy, the used crane-routing strategy and the predictability of container-arrival and collection times are identified to influence the operational performance of RMGC systems by affecting the available crane resources to handle the workload an RMGC system is faced with.

Apart from the number of cranes deployed per yard block, which is defined by the design of the RMGC systems, the available crane resources are, to a great extent, determined by the kinematics of the cranes (see Sect. 3.4.2). Higher velocities as well as faster accelerations and decelerations of portal, trolley and/or spreader are generally connected with shorter execution times for individual jobs. As a consequence, each executed job is finished more quickly, thus reducing the risk for and the extent of vehicle-waiting times in the handover areas of the yard blocks for these jobs and allowing an earlier start of subsequent jobs, which again reduces the risk for and the extent of vehicle-waiting times for these jobs. The terminal operator may at most be able to influence the crane kinematics by deciding on the block width and height, which implicate the corresponding crane dimensions (see Sect. 3.4.2). However, also this scope of influence of the terminal is rather limited. Taking into account that there are no other options for the terminal operator to control the crane kinematics, this crane-resource-defining parameter of the RMGC systems has to be regarded as mainly externally given.

The time required by the cranes for the final handovers of containers can be expected to have similar effects on the available crane resources as the crane kinematics. In contrast to the movements of portal, trolley and spreader that are given deterministically by the crane kinematics, here, the final-handover times are assumed to comprise all non-deterministic time components of a container handover, like fine positioning of the crane (see Sect. 3.4.2), bolting and unbolting of the twist locks and waiting time for the remote operators at the landside handover area (see Sect. 3.3.3). The precise duration of these time components vary from handover to handover depending on several random influence factors like wind conditions, positioning accuracy of containers, XTs and AGVs as well as the remote operators' workload and skills. The less time is spent on these stochastic time components of the final container handover, the earlier a job is finished and the sooner the next job can be started, which both reduce the risk for and the extent of vehicle-waiting times. Owing to different positioning accuracies of containers and vehicles in the handover areas and in the stack (see Sect. 3.4.2), the final-handover times may vary notably between the landside handover area, the waterside handover area and the stack. Considering that a final handover in the landside handover areas cannot be started before a remote operator is assigned, which may take some time depending on the landside crane workload and the available number of remote operators, it can be expected that the handover times in the landside handover area are notably longer than in the waterside handover area and inside the block. While the waiting times for the remote operators can at least partly be controlled by the terminals themselves by changing the number of deployed remote operators, the other time components of the final-handover times are mostly given by external factors and framework conditions.

In contrast to the crane-resource-defining kinematics and final-handover times of the cranes, type, number and control of the deployed equipment for the waterside horizontal transport are usually directly defined by the terminal operators themselves. The type of the horizontal-transport equipment, which can either be an active or a passive vehicle (see Sect. 2.2.3.2), is of particular importance for the operational performance of RMGC systems in two aspects: Firstly, by defining type and quantity of crane processes which may induce some waiting time for the horizontal-transport vehicles. While a passive vehicle always needs to wait in the waterside handover area for a not yet arrived crane, independently of delivering or collecting a container, active vehicles only need to wait when collecting a container (i.e., waterside retrieval processes of the cranes), but never when delivering (i.e., waterside storage processes of the cranes). As a consequence, the risk for vehicle-waiting times in the waterside handover areas of the yard blocks is much greater for passive vehicles than for active vehicles. Secondly, also type and quantity of crane processes which may be connected with unproductive waiting times for the cranes themselves are determined by the type of the deployed horizontal-transport equipment. Similar to the waiting times of the vehicles, a crane always needs to wait for a passive vehicle that has not yet arrived, while it only needs to wait for active vehicles that deliver a container but never for active vehicles that collect a container. Thus, the risk for unproductive crane-waiting times in the waterside handover areas of the yard blocks is much greater for passive vehicles than for active vehicles. The longer these unproductive crane-waiting times are, the more time is spent on the execution of crane-transport jobs, thus wasting crane resources and reducing the crane resources actually available for performing other storage and retrieval jobs. Altogether, the type of the deployed horizontal-transport equipment has both direct and indirect effects on the resulting vehicle-waiting times of RMGC systems.

Apart from the deployed vehicle type for the waterside horizontal transport, there may be two reasons for unproductive crane-waiting times in the waterside handover areas of the yard blocks: Firstly, the crane may arrive too early in comparison to the announced arrival time of the transport vehicle—which is the due date of the corresponding job. And secondly, the transport vehicle may arrive too late in comparison to its originally announced arrival time. While the first reason for crane-waiting times is determined by the scheduling and routing of the cranes, which is discussed subsequently, the second cause for crane-waiting time is dependent on the number of deployed horizontal-transport vehicles and the applied dispatching and routing strategies to control these vehicles (see Sects. 2.4.3.5 and 2.4.3.6). Usually, it can be expected that a greater number of horizontal-transport machines and improved operational planning strategies lead to more timely arrivals of the vehicles at the yard blocks, thus reducing the crane-waiting times and increasing the actually available crane resources.

In addition to the waiting times of the cranes in the handover areas of the yard blocks, the waste of crane resources also consists of the amount of crane resources that is tied up by unproductive shuffle moves, empty-movement times of the cranes and interferences between the cranes. Usually, these reasons for a reduction of the actually available amount of crane resources are greatly determined by operational decisions on the stacking of containers, scheduling of crane-transport jobs and routing of cranes, which depend on the configuration of the underlying planning strategies for these operational decisions. Throughout this analysis, it is distinguished between the selection and the parametrisation of container-stacking, crane-scheduling and crane-routing strategies, which are all in detail addressed in Chap. 5. Each of these strategies can be helpful to reduce the waste of crane resources and to minimise the vehicle-waiting times in the handover areas. The number of required shuffle moves, which is of great importance for the operational performance of container-storage yards (see Sect. 3.2), is to a great extent determined by the quality of the used stacking strategy. For multi-crane systems, the extent of mutual interferences between the cranes of a yard block is greatly affected by the applied routing strategy. The crane-scheduling strategy is of particular relevance for the operational performance of RMGC systems, as not only the waste of crane resources in terms of crane-waiting, empty-movement and interference times is determined by the configuration of this operational planning strategy, but also the starting time of individual crane-transport jobs. This directly affects the resulting vehicle-waiting times. Altogether, each of these operational planning strategies for RMGC systems can be regarded as another crane-resource-defining parameter of the RMGC-design-planning problem.

In Sect. 2.4.3.1, it is illustrated that most operational planning decisions at seaport container terminals are usually based on only incomplete and/or uncertain information. This means they belong to the class of online-planning problems. The operational planning problems of container stacking, crane scheduling and crane routing require information on the times of prospective container arrivals and collections in order to make good decisions (see Chap. 5). Since the container arrivals and collections are usually not completely known in advance and also uncertain to some degree, the operational planning problems of RMGC systems also belong to the class of online-planning problems (see Sects. 2.4.3.7 and 2.4.3.8). Additionally, considering the fact that the ex post realised solution quality of an online-planning problem usually is the better the more reliable information are ex ante available for taking the necessary decisions, it can be expected that the waste of crane resources is not only determined by the selected planning strategies and their parametrisations, but also by the predictability of the container-arrival and collection times at the waterside and landside ends of the yard blocks. Provided that the applied planning strategies make use of all available information, it can be expected that the waste of crane resources is the smaller, the more container arrivals and collections are known in advance and the more reliably the arrival times of the corresponding transport vehicles at the yard blocks are known.

Similar to the distributions of container-arrival and collection times, it has to be distinguished between the predictability of arrivals and collections by XT, train, deep-sea vessel and feeder vessel. As explained before, individual XT arrivals are so far not at all predictable. Moreover, container arrivals and collections by XTs just become known at the moment when the corresponding XT arrives at the terminal gate. Even with a properly working truck-appointment system the realised XT-arrival times can differ from the agreed ones, due to traffic congestions and/or other external events. In addition, even after an XT arrives at the gate, the container-arrival or collection time at the corresponding yard block is still difficult to predict for the terminal, as it cannot be reliably controlled when the corresponding RMGC job is triggered by the trucker. Hence, individual container arrivals and collections by XTs can hardly be predicted by the terminals and there is only little room for the terminal operator to improve/control this predictability.

The predictability of container arrivals and collections by trains is much better, as the arrival times and loading lists of the trains are usually submitted to the terminal a few hours or even days before the actual arrival. Furthermore, the container transports between the rail station and the yard blocks are usually performed by terminal equipment, which allows reliable predictions of the container-arrival and collection times at the yard blocks. But due to human influences and dynamic effects, the quality of such predictions may differ depending on the planning and IT systems of the terminal. Therefore, the predictability of container arrivals and collections by train as well as its controllability by the terminal are regarded as substantially better than for arrivals and collections by XTs.

For the predictability of container arrivals and collections by deep-sea and feeder vessel, it has to be distinguished between a rough estimation of container arrivals and collections and the prediction of exact arrival and collection times at the yard blocks. While arrivals of deep-sea vessels usually follow a periodically repeated vessel-call pattern, thus allowing a rough estimation of future container arrivals and collections, the arrivals of feeder vessels become known only shortly before the actual arrival time. However, owing to stochastic influences like weather conditions and disturbances of the vessel operations in prior ports on the route of a vessel, the announced arrival times of both deep-sea and feeder vessels may still vary substantially. Only when a vessel arrives at the quay of the terminal, it is possible for the terminal to predict the exact arrival and collection times of individual containers at the yard block, as vessel-loading and unloading operations as well as the waterside horizontal transport between the quay and the yard blocks are controlled by the terminal itself. How far in advance the exact arrival and collection times can actually be predicted, is greatly dependent on the terminal operations and the abilities of the applied TOS, which are both determined by the terminal operator. But considering the fact that the QC operations are manually controlled, thus leading to stochastic variations of the vessel-unloading and loading processes, the precise arrival and collection times of individual containers at the yard block can usually only be predicted once the corresponding horizontal-transport vehicle has started the drive to the yard block, which typically is only a few minutes or even seconds before its actual arrival time.

4.2 Literature Overview

In total, far more than 300 references on container-terminal issues are available and this number is steadily growing. However, the RMGC-design-planning problem is hardly addressed in the literature so far. In this section, an overview on literature relevant to this topic is given, which does not just comprise papers on container terminals which discuss RMGC-design planning, but also storage-yard-design planning in general and design planning of RTGC systems. In total, 19 relevant references on the strategical design of container-storage yards at seaport container terminals can be found in the literature, whereof seven address the design problem of container-storage yards in general, six address the problem of designing RTGC systems and another six address the previously introduced RMGC-design-planning problem. Subsequently, the objectives, the research approaches and the most important findings of these papers are summarised.

4.2.1 Storage-Yard Design

All seven references on the design of the container-storage yard in general have in common that different types of stacking equipment are compared. Nam and Ha (2001) present a comparison study of automated and conventional terminal equipment with regard to several evaluation criteria. In particular, a conventional container terminal with TTUs and sideway-loading yard cranes is compared with an innovative terminal that deploys automated terminal equipment like AGVs and RMGCs. In the first part of the paper, automated and conventional terminals are just qualitatively compared. Numerous evaluation criteria are introduced by Nam and Ha (2001), ranging from cost and productivity figures to terminal characteristics and the skills of the labour. They find the conventional terminal to be superior in almost all considered aspects. In the second part of the paper, these qualitative findings are confirmed by results of a simulation-based commercial case study by PNC (1999) on the equipment selection for the Busan New Port project in South Korea. In detail, the conventional terminal is found to be superior for the considered case in terms of land-use efficiency, equipment productivity, investment costs and annual operation costs. However, due to the technological progress in the field of automated terminal equipment, several assumptions and conclusions of Nam and Ha (2001) seem to be questionable and/or outdated from a present-day perspective.

Liu et al. (2002) compare four innovative concepts for automated container terminals by means of a simulation study with regard to several performance indicators like the GCR, the standardised storage-handling capacity and the container-cost index. The concepts differ in the used equipment for both the storage yard and the horizontal transport: Firstly, AGVs and RTGCs are combined. Secondly, a linear motor-conveyance system for the horizontal transport is combined with RTGCs. Thirdly, a combination of AGVs and grid-rail systems (i.e., a yard-block-overhead-rail system with several shuttles) is considered. Fourthly, AGVs are combined with an AS/RS system (i.e., a storage-rack system with several automated storage and retrieval machines). It is found that automation could dramatically increase the terminals throughput and reduce its costs. The highest standardised storage-handling capacity is obtained for the combination of AGVs and an AS/RS system, while the AGV-RTGC combination leads to the lowest container-cost index.

Chu and Huang (2005) present an analytical comparison of SCs, RTGCs and sideway-loading RMGCs as stacking equipment. Their paper mainly aims at supporting decisions on the employed stacking equipment and yard-block layout with respect to the container-handling capacity of the terminal. In order to compute this figure, a general equation is proposed by Chu and Huang (2005) that takes into account the space requirements of the stacking system, the dimensions of the yard block, the transshipment factor, the average container-dwell time and the terminal size. It is found that the container-handling capacities increase from SC over RTGC to RMGC. Furthermore, Chu and Huang (2005) show that the handling capacities increase with decreasing container-dwell time and increasing transshipment factor. Apart from the container-handling capacity, no other performance criteria are considered.

In contrast, Vis (2006a) compares the performance of an automated SRMGC system and a manned SC system with regard to the movement times required to handle storage and retrieval requests at both sides of the blocks. In particular, the influence of the yard-block layout, the number of storage and retrieval requests as well as the arrival pattern of these requests on the comparative performance of SRMGCs and SCs are investigated by Vis (2006a). It is found for the used experimental setup that the SRMGC system is superior in terms of total movement time up to a block width of 9 TEUs, while for broader yard blocks the SC system performs better.

Saanen (2006) presents a performance comparison of an RTGC system and an automated TRMGC system with regard to the yard density, the equipment productivity and the container-cost index. While quite detailed information on the cost-efficiency analysis are provided, hardly any information about the simulation model and the experimental setup are given, that are used to obtain the productivity figures. However, the TRMGC system is found to yield higher yard densities but lower productivities than RTGC systems for the considered experimental setup. From the cost perspective, the TRMGC system is found to be greatly preferable for the assumed cost parameters.

Lee and Kim (2010) have looked at estimating the optimal block dimensions for RTGC and SRMGC systems with regard to the equipment productivity. To estimate this performance figure, several cycle-time models of various crane operations are analytically derived. It is found that the optimal number of bays per yard block is larger for the RTGC systems than for the SRMGC system, while the optimal number of rows per yard block is larger for the SRMGC system than for the RTGC system.

Unlike all other papers on the design of the container-storage yard in general, Pirhonen (2011) compares two different terminal systems—a conventional terminal with RTGCs and TTUs and a new terminal concept using an automated front-end-loading TRMGC system in combination with automated shuttle carriers (see Sect. 2.2.3.2)—not just with regard to cost, area and operational-performance figures, but mainly regarding energy consumption and exhaust emissions of the compared equipment combinations. These figures are analytically computed based on the power use and emissions of individual machines and the numbers of machines needed to yield similar GCRs with both terminal systems, which are determined by means of a simulation study. It is found that slightly more energy is needed by the automated terminal system compared to the conventional system, while local exhaust emissions are substantially reduced by the combination of automated TRMGC system and shuttle carriers.

4.2.2 RTGC Design

Most references on the design of RTGC-operated container-storage yards deal with the layout planning for that type of storage systems. While Kim et al. (2008); Wiese et al. (2009b) and Wiese et al. (2010) suggest analytical equations as well as optimisation models and methods to derive the optimal layout for a given yard shape, Petering and Murty (2009) as well as Petering (2009) investigate the influence of the yard-block dimensions by means of simulation studies. In contrast, both the optimal layout and the needed number of RTGCs are determined by Kim and Kim (1998) using analytical equations.

In detail, Kim and Kim (1998) develop a model to determine the optimal dimensions and numbers of needed RTGCs for an import-container-storage yard, with respect to space costs, fixed investment costs for the cranes, variable crane costs and outside truck costs in terms of time spent for the transfer of containers. Crane-transfer times between different bays, container loading and unloading times, the number of required shuffle moves as a function of the stacking height and the initial filling rate of the yard blocks are taken into account. A numerical example is solved and the sensitivity of the optimal solution to the change of cost parameters is investigated, but no general recommendations for the design of RTGC storage yards are provided.

Kim et al. (2008) present a method to determine the optimal number of bays, rows and tiers per yard block for a container terminal that makes use of RTGCs and TTUs. For both types of yard-block layouts—parallel and perpendicular to the quay wall—optimisation models are suggested that aim at minimising the weighted sum of the expected TTU driving distances and the expected number of shuffle moves. Kim et al. (2008) derive analytical formulae to estimate both values. The optimal layout for given parameters is then computed by enumerating different numbers of horizontal and vertical driving lanes (i.e., different block widths and lengths). Finally, numerical examples for the suggested design method are provided for real-world container terminals, and the layout with parallel laid-out yard blocks is shown to be superior for the considered parameter settings and assumptions.

Wiese et al. (2009b) make use of parallels between the layout-planning problem for container terminals and the FLP (facility-layout problem), which is frequently investigated. Recent surveys of the FLP are provided by Singh and Sharma (2006) as well as Drira et al. (2007). Wiese et al. (2009b) propose an FLP-based MIP model to find optimal positions for the elements of a container terminal that deploys RTGCs. The adequacy and the performance of the attained layouts are evaluated and analysed by means of a simulation model. Two shortcomings of this layout-planning approach are the restrictive assumptions on rectangularly shaped layouts and on block lengths, which are assumed to be given for the MIP model.

In a subsequent paper, Wiese et al. (2010) present a layout-planning method for arbitrarily shaped terminals with RTGCs and variable block lengths. Firstly, they show that the layout-planning problem for rectangular terminals can be reformulated as a resource-constrained-shortest-path problem. Secondly, for terminals with an arbitrary shape, Wiese et al. (2010) develop a variable-neighbourhood-search heuristic, as the problem is non-linear for non-rectangular terminals. By means of a computational study it is shown that the heuristic leads to competitive results for rectangular terminals, as the optimal solution is obtained for 43% of the tested instances and the optimality gap is less than 1.5% for all remaining instances.

In contrast to these analytical studies of layout planning for RTGC systems, Petering (2009) presents a simulation approach that seeks to investigate the influence of different block widths on the total terminal performance in terms of the GCR. For a pure transshipment terminal and dozens of terminal scenarios, block widths ranging from two to fifteen rows are evaluated by means of a discrete-event simulation model. It is found that the GCR is 'concave' with respect to the block width for constant storage capacities and equipment numbers. In addition, the results show that the optimal block width ranges from six to twelve rows depending on the terminal characteristics.

In a further simulation study, Petering and Murty (2009) analyse the influence of the block length and the influence of the crane-deployment strategy on the GCR of pure transshipment terminals. For four different terminal scenarios, block lengths in the range from 14 to 360 TEUs are investigated by means of the same simulation model that is used by Petering (2009). Results on the effects of the block length indicate that RTGC-operated yard blocks with a length between 56 and 72 TEUs, which is longer than the common blocks in use today, lead to the highest GCR.

4.2.3 RMGC Design

In contrast to the references on the design of RTGC-operated storage yards, most studies on the RMGC-design-planning problem are based on simulation experiments. Like the problem itself, the six simulation studies on the RMGC-design-planning problem can be classified into different groups, depending on which main decisions are addressed. There are three papers that compare different types of RMGC systems for a given yard-block layout (Valkengoed 2004; Saanen and Valkengoed 2005; Saanen 2007), two papers that compare different block layouts for a given type of RMGC system (Duinkerken et al. 2001; Wiese et al. 2011) and one paper that roughly addresses both main decisions of the RMGC-design-planning problem (Zyngiridis 2005).

Both operational and strategical planning problems of an automated container terminal that makes use of AGVs and SRMGCs are addressed by Duinkerken et al. (2001). Besides the influence of the stacking height on the QC performance, they also investigate the effects of different stacking strategies and different numbers of AGVs. With regard to the block-layout problem, the stacking height is varied in the range from two to nine tiers for yard blocks with constant width and capacity, which means that the block length is adapted appropriately to the stacking height. Therefore, two different performance effects of an increasing stacking height are identified. Firstly, more tiers are involved with more shuffle moves for the cranes and reductions of the GCR. Secondly, more tiers require shorter blocks and lead to shorter crane-driving distances, thus facilitating GCR improvements. Duinkerken et al. (2001) find the second effect to be superior up to a stacking height of five tiers.

Similarly, also Zyngiridis (2005) addresses operational and strategical planning problems of an automated container terminal with RMGCs and SCs. In the first part of his work, MIP models for the SRMGC and TRMGC-scheduling problems are developed, while in the second part of the study, these models are used to compare the performance of yard blocks with different lengths and filling rates. In detail, for single and twin-crane systems a yard block with six rows and four tiers is tested over a period of four hours for yard lengths of 20 and 60 bays as well as filling rates of 22% and 66%. It is observed that the twin-crane system performs better than the single-crane system for all considered tests. In addition, Zyngiridis (2005) finds for the considered parameter settings and assumptions that increasing the block length and/or fullness of the yard block have substantially negative performance effects for SRMGC systems, while TRMGC systems are only affected by the block length. However, due to the short simulation period and the small number of experiments, the general validity of these findings is at least statistically questionable.

An extensive simulation study on the performance effects of the TRMGC and DRMGC systems is provided by Valkengoed (2004). She considers a container terminal with AGVs and yard blocks that are 40 bays long, 8 rows wide and 4 tiers high. Several different criteria are used to compare both types of RMGC systems, such as the GCR, the equipment productivities and mutual blocking times of the cranes. In addition, both crane systems are compared for different types of crane-scheduling strategies and different workload scenarios. The results are somehow ambivalent, as the TRMGC system seems to have a slightly higher productivity than the DRMGC system when regarding a single yard block, while when regarding the entire terminal operations, the DRMGCs are able to produce higher GCRs at the cost of longer truck-service times by serving the waterside handover areas with both cranes. Valkengoed (2004) explains the surprising productivity lack of the double-crane systems with the time-intensive crane-crossing processes and the slower crane velocity that is assumed for the outer large cranes.

A similar simulation study is presented by Saanen and Valkengoed (2005). For a container terminal that deploys AGVs, they compare SRMGC, TRMGC and DRMGC systems with regard to several criteria, such as the GCR, the equipment productivities, the container-handling capacity and costs. The considered yard blocks are 40 bays long and 4 tiers high. While SRMGC-operated blocks are only 6 rows wide, the blocks of TRMGC and DRMGC systems are 10 rows wide. Comparable to the results of Valkengoed (2004), no advantage in terms of the block productivity is found for the double-crane system, while it leads to the highest GCR when regarding the entire terminal operations. However, according to Saanen and Valkengoed (2005), this small performance benefit of the DRMGC system does not seem to outweigh the smaller container-handling capacity in comparison to the TRMGC system, which is induced by the lower storage capacity due to the additional space requirements (see Sect. 3.4.1.3). The single-crane system is the most attractive type of RMGC system from a cost perspective, but it is clearly outperformed by the two-crane systems in terms of productivities and GCR.

Different automation technologies for both the storage subsystem and the horizontal-transport subsystem are presented and compared by Saanen (2007). Regarding the storage yard, TRMGC, DRMGC and TriRMGC systems are evaluated with respect to the equipment productivity, the storage capacity and the investment costs. In particular, the equipment productivity is studied by means of a simulation study for different transshipment factors. But only very little information on the simulation model and the used experimental setup is provided. However, for yard blocks that are 40 bays long, 10 rows wide and 5 tiers high, the results show that the TriRMGC system leads to a two-moves-per-hour higher productivity than the other types of RMGC systems, independently of the transshipment factor. In addition, Saanen (2007) reveals that the DRMGC system is outperformed by the TRMGC system for transshipment factors below 70%, while for transshipment factors above 70%, the DRMGC system performs better than the TRMGC system. With regard to the storage capacity and the investment costs, Saanen (2007) finds the TRMGC system to be clearly better than DRMGC and TriRMGC systems.

Wiese et al. (2011) address the block-layout problem for the SRMGC system in an analytical way. They aim at identifying the optimal width, length and number of yard blocks with respect to the cost performance and the operational performance of a rectangular seaport container terminal with a given stacking height, a fixed total width, but a variable depth. The cost performance of a yard-block layout is evaluated in terms of the corresponding need for area and yard blocks, while the operational performance is measured by the time required to perform a given number of storage and retrieval jobs in the container-storage yard. Wiese et al. (2011) compute this time based on the estimated crane-cycle time for performing a storage or retrieval job, which can be calculated by taking several simplifying assumptions into account, such as assuming equally distributed containers over yard blocks and bays, neglecting shuffle and housekeeping jobs as well as ignoring trolley and spreader-movement times. By enumerating the performance effects of block widths in the range from 3–15 rows, the cost performance of a yard-block layout is found to improve with increasing block width, while the operational performance is found to worsen. For a more precise analysis of the operational-performance effects of different yard-block layouts—in particular for multi-crane systems—Wiese et al. (2011) suggest the usage of simulation models.

In addition to these six references that directly address RMGC-design-planning issues, there are several other papers with different purposes that only deal with these issues en passant. Strategical design-planning problems for horizontal-transport systems that interact with RMGC systems are regarded, for example, by Vis et al. (2001); Saanen et al. (2003); Yang et al. (2004); Vis and Harika (2004); Liu et al. (2004) and Duinkerken et al. (2006). Furthermore, simulation-based case studies on design planning of automated container terminals as a whole—including RMGC issues—are provided by Duinkerken and Ottjes (2000); Ottjes et al. (2002) and Ottjes et al. (2007).

4.2.4 Concluding Summary

A summarising overview of all previously presented references on the design-planning problem for container-storage yards at seaport container terminals is provided in Table 4.1. There, each reference is characterised with respect to the investigated and/or compared storage system, the addressed aspect of the design-planning problem, the considered planning objectives and/or criteria as well as the applied research approach. It can be seen that so far only few references are directly related to the system-choice and block-layout problems of RMGC systems at seaport container terminals. In particular, the operational-performance effects of the TriRMGC system and the joint performance effects of decisions on the system choice and the block layout are hardly investigated in the relevant literature. Although the performance of the TriRMGC system is analysed by Saanen (2007), the results do not provide any scientific insights as no information on the experimental setup and the implementation of the used simulation model is given. Most references on the design of RMGC systems either compare different types of RMGC systems for a given layout or compare different layouts for a given type of RMGC system, but the interaction of system-choice and block-layout decisions have not been reliably quantified. Only two types of RMGC systems and two yard-block layouts are considered by Zyngiridis (2005), thus not providing statistically significant results of practical relevance for the joint system-choice and block-layout problem. Upon closer investigation of the listed references, it is additionally found that the operational-performance effects of the discussed parameters (see Sect. 4.1.3) are virtually not analysed. Only some operational-performance effects of the transshipment factor are en passant mentioned by Saanen (2007), while the effects of all other parameters on the performance and the design of RMGC systems appear not to be investigated at all.

From the two rightmost columns of Table 4.1, it can be observed that about 70% of all identified references on the design of container-storage yards address that problem by means of a simulation-based research approach. In the following section, simulation as well as other well-known research approaches are briefly introduced and discussed with respect to their suitability for addressing the research objectives pursued here.

Table 4.1 Summary of references on the design-planning problem for container-storage yards at seaport container terminals

	Storage system						Problem		Performance criteria			Research approach	
Reference	SC	RTGC	SRMGC	TRMGC	DRMGC	TriRMGC	System choice	Block layout	Cost	Operational	Area	Analytical	Simulation
Kim and Kim (1998)	–	√	–	–	–	–	–	√	√	√	–	√	–
Duinkerken et al. (2001)	–	–	√	–	–	–	–	√	–	√	–	–	√
Nam and Ha (2001)	–	√	–	√	–	–	√	–	√	√	–	–	√
Liu et al. (2002)	–	√	(√)	–	–	–	√	–	√	√	√	–	√
Valkengoed (2004)	–	–	–	√	√	–	√	–	–	√	–	–	√
Chu and Huang (2005)	√	√	–	–	–	–	√	–	–	–	√	√	–
Saanen and Valkengoed (2005)	–	–	√	√	√	–	√	–	√	√	√	–	√
Zyngiridis (2005)	–	–	√	√	–	–	(√)	(√)	–	√	–	√	–
Vis (2006a)	√	–	√	–	–	–	√	–	–	√	–	–	√
Saanen (2006)	–	√	–	√	–	–	√	–	√	√	√	–	√
Saanen (2007)	–	–	–	√	√	√	√	–	√	√	√	–	√
Kim et al. (2008)	–	√	–	–	–	–	–	√	–	√	–	√	–
Petering (2009)	–	√	–	–	–	–	–	√	–	√	–	–	√
Petering and Murty (2009)	–	√	–	–	–	–	–	√	–	√	–	–	√
Wiese et al. (2009b)	–	√	–	–	–	–	–	√	–	√	–	√	√
Lee and Kim (2010)	–	√	√	–	–	–	(√)	√	–	√	–	√	–
Wiese et al. (2010)	–	√	–	–	–	–	–	√	–	√	–	√	√
Pirhonen (2011)	–	√	–	√	–	–	√	–	(√)	(√)	–	√	√
Wiese et al. (2011)	–	–	√	–	–	–	–	√	√	√	–	√	–

4.3 Types of Research Approaches

In order to derive generally valid findings for the RMGC-design-planning problem, an appropriate research approach has to be selected, which ensures a target-oriented and systematic procedure for the whole research project. According to Homburg (2007), there are four dominating research methods: empiricism, morphology, pure theory and modelling.

Empiricism comprises all kinds of research projects that gather, preprocess and analyse external data in order to tackle the formulated research objectives. More abstractly spoken, the use of external data means that conclusions of empirical research projects are based on real-world experience. Within the field of empiricism, usually no valid conclusions are derived just from logical reasoning. Nevertheless, theory and/or logical reasoning are needed as the basis for systematic empirical projects. The other three research methods clearly have to be distinguished from empiricism, although project-specific interdependencies may be possible (Homburg 2007).

Similarly to empiricism, also the research method morphology is based on real-world experience. But here it is used to derive definitions and classifications of observed phenomena within a research field. Frequently, the experience that is used for morphology is based on empirical research. The main difference between empiricism and morphology is that empirical research is defined as a transparent process. Within empiricism, all steps of gaining insight and/or conclusions of a research project are described such that other scientists can objectively understand the findings. Whereas, morphology does not require a transparent process, moreover only the conclusion itself is of interest (Homburg 2007).

The research method that is named pure theory may use empirical phenomena as starting point for theoretical reasoning. But all conclusions and findings are only based on logical reasoning with respect to certain premises. Neither the premises nor the conclusions are checked for real-world validity (Homburg 2007).

Modelling is mainly used to investigate systems. Here, a system is defined as a collection of entities (e.g., people, machines) that act and interact together toward the accomplishment of some logical end (Schmidt and Taylor 1970, p. 4). Usually, it is too costly or too disruptive to experiment with the actual system. In some cases the system might even not exist (e.g., a terminal greenfield project). For these reasons, a model has to be built as a representation of the actual system. The model can then be investigated as a surrogate of the actual system (Law and Kelton 2000, p. 4). Similar to pure theory, modelling is based on logical reasoning and premises that are usually not all checked for real-world validity (Homburg 2007).

In general, two types of models have to be distinguished: mathematical models and physical models. Examples of physical models are clay cars in wind tunnels, cockpits disconnected from their aeroplanes to be used in pilot training or miniature vessels scurrying around in a swimming pool. However, these physical models are not typical kinds of models that are usually of interest in system analysis. The vast majority of models that are built for system analysis are mathematical ones that represent the logical and quantitative relationships of entities in a system. These entities and the relationships between them can then be changed in order to derive some conclusions on the reaction of the system to such changes (Law and Kelton 2000, pp. 4–5).

Depending on the degrees of complexity, the dynamics and the stochastic relations of a system, two types of mathematical models have to be distinguished: analytical models and simulation models (Valkengoed 2004, p. 18). Analytical models are usually applied to obtain exact analytical solutions for planning problems of rather simple systems. If a solution of such a mathematical model is available and is computationally efficient, it is usually recommended to study the model analytically rather than by a simulation model (Law and Kelton 2000, p. 5). However, many real-world systems are highly complex and far from trivial. As a consequence, mathematical models of such systems either are themselves complex, requiring vast computing resources that preclude any analytical solution (Law and Kelton 2000, p. 5), or require so many simplifying assumptions that the solutions are likely to be inferior or inadequate for implementation (Winston 2004, p. 1145). In this case, the system should be studied by means of a simulation model, which roughly means

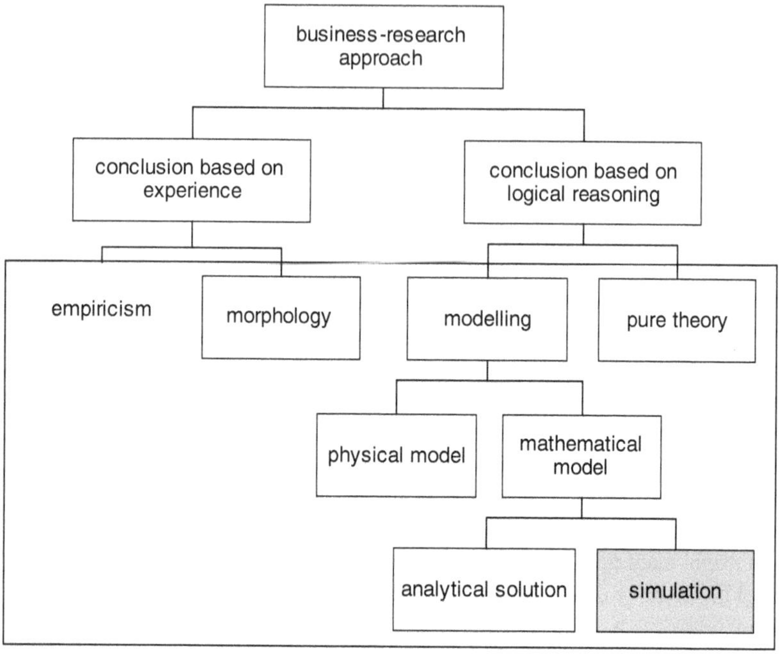

Fig. 4.2 Classification of business-research approaches (based on Law and Kelton 2000, p. 4; Homburg 2007)

that the model inputs in question are evaluated by exercising the model for different values of the inputs and analysing the resulting outputs of certain performance measures. In Sect. 6.1, the field of mathematical simulation is addressed in some more detail. A summarising overview and classification of all business-research approaches introduced before is shown in Fig. 4.2.

Altogether, simulation is a useful technique for problems that cannot be investigated with the real system and/or adequately be solved by an analytical model, which is usually the case for systems with high degrees of complexity, dynamics and stochastic relations (Winston 2004, p. 1145). In general, all seaport container terminals can be regarded as such a system (Böse 2011), but for several reasons especially container-storage yards with automated RMGC systems are stochastic, complex and highly dynamic systems (Saanen 2011): Firstly, a lot of stochasticity is involved in the operations of container-storage yards: XT arrivals are completely unpredictable, the duration of terminal operations is dependent on many human-influenced factors and despite the planned vessel-call patterns for deep-sea vessels, their arrival times are also uncertain to some degree (see Sect. 2.4.3.1). Secondly, container-storage yards are complex facilities with several types and numbers of equipment that can be in several dozens of possible states and can be located in a large number of yard locations. In particular, automated RMGC systems are highly complex systems due to the absence of a crane driver and the resulting need to control all crane movements by means of computer systems. Thirdly, considering shuffle moves and the possibility for mutual blocking of RMGC movements, the system state of a terminal may be continuously changing without any external event involved. Therefore, a container-storage yard can also be regarded as a dynamic system. In addition, it is usually not possible to experiment with real RMGC systems to derive optimal decisions about their design. Based on this, simulation appears to be the method of choice to investigate the design of automated RMGC systems at seaport container terminals. This is also confirmed by the fact that 13 of 19 design studies, which are presented in Sect. 4.2, are based on simulation.

4.4 Concluding Remarks

In this chapter, the design-planning problem for RMGC-operated storage yards at seaport container terminals is addressed in detail. Firstly, the RMGC-design-planning problem is described in all its aspects. Here, the system-choice problem and the block-layout problem are identified as the most relevant RMGC-design-planning subproblems for the performance of RMGC systems. Thereafter, relevant literature on these as well as related topics are summarised and discussed. Finally, different types of research approaches are compared and the most appropriate one for the RMGC-design-planning problem is identified.

Although the strategical design of RMGC systems is found to be of particular importance for the performance of seaport container terminals as a whole (see Sect. 4.1), the literature overview on the RMGC-design-planning problem reveals that so far only very few references are directly related to the system-choice and block-layout problems of RMGC systems (see Sect. 4.2). In particular, to the author's knowledge, three aspects of the RMGC-design-planning problem have either not at all or only insufficiently been investigated by today: Firstly, the triple-crane system has so far not been comprehensibly compared with single, twin and double-crane systems. Secondly, most known yard-design studies either compare different types of RMGC systems for a given layout or compare different layouts for a given type of RMGC system, but the interaction of system-choice and block-layout decisions have not been quantified until now. Thirdly, the influence of other parameters on the decisions on system choice and block layout has also almost not been investigated.

Among others, the selection and parametrisation of container-stacking, crane-scheduling and crane-routing strategies are identified as parameters that are expected to have substantial influence on the operational performance and the design of RMGC systems at seaport container terminals. But in contrast to the other identified parameters, which can often be expressed by a single value, these operational planning strategies are rather complicated parameters of the RMGC-design-planning problem that may be composed of several definable procedures and dozens of individual value settings. For that reason, the operational problems of

RMGC systems as well the corresponding planning strategies are comprehensively addressed in Chap. 5.

A further look at the relevant literature reveals that different research approaches can be used to investigate the design-planning problems of container-storage yards. Most design studies are based on simulation (see Sect. 4.2). The comparison of different research approaches in Sect. 4.3 confirms that simulation is the most suited research approach to analyse the operational-performance effects of the RMGC design. The simulation model that is designed here to investigate the so far insufficiently addressed aspects of RMGC-design planning is introduced in Chap. 6. Thereafter, in Chap. 7, the simulation model is deployed for an extensive study on these aspects. Within this simulation study, the implemented simulation model is exercised for various combinations of different types of RMGC systems and yard-block layouts in order to quantify their influence on the operational performance of the container-storage yard. In addition, owing to the fact that the operational performance of RMGC systems is not only determined by the design of these systems, but also by several crane-workload and crane-resource-defining parameters (see Sect. 4.1.3), several further simulation experiments are conducted with varying settings for these parameters in order to evaluate the sensitivity of the RMGC-design-planning problem with respect to these changes.

Chapter 5
Operational RMGC-Planning Problems

In this chapter, operational planning problems of automated RMGC systems are explicitly addressed. In particular, it is focused on the container-stacking and crane-scheduling problems, which are briefly introduced in Sect. 3.4.4. Both planning problems are frequently addressed in the OR literature. In addition, also the less familiar operational planning problem of routing RMGCs is considered. In the forgone chapter, it is argued that the solution approaches for these planning problems are of great importance for the operational performance and the design of RMGC systems. Here in this chapter, different types of solution approaches are presented, discussed, modified and developed for each of these three planning problems. After some basic terms and notations needed to formalise the planning problems are introduced in Sect. 5.1, first of all, the container-stacking problem is addressed in Sect. 5.2. Thereafter, in Sect. 5.3, the crane-scheduling problem is dealt with and finally, the routing problem of RMGC systems is regarded. The way these planning problems are addressed in this chapter is very similar for all problems: Firstly, a detailed problem description is given. Secondly, an extensive overview on literature relevant to that planning problem is provided. Thirdly, known types of solution approaches are discussed and classified, before finally, new and/or modified solution approaches for the relevant problem are presented in detail. The chapter is closed with some concluding remarks on the discussed problems and solution approaches.

5.1 Basic Terms and Notations

In this section, several important notations and terms are introduced that are needed in order to ensure a precise description of the addressed problems and solution approaches. Among others, several notations are introduced that define the crane kinematics, the container, the crane-transport job, the crane-movement times and the resulting crane and vehicle-waiting times in the handover areas of the yard blocks.

N. Kemme, *Design and Operation of Automated Container Storage Systems*, Contributions to Management Science, DOI 10.1007/978-3-7908-2885-6_5,

A yard block has three dimensions. Here, it is referred to the block length, width and height as the x-, y- and z-dimension of a yard block, respectively. By movements of portal, trolley and spreader, the crane can move along all these dimensions. The maximum velocity as well as acceleration and deceleration of gantry crane $g \in G$, with G defining the set of all gantry cranes of a yard block, depends on its load status. Throughout this work, a laden gantry crane g moves along the x-, y- and z-axis at velocities v_g^{xf}, v_g^{yf} and v_g^{zf}, accelerates with acceleration values a_g^{xf}, a_g^{yf} and a_g^{zf} and decelerates with deceleration values b_g^{xf}, b_g^{yf} and b_g^{zf}, while an empty cranc g moves, accelerates and decelerates along the x-, y- and z-axis with v_g^{xe}, v_g^{ye}, v_g^{ze}, a_g^{xe}, a_g^{ye}, a_g^{ze}, b_g^{xe}, b_g^{ye} and b_g^{ze}, respectively.

The object of all yard-block operations is the container $c \in C$, with C defining the set of all containers that are stored in a yard block during the considered time frame T. Each container c is delivered to a handover area of the yard block by a horizontal-transport vehicle for temporary storage at time t_c^{in} and at a later point in time t_c^{out}, it is collected from the yard block by another vehicle. The period of time in between the delivery and the collection of container c is its dwell time $\delta_c = t_c^{\text{out}} - t_c^{\text{in}}$, which is usually measured as the number of days. A storage position for container c in yard block $p_c^{\text{b}} \in \{1, 2, \ldots, n^{\text{b}}\}$ is addressed by the coordinate triple $(p_c^{\text{x}}, p_c^{\text{y}}, p_c^{\text{z}}) \in \{1, 2, \ldots, n^{\text{x}}\} \times \{1, 2, \ldots, n^{\text{y}}\} \times \{1, 2, \ldots, n^{\text{z}}\}$, that gives the bay, row and tier where container c is positioned in the yard block. For containers that occupy storage slots in two or even three adjacent bays (i.e., 40′ or 45′ containers), the coordinate triple addresses the bay covered by that container which is closest to the waterside handover area. Furthermore, there are several other attributes that can be used to characterise a container c. Firstly, a container can be characterised by its length (e_c^{size}), which usually either is $e_c^{\text{size}} = 20$ or $e_c^{\text{size}} = 40$ feet. Secondly, each container c will leave the terminal by a certain mode of transportation (e_c^{outmode}), which is either a deep-sea vessel, a feeder vessel, a train or an XT. Finally, each container that will leave the terminal by deep-sea vessel (i.e., $e_c^{\text{outmode}} = \text{deep} - \text{sea}$) can additionally be characterised on the basis of its container category (e_c^{cat}). A certain category e_c^{cat} comprises all containers that are of similar weight and that leave the terminal with the same vessel to the same PoD.

In this work, a transport job $j \in J$ for gantry crane g, with J defining the set of all jobs that occur in a yard block during the considered time frame T, is always associated with the transport of a container c from its current position to a new position. As a consequence, origin and destination of a transport job j are equivalent to the current and the new position of that container. Here, current and new position of container c as well as origin and destination of the corresponding transport job j are defined by the coordinate triples $\left(o_j^{\text{x}}, o_j^{\text{y}}, o_j^{\text{z}}\right) \in [0, \theta^{\text{x}}] \times [0, \theta^{\text{y}}] \times [0, \theta^{\text{z}}]$ and $\left(d_j^{\text{x}}, d_j^{\text{y}}, d_j^{\text{z}}\right) \in [0, \theta^{\text{x}}] \times [0, \theta^{\text{y}}] \times [0, \theta^{\text{z}}]$, with θ^{x}, θ^{y} and θ^{z} defining the end of the portal-driving range (which ranges from the beginning of the waterside handover area to the end of the landside handover area), the width of the yard block and the stacking height of the yard block, respectively. The shortest portal and trolley-driving distances between the origin and the destination of transport job j are

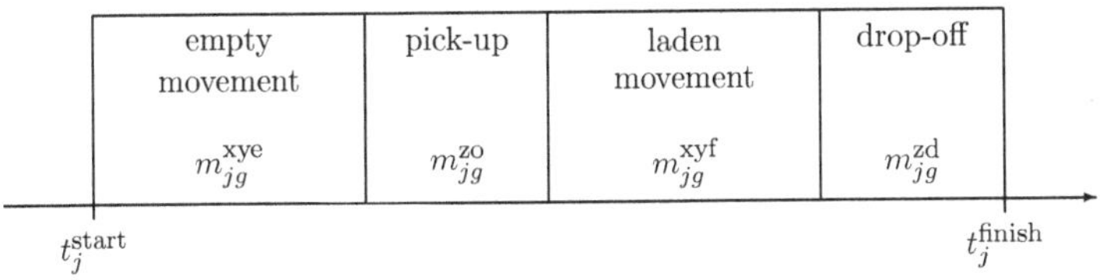

Fig. 5.1 Schematic illustration of the subtask sequence for crane-transport job j

defined by $l_j^{\text{x}} = \left|o_j^{\text{x}} - d_j^{\text{x}}\right|$ and $l_j^{\text{y}} = \left|o_j^{\text{y}} - d_j^{\text{y}}\right|$, respectively. Similarly, the portal and trolley empty-driving distances between the destination of job i and the origin of job j are defined by $l_{ij}^{\text{x}} = \left|d_i^{\text{x}} - o_j^{\text{x}}\right|$ and $l_{ij}^{\text{y}} = \left|d_i^{\text{y}} - o_j^{\text{y}}\right|$, respectively. However, for multi-crane systems prolonged driving distances may result due to crane-crossing and evasive manoeuvres that are induced by interferences among the cranes. In order to perform a crane-crossing manoeuvre in the double and triple-crane systems, the outer large crane g has to be moved to its crossing position p_g^{cross}.

For the cranes of the single and twin system as well as for the inner small cranes of the double and triple-crane systems, it is assumed that portal and trolley are always moved simultaneously, while the movements of the outer large crane are dependent on the occurrence of crane interferences and the applied crane-routing strategy. Different types of crane-routing strategies and the resulting portal and trolley movements are described in detail in Sect. 5.4. In addition, both portal and trolley of gantry crane g are only allowed to move if the spreader is brought to its driving position p_g^{drive}, which is at least one tier above the maximum stacking height of the yard block, since otherwise collisions with containers in the top layer of the yard block might occur. As a consequence, the spreader has to be lowered and lifted at both the pick-up and drop-off position of job j. The spreader-hoisting distances at origin and destination of job j are then given by $l_j^{\text{zo}} = \left|p_g^{\text{drive}} - o_j^{\text{z}}\right|$ and $l_j^{\text{zd}} = \left|p_g^{\text{drive}} - d_j^{\text{z}}\right|$, respectively. The expected final-handover times for picking up or dropping off containers in the yard block and in the waterside and landside handover areas (see Sect. 4.1.3) are defined by h^{b}, h^{ws} and h^{ls}, respectively.

Altogether, a gantry crane g has to perform several subtasks between the starting time t_j^{start} and the finishing time t_j^{finish} of job j. Firstly, portal and trolley of crane g have to be moved empty to the respective origin position of that job, which is at $\left(o_j^{\text{x}}, o_j^{\text{y}}\right)$. Such an empty crane movement takes m_{jg}^{xye} time units. Secondly, the container is picked up by the crane, which takes m_{jg}^{zo} time units. Thereafter, portal and trolley of crane g are moved laden to the respective destination positions of job j, which is at $\left(d_j^{\text{x}}, d_j^{\text{y}}\right)$ and takes m_{jg}^{xyf} time units. Finally, the container is dropped off by the crane and the spreader is hoisted back up to the driving position p_g^{drive}, which takes m_{jg}^{zd} time units. These subtasks of job j are summarised in chronological order in Fig. 5.1.

The time duration m_{jg}^{xye} for an empty movement of crane g to the origin of job j is determined by the crane kinematics, the last position of crane g, the distance to the origin of job j, the occurrence of crane interferences during that empty movement and the applied crane-routing strategy. Considering that crane g is in most cases located at the destination of the previous job i and ignoring possible crane interferences, the duration m_{jg}^{xye} is simply defined by the maximum of trolley and portal-movement times of crane g between the destination of job i and the origin of job j. By basic physical principles,[1] the duration m_{jg}^{xye} can then be computed as

$$m_{jg}^{\text{xye}} = \max\left\{\frac{l_{ij}^{\text{x}}}{v_g^{\text{xe}}} + \frac{v^{\text{xe}}}{2a_g^{\text{xe}}} + \frac{v^{\text{xe}}}{2b_g^{\text{xe}}}, \frac{l_{ij}^{\text{y}}}{v_g^{\text{ye}}} + \frac{v^{\text{ye}}}{2a_g^{\text{ye}}} + \frac{v^{\text{ye}}}{2b_g^{\text{ye}}}\right\}, \tag{5.1}$$

where the portal and trolley-movement times are given by the first and second element of the maximum function, respectively. Similarly, the duration m_{jg}^{xyf} for the laden movement of crane g between the origin and the destination of job j are given as

$$m_{jg}^{\text{xyf}} = \max\left\{\frac{l_{j}^{\text{x}}}{v_g^{\text{xf}}} + \frac{v^{\text{xf}}}{2a_g^{\text{xf}}} + \frac{v^{\text{xf}}}{2b_g^{\text{xf}}}, \frac{l_{j}^{\text{y}}}{v_g^{\text{yf}}} + \frac{v^{\text{yf}}}{2a_g^{\text{yf}}} + \frac{v^{\text{yf}}}{2b_g^{\text{yf}}}\right\}, \tag{5.2}$$

which mainly differs in the driving distance and the kinematics for laden cranes from the computation of m_{jg}^{xye}.

The durations of the pick-up and drop-off operations of containers are not affected by crane interferences and the applied crane-routing strategy. Moreover, the duration of both operations only depends on the spreader kinematics and the respective hoisting distance as well as on the position where the pick-up or drop-off operation takes place. The durations of pick-up and drop-off operations inside the yard block are calculated by

---

[1]The kinematic equations for the computation of driving, acceleration and deceleration times as well as for acceleration and deceleration distances (Hering et al. 2009) can be used to compute the time duration for movements of a steadily accelerated/decelerated portal, trolley and spreader between two positions as

$$m = \frac{v}{a} + \frac{1}{v} \times \left(l - \frac{v^2}{2a} - \frac{v^2}{2b}\right) + \frac{v}{b},$$

where the time for acceleration to the maximum velocity, the driving time with the maximum velocity and the time for deceleration to the stop are given by the first, second and third terms of the sum. Simplifying this equation yields

$$m = \frac{l}{v} + \frac{v}{2a} + \frac{v}{2b}.$$

$$m_{jg}^{\mathrm{zo}} = \frac{l_j^{\mathrm{zo}}}{v_g^{\mathrm{ze}}} + \frac{v^{\mathrm{ze}}}{2a_g^{\mathrm{ze}}} + \frac{v^{\mathrm{ze}}}{2b_g^{\mathrm{ze}}} + h^{\mathrm{b}} + \frac{l_j^{\mathrm{zo}}}{v_g^{\mathrm{zf}}} + \frac{v^{\mathrm{zf}}}{2a_g^{\mathrm{zf}}} + \frac{v^{\mathrm{zf}}}{2b_g^{\mathrm{zf}}} \text{ and} \tag{5.3}$$

$$m_{jg}^{\mathrm{zd}} = \frac{l_j^{\mathrm{zd}}}{v_g^{\mathrm{zf}}} + \frac{v^{\mathrm{zf}}}{2a_g^{\mathrm{zf}}} + \frac{v^{\mathrm{zf}}}{2b_g^{\mathrm{zf}}} + h^{\mathrm{b}} + \frac{l_j^{\mathrm{zd}}}{v_g^{\mathrm{ze}}} + \frac{v^{\mathrm{ze}}}{2a_g^{\mathrm{ze}}} + \frac{v^{\mathrm{ze}}}{2b_g^{\mathrm{ze}}}, \tag{5.4}$$

respectively. To compute the durations of pick-up and drop-off operations in the waterside and landside handover areas, only h^{b} needs to be replaced by h^{ws} and h^{ls} in (5.3) and (5.4).

All main jobs of RMGC systems are induced by the arrivals of horizontal-transport vehicles in the waterside and landside handover areas of a yard block (see Sect. 3.4.3). Storage jobs are induced by vehicles that arrive laden at the yard block with a certain container c, while retrieval jobs are induced by vehicles that arrive empty at the yard block in order to collect a certain container c. For each main job j, a handover-area due date t_j^{hd} can be defined as the point in time at which the corresponding transport vehicle has to be served in the handover area (i.e., loaded or unloaded) in order to ensure the shortest possible waiting time for that transport vehicle. Here, the handover-area due date t_j^{hd} is defined by the planned arrival time of the corresponding transport vehicle in the handover area and all vehicles are assumed to arrive as planned before—late and early vehicle arrivals are neglected. For each storage job, t_j^{hd} defines the target time for the start of the pick-up operation at the origin of the job, whereas, for each retrieval job, the target time for the start of the drop-off operation at the destination of the job is given by t_j^{hd}. A common pick-up due date t_j^{pd} for all jobs defining the time a crane has to start the pick-up operation in order to ensure the shortest possible waiting time for the corresponding vehicle in the handover area can then be determined by

$$t_j^{\mathrm{pd}} = \begin{cases} t_j^{\mathrm{hd}} & \text{for storage jobs} \\ t_j^{\mathrm{hd}} - m_{jg}^{\mathrm{xyf}} - m_{jg}^{\mathrm{zo}} & \text{for retrieval jobs.} \end{cases} \tag{5.5}$$

These different time relations between the handover-area and pick-up due dates are illustrated in Fig. 5.2.

For shuffle and housekeeping jobs, no handover-area due date can be defined, as neither pick-up nor drop-off operations of these jobs take place in one of the handover areas. Hence, the pick-up due dates for these jobs can be freely specified. However, a shuffle job is usually a direct predecessor ρ_j of another job j, that cannot be performed before the container of the shuffle job is picked up. Thus, the pick-up due date of shuffle jobs should be set a certain time before the pick-up due date of the causative retrieval job in order to allow a smooth retrieval of that job.

Due to the online character of seaport container terminals, the arrival time of a vehicle in the handover area and the corresponding handover-area due date t_j^{hd} usually become reliably known only a short period of time—a so-called look-ahead time m_j^{lat}—before the actual vehicle-arrival time in the handover area (see Sect. 4.1.3). The moment the arrival of job j is qualified as plannable (i.e., it becomes reliably known) is its announcement time t_j^{a}, with $t_j^{\mathrm{a}} = t_j^{\mathrm{hd}} - m_j^{\mathrm{lat}}$.

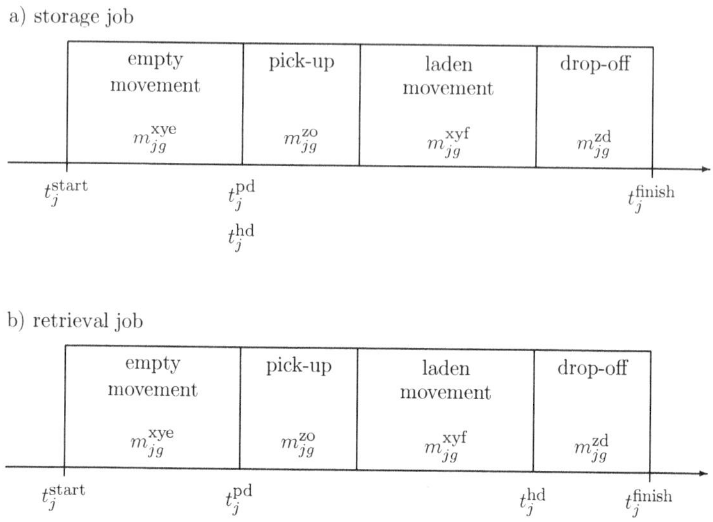

Fig. 5.2 Job-dependent time relations between handover-area and pick-up due dates

As a consequence, not all jobs in J are plannable at a certain point in time t. Instead only a subset of all jobs $J_t^{\mathrm{p}} \subset J$ with

$$J_t^{\mathrm{p}} = \left\{ j \epsilon J \,|\, t_j^{\mathrm{a}} \leq t < t_j^{\mathrm{start}} \right\} \tag{5.6}$$

is defined as plannable at time t, which includes all announced jobs that have not yet been started. In addition, some main jobs may be non-executable for a crane g, as the relevant handover area, can for instance, not be accessed by that crane due to having no crossing ability (see Sects. 3.4.1.2 and 3.4.1.4). Of course, all auxiliary jobs can theoretically be performed by all cranes. The subset of plannable jobs for crane g at time t is denoted by J_{tg}^{p} with $\bigcup_g J_{tg}^{\mathrm{p}} = J_t^{\mathrm{p}}$.

Besides the due dates, which define target times for the crane arrivals at the handover areas and pick-up positions, there are also planned and realised crane-arrival times at these positions. Differences between the due dates and the planned and/or realised crane-arrival times can then be used to evaluate the quality of scheduling decisions ex ante and ex post, respectively. The planned arrival time t_{jg}^{pp} of crane g at the pick-up position of job j is defined as the planned point in time both portal and trolley of crane g have arrived at the origin of job j and are ready to start the corresponding pick-up operation. Based on the definition of the planned pick-up arrival time t_{jg}^{pp}, the planned arrival time in the handover area can be easily computed for main jobs by appropriate forward calculations (see (5.5)). As a pick-up due date is defined for all jobs (i.e., also for shuffle and housekeeping jobs), the difference between this figure and the planned pick-up arrival time can ideally be used to evaluate the quality of all scheduling decisions ex ante. However,the planned arrival times are not necessarily in line with the realised arrival times. The planned arrival times are usually based on reasonable estimations for the duration of certain crane movements and operations, but the duration of some operations is involved with some hardly predictable uncertainty. Hence, some crane movements take longer or shorter than planned before, which leads to later or earlier realised crane-arrival times. Here, the realised handover-area-arrival time t_{jg}^{hr} is defined as the actually realised point in time at which both portal and trolley of crane g are ready to start the hoisting operation of main job j in the relevant handover area. Considering that the realised handover-area-arrival times refer to the interfaces of an RMGC system, thus having direct effects on the waiting times of the related horizontal-transport vehicles in the handover areas, they are more suited to evaluate the ex post performance of an RMGC system than the realised arrival times at the pick-up positions.

In most cases, neither the planned pick-up arrival time t_{jg}^{pp} nor the realised handover-area-arrival time t_{jg}^{hr} of job j are completely identical with the respective due dates. Usually, the cranes are planned to arrive and they actually do arrive either prior or after the corresponding due dates. The extent of early and late planned arrivals of crane g at the pick-up position of job j is for all jobs measured by the planned pick-up earliness $\Delta_{jg}^{\text{pp}-}$ and the planned pick-up lateness $\Delta_{jg}^{\text{pp}+}$, which are computed by

$$\Delta_{jg}^{\text{pp}-} = \max(t_j^{\text{pd}} - t_{jg}^{\text{pp}}, 0) \text{ and} \tag{5.7}$$

$$\Delta_{jg}^{\text{pp}+} = \max(t_{jg}^{\text{pp}} - t_j^{\text{pd}}, 0), \tag{5.8}$$

respectively. The extent of punctual realised crane arrivals in the handover areas can basically be measured in a very similar way for all main jobs. However, at the interfaces to the horizontal-transport systems, the pure earliness and lateness of the RMGCs are of only minor interest. Moreover, the effects of late and early crane arrivals for the RMGCs themselves as well as for the related horizontal-transport vehicles are of importance in this context (see Sects. 3.2 and 4.1.2). A late realised arrival ($t_{jg}^{\text{hr}} > t_j^{\text{hd}}$) of crane g in the relevant handover area of job j may lead to a prolonged waiting time for the related horizontal-transport vehicle, while an early arrival ($t_{jg}^{\text{hr}} < t_j^{\text{hd}}$) may result in waiting time for crane g until the corresponding vehicle arrives and the corresponding hoisting operation can be started. Here, the realised crane and vehicle-waiting times in the handover areas are denoted by $\omega_{jg}^{\text{hr}-}$ and $\omega_{jg}^{\text{hr}+}$, respectively.

The specific effects of late and early realised crane arrivals at the handover areas differ in the type of the horizontal-transport equipment and the considered job type (see Sect. 4.1.3). Passive vehicles like AGVs and XTs need to wait ($\omega_{jg}^{\text{hr}+}$) for both storage and retrieval jobs when the relevant crane arrives late (see (5.10) and (5.12)), since these vehicles are unable to load and discharge themselves. For the same reason, a crane g always has to wait ($\omega_{jg}^{\text{hr}-}$) for passive vehicles in the handover area, when arriving too early (see (5.9) and (5.11)). For active vehicles like SCs the situation is different, as these vehicles are able to load and unload themselves. As a consequence, no SC-waiting time is resulting when the crane arrives too late for a waterside storage job (see (5.14)) and no crane-waiting time results when the crane arrives too early for a waterside retrieval job (see (5.15)). The corresponding containers are simply placed in the handover area by the delivering machine, independently of the availability of the collecting machine. Nevertheless, early crane arrivals for storage jobs and late crane arrivals for retrieval jobs lead to the same waiting times for the cranes ($\omega_{jg}^{\mathrm{hr}-}$) and the active horizontal-transport vehicles ($\omega_{jg}^{\mathrm{hr}+}$), respectively, as with passive transport machines (see (5.13) and (5.16)). In summary, this yields for

storage jobs with passive vehicles,

$$\omega_{jg}^{\mathrm{hr}-} = \max(t_j^{\mathrm{hd}} - t_{jg}^{\mathrm{hr}}, 0) \quad (5.9)$$

$$\omega_{jg}^{\mathrm{hr}+} = \max(t_{jg}^{\mathrm{hr}} - t_j^{\mathrm{hd}}, 0) \quad (5.10)$$

retrieval jobs with passive vehicles,

$$\omega_{jg}^{\mathrm{hr}-} = \max(t_j^{\mathrm{hd}} - t_{jg}^{\mathrm{hr}}, 0) \quad (5.11)$$

$$\omega_{jg}^{\mathrm{hr}+} = \max(t_{jg}^{\mathrm{hr}} - t_j^{\mathrm{hd}}, 0) \quad (5.12)$$

storage jobs with active vehicles,

$$\omega_{jg}^{\mathrm{hr}-} = \max(t_j^{\mathrm{hd}} - t_{jg}^{\mathrm{hr}}, 0) \quad (5.13)$$

$$\omega_{jg}^{\mathrm{hr}+} = 0 \quad (5.14)$$

retrieval jobs with active vehicles.

$$\omega_{jg}^{\mathrm{hr}-} = 0 \quad (5.15)$$

$$\omega_{jg}^{\mathrm{hr}+} = \max(t_{jg}^{\mathrm{hr}} - t_j^{\mathrm{hd}}, 0) \quad (5.16)$$

Altogether, the relations between all aforementioned points in time and durations of crane-transport-job operations are schematically summarised in Fig. 5.3. In particular, four different cases are shown, that illustrate the reasons and the results of late and early crane arrivals for storage and retrieval jobs. The differences between active and passive vehicles are indicated by the dashed lines in Fig. 5.3b and c.

Considering the fact that the operational performance of RMGC systems can hardly be evaluated on the basis of vehicle-waiting times for individual jobs $j \in J$, but only with respect to the vehicle-waiting-time effects of greater numbers of performed main jobs, it is reasonable to evaluate the operational performance of RMGC systems based on the average of the vehicle-waiting time in the waterside and landside handover areas, which can be computed as

$$\overline{\omega}_{\mathrm{ws}}^{\mathrm{hr}+} = \frac{\sum_{g \in G} \sum_{j \in J | \tau(j) \in \{\mathrm{wsin}, \mathrm{wsout}\}} \omega_{jg}^{\mathrm{hr}+}}{|\{j \in J | \tau(j) \in \{\mathrm{wsin}, \mathrm{wsout}\}\}|} \text{ and} \quad (5.17)$$

$$\overline{\omega}_{\mathrm{ls}}^{\mathrm{hr}+} = \frac{\sum_{g \in G} \sum_{j \in J | \tau(j) \in \{\mathrm{lsin}, \mathrm{lsout}\}} \omega_{jg}^{\mathrm{hr}+}}{|\{j \in J | \tau(j) \in \{\mathrm{lsin}, \mathrm{lsout}\}\}|}, \quad (5.18)$$

respectively, where $\tau(j) \in \{\mathrm{wsin}, \mathrm{lsin}, \mathrm{wsout}, \mathrm{lsout}, \mathrm{wsshu}, \mathrm{lsshu}, \mathrm{wshk}, \mathrm{lshk}\}$ specifies the job type of job j, which can either be a waterside storage job (wsin), a landside storage job (lsin), a waterside retrieval job (wsout), a landside retrieval job(lsout), a shuffle job induced by a waterside retrieval job (wsshu), a shuffle job

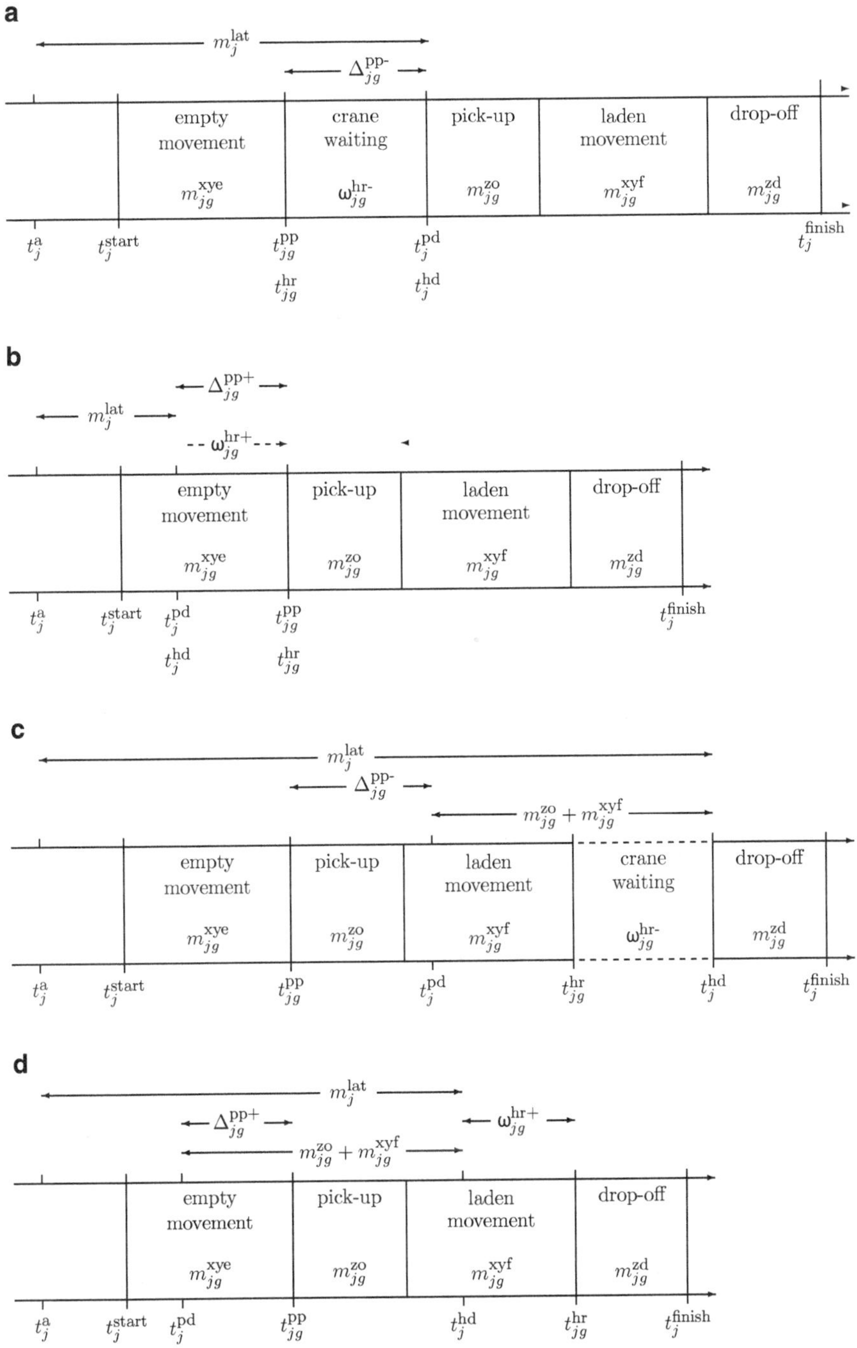

Fig. 5.3 Schematic illustration of points in time and durations of crane-transport jobs. (**a**) Early storage job. (**b**) Late storage job. (**c**) Early retrieval job. (**d**) Late retrieval job

induced by a landside retrieval job (lsshu), a housekeeping job for a waterside-departing container (wshk) or a housekeeping job for a landside-departing container (lshk) (see Sect. 3.4.3).

5.2 Container-Stacking Problem

A general introduction to the container-stacking problem for all types of container-storage yards is provided in Sect. 2.4.3.7. In this section, the problem of finding well-suited stacking positions for containers in a single RMGC-operated yard block is addressed in-depth. In Sect. 5.2.1, it is started with a description of the container-stacking problem for RMGC systems. Thereafter, an overview on literature relevant to this problem is provided, which is used as a starting point for the following classification and evaluation of known stacking approaches. In Sect. 5.2.4, a new cost-function-based stacking concept is introduced that is inspired by the beforehand discussed stacking approaches. Finally, in Sect. 5.2.5, a housekeeping concept is presented that is designed to smooth the crane workload in close collaboration with the aforementioned cost-function-based stacking.

5.2.1 Problem Description

Each day, thousands of new containers arrive at medium- to large-sized seaport container terminals and need to be temporarily stored in the container-storage area. In addition, even more containers are usually already located inside the storage yard, which sometimes need to be relocated to other storage positions as containers stored below them have to be retrieved. Each time a new container c is announced to arrive at the terminal or an already stored container c needs to be relocated, it has to be decided where to place it in the container-storage yard with respect to certain objectives.

For RMGC-operated storage yards, like considered here, a storage position for container c is addressed by the number p_c^{b} of the yard block and the bay-row-tier coordinate triple $\left(p_c^{\mathrm{x}}, p_c^{\mathrm{y}}, p_c^{\mathrm{z}}\right)$. However, the selection of a certain yard block p_c^{b} for container c is beyond the scope of this work. Here, only a single yard block is considered and each arriving container $c \in C$ is assumed to be assigned to that yard block in advance by a certain planning procedure. Furthermore, decision variables of the container-stacking problem are only p_c^{x} and p_c^{y}, while the stacking height (p_c^{z}) for container c cannot directly be decided. Rather, it is implicitly given by the current stacking height of the considered container pile $\phi_c^{\mathrm{xy}} = \phi\left(p_c^{\mathrm{x}}, p_c^{\mathrm{y}}\right)$, which is determined by the number of the bay and row. As a consequence, only the pile $\phi_c^{\mathrm{xy}} \in \Phi$ has to be selected in order to define the stacking position for container c, with Φ defining the set of all piles in the considered yard block. But in most cases not each pile $\phi_c^{\mathrm{xy}} \in \Phi$ can be selected as stacking position for container c, since several physical constraints have to be regarded (Dekker et al. 2006): Firstly, 20′ containers occupy one TEU slot, while 40′ and 45′ containers occupy two and three slots in adjacent bays, respectively. Secondly, containers of different sizes must not be stacked on top of each other. Thirdly, the containers have to be stacked precisely on top of each other. A container is not allowed to be stacked in such a way that overhang or a position on top of two adjacent containers results. Fourthly, containers can only be stacked in the direction along the length of the yard block. Finally, a container can only be placed on top of piles, which have not yet reached the maximum allowed stacking height. Altogether, stacking of container c is physically only possible for each pile $\phi_c^{\mathrm{xy}} \in \Phi_c^{\mathrm{allowed}}$, with $\Phi_c^{\mathrm{allowed}}$ defining the set of allowed stacking positions for that container with respect to the aforementioned constraints.

Owing to the fact that the cost and land performance of RMGC systems cannot be directly influenced by the solutions of operational planning problems for these systems, the superior objective for operational planning problems of RMGC systems usually is the optimisation of the operational performance of the container-storage yard, which is realised by minimising the waiting times for horizontal-transport vehicles in the handover areas of the considered yard block (see Sect. 4.1.2). However, this objective is usually not directly operationable for the container-stacking problem. Instead, it needs to be operationalised by supporting subgoals that foster the realisation of the superior main goal. In Sect. 3.2, it is already argued that minimising the number of required shuffle moves—which is usually used as the objective of the container-stacking problem (Steenken et al. 2004)—is well suited to facilitate the minimisation of the vehicle-waiting times in the handover areas.

Additionally, there is a further linkage between the stacking decisions and the operational performance of RMGC systems, as the crane-driving distances and perhaps the resulting lateness of all jobs are implicitly given by the preceding stacking decisions. The selection of a stacking position $(p_c^{\mathrm{x}}, p_c^{\mathrm{y}}, p_c^{\mathrm{z}})$ for container c in the yard block specifies both the destination coordinates $(d_j^{\mathrm{x}}, d_j^{\mathrm{y}}, d_j^{\mathrm{z}})$ of the crane-transport job to the stacking position and the origin coordinates $(o_j^{\mathrm{x}}, o_j^{\mathrm{y}}, o_j^{\mathrm{z}})$ of the transport job from that stacking position to another position. Transshipment containers arrive at and depart from the waterside block end. Thus, the stacking position for an arriving transshipment container should be close to the waterside handover area in order to reduce the laden crane-movement times m_{jg}^{xyf} for the corresponding storage and retrieval jobs. By avoiding unnecessary long laden crane movements, crane resources are saved for an earlier execution of other jobs, thus minimising the risk for and the extent of crane lateness for these jobs. In contrast, there is no generally preferred stacking position for import and export containers, as these containers always enter and leave the yard block at opposite block ends. Therefore, the sum of laden storage and retrieval movements can hardly be influenced by stacking decisions (Borgman et al. 2010). However, the split of the sum of laden crane movements for a certain import or export container between the storage and retrieval job is dependent on the selected stacking position (neglecting intermediate shuffle and housekeeping moves). In order to smooth the workload for the cranes of a yard block, it may be advisable to determine the initial stacking position for import and export containers with respect to the workload situation at the arrival of the respective container. During situations of high crane workload, an arriving container should be positioned close to the incoming side in order to preserve as much crane resources as possible for the execution of other jobs. In contrast, during times of low crane workload, stacking positions close to the outgoing handover area should be preferred in order to use the available crane resources as efficiently as possible. In addition, the yard block may be reorganised during times of low workload by repositioning containers, that are initially stacked close to the incoming side, to a stacking position near the departing handover area (see Sect. 5.2.5). However, the positioning of most containers near the handover areas would lead to very high stacked piles near the block ends compared to rather low stacking heights in the middle of the yard block. Usually, such imbalanced stacking heights are expected to increase the risk for shuffle moves (De Castilho and Daganzo 1993; Taleb-Ibrahimi et al. 1993). Thus, there is a trade-off between stacking close to the handover areas for reasons of driving-distance minimisation and workload smoothing and stacking somewhere further away from both handover areas for reasons of stacking-height levelling and shuffle-move minimisation.

The problem of finding well-suited stacking positions for arriving and to-be-relocated containers is additionally complicated by the underlying online nature of the container-stacking problem which is characterised by incompleteness and uncertainty of the needed information (2.4.3.1). While accurate data on container-departure times is the most crucial information that is needed in order to avoid shuffle moves, the smoothing of the crane-workload distribution requires information on the outgoing handover areas of the containers. Throughout this work it is assumed that the outgoing mode of transportation (e_c^{outmode}) for each container $c \in C$ is known at its arrival, which directly defines the needed information on the outgoing handover area for that container. Likewise, also size and weight are supposed to be known upon the arrival of each container $c \in C$. For each container $c \in C^{\text{deep}}$, where $C^{\text{deep}} = \{c \in C \,|\, e_c^{\text{outmode}} = \text{deep} - \text{sea}\}$ is the set of all containers that are planned to depart by deep-sea vessel, it is additionally assumed that also the collecting vessel and the port of destination are known at the arrival of the container. However, the precise container-departure time, that is needed to stack the containers with respect to the retrieval sequence from the yard block, is not directly provided for any container $c \in C$. It can only be anticipated depending on knowing the collecting mode of transportation and the arrival time of that vehicle at the arrival of container c. As mentioned before, the departing vessel is only known for each container $c \in C^{\text{deep}}$, while the specific collecting vehicle is completely unknown at the arrival of each container $c \in C^{\text{feeder}}$ and $c \in C^{\text{xt}}$, where $C^{\text{feeder}} = \{c \in C \,|\, e_c^{\text{outmode}} = \text{feeder}\}$ and $C^{\text{xt}} = \{c \in C \,|\, e_c^{\text{outmode}} = \text{xt}\}$ are the sets of all containers that are planned to depart by feeder vessel and XT, respectively. Likewise, the arrival time of the collecting vehicle is only known far in advance for containers departing by deep-sea vessel, while the arrival times of feeder vessels and XTs only become known shortly before the actual arrival date at the terminal (see Sect. 4.1.3). As a consequence, the departure times of containers departing by deep-sea vessels can best be anticipated at their arrival, thus allowing the use of elaborated shuffle-move-minimising stacking approaches. In contrast, for all other containers, the shuffle-move-minimising container stacking is greatly complicated as hardly any information on their departure times is available.

Altogether, the container-stacking problem for RMGC systems at seaport container terminals can be summarised as an operational online-planning problem that aims to support the minimisation of the vehicle-waiting times in the handover areas of a yard block by selecting storage positions for newly arriving and to-be-relocated containers in such a way that the number of shuffle moves needed is minimised and the crane workload is smoothed over time.

5.2.2 *Literature Overview*

In contrast to the strategical design-planning problem of storage yards, the operational container-stacking problem has attracted more attention in the OR community so far. However, the container-stacking problem for front-end-loading RMGC systems—which is considered here—is only addressed by very few papers. The majority of works deals with sideway-loading systems—mostly RTGCs—for which container stacking is different from front-end-loading systems (see Sect. 3.3), in particular with regard to the pursued objectives. In sideway-loading systems, the containers are handed over to other vehicles alongside the block without long laden crane movements, which does not allow to smooth crane workloads by stacking decisions as is the case for front-end-loading RMGC systems. Nonetheless, the papers on the sideway-loading system may provide useful approaches for minimising the number of shuffle moves that can also be applied to front-end-loading systems. In total, 28 relevant references on the container-stacking problem at seaport container terminals are identified, whereof 21 deal with stacking for sideway-loading systems, only five address the container-stacking problem for front-end-loading systems and two references introduce some basic stacking approaches, like category stacking, remarshalling stacking and scattered stacking, that are applicable to all types of storage systems. In this subsection, the papers on sideway and front-end-loading systems are briefly summarised, whereas the generally applicable stacking approaches, that are described by Chen (1999) and Steenken et al. (2004), are addressed in more detail in Sect. 5.2.3.

5.2.2.1 Stacking in Sideway-Loading Systems

The references on sideway-loading systems that are described in this subsection mainly differ in the research approach applied. According to Dekker et al. (2006), most references on container stacking are based on analytical calculations or detailed simulation studies. The works of Taleb-Ibrahimi et al. (1993), De Castilho and Daganzo (1993), Kim (1997), Kim and Bae (1998), Kim and Kim (1999a),

Kim et al. (2000), Kim and Hong (2006), Kang et al. (2006), Kang et al. (2006a,b), Hirashima et al. (2006), Lee et al. (2006), Aydin (2007), Lee and Hsu (2007), Han et al. (2008) and Caserta et al. (2011) are based on analytical calculations. Simulation studies are only conducted by Saanen and Dekker (2006a,b). Furthermore, an empirical analysis on container stacking in sideway-loading systems is presented by Chen et al. (2000). In addition, all these references are characterised by the specific problem setting and the considered objective.

Taleb-Ibrahimi et al. (1993) and De Castilho and Daganzo (1993) are among the first to investigate the relation between the stacking height and the resulting number of shuffle moves. While Taleb-Ibrahimi et al. (1993) discuss this relation for export containers only, the discussion is continued by De Castilho and Daganzo (1993) for stacking of import containers. Taleb-Ibrahimi et al. (1993) propose a remarshalling stacking approach (see Sect. 5.2.3) with the intention to stack arriving export containers in an unsorted pile at first and to relocate them later to a stack near the relevant berthing place in the required retrieval sequence. Analytical procedures are presented to calculate the maximum and average container-stacking capacity as well as the number of container slots that must be reserved for storing future container arrivals as a function of time. De Castilho and Daganzo (1993) develop analytical expressions for the expected number of moves required to retrieve an import container from the stack under two different storage strategies. They propose variants of levelling stacking (see Sect. 5.2.3), which keeps stacks of the same stacking height, and retrieval-time stacking (see Sect. 5.2.3), that segregates containers with respect to their retrieval times.

The problem of estimating the number of required shuffle moves both to retrieve a single import container from a stack and to retrieve all containers of a bay in a given sequence is addressed by Kim (1997). He proposes several tables and equations to estimate these numbers as a function of the block width, stacking height and initial filling rate of the bay.

Kim and Bae (1998) address the problem of remarshalling (see Sect. 5.2.3) export containers from an unsorted stack configuration to a stowage-plan-compliant configuration with the objective of minimising the number of relocated containers and the resulting driving distances. The problem is decomposed into three subproblems that are solved in a two-stage process. On the first stage, the bay-matching problem and the move-planning problem are solved simultaneously, while the task-sequencing problem is solved on the second stage. Both the bay matching-problem and the task-sequencing problem are solved by dynamic programming, while the move-planning problem is formulated and solved as a transportation problem.

Kim and Kim (1999a) aim for stacking arriving import containers in a shuffle-move-minimising way with respect to given space constraints for a container terminal using a retrieval-time stacking strategy (see Sect. 5.2.3), which does not allow to stack newly arrived containers on top of containers that are planned to depart earlier. The problem is mathematically formulated for constant, cyclic and dynamic arrival rates of import containers. A Lagrangian-relaxation-based solution method is suggested to solve these problems to optimality.

In contrast to the preceding references, Chen et al. (2000) study the causes for unproductive moves in yard operations by means of empirical analysis of real-world data from the Yang Ming Terminal in the Port of Kaohsiung (Taiwan). Shuffle and housekeeping moves are classified as major categories of unproductive moves. They identify a significant correlation between the number of required shuffle moves and the yard density, the volume of containers loaded onto vessels and the volume of containers discharged from vessels both for RTGC and SC systems. In contrast, the number of housekeeping moves is shown to be mainly determined by the volume of containers discharged only.

The problem how to stack export containers with an unknown arrival sequence and unknown departure times in such a way that the number of shuffle moves is minimised during the future vessel-loading processes is addressed by Kim et al. (2000) and Kang et al. (2006a,b). Kim et al. (2000) try to exploit the fact that heavy containers are usually stored below lighter ones on the vessel. Therefore, it is expected that heavy containers have to be retrieved from the stack before lighter ones. Based on this analysis, decision rules to use weight groups for stacking export containers are derived by Kim et al. (2000). These rules are evaluated by comparing the resulting decisions with optimal decisions from a dynamic-programming method. Zhang et al. (2010) show that this dynamic-programming method is incorrect with respect to its key model transformation. They analyse the errors in the original derivation of the model transformation and present the correct form. In contrast to Kim et al. (2000), it is argued by Kang et al. (2006a,b) that the weight information available at the time of container arrival is only an estimate, which may lead to disadvantageous stacking decisions depending on the estimation quality. They propose as an alternative an SA algorithm in order to find shuffle-move-minimising stacking positions for arriving export container with uncertain weight information.

In another paper of a similar group of authors, Kang et al. (2006) study the problem of remarshalling (see Sect. 5.2.3) export containers in a yard block with multiple non-crossing RTGCs. In order to minimise the required time for all remarshalling operations in a yard block, it is aimed for finding a remarshalling plan that minimises the number of relocated containers and the crane interferences during remarshalling. They propose an SA algorithm to solve this problem and show that this algorithm is able to produce an efficient remarshalling plan in reasonable time.

The remarshalling problem is also addressed by Hirashima et al. (2006), Hirashima (2008, 2009) as well as Lee and Hsu (2007). In order to reduce the vessel-turn-around times, they all strive to find a remarshalling plan that minimises the number of relocated containers during the remarshalling operations. For solving this remarshalling problem, Hirashima et al. (2006) and Hirashima (2008, 2009) consider the use of a Q-Learning algorithm that belongs to the class of reinforcement learning techniques, while Lee and Hsu (2007) develop an IP formulation and a heuristic for this purpose. The model formulation is based on a multi-commodity network flow model and a set of additional constraints, representing physical restrictions of the containers.

Different from all other studies on the container-stacking problem for sideway-loading gantry-crane systems, Lee et al. (2006) and Han et al. (2008) do not only consider the consequences of stacking decisions for the cranes, but also for the horizontal-transport machines. They study a transshipment terminal with RTGCs as stacking equipment and TTUs for the horizontal transport. The containers are allocated to different yard blocks using a scattered stacking strategy (see Sect. 5.2.3) that groups incoming transshipment and export containers according to their destination vessel. Consequently, many TTUs are located in the same part of the storage yard during the loading of a certain vessel, which may cause heavy traffic congestion in the yard. Therefore, in order to avoid prolonged vessel-loading operations, stacking methods are proposed by Lee et al. (2006) and Han et al. (2008) that aim at minimising both the number of shuffle moves and the traffic congestion in the yard. Corresponding MIP models are formulated by both of them. In addition, a sequential heuristic and a column-generation heuristic are proposed by Lee et al. (2006), whereas Han et al. (2008) present a TS-based heuristic to solve the formulated problem.

Saanen and Dekker (2006a,b) are the first to investigate different stacking strategies by means of a fully integrated simulation model of a complete transshipment terminal using RTGCs and TTUs in the yard. The stacking performance is evaluated with respect to several performance figures like the GCR, the TTU-service times as well as RTGC and TTU productivities. The simulation results show, among others, a negative correlation between the average yard-filling rate and the GCR, the number of shuffle moves and the GCR, the RTGC travel time per job and the GCR as well as a positive correlation between the average yard-filling rate and the RTGC travel time per job. It is found that the performance differences between more sophisticated stacking strategies, that make use of several stacking criteria, and a simple random stacking strategy (see Sect. 5.2.3) are rather small.

In contrast to all other references on container stacking for sideway-loading systems, Kim and Hong (2006), Aydin (2007) and Caserta et al. (2011) do not address stacking of newly arriving containers. Moreover, they address the so-called block-relocation problem, that strives to minimise the number of unproductive shuffle and housekeeping moves for retrieving all containers of a yard bay with a given initial configuration in a fixed sequence. It is assumed that containers are only allowed to be relocated to other piles within the same bay. Kim and Hong (2006) propose a B&B algorithm and a heuristic to solve the block-relocation problem. The B&B algorithm is found to be inappropriate for practical real-time applications due to a comparably high computational effort, whereas near optimal solutions (7.3% optimality gap) are produced in real-time (less then 2 s) by the heuristic method. The heuristic is based upon an estimation of the expected number of additional shuffle moves that result from relocating a certain container to other piles of the same bay. Another B&B algorithm and three alternative heuristics for the solution of the block-relocation problem are presented by Aydin (2007). In addition, housekeeping moves, which are not considered by Kim and Hong (2006), are introduced as a promising tool for the further reduction of the total number of unproductive crane moves. In contrast to the previous works, Caserta et al. (2011) solve the block-relocation problem using a dynamic-programming-inspired meta-heuristic called corridor method (Sniedovich and Voß 2006). Firstly, a dynamic-programming algorithm is developed, which is impractical for solving real-world instances of the block-relocation problem in reasonable time. But, by applying the corridor method, which imposes exogenous constraints onto the target problem, the size of the solution space of the dynamic-programming algorithm can be reduced, which makes it useful even for very large problem instances.

5.2.2.2 Stacking in Front-End-Loading Systems

Academic literature on container stacking for front-end-loading gantry-crane systems is not very common yet, perhaps because the problem does not easily lend itself to analytical solutions (Dekker et al. 2006). In fact, contrary to sideway-loading systems, all five identified stacking references on front-end-loading systems are based on simulation studies. While Duinkerken et al. (2001), Park et al. (2006), Dekker et al. (2006) and Borgman et al. (2010) consider stacking for SRMGC systems, Park et al. (2011) are the first to investigate container-stacking strategies for multi-crane systems.

Duinkerken et al. (2001) compare different stacking strategies like simple random stacking, category stacking, positional stacking, retrieval-time stacking and levelling stacking (see Sect. 5.2.3) by means of a detailed simulation model of the Delta Sealand Terminal in Rotterdam (Netherlands). The strategies are evaluated with respect to several performance figures like the number of shuffle moves, the QC productivity as well as the average execution times for storage and retrieval jobs. They find the random stacking strategy to perform worst among the tested strategies, while category stacking leads to the best results for all considered performance figures, even for situations of only imperfect knowledge about the container characteristics.

Various combinations of container-stacking strategies and dispatching rules for the horizontal-transport equipment are compared by Park et al. (2006) with respect to the makespan of the loading operations for certain amounts of containers. Comparable to Duinkerken et al. (2001), the stacking strategies of random stacking, positional stacking and category stacking (see Sect. 5.2.3) are tested for a container terminal with SRMGCs and AGVs. The findings of Duinkerken et al. (2001) are confirmed by the results of Park et al. (2006) for their simulation of a small-sized terminal with only one berth and four yard blocks. Likewise, category stacking is found to perform best in most cases, while random stacking mostly leads to the worst performance.

A simulation study on stacking strategies for an automated SRMGC system with 27 blocks, each 40 TEUs long, 6 wide and 3 high is carried out by Dekker et al. (2006). The horizontal transport at the waterside is done by AGVs. In order to simplify, the crane capacities are not realistically mapped and the average filling rate of the container-storage yard has been set to only 50% of the physical capacity. Several enhancements and modifications of category stacking are examined and compared with a base case in which containers are stacked randomly. The proposed enhancements of category stacking are mainly inspired by other stacking strategies like levelling stacking, positional stacking and retrieval-time stacking (see Sect. 5.2.3). Once again, category stacking is found to clearly outperform random stacking in terms of the number of shuffle moves, while the retrieval-time feature appears to be the most promising enhancement for the category-stacking strategy.

Borgman et al. (2010) use the same simulation model as Dekker et al. (2006) to investigate the trade-off between minimising the retrieval time of containers by stacking close to the outgoing handover area and minimising the number of shuffle moves by stacking containers only on top of containers that are expected to depart later. Variants and combinations of the positional and retrieval-time stacking strategies are compared to the benchmark strategies random and levelling stacking (see Sect. 5.2.3). The performance is evaluated with respect to the number of shuffle moves and the average time needed to retrieve a container from the stack. It is found that avoiding shuffle moves is more important than stacking close to the outgoing handover area. Even in case of only imperfect knowledge about the container departure times, retrieval-time stacking is shown to be superior to positional stacking.

Finally, container stacking in the field of front-end-loading multi-crane systems is so far only addressed by Park et al. (2011). An online search algorithm is proposed which dynamically adjusts and optimises a stacking strategy by continuously generating and evaluating different variants of stacking strategies while they are actually applied to determine the stacking positions. Simulation results for a TRMGC system show that the operational performance of the container-storage yard in terms of the vehicle-waiting times in the handover areas can be substantially improved by the proposed algorithm.

5.2.2.3 Concluding Summary

A summarising overview of all previously presented references on the container-stacking problem at seaport container terminals is provided in Table 5.1. There, each reference is characterised with respect to several criteria on the considered crane system, the investigated problem setting, the stacking objective as well as the used stacking and research approaches. It is illustrated that the vast majority of references deals with sideway-loading crane systems while only very few papers address the container-stacking problem for front-end-loading systems that are considered in this work. Moreover, two shortcomings are observed for the available papers on front-end-loading systems. Firstly, the performance of the proposed stacking strategies is so far not evaluated with respect to the operating type of RMGC system and the considered yard-block layout. In particular, container stacking within DRMGC and TriRMGC systems has so far not been addressed by any available reference. Secondly, most presented references only investigate and/or

Table 5.1 Summary of container-stacking references

	Crane system			Problem				Objective				Approach	
Reference	Loading	Cranes per block	Crossing ability	Import stacking	Export stacking	Block relocation	Remarshalling	Unprod. moves	Retrieval time	Yard congestion	Workload smoothing	Stacking	Research
De Castilho and Daganzo (1993)	s	1	–	√	–	–	–	√	–	–	–	RTS, LeS	a
Taleb-Ibrahimi et al. (1993)	s	1	–	–	√	–	√	√	–	–	–	ReS	a
Kim (1997)	s	1	–	√	–	–	–	√	–	–	–	-	a
Kim and Bae (1998)	s	1	–	–	√	–	√	√	√	–	–	ReS	a
Chen (1999)	–	–	–	√	√	–	√	√	–	–	–	CaS, ReS	t
Kim and Kim (1999a)	s	1	–	√	–	–	–	√	–	–	–	RTS	a
Chen et al. (2000)	s	1	–	√	√	–	–	√	–	–	–	–	e
Kim et al. (2000)	s	1	–	–	√	–	–	√	–	–	–	CaS	a
Duinkerken et al. (2001)	f	1	–	(√)	√	–	–	√	√	–	–	CaS, RTS, LeS, PoS, RaS	s
Steenken et al. (2004)	–	–	–	–	–	–	–	√	–	–	–	CaS, ReS, RvS, ScS	t
Dekker et al. (2006)	f	1	–	(√)	√	–	–	√	√	–	–	CaS, RTS, PoS, RaS	s
Hirashima et al. (2006)	s	1	–	–	√	–	√	√	–	–	–	ReS	a
Kang et al. (2006a,b)	s	1	–	–	√	–	-	√	–	–	–	CaS	a
Kang et al. (2006)	s	Any	–	–	√	–	√	√	√	–	–	ReS	a
Kim and Hong (2006)	s	1	–	–	–	√	–	√	–	–	–	–	a
Lee et al. (2006)	s	1	–	–	√	–	–	√	–	√	–	ScS	a
Park et al. (2006)	f	1	–	(√)	√	–	–	√	√	–	–	CaS, PoS, RaS	s
Saanen and Dekker (2006a,b)	s	1	–	√	√	–	–	√	√	√	–	CaS, RaS	s
Aydin (2007)	s	1	–	–	–	√	–	√	–	–	–	–	a
Lee and Hsu (2007)	s	1	–	–	√	–	√	√	–	–	–	ReS	a
Han et al. (2008)	s	1	–	–	√	–	–	√	–	√	–	ScS	a
Hirashima (2008, 2009)	s	1	–	–	√	–	√	√	–	–	–	ReS	a
Borgman et al. (2010)	f	1	–	(√)	√	–	–	√	√	–	–	RTS, LeS, PoS, RaS	s
Caserta et al. (2011)	s	1	–	–	–	√	–	√	–	–	–	–	a
Park et al. (2011)	f	2	–	(√)	√	–	–	√	√	–	–	–	s

Loading: front end (f) vs. sideway (s); stacking: category stacking (CaS), retrieval-time stacking (RTS), levelling stacking (LeS), positional stacking (PoS), random stacking (RaS), remarshalling stacking (ReS), reservation stacking (RvS), scattered stacking (ScS); research: analytical (a), empirical (e), simulation (s), theory (t) compare the use of certain stacking approaches in isolation, but do not consider in which way these approaches may be combined and may be helpful to reduce the vehicle-waiting times in the handover areas. In particular, possible differences in the combinations of stacking approaches between waterside and landside-departing containers have so far not been investigated. In this work, both shortcomings are addressed: Subsequently, an integrated stacking concept is presented, that is based on different combinations of the aforementioned stacking principles for waterside and landside-departing containers, and a simulation-based comparison of different stacking strategies for different types of RMGC systems and yard-block layouts is provided in Chap. 7.

5.2.3 Classification of Stacking Strategies

The preceding literature overview on the container-stacking problem reveals that several different types of solution methods are already proposed and tested for this operational terminal-planing problem. But the container-stacking problem—as addressed in this work (see Sect. 5.2.1)—is not solved by each of the mentioned solution methods. By means of remarshalling stacking, reservation stacking and scattered stacking, no precise storage position is determined for an incoming and/or to-be-shuffled container. Moreover, only a preselection of potential storage positions for incoming containers is provided by these stacking approaches with respect to the part of the storage area and/or yard block in which the relevant container can be stacked. Depending on the characteristics of an incoming container and the usage of remarshalling, reservation or scattered stacking, it may only be allowed to store an incoming container in certain parts or blocks of the storage yard. Thus, the storage yard is virtually subdivided into different parts by these stacking approaches, which are therefore referred to as storage-area-division policies throughout this work.

In contrast, retrieval-time stacking, category stacking, levelling stacking, positional stacking and random stacking can be used to solve the container-stacking problem the way it is addressed in this work. These stacking approaches determine precise storage positions for incoming and to-be-shuffled containers with respect to the allowed storage areas for the relevant container. Therefore, these stacking approaches are referred to as container-positioning methods throughout this work. Altogether, a container-stacking strategy is then defined by the used combination of storage-area-division policy and container-positioning method. A classification and summarising overview on the functional interaction of storage-area-division policies and container-positioning methods is illustrated in Fig. 5.4. However, not all mentioned storage-area-division policies and container-positioning methods are similarly well suited for front-end-loading RMGC systems. Subsequently, the underlying ideas of these policies and methods are introduced and they are evaluated with respect to their applicability to the RMGC systems examined in this work.

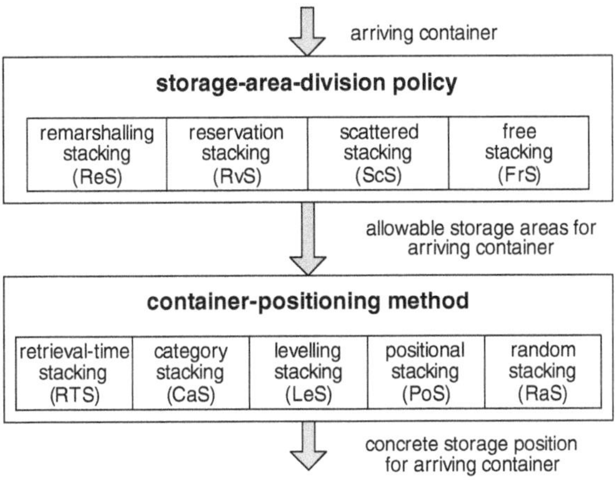

Fig. 5.4 Classification of container-stacking strategies

5.2.3.1 Storage-Area-Division Policies

Remarshalling stacking (ReS) is a storage-area-division policy which addresses the stacking of incoming export containers only. The storage area for export containers is subdivided into rough piles and remarshalling areas for each berthing deep-sea vessel. Based on the assumption that often hardly any suitable information on the future departure times of export containers is known at their arrivals, the containers are firstly stored in an unsorted way in rough piles, without considering the consequences of selecting certain storage positions. Once a stowage plan for a deep-sea vessel is available (e.g., 24 h before its arrival), the export containers are retrieved from the rough piles and brought to the remarshalling area, where they are stacked according to the loading sequence that results from the stowage plan. During the loading operations of a deep-sea vessel the containers are retrieved from the remarshalling area in the stacked order and loaded onto the vessel. As a consequence, time-intensive shuffle moves during the vessel-loading operations are minimised as far as possible by remarshalling stacking (Steenken et al. 2004).

The merit of remarshalling stacking is the simplification of the stacking problem. Sophisticated container-positioning methods are not required for incoming containers since they are firstly stacked more or less randomly in a temporary storage area and only afterwards stacked in the remarshalling area in the order of the stowage plan. The major drawbacks of this stacking approach are the additional storage-space requirements for the remarshalling area and the high yard-crane-resource requirements that are induced by the huge number of remarshalling moves from the rough pile to the remarshalling area. A remarshalling-stacking strategy is particularly useful for SC or RTGC-operated yards, when accurate information on the containers and stowage plans are missing and thus, many shuffle moves during the loading processes are expected anyway. For RMGC systems, remarshalling is only partly or even not at all applicable. Either temporary storage areas have to be defined in each block or special temporary yard blocks have to be installed. Both are connected with operational problems, like the reduced exchangeability of containers between the RMGC blocks and the huge equipment-resource requirements involved (Kemme 2011b).

Within the framework of reservation stacking (RvS), the storage area is subdivided into several vessel-arrival-related areas. These areas result from allocating certain amounts of unused storage space to prospectively arriving vessels a few days or weeks before their actual arrival. The size of the reserved storage area for an arriving vessel is determined by the expected numbers of import and export containers that are delivered and picked up by that vessel, respectively. All arriving export containers for that vessel are stored in the previously reserved area until they are loaded onto the vessel. After all containers have been loaded from and unloaded to the reserved area for that vessel, the delivered containers are one by one collected by other vehicles, thus continuously deallocating the reserved area for a vessel arrival (Steenken et al. 2004).

The benefits of reservation stacking are the separation of containers for/from different vessels, thus reducing the number of required shuffle moves. Furthermore, a realistic evaluation of the future yard capacity is always available, since prospectively arriving containers are already incorporated in the storage statistics. But at the same time, this is also the main disadvantage of reservation stacking, because physically available slots are blocked for other usage. Thus, flexibility and a potentially higher yard utilisation is lost. This strategy is theoretically applicable for RMGC systems (Kemme 2011b).

Scattered stacking (ScS) is a storage-area-division policy, dividing the storage yard into several berth-related areas for import and export containers. In contrast to reservation stacking, no storage capacities are allocated to each individual vessel arrival. Instead, each part of the storage yard is uniquely assigned to a certain berth of the terminal. For all containers that are transshipped at a certain berth, stacking is only allowed in the storage areas that are allocated to that berth. All incoming export containers which arrive in the run-up to a vessel are stacked in the storage areas that are assigned to the berthing place at which that vessel is planned to moor. Similarly, upon arrival of a certain vessel, a location for each container to-be-unloaded is searched in real-time within the dedicated storage area of the used berthing place (Steenken et al. 2004).

The scattered-stacking concept results in a higher yard utilisation than reservation stacking, as no slots are virtually occupied before the arrival of a vessel. Since it is possible to assign a yard block to a certain berthing place, scattered stacking can theoretically be applied to front-end-loading RMGC systems. But assigning each yard block only to a single berth may lead to an uneven utilisation of the different yard blocks over time. During the processing of a certain vessel, the relevant yard blocks may be overcharged in terms of handover-area and yard-crane capacity, resulting in disturbed loading and unloading operations for that vessel. Furthermore, an uneven yard-block utilisation leads to a concentration of horizontal-transport equipment in certain parts of the yard, which may cause blocking or even deadlock situations (Kemme 2011b).

To avoid these shortcomings, container terminals using front-end-loading RMGC systems are expected not to assign storage capacities to vessel arrivals or berthing places. Instead, stacking should be allowed in all parts of the yard and not be restricted to certain blocks. In this work, a storage-area-division policy which allows stacking of each incoming container in each block (i.e., the storage yard is not subdivided) is called free stacking (FrS) (see Fig. 5.4). Such a policy is not explicitly described, but implicitly assumed by Dekker et al. (2006) due to the configuration of the presented container-positioning methods. Altogether, free stacking seems to be the most suitable storage-area-division policy for the automated RMGC systems examined here (Kemme 2011b).

5.2.3.2 Container-Positioning Methods

The probably most straightforward container-positioning methods are random stacking and levelling stacking. Both methods are frequently used as benchmark algorithms for more elaborated positioning methods (Borgman et al. 2010). Within the framework of random stacking (RaS), a new container is basically placed at a randomly chosen allowed location. Neglecting the problem of selecting a yard block for an incoming container, as done in this work, random stacking can be implemented as follows (Dekker et al. 2006; Borgman et al. 2010): Firstly, all allowed positions $\phi_c^{xy} \in \Phi_c^{\text{allowed}}$ for container c, that has to be stacked, are determined. Thereafter, based on the set of allowed stacking positions, one position is randomly selected for container c, with every allowed position having an equal probability of being selected.

A possible advantage of random stacking—if there is any—is the probably even distribution of containers among different piles. Thus, the drawbacks of uneven pile heights can be avoided. However, the objectives of the container-stacking problem are not all taken into account for the stacking decisions by the random-stacking method. In particular, information on the retrieval sequence of containers to-be-stacked are not taken into account. Therefore, comparably large numbers of shuffle moves and a rather poor operational performance of the container-storage yard are expected by applying random stacking.

The basic idea of levelling stacking (LeS) is to fill the yard blocks layer by layer in order to avoid an uneven distribution of pile heights, with some very high stacked piles that can be expected to cause many more shuffle moves than more levelled stacks (De Castilho and Daganzo 1993). Based on Duinkerken et al. (2001) and Borgman et al. (2010), levelling stacking can be implemented in the following way: It is started with the determination of all generally allowed positions $\phi_c^{xy} \in \Phi_c^{\text{allowed}}$ for container c in the considered yard block. Thereafter, the layer of each allowed position is determined with ground positions having layer one. In the next step, all allowed positions are sorted in increasing order of their layers. Finally, a position for container c is randomly selected out of the set of all allowed positions in the lowest available layer, with each of these positions having an equal probability of being chosen.

The benefit of levelling stacking is an even distribution of pile heights which is expected to cause fewer shuffle moves than unlevelled yard blocks with some rather highly stacked piles. On the one hand, this intuitive container-positioning method is expected to cause fewer shuffle moves and to yield a better operational performance than random stacking. On the other hand, the container-retrieval sequences are not respected for stacking decisions, thus raising potential for further shuffle-move reductions. In addition, the containers are not stacked with respect to smoothing the crane workload. Altogether, levelling stacking is expected to still cause a large number of evitable shuffle moves and to lead to an operational performance of the container-storage yard that can only be used as benchmark for other container-positioning methods.

In contrast to random and levelling stacking, the containers are stacked with respect to their retrieval sequences within the framework of retrieval-time stacking (RTS). Basically, a container should only be stacked on top of containers that all have a retrieval time that is later than the retrieval time of the new container. Based on Borgman et al. (2010), retrieval-time stacking can be implemented as follows: Firstly, all generally allowed positions $\phi_c^{xy} \in \Phi_c^{\text{allowed}}$ for container c are determined. Secondly, the time of the next planned retrieval of each allowed pile needs to be looked up and/or estimated. While no next retrieval time can be determined for a ground position, the next retrieval time for a non-empty pile can be determined as the pick-up due date $t_{j'}^{\text{pp}}$ of the retrieval job j', which belongs to the container c' that is currently stored on top of that pile. Thereafter, it is searched for allowed positions in non-empty piles where the current top container c' is expected to depart later than the new container c. If such positions are found, container c is stacked in the pile where $t_{j'}^{\text{pp}} - t_j^{\text{pp}}$ is minimal, with job j denoting the retrieval job of container c, in order to preserve as many stacking positions as possible for containers to-be-stacked in the future. If no such position is found, it is firstly tried to randomly stack container c in an allowed ground position, and if no allowed ground position is available either, one of the generally allowed positions is randomly selected as stacking position for container c.

Principally, retrieval-time stacking is an interesting concept, since the number of shuffle moves can theoretically be reduced to an unavoidable minimum by observing the exact container-retrieval sequences. However, as discussed in Sect. 5.2.1, it is usually impossible to anticipate the retrieval time of each container $c \in C$ at its arrival. In particular, the retrieval time for an import container is usually completely unknown until the arrival of the collecting vehicle in the landside handover area, and even the exact retrieval times of export and transshipment containers are usually only known a few minutes before the relevant vehicle arrives in the waterside handover area (see Sect. 4.1.3). Therefore, retrieval-time stacking is solely inapplicable to practical situations without further concepts to anticipate and/or estimate the container-retrieval times.

Category stacking (CaS) is a container-positioning method that aims to minimise the number of shuffle moves—in particular for containers departing by deep-sea vessel—by combining two concepts: Firstly, it is tried to stack waterside-departing containers with respect to the load plans of the collecting vessels by utilising some general patterns of the vessel stowage plans. Primarily, containers to-be-loaded are distinguished for stowage planning with respect to their PoD and their weight. Basically, only containers destined for the same PoD are stowed in the same pile of the vessel in order to avoid QC-shuffle moves in the following ports. For reasons of stability, heavy containers are usually stowed below lighter ones. Usually, not the exact container weights are regarded for stowage planning, but all containers are classified into a defined number of weight groups that is needed by the ship planners in order to ensure the vessel stability (e.g., 3–5 groups). Secondly, it is tried to exploit the free exchangeability of containers during the vessel-loading process with respect to these container attributes, if online stowage planning is applied (see Sect. 2.4.3.2). This means that each time a container with certain weight group and PoD is required for loading onto a deep-sea vessel, an arbitrary container with the same attributes is retrieved from the yard block that is expected to cause the fewest shuffle moves. Hence, it is advisable to stack containers that are planned for loading onto the same vessel, that are destined for the same PoD and that belong to the same weight group on top of each other (Chen 1999; Dekker et al. 2006).

Within the framework of category stacking, newly arriving containers that are planned to depart by deep-sea vessel (i.e., $c \in C^{\text{deep}}$) are basically classified into several categories according to their collecting vessel, their PoD and their weight group (see Sect. 5.2.1). Then it is tried to stack them in such a way that only boxes of the same category are positioned on each other. For containers that are planned to be collected by other modes of transportation, like feeder vessels and XTs, such a detailed categorisation is usually not possible and/or unhelpful, since neither the collecting vehicle nor its arrival time are known at the arrival of these containers (see Sect. 5.2.1). Instead, all containers departing by feeder vessel and XT may be regarded as two big separate categories that have to be stacked by applying other container-positioning methods (Chen 1999; Dekker et al. 2006).

According to Dekker et al. (2006), category stacking can be implemented in the following way: Firstly, all generally allowed positions $\phi_c^{xy} \in \Phi_c^{\text{allowed}}$ for an arriving container $c \in C^{\text{deep}}$ are determined. Thereafter, the category e_c^{cat} of container c is determined and all allowed positions are searched for non-empty piles where the current top container is of the similar category. If such positions are found, one of these positions is randomly selected for container c, with every position having an equal probability of being selected. If no such position is found, it is firstly tried to randomly stack container c in an allowed ground position. If no allowed ground position is available either, one of the generally allowed positions is randomly selected as stacking position for container c.

In summary, applying category stacking in combination with online stowage planning appears to be a practical approach to reduce the number of shuffle moves for containers departing by deep-sea vessel (Dekker et al. 2006). However, without the simultaneous use of online stowage planning, category stacking is expected to be hardly helpful to reduce the number of shuffle moves, as the container-retrieval sequence could not be adapted to the stacking situation in the storage yard. In addition, category stacking is unhelpful for containers departing by feeder vessel and XT. Therefore, still great numbers of shuffle moves are expected to occur for these containers. Finally, it has to be noted that category stacking is well-suited for a combined application with retrieval-time stacking, as both concepts are greatly complementing each other (Dekker et al. 2006; Borgman et al. 2010). The retrieval times of containers $c \in C^{\text{deep}}$ can be roughly anticipated on the basis of the estimated time of departure (ETD) of the collecting vessels. In order to increase the yard utilisation within the framework of category stacking, it may be allowed to stack container c on top of piles that are used for different categories if the collecting vessel of the new container is expected to depart earlier than the vessel of the already stacked containers. However, unwanted shuffle moves may be resulting in the case of overlapping berthing times of deep-sea vessels. This problem can be fixed by introducing a sufficiently large buffer time between the ETDs when stacking container c on piles with different categories (Kemme 2011b).

Finally, several variants of positional-stacking methods (PoS) are described in the literature on container stacking. All these positional-stacking approaches have in common that they are not designed to minimise the number of shuffle moves. Moreover, the crane-driving distances and/or times that result from selecting a certain stacking position for an incoming container are mainly considered by these methods. The different variants of positional stacking can be distinguished with respect to the pursued objective and the preferred stacking positions for import, export and transshipment containers. The simplest variant of positional stacking, as described by Duinkerken et al. (2001), aims for minimising the crane-driving distances for future retrieval jobs in order to reduce the vehicle-waiting times in the handover areas for these jobs. Therefore, incoming import containers should be stacked on the allowed position that is closest to the landside handover area, while export and transshipment containers are preferably stacked on the allowed positions that are nearest to the waterside handover area. Possibly resulting shuffle moves are not considered.

In contrast, Dekker et al. (2006) and Park et al. (2006) only use positional stacking as an enhancing feature within the framework of category stacking, since it is primarily aimed to minimise the number of shuffle moves for containers departing by deep-sea vessel. To minimise the crane-driving distance for retrieval jobs is only considered as subordinate objective. An incoming container $c \in C^{\text{deep}}$ should be stacked on the allowed position of the same category e_c^{cat} that is located closest to the waterside handover area.

A positional-stacking method that only aims at minimising the crane-driving distances for storage and retrieval moves of transshipment containers is presented by Borgman et al. (2010). It is argued that it is irrelevant for the operational performance of the container-storage yard to stack either import or export containers close to the landside or waterside handover areas, as these containers have to be transferred through the entire block anyway (see Sect. 5.2.1). However, the best positions for transshipment containers should not be blocked by import and/or export containers. Therefore, transshipment containers should be stacked close to the waterside handover area, while both import and export containers should be stacked near the landside handover area. Borgman et al. (2010) propose to consider these deliberations on preferred stacking positions for containers with respect to crane-movement time reasons within a weighted cost function of the resulting crane-movement times and the expected probability of shuffle moves for allowed positions. The allowed position which leads to the lowest cost with respect to this trade-off is selected. In addition, Borgman et al. (2010) are the first to propose a crane-workload-dependent positioning of containers. It is suggested to stack import containers not close to the landside handover area during peak workloads of the cranes, but somewhere further away in order to save crane resources for other jobs.

Altogether, positional stacking should be used as an enhancement for other container-positioning methods only. Huge numbers of shuffle moves are expected to occur, if containers are only stacked with regard to the crane-driving distances without taking into account that there may result shuffle moves (Duinkerken et al. 2001). Among the other works on positional stacking, the container-positioning methods by Dekker et al. (2006) and by Park et al. (2006) seem to be most suitable with regard to the simultaneous consideration of shuffle moves and crane-driving distances, as fewer shuffle moves are expected to occur in comparison to the approach presented by Borgman et al. (2010). This can be explained by the use of deterministic information on the container-retrieval sequence in category stacking as compared to Borgman et al. (2010) who only consider stochastic shuffle-move probabilities. With regard to the aimed objective, however, the approach presented by Borgman et al. (2010) appears to be better suited than the methods by Dekker et al. (2006) and Park et al. (2006). To minimise the crane-driving distances for future retrieval moves, like Dekker et al. (2006) and Park et al. (2006) do, is not always helpful. In particular, during situations of high crane workload the crane resources are too precious to be used for long crane-driving distances to store incoming import and export containers close to their outgoing handover areas (see Sect. 5.2.1). In contrast, only to minimise the crane-driving distances for storage and retrieval jobs of transshipment containers and to additionally smooth the crane workload with respect to stacking of import containers, like Borgman et al. (2010) do, are suitable objectives for positional stacking (see Sect. 5.2.1). But stacking of export containers with respect to the crane workload, which may also be useful to smooth the crane workload over time, is not considered by Borgman et al. (2010).

5.2.4 Combined-Cost-Function Stacking

In the preceding subsection, several stacking concepts are classified and evaluated with respect to their applicability to front-end-loading RMGC systems. Based on the discussed advantages and disadvantages, it is concluded that free stacking is the most suitable storage-area-division policy for the kind of RMGC systems analysed here. However, such a policy cannot be explicitly investigated in this work, but only implicitly assumed, as only a single yard block is considered here. In contrast to the storage-area-division policy, there is no apparently most suitable container-positioning method for RMGC systems. Each of the discussed methods has its advantages and disadvantages for stacking of certain containers with respect to certain stacking objectives: Retrieval-time stacking is an interesting theoretical concept to minimise the number of shuffle moves. Category stacking is a practically useful approach to reduce the number of shuffle moves for containers departing by deep-sea vessel. Positional stacking is a reasonable endorsement for other container-positioning methods in order to smooth the crane workload over time and to reduce crane-movement times.

In this subsection, an alternative container-positioning method is presented that aims at both minimising the number of shuffle moves and smoothing the crane workload over time by combining the principles of category, positional and retrieval-time stacking within the framework of a weighted cost function. The method is based on the idea to compute cost values for each allowed stacking position, with respect to weighable cost components that represent the trade-off between the aforementioned stacking principles, and to select the stacking position with minimal costs. Due to the fact that category stacking is only applicable to minimise the number of shuffle moves for containers departing by deep-sea vessel, two different cost functions are needed. While stacking positions for containers departing by deep-sea vessel are evaluated by a cost function combining the principles of category and positional stacking, a cost function that is based on retrieval-time stacking and positional stacking is used to evaluate the stacking positions for all other containers. Referring to the main idea of this container-positioning method, it is called combined-cost-function stacking (CCFS).

The objective of smoothing the crane workload over time is reflected by a single positional stacking-based cost component, that is always computed in the same way, independently of the mode of transportation a container $c \in C$ is planned to depart with. Briefly worded, the workload-smoothing costs of a stacking position are calculated as the crane-driving distances for the resulting storage and retrieval jobs which are weighted with the current and the future price of the crane resources, respectively. In contrast, the shuffle-move-minimisation objective is reflected by two cost components whereof one is computed in different ways with respect to the mode of transportation a container $c \in C$ is planned to depart with. First of all, the costs of stacking container c intermingled with containers that are planned to depart with other modes of transportation than e_c^{outmode} are computed in the same way for each container $c \in C$. It is advisable to stack only containers that are planned to depart by the same mode of transportation in the same piles (Chen 1999), as other containers may be stacked differently (category vs. retrieval time), may depart at different handover areas (waterside vs. landside) and may have different departure-time distributions (see Sect. 4.1.3). For each container $c \in C^{\text{deep}}$, the second cost component reflecting the shuffle-move-minimisation objective is computed referring to category stacking, whereas a retrieval-time-stacking-based cost component is calculated for all other containers (i.e., $c \in C^{\text{feeder}}$ and $c \in C^{\text{xt}}$). The category-based shuffle-move costs of a stacking position are computed as the weighted number of containers in that pile, which are of different category than e_c^{cat}. The retrieval-time-based shuffle-move costs of a pile are computed assuming that container c and all already stacked containers in that pile are retrieved $\overline{\delta}$ days after their delivery time t_c^{in}. Taking into account that hardly anything is known about the individual retrieval time of all containers that are planned to depart by feeder vessel or XT, the mean dwell time $\overline{\delta}$ can be used as a reasonable estimator to anticipate the container-retrieval times and the resulting retrieval sequences for these containers. Finally, a further cost component is added to the cost function penalising the use of ground positions. As long as there are comparably well-suited stacking positions for container c on top of other containers, the use of ground positions should be avoided in order to preserve them for other containers that cannot be stacked on top of existing piles (Dekker et al. 2006).

Altogether, the quality of each allowed stacking position $\phi_c^{\text{xy}} \in \Phi_c^{\text{allowed}}$ for a container $c \in C$ is evaluated with respect to a cost function $f^{\text{ccfs}}(c, \phi_c^{\text{xy}})$ providing the stacking costs of positioning container c on top of pile ϕ_c^{xy}, and the position

$$\phi_c^{\text{xy}*} = \arg \min_{\phi_c^{\text{xy}} \in \Phi_c^{\text{allowed}}} f^{\text{ccfs}}(c, \phi_c^{\text{xy}}) \tag{5.19}$$

leading to the minimal sum of cost components is selected as new stacking position for container c. Here, the cost function is in general composed of four cost components: workload-smoothing costs, modality-intermingling costs, shuffle-move costs and ground-position costs. In order to formulate the cost function with all its cost components, the variables

$$w_{c,c'}^{\text{mod}} = \begin{cases} 1 & \text{if } e_c^{\text{outmode}} \neq e_{c'}^{\text{outmode}}, \\ 0 & \text{otherwise.} \end{cases}$$

$$w_{c,c'}^{\text{cat}} = \begin{cases} 1 & \text{if } e_c^{\text{cat}} \neq e_{c'}^{\text{cat}}, \\ 0 & \text{otherwise.} \end{cases}$$

$$w_{\phi_c^{\text{xy}}}^{\text{gs}} = \begin{cases} 1 & \text{if stacking position } \phi_c^{\text{xy}} \text{ is a ground position,} \\ 0 & \text{otherwise.} \end{cases}$$

need to be defined. In addition, the laden portal-driving distance between the current position of container c (which is a handover area for newly arriving containers) and pile ϕ_c^{xy} as well as the portal-driving distance between pile ϕ_c^{xy} and the handover area container c is planned to be collected from in the future are denoted by $l_{\text{in}}^{\text{x}}(\phi_c^{\text{xy}})$ and $l_{\text{out}}^{\text{x}}(\phi_c^{\text{xy}})$, respectively. Based on these definitions, the costs of stacking an incoming or to-be-repositioned container $c \in C^{\text{deep}}$ on top of pile ϕ_c^{xy} are computed as

$$\begin{aligned} f^{\text{ccfs}}(c, \phi_c^{\text{xy}}) = \lambda_{\tau(j)}^{\text{mod}} & \sum_{c' \in C(\phi_c^{\text{xy}})} w_{c,c'}^{\text{mod}} \\ + \lambda_{\tau(j)}^{\text{cat}} & \sum_{c' \in C(\phi_c^{\text{xy}})} w_{c,c'}^{\text{cat}} \end{aligned} \tag{5.20}$$

$$+\lambda^{\text{dist}}_{\tau(j)}\left(\frac{\left|J^{\text{p}}_{t}\right|}{\left|\overline{J^{\text{p}}}\right|}\times l^{\text{x}}_{\text{in}}\left(\phi^{\text{xy}}_{c}\right)+\frac{\left|\overline{J^{\text{p}}}\right|}{\left|J^{\text{p}}_{t}\right|}\times l^{\text{x}}_{\text{out}}\left(\phi^{\text{xy}}_{c}\right)\right)$$
$$+\lambda^{\text{gs}}_{\tau(j)}w^{\text{gs}}_{\phi^{\text{xy}}_{c}}$$

with $\lambda^{\text{mod}}_{\tau(j)}$, $\lambda^{\text{cat}}_{\tau(j)}$, $\lambda^{\text{dist}}_{\tau(j)}$ and $\lambda^{\text{gs}}_{\tau(j)}$ denoting the user-specified weighting factors with respect to the type of job that is induced by stacking container c, for the modality-intermingling costs, the category-based shuffle-move costs, the workload-smoothing costs and the ground-position costs, respectively. Similarly, the stacking costs for a container that is planned to depart by feeder vessel or XT are defined by

$$f^{\text{ccfs}}(c,\phi^{\text{xy}}_{c})=\lambda^{\text{mod}}_{\tau(j)}\sum_{c'\in C(\phi^{\text{xy}}_{c})}w^{\text{mod}}_{c,c'} \tag{5.21}$$
$$+\lambda^{\text{rts}}_{\tau(j)}\sum_{c'\in C(\phi^{\text{xy}}_{c})}\left(t^{\text{in}}_{c}-t^{\text{in}}_{c'}\right)$$
$$+\lambda^{\text{dist}}_{\tau(j)}\left(\frac{\left|J^{\text{p}}_{t}\right|}{\left|\overline{J^{\text{p}}}\right|}\times l^{\text{x}}_{\text{in}}\left(\phi^{\text{xy}}_{c}\right)+\frac{\left|\overline{J^{\text{p}}}\right|}{\left|J^{\text{p}}_{t}\right|}\times l^{\text{x}}_{\text{out}}\left(\phi^{\text{xy}}_{c}\right)\right)$$
$$+\lambda^{\text{gs}}_{\tau(j)}w^{\text{gs}}_{\phi^{\text{xy}}_{c}}$$

with $\lambda^{\text{rts}}_{\tau(j)}$ denoting the job-type-specific weighting factor for the retrieval-time-based shuffle-move costs. The first term of (5.20) and (5.21) defines the modality-intermingling costs of stacking container c on top of pile ϕ^{xy}_{c}, which are computed as the sum of all containers stored in that pile that are not planned to depart with e^{outmode}_{c}. The more containers, which are planned to depart by other modes of transportation, are stacked in pile ϕ^{xy}_{c}, the higher is the risk for shuffle moves and the higher should be the stacking costs for that pile in order to reduce its attractiveness of being selected as the stacking position for container c.

The shuffle-move costs are defined by the second term of (5.20) and (5.21). For each container $c \in C^{\text{deep}}$, they are computed similarly to the modality-intermingling costs as the number of containers that are stored in the evaluated pile ϕ^{xy}_{c} and that are not categorised as e^{cat}_{c}. Thus, the shuffle-move costs increase with a growing number of differently categorised containers in pile ϕ^{xy}_{c}, since more shuffle moves are expected to occur if containers of different categories are stacked on top of each other. In contrast to the category-stacking approach described by Dekker et al. (2006), which is only based on the top containers of the piles, here all containers stored in a considered pile are taken into account for the computation of the category-based cost component in order to allow a more profound selection of stacking positions—in particular if there is no pile available for container c which consists entirely of containers of the same category. For each container that is planned to depart by feeder vessel or XT, the shuffle-move costs of stacking container c on top of pile ϕ^{xy}_{c} are computed as the sum of delivery-time differences between container c and all containers already stacked in that pile. The more containers are already stacked in a pile ϕ_c^{xy} and the earlier these containers have been stored in the block, the higher is the risk for shuffle moves if container c is stacked on top of that pile. Hence, the stacking costs need to increase with a growing sum of delivery-time differences in order to reduce the attractiveness of stacking positions with high shuffle-move risks.

The third term of (5.20) and (5.21) is used to compute the workload-smoothing costs of pile $\phi_c^{xy} \in \Phi_c^{\text{allowed}}$ with respect to the current crane workload and the laden-portal-driving distances resulting from stacking container c on top of that pile. The current crane workload is represented by a workload factor that is calculated as the number $\left|J_t^{\text{p}}\right|$ of currently plannable jobs in relation to the average number $\left|\overline{J^{\text{p}}}\right|$ of plannable jobs. By multiplying the crane-driving distance for the upcoming movement of container c ($l_{\text{in}}^{\text{x}}\left(\phi_c^{xy}\right)$) with this workload factor and multiplying the crane-driving distance for the future retrieval movement of container c ($l_{\text{out}}^{\text{x}}\left(\phi_c^{xy}\right)$) with the reciprocal workload factor, stacking far away from the departing handover area is penalised more than stacking far away from the current position of container c during below-average workload situations (i.e.,$\left|J_t^{\text{p}}\right|/\left|\overline{J^{\text{p}}}\right| < 1$), while this is reversed for above-average workload situations. For incoming transshipment containers, the workload-smoothing costs are the smaller, the closer pile ϕ_c^{xy} is located to the waterside handover area, independently of the current workload situation since storage and retrieval distances are identical (i.e., $l_{\text{in}}^{\text{x}}\left(\phi_c^{xy}\right) = l_{\text{out}}^{\text{x}}\left(\phi_c^{xy}\right)$). In contrast, the workload-smoothing costs for import and export containers are greatly dependent on the current workload situation. For below-average workloads, piles located closer to the outgoing handover area are connected with lower costs in order to facilitate longer crane movements and to work against an under-utilisation of available crane resources. Whereas for above-average workloads, lower costs are induced by stacking positions closer to the current position of container c in order to avoid long crane-driving distances and to preserve crane resources for the execution of other jobs.

The ground-position costs of stacking position ϕ_c^{xy} are included by the last term of (5.20) and (5.21). Ground-position costs are only incurred for a stacking position if it is actually a ground position. The amount of costs incurred is only determined by the relevant cost factor $\lambda_{\tau(j)}^{gs}$. In general, the higher the cost factor of a cost component, the more attention is given to the underlying stacking objective of that cost component in comparison to other objectives. For example, in order to primarily aim at minimising the number of shuffle moves, $\lambda_{\tau(j)}^{\text{mod}}$ and $\lambda_{\tau(j)}^{\text{cat}}$ or $\lambda_{\tau(j)}^{\text{rts}}$ should be given comparably high weights to ensure that workload-smoothing or ground-slot preferences do not have a bigger impact on the stacking costs than the avoidance of shuffle moves.

Finally, it also needs to be defined, how to deal with containers for which no allowed stacking position is available at all (i.e., $\Phi_c^{\text{allowed}} = \{\}$). This is the case if the maximum allowed filling rate of the yard block is already reached and/or if all piles with same-sized containers are already filled to the maximum stacking height and no adequate ground position is available either. Usually, such a situation should

```
begin
   determine set Φ_c^allowed of allowed positions for c
   if Φ_c^allowed ≠ {} then
      for all φ_c^xy ∈ Φ_c^allowed do
         if e_c^outmode = deep-sea then
            compute stacking cost f^ccfs(c, φ_c^xy) based on (5.20)
         else
            compute stacking cost f^ccfs(c, φ_c^xy) based on (5.21)
         end-if
      end-do
      select position φ_c^xy* = arg min_{φ_c^xy ∈ Φ_c^allowed} f^ccfs(c, φ_c^xy)
   else
      if c is already stored inside the yard block then
         relocate c to another yard block
      else
         redirect c to another yard block
      end-if
   end-if
end
```

Algorithm 5.1: Pseudocode formulation of combined-cost-function stacking (CCFS)

only be expected for yard blocks that are (almost) entirely filled. In particular, for 40′ containers it may be increasingly difficult to find allowed stacking positions with increasing yard-block-filling rates, as, compared to 20′ containers, two adjacent ground positions are needed if no non-full pile with 40′ containers is available. Here, newly arriving containers are simply assumed to be redirected to other yard blocks if no allowed stacking position is available, while already stored containers (that need to be shuffled) need to be removed from the yard block in order not to block other yard operations. Therefore, all such containers that need to be shuffled are retrieved at the waterside end of the yard block and assumed to be taken to neighbouring yard blocks if no allowed stacking position is available. Altogether, a summarising overview on the implementation of combined-cost-function stacking is given by the pseudocode formulation of Algorithm 5.1.

5.2.5 *Heuristical Housekeeping Stacking*

In contrast to the preceding stacking strategies, the housekeeping concept presented in this subsection does not deal with the selection of stacking positions for incoming or to-be-shuffled containers. Moreover, the relocation of containers inside the yard blocks without any direct requirements is addressed. Except for shuffle moves, containers are usually relocated inside the yard block in order to smooth the crane workload over time by improving the stacking positions of containers before they actually need to be retrieved or shuffled. For front-end-loading RMGC systems, the stacking position of a container may be improved in two ways: Firstly, a container may be restacked in such a way that it less likely needs to be shuffled in the future. Secondly, a container may be relocated closer to its outgoing handover area in order to reduce the execution time and the vehicle-waiting time for the corresponding future retrieval job. In this sense, both improvements are helpful to reduce the future crane workload, as fewer shuffle moves have to be performed and shorter laden crane-movement times can be expected in the future. Thus, future crane workload can optionally be shifted to the present by performing additional crane movements in the present that avoid future shuffle moves and/or long laden crane movements to the outgoing handover area. However, this is only advisable if the available crane resources are currently 'under-used' or even idle. Otherwise, yard-performance-reducing peak crane workloads may be caused or amplified in the present, which is not in line with the crane-workload-smoothing objective. Therefore, stacking-position-improving container relocations, which are called housekeeping jobs here (see Sect. 3.4.3), should only be performed if the execution of more urgent main jobs is not delayed by relocating other containers, which can only be ensured in case that the cranes are not already working to capacity at the moment.

The main idea and the benefits of the housekeeping concept, which is sometimes also referred to as repositioning and/or prepositioning (e.g., Choe et al. 2007; Park et al. 2010), are described by several authors (e.g., Chen et al. 2000; Saanen 2004, p. 112; Valkengoed 2004, p. 15). However, hardly any detailed information on the implementation of the housekeeping concept have been provided so far—in particular, the generation of housekeeping jobs is so far not addressed to the author's knowledge. In order to generate a new housekeeping job, both a container for relocation and a new position for that container have to be selected. Usually, each container $c \in C^{\text{top}}$ can be selected for relocation, with C^{top} defining the set of all currently stored containers that are located on top of a pile. A selected container c can be relocated to each allowed position $\phi_c^{\text{xy}} \in \Phi_c^{\text{allowed}}$. In order to comply with the objective of workload smoothing, as much future workload as possible should be shifted to the present, which means the container $c^* \in C^{\text{top}}$ should be selected, whose stacking position can be improved most by relocating it to the best allowed position, and that position should be selected as new stacking position for c^*. Taking into account that—depending on the block dimensions—several hundred containers (i.e., all $c \in C^{\text{top}}$) and several hundred positions (i.e., all $\phi_c^{\text{xy}} \in \Phi_c^{\text{allowed}}$) can be selected for relocation, several tens of thousands of different housekeeping jobs can be generated. Thus, the enumeration of all possible combinations of $c \in C^{\text{top}}$ and $\phi_c^{\text{xy}} \in \Phi_c^{\text{allowed}}$ in order to find the best housekeeping job is expected to be a very time-consuming approach, which is not applicable in practice since housekeeping jobs usually need to be generated in real-time.

Within the framework of this subsection, a housekeeping concept is introduced that is based on a greedy two-phase heuristic method to generate new housekeeping jobs in real-time whenever no other plannable job is available for an idle crane $g \in G$ (i.e., $J_{tg}^{p} = \{\}$). In the first phase of the heuristic, each container $c \in C^{\text{top}}$

1. begin
2.   wait until a crane $g \in G$ is idle and $J_{tg}^{\mathrm{p}} = \{\}$
3.   for all containers $c \in C^{\mathrm{top}}$ do
4.   compute $f^{\mathrm{ccfs}}\left(c, \phi_c^{\mathrm{xy,cu}}\right)$ of container c
5.   if $f^{\mathrm{ccfs}}\left(c, \phi_c^{\mathrm{xy,cu}}\right) \geq \kappa_{\mathrm{hhs}}^{\mathrm{al}}$ then
6.   add c to C^{relocate}
7.   end-if
8.   end-do
9.   sort set C^{relocate} in decreasing order of $f^{\mathrm{ccfs}}\left(c, \phi_c^{\mathrm{xy,cu}}\right)$
10.   for all containers $c \in C^{\mathrm{relocate}}$ do
11.   determine $\phi_c^{\mathrm{xy}*}$ and $f^{\mathrm{ccfs}}\left(c, \phi_c^{\mathrm{xy}*}\right)$ by use of CCFS
12.   if $\left(f^{\mathrm{ccfs}}\left(c, \phi_c^{\mathrm{xy,cu}}\right) - f^{\mathrm{ccfs}}\left(c, \phi_c^{\mathrm{xy}*}\right)\right) / f^{\mathrm{ccfs}}\left(c, \phi_c^{\mathrm{xy,cu}}\right) \geq \kappa_{\mathrm{hhs}}^{\mathrm{mci}}$ then
13.   create housekeeping job moving c to $\phi_c^{\mathrm{xy}*}$
14.   terminate heuristical housekeeping stacking
15.   end-if
16.   end-do
17. end

Algorithm 5.2: Pseudocode formulation of heuristical housekeeping stacking (HHS)

is evaluated with respect to the quality of its current stacking position $\phi_c^{\mathrm{xy,cu}}$, which is measured by the CCFS cost functions (5.20) and (5.21). Only a container exhibiting a sufficiently high room for improvement is added to a set C^{relocate} of relocation candidates. In the second phase, all relocation candidates are investigated in decreasing order of room for improvement with respect to the actually attainable improvement of the stacking quality. Once a preset relative improvement level is reached by an investigated candidate container, a housekeeping job is created relocating that container to the best available stacking position and the search process for a housekeeping job is terminated. Before some issues of this housekeeping concept—which is referred to as heuristical housekeeping stacking (HHS) here—are addressed in more detail, a summarising overview on its implementation is provided by the pseudocode formulation of Algorithm 5.2.

Within the framework of heuristical housekeeping stacking, it is only searched for a new housekeeping job as long as there are no other plannable jobs for an idle crane $g \in G$ (see pseudocode line 2). In this way, a smoothing of the crane workload can best be guaranteed as it is ensured that the execution of plannable main and shuffle jobs cannot be delayed by the creation of operationally less important housekeeping jobs. Once a new housekeeping job is needed by one of the cranes, each container $c \in C^{\mathrm{top}}$ is evaluated in the first phase of the heuristic with respect to its basic suitability for relocation (see pseudocode lines 3–8). Here, a container $c \in C^{\mathrm{top}}$ is regarded as suitable for relocation if the quality of its current position $\phi_c^{\mathrm{xy,cu}}$ can theoretically be improved by a sufficiently high degree. Containers that are already stacked on comparable good positions do not need to be considered for relocation as hardly any positive workload-smoothing effect is expected by relocating such containers. Here, the quality of a current stacking position is evaluated on the basis of stacking costs $f^{\mathrm{ccfs}}\left(c, \phi_c^{\mathrm{xy,cu}}\right)$ with higher stacking costs representing more room for improvement (see pseudocode line 4). Therefore, only containers with stacking costs $f^{\text{ccfs}}\left(c, \phi_c^{\text{xy,cu}}\right)$ exceeding a user-defined acceptance level $\kappa_{\text{hhs}}^{\text{al}}$ are considered as containers suitable for relocation. They are added to the set C^{relocate} of relocation candidates, whereas all other containers (i.e., $c \in C^{\text{top}} | f^{\text{ccfs}}\left(c, \phi_c^{\text{xy,cu}}\right) < \kappa_{\text{hhs}}^{\text{al}}$) are neglected for the further process (see pseudocode lines 5–7). Because the quality of the container positions is measured by the CCFS cost functions (5.20) and (5.21), shuffle-move risks, crane-driving distances and use of ground-positions are simultaneously taking into account for the decision on the creation of housekeeping jobs. Thus, the stacking costs $f^{\text{ccfs}}\left(c, \phi_c^{\text{xy,cu}}\right)$ of the current stacking position of a container $c \in C^{\text{top}}$ are the higher, the greater the risk of the need container c to be shuffled in the future and the further afar container c is stacked from its outgoing handover area. Since low crane workloads are required to initiate the generation of housekeeping jobs, comparably high workload-smoothing costs are assigned to containers with long driving distances $l_{\text{out}}^{\text{x}}\left(\phi_c^{\text{xy}}\right)$, thus increasing the improvement potential for containers stacked far away from their outgoing handover area (see Sect. 5.2.4).

In the second phase of heuristical housekeeping stacking, the set C^{relocate} of relocation candidates is searched for a container to-be-relocated and a new position for that container (see pseudocode lines 9–16). In order to shorten this search process and the required computation time, the first container fulfilling a certain criterion is greedily selected for relocation. Here, a minimum relative stacking cost improvement $\kappa_{\text{hhs}}^{\text{mci}}$ has to be actually met by a candidate container $c \in C^{\text{relocate}}$ to be selected (see pseudocode line 12). The actually attainable relative stacking-cost improvement for each container $c \in C^{\text{relocate}}$ is computed by dividing the cost savings $f^{\text{ccfs}}\left(c, \phi_c^{\text{xy,cu}}\right) - f^{\text{ccfs}}\left(c, \phi_c^{\text{xy*}}\right)$ of relocating container c to the best allowed stacking position for that container ($\phi_c^{\text{xy*}}$) by the stacking costs $f^{\text{ccfs}}\left(\phi_c^{\text{xy,cu}}\right)$ of its current stacking position, which is its theoretical potential for improvement. Both the best allowed stacking position $\phi_c^{\text{xy*}}$ for container $c \in C^{\text{relocate}}$ and the associated minimum stacking costs $f^{\text{ccfs}}\left(c, \phi_c^{\text{xy*}}\right)$ are determined by applying the CCFS container-positioning method (see pseudocode line 11, see Sect. 5.2.4). Once a certain container c is found to have an actually attainable relative stacking-cost improvement exceeding $\kappa_{\text{hhs}}^{\text{mci}}$, a housekeeping job relocating that container to its best stacking position $\phi_c^{\text{xy*}}$ is created (pseudocode line 13) and the search for a container to-be-relocated is terminated (pseudocode line 14). In order to select a container for relocation whose actually attainable stacking-cost improvement is not only high in relative terms, but also in absolute values, the candidate containers are checked in decreasing order of current stacking costs $f^{\text{ccfs}}\left(c, \phi_c^{\text{xy,cu}}\right)$ for fulfilling the termination criterion. This is ensured by sorting the set $c \in C^{\text{relocate}}$ of candidate containers in decreasing order of their current stacking costs $f^{\text{ccfs}}\left(c, \phi_c^{\text{xy,cu}}\right)$ before this set is searched for a suitable container for relocation (see pseudocode line 9). No housekeeping job at all is created if none of the candidate containers $c \in C^{\text{relocate}}$ is found to have an actually attainable relative stacking-cost improvement exceeding $\kappa_{\text{hhs}}^{\text{mci}}$.

The effects of heuristical housekeeping stacking on the operational performance of RMGC systems greatly depend on the user-specified parameter settings for $\kappa_{\text{hhs}}^{\text{al}}$ and $\kappa_{\text{hhs}}^{\text{mci}}$. The smaller values are defined for $\kappa_{\text{hhs}}^{\text{al}}$ and $\kappa_{\text{hhs}}^{\text{mci}}$, the greater the set C^{relocate} of candidate containers is and the more likely a container is selected to be relocated, respectively. Thus, on the one hand, the probability of actually creating a housekeeping job increases with decreasing values for $\kappa_{\text{hhs}}^{\text{al}}$ and $\kappa_{\text{hhs}}^{\text{mci}}$, but on the other hand, the probability for relocating a container that can only be improved by a rather small amount of stacking costs increases as well.

5.3 Crane-Scheduling Problem

After a storage position has been chosen for a container, it has to be decided which crane transports the container to its designated pile and at what time this transport job takes place. The underlying planning problem is the crane-scheduling problem, which is generally introduced in Sect. 2.4.3.8 and addressed in-depth throughout this section for the special application area of RMGC systems. Firstly, the RMGC-specific problem settings including the objectives and constraints of the crane-scheduling problem are introduced. Secondly, a survey on literature relevant to this planning problem is provided, which is used as the basis for the following classification of scheduling strategies. Thereafter, different variants for each of the classified strategy types are presented in detail. It is started with a discussion of some preselection methods that might be helpful to reduce the planning effort for the original crane-scheduling problem, which is followed by the introduction of two multi-criteria priority rules. In Sect. 5.3.6, the first IP models for all types of RMGC systems are presented and evaluated on the basis of some numerical investigations. As a consequence of the unpromising results of the integer models, this section is closed with two heuristical strategies to create complete schedules for several jobs and cranes. While the first strategy is an enumerative approach, the second one is based on a GA.

5.3.1 Problem Description

Each time a job i is finished by a gantry crane g at time t_{ig}^{finish}, it has to be decided, which job $j \in J_{tg}^{\text{p}}$ should be performed next by that crane. In case, no plannable job is available for crane g (i.e., $J_{tg}^{\text{p}} = \{\}$), the crane has to wait until an appropriate job becomes available. Usually, the next job is submitted to a crane indirectly by a job-management module of the TOS that is alerted by a crane when it becomes idle. A scheduler module of the TOS is then called by the job-management module, each time a new job needs to be determined for a crane. Although the crane actions are not directly controlled by these modules as these actions are performed autonomously, the operational performance of an RMGC system is greatly influenced by the sequence of submitted jobs that results in a particular sequence of crane movements. Which job $j \in J^{\mathrm{p}}_{tg}$ is submitted next to a crane g by the job-management module is determined by the applied strategy for the RMGC-scheduling problem (Stahlbock and Voß 2010).

The RMGC-scheduling problem deals with the crane assignment and sequencing of jobs within the same yard block. In case of multiple cranes per yard block, the solution of the RMGC-scheduling problem requires two decisions that can be made either successively or simultaneously: Firstly, it has to be scheduled, which known jobs should be performed by which crane. And secondly, a decision is needed, in which sequence the assigned jobs should be performed by the respective crane. For SRMGC systems, only the sequence of known jobs and no crane assignment is required. The scheduling problem for SRMGC systems is thus equivalent to the well known TSP, which is characterised as NP-hard (Garey and Johnson 1979, pp. 27–29). With two or three cranes per block the scheduling problem is even more complicated, not just because of the additional crane-assignment problem, which makes RMGC scheduling similar to a type of the VRP (see Sect. 3.4.5), but especially due to the need to consider the dynamic interferences between the cranes of a yard block. In order to realistically evaluate a schedule, resulting crane interferences have to be reasonably anticipated. In this study, crane-routing and crossing manoeuvres are decided in real-time on the basis of certain rules that are described in detail in Sect. 5.4. These rules can be taken into account implicitly by the solution approaches of the crane-scheduling problem for the evaluation of different scheduling decisions.

Another difficulty of the RMGC-scheduling problem is its online character, which means the arrival of a vehicle in the handover area and the corresponding job j usually becomes known only shortly before its actual handover-area due date t^{hd}_j. Throughout this work, it is assumed that each main job becomes known at time t^{a}_j, a randomly distributed look-ahead time m^{lat}_j before the actual handover-area due date t^{hd}_j of that job. Owing to differences in the predictability of vehicle arrivals in the waterside and landside handover areas (see Sect. 4.1.3), the length of the look-ahead time differs between waterside and landside jobs. XT arrivals at the landside interface of the yard block are usually completely unknown until the actual arrival of the vehicle, thus leading to a rather short look-ahead time m^{lat}_j for landside storage and retrieval jobs (i.e., $m^{\mathrm{lat}}_j = t^{\mathrm{hd}}_j - t^{\mathrm{a}}_j \approxeq 0$). In contrast, the container flow at the waterside ends of the yard blocks is somewhat more predictable, thus leading to a longer look-ahead time m^{lat}_j for waterside storage and retrieval jobs (i.e., $m^{\mathrm{lat}}_j = t^{\mathrm{hd}}_j - t^{\mathrm{a}}_j > 0$). Depending on the quality of the underlying TOS and some stochastic influences, like disturbances of the manually controlled ship-to-shore processes, it is usually possible to predict the arrival of a vehicle in the waterside handover area of a yard block several seconds or minutes prior to the actual arrival time. Owing to this online-planning situation, reasonable scheduling decisions that are based on up-to-date information, can usually only be made shortly before the next crane is calling the job-management module.

Therefore, RMGC-scheduling strategies with very short runtimes are needed in order to immediately deliver results.

Of great importance for the performance of a scheduling strategy is the used objective. In this work, the minimisation of waiting times for horizontal-transport vehicles in the handover areas of a yard block—in particular in the waterside handover area—is identified as the main objective for the crane-scheduling problem (see Sect. 3.2). As a consequence, the jobs have to be scheduled in such a way that the realised vehicle-waiting times in the waterside and landside handover areas are minimised. But as the realised vehicle-waiting time $\omega_{jg}^{\text{hr}+}$ of a certain job j is not known at the point in time at which the relevant scheduling decisions are made, the minimisation of $\overline{\omega}_{\text{ws}}^{\text{hr}+}$ and $\overline{\omega}_{\text{ls}}^{\text{hr}+}$ is not directly operationable. Instead, the planned lateness $\Delta_{jg}^{\text{pp}+}$ of crane g at the pick-up position of job j is a reasonable estimate for the actually realised vehicle-waiting time which can be computed in advance of a scheduling decision (see Sect. 5.1). Therefore, the minimisation of the total planned lateness

$$\sum_{g\in G}\sum_{j\in J_{tg}^{\text{p}}} \Delta_{jg}^{\text{pp}+} \tag{5.22}$$

may be regarded as the most important objective of the crane-scheduling problem.

In addition, it may be helpful to deploy the available crane resources as efficiently as possible in order to have sufficient resources available for a timely execution of other jobs. This is facilitated by minimising the duration of the execution of each job j with respect to its time components that are controllable by scheduling decisions. Referring to the time components that are shown in Fig. 5.3, the duration of pick-up and drop-off operations cannot be influenced by scheduling decisions, while the duration of all other time components of job j are—at least to some extent—determined by the crane-assignment and job-sequencing decisions.

The duration m_{jg}^{xye} of an empty movement is greatly influenced by scheduling decisions in two ways: Firstly, the empty-driving distances l_{ij}^{x} and l_{ij}^{y} of a crane g between the destination of job i and the origin of its successor j are determined by the scheduled sequence of jobs for that crane. Secondly, the extent of crane interferences during an empty movement is controlled by the sequences of movements for the cranes of a yard block that also result from the scheduled job sequences. In general, two types of crane interferences can be distinguished regarding their consequences for the involved crane g. On the one hand, crane g may be required to stop its movement and to wait until another crane has finished a certain operation on its way, which leads to unproductive waiting times for crane g. And on the other hand, crane g may be required to stop and to evade as the interfering crane is granted the right of way, which leads to both unproductive movements and waiting times for crane g. The total crane-interference time during the performance of job j is denoted by m_j^{cit}. The controllability of the laden crane-movement time m_{jg}^{xyf} is far smaller than for empty movements, as the driving distances l_j^{x} and l_j^{y} are given by the origin and destination of the job itself. Nevertheless, the duration of m_{jg}^{xyf} is partly influenced by scheduling decisions, since the extent of crane interferences results from the crane movements of scheduled job sequences.

The realised waiting time $\omega_{jg}^{\text{hr}-}$ of crane g for job j in the handover area is also greatly determined by scheduling decisions, as the realised arrival time at the handover area depends on the assigned crane g and the scheduled starting time t_{jg}^{start} for that job. Taking into account that crane resources are wasted when waiting for horizontal-transport vehicles, not just the vehicle-waiting time $\omega_{jg}^{\text{hr}+}$, but also the crane-waiting time $\omega_{jg}^{\text{hr}-}$ in the handover areas should be minimised. However, analogously to the realised vehicle-waiting times, the realised crane-waiting times are also unknown for scheduling decisions, but the planned arrival time t_{jg}^{pp} at the pick-up position of job j is available, such that the planned earliness $\Delta_{jg}^{\text{pp}-}$ of crane g at the pick-up position of job j can be used as a reasonable substitute for scheduling decisions.

Altogether, the main objectives of the crane-scheduling problem are

$$\min \overline{\omega}_{\text{ws}}^{\text{hr}+} \qquad (5.23) \qquad \text{and} \qquad \min \overline{\omega}_{\text{ls}}^{\text{hr}+} . \qquad (5.24)$$

But, in view of the fact that both objectives are not directly operationable, they are operationalised for the solution of the crane-scheduling problem by

$$\min \Delta_{jg}^{\text{pp}+} , \qquad (5.25) \qquad\qquad \min m_{jg}^{\text{xye}} , \qquad (5.27)$$

$$\min \Delta_{jg}^{\text{pp}-} \qquad (5.26) \qquad \text{and} \qquad \min m_{j}^{\text{cit}} . \qquad (5.28)$$

The preceding explanations and thoughts of the crane-scheduling problem can be illustrated by an example of a simplified planning situation for a TRMGC system with 38 bays. But only bays 2–37 are actual bays of the yard block where the containers can be stacked, while the waterside and landside handover areas are represented by bays 1 and 38, respectively, where the respective cranes are positioned initially. All relevant data of the example planning situation are summarised in Table 5.2. For simplifying reasons, origin and destination are only given as x-coordinates in terms of bays. In addition, the time is measured in terms of the required constant crane-movement time for a single bay and five time units are needed for all pick-up and drop-off operations. As the cranes are not able to cross each other, jobs 1, 2, 5 and 8 can only be performed by the waterside crane, while jobs 3 and 6 can only be performed by the landside crane and the shuffle jobs 4 and 7 can be performed by both cranes. Finally, a minimum distance between the RMGCs of two bays is assumed for safety reasons and the right of way is always granted to the crane which is closer to its current driving target (i.e., origin or destination).

Applying the First-In-First-Out (FIFO) method, which assigns the jobs in the order they become known to suitable and available cranes, yields that jobs 1, 2, 5, 7 and 8 are performed in that order by the waterside crane, while jobs 3, 4 and 6 are performed by the landside crane. The corresponding crane-movement paths are illustrated by the solid lines in Fig. 5.5. With regard to the identified objectives of the crane-scheduling problem, this solution leads to $\sum_{j \in J} \Delta_{jg}^{\text{pp}+} = 252$ time units crane lateness at the pick-up positions of the jobs, $\sum_{j \in J} m_{jg}^{\text{xye}} = 96$ time units empty

Table 5.2 Data set of an example crane-scheduling problem

j	o_j^x	d_j^x	t_j^a	t_j^{pd}	ρ_j
1	1	8	−9	21	
2	18	1	−1	17	
3	12	38	0	0	
4	16	16	36	36	
5	16	1	36	56	4
6	25	38	67	67	
7	15	15	88	88	
8	15	1	88	121	7

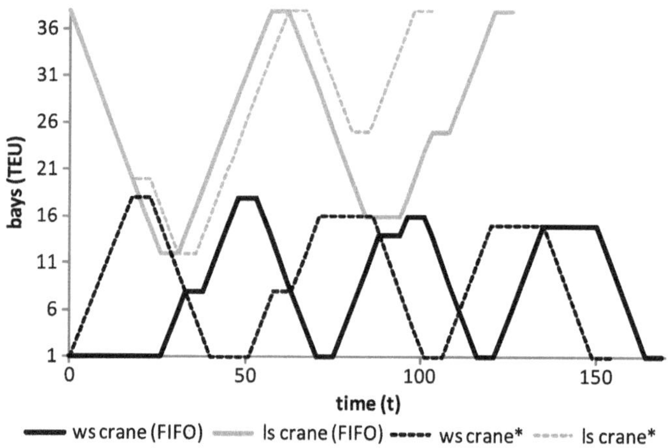

Fig. 5.5 Schematic illustration of crane-movement paths

movements, $\sum_{j \in J} \Delta_{jg}^{pp-} = 21$ time units crane earliness at the pick-up positions of the jobs and $\sum_{j \in J} m_j^{cit} = 6$ time units crane interference. In contrast, another schedule, that assigns jobs 2, 1, 4, 5, 7 and 8 in that order to the waterside crane and only jobs 3 and 6 to the landside crane, as illustrated by the dashed lines in Fig. 5.5, would yield crane lateness, empty-movement times, crane earliness and interference times of only 171, 72, 0 and 5 time units, respectively. These results illustrate the potential for performance improvements and provide the motivation for the development of more elaborated scheduling strategies than myopic priority rules. An overview on the current state of research in the field of crane scheduling at seaport container terminals is provided in the following subsection.

5.3.2 *Literature Overview*

Similar to the container-stacking problem, the scheduling problem of storage machines has been addressed by a great number of papers so far. In particular, dozens of relevant papers on crane scheduling at seaport container terminals are available. But similar to the container-stacking problem, only very few authors address the crane-scheduling problem for front-end-loading RMGC systems, while plenty of papers deal with the logistically different sideway-loading systems. Within these sideway-loading systems, the cranes do not need to move long distances along the block each time a container is transferred to or from a vehicle (see Sect. 3.3). As a consequence, empty crane movements, crane interferences and cooperation among the cranes are less important issues than for the front-end-loading RMGC systems. Nevertheless, the references on sideway-loading systems may provide useful modelling and solution approaches for the crane-scheduling problem addressed here. Altogether, 29 relevant references on the crane-scheduling problem at seaport container terminals can be found, whereof 21 deal with scheduling problems for sideway-loading systems and only eight address the crane-scheduling problem for different types of front-end-loading systems. Subsequently, the scheduling objectives, the considered planning restrictions, the modelling and solution approaches as well as the most important findings of these papers are summarised.

5.3.2.1 Scheduling of Sideway-Loading Systems

The papers on sideway-loading systems that are presented throughout this subsection can be distinguished with respect to the considered number of yard cranes per yard block and the applied research method. While Kim and Kim (1997, 1999b), Kozan and Preston (1999), Narasimhan and Palekar (2002), Kim and Kim (2003), Kim et al. (2004) and Ng and Mak (2005a,b) address scheduling of a single crane per yard block, crane scheduling for two or more cranes per yard block is addressed by Kim et al. (2002), Zhang et al. (2002), Linn and Zhang (2003), Murty et al. (2005), Ng (2005), Bohrer (2010), Lee et al. (2006), Jung and Kim (2006), Lee et al. (2007), Froyland et al. (2008), Cao et al. (2008), Li et al. (2009) and Petering et al. (2009). Apart from Kim et al. (2002) and Petering et al. (2009), who compare different scheduling methods by means of simulation studies, analytical solution approaches and investigations are presented by all other references.

Kim and Kim (1997, 1999b) address the problem of routing a single gantry crane in a yard block during loading operations of export containers out of the stack onto waiting vehicles. Their objective is the minimisation of the total container-handling time of the crane with respect to the setup times at the bay and the travelling times between consecutive bays. In both papers, an MIP formulation as well as an optimal solution algorithm is presented, that is based on dynamic programming and solves the problem in real-time. The solution provides the optimal sequence of bay visits and the number of container retrievals in each bay, but the handling sequence of individual containers within a specific bay is not determined.

Comparable to Kim and Kim (1997, 1999b), Narasimhan and Palekar (2002) address the problem of finding an optimal sequence of bay visits and container pick-ups for a single gantry crane with the objective of minimising the total container-handling time of the crane for executing a given load plan with a given bay plan of export containers. Firstly, an IP formulation is provided and the problem is proven to be NP-hard. Thereafter, an optimal B&B algorithm and a heuristic method are developed. Finally, computational tests on randomly generated problems are conducted, which show the heuristic to be more applicable to real-world problems.

In contrast to Kim and Kim (1997, 1999b), scheduling of both sideway-loading gantry cranes and SCs, is addressed by Kim and Kim (2003). Likewise their objective is the minimisation of the total container-handling time. Two alternative scheduling algorithms are presented which are able to determine the route of the yard equipment and the number of containers picked up at each bay simultaneously. As in Kim and Kim (1997, 1999b), the handling sequence of individual containers within a specific bay remains undetermined. Numerical investigations are conducted to compare the suggested GA and the beam-search algorithm against each other and against the optimal solution. It is found that the beam-search algorithm outperforms the GA.

Kozan and Preston (1999) as well as Kim et al. (2004) do not only address the problem of scheduling the crane route and the number of container pick-ups at each bay, but also the problem of determining the handling sequences within specific bays. Kozan and Preston (1999) present an MIP model with the objective of minimising the vessel-berthing times with respect to the container-handling and transport times of both gantry cranes and TTUs. Owing to the NP-hardness of the problem, a GA is suggested by them, which is tested with real-world data from the Fisherman Islands Port in Brisbane (Australia). Several sensitivity analyses with respect to the moves per call, the stacking capacity and strategy as well as the yard layout are conducted. In comparison to Kozan and Preston (1999), several additional real-world constraints with regard to the crane-driving distances, the stacking height and the container weights are incorporated into the scheduling problem that is suggested by Kim et al. (2004). They formulate an MIP model with a multi-objective quadratic function. In summary, the objective is the minimisation of QC and yard-crane-handling times. Individual yard-crane-related objectives are among others the minimisation of crane-driving distances and the minimisation of shuffle moves. In order to produce near optimal solutions for the formulated problem in reasonable time, a beam-search algorithm is suggested by Kim et al. (2004). Through numerical experiments, the beam-search algorithm is found to perform better for this problem than an ant-colony-system approach and a neighbourhood-search algorithm.

Ng and Mak (2005a,b) study a problem that is different from the previously discussed papers in so far as not only the retrieval of export containers is scheduled. Moreover, the problem of scheduling a single gantry crane to perform a given set of storage and retrieval jobs with different due dates is addressed. This problem is formulated as an IP model with the objective of minimising the lateness of the crane compared to the due dates. While a B&B algorithm is proposed by Ng and Mak (2005b) to solve the scheduling problem optimally, Ng and Mak (2005a) develop a heuristical algorithm for the same problem. Finally, numerical investigations are conducted for both solution approaches. It is found that the B&B algorithm can provide the optimal solution for most problems of realistic size, whereas near optimal solutions are produced within seconds by the heuristic algorithm.

In contrast to the preceding references, Zhang et al. (2002) and Linn and Zhang (2003) as well as Murty et al. (2005) do not address the crane-scheduling problem for a single yard block. Moreover they analyse the dynamic deployment of gantry cranes among different yard blocks with one or two cranes per block. In Zhang et al. (2002), the objective is to find the times and routes of crane movements among blocks with forecasted workloads over a four-hour planning period so that the total delayed workload in the yard is minimised. The problem is formulated as an MIP model and solved by a modified Lagrangian relaxation. The same problem is solved by Linn and Zhang (2003) in a different way. They suggest a heuristic solution approach that is based on the idea of classifying the yard blocks into different categories in order to reduce the problem size. Additional cranes are required in the first category of yard blocks, while these cranes are provided by yard blocks of the second category. All yard blocks that need additional cranes but have no capacity left for a further crane are summarised in another category of yard blocks that is excluded from the scheduling problem. Finally, the heuristic is tested with real-world data from the port of Hong Kong (China). In contrast to Zhang et al. (2002) and Linn and Zhang (2003), Murty et al. (2005) do not regard the dynamic crane deployment among different blocks as an isolated subproblem of the total terminal-planning problem. Moreover, this problem is solved as an integrated part of several interrelated terminal-planning problems like berth allocation, waterside horizontal-transport-vehicle dispatching and routing as well as container stacking (see Sect. 2.4.3).

Lee et al. (2007) investigate the problem of scheduling two gantry cranes working in two different yard blocks during retrieval operations of export containers. Similar to Kim and Kim (1997, 1999b) as well as Narasimhan and Palekar (2002), they aim at optimising the sequence of bay visits and the number of container retrievals at each bay with respect to the total container-handling time of the cranes for a given vessel load plan. In contrast to all following references, no interferences among the two cranes need to be taken into account by Lee et al. (2007) as they are operating in different blocks. Nevertheless, the schedules of the two cranes are interrelated due to the precedence constraints among the jobs that result from the loading order at the QCs. The scheduling problem is formulated as an IP model and an SA algorithm is developed, which is evaluated by means of comparison with a loosely estimated lower bound for that problem.

Kim et al. (2002) are the first, who address the crane-scheduling problem with two cranes working in the same yard block. They present a simulation study on operation rules for automated container terminals with sideway-loading DRMGCs that load and unload AGVs in parallel to the yard block. In particular, two different crane-dispatching rules and two job-sequencing rules are compared. While the tested crane-dispatching rules, that are based on the crane capabilities, can be regarded as problem-specific operation rules, the tested job-sequencing rules are well-known priority rules for all types of routing and scheduling problems. These sequencing rules are the FIFO rule and the NN rule that assigns the jobs with respect to the minimisation of the driving distances of empty cranes.

The problem of scheduling multiple sideway-loading gantry cranes to perform a given set of jobs with different due dates in a yard block is studied by Ng (2005). These gantry cranes are not able to cross each other, which is comparable to TRMGCs. Ng (2005) formulates the scheduling problem, which is noted to be NP-complete, as an integer discrete-time programme with the objective of minimising the sum of total crane delays in comparison to the due dates of the jobs. In order to allow exact modelling of interferences among the cranes, the time is discretised with respect to the required crane-movement time for a single bay. Sequence relations among jobs that result from the need for shuffle moves are not taken into account. A dynamic-programming-based heuristic to solve the problem and an algorithm to find lower bounds for benchmarking the schedules found by the heuristic are developed by Ng (2005). Finally, computational experiments are carried out to evaluate the performance of the heuristic.

The problem of scheduling multiple sideway-loading RTGCs and RMGCs over a certain period in such a way that the unfinished crane tasks at the end of a period are minimised is addressed by Bohrer (2010). Two alternative discrete-time MIP formulations are proposed for both RTGC and RMGC systems. In all models, the time is discretised, as in Ng (2005), with respect to the crane-movement time for a single bay. In the first model formulation, the crane tasks are interpreted as jobs with due dates and processing times, while in the second formulation, the tasks are modelled as generic workload. The RTGC and RMGC-model formulations differ with respect to whether interferences between different cranes are included. While crane-interference restrictions are included in the RMGC model, the RTGC model negligently does not contain such interference restrictions, although multiple cranes are allowed to work in the same yard block. The crane-scheduling problems are shown to be NP-hard. Therefore, two myopic priority rules are developed for the solution of these problems and evaluated by numerical results.

Jung and Kim (2006) and Lee et al. (2006) address a very similar scheduling problem as Kim and Kim (1997, 1999b) and Narasimhan and Palekar (2002) do. But instead of routing a single gantry crane per yard block, Jung and Kim (2006) and Lee et al. (2006) analyse the problem of routing multiple cranes per yard block. They aim to find a near optimal routing schedule for each crane of a yard block during retrieval operations of export containers in reasonable time. While the sequence of bay visits as well as the number of container retrievals at each bay is determined by a routing schedule, the retrieval sequence of individual containers within a specific bay is outside their focus. The optimisation problem is formulated as an IP model with the objective of minimising the makespan of all crane operations for executing a given vessel load plan. The objective function includes the crane-movement times between different bays, the container-handling times at each visited bay and the crane-waiting times caused by crane interferences. A GA and an SA algorithm are designed by Jung and Kim (2006) for the solution of the problem. By means of numerical tests, the SA algorithm is shown to perform better in terms of computation time and objective value. In contrast, Lee et al. (2006) develop a problem-specific priority rule and an SA algorithm, whereof the priority rule is shown to perform better.

Similar to Jung and Kim (2006) and Lee et al. (2006), also Cao et al. (2008) address the scheduling of multiple gantry cranes in a yard block during loading of export containers onto waiting vehicles with the objective of minimising the makespan of all crane operations. But in contrast to Jung and Kim (2006) as well as Lee et al. (2006), no arbitrary number of same-sized cranes per yard block are scheduled by Cao et al. (2008). Instead, a sideway-loading DRMGC system with two cranes of different sizes which can cross each other is analysed. An IP model is developed, including restrictions that prevent the cranes from working at the same bay at the same time and that prevent the inner small crane from crossing the outer large crane when the large crane is loading a container. Three heuristic solution approaches, including an SA algorithm, are designed to solve the problem. These heuristics are compared by means of numerical experiments and it is shown that a problem-specific heuristic performs best.

Froyland et al. (2008) address the scheduling of multiple sideway-loading gantry cranes at seaport container terminals in a different context. They consider the operation of a landside container-exchange facility which is served by multiple gantry cranes that cannot cross each other. The cranes are used to transfer the containers between the rail interface and the intermediate-container-stacking area, which are both located inside the crane portal, as well as between the terminal-side SC interface and the landside truck interface that are located underneath the cantilevers of the cranes at both sides. Interferences among the cranes do not need to be included as the movements of each crane are restricted to a certain non-overlapping corridor of the total container-exchange facility. The planning objectives of such a facility are different from those of yard-crane systems. Froyland et al. (2008) introduce several objectives like the minimisation of XT-waiting times and the balancing of crane workloads. Nevertheless, the crane-scheduling problem is comparable to that of sideway-loading yard cranes in so far as most crane movements are performed in the same bay—laden gantrying is usually avoided. A multi-stage IP approach is suggested for the solution of the problem and tested with real-world data.

A problem setting that is very similar to that of Ng (2005) is investigated by Li et al. (2009). They address the problem of scheduling multiple sideway-loading gantry cranes in a single yard block to perform a given set of storage and retrieval jobs with certain due dates. Likewise, the problem is formulated as an IP model with the objective of minimising the sum of total crane delays in comparison to the due dates of the jobs. But in contrast to Ng (2005), the time axis is discretised into rather long intervals of 3.5 min, and minimum safety distances between the cranes are additionally included. In order to reduce the computation time for the problem solution, two heuristical programme modifications are developed: Firstly, restrictive time windows around the due dates are implemented to narrow the search space of the programme. Secondly, the IP model is embedded into a rolling-horizon algorithm that repeatedly solves the programme for smaller instances.

Finally, a simulation-based investigation of several yard-crane dispatching rules is provided by Petering et al. (2009). They discuss the use of look-ahead times and IP approaches for yard-crane scheduling and come to the conclusion that they are mostly inappropriate for yard-crane scheduling, as the planning horizon has to be kept short in order to avoid deadlocks. Therefore, twelve different yard-crane-dispatching rules are proposed that differ with respect to the considered priority-rule principle (e.g., NN, FIFO) and the prioritisation of certain types of jobs. A simulation model of a pure transshipment terminal with dozens of yard blocks and multiple sideway-loading gantry cranes per yard block is then used to evaluate the suggested crane-dispatching rules with respect to the resulting GCR over a 3-week period. The numerical results show a strong negative correlation between the GCR and the average vehicle-waiting times alongside the yard blocks.

5.3.2.2 Scheduling of Front-End-Loading Systems

In this subsection, several references on the crane-scheduling problem of front-end-loading gantry-crane systems are addressed. These references can mainly be distinguished with respect to the types of RMGC systems studied. While the SRMGC system is only analysed by Zyngiridis (2005), scheduling of TRMGC systems is addressed by Zyngiridis (2005), Choe et al. (2007), and Carlo and Vis (2008) as well as Park et al. (2010). Carlo and Vis (2008), Stahlbock and Voß (2010), and Vis and Carlo (2010) as well as Speer et al. (2011) deal with crane scheduling for DRMGC systems. Scheduling of TriRMGC systems is so far only addressed by Dorndorf and Schneider (2010).

An IP-based three-step solution procedure for scheduling of both SRMGC and TRMGC systems is developed by Zyngiridis (2005). He considers a single yard block that is served by SCs in the waterside and landside handover areas. In contrast to other studies, the crane-scheduling problem is not solved as an isolated problem. Moreover, an integrated solution of the container-stacking and crane-scheduling problems is aimed for by Zyngiridis (2005). This integrated planning problem is solved by two similar three-step solution procedures for SRMGC and TRMGC systems that are based on solving consecutive IP models. In the first step, stacking positions for inbound containers and the crane movements for storage and retrieval jobs are scheduled. In the second step, stacking of shuffle containers and the related crane movements are scheduled. In step three, housekeeping jobs are scheduled and potential crane interferences are identified and repaired. Although, the avoidance of any delays in the handover areas is formulated as primary objective, the objective functions of the solution procedures aim at minimising the penalties for the stacking positions of incoming containers, while delays in the handover areas above a certain limiting value are prohibited by model restrictions. Finally, several computational experiments and sensitivity analyses are conducted by Zyngiridis (2005).

Choe et al. (2007) address the crane-scheduling problem for a single TRMGC yard block that is served by AGVs and XTs in the waterside and landside handover areas, respectively. Whenever a new job is requested by an idle crane it has to be decided which job out of a given set of jobs with different due dates should be assigned next in order to minimise the AGV and XT-waiting times in the handover areas. In a more detailed paper of the same group of authors, Park et al. (2010) provide an IP formulation for this scheduling problem. The programme does not contain any restrictions on the avoidance of crane interferences. Due to not being real-time compliant, both Choe et al. (2007) and Park et al. (2010) propose heuristic solution approaches for this scheduling problem. Different degrees of cooperation among the cranes and different scheduling methods are developed by them. The degree of crane cooperation is defined by the yard-block zone in which a crane is allowed to perform shuffle jobs required by main jobs of the other crane – the greater the zone, the more crane cooperation. Besides myopic priority rules, an SA algorithm and a hill-climbing algorithm are proposed as scheduling methods. Finally, several simulation experiments are conducted to evaluate different combinations of crane cooperation and scheduling methods. The results reveal performance advantages for a higher degree of cooperation and for the application of meta-heuristics.

The crane-scheduling problem of both TRMGC and DRMGC systems is addressed by Carlo and Vis (2008). They look at the scheduling of two gantry cranes performing a given set of storage and retrieval jobs—but no shuffle jobs—in a single yard block with the objective of minimising the makespan. The scheduling problems for both types of RMGC systems and its system-specific restrictions are verbally described in detail, but no optimisation programmes for these problems are formulated. Different heuristic solution methods are developed for both types of RMGC systems, which are based on a transformation of the two-crane-scheduling problem into a standard TSP. The transformed problem can then be solved with the methodology from Vis and Roodbergen (2009), which yields the optimal solution with respect to the total movement time of the cranes, but not necessarily with respect to the makespan. The heuristic for TRMGC systems is completed by a repair procedure which has to ensure that the final crane routes do not cross at any point in time. However, some variants of crane interferences are not realistically modelled, in particular the fact that crossing manoeuvres are not possible in the DRMGC system during hoisting operations of the outer large crane is completely neglected by Carlo and Vis (2008).

In a more recent paper on a similar problem setting, Vis and Carlo (2010) only address the crane-scheduling problem for DRMGC systems with the objective of minimising the makespan of the crane operations. In contrast to Carlo and Vis (2008), an MIP formulation is provided for the DRMGC-scheduling problem, but the crane interferences are likewise not modelled correctly. Due to the complexity of the modelled problem, an SA algorithm is proposed for its solution which can be evaluated on the basis of a derived lower bound for the makespan. Numerical experiments demonstrate that the proposed SA algorithm is capable of solving large problem instances with up to 50 jobs very close to optimality within seconds.

The crane-scheduling problems for DRMGCs is also addressed by Stahlbock and Voß (2010). They investigate the problem of scheduling two cranes in a single yard block performing a given set of jobs with certain due dates in such a way that the waiting times for the AGVs in the waterside handover area are minimised. An optimisation programme for that problem is not formulated by Stahlbock and Voß

(2010). Instead, quite detailed formulae for the computation of movement times and crane interferences are presented which can be used to calculate the resulting vehicle-waiting times of certain schedules. An SA algorithm, that is based on these formulae, is proposed to replan the crane-scheduling problem each time a crane becomes idle. Several extensive simulation experiments are conducted to compare this SA algorithm with other priority-rule-based scheduling methods. It is shown that these myopic rule-based methods are outperformed by the SA algorithm—in particular for situations with high workloads.

A similar setting of the crane-scheduling problem for the DRMGC system is addressed by Speer et al. (2011). But in contrast to Stahlbock and Voß (2010), they aim at minimising the weighted sum of the vehicle-waiting times in the handover areas, the crane cycle times and the makespan of the crane operations. An optimisation programme for that problem is not formulated either, but several practical insights into scheduling issues and approaches at the CTA in Hamburg (Germany) are given. In contrast to the greedy priority rule used at the CTA, Speer et al. (2011) propose a B&B algorithm, that is based on accurate estimations of crane-movement times, to schedule a user-defined number of urgent jobs to optimality with respect to the weighted objective function each time relevant scheduling information becomes known. By means of simulation experiments, the B&B algorithm is tested against different priority rules for a real-world problem instance from the CTA. It is found that the operational performance of the container-storage yard can greatly be improved with the B&B algorithm—in particular during peak workloads and even when considering only a small number of most urgent jobs.

To the author's knowledge, the crane-scheduling problem for TriRMGC systems is so far only studied by Dorndorf and Schneider (2010). They analyse the problem of scheduling and routing three gantry cranes in a single yard block to perform a given set of jobs with the objective of maximising the crane productivities. In contrast to the other studies on front-end-loading gantry-crane systems, Dorndorf and Schneider (2010) do not only address the crane assignment and sequencing. In addition, quite detailed crane-routing decisions on the right of way in interfering situations and the execution of crane-crossing manoeuvres are connected with the crane-assignment and sequencing problem. But no optimisation programme for the joint crane-scheduling and routing problem is formulated. Instead, the problem to route cranes for a given, fixed sequence of assigned jobs so that the cranes do not interfere, is modelled as a separate discrete-time programme which can be linearised. For the solution of the whole scheduling and routing problem, a heuristic is developed by Dorndorf and Schneider (2010) that is based on a combination of beam search for finding promising schedules and B&B for optimal crane routing of promising schedules. The performance of this heuristic solution procedure is tested and evaluated in extensive simulation experiments. It is shown that commonly used rule-based scheduling and routing methods are clearly outperformed by the proposed heuristic.

5.3.2.3 Concluding Summary

A summarising overview of all previously discussed references on the scheduling problem for sideway and front-end-loading gantry-crane systems is given in Table 5.3. Similar to the summarising overview on the container-stacking problem in Table 5.1, each reference is characterised with respect to the studied crane systems, the investigated problem setting, the pursued scheduling objective as well as the used research and solution approaches. It is illustrated that 75% of the references on the crane-scheduling problem pertain to sideway-loading crane systems while only 25% of the papers address the crane-scheduling problem for front-end-loading systems that are investigated here. In addition, some shortcomings can be found in each of the mentioned references on crane scheduling for front-end-loading systems: In the works of Zyngiridis (2005) as well as Dorndorf and Schneider (2010) it is not aimed for minimising the vehicle-waiting times in the handover areas, which is identified as the main objective here (see Sect. 3.2). Carlo and Vis (2008) as well as Vis and Carlo (2010) do not include all types of crane interferences correctly and do not provide any simulation results. Finally, Park et al. (2010) formulate an optimisation programme for the crane-scheduling problem without crane interferences, while no programme formulations are provided at all by Choe et al. (2007) and Stahlbock and Voß (2010) as well as Speer et al. (2011).

Altogether, the crane-scheduling problem for front-end-loading RMGC systems has not yet been completely addressed in all its facets satisfactorily. In particular, to the author's knowledge, the joint crane-scheduling and routing problem has so far not been adequately formulated as an IP model including all relevant restrictions. In addition, no analysis of the performance effects of different crane-scheduling strategies for different types of RMGC systems is available. In this work, both shortcomings are addressed: A suitable IP formulation is provided for each type of RMGC system and some generic scheduling methods are introduced, which are tested for all four types of RMGC systems.

5.3.3 *Classification of Scheduling Strategies*

Before different design alternatives of crane-scheduling strategies are in detail presented in the following subsections, first of all the functionality and the classifying characteristics of crane-scheduling strategies need to be defined. This is necessary as the term crane-scheduling strategy is beyond the scope of the applied solution method for the crane-scheduling problems of RMGC systems. The scheduling approaches that are summarised in the preceding subsection are not just characterised by the applied solution method, but also by the applied online policy (see Sect. 2.4.3.1). In addition, Choe et al. (2007) and Park et al. (2010) suggest to filter sets of plannable jobs for each crane in order to control the degree of cooperation among the cranes. This is trivial or even unnecessary for SRMGC systems, but for multi-crane systems different variants of filtering

Table 5.3 Summary of crane-scheduling references

Reference	Crane system			Problem							Objective				Approach		
	Loading	Cranes per block	Crossing ability	Storage jobs	Retrieval jobs	Block allocation	Bay sequence	Ct. per bay	Ct. sequence	Interferences	Makespan	Vehicle waiting time	Productivity	Opt. model	Simulation	Algorithm
Kim and Kim (1997, 1999b)	s	1	–	–	√	–	√	√	–	–	√	–	–	√	–	DP
Kozan and Preston (1999)	s	1	–	–	√	–	√	√	√	–	√	–	–	√	–	GA
Kim et al. (2002)	s	2	√	√	√	–	√	√	√	√	√	–	–	–	√	prio
Narasimhan and Palekar (2002)	s	1	–	–	√	–	√	√	–	–	√	–	–	√	–	Lagrange
Zhang et al. (2002)	s	≤ 2	–	√	√	√	–	–	–	–	√	–	–	√	–	B&B, heu
Kim and Kim (2003)	s	1	–	–	√	–	√	√	–	–	√	–	–	√	–	GA, BS
Linn and Zhang (2003)	s	≤ 2	–	√	√	√	–	–	–	–	√	–	–	√	–	heu
Kim et al. (2004)	s	1	–	–	√	–	√	√	√	–	√	–	–	√	–	BS
Murty et al. (2005)	s	≤ 2	–	√	√	√	–	–	–	–	√	–	–	√	–	heu
Ng (2005)	s	Any	–	√	√	–	√	√	√	√	–	√	–	√	–	DP
Ng and Mak (2005a,b)	s	1	–	√	√	–	√	√	√	–	–	√	–	√	–	B&B, heu
Zyngiridis (2005)	f	2	–	√	√	–	√	√	√	√	–	–	–	√	–	heu
Jung and Kim (2006)	s	Any	–	–	√	–	√	√	–	√	√	–	–	√	–	GA, SA
Lee et al. (2006)	s	Any	–	–	√	–	√	√	–	√	√	–	–	√	–	prio, SA
Choe et al. (2007)	f	2	–	√	√	–	√	√	√	√	–	√	–	–	√	prio, SA
Lee et al. (2007)	s	1	–	–	√	–	√	√	–	–	√	–	–	√	–	SA
Cao et al. (2008)	s	2	√	–	√	–	√	√	–	√	√	–	–	√	–	SA, heu
Carlo and Vis (2008)	f	2	√	√	√	–	√	√	√	(√)	√	–	–	–	–	heu
Froyland et al. (2008)	s	Any	–	√	√	–	√	√	√	–	–	√	–	√	–	heu
Li et al. (2009)	s	Any	–	√	√	–	√	√	√	√	–	√	–	√	–	heu
Petering et al. (2009)	s	Any	–	√	√	–	√	√	√	√	–	√	–	–	√	prio
Bohrer (2010)	s	Any	–	√	√	√	√	√	√	√	√	–	–	√	–	prio
Dorndorf and Schneider (2010)	f	3	√	√	√	–	√	√	√	√	–	–	√	√	√	heu
Park et al. (2010)	f	2	–	√	√	–	√	√	√	√	–	√	–	√	√	prio, SA
Stahlbock and Voß (2010)	f	2	√	√	√	–	√	√	√	√	–	√	–	–	√	prio, SA
Vis and Carlo (2010)	f	2	√	√	√	–	√	√	√	(√)	√	–	–	√	–	SA
Speer et al. (2011)	f	2	√	√	√	–	√	√	√	√	√	√	√	–	√	prio, B&B

Loading: front end (f) vs. sideway (s); algorithm: branch and bound (B&B), beam search (BS), dynamic programming (DP), genetic algorithm (GA), problem-specific heuristic (heu), Lagrangian relaxation (Lagrange), priority rule (prio), simulated annealing (SA)

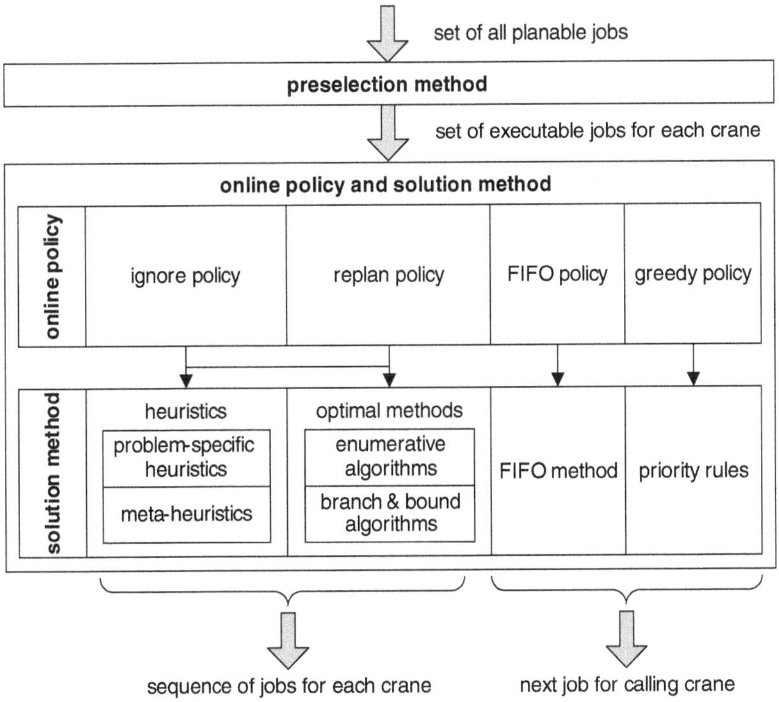

Fig. 5.6 Classification of crane-scheduling strategies

approaches are possible. In the following, these approaches are referred to as preselection methods. Altogether, each crane-scheduling strategy is defined here by a certain combination of preselection method, online policy and solution method. A rough classification and the interaction of these scheduling strategy components are illustrated in Fig. 5.6.

Each time a new job and/or sequence of jobs is required by the job-management module of the TOS, it is first of all decided for all currently plannable jobs $j \in J_t^{\mathrm{p}}$ which crane(s) is (are) allowed to perform a certain job. As a result, sets of plannable jobs J_{tg}^{p} are obtained for each crane g. Depending on the applied preselection method, the resulting sets of plannable jobs J_{tg}^{p} may be overlapping, which means some jobs may be plannable by several cranes, while others may only be performed by a single crane. Different design alternatives of preselection methods are presented in Sect. 5.3.4.

The sets of plannable jobs for each crane g are then used as input for the actual sequencing process. Depending on the applied online policy and/or solution method, either sequences of several jobs are determined for all cranes of a yard block or only a single job is determined for the calling crane. According to Grötschel et al. (2001), FIFO, greedy, ignore and replan online policies have to be distinguished (see Sect. 2.4.3.1). Both the application of the FIFO and greedy policy directly determine the applicable type of solution method. The FIFO online policy is equivalent to the FIFO solution method and the greedy online policy is equivalent to the use of a certain priority rule. The result of both online policies and/or solution methods is the next job for the calling crane. In contrast, if the replan or ignore policy is applied, new sequences of several jobs are determined for all cranes of a yard block. Such sequences can either be computed by an optimal method or a heuristic. If the replan policy is applied, completely new sequences of jobs are computed each time the scheduler module of the TOS is called. Whereas in case of the ignore policy, no new sequences of jobs are computed as long as there are still unexecuted jobs of the lastly determined job sequence for the calling crane. New sequences of jobs are then computed for all cranes of a yard block if all jobs in the current sequence of the calling crane have already been executed.

In the following subsections, solution methods for all types of online policies introduced are developed. In Sect. 5.3.5, priority rules for greedy online policies are addressed. Thereafter, in Sect. 5.3.6, IP models are developed that can be solved to optimality by common solvers. Finally, two heuristic solution methods are proposed: a meta-heuristic-based and a problem-specific algorithm. Both the IP formulations and the heuristics, can be applied in the style of the ignore and replan policies.

5.3.4 Preselection Methods

The purpose of preselection methods is to compute sets of plannable jobs J_{tg}^{p} for each crane g of a yard block at time t on the basis of all currently plannable jobs J_t^{p}. Here, two functions are fulfilled by computing sets of plannable jobs J_{tg}^{p} in a rule-based way prior to the application of certain solution methods: Firstly, ensuring the technical feasibility of resulting crane-job assignments, and secondly, restricting the potential crane-job assignments with regard to the operational scheduling objectives (see Sect. 5.3.1). While there is no design flexibility in the implementation of the first function, as the technical feasibility always has to be ensured, preselection methods can differ in the way and the degree in which potential crane-job assignments are restricted for operational reasons.

The technical feasibility of assigning job j to crane g is determined by the accessibility of the origin and destination of the job by crane g. Of course, for SRMGC systems all positions are accessible by the only crane, but for multi-crane systems situations need to be distinguished with respect to the accessibility of the x-coordinates of a job by the portal of a crane. Depending on the crossing ability of the cranes, not each crane can serve each handover area (see Sect. 3.4.1). As a consequence, a job j is technically infeasible for crane g if its origin or destination

Table 5.4 Technical feasibility of assigning job j to crane g

	RMGC system (crane g)							
	SRMGC	TRMGC		DRMGC		TriRMGC		
$\tau(j)$	1	1	2	1	2	1	2	3
wsin	√	√	–	√	√	√	–	√
wsout	√	√	–	√	√	√	–	√
lsin	√	–	√	√	√	–	√	√
lsout	√	–	√	√	√	–	√	√
wsshu	√	√	√	√	√	√	√	√
lsshu	√	√	√	√	√	√	√	√
wshk	√	√	√	√	√	√	√	√
lshk	√	√	√	√	√	√	√	√

is located in an inaccessible handover area for that crane. But only main jobs are either picked up or dropped off in one of the handover areas, while all auxiliary jobs are neither picked up nor dropped off in the handover areas. Therefore, all auxiliary jobs are technically feasible for all cranes of a yard block independently of the operating type of RMGC system and its crossing ability. In contrast, main jobs that are related to a certain handover area cannot be performed by cranes that cannot access this handover area. A crane that cannot access the waterside handover area is, for instance, unable to perform waterside storage or retrieval jobs. A summarising overview on the technical feasibility of crane-job assignments with respect to types of jobs and RMGC systems is given in Table 5.4. Here and throughout the rest of this work, the following numbering of cranes is used for the different types of RMGC systems. For TRMGC systems, $g = 1$ and $g = 2$ are the waterside and landside cranes, respectively, while for DRMGC systems the inner small crane and the outer large crane are denoted by $g = 1$ and $g = 2$, respectively. For TriRMGC systems, $g = 1$ and $g = 2$ are the same-sized waterside and landside cranes, respectively, and the outer large crane is denoted by $g = 3$.

The idea of restricting potential crane-job assignments with regard to the operational scheduling objectives, is the support and the simplification of the crane-assignment and sequencing problem for the following solution method. The more potential crane-job assignments are excluded in advance, the smaller is the intersection $J^{\mathrm{p}}_{tg} \bigcap J^{\mathrm{p}}_{tg'}$ of the sets of plannable jobs for two different cranes g and g'. On the one hand, the crane assignment problem is simplified a lot by small intersections of the job sets, but on the other hand, the scope of action and the potential for optimisation by the following solution method may be reduced. Very restrictive preselection methods may in an extreme case even lead to empty intersections $J^{\mathrm{p}}_{tg} \bigcap J^{\mathrm{p}}_{tg'}$ and crane-scheduling problems that are reduced to separate job-sequencing problems. In order to ensure that each job j can be performed by a crane, the potential crane-job assignments can only be restricted in such a way that each job j is assignable for at least one crane (i.e., $\bigcup_g J^{\mathrm{p}}_{tg} = J^{\mathrm{p}}_t$).

Two main concepts are proposed to restrict the potential crane-job assignments with regard to the operational scheduling objectives: dedicated preselection and zoning-based preselection. Both concepts are mainly designed to reduce the risk for interferences among different cranes of a yard block. In addition, both preselection approaches can be parametrised in such a way that certain handover areas, types of jobs or gantry cranes are given priority by the crane-scheduling strategy.

The dedicated concept is a derivative of filtering technically assignable jobs with respect to the types of jobs. Above and beyond the technical feasibility of assigning job j with $\tau(j)$ to crane g, there may be operational objectives to restrict jobs of a certain type from being assigned to a crane g. For the TRMGC system, it may, for instance, be advisable to restrict the waterside crane from performing shuffle and housekeeping jobs for landside-departing main jobs in order to have more crane resources available for waterside jobs (i.e., $J_{t1}^{\mathrm{p}} = \{j \in J_t^{\mathrm{p}} | \tau(j) \notin \{\mathrm{lsin}, \mathrm{lsout}, \mathrm{lsshu}, \mathrm{lshk}\}\}$). Similarly, it may be decided that the outer large crane in the TriRMGC system is only allowed to perform auxiliary jobs in order to avoid interferences with smaller cranes in the handover areas (i.e., $J_{t3}^{\mathrm{p}} = \{j \in J_t^{\mathrm{p}} | \tau(j) \notin \{\mathrm{wsin}, \mathrm{lsin}, \mathrm{wsout}, \mathrm{lsout}\}\}$). These are just examples, but in total there are hosts of theoretically possible combinations for each multi-crane system of restricting a certain job type from being performed by a certain crane. In particular for the TriRMGC system, dozens of combinations can be parametrised, but not each combination does comply with the objectives of the crane-scheduling problem.

The zoning concept is based on the idea of Choe et al. (2007) and Park et al. (2010) for TRMGC systems to divide the length of a yard block into three non-overlapping equal-sized zones—a waterside zone, a landside zone and an intermediate zone—determining the set of assignable jobs for each crane. Jobs having both origin and destination in a specific zone of the yard block are then exclusively assignable to the crane that is allocated to that zone, while jobs having origin and destination in different yard zones can be assigned to different cranes. In case no specific crane is defined for a certain zone, all cranes of a yard block are assignable for jobs having origin and destination in that zone. The intention of filtering sets of assignable jobs in such a way is mainly the avoidance of crane interferences.

In contrast to the basic concept proposed by Choe et al. (2007) and Park et al. (2010), the zones of a yard block are here scalable and allowed to overlap in order to have more flexibility in designing efficient preselection methods. The sizes of the yard zones are determined by user-specified zone borders $\kappa_{\mathrm{zb}}^{\mathrm{ws}}$ and $\kappa_{\mathrm{zb}}^{\mathrm{ls}}$, which define the end of the waterside zone and the beginning of the landside zone, respectively. As a consequence, the waterside and landside zones are defined by all x-coordinates in the intervals $[0, \kappa_{\mathrm{zb}}^{\mathrm{ws}}]$ and $[\kappa_{\mathrm{zb}}^{\mathrm{ls}}, \theta^{\mathrm{x}}]$, respectively. In case the whole portal-driving range is not already covered by the waterside and landside zones (i.e., $\kappa_{\mathrm{zb}}^{\mathrm{ws}} < \kappa_{\mathrm{zb}}^{\mathrm{ls}}$), the intermediate zone is defined by the interval $(\kappa_{\mathrm{zb}}^{\mathrm{ws}}, \kappa_{\mathrm{zb}}^{\mathrm{ls}})$. Within TRMGC systems the waterside and landside cranes are allocated to the waterside and landside zones, respectively, while no crane is assigned to the intermediate zone. Similarly, no crane is allocated for DRMGC systems to the intermediate zone, while the inner small

Table 5.5 Zone-dependent assignability of job j to sets of plannable jobs for different cranes

TRMGC and DRMGC systems			
	$d_j^x \leq \kappa_{zb}^{ws}$	$d_j^x > \kappa_{zb}^{ws}$ and $d_j^x < \kappa_{zb}^{ls}$	$d_j^x \geq \kappa_{zb}^{ls}$
$o_j^x \leq \kappa_{zb}^{ws}$	J_{t1}^p	J_{t1}^p, J_{t2}^p	J_{t1}^p, J_{t2}^p
$o_j^x > \kappa_{zb}^{ws}$ and $o_j^x < \kappa_{zb}^{ls}$	J_{t1}^p, J_{t2}^p	J_{t1}^p, J_{t2}^p	J_{t1}^p, J_{t2}^p
$o_j^x \geq \kappa_{zb}^{ls}$	J_{t1}^p, J_{t2}^p	J_{t1}^p, J_{t2}^p	J_{t2}^p

TriRMGC system			
	$d_j^x \leq \kappa_{zb}^{ws}$	$d_j^x > \kappa_{zb}^{ws}$ and $d_j^x < \kappa_{zb}^{ls}$	$d_j^x \geq \kappa_{zb}^{ls}$
$o_j^x \leq \kappa_{zb}^{ws}$	J_{t1}^p	J_{t1}^p, J_{t3}^p	$J_{t1}^p, J_{t2}^p, J_{t3}^p$
$o_j^x > \kappa_{zb}^{ws}$ and $o_j^x < \kappa_{zb}^{ls}$	J_{t1}^p, J_{t3}^p	J_{t3}^p	J_{t2}^p, J_{t3}^p
$o_j^x \geq \kappa_{zb}^{ls}$	$J_{t1}^p, J_{t2}^p, J_{t3}^p$	J_{t2}^p, J_{t3}^p	J_{t2}^p

crane and the outer large crane are assigned to the waterside and landside zones, respectively. For TriRMGC systems, the waterside, landside and outer large crane are allocated to the waterside, landside and intermediate zones, respectively. A job j is then assignable to different cranes depending on the position of its x-coordinates o_j^x and d_j^x in relation to the zone borders κ_{zb}^{ws} and κ_{zb}^{ls}. A job j having both origin and destination in the waterside zone (i.e., $o_j^x \epsilon [0, \kappa_{zb}^{ws}]$ and $d_j^x \epsilon [0, \kappa_{zb}^{ws}]$) can, for instance, only be assigned to crane 1 (i.e., $j \in J_{t1}^p$ and $j \notin J_{tg}^p$ for $g = 2, 3$), whereas job j would be assignable to all cranes of the yard block (i.e., $j \in J_{tg}^p$ for all $g \in G$) if its origin and destination are located in the waterside and landside zones, respectively (i.e., $o_j^x \epsilon [0, \kappa_{zb}^{ws}]$ and $d_j^x \epsilon [\kappa_{zb}^{ls}, \theta^x]$).

Altogether, the assignability of job j to different cranes $g \in G$ is summarised in Table 5.5 with respect to the considered RMGC system and the origin and destination of job j. The aforementioned technical restrictions on the assignability of jobs are, of course, not invalidated by the zoning concept. The waterside and landside cranes are still restricted not to perform jobs that belong to the opposite handover area (see Table 5.4).

5.3.5 *Multi-Criteria Priority Rules*

Priority rules are used to determine only the next job for a calling crane g. In general terms, the next job for crane g is computed with respect to certain assignment costs $f^{ac}(j)$, which give the costs for job j being assigned next to crane g with respect to previously defined assignment criteria. The next job for crane g is then simply computed as

$$j^* = \arg\min_{j \in J_{tg}^p} f^{ac}(j) \tag{5.29}$$

with job j^* leading to the lowest assignment costs $f^{ac}(j)^*$ among the set J_{tg}^p of all plannable jobs for crane g at time t.

An inherent characteristic of each priority rule is the greedy approach. Decisions on the next job j^* for crane g are made unmindful of negative consequences for prospective assignments for one of the cranes of the considered yard block. Therefore, priority rules are usually not expected to perform as good as optimal solution methods—in particular in offline situations. But in online environments like container terminals, the performance disadvantages of priority rules may be reduced due to the continuously obtained information on new jobs that may require frequent replanning (see Sect. 2.4.3.1). In addition, priority rules are usually intuitively understandable in contrast to most optimal solution methods, which may be an important reason for the acceptance and the common application of priority rules at seaport container terminals.

Several references on operational terminal-planning problems make use of different types of priority rules—mostly as easily understandable benchmarks for more sophisticated solution methods (e.g., Böse et al. 2000; Briskorn et al. 2006). In the context of the crane-scheduling problem for RMGCs, Park et al. (2010) as well as Dorndorf and Schneider (2010) apply the well-known NN and EDD (earliest due date) priority rules. The assignment criterion of the NN rule is the empty-movement time m_{jg}^{xye} between the current position of the calling crane g and the origin of an assignable job $j \in J_{tg}^{\mathrm{p}}$, which should be minimised in order to save crane resources for inevitable laden crane movements. This is equivalent to objective (5.27). Hence, the next job for crane g is defined as

$$j^* = \arg\min_{j \in J_{tg}^{\mathrm{p}}} m_{jg}^{\mathrm{xye}} \tag{5.30}$$

with job j^* leading to the shortest empty-movement time among all assignable jobs for crane g. In contrast, the next job of crane g is determined by the EDD rule with respect to the pick-up due date t_j^{pd} of each job $j \in J_{tg}^{\mathrm{p}}$, which should be minimised as well in order to reduce the risk for and the extent of jobs being performed lately. Hence, for the EDD rule the next job of crane g is defined by

$$j^* = \arg\min_{j \in J_{tg}^{\mathrm{p}}} t_j^{\mathrm{pd}}, \tag{5.31}$$

which is consistent with objective (5.25) that aims for minimising the crane lateness.

Although both the EDD rule and the NN rule are based on reasonable intentions, taking into account only one of several possible assignment criteria each (see objectives (5.25)–(5.28)) may be too shortsighted—especially in the context of a greedy approach. On the one hand, the NN rule is expected to yield at least short empty-movement times, but this is not necessarily aligned with short vehicle-waiting times in the handover areas as the due dates are not considered in any form. On the other hand, only looking at the due dates in a greedy way may be too shortsighted as well, since this may be connected with a waste of crane resources caused by very early crane arrivals in the handover areas and/or far too long empty-movement times, which may in turn lead to unnecessarily prolonged vehicle-waiting times for the following jobs. Therefore, it may be advisable to apply multi-criteria priority rules instead of only considering a single assignment criterion. Here, two intuitively understandable multi-criteria priority rules are proposed: PRIO1 and PRIO2. While the PRIO1 rule is some kind of combination of the EDD and NN rules, the PRIO2 rule makes use of a common due-date-based earliness-lateness objective (e.g., Briskorn et al. 2006; Stahlbock and Voß 2010).

For the PRIO1 rule, the next job of crane g is determined on the basis of the weighted sum of the pick-up due dates t_j^{pd} and the resulting empty-movement times m_{jg}^{xye} for all assignable jobs $j \in J_{tg}^{\text{p}}$. The longer the empty-movement time m_{jg}^{xye} for a certain job j and/or the later the pick-up due date t_j^{pd} of job j in comparison to other assignable jobs, the more unlikely this job is assigned next to crane g. In order to avoid an unjustified increase in the importance of pick-up due dates with the mere passing of time for the selection of the next job-crane assignment, the pick-up due date t_j^{pd} should not be used directly as assignment criterion. Moreover, the difference between the pick-up due date t_j^{pd} of the currently considered job j and the earliest pick-up due date $\min_{i \in J_{tg}^{\text{p}}} t_i^{\text{pd}}$ among all assignable jobs $i \in J_{tg}^{\text{p}}$ should be used in order to ensure an unbiased influence of the pick-up due date on the job-crane assignments. As a consequence, for the PRIO1 rule, the next job of crane g is given by

$$j^* = \arg \min_{j \in J_{tg}^{\text{p}}} \left(\lambda_{\tau(j),g}^{\text{empty}} m_{jg}^{\text{xye}} + \lambda_{\tau(j),g}^{\text{dd}} \left(t_j^{\text{pd}} - \min_{i \in J_{tg}^{\text{p}}} t_i^{\text{pd}} \right) \right) \tag{5.32}$$

with $\lambda_{\tau(j),g}^{\text{empty}}$ and $\lambda_{\tau(j),g}^{\text{dd}}$ denoting user-specified weighting factors for both assignment criteria with respect to the considered job type and crane. The greater $\lambda_{\tau(j),g}^{\text{empty}}$ ($\lambda_{\tau(j),g}^{\text{dd}}$), the more important is the empty-movement time (pick-up due date) for the selection of the next job-crane assignment and the more this rule is used in the original sense of the NN (EDD) rule. By specifying different weights $\lambda_{\tau(j),g}^{\text{empty}}$ and $\lambda_{\tau(j),g}^{\text{dd}}$ for different job types and/or cranes, certain jobs and/or handover areas may be assigned with higher priority. Waterside retrieval jobs are, for instance, prioritised by defining lower weights for $\lambda_{\text{wsout},g}^{\text{empty}}$ and $\lambda_{\text{wsout},g}^{\text{dd}}$.

By using the weighted sum of the assignment criteria of the EDD and NN rules, the aforementioned shortcomings of these rules may be partially overcome by the PRIO1 rule, since both the greedy minimisation of vehicle-waiting times and the efficient use of crane resources, are regarded simultaneously. However, only two of four previously identified crane-scheduling objectives are considered by the PRIO1 rule (i.e., objectives (5.25) and (5.27)). In particular, the objective of minimising the crane earliness $\Delta_{jg}^{\text{pp}-}$ (i.e., objective (5.27)) in order to avoid unproductive crane-waiting times in the handover areas is not included. In contrast, the PRIO2 rule is based on the objectives (5.25)–(5.27), which means the next job of crane g is determined with respect to the weighted sum of the empty-movement time, the lateness and the earliness of all assignable jobs $j \in J^{\mathrm{p}}_{tg}$. This is job

$$j^* = \arg\min_{j \in J^{\mathrm{p}}_{tg}} \left(\lambda^{\mathrm{empty}}_{\tau(j),g} m^{\mathrm{xye}}_{jg} + \lambda^{\mathrm{late}}_{\tau(j),g} \Delta^{\mathrm{pp}+}_{jg} + \lambda^{\mathrm{early}}_{\tau(j),g} \Delta^{\mathrm{pp}-}_{jg} \right) \tag{5.33}$$

where $\lambda^{\mathrm{late}}_{\tau(j),g}$ and $\lambda^{\mathrm{early}}_{\tau(j),g}$ denote job-type and crane-specific user-specified weighting factors for the assignment criteria crane lateness and earliness, respectively. Of course, the more earliness $\Delta^{\mathrm{pp}-}_{jg}$ and/or the more empty-movement time m^{xye}_{jg} is connected with the assignment of a certain job j, the higher the assignment costs for this job should be in order to avoid this job from being assigned next. But the situation is different with respect to the crane lateness $\Delta^{\mathrm{pp}+}_{jg}$, which—contrary to the crane earliness $\Delta^{\mathrm{pp}-}_{jg}$—cannot be expected to decrease with passing of time. An already delayed job j should be performed as soon as possible, in order to avoid a further increase in the crane lateness $\Delta^{\mathrm{pp}+}_{jg}$ for this job. Therefore, the assignment costs should decrease with increasing lateness in order to make a job more attractive for being assigned next, the more delayed it is. As a consequence, the resulting crane lateness of assigning job j to crane g should be weighted with $\lambda^{\mathrm{late}}_{\tau(j),g} < 0$ in order to comply with the intention of objective (5.25).

5.3.6 *IP Scheduling Models*

In this subsection, the RMGC-scheduling problem described in Sect. 5.3.1 is formulated as a discrete-time IP model, which can be solved to optimality using different solver software. The programme formulation is partly inspired by some of the aforementioned integer models for sideway-loading crane systems (e.g., Ng 2005; Bohrer 2010). But several additional constraints are needed in order to model the more complicated logistical processes of front-end-loading RMGC systems appropriately. In particular, it has to be taken into account that the execution of most transport jobs consists of crane operations in two different positions along the x-axis of the yard block and laden movements between these positions. The proposed model is nearly identical for all types of RMGC systems. Only very few system-specific collision-avoidance restrictions are needed in order to model crane interferences correctly for each type of multi-crane system.

This subsection is opened with a presentation of the basic programme formulation, including the introduction of all needed parameters, variables and restrictions. Thereafter, the system-specific collision-avoidance restrictions are introduced which is followed by some suggestions on alternative objectives and the computation of upper bounds. Finally, this subsection is closed with a numerical study on the required computation times for the solution of the programme in order to evaluate its applicability to real-world problem settings.

5.3.6.1 Basic Programme Formulation

Subsequently, the problem of scheduling multiple RMGCs in a single yard block to perform a given set of jobs with different due dates is formulated as a discrete-time IP model. In contrast to the remainder of this work, only movements of the crane portal from bay to bay along the x-axis are explicitly modelled here, while the trolley and spreader movements along the y- and z-axes are considered as crane and job-specific handling time h_{jg} to pick up and/or drop off a container in a certain bay of the block. This simplifying assumption can be made without considerable consequences for the practical validity of the model as the crane-movement and interference times are mostly determined by the portal movements along the x-axis. Based on the assumption that all cranes move at the same speed and the length of the planning period is given by an upper bound for the makespan of the optimal schedule, it is possible to partition the planning period into a number Γ of periods with the length of each period being equal to the required crane-movement time for a single bay. Consequently, all dates and periods of time are measured in terms of bay-movement time units.

There are n^{J} jobs to be scheduled for $|G|$ cranes in a yard block with $n^{\mathrm{zo}} = n^{\mathrm{x}}+2$ zones, which are of equal size like a single bay of the yard block. The zones in the yard block are numbered sequentially from 1 to n^{zo} with zone 1 and zone n^{zo} representing the waterside and landside handover areas, respectively. It is assumed that each crane g, $g = 1, 2, \ldots, |G|$ always occupies one zone r, $r = 1, 2, \ldots, n^{\mathrm{zo}}$ in each period γ, $\gamma = 1, 2, \ldots, \Gamma$. The number n^{J} of jobs to be scheduled results from the number $\left|J_t^{\mathrm{p}}\right|$ of plannable jobs at time t and the number $|G|$ of dummy jobs representing the current crane position in period $\gamma = 1$. Hence, there are $n^{\mathrm{J}} = |G| + \left|J_t^{\mathrm{p}}\right|$ jobs to be scheduled in total, with each job $j = 1, 2, .., |G|$ representing the dummy job of the corresponding crane. For each job $j = 1, 2, \ldots, n^{\mathrm{J}}$, the handover-area due dates, the pick-up zone and the drop-off zone of job j are denoted by t_j^{hd}, o_j^{x} and d_j^{x}, respectively. In order to simplify, shuffle moves and resulting precedence constraints among the jobs are first of all neglected. The following decision variables are needed to formulate the multi-crane-scheduling problem for RMGC systems:

$$x_{ijg} = \begin{cases} 1 & \text{if crane } g \text{ performs job } j \text{ directly after job } i, \\ 0 & \text{otherwise.} \end{cases}$$

$$y_{r\gamma g} = \begin{cases} 1 & \text{if crane } g \text{ is located in bay } r \text{ in period } \gamma, \\ 0 & \text{otherwise.} \end{cases}$$

$$z_{j\gamma g}^{\mathrm{pick}} = \begin{cases} 1 & \text{if crane } g \text{ finishes pick-up operation of job } j \text{ in period } \gamma, \\ 0 & \text{otherwise.} \end{cases}$$

$$z_{j\gamma g}^{\mathrm{drop}} = \begin{cases} 1 & \text{if crane } g \text{ finishes drop-off operation of job } j \text{ in period } \gamma, \\ 0 & \text{otherwise.} \end{cases}$$

The values of several variables concerning the dummy jobs are fixed a priori. Firstly, as each crane g, $g = 1, 2, \ldots, |G|$ is initially located in zone $o^{\mathrm{x}}_g = d^{\mathrm{x}}_g$, the positioning variables are set to $y_{o^{\mathrm{x}}_g 1g} = 1$ and $y_{r1g} = 0$ for all $r \neq o^{\mathrm{x}}_g$ and $g = 1, 2, \ldots, |G|$. Secondly, in order to avoid any influence of the dummy jobs on the optimisation problem, all dummy jobs $j = 1, 2, .., |G|$ are quasi picked up and dropped off in the first period by the respective crane, which means the pick-up and drop-off variables are set to $z^{\mathrm{pick}}_{g1g} = z^{\mathrm{drop}}_{g1g} = 1$ for all g, $g = 1, 2, \ldots, |G|$. Finally, the sequence variables are set to $\sum_{j=1}^{n^{\mathrm{J}}} x_{gjg} = 1$ for all g, $g = 1, 2, \ldots, |G|$ in order to ensure that each dummy job is performed by the respective crane.

The main objective of the crane-scheduling problem is to minimise the waiting times for AGVs/SCs and XTs in the handover areas (see Sect. 5.3.1). Here, the waiting time for the vehicle dispatched to job j is given by $\sum_{\gamma=1}^{\Gamma} \sum_{g=1}^{|G|} z^{\mathrm{pick}}_{j\gamma g} \left(\gamma - t^{\mathrm{hd}}_j\right)$ and $\sum_{\gamma=1}^{\Gamma} \sum_{g=1}^{|G|} z^{\mathrm{drop}}_{j\gamma g} \left(\gamma - t^{\mathrm{hd}}_j\right)$ for storage and retrieval jobs, respectively. Since the handover-area due dates t^{hd}_j are given parameters, the sum of all vehicle-waiting times is also minimised by the schedule that minimises the sum of completion times of pick-up and drop-off operations in the handover areas for all jobs $j = 1, 2, \ldots, n^{\mathrm{J}}$, which is $\sum_{j=1|o^{\mathrm{x}}_j \in \{1,n^{\mathrm{zo}}\}}^{n^{\mathrm{J}}} \sum_{\gamma=1}^{\Gamma} \sum_{g=1}^{|G|} z^{\mathrm{pick}}_{j\gamma g}\gamma + \sum_{j=1|d^{\mathrm{x}}_j \in \{1,n^{\mathrm{zo}}\}}^{n^{\mathrm{J}}} \sum_{\gamma=1}^{\Gamma} \sum_{g=1}^{|G|} z^{\mathrm{drop}}_{j\gamma g}\gamma$. Nevertheless, minimising the sum of all vehicle-waiting times is selected as the objective for the IP model due to being intuitively more informative. Altogether, the crane-scheduling problem for front-end-loading RMGC systems can be formulated as

$$\min \quad \sum_{j=1|o^{\mathrm{x}}_j \in \{1,n^{\mathrm{zo}}\}}^{n^{\mathrm{J}}} \sum_{\gamma=1}^{\Gamma} \sum_{g=1}^{|G|} z^{\mathrm{pick}}_{j\gamma g} \left(\gamma - t^{\mathrm{hd}}_j\right) \tag{5.34}$$

$$+ \sum_{j=1|d^{\mathrm{x}}_j \in \{1,n^{\mathrm{zo}}\}}^{n^{\mathrm{J}}} \sum_{\gamma=1}^{\Gamma} \sum_{g=1}^{|G|} z^{\mathrm{drop}}_{j\gamma g} \left(\gamma - t^{\mathrm{hd}}_j\right)$$

$$\text{subject to} \quad \sum_{g=1}^{|G|} \sum_{j=1}^{n^{\mathrm{J}}} x_{ijg} = 1, \ \forall\, i = 1, 2, \ldots, n^{\mathrm{J}},\ i \neq j \tag{5.35}$$

$$\sum_{g=1}^{|G|} \sum_{i=1}^{n^{\mathrm{J}}} x_{ijg} = 1, \ \forall\, j = 1, 2, \ldots, n^{\mathrm{J}},\ i \neq j \tag{5.36}$$

$$M \left(1 - \sum_{i=1}^{n^{\mathrm{J}}} x_{ijg}\right) \geq \sum_{i=1}^{n^{\mathrm{J}}} x_{jig'}, \forall\, j = 1, 2, \ldots, n^{\mathrm{J}}, \quad g, g' = 1, 2, \ldots, |G|,\ g \neq g' \tag{5.37}$$

$$\sum_{r=1}^{n^{\mathrm{zo}}} y_{r\gamma g} = 1, \ \forall \, \gamma = 1, 2, \ldots, \Gamma, \ g = 1, 2, \ldots, |G| \tag{5.38}$$

$$\sum_{r=\max\{q-1,1\}}^{\min\{n^{\mathrm{zo}},q+1\}} y_{r,\gamma+1,g} \geq y_{q\gamma g}, \ \forall \, \gamma = 1, 2, \ldots, \Gamma - 1, \tag{5.39}$$

$$q = 1, 2, \ldots, n^{\mathrm{zo}}, \ g = 1, 2, \ldots, |G|$$

$$\sum_{r=\max\{q-1,1\}}^{\min\{n^{\mathrm{zo}},q+1\}} y_{r,\gamma-1,g} \geq y_{q\gamma g}, \ \forall \, \gamma = 2, 3, \ldots, \Gamma, \tag{5.40}$$

$$q = 1, 2, \ldots, n^{\mathrm{zo}}, \ g = 1, 2, \ldots, |G|$$

$$\sum_{g=1}^{|G|} \sum_{\gamma=1}^{\Gamma} z_{j\gamma g}^{\mathrm{pick}} = 1, \ \forall \, j = 1, 2, \ldots, n^{\mathrm{J}} \tag{5.41}$$

$$\sum_{g=1}^{|G|} \sum_{\gamma=1}^{\Gamma} z_{j\gamma g}^{\mathrm{drop}} = 1, \ \forall \, j = 1, 2, \ldots, n^{\mathrm{J}} \tag{5.42}$$

$$\sum_{i=1}^{n^{\mathrm{J}}} x_{ijg} = \sum_{\gamma=1}^{\Gamma} z_{j\gamma g}^{\mathrm{pick}}, \ \forall \, j = 1, 2, \ldots, n^{\mathrm{J}}, \tag{5.43}$$

$$g = 1, 2, \ldots, |G|$$

$$\sum_{\eta=0}^{h_{jg}} y_{o_j^{\mathrm{x}},\gamma-\eta,g} - h_{jg} - 1 \geq M \left(z_{j\gamma g}^{\mathrm{pick}} - 1 \right), \tag{5.44}$$

$$\forall \, j = |G| + 1, |G| + 2, \ldots, n^{\mathrm{J}},$$

$$\gamma = h_{jg} + 1, \ldots, \Gamma, \ g = 1, 2, \ldots, |G|$$

$$\sum_{\eta=0}^{h_{jg}} y_{d_j^{\mathrm{x}},\gamma-\eta,g} - h_{jg} - 1 \geq M \left(z_{j\gamma g}^{\mathrm{drop}} - 1 \right), \tag{5.45}$$

$$\forall \, j = |G| + 1, |G| + 2, \ldots, n^{\mathrm{J}},$$

$$\gamma = h_{jg} + 1, \ldots, \Gamma, \ g = 1, 2, \ldots, |G|$$

$$\sum_{\gamma=1}^{\Gamma} z_{i\gamma g}^{\mathrm{drop}} (\gamma + l_{ij}^{\mathrm{x}} + h_{jg}) \leq M \left(1 - x_{ijg}\right) + \sum_{\eta=1}^{\Gamma} \eta z_{j\eta g}^{\mathrm{pick}}, \tag{5.46}$$

$$\forall \, i = 1, 2, \ldots, n^{\mathrm{J}}, \ g = 1, 2, \ldots, |G|$$

$$j = |G| + 1, |G| + 2, \ldots, n^{\mathrm{J}}$$

$$\sum_{\gamma=1}^{\Gamma} z_{j\gamma g}^{\text{pick}} \left(\gamma + l_j^{\text{x}} + h_{jg}\right) \leq \sum_{\eta=2}^{\Gamma} \eta z_{j\eta g}^{\text{drop}}, \tag{5.47}$$

$$\forall\, j = |G| + 1, |G| + 2, \ldots, n^{\text{J}},$$

$$g = 1, 2, \ldots, |G|$$

$$\sum_{g=1}^{|G|} \sum_{\gamma=1}^{\Gamma} \gamma z_{j\gamma g}^{\text{pick}} \geq t_j^{\text{hd}}, \ \forall\, j = 1, 2, \ldots, n^{\text{J}} | o_j^{\text{x}} \in \{1, n^{\text{zo}}\} \tag{5.48}$$

$$\sum_{g=1}^{|G|} \sum_{\gamma=1}^{\Gamma} \gamma z_{j\gamma g}^{\text{drop}} \geq t_j^{\text{hd}}, \ \forall\, j = 1, 2, \ldots, n^{\text{J}} | d_j^{\text{x}} \in \{1, n^{\text{zo}}\} \tag{5.49}$$

$$x_{ijg},\ y_{r\gamma g},\ z_{j\gamma g}^{\text{pick}},\ z_{j\gamma g}^{\text{drop}} \in \{0, 1\},\ \forall\, i, j = 1, 2, \ldots, n^{\text{J}}, \tag{5.50}$$

$$g = 1, 2, \ldots, |G|,$$

$$r = 1, 2, \ldots, n^{\text{zo}},\ \gamma = 1, 2, \ldots, \Gamma$$

where M is a big positive number.

The objective of the scheduling problem is to minimise the total vehicle-waiting time in both handover areas. The total vehicle-waiting time induced by late execution of storage jobs is given by the first term of objective (5.34), while the second term gives the vehicle-waiting time caused by late execution of retrieval jobs. Constraints (5.35), (5.36) and (5.37) are tour constructing constraints. By means of constraints (5.35) and (5.36) it is stated that each job is succeeded and preceded by exactly one other job, while constraints (5.37) are required to ensure that each job is performed by the same crane as its predecessor and successor. Constraints (5.38), (5.39) and (5.40) can be summarised as crane-positioning constraints. While constraints (5.38) simply state that each crane can only be located in one of the zones in each period, constraints (5.39) and (5.40) are used to ensure that all cranes do not travel more than one zone per period. By means of constraints (5.41) and (5.42), it is guaranteed that the pick-up and drop-off operations connected with each job are finished exactly once. Constraints (5.43) give the logical relationship between the variables x_{ijg} and $z_{j\gamma g}^{\text{pick}}$. Only if job j is part of the tour of crane g, it is also picked up by that crane. Constraints (5.44) and (5.45) are needed to ensure that a crane stays at the pick-up and drop-off position of a job while performing the respective operations. A crane g has to stay for at least h_{jg} periods at the pick-up and drop-off position of job j before the respective operations are finished. By means of constraints (5.46) and (5.47), logically required time lags between different pick-up and drop-off operations are guaranteed. Constraints (5.46) state that a crane g can just finish the pick-up operation of job j, after the predecessor i has been dropped off, the crane has travelled the empty-driving distance l_{ij}^{x} and the handling at the pick-up position of job j has been done. Similarly, constraints (5.47) state that a crane g can just finish the drop-off operation of job j, after the corresponding pick-up operation has been finished, the crane has travelled the laden-driving distance l_j^{x} and the handling at the drop-off position has been done. For handovers to passive vehicles, like assumed here for both handover areas, the vehicle dispatched to a certain job has to be in place before the crane can perform the relevant pick-up or drop-off operation. As a consequence, constraints (5.48) and (5.49) are required to ensure that pick-up and drop-off operations in the handover areas are not performed before the due date of the corresponding job. However, the constraints can easily be adapted to the use of active waterside horizontal-transport machines, by relaxation of the constraints for the respective handover area. Constraints (5.50) are simple binary constraints.

5.3.6.2 RMGC-System-Specific Restrictions

The objective function (5.34) and the constraints (5.35)–(5.50) are structurally all needed for modelling the crane-scheduling problem of all types of multi-crane RMGC systems. Theoretically, the IP formulation is also applicable for SRMGC systems (i.e., with $|G| = 1$), but crane-scheduling of SRMGC systems can usually be modelled a whole lot simpler as a TSP (Bohrer 2010, pp. 13–17). The crane-scheduling problem of the SRMGC system does not need to be modelled as a discrete-time programme with constant control of crane positions as there is no risk for collisions between different cranes. In contrast, for multi-crane systems the avoidance of crane collisions is an important topic. But so far, the IP model (5.34)–(5.50) does not contain any constraint on the avoidance of crane collisions and the correct incorporation of crane-interference times. Therefore, some additional constraints are needed that look at the system-specific risks for crane collisions.

The cranes of TRMGC systems cannot cross each other. Thus, it is additionally required for an IP model on the scheduling problem of TRMGC systems that

$$\sum_{r=1}^{n^{\mathrm{zo}}} r y_{r\gamma 2} - 1 \geq \sum_{r=1}^{n^{\mathrm{zo}}} r y_{r\gamma 1}, \ \forall\, \gamma = 1, 2, \ldots, \Gamma \tag{5.51}$$

in order to ensure that the waterside crane $g = 1$ is always located closer to the waterside handover area than the landside crane $g = 2$.

In contrast, the cranes of DRMGC systems are able to cross each other. But crossing is only possible as long as the outer large crane is not working in a certain zone. Then, the inner small crane has to wait until trolley and spreader of the larger crane have been brought back to the crossing and driving positions, respectively. Therefore, IP models for the crane-scheduling problem of DRMGC systems additionally require that

$$M\left(1 - z_{j\eta 2}^{\mathrm{pick}}\right) \geq \sum_{\gamma=\eta-h_{j2}}^{\eta} y_{o_j^{\mathrm{x}}\gamma 1}, \tag{5.52}$$

$$\forall\, j = 1, 2, \ldots, n^{\mathrm{J}},\ \eta = h_{j2} + 1, \ldots, \Gamma \text{ and}$$

$$M\left(1 - z_{j\eta 2}^{\text{drop}}\right) \geq \sum_{\gamma=\eta-h_{j2}}^{\eta} y_{d_j^{\text{x}}\gamma 1}, \tag{5.53}$$

$$\forall\, j = 1, 2, \ldots, n^{\text{J}},\ \eta = h_{j2} + 1, \ldots, \Gamma$$

in order to include the system-specific crane-interferences correctly. By means of constraints (5.52), it is ensured that the inner small crane cannot be located in the same zone as the outer large crane when this crane is currently performing a pick-up operation. Similarly, the same issue is stated for drop-off operations by constraints (5.53).

The TriRMGC system combines characteristics of TRMGC and DRMGC systems. The waterside and landside cranes cannot cross each other while they are both able to cross the outer large crane when it is not working in a zone. Thus, IP models for the crane-scheduling problem of TriRMGC systems additionally require that

$$\sum_{r=1}^{n^{\text{zo}}} r y_{r\gamma 2} - 1 \geq \sum_{r=1}^{n^{\text{zo}}} r y_{r\gamma 1},\ \forall\, \gamma = 1, 2, \ldots, \Gamma, \tag{5.54}$$

$$M\left(1 - z_{j\eta 3}^{\text{pick}}\right) \geq \sum_{\gamma=\eta-h_{j3}}^{\eta} y_{o_j^{\text{x}}\gamma g},\ \forall\, j = 1, 2, \ldots, n^{\text{J}}, \tag{5.55}$$

$$\eta = h_{j3} + 1, \ldots, \Gamma,\ g = 1, 2 \text{ and}$$

$$M\left(1 - z_{j\eta 3}^{\text{drop}}\right) \geq \sum_{\gamma=\eta-h_{j3}}^{\eta} y_{d_j^{\text{x}}\gamma g},\ \forall\, j = 1, 2, \ldots, n^{\text{J}}, \tag{5.56}$$

$$\eta = h_{j3} + 1, \ldots, \Gamma,\ g = 1, 2$$

in order ensure a realistic modelling of system-specific interference times for the computation of the optimal schedule. While constraints (5.54) state that the landside crane always has to be located closer to the landside handover area than the waterside crane, constraints (5.55) and (5.56) are used to ensure that neither the waterside crane nor the landside crane can be located in the same zone as the outer large crane when this crane is performing a pick-up or drop-off operation.

Altogether, the crane-scheduling problem for TRMGC systems, that aim for minimising the total vehicle-waiting time in the handover areas, can be formulated by objective (5.34) and constraints (5.35)–(5.51). The IP formulation of the crane-scheduling problem for DRMGC systems comprises objective (5.34), constraints (5.35)–(5.50) as well as constraints (5.52) and (5.53). Finally, the crane-scheduling problem for TriRMGC systems can be formulated by objective (5.34) and constraints (5.35)–(5.50) and (5.54)–(5.56).

5.3.6.3 Programme Extensions and Modifications

The presented IP models can easily be modified and extended to accommodate alternative objectives and/or additional restrictions. Firstly, it may be helpful to constrain the solution space to shorten the computation times for the solution of realistic instances, which are expected to be long due to the experience of Ng (2005) with a similar model for sideway-loading systems. Secondly, it may be interesting to use the basic programme formulations with other objectives, as several other references on crane scheduling at seaport container terminals aim for different objectives (see Table 5.3).

By introducing an upper bound U^{late} on the total vehicle-waiting time in the handover areas of a yard block, the solution space may be greatly restricted depending on the quality of the upper bound. The upper bound U^{late} is implemented by adding the constraint

$$U^{\text{late}} \geq \sum_{j=1 | o_j^{\text{x}} \in \{1, n^{\text{zo}}\}}^{n^{\text{J}}} \sum_{\gamma=1}^{\Gamma} \sum_{g=1}^{|G|} z_{j\gamma g}^{\text{pick}} \left(\gamma - t_j^{\text{hd}} \right) + \sum_{j=1 | d_j^{\text{x}} \in \{1, n^{\text{zo}}\}}^{n^{\text{J}}} \sum_{\gamma=1}^{\Gamma} \sum_{g=1}^{|G|} z_{j\gamma g}^{\text{drop}} \left(\gamma - t_j^{\text{hd}} \right) \quad (5.57)$$

to the IP models. There are several ways to determine an upper bound U^{late}. Here, it is computed using a simple discrete-time simulation applying the EDD rule as a greedy solution approach. Each time a crane g becomes idle, the job j with the earliest due date t_j^{hd} is assigned to that crane. Then, the crane is moved from one zone to the next zone each period of time approaching the pick-up position of job j, unless no other crane is already working in the next zone. Conflicts between different cranes during movements are resolved in a rule-based manner. The right of way is granted to the crane that is closer to its pick-up or drop-off position. After reaching the pick-up position, the crane stays there for h_{jg} time units and then continues its movement to the drop-off position, where it also stays for h_{jg} time units until it becomes idle again. Due to the comparably rough discretisation of time and the simple solution method, an upper bound can be computed within milliseconds. In addition, the resulting makespan of the EDD-based solution can be used as a reference point for the length of the planning period and thus for the number Γ of periods in the IP models.

Some other references on scheduling of stacking equipment aim for minimising the empty-movement times of the stacking equipment (e.g., Vis and Roodbergen 2009) or the makespan W of the stacking operations (e.g., Cao et al. 2008). The proposed programme formulation can also be applied with respect to these objectives. By replacing objective (5.34) by objective

$$\text{minimise} \sum_{g=1}^{|G|} \sum_{i=1}^{n^{\mathrm{J}}} \sum_{j=1}^{n^{\mathrm{J}}} l_{ij}^{\mathrm{x}} x_{ijg} \tag{5.58}$$

the IP models are no longer aiming for minimising the total vehicle-waiting time in the handover areas. Instead, the solution is computed that minimises the total empty-movement time. In contrast, by replacing objective (5.34) by objective

$$\text{minimise } W \tag{5.59}$$

and adding the makespan-defining constraints

$$\sum_{\gamma=1}^{\Gamma} \gamma z_{j\gamma g}^{\mathrm{drop}} \leq W, \ \forall \ j = 1, 2, \ldots, n^{\mathrm{J}}, \ g = 1, 2, \ldots, |G| \tag{5.60}$$

to the IP model, the optimal solution with regard to the makespan minimisation objective is computed.

5.3.6.4 Numerical Experiments and Conclusions

Considering the fast changing online environment of container-storage yards at seaport container terminals, a new crane schedule usually needs to be generated within very short time frames of only several seconds or a few minutes—in particular when the replan online policy is applied. Therefore, in order to evaluate the applicability of the formulated IP models for solving realistic instances of the joint crane-scheduling and routing problem of RMGC-multi-crane systems, some computational experiments on the computation times required to solve these models need to be conducted. Upon closer examination of the introduced IP models it can be noticed that the numbers of variables and restrictions needed to model the crane-scheduling and routing problems of different types of RMGC systems as integer programmes are mostly determined by the number n^{zo} of yard zones and the number n^{J} of jobs to be scheduled. Thus, it is reasonable to investigate the computation times required to solve the IP models with respect to scheduling problems that differ in the number $\left|J_t^{\mathrm{p}}\right|$ of plannable jobs and the number n^{x} of bays in the yard block.

In order to shortly illustrate the computation-time effects of the block length and the crane workload, the problems of scheduling and routing the cranes of TRMGC, DRMGC and TriRMGC systems in such a way that the sum of the vehicle-waiting times in the handover areas is minimised, are tested with two different block lengths—either $n^{\mathrm{x}} = 16$ or $n^{\mathrm{x}} = 28$—and two different numbers of plannable jobs—$\left|J_t^{\mathrm{p}}\right| = 4$ or $\left|J_t^{\mathrm{p}}\right| = 8$. Thus, a total of four different scheduling scenarios is considered for each type of multi-crane system. Ten different problem instances of the crane-scheduling and routing problem are generated for each combination of multi-crane system and scheduling scenario, thus leading to 120 individual scheduling instances in total. These instances of the crane-scheduling problems

Table 5.6 Details and numbers of solved instances with computing times of the IP models (in brackets: the average computation times and the optimality gap of only integer solutions)

Crane system	Scenario		Average number of		Instances solved within 15 min		
	n^{x}	$\lvert J_t^{\text{P}} \rvert$	Restrictions	Variables	Optimal	Integer	No
TRMGC	16	4	8,963.1	4,697.9	10 (99.19 s)	0 (–)	0
	28	4	18,476.5	9,480,0	6 (237.70 s)	0 (–)	4
	16	8	20,454.1	11,612.1	3 (641.87 s)	0 (–)	7
	28	8	41,018.8	22,197.0	0 (–)	0 (–)	10
DRMGC	16	4	9,128.8	4,739.2	10 (259.28 s)	0 (–)	0
	28	4	19,314.2	9,864.1	3 (367.40 s)	2 (35%)	5
	16	8	22,959.2	12,453.6	0 (–)	0 (–)	10
	28	8	45,684.0	24,139.6	0 (–)	0 (–)	10
TriRMGC	16	4	12,030.0	5,929.0	10 (184.98 s)	0 (–)	0
	28	4	26,748.6	13,248.4	8 (401.01 s)	2 (73%)	0
	16	8	27,546.2	13,646.4	4 (370.02 s)	2 (95%)	4
	28	8	58,880.0	29,215.9	0 (–)	0 (–)	10

differ with respect to the origin (o_j^{x}), destination (d_j^{x}) and handover-area due date (t_j^{hd}) of the jobs, while the crane and job-specific handling times to pick up and drop off a container in a certain zone of the block are set to $h_{jg} = 10, \ \forall\, j = |G+1|, |G+2|, \ldots, n^{\text{J}}, \ g = 1, 2, \ldots, |G|$ for all instances. For each individual instance of the crane-scheduling problem, both the number Γ of periods and the upper bound U^{late} on the total vehicle-waiting time in the handover areas are determined by means of a discrete-time simulation model applying the EDD rule. Based on the data generated and determined for all problem instances, each instance of the crane-scheduling and routing problem is modelled as an integer programme, just as described in the preceding subsections, and tried to be solved to optimality by Xpress MP running on a 2.2 GHz Pentium Dual Core 2 machine with 4 GB of RAM within a time limit of 15 min. Owing to the performance capabilities of the test computer and the real-time requirements of the crane-scheduling problem, computing times exceeding 15 min are considered to be far away from any practical use, thus suggesting to restrict the investigation on the computing times of the IP models to solutions obtained within that time limit.

The results of the numerical experiments conducted on the computing times of the IP models are summarised in Table 5.6. There, the average problem sizes of the crane-scheduling problems in terms of the numbers of restrictions and variables as well as the number of instances, for which the optimal solution, at least an integer solution or no solution at all is determined within 15 min, are provided for all combinations of multi-crane systems and scheduling scenarios. The average computing times to obtain the optimal solution and the optimality gap of only integer, but not optimal solutions are noted in brackets. It can be seen from the numerical results of Table 5.6 that the numbers of scheduling instances solved to optimality within 15 min decrease and the average computing times to solve the instances to optimality increase with the length of the yard block and the number of plannable jobs for all considered types of RMGC systems. While all instances of the most small-sized scheduling scenario with only $n^x = 16$ bays and $|J_t^p| = 4$ plannable jobs can be solved to optimality within the time prescribed, none of the problem instances of the largest scheduling scenario with $n^x = 28$ bays and $|J_t^p| = 8$ plannable jobs can be solved to optimality within the framework of these numerical experiments. Even solving the instances of the smallest scheduling scenario to optimality is observed to take a few minutes on average, which often is not available during situations of typical crane workload for RMGC systems. Further, considering the fact that the yard blocks of currently operating front-end-loading RMGC systems at seaport container terminals are between 28 and 42 bays long (see Sect. 3.4.1) and the cranes of these systems are often faced with a crane workload of much more than only four plannable jobs, the computing times of the introduced IP models are expected to be far too long to comply with the real-time requirements of these problems. Therefore, the introduced IP models are found not be suitable for practical applications and extensive simulation experiments in that field, as conducted here subsequently.

5.3.7 *Alternative Solution Methods*

In view of the much too long computing times rendering the previously introduced IP models unsuitable for the generation of optimal crane schedules, some heuristic algorithms are needed to evaluate the effects of crane-scheduling strategies on the RMGC-design-planning problem not just with respect to greedy priority rules, but also with respect to elaborated ignore and replan approaches. In this subsection, two alternative heuristic algorithms are presented that can both be applied in the style of the ignore and replan online policies: a subset full enumeration (SFE) and a GA-based method (GAM). The outputs of both heuristics are sequences of jobs for each crane of a yard block, but contrary to the IP models, no routing decisions are computed—the crane routing is decided by the crane-control module of the TOS in a rule-based way (see Sect. 5.4). The algorithms mainly differ with respect to the generation procedure of the crane schedules, while they are based on the same solution-representation scheme and the same solution-inspection and evaluation procedure. Subsequently, the common basics of both heuristics are introduced first, while thereafter SFE and GAM are described in detail.

5.3.7.1 Common Basics of the Solution Methods

An essential prerequisite for the implementation of several heuristics on combinatorial optimisation problems—like crane scheduling—is the definition of a scheme to represent individual solutions $s \in S$, with S denoting the solution space of feasible (or even infeasible) solutions. In particular, for the design of a GA the choice of a solution-representation scheme is of crucial importance, because the size and the shape of the search space S as well as the configuration and the performance of the GA are greatly affected by the scheme used to represent different solutions (Voß 2001). There are many representation schemes used in GA-based approaches to scheduling problems (e.g., binary, permutation), but simple permutation schemes that represent solutions $s \in S$ as arrays of tasks ordered in the planned execution sequence are most common. Furthermore, solution representation schemes may also differ with respect to their dimensionality, as additional information needs to be represented besides the execution sequence. If, for instance, multiple machines are available—like it is the case here for multi-crane systems—a second dimension may be used to represent the assignment of tasks to machines (Urlings et al. 2010). By applying a two-dimensional permutation scheme, the FIFO-based schedule of the numerical example for the crane-scheduling problem provided in Sect. 5.3.1 can, for example, be represented by solution

$$s = \begin{pmatrix} 3\ 1\ 2\ 4\ 5\ 6\ 7\ 8 \\ 2\ 1\ 1\ 2\ 1\ 2\ 1\ 1 \end{pmatrix} \begin{matrix} \text{job permutation} \\ \text{crane assignment} \end{matrix} \tag{5.61}$$

indicating that jobs 1, 2, 5, 7 and 8 are performed in that order by the waterside crane, while jobs 3, 4 and 6 are performed by the landside crane.

In contrast, a solution $s \in S$ of the crane-scheduling problem is represented here for the SFE and GAM heuristics by a one-dimensional vector that contains the scheduled jobs in the order of execution. In order to represent the scheduled crane-job assignment for multi-crane systems, the solution vector $s \in S$ is virtually subdivided into an RMGC-system-dependent number $|G|$ of crane-related job sequences, by inserting $|G| - 1$ separator tasks $k \in K$ between the crane-related sequences of jobs. A schedule for TRMGC and DRMGC systems is schematically represented by the solution vector

$$s_v = (\text{job sequence 1},\ k_1,\ \text{job sequence 2})\,, \tag{5.62}$$

while a schedule for TriRMGC systems is represented by the solution

$$s_v = (\text{job sequence 1},\ k_1,\ \text{job sequence 2},\ k_2,\ \text{job sequence 3}) \tag{5.63}$$

with index $\upsilon \in \Upsilon$ denoting the υ−th solution among the set of all generated solution vectors $\Upsilon \subseteq S$. Jobs before the first separator task k_1 are assigned to crane 1, while jobs after the first separator task k_1 and—if applicable—before the second separator task k_2 are assigned to crane 2. For TriRMGC systems, jobs after the second separator task k_2 are assigned to crane 3. As a consequence, an extended set $J_t^{\text{pe}} = J_t^{\text{p}} \bigcup K$ of all currently plannable jobs is defined, including all real jobs $j \in J_t^{\text{p}}$ and all needed separator tasks $k \in K$. The two-dimensional solution (5.61) is for instance represented by

$$s = (1, 2, 5, 7, 8, k_1, 3, 4, 6) \tag{5.64}$$

in terms of the representation scheme that is applied here for the SFE and GAM heuristics.

Both the SFE and the GAM heuristic apply the same procedures to check for feasibility of the generated solutions and to evaluate the quality of feasible solutions. An inspection of the feasibility of solutions is necessary as the solution generation processes of the SFE and GAM heuristics cannot guarantee that the generated solutions are actually feasible. A generated solution $s_\upsilon \in \Upsilon$ might be infeasible due to invalid crane-job assignments and/or invalid job sequences with respect to the precedence constraints. Here, a crane-job assignment is denoted to be invalid if a job $j \notin J^{\mathrm{p}}_{tg}$ is impermissibly planned to be assigned to crane g. In the simplest case, a planned job sequence for crane g can be termed as invalid, if both job $j \in J^{\mathrm{p}}_{tg}$ and its predecessor ρ_j are planned to be assigned to crane g, but job j is scheduled before job ρ_j. Another problem with regard to the precedence constraints can be observed for multi-crane systems if job j and its predecessor ρ_j are allowed to be performed by different cranes, which depends on the parametrisation of the applied preselection method. However, if allowed, crane g may be scheduled to perform job j before job $\rho_{j'}$ and crane g' may be scheduled to perform job j' before job ρ_j. In such a case, crane g having assigned job j is waiting for crane g' to perform job ρ_j while crane g' having assigned job j' is waiting for crane g to perform job $\rho_{j'}$. As a consequence, such solutions are also invalid with regard to the precedence constraints, since neither crane g nor crane g' would be able to continue the execution of its planned job sequence.

If a solution $s_\upsilon \in \Upsilon$ is found to be invalid, there is no need to evaluate this solution, whereas the quality of valid solutions needs to be evaluated with respect to certain criteria in order select the best solution $s^*_\upsilon \in \Upsilon$ for realisation. Here, the quality of a solution s_υ is evaluated with respect to a cost function $f^{\mathrm{sc}}(s_\upsilon)$ providing the crane-assignment and job-sequencing costs of that solution. The best solution is then computed as

$$s^*_\upsilon = \arg\min_{s_\upsilon \in \Upsilon} f^{\mathrm{sc}}(s_\upsilon) \tag{5.65}$$

where the exact configuration of the cost function needs to be specified by the user. Although the minimisation of the vehicle-waiting times in the handover areas is identified as the main objective of the crane-scheduling problem, multi-criteria cost functions are defined in Sect. 5.3.5 to determine the next job for a calling crane in order to counterbalance the myopic nature of greedy priority rules. But the situation is different for solution methods that create complete schedules for several jobs and cranes like the SFE and GAM heuristics. There is no need to consider other objectives than minimising lateness of the cranes at the origins of the plannable jobs (see objective (5.25)), since an efficient use of crane resources (see objectives (5.26)–(5.28)) is a necessary prerequisite that has to be implicitly fulfilled in order to generate schedules with short vehicle-waiting times. Hence, both the SFE and GAM heuristics evaluate the quality of a solution s_υ with respect to the cost function

$$f^{\mathrm{sc}}(s_\upsilon) = \sum_{j \in J^{\mathrm{p}'}_t} \lambda^{\mathrm{late}}_{\tau(j),g} \Delta^{\mathrm{pp}+}_{jg} \tag{5.66}$$

with $J_t^{\mathrm{p}'} \subseteq J_t^{\mathrm{p}}$ (and $J_t^{\mathrm{pe}'} \subseteq J_t^{\mathrm{pe}}$) denoting the set of all scheduled jobs as a subset of all plannable jobs at time t. As a consequence, the solution s_υ^* is selected that minimises the weighted sum of late crane arrivals at the pick-up positions of all scheduled jobs $J_t^{\mathrm{p}'}$. The user-specified weighting factors $\lambda_{\tau(j),g}^{\mathrm{late}}$ can be used to schedule certain types of jobs and/or cranes in such a way that vehicle-waiting times connected with these jobs and/or cranes are minimised with higher priority. Waterside retrieval jobs can be, for instance, prioritised by increasing $\lambda_{\mathrm{wsout},g}^{\mathrm{late}}$ in comparison to all other weighting factors.

An important prerequisite for the evaluation and selection of certain solutions is to look at all crane movements and operations as realistically and accurately as possible. Otherwise, dynamic effects may lead to completely different crane movements for the selected solution as planned before, resulting in notably longer vehicle-waiting times for the previously computed best solution. In particular, for multi-crane systems, the evaluation of solutions $s_\nu \in \Upsilon$ is a challenging task due to the problem of mutual interferences among the cranes. In order to calculate the crane-movement times and the resulting crane lateness at the pick-up positions of the jobs as exactly as possible, it is necessary to anticipate possible crane interferences and to take the resulting time shifts (i.e., waiting times and evasion times) in the crane operations into account.

In this work, the solutions generated by the SFE and GAM heuristics are evaluated by a two-step evaluation procedure. In the first step, a solution is decoded into a chronological sequence of crane operations (i.e., movements, pick-up, drop-off) neglecting possible crane collisions and interferences. In the second step, the resulting sequence of crane operations is inspected for crane collisions and, if necessary, amended by shifting crane operations such that a collision-free sequence of crane operations is yielded. The exact configuration of the evaluation procedure differs with respect to the operating type of RMGC system in order to incorporate the system-dependent possibilities for and characteristics of crane interferences as accurately as possible. However, the procedure works in principle identically, independently of the operating type of RMGC system.

The input data for the first step are the scheduled job sequences for each crane as well as the positions of currently idle cranes or the remaining operations of currently assigned cranes. Based on these input data, a chronological sequence of operations is calculated for each crane of a yard block neglecting the operations of other cranes. For each assigned and currently executed job of a crane, the chronological sequences of operations comprise information about the start times and positions of crane movements to the pick-up and drop-off positions, the standing times at these positions including non-productive waiting times as well as empty and laden-movement times. The times needed for all crane movements as well as pick-up and drop-off operations are simply calculated by means of (5.1)–(5.4), that are only based on the job coordinates and the crane kinematics. As a result, a chronological sequence of operations is obtained for each crane, which might still be infeasible due to overlapping of certain crane-movement paths and/or operations.

The input data for the second step of the solution-evaluation procedure are the potentially infeasible sequences of crane operations of the first step which are used as the basis for inspection and repair of crane interferences in this step. The inspection and repair process is implemented in such a way that all crane movements and operations are chronologically inspected for conflicts with other crane movements and/or operations. If a conflict with another crane movement and/or operation is detected, it is firstly determined where and when the overlapping is expected to occur. Based on the expected conflict position and time, it is next decided with respect to the crane-routing rules (see Sect. 5.4) which crane is granted the right of way for the detected conflicting situation. Thereafter, the interference time of the unselected crane is determined as the time it has to wait and/or the time lost by evasive manoeuvres in order to grant the right of way to the other crane. Finally, both the currently considered and all following operations and/or movements of the unselected crane are shifted backwards by the determined interference time. By successively applying this inspection and repair process to all crane movements and operations, this yields a conflict-free chronological sequence of operations for each crane. The computed pick-up arrival time t_{jg}^{pp} and the resulting lateness $\Delta_{jg}^{\mathrm{pp}+}$ of each scheduled job $j \in J_t^{\mathrm{p}'}$ can then be used to calculate the combined crane-assignment and job-sequencing costs $f^{\mathrm{sc}}(s_\upsilon)$ of the obtained feasible solution s_υ.

5.3.7.2 Subset Full Enumeration

Of course, the optimal schedule for all currently plannable jobs can be determined by generating and evaluating all possible permutations of the extended set J_t^{pe} of plannable jobs. But this can take a rather long time—even for realistic instance sizes up to only ten plannable jobs—due to the growth of the number of possible permutations as the factorial $\left|J_t^{\mathrm{pe}}\right|!$ in the number $\left|J_t^{\mathrm{pe}}\right|$ of plannable jobs and separator tasks. Hence, the full enumeration of all possible permutations of the extended set of plannable jobs is not a suitable solution method for the crane-scheduling problem because it would not be real-time compliant.

The SFE heuristic is aimed at computing near optimal solutions for the online crane-scheduling problem in reasonable time. This is facilitated by considering only a fixed number of urgent jobs and computing an optimal solution for this subset of plannable jobs by means of full enumeration. The SFE heuristic can undoubtedly fulfil the real-time requirements of the crane-scheduling problem by defining a reasonable small maximum number $\kappa_{\mathrm{sfe}}^{\mathrm{jobs}}$ of plannable jobs for the full enumeration. For two reasons, the SFE heuristic can be expected to perform quite well: Firstly, for $\left|J_t^{\mathrm{p}}\right| \leq \kappa_{\mathrm{sfe}}^{\mathrm{jobs}}$ the optimal solution for the set of plannable jobs at time t is computed by the SFE heuristic. Secondly, even for $\left|J_t^{\mathrm{p}}\right| > \kappa_{\mathrm{sfe}}^{\mathrm{jobs}}$ the first jobs of the optimal job sequences of the cranes can be expected to be very similar to the solution of the SFE heuristic, as urgent jobs are usually scheduled before less

```
begin
    determine subset $J_t^{p'} \subseteq J_t^p$ of $\kappa_{sfe}^{jobs}$ most urgent jobs
    extend $J_t^{p'}$ to $J_t^{pe'}$
    generate the set $\Upsilon$ of all permutations on $J_t^{pe'}$
    for all generated schedules $s_\upsilon \in \Upsilon$ do
        inspect schedule $s_\upsilon$ for feasibility
        if feasible=true then
            evaluate schedule $s_\upsilon$ (compute $f^{sc}(s_\upsilon)$)
        else
            delete schedule $s_\upsilon$
        end-if
    end-do
    select schedule $s^* = \arg\min_{s_\upsilon \in \Upsilon} f^{sc}(s_\upsilon)$
end
```

Algorithm 5.3: Pseudocode formulation of subset full enumeration (SFE)

urgent jobs. In particular, when the replan online policy is applied, the SFE heuristic can be expected to perform nearly as good as an optimal solution method, as only the first job in the scheduled sequence of the calling crane is actually realised. A summarising overview on the implementation of this heuristic is provided by the pseudocode formulation of Algorithm 5.3.

The urgency of job $j \in J_t^{\mathrm{p}}$ is evaluated with respect to its pick-up due date t_j^{pd}. Hence, the subset $J_t^{\mathrm{p}'}$ of jobs used by the SFE heuristic is basically determined by selecting the $\kappa_{\mathrm{sfe}}^{\mathrm{jobs}}$ jobs with the earliest due dates. But in order to ensure feasible solutions that yield high operational performances of the RMGC systems, two important requirements have to be fulfilled by the job-selection process. Firstly, for each job $j \in J_t^{\mathrm{p}'}$ that requires a predecessor job to be performed prior to its own execution, the predecessor job ρ_j likewise has to be a part of the set $J_t^{\mathrm{p}'}$. Otherwise, each generated schedule would be operationally infeasible. Secondly, in order to ensure an efficient use of the available crane resources, solutions have to be generated that assign at least one job $j \in J_t^{\mathrm{p}}$ to each crane $g \in G$, provided that there are plannable jobs for that crane (i.e., $J_{tg}^{\mathrm{p}} \neq \{\}$). Thus, for each crane $g \in G$ a plannable job $j \in J_{tg}^{\mathrm{p}}$ has to be selected for the subset $J_t^{\mathrm{p}'}$ if $J_{tg}^{\mathrm{p}} \neq \{\}$ (even if other jobs with earlier due dates are available). In most cases, both requirements can be fulfilled by replacing urgent jobs intended for the subset $J_t^{\mathrm{p}'}$ by less urgent jobs. But in the worst case, it is also allowed to use a few more jobs in the set $J_t^{\mathrm{p}'}$ than originally planned (i.e., $\left|J_t^{\mathrm{p}'}\right| > \kappa_{\mathrm{sfe}}^{\mathrm{jobs}}$) in order to comply with the requirements. At the end of the job-selection process, the subset $J_t^{\mathrm{p}'}$ of jobs used by the SFE heuristic is determined, which is then extended to the set $J_t^{\mathrm{pe}'}$ by adding all needed separator tasks $k \in K$. Thereafter, all possible permutations of the set $J_t^{\mathrm{pe}'}$ are generated, which are then successively inspected for feasibility and, if feasible, evaluated.

Altogether, the implementation of the SFE heuristic can be described as six-step procedure. Firstly, the subset $J_t^{p'} \subseteq J_t^{p}$ of the $\kappa_{\text{sfe}}^{\text{jobs}}$ most urgent jobs is determined (see pseudocode line 2) and thereafter extended to the subset $J_t^{pe'}$ of plannable jobs (see pseudocode line 3). In the third step, all possible permutations on this subset are generated (see pseudocode line 4). Thereafter, all generated solutions are inspected for feasibility (see pseudocode line 6) and, depending on its feasibility, either deleted (see pseudocode line 10) or evaluated on the basis of cost function $f^{\text{sc}}(s_\upsilon)$ as described in the preceding subsection (see pseudocode line 8). Finally, the schedule leading to the lowest costs is selected for realisation (see pseudocode line 13).

5.3.7.3 Genetic Algorithm

Genetic algorithms (GA) belong to the class of meta-heuristics, which can basically be defined as top-level strategies for the design of underlying heuristics on a given problem. Meta-heuristics are typically used for problems that are too difficult to be solved exactly within a reasonable amount of time, like it is the case here for the crane-scheduling problem (Voß 2001). For this reason, it is observed that a lot of references on the crane-scheduling problem apply meta-heuristics like TS, SA and GA (see Table 5.3). GAs are a class of random-search algorithms that are inspired by principles derived from the dynamics of natural population genetics (Mühlenbein and Schlierkamp-Voosen 1995). Detailed explanations and further references on GAs are given by Goldberg (1989), Holland (1992) and Mühlenbein (1997).

In general, the starting point of each GA is a population of initially generated individuals (i.e., a set of initial solutions). The individuals of this initial population can be regarded as the ancestors of all subsequent populations, as the following solutions are all generated by rules of genetics on the basis of the set of initial solutions. New solutions are generated by copying solutions of previous populations and partly exchanging information between them (Voß 2001). A typical inheritance process from one population to the next consists of three main concepts that are named according to the corresponding genetic principles (Mühlenbein and Schlierkamp-Voosen 1995): selection, recombination and mutation. Firstly, certain parental individuals are selected from the current population according to their fitness values with respect to the objective function of the underlying problem. Thereafter, descendants of the parental individuals are created by copying and recombining them in a new way. Finally, some descendants are stochastically mutated in order to protect the search from premature lack of versatility (Voß 2001). Usually, this inheritance process is continued until a certain termination condition is fulfilled.

The GAM heuristic proposed here to solve the crane-scheduling problem is based on the typical mechanisms of a simple GA. At the beginning, some initial solutions are generated and evaluated with respect to cost function $f^{\text{sc}}(s_\upsilon)$. Thereafter, new solutions are generated by repeatedly applying the aforementioned

1. begin
2.   generate initial schedules
3.   evaluate initial schedules
4.   repeat
5.   select $s_{\text{parent}_1} \in \Upsilon$ and $s_{\text{parent}_2} \in \Upsilon$
6.   recombine s_{parent_1} and s_{parent_2} to $s_{\text{descendant}_1}$ and $s_{\text{descendant}_2}$
7.   mutate $s_{\text{descendant}_1}$ and $s_{\text{descendant}_2}$ with probability $\kappa_{\text{gam}}^{\text{mut}}$
8.   for $\upsilon \in \{\text{descendant}_1, \text{descendant}_2\}$ do
9.   inspect schedule s_υ for feasibility
10.   if feasible=true then
11.   evaluate schedule s_υ (compute $f^{\text{sc}}(s_\upsilon)$)
12.   else
13.   delete schedule s_υ
14.   end-if
15.   end-do
16.   reorganise population Υ
17.   until convergence criterion is reached
18.   select schedule $s^* = \arg\min_{s_\upsilon \in \Upsilon} f^{\text{sc}}(s_\upsilon)$
19. end

Algorithm 5.4: Pseudocode formulation of the GA-based method (GAM)

inheritance process until one of two termination conditions is fulfilled. Finally, the best generated solution with respect to the cost function $f^{\text{sc}}(s_\upsilon)$ is selected for realisation. A summarising overview on the implementation of this solution method is provided by the pseudocode formulation of Algorithm 5.4.

In order to obtain both a good quality of the initial solutions and a great diversity in the genes of the initial population, the solutions are generated by means of different priority rules and random creation (see pseudocode line 2). Only feasible solutions s_ν are included in the subset Υ of solutions (i.e., the population), whereas generated solutions that are either infeasible or identical to already included solutions are neglected. Feasible initial solutions s_ν are generated by applying the FIFO, NN and EDD rules to schedule all plannable jobs $j \in J_t^{\text{p}}$ observing preselection and precedence constraints. Further initial solutions are randomly generated until either a certain number $\kappa_{\text{gam}}^{\text{itinit}}$ of solutions has been generated or a certain number $\kappa_{\text{gam}}^{\text{noinit}}$ of different feasible solutions has been included in the population Υ. Thereafter, all solutions $s_\upsilon \in \Upsilon$ initially included in the population are evaluated using the evaluation procedure described in Sect. 5.3.7.1 (see pseudocode line 3). The initially best solution with respect to cost function $f^{\text{sc}}(s_\upsilon)$ is denoted as $s^{*\text{init}}$.

At the beginning of the inheritance process (pseudocode lines 5-16), two parental solutions s_{parent_1} and s_{parent_2} are first of all selected from the current population Υ (see pseudocode line 5). Here, the roulette wheel strategy is applied, which means that the parental solutions are chosen randomly with respect to their fitness values (Goldberg and Deb 1991). In the next step, two descendant solutions $s_{\text{descendant}_1}$ and $s_{\text{descendant}_2}$ are generated by randomly recombining the selected parental solutions s_{parent_1} and s_{parent_2} according to a two-point crossover strategy (Mühlenbein and

Schlierkamp-Voosen 1995) (see pseudocode line 6). Right at the start of this crossover strategy, two positions in the solution vector are randomly selected, in between which exchange of the parental genes (i.e., individual jobs) is allowed only. Thus, the genes of $s_{\text{descendant}_1}$ and $s_{\text{descendant}_2}$ before the first and after the second selected position equal those of s_{parent_1} and s_{parent_2}, respectively, while the genes of $s_{\text{descendant}_1}$ and $s_{\text{descendant}_2}$ in between the randomly selected positions are taken from s_{parent_2} and s_{parent_1}, respectively. But in order not to select genes from s_{parent_2} and s_{parent_1} that are already included in $s_{\text{descendant}_1}$ and $s_{\text{descendant}_2}$, respectively, only not yet included genes from the relevant parental solution are added in chronological order in between the selected positions. Thereafter, each of these descendant solutions generated is modified with mutation probability $\kappa_{\text{gam}}^{\text{mut}}$ (see pseudocode line 7). For this purpose, a swap mutation is applied that randomly chooses two jobs and exchanges their positions in the solution vector (Croce et al. 1995). The following inspection and evaluation of both descendant solutions $s_{\text{descendant}_1}$ and $s_{\text{descendant}_2}$ is carried out again in the same way as described in Sect. 5.3.7.1 (see pseudocode lines 8–15). At the end of the inheritance process, the population Υ is reorganised (see pseudocode line 16). Firstly, newly generated solutions (i.e., $s_{\text{descendant}_1}$, $s_{\text{descendant}_2}$), that have not been deleted before, are added to the population Υ. Thereafter, the $|\Upsilon|-\kappa_{\text{gam}}^{\max\Upsilon}$ solutions $s_{\upsilon} \in \Upsilon$ which exhibit the worst cost function values are deleted from the population if its size $|\Upsilon|$ exceeds the user-specified maximum allowed size $\kappa_{\text{gam}}^{\max\Upsilon}$ of thc population. Finally, the repeated generation of new solutions is terminated if either the maximum allowed number $\kappa_{\text{gam}}^{\text{maxit}}$ of repetitions of the inheritance process is reached or a certain improvement of the solution quality is reached in comparison to the initially best solution $s^{*\text{init}}$ (pseudocode line 17). The quality improvement is evaluated with respect to the quality ratio of the current best solution $f^{\text{sc}}(s^*)$ and the initial best solution $f^{\text{sc}}\left(s^{*\text{init}}\right)$ compared to the user-defined aspiration level $\kappa_{\text{gam}}^{\text{al}}$. Hence, the generation process is terminated if $f^{\text{sc}}(s^*)/f^{\text{sc}}\left(s^{*\text{init}}\right) < \kappa_{\text{gam}}^{\text{al}}$.

Altogether, the performance of the GAM heuristic depends on the setting of the parameters $\kappa_{\text{gam}}^{\text{itinit}}$, $\kappa_{\text{gam}}^{\text{noinit}}$, $\kappa_{\text{gam}}^{\text{mut}}$, $\kappa_{\text{gam}}^{\max\Upsilon}$, $\kappa_{\text{gam}}^{\text{maxit}}$ and $\kappa_{\text{gam}}^{\text{al}}$. It can be expected to produce high-quality solutions within reasonable amounts of time. In comparison to the SFE heuristic, high-quality (but not necessarily optimal) solutions for all currently plannable jobs $j \in J_t^{\text{p}}$ are generated by the GAM heuristic, whereas the SFE heuristic solves the crane-scheduling problem to optimality for only a subset $J_t^{\text{p}'} \subseteq J_t^{\text{p}}$ of plannable jobs.

5.4 Crane-Routing Problem

After a new job has been assigned to a crane, the portal and the trolley of that crane have to be moved to the corresponding pick-up and drop-off position in the shortest possible way such that neither collisions nor unnecessarily long interference times with other cranes will occur in the case of multi-crane systems.

Here,the underlying planning problem is referred to as the crane-routing problem, which is—in contrast to the container-stacking and crane-scheduling problems—only briefly addressed throughout this section. It is started with an introduction to the crane-routing problem including its RMGC-specific objectives and constraints. Thereafter, a comparably short overview on literature relevant to this problem is provided in Sect. 5.4.2. This section is closed with the description of different design variants of a claiming-based crane-routing strategy.

5.4.1 Problem Description

Typically, routing problems address the issue of finding a shortest way and/or movement time between two or even more locations. For front-end-loading RMGC systems, a crane $g \in G$ has to be driven from its current position to the origin and from the origin to the destination in order to perform a newly assigned job $j \in J_{tg}^{\mathrm{p}}$. The corresponding crane movements have to be performed in the shortest possible way in order to realise a short execution time for job j without any avoidable vehicle-waiting time. Thus, the cranes have to be routed in a movement-time-minimising way, which is generally facilitated by selecting the shortest possible direct connection between two different locations. For single-crane systems, these direct connections can always be realised without any restrictions and the execution time of a job j only depends on the driving distances of the direct connections and the kinematics of crane g (see Sect. 5.1). Therefore, crane routing for single-crane systems may be regarded as a hardly restricted planning problem with no potential for optimisation and no scope for decision-making.

In contrast, crane routing for multi-crane systems is a restricted planning problem with potential for optimisation and scope for decision-making, as the job-execution times and the resulting vehicle-waiting times are dependent on the routing decisions to ensure a collision-free routing of the cranes. In order to avoid a collision with a conflicting crane g' during the execution of job j, it may be necessary to temporarily stop or to redirect the movement of crane g (i.e., to a shunting position), thus leading to interference time m_j^{cit} and a prolonged execution time for job j in comparison to the theoretically shortest possible execution time. Similarly, it may also be possible that the conflicting crane g', that performs job j', is stopped and/or moved out of the way in order to avoid a crane collision. In that case, the movements of crane g' and the execution time of job j' are prolonged in comparison to the shortest possible times, while no interference time is induced for job j. By deciding on which crane is given the right of way and which crane has to stop and/or to evade in conflicting situations, not just the interference times for individual jobs are controlled, but also the total amount of crane-interference and vehicle-waiting times in the handover areas can be influenced. In fact, conflicting situations may occur between the cranes of a yard block where none of the conflicting cranes can reach its destination without the other crane being moved to a shunting position. To resolve such a conflict, different driving distances and durations of the evasive moves—and thus different interference times—are possible, depending on which crane is selected to evade. Assuming, for instance, that within the framework of a TRMGC system crane 1 has to be moved from bay 8 to bay 30, while crane 2 needs to drive from bay 10 to bay 6. In order to avoid crane collisions and deadlocks, either crane 1 has to evade firstly to bay 5 (neglecting the minimum safety distance between cranes) before moving to its destination or crane 2 has to evade to bay 31 before moving to bay 6. If crane 1 is granted the right of way, an additional portal-evasion distance of $2 \times (31 - 10) = 42$ bays is induced for crane 2 compared to the shortest possible driving distance to its destination, whereas granting the right of way to crane 2 yields only $2 \times (8 - 5) = 6$ bays additional portal-evasion distance for crane 1. The consequences of interference time m_j^{cit} for the waiting time $\omega_{jg}^{\text{hr+}}$ of the related vehicle in the handover area greatly depends on the extent to which additional vehicle-waiting time is induced by temporarily stopping and/or redirecting crane g during the execution of job j. If job j is expected to arrive early in comparison to the handover-area due date t_j^{hd}, the consequences of additional interference times are less negative than for jobs which are already expected to arrive late, even without any interference times involved.

Considering the diverse characteristics of different types of multi-crane systems (see Sect. 3.4.1), basically two main types of crane collisions and interference times have to be distinguished with respect to the crossing ability of the conflicting cranes. A conflict can either occur between two small same-sized cranes or two differently sized cranes with crossing ability. A collision between two same-sized cranes can only occur if both portals come too close to each other alongside the x-axis of the yard block (i.e., being located in adjacent bays, see Sect. 3.4.1.2). Thus, a minimum safety distance between the portals of two same-sized cranes always has to be ensured in order to avoid such collisions. A conflict between these cranes can only be resolved by prompting one of the cranes to evade and/or to wait until the other crane has finished a certain operation. The amount of interference time for the crane that is not granted the right of way is defined by the amount of waiting time for the other crane and the additional crane-movement time to and from the required shunting position.

In contrast, a collision between two differently sized cranes with crossing capability can only occur, if the portals of both cranes come very close to each other (e.g., for performing a crossing manoeuvre) while the trolley of the outer large crane is not located in its crossing position p_g^{cross} (see Sect. 3.4.1.3). Hence, it has to be ensured that the trolley of the outer large crane is always located in the crossing position when a minimum safety distance between the portals is undershot alongside the x-axis of the yard block. Due to the crossing possibility, a conflict between two differently sized cranes cannot only be resolved by stopping and/or redirecting one of the cranes, but also by performing a crossing manoeuvre. As a consequence, there is more scope for decision-making concerning the routing problem for differently sized cranes—not only the right of way has to be decided but also the performance of crossing manoeuvres. The amount of interference time that is induced for the inner small crane and/or the outer larger crane by performing a crossing manoeuvre is mainly determined by the technical implementation of the crossing process. In principle, a crossing manoeuvre can either be implemented by not moving the portal of the outer large crane until its trolley is located in the crossing position or by moving the trolley to the crossing position while also moving the portal to its destination if no collision is expected during the trolley movement. Of course, it can be expected that the second implementation is connected with shorter interference times, thus inducing a more efficient use of crane resources than the first implementation.

In addition to the crane-interference times caused by crane-crossing manoeuvres, there is a further possible source for inefficient use of crane resources of DRMGC and TriRMGC systems—regardless of the way crane-crossing manoeuvres are performed: unnecessary blocking of handover areas. Once a handover area is claimed and accessed by the outer large crane (inner small crane), the handover area is blocked for claiming and access by the inner small crane (outer large crane without the trolley being located in the crossing position) until the outer large crane (inner small crane) finishes its pick-up and/or drop-off operation in that handover area and releases it for claiming and access by the inner small crane (outer large crane). In case the relevant container and/or horizontal-transport vehicle required to perform the pick-up and/or drop-off operation in the handover area has not yet arrived, because the crane arrives too early compared to the corresponding handover-area due date t_j^{hd}, the handover area is unnecessarily blocked for operations of other cranes, thus possibly leading to a waste of crane resources due to avoidable waiting times for these cranes. For TRMGC systems, there is no problem of handover area blocking, as each handover area can only be served by one crane anyway. Thus, in order to improve the crane-use efficiency of DRMGC and TriRMGC systems, it might be advisable to prevent a crane of these multi-crane systems from claiming and/or entering a handover area when it arrives much too early.

Besides ensuring collision-free movements of the cranes, crane routing in multi-crane systems additionally has to be made with respect to the job-precedence constraints that are induced by the stacking order. The pick-up operation of job j, having a predecessor job ρ_j, cannot be started by crane g before the relevant container of job ρ_j, that is stored on top of the container associated with job j, has been picked by another crane g'. Hence, for conflicting situations between two different cranes g and g' that are both going to perform the pick-up operations of two precedence-related jobs j and ρ_j, respectively, the right of way always has to be granted to the crane g' that is going to perform the predecessor job ρ_j, regardless of any optimisation objectives. Otherwise, the RMGC system may be caught in a deadlock situation.

Altogether, the crane-routing problem for front-end-loading RMGC systems can be summarised as an optimisation problem for multi-crane systems only, aiming to minimise the amount of crane-interference and vehicle-waiting times with respect to avoiding system-specific crane collisions and to being compliant with job-precedence constraints caused by the stacking order.

5.4.2 Literature Overview

In contrast to the container-stacking and crane-scheduling problems, the crane-routing problem has so far not attracted a great deal of attention in the logistics and OR literature on yard-crane systems for seaport container terminals. While some papers on scheduling of sideway-loading crane systems deal with the crane routing en passant (see Sect. 5.3.2), this problem is directly addressed by only very few works on front-end-loading crane systems. This can be explained as the issue of collision avoidance is mainly of importance for automated front-end-loading crane systems. Compared to manual sideway-loading crane systems, far more potential for collisions is induced by the long crane movements alongside the length of the yard block and no crane drivers are in place to prevent the cranes from colliding with each other.

All papers on the scheduling of sideway-loading crane systems, that address the problem of finding optimal sequences of bay visits for container pick-ups by the scheduled crane(s), implicitly also aim for finding an optimal collision-free routing of the crane(s). The problem of finding optimal sequences of bay visits for yard blocks with a single gantry crane—without the need to consider crane collisions—is for example addressed by Kim and Kim (1997, 1999b, 2003), Kozan and Preston (1999), Narasimhan and Palekar (2002) as well as Ng and Mak (2005a,b), while, among others, Ng (2005), Jung and Kim (2006) and Lee et al. (2006) look for optimal collision-free sequences of bay visits for yard blocks with two or more cranes. A detailed overview on the papers simultaneously addressing the crane-scheduling and routing problems is provided in Sect. 5.3.2. In the majority of these papers, the problem of finding optimal sequences of bay visits is formulated as IP model, that is discrete in time and position, and solved by means of heuristic methods.

Within the framework of Sect. 5.3.6, it is shown that the crane-scheduling problem for front-end-loading multi-crane systems can likewise be formulated as an IP model, that is discrete in time and position, for finding a collision-free sequence of bay visits for the cranes of a yard block that minimises the vehicle-waiting times in the handover areas. Thus, solving such models does not only provide the optimal job sequences for the cranes (i.e., the solution of the crane-scheduling problem) but also the optimal crane routing. However, it is also shown in Sect. 5.3.6 that the computation times to solve these models to optimality are much too long to be applied for real-time crane scheduling and routing in practical applications. In the relevant literature, scheduling and routing of multi-crane RMGC systems are therefore mostly addressed as two distinct planning problems. An overall solution approach for the joint crane-scheduling and routing problem of TriRMGC systems is for example proposed by Dorndorf and Schneider (2010) (see Sect. 5.3.2). When treated as a distinct problem, the crane routing for front-end-loading multi-crane systems is mostly handled by applying fixed rules (e.g., Saanen et al. 2003; Valkengoed 2004, pp. 22–26). But before certain rules can be used to resolve conflicting situations between different cranes, first of all avoidance of crane collisions has to be ensured for all possible crane movements.

A basic approach to ensure collision-free routing in multi-crane systems, that is usually used in conjunction with rule-based crane-routing decisions, is the claiming concept (Saanen 2004, p. 217), which can also be used to ensure a collision-free routing of AGVs at seaport container terminals (Meersmans 2002, p. 32). The basic idea of the claiming concept for front-end-loading yard-crane systems is to divide the yard block into several sections alongside the length of the x-axis and to only allow a crane to drive into such a section if it has previously been exclusively claimed for the respective crane. Otherwise, the crane cannot start driving into the section or it has to stop. Of course, no overlap is allowed between claimed sections of different cranes. Therefore, a crane can move freely within claimed sections without the risk of colliding with other cranes. The size and the arrangement of claimable sections can be freely selected, but usually the length of the yard block is divided into n^x equally-sized sections, such that each bay of a yard block is a section which can be separately claimed (Valkengoed 2004, p. 25).

Basically, two types of claiming approaches for front-end-loading RMGC systems are distinguished by Saanen (2004, pp. 217–218), that differ with respect to the time at which a section is claimed by a crane. In static claiming, it is tried to claim the entire block length to the next destination position of a crane upon starting a movement. If this is not possible, it has to be decided on the basis of certain rules whether to wait until the entire length becomes claimable or to immediately claim the sections up to as close to the destination position as possible. In contrast, in first-win claiming, only the minimally required stopping distance of a crane is repeatedly claimed in advance during a crane movement. The crane that arrives first at its destination is the winner, while the other crane possibly has to wait. If none of the cranes can reach their destination positions, it has to be decided with respect to certain decision rules, which crane is granted the right of way and which crane is sent away. With regard to the yard-crane productivities, no significant performance differences between both types of claiming approaches are found by Saanen (2004, p. 218). Independently of whether static or first-win claiming is applied, conflicts are resolved by means of certain decision rules that are, for instance, based on the remaining driving distances to the destinations of the cranes and/or the urgencies of the currently performed jobs (Valkengoed 2004, pp. 22–26).

Only very little has been published so far on crane routing and crossing for front-end-loading systems with crossing ability. In a study on crane scheduling for DRMGCs, Stahlbock and Voß (2010) assume that the trolley of the outer large crane should generally move to the crossing position before starting a portal movement. On the one hand, collision avoidance and crane-crossing are greatly facilitated by such a crane-routing strategy. But on the other hand, a lot of time is wasted, since not all crane movements necessarily require the trolley to be moved to the crossing position in order to avoid collisions, and sometimes it may also be possible to move portal and trolley simultaneously.

Quite detailed descriptions of the implementation of claiming-based collision-avoidance processes for TRMGC and DRMGC systems are provided by Valkengoed (2004, pp. 22–26). In contrast to Stahlbock and Voß (2010), a general trolley movement to the crossing position of the outer large crane is rejected for

DRMGC systems. Instead, it is proposed to neglect the crossing ability of DRMGC systems until a conflict between the cranes occur. Then it has to be decided whether it is beneficial, with regard to the crane productivity, to perform a crossing manoeuvre or to stop and/or move one of the cranes out of the way. These decisions are made in a rule-based way with respect to several criteria like the current and next destination positions of the cranes.

5.4.3 Claiming-Based Crane Routing

In view of the fact that the IP models introduced in Sect. 5.3.6 for jointly solving the crane-scheduling and routing problems to optimality are shown to be inapplicable for real-world problems as well as simulation studies in that field, crane routing still needs to be addressed as a problem of its own. In this subsection, different design variants of claiming-based crane-routing strategies are introduced to address the routing problem of RMGC-multi-crane systems, which mainly differ in the way in which crane-crossing manoeuvres are performed. While the claiming concept is used to ensure collision-free crane movements for all types of multi-crane systems, conflicts between the cranes are resolved with respect to system-specific decision rules. These rules and the resulting crane movements can implicitly be considered by elaborated crane-scheduling strategies in order to allow forward-looking scheduling decisions that are based on profound estimates of job-execution times (see Sect. 5.3.7). Both the claiming-based collision-avoidance mechanism as well as the considered criteria for the rule-based routing decisions are inspired by Saanen (2004, pp. 217–218) and Valkengoed (2004, pp. 22–26).

For the implementation of the collision-avoidance mechanism, the yard block is divided into equally-sized sections with the length of a yard bay, such that each yard bay and both handover areas can be claimed separately. Here, a section only needs to be claimed by a crane, when the corresponding yard bay is blocked by that crane for storage and/or retrieval operations of other cranes. While an inner small crane always blocks the yard bays it is located in, an outer large crane only blocks these bays when its trolley is not located in the crossing position. Otherwise, containers below the portal of the outer large crane are still accessible for an inner small crane. Taking into account the crane dimensions and some additional safety distance, it is assumed that the claimed area of a blocking yard crane always has a size of three sections when standing still. Besides the section the middle of the crane portal is located in, also the sections to the right and to the left are claimed by that crane. Upon the start of a crane movement to another position in the yard block, it is tried to claim a bigger area of the block, ahead of it. While the claiming process for TRMGC systems is based on the static claiming concept, the idea of first-win claiming is used for DRMGC and TriRMGC systems. Subsequently, only the basic ideas of these system-specific routing strategies are explained. In particular, it is focused on the decision rules for resolving conflicts between the cranes and the different possibilities for performing crane-crossing manoeuvres. Detailed information on the implementation of these claiming-based routing strategies are given by Kemme (2011c, pp. 19–25).

Within the framework of TRMGC systems, it is always tried to claim the entire block area up to the next destination position of a crane (i.e., static claiming) subject to job-precedence constraints and sections that are claimed by other cranes. If the currently routed crane has to wait for the pick-up of a predecessor job, the crane is either moved to an adequate shunting position or as close to its destination as possible without blocking the other crane. In case the cranes conflict in such a way that neither the currently routed crane nor the other one can reach its destination, the right of way is granted to the crane that is located closer to its target position, while the other crane is moved to an adequate shunting position.

For the inner small cranes of DRMGC and TriRMGC systems, it is only tried to claim at most ten sections in the direction of the next destination position of a crane in order to prevent the inner small cranes from blocking too many yard bays far in advance for storage and retrieval operations of the outer large crane. Basically, the right of way is granted to the crane that firstly claims the relevant sections (i.e., first-win claiming). However, precedence conflicts between the inner small crane(s) and the outer large crane are resolved such that the pick-up position of a predecessor job can be reached by the relevant crane, while claiming conflicts between both inner small cranes of TriRMGC systems are resolved similarly to TRMGC systems looking at the distances to the destination positions.

The desired claiming area for an outer large crane greatly depends on the way in which crane-crossing manoeuvres are performed. Here, four configuration levels of crane-crossing processes are proposed that are based on one another. Comparable to Stahlbock and Voß (2010), portal and trolley of the outer large crane are not allowed to move simultaneously within the framework of the simplest crane-crossing process (CCP1). The trolley of the outer large crane always has to be located in the crossing position p_g^{cross} before the portal is allowed to gantry. Thus, only the three sections around the next pick-up and/or drop-off position of the outer large crane have to be claimed upon arrival at that position. Other sections never need to be claimed for the outer large crane.

In order to shorten the crane-movement and job-execution times compared to CCP1, the second crane-crossing process (CCP2) allows simultaneous trolley and portal movements of the outer large crane if certain conditions are fulfilled. The trolley also has to be moved to its crossing position p_g^{cross} for each crane movement to the next destination position, but the portal is allowed to start to move as well, if the sections, that would be passed by the crane while its trolley has not yet reached the crossing position p_g^{cross}, can be claimed in advance by that crane. The number of sections that need to be claimed upon starting a portal movement are determined by computing the required trolley-movement time to the crossing position and computing the portal distance covered in that time. Similarly, the required trolley-movement time from the crossing position to the next trolley destination as well as the portal distance covered in that time can be computed as well. Once the remaining distance to the portal destination is smaller than the distance covered during the time needed to move the trolley to its destination, it is checked if the relevant sections up to the destination position can be claimed by that crane and the trolley can start to move to its destination as well. If the required sections for simultaneous portal and trolley movement to (from) the crossing position cannot be claimed by the outer large crane, the start of the portal (trolley) movement is firstly denied, but it is constantly checked if the simultaneous movement becomes possible with fewer numbers of sections to be claimed due to the decreasing trolley (portal) driving distance to the crossing (destination) position.

Similar considerations as with CCP2 for the trolley may also apply for the spreader, which usually has to be lifted to the driving position p_g^{drive} before portal and/or trolley are allowed to move. In contrast to this current practice, which is also assumed here (see Sect. 5.1), future crane routing strategies may allow portal and/or trolley movements without the spreader being located in the driving position p_g^{drive} if certain requirements concerning the stacking heights of neighbouring piles are fulfilled.

The next configuration level of crane-crossing processes (CCP3) is designed to further shorten the crane-movement and job-execution times by additionally allowing the trolley of the outer large crane to move directly to the next trolley destination without prior movement to the crossing position. But in order to avoid unnecessary conflicts with the small crane(s), such a direct trolley movement of the outer large crane is only allowed if possible and beneficial. A direct trolley movement is possible if the whole portal-driving distance from the current position to the next portal destination can be claimed for that crane when the relevant spreader has just reached the driving position p_g^{drive} after performing the prior pick-up or drop-off operation. In addition, a direct movement of the trolley is regarded as beneficial only if the portal-movement time to the next destination position is shorter than the sum of the trolley-movement times from the current trolley position to the crossing position p_g^{cross} and from the crossing position p_g^{cross} to the next trolley destination. Otherwise, portal and trolley can also be moved simultaneously in the style of CCP2 to/from the crossing position without any prolongation of the total crane-movement time to the next destination, but with the additional opportunity for crane-crossing manoeuvres while the crane moves to that destination. In case a direct trolley movement is not possible and/or beneficial, portal and trolley are either moved simultaneously (CCP2) or successively (CCP1), depending on whether the required sections can be claimed.

The last configuration level of crane-crossing processes (CCP4) is designed to facilitate direct (CCP3) and simultaneous (CCP2) trolley movements of the outer large crane by moving conflicting inner small cranes out of the way whenever possible. Each time a desired direct and/or simultaneous trolley movement is disabled by an inner small crane, that has claimed sections required by the outer large crane, it is checked whether the conflicting small crane is currently idle or occupied. In case the conflicting crane is currently idle, it is moved to an adequate shunting position and the outer large crane is allowed to start the desired direct or simultaneous trolley movement in the style of CCP3 or CCP2, respectively, even though not all required sections up to its next destination are immediately claimable upon the start of the movement. If the conflicting crane is currently occupied, evading of the blocking inner small crane is denied and the trolley of the outer large crane can for the moment not be moved directly and/or simultaneously.

In order to avoid any unnecessary blocking of handover areas for DRMGC and TriRMGC systems, just as described in Sect. 5.4.1, a so-called handover-area access control (HAC) mechanism can optionally be used in connection with each of the aforementioned crossing processes. Basically, the HAC mechanism is based on the idea to only allow a crane to claim and/or access a handover area if no long crane-waiting time in the handover area is to be expected, thus keeping the handover area free for operations of other cranes. Each time a crane is going to claim and/or access a handover area, it is checked on the basis of the estimated remaining movement time to the pick-up or drop-off position in that handover area, whether the crane will arrive too early compared to the handover-area due date of the currently assigned job. For inner small cranes, this arrival time check is carried out when passing the last possible stop position for the crane before accessing the handover area, while for the outer large crane, place and point in time of that check are determined by the applied crane-crossing process. If portal and trolley of the outer large crane are moved successively (CCP1), the arrival time check is just made when the portal arrives in the handover area, whereas this check is carried out before starting a simultaneous (CCP2) or direct trolley move (CCP3) to the handover area. Because of the differences in the lifting capabilities of the horizontal-transport vehicles, however, not each early crane arrival in the handover area will directly lead to an unproductive crane-waiting time and an unnecessary blocking of that zone (see Sect. 5.1). In case no crane-waiting time in the handover area is to be expected for an inner small crane (outer larger crane), the crane is allowed to proceed (start) the movement to the pick-up or drop-off position in the handover area without any delay. If, however, any crane-waiting time is to be expected, an inner small crane (outer large crane) is forced to stop (not to start) the movement to the handover area and claiming of that zone is revised (denied), until the remaining movement time will lead to an on-time arrival at the pick-up or drop-off position in the handover area without any crane or vehicle-waiting time involved.

5.5 Concluding Remarks

In this chapter, the operational planning problems of RMGC systems at seaport container terminals are addressed in detail. After introducing some basic terms and notations for the formal representation of the operational planning problems, the container-stacking problem, the crane-scheduling problem and the crane-routing problem are successively analysed in Sects. 5.2–5.4, respectively. For each of these operational planning problems, a detailed problem description is given, an extensive survey on literature relevant to that planning problem is provided, known types of solution approaches are classified and new/modified solution approaches are proposed.

Table 5.7 Summary of introduced operational planning strategies

Container-stacking strategy		Crane-scheduling strategy			Crane-routing strategy
Division policy	Positioning method	Preselection method	Solution method	Online policy	
ReS	RaS	dedicated[a]	FIFO	FIFO	CCP1[b]
RvS	LeS	zoning[a]	NN	greedy	CCP2[b]
ScS	RTS		EDD	replan	CCP3[b]
FrS	PoS		PRIO1	ignore	CCP4[b]
	CaS		PRIO2		HAC[b]
	CCFS		SFE		
	HHS		GAM		

[a]Only needed for TRMGC, DRMGC and TriRMGC
[b]Only needed for DRMGC and TriRMGC

The way the container-stacking problem is addressed at seaport container terminals is determined by the applied stacking strategy, which is composed of a storage-area-division policy and a container-positioning method. In this chapter, a new cost-function-based container-positioning method (CCFS) is introduced that is based on the ideas of category stacking (CaS), retrieval-time stacking (RTS) and positional stacking (PoS) (see Sect. 5.2.4). In addition, a detailed implementation of a housekeeping concept (HHS) for front-end-loading RMGC systems is presented, that is designed to smooth the crane workload over time (see Sect. 5.2.5).

In Sect. 5.3.6, the combined crane-scheduling and routing problem is formulated as an IP model that correctly takes into account all risks for crane interferences for each type of RMGC system. But due to the prohibitively long computation times needed to solve these programmes to optimality, they are usually not applicable to practical applications and extensive simulation experiments. Thus, the crane-scheduling and routing problems are addressed separately in the following simulation study by means of different approaches. For the crane-scheduling problem, different types of preselection methods (dedicated, zoning), online policies (FIFO, greedy, replan, ignore) and solution methods (optimal, heuristic, FIFO, priority) are introduced, which, if combined, jointly define different crane-scheduling strategies. In particular, several new/modified solution methods are proposed, ranging from multi-criteria priority rules (PRIO1, PRIO2) to more elaborated (meta-) heuristic scheduling methods (SFE, GAM), which can both be applied in the style of the ignore and replan online policies. The crane-routing problem is basically addressed by RMGC-type-specific routing rules that are all based on a claiming concept to avoid crane collisions. For RMGC systems with crane-crossing capabilities, four different crane-crossing processes are introduced (CCP1–4), that differ with regard to the way in which crane-crossing manoeuvres are performed, and a handover-area access control (HAC) mechanism is proposed to avoid unnecessary blocking times of the handover areas. A summarising overview on all previously introduced planning approaches for the operational planning problems of RMGC systems at seaport container terminals is provided in Table 5.7.

Chapter 6
Simulation as a Terminal-Planning Approach

The availability of simulation languages, the progress in the field of simulation methods and, in particular, the steadily improving performance capabilities of computer technology have led computer-based simulation to become one of the most widely-used and most accepted tools within the field of OR and system analysis (Banks et al. 2004, p. 4; Domschke and Drexl 2011, p. 225). It is typically used for problems that cannot be adequately solved by an analytic model and where experiments with the real system are too costly, too dangerous, too time-consuming and/or not possible at all (Winston 2004, p. 1145). For these reasons, computer-based simulation is already identified in Sect. 4.3 as the method of choice to investigate the stochastic real-time operations of automated RMGC systems at seaport container terminals. In this chapter, the use of simulation for investigating strategical and operational planning problems of automated RMGC systems is addressed in more detail. In particular, a detailed simulation model of a front-end-loading RMGC system is introduced that is designed to compare both alternative RMGC designs and different types of operational planning strategies.

This chapter is started in Sect. 6.1 with a brief introduction to the field of simulation analysis, including a description of typical steps in a sound simulation study and a classification of different types of computer-based simulations. Thereafter, known simulation studies of seaport container terminals—in particular those concerning front-end-loading RMGC systems—are reviewed with respect to the concepts, assumptions and possible shortcomings of the implemented simulation models. Based on this literature review as well as generally accepted guidelines for the design of simulation models, some basic principles for a new simulation model addressing the research questions of this work are summarised in Sect. 6.3. The RMGC-simulation model that is actually used for the simulation study of this work is then introduced in Sect. 6.4. The chapter is closed with some concluding remarks.

N. Kemme, *Design and Operation of Automated Container Storage Systems*, Contributions to Management Science, DOI 10.1007/978-3-7908-2885-6_6,

6.1 Introduction to Simulation Analysis

In general, simulation can be defined as 'the process of designing a model of a real system and conducting experiments with this model for the purpose of understanding the behaviour of the system and/or evaluating various strategies for the operation of the system' (Oakshott 1996, p. 121). A system is composed of a number of acting and interacting entities. Depending on whether the system has one or more interface(s) to its environment, it is either an open or a closed system (Voß and Gutenschwager 2001, p. 6). A model is a representation of a real system that is designed for a certain purpose. Usually, only structures and/or functions of the real systems are realistically modelled that are essential for the purpose of a simulation, while system entities and capabilities that are unimportant for that purpose are neglected and/or only incorporated into a model in a simplified way. The main purpose of modelling is to understand, to explain and to illustrate the behaviour of the real system (Fink et al. 2005, p. 91).

With regard to the characteristics of the underlying system, simulation models can be classified along three dimensions (Law and Kelton 2000, pp. 5–6): static vs. dynamic, continuous vs. discrete and deterministic vs. stochastic. A static simulation model is used if no changes of the system status over time need to be regarded, while a dynamic simulation model is employed to represent changes of the system over time. Systems for which the state variables are changing instantaneously at separate points in time are usually represented by discrete simulation models. If these points in time are determined by a given number of specified time intervals (e.g., seconds, minutes), the model is denoted as a discrete-period simulation model, while the model is termed to be a discrete-event simulation model if the points in time are determined by certain events in the model. In contrast, continuous simulation models are used to represent systems for which the state variables change continuously over time. Although most real systems are to some extent both discrete and continuous, one type of change usually predominates for most systems. The majority of production and logistic problems is represented by discrete-event simulation models (Fink et al. 2005, p. 120). A simulation model without any probabilistic components is called deterministic. Once all inputs of a deterministic simulation model have been specified, the output is determined as well, even though it might take a lot of computation time to obtain the actual results. However, most real systems have to be represented by stochastic simulation models, that are characterised by having some random input components (Law and Kelton 2000, p. 6). Of course, the output of a stochastic model is itself random and therefore has to be regarded as an estimate of the real system behaviour, which is probably one of the most important disadvantages of simulation.

Besides the pure implementation of a simulation model and the conduct of experiments with that model, a simulation study is usually composed of several further steps with regard to planning and realisation of both modelling and experimenting (Banks et al. 2004, p. 354; Domschke and Drexl 2011, p. 228–239). A listing of typical steps in a sound simulation study—ranging from the problem

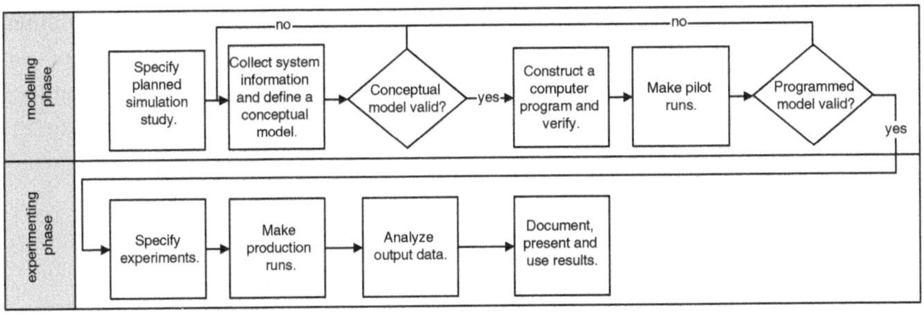

Fig. 6.1 Steps in a sound simulation study (based on Law and Kelton 2000, p. 84)

formulation to the result documentation—is provided by Law and Kelton (2000, pp. 83–86). As illustrated in Fig. 6.1, these successive steps can be divided into a two-phase simulation process, which is also used as guiding principle for the simulation study on RMGC systems at seaport container terminals conducted in this work. In the modelling phase, a simulation model is constructed that can be used to conduct meaningful experiments with respect to the purpose of a simulation study, while these experiments are actually conducted, analysed and discussed in the experimenting phase of the simulation process.

The modelling phase is started with a specification of the simulation study, including, among others, the definition of overall study objectives, specific research questions to be answered, considered performance measures and system configurations to be modelled. In the following step, required information on system layout, procedures, model parameters and input probability distributions are collected and delineated in a document on the conceptual model design. Thereafter, the conceptual model is evaluated with respect to its validity by experts on the considered system. Once the conceptual model is qualified as valid, it is implemented in a programming language (e.g., C or JAVA) or in simulation software (e.g., Arena, Plant Simulation) and the resulting simulation computer programme is verified with respect to its general functionality. Finally, pilot runs are conducted with the programmed model for validation purposes. The validation of the programmed model is composed of reviews of the model results by experts (i.e., expert validation) as well as comparisons of real performance figures with simulation results (i.e., statistical validation) (Law and Kelton 2000, p. 86). Usually, only a valid simulation model should be used for conducting simulation experiments, as otherwise correct decisions for the real system cannot be expected to be made on the basis of the simulation results (Law 2009).

The experimenting phase of the simulation process is started with a specification of the experiments that are needed in order to answer the research questions on the modelled system. Besides the detailed definition of the different system configurations to be simulated, also the length T of each simulation run, the length T^{warm} of the warm-up period and the number n^{run} of independent simulation runs using different random numbers need to be specified for each planned experiment. Thereafter, all previously specified simulation experiments are actually conducted and the resulting performance figures are statistically evaluated and explained with respect to the system modelled. Finally, all results and findings of the simulation study need to be documented together with the model assumptions and implementations in order to allow a transparent evaluation of the conducted simulation study (Law and Kelton 2000, p. 86).

6.2 Review of Simulation Approaches Within Seaport Container Terminals

In Sect. 4.3, simulation is identified as a well-suited decision support technique for planning problems at seaport container terminals. This is also confirmed by the fact that simulation is nowadays frequently used to address all types of terminal-planning problems, on all levels of a terminal lifecycle (Saanen et al. 2000; Schütt 2011). As a consequence, dozens of simulation studies and papers addressing simulation topics can be found in the literature on container terminals. In total, 41 container-terminal simulation models are identified by Petering et al. (2009). A general guide on the use of simulation models at seaport container terminals—in particular for designing automated terminals—is provided by Saanen (2004, 2011). Some recent models are given by Duinkerken and Ottjes (2000), Legato and Mazza (2001), Liu et al. (2002), Vis and Harika (2004), Nazari (2005), Parola and Sciomachen (2005), Zauner (2005), Briskorn et al. (2006), Alessandri et al. (2007), Ottjes et al. (2007), Dai et al. (2008), Petering (2009), and Wiese et al. (2009b). These simulation models and studies differ with respect to the investigated planning problem (see Sect. 2.4), the terminal configuration (e.g., size, equipment), the modelled subsystem(s) of the terminal (see Sect. 2.2.2), the modelled level of detail, the used programming language/software, the visualisation options and various other criteria. According to Petering et al. (2009), the major limitations of most simulation models on container terminals are rather short simulation horizons (often only 1 day) and the restriction to look at the processing of only a single vessel in isolation. In addition, Bruzzone et al. (1999) argue that isolated models of certain subsystems are expected to produce only useless simulation results, as interdependencies to connected subsystems are neglected. Thus, it is recommended to either develop models of the entire terminal system (Bruzzone et al. 1999) or to consider the interfaces of an isolatedly modelled subsystem as realistically as possible, for instance by means of relevant real-world probability distributions, imitating the behaviour of the connected subsystems (Hartmann et al. 2007).

Problems on the design and the operation of front-end-loading RMGC systems are also mostly addressed by means of simulation studies. Based on the literature overviews provided on all types of RMGC-planning problems (see Sects. 4.2, 5.2.2, and 5.3.2), altogether 17 simulation studies and eleven different simulation models on front-end-loading RMGC systems can be identified. Subsequently, some selected simulation models and studies on RMGC systems are reviewed with respect to their conceptual design.

The simulation studies on RMGC-design planning of Valkengoed (2004), Saanen and Valkengoed (2005) as well as Saanen (2007) are based on the commercial TIMESquare simulation model library of the Dutch port consulting company TBA, that has been used for several consultancy and simulation projects all over the world. Therefore, it is, on the one hand, expected to be one of the most elaborated simulation models for seaport container terminals—in particular with regard to the visualisation abilities. But, on the other hand, only little information on the implementation of this model library is available. The most detailed information on the conceptual design of that model library with regard to yard-crane modelling is provided by Valkengoed (2004). The precise level of detail can be largely defined for each simulation study with respect to the included subsystem(s), the equipment kinematics, the stochastics and various other topics. The studies of Valkengoed (2004) and Saanen and Valkengoed (2005) are, for instance, based on different simulation experiments with an isolated yard block and with the entire terminal system. With regard to the yard-crane operations, only 20′ containers are modelled, all crane movements are realistically mapped using their kinematics and the container handovers to horizontal-transport vehicles are not explicitly modelled but only included as fixed times (30 s to XT, 10 s to AGV). For the experiments with the isolated yard block (entire terminal), the presented simulation results are based on $n^{\mathrm{run}} = 10$ (8) stochastically independent simulation runs of only $T = 24\,\mathrm{h}$ (8 h) of terminal operations.

The simulation model that is used by Dekker et al. (2006) and Borgman et al. (2010) to investigate different types of container-stacking strategies is implemented in the MUST and JAVA programming languages, respectively. It is composed of a generator and an evaluator programme. Firstly, relevant data on all individual containers that arrive at the terminal over a user-defined simulation horizon are stochastically produced, including information on each container such as planned arrival and departure time, arriving and departing transport mode, PoD, weight and size. This data is used as input for a deterministic evaluation programme on the stacking operations of the entire storage subsystem. Both the QC and horizontal-transport operations are only included in terms of fixed transfer and handling times. The movements of the yard cranes are modelled more precisely as deterministic movement times that are based on the crane kinematics, but stochastic influences are neglected and the exact crane locations in time are not always captured. In addition, no visualisation possibilities are provided. The results of each experiment conducted by Dekker et al. (2006) and Borgman et al. (2010) are based on $n^{\mathrm{run}} = 10$ stochastically independent simulation runs with a length of $T = 15$ weeks and a warm-up period of $T^{\mathrm{warm}} = 3$ weeks to fill the yard blocks.

The studies of Choe et al. (2007), Park et al. (2010) as well as Park et al. (2011) on container stacking and crane scheduling are based on a discrete-period simulation model of an entire container terminal of small size (only three QCs and seven RMGC blocks). Only little information about the model design is provided with regard to the scenario generation, the stochastic components as well as the modelling of QC and AGV operations. The RMGC operations are modelled in comparably great detail. The exact positions in time of the crane portals are always traced, but not visualised, whereas trolley and spreader movements are not explicitly modelled. The results of each simulation experiment conducted by Choe et al. (2007) and Park et al. (2010) are obtained by conducting $n^{\mathrm{run}} = 10$ stochastically independent simulation runs. The length T of each simulation run is determined by the time required to load and unload 1,000 containers of a berthing vessel, respectively.

The simulation model used by Stahlbock and Voß (2010) to investigate the crane-scheduling problem for DRMGCs is implemented with Tecnomatix Plant Simulation and JAVA. While the crane operations of a single yard block are modelled in great detail—including the visualisation of all kinematic-based crane movements—the other terminal operations are only roughly imitated as required for the yard-block operations. Each simulation experiment is composed of $n^{\mathrm{run}} = 5$ stochastically independent simulation runs, which are terminated when a total number of 2,000 jobs have been performed by the yard cranes.

Meaningful results for practical terminal planning and operation do not just require quite realistic simulation models, but also quite realistic input data for the simulation model in terms of individual vessels, XTs and containers that have to be handled at the terminal. Considering that such real-world data of seaport container terminals is not always available—in particular not for terminals that are still being planned and/or built, as typically addressed by simulation studies on the terminal design—data generators are needed in order to create close to reality scenarios for the modelled terminal. In fact, parameter-based data generation is a discipline on its own within the field of OR. Several works covering this problem in general (e.g. Hall and Posner 2001) or for problem-specific settings (e.g. Kolisch and Sprecher 1995) are available, but there is not a whole lot of literature on data generators for the special application of seaport container terminals. Since data generation is usually not the primary focus of OR references on container-terminal issues, only little insight into the data generation processes is given. So far, only Hartmann (2004) and Voogd et al. (1999) cover directly aspects of data generation for container-terminal simulation and optimisation.

6.3 Principles for Modelling RMGC Systems

As illustrated in Fig. 6.1, there are many important steps for the success of simulation studies, but the conceptual design and the implementation of simulation models are often regarded as the most critical issues of each simulation study (Musselman 1994). Thus, several general guidelines for modelling all kinds of systems are described in the relevant simulation literature. Here, based on Musselman (1994), Law and Kelton (2000, pp. 264–289) as well as Saanen (2004, pp. 87–93, 2011) the generally applicable modelling guidelines

- Formulate clear objective,
- Define appropriate level of detail,
- Use real system/operations as leitmotif,

- Allow for flexibility,
- Consider stochastic elements,
- Ensure reproducibility of simulation results,
- Define and measure appropriate figures and
- Consider animation possibility

are identified. Compliance with these guidelines is usually expected to increase the probability of success of simulation studies if adopted appropriately for the systems under investigation. Subsequently, these guidelines are discussed with regard to their implications for modelling of front-end-loading RMGC systems, thus resulting in some RMGC-specific basic modelling principles as needed for the purpose of this work.

Target-oriented decisions usually require the formulation of a clear objective, otherwise decisions are made arbitrarily and/or may turn out to be harmful in the future. Therefore, the modelling process should be started with a clear formulation of the purpose of the simulation model in order to allow target-oriented decision-making on the level of detail, the performance figures and other modelling decisions. Referring to the research objectives of this work (see Sect. 1.2), the purpose of the needed simulation model is to investigate the effects of decisions on the design and the operation of RMGC systems for the operational performance of seaport container terminals as a whole. Thus, it is insufficient to consider the operations of container-storage yards in isolation due to their great interdependencies with other terminal subsystems. Moreover, the effects of the container-storage yard for the operational performance of the connected terminal subsystems either need to be explicitly modelled or implicitly taken into account.

Before a certain system is modelled, it needs to be decided on the required level of detail for each object and process of that system with respect to both the previously formulated model objectives and the simulation costs resulting from a model with a certain level of detail. While some objects and/or processes essentially need to be modelled in great detail, as the simulation study is primarily devoted to their investigation, other objects and/or processes are less important with regard to the model objectives and can therefore be modelled in a simplified way. Here, the RMGCs, the stored containers and the storage-yard processes are the central research objects and therefore need to be modelled in great detail. In contrast, the ship-to-shore and waterside horizontal-transport subsystems are only of minor importance for the purpose of this work, since the effects of the RMGC system on the operational performance of the total terminal system can be anticipated to a large extent from the vehicle-waiting times in the handover areas of the yard blocks (see Sect. 3.2), and therefore require a much less detailed modelling—in particular when the simulation costs in terms of modelling and experimenting times are additionally taken into account. In fact, it can be expected that several weeks of container-storage-yard operations need to be repeatedly simulated in several stochastically independent simulation runs in order to produce statistically meaningful simulation results for real RMGC systems. However, modelling and simulating all terminal operations in great detail is expected to take too much time in relation to the additional insights gained in the effects of RMGC systems on the operational performance of seaport container terminals as a whole. For similar reasons, modelling a single yard block appears to be sufficient, as only little additional insights for the research objectives of this work can be expected by modelling several identical yard blocks compared to the required computation costs.

The starting point of simulation modelling for all kinds of systems should be the real system operations. In particular, the greater the level of detail planned for certain objects or processes, the more precisely the original processes should be mirrored in the model. At a first glance, modelling different and/or simplified processes compared to the real operations may even lead to realistic performance figures, in particular when using well-defined input parameters. But such a model can hardly be used to investigate any changes of the real system—which usually is the original purpose of simulation studies—as the validity of simulation results for the real systems has to be regarded as greatly doubtful for models that are not based on the real operations. Hence, it is advisable to model all storage-yard operations as realistically as possible when primarily aiming for the investigation of the container-storage yard—as is the case here. Usually, the container business and its related processes are full of exceptions, therefore a profound knowledge of the operational processes is even more important than for other systems (Saanen 2011). Here, all information on RMGC systems that are provided in the preceding chapters should be used as a starting point for the model implementation.

In order to facilitate the experimenting with a simulation model, it should be implemented in a way that allows simple model changes with regard to the investigated objects and/or operations. Ideally, all investigated processes and operational strategies of a system are modelled as exchangeable modules, leading to reduced implementation times for new processes, improved usability of the model and directly assignable performance effects of model changes. In addition, the items of a system to be investigated should be implemented object-oriented such that both number and properties of these items can easily be changed from experiment to experiment. Altogether, the RMGC system should be modelled in a way that allows easy changes of the RMGC design and of other parameters that may affect the operational performance of RMGC systems (see Sect. 4.1.3).

An important property of most systems is the presence of stochastic operations. In order to come to valid simulation results, all stochastic elements of a system should be modelled by appropriately distributed random variables. Otherwise, invalid simulation results are yielded as the controllability of the system performance by decision makers may be systematically overestimated. Despite the inclusion of stochastic elements, it should at the same time be ensured by a simulation model that identical simulation results can be reproduced by repeatedly conducting a simulation run with the same parameter settings. This is necessary in order to facilitate the search for implementation errors and/or illogical processes as well as to allow a meaningful comparison between simulation experiments with regard to the influence of the changed parameter. Here, the container properties, in particular the arrival and departure times of containers, the announcement times of vehicle arrivals in the handover areas and the final-handover times for picking up or dropping off containers are identified as stochastic elements that need to be modelled as random (but reproducible) variables (see Sect. 4.1.3).

In order to be able to evaluate and/or compare the outcome of simulation experiments with alternative parameter settings afterwards, both the objectives of the investigated system and the associated KPIs have to be clearly specified in advance. Of course, the KPIs should be in line with the objectives in order to be able to determine to what extent the objectives are accomplished when analysing the performance indicators (Saanen 2004, pp. 92–93). On top of that, not only the KPIs might be of interest for analysing simulation experiments, but also further explanatory indicators are required for an in-depth analysis of simulation experiments with regard to the reasons for certain performance changes. Hence, it is required for good simulation modelling that both the KPIs and possible explanatory indicators of the investigated system are defined before starting its model implementation. The model should be implemented in such a way that all needed data for the defined indicators is continuously collected during each simulation run and the defined indicators are computed at the end of each run. Here, the average vehicle-waiting times in the handover areas of the yard blocks are identified as the KPIs of RMGC systems that definitely need to be measured for each simulation run. In addition, several other indicators like the crane productivities, the empty-movement times of the cranes, the interference times, the accessibility of containers in the yard block and a detailed breakdown of all these indicators with regard to job types and cranes might be helpful for a differentiated explanation of certain simulation results.

Finally, for several reasons, the feature to optionally animate a modelled system is likewise regarded as a desired feature for most simulation models. In an animation of a computer-based simulation model, the most important items of a system are represented on the screen by icons that dynamically change position, colour and other outer appearances as the simulation model evolves through time. An animation is in particular useful for debugging a simulation computer programme, showing the invalidity of a simulation model, suggesting operational procedures to be improved for a system (i.e, not all potential for improvement can be identified by analysing the numerical results only) and facilitating the discussion about the simulation model. Several investigations show that graphical methods for representing information, systems or alternative solutions improve performance, understanding and solution quality for users (Pirkul et al. 1999; Carrol et al. 1980). For these reasons, it is advisable to implement a simulation model for the purpose of this work that includes an option to animate all crane movements.

6.4 Applied Simulation Model

Based on the previously discussed modelling principles, a new discrete-event simulation model of RMGC systems at seaport container terminals is introduced in this section that is exclusively developed to reproduce the multi-objective, stochastic, real-time environment of these systems at a multi-berth facility for the special purpose of this investigation. The model is implemented and validated based on the author's work experience at several container terminals and on discussions with managers and staff members of these terminals. In this section, the newly designed RMGC-simulation model is only briefly introduced as required for the understanding and evaluation of the following simulation study. A comprehensive description of this simulation model with respect to all its functionalities, events, inputs and outputs as well as details on the implementation of all simulated processes and stochastic distributions is provided in Kemme (2011c). This section is started with a summary of the conceptual design of the newly designed simulation model, followed by a description of its main features. Thereafter, the most important model assumptions and limitations are addressed and finally, the validity of the model for real-world RMGC systems is briefly discussed.

6.4.1 Conceptual Design

The simulation model developed for the purpose of this work is able to reproduce the operations of a single RMGC yard block along with the corresponding handover areas in great detail over a user-defined period of time. The up- and downstream processes are only modelled in a very simplified way in order to keep the model at a manageable size in terms of parametrisation possibilities, simulation costs and interpretation effort. Basically, the number of bays, rows and tiers as well as the capacities of the handover areas are freely scalable and the SRMGC, TRMGC, DRMGC and TriRMGC system can be selected as the operating type of the RMGC system for the yard block.

Altogether, the implemented simulation model comprises hundreds of variables, parameters, tables, methods, dialogues and other items—each of them connected with a certain module of the simulation model that is designed to fulfil a certain function within the entire model. In total, six modules and several submodules can be distinguished. An overview of the architecture of the implemented simulation model and the interactions between its modules is given in Fig. 6.2. The simulation model is implemented using the simulation model library Tecnomatix Plant Simulation 8.2. A detailed introduction to this model library is given, for instance, by Bangsow (2008).

The scenario-creation module comprises all functions concerning the generation of reproducible container arrivals and departures for the modelled yard block. While individual containers as well as vessel and XT arrivals are randomly generated by a parameter-based data generator, the time of container arrivals and departures at the modelled yard block are determined by a data-preprocessing submodule which imitates the operations of QCs and waterside horizontal-transport machines in a simplified way.

The administration module and the drive-control module are the core of the simulation model. While the latter one executes and controls all crane movements,

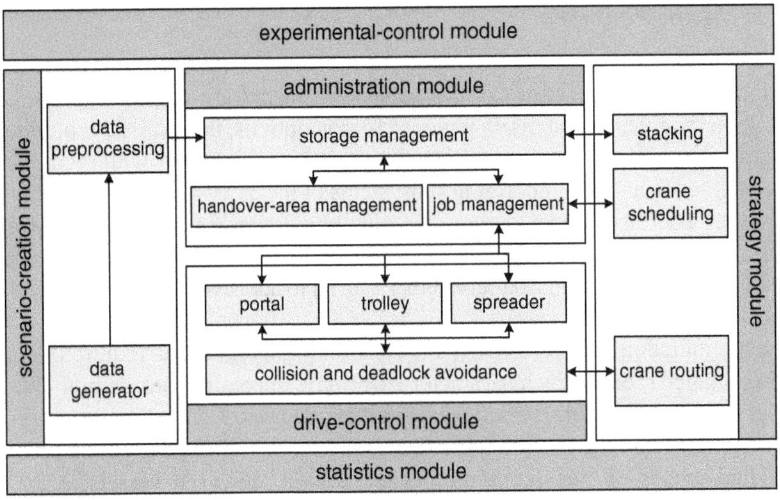

Fig. 6.2 Architecture of newly implemented RMGC-simulation model

the administration module has many functions. Firstly, the yard-block capacities are managed by the storage-management submodule. Secondly, the job-management submodule generates and manages transport jobs for the gantry cranes, initiates their scheduling and initiates the execution in the scheduled order. Thirdly, the handover-area-management submodule controls the occupancy of the handover-area capacities.

The strategy module is closely linked with the administration and drive-control modules as it contains exchangeable decision procedures for these modules. The stacking submodule decides on stacking locations for containers and returns its decision to the storage-management submodule. The crane-scheduling submodule schedules the crane assignment and sequencing of transport jobs and returns the next job for a calling crane to the job-management submodule. The crane-routing submodule decides on the routing of the RMGCs with respect to granting the right of way and executing crane-crossing manoeuvres and returns the decision to the collision and deadlock-avoidance submodule that is designed to ensure collision-free crane movements.

The experimental-control and the statistics modules have assisting cross-sectional functions for the main modules. The experimental-control module is designed to facilitate the conduct of experiments by automatic parameter changes according to a prespecified change pattern. Statistical data that is needed to evaluate simulation experiments with different parameter settings is continuously gathered and processed by the statistics module.

6.4.2 Main Features

The most noteworthy features of the simulation model are the detailed scenario-generation module, the extensive parametrisation options, the realistic reproduction of highly dynamic and stochastic RMGC systems—in particular with regard to the crane operations and the underlying subsystems of the TOS—as well as quality and quantity of provided model outputs for each simulation run. Subsequently, these features are shortly explained in order to give an impression on the quality and the level of detail of the simulation model that is used to address the research objectives of this investigation.

Each simulation run is started with the initial generation of required data for the investigated scenario by a parameter-based data-generation programme (i.e., the data-generator submodule) which is inspired by the basic data-generation approach for container terminals of Hartmann (2004). The generation programme produces individual means of transportation (feeder vessels, deep-sea vessels, XTs) and containers. The number of container arrivals at the modelled yard block (i.e., the workload) is determined by the user-specified planned average filling rate of the block $\left(\pi^{\text{fillavg}}\right)$ and its capacity $(n^{\text{x}} \times n^{\text{y}} \times n^{\text{z}})$. Hence, the workload is always adjusted to its capacity, thus allowing for meaningful comparisons of the simulation results for different yard-block layouts. For each individual vessel, the arrival times and the number of containers to-be-loaded and unloaded are randomly chosen with respect to the available berthing capacity (that is defined by the length of the quay wall) according to distributions which can be specified by the user. While the arrivals of deep-sea vessels are mainly determined by a user-specified, weekly repeated vessel-call pattern and only the exact arrival times vary by a few hours from week to week, the arrival times of XTs and feeder vessels are generated at random without any weekly repetition. Feeder vessels arrive completely at random throughout the simulation horizon with respect to the remaining berthing capacity after certain berthing windows have been reserved for deep-sea vessels. In order to realistically reproduce XT-arrival patterns (e.g., more XT arrivals at daytime than at night), the arrival times of XTs are generated such that certain user-specified fractions of XT arrivals for user-specified daily time windows are met. The exact XT-arrival times within the time windows are rectangular-distributed random variables. The randomly generated attributes for each container comprise information on the ingoing and outgoing mode of transportation, the size, the weight and the port of destination. In addition, the programme provides data generation for variable fractions of transshipment containers. Thus, pure transshipment terminals, import-export terminals and hybrid terminals can be modelled. Taking into account typical distributions of container-dwell times (see Sect. 2.3.1), each individual container c is assumed to stay $\delta_c = 1+x$ days on the terminal, where x is a random exponential-distributed variable. This yields the probability density function for δ_c

$$f\left(\delta_c\right) = \begin{cases} \frac{1}{\bar{\delta}-1} \exp(\frac{-\delta_c-1}{\bar{\delta}-1}) & \delta_c \geq 1 \\ 0 & \delta_c < 1 \end{cases} \tag{6.1}$$

which is specified by the mean container-dwell time $\overline{\delta}$. In this way, both a minimum dwell time of 1 day for each container c (i.e., $\delta_c \geq 1.0$ days, $\forall c \in C$) and an expected value for the container-dwell time of $\overline{\delta}$ days are ensured. Owing to possible differences between the dwell-time distributions of transshipment containers and import/export containers (Saanen 2004, pp. 42–43), a mean dwell time $\overline{\delta}^{\text{ts}}$ for transshipment containers and a mean dwell time $\overline{\delta}^{\text{ie}}$ for import/export containers can separately be specified by the user with the mean container-dwell time over all types of containers $\overline{\delta} = \frac{\pi^{\text{ts}}}{2} \times \overline{\delta}^{\text{ts}} + \left(1 - \frac{\pi^{\text{ts}}}{2}\right) \times \overline{\delta}^{\text{ie}}$. In summary, the data generator produces individual means of transportation and containers and assigns each container to a transport mode for delivery and pick-up in such a way that the specified distributions for means of transportation, vessel sizes, transport-mode arrival times and dwell times are matched simultaneously.

Besides the stochasticity provided by the data-generation programme, the simulation naturally contains some other stochastic components. The announcement time for each vehicle arrival at the handover area is defined to be a random triangular-distributed look-ahead time before the corresponding AGV/SC or XT is due to arrive at the block. After a vehicle has been unloaded or loaded in the handover area, the corresponding lane is not immediately released for new vehicle arrivals, but only after a random exponential-distributed period of time, in order to represent the uncertainty in the operations of manual-controlled vehicles. Owing to different degrees of uncertainty in the arrivals and operations of waterside and landside transport vehicles, different stochastic distributions for the look-ahead time and residence time of waterside and landside-arriving vehicles can be specified. Furthermore, the final-handover times at the pick-up and drop-off locations are random gamma-distributed variables. Different parameters can be defined for final-handover-time distributions in the yard block and in the waterside and landside handover areas. In order to ensure the reproducibility of simulation results when applying identical parameter settings, the random variables are implemented as seed-initialised stochastic distributions. In this way, identical random numbers are used in simulating different systems with the same seed initialisation (Park and Miller 1988).

Even though the final-handover times at the pick-up and drop-off locations are stochastic components, all crane operations including portal, trolley and spreader movements are realistically mapped in great detail. For all three crane components, the exact location in time is always captured and the load-dependent crane kinematics are explicitly modelled—not just in the form of velocities but also in terms of acceleration and deceleration times and distances for portal, trolley and spreader. In order to avoid collisions and deadlocks for TRMGC, DRMGC and TriRMGC systems, a claiming-based collision-avoidance mechanism as described in Sect. 5.4.3 is implemented. All crane movements are continuously observed and managed by the drive-control module of the simulation model.

In order to yield smooth crane operations and realistic simulation results, not just the crane operations themselves need to be realistically modelled, but also the subsystems of the TOS that are responsible for the management of the yard-block capacities and the crane-transport jobs need to be mapped in detail. In particular, the occupancy of each individual pile and the exact position of each stored container need to be known at each point in time, storage positions have to be determined and reserved for newly arriving containers, storage positions and capacities of retrieved containers have to be released, required shuffle moves need to be identified and planned and finally, all resulting types of transport jobs need to be scheduled, checked for feasibility and initiated. Within the implemented simulation model, all these tasks of the TOS are precisely mirrored by the administration module in combination with the relevant submodules of the strategy module.

In summary, the model inputs consist of parameters that specify the scenario creation, the technical crane data, the yard-block dimensions, the handover areas, the automatic experiment execution and the yard operations. The inputs for the scenario creation comprise all parameters that define the distribution of container arrivals and container attributes (e.g., mean container-dwell time, VCP –vessel-call pattern, vessel sizes, XT-arrival distribution, container-weight distributions, TEU-factor, transshipment factor). Different values for velocity, acceleration and deceleration can be individually set for portal, trolley and spreader of each crane depending on whether or not the crane is laden. The yard-block dimensions are specified by parameters on the number of bays, rows and tiers as well as on the length, width and height of a single storage slot. For both handover areas, the capacities can be specified by the user and distributions for the final handover times, the look-ahead times of vehicle arrivals and the residence time of vehicles in the handover area can be parametrised. In addition, it can be selected whether the waterside transport vehicles are either AGVs or SCs. For the automatic execution of experiments, the parameters to be changed and the corresponding change pattern as well as the number of different data realisations for the experiments have to be specified by the user. Finally, dozens of parameters for the yard operations have to be specified by the user. Most of theses parameters pertain to the container-stacking and crane-scheduling strategies, which may be individually parametrised for each crane and for each job type. The user can choose between the operational strategies listed in Table 5.7. Altogether, depending on the selected crane system between 100 and 200 parameters can be specified per simulation run.

Finally, the outputs of the simulation model are twofold. Firstly, several figures are recorded and computed for each single simulation run and each experiment. These figures include, among others, the number of performed jobs, the average filling rate, different types of crane productivities, average execution, interference and empty-movement times per job as well as average crane and vehicle-waiting times per job in the handover areas. Most of theses figures are distinguished according to the relevant crane and job type. Thus, depending on the investigated crane system between 60 and 220 figures are collected and computed for each simulation run and experiment. Secondly, during each simulation run all crane movements can be graphically displayed in a two dimensional model in any desired simulation speed. Thus, the driving behaviour of the cranes can easily be observed, which simplifies the verification and validation of the simulation model and the interpretation of performance figures. Some screenshots of the implemented simulation model, that illustrate the way crane movements are animated and that show the menu windows for specifying the scenario creation, the yard-block dimensions, the system operations, the handover areas and the crane kinematics, are provided in Appendix A.1.

6.4.3 Assumptions and Limitations

Although the great level of detail and the extensive parametrisation options of the simulation model are positively emphasised before, still several assumptions are required in order to keep the model manageable in terms of parametrisation possibilities, simulation costs and interpretation effort. Here, complying with the modelling principles (see Sect. 6.3), only simplifying model assumptions are made that do not adversely affect the validity of the entire simulation model. Most of these assumptions are made with respect to the scenario generation and the modelling detail of the up- and downstream terminal processes.

Both the QCs and the waterside horizontal-transport machines are not explicitly modelled. Instead, it is assumed that the related processes are deterministic and that a sufficient number of handling and/or transport equipment is always available, so that no waiting times for the RMGCs are induced due to late arrivals of horizontal-transport vehicles. In addition, only one yard block is modelled. Therefore, the interdependencies between processes of the whole container-storage yard, the horizontal-transport subsystem and the ship-to-shore subsystem are neglected here and the GCR cannot be used as a performance indicator. However, with respect to the purpose of this work, no crucial limitations of the simulation model are involved with these simplifying assumptions, as the measured vehicle-waiting times in the handover areas of the modelled yard block are reasonably good indicators for the effects of strategical and operational planning decisions on RMGC systems on the operational performance of seaport container terminals as a whole (see Sects. 3.2 and 6.3).

Owing to the fact that only limited, user-specified capacities for arriving vehicles are available in the waterside and landside handover areas, it needs to be defined, how to deal with arriving vehicles if the relevant handover area is fully occupied by other vehicles. Here, it is assumed that vehicles arriving to deliver a container are redirected to another yard block (i.e., the delivered container is not stored in the modelled yard block), while vehicles arriving to collect a certain container are placed in a waiting position near the yard block until the next lane in the relevant handover area becomes available (i.e., a lane in the relevant handover area is released by departure of another vehicle).

In addition, several assumptions (not necessarily real limitations) have to be made for the scenario creation. Firstly, trains and land-land movements are ignored within the model. The former assumption can be made without loss of generality since the transport between a rail station and the landside handover areas of the yard block would be performed by TTUs. Hence, the processes are similar to that for XTs, only the look-ahead time for arrivals of TTUs may be longer since the transport is controlled by the terminal. Also, no noteworthy limitation is involved with the latter assumption, since containers arriving and departing by XT are usually not desired by the terminals and only make up for very small fractions of the overall cargo volume. Secondly, some simplifying assumptions on the relations of import, export and transshipment containers are made for the creation of container flows between all considered modes of transportation in order to avoid the need for explicit specifications of all these container flows. It is assumed that transshipment containers arrive with equal shares by deep-sea and feeder vessel and that they are either going from feeder to deep-sea vessel or vice versa, but never from deep-sea to deep-sea or feeder to feeder. Furthermore, it is assumed that equal numbers of import and export containers are handled in the considered yard block. All import containers are assumed to arrive by deep-sea vessel and to depart by XT, and vice versa for export containers. Thirdly, only two different types of deep-sea and feeder vessels are modelled, which differ in length and moves per call. While the length of these vessel types are user-specified fixed parameters, the exact number of moves per call of each arriving vessel is a random rectangular-distributed variable within a vessel-type-specific interval. Fourthly, vehicle arrivals around the clock are generated as 'twenty-four-seven' terminal operations are assumed. With regard to the waterside processes, this may be a reasonable assumption for most terminals, but the landside working hours differ between terminals—often with respect to the relevant legislative provisions of the country where the terminal is located (e.g., XT-driving ban on weekends).

Finally, only 20′ and 40′ standard dry containers are created. Containers of other sizes (e.g., 45′ long, high cubes, foldable) and boxes for special goods (e.g., refrigerated goods, liquids, dangerous goods), which are accountable for about 15% of the annual throughput of a container terminal (Petering et al. 2009), are neglected. In addition, it is assumed that only a single container is either delivered or collected by each arriving vehicle in the waterside and landside handover areas. Technical errors and machine breakdowns are ignored for the RMGCs.

6.4.4 Validation and Verification

In order to use the results of a simulation model for supporting real-world planning decisions on the design and the operation of RMGC systems at seaport container terminals, it is of utmost importance that the model is without errors and valid for that purpose. This holds in particular for the simulation model developed here, as it is built from scratch without any reused simulation modules that have already been verified and/or validated before.

In general, a simulation model can be validated by applying statistical and expert validation to the graphical and numerical outputs of that model (Kleijnen 1999). In the context of automated container terminals, the use of both statistical and expert validation is recommended by Saanen (2004, pp. 159–160). However, the new simulation model developed for the purpose of this work is not designed to represent actually existing container terminals, but to support the planning of new constructions of RMGC systems. Therefore, it would be improper for validating this model to focus on the comparison of simulation results of a certain real-world model configuration with the actual performance figures of the corresponding real system. Instead, the developed model has mainly been validated by a multi-stage expert analysis of the graphical and numerical model outputs, while only some statistical validations are conducted to underpin the expert validation. The expert analysis is mainly based on the author's professional experience on design planning and operation of international seaport container terminals. In addition, several discussions with operational terminal staff (e.g., yard planner, ship planner), terminal managers (e.g., operations manager, head of terminal development, head of terminal extension project, managing director) and experienced terminal simulation people (e.g., employees and researchers in that field)—mostly current and former employees of container terminals in the port of Hamburg (Germany)—are used for the expert validation of this model.

The multi-stage expert validation of the developed simulation model is organised in several iteratively repeated steps. It is started with an inspection of the numerical simulation results of pilot runs with different model configurations. Whenever relatively extreme performance measurements are found (based on the expert evaluation), the relevant model configuration is rerun and the animation is carefully inspected for errors and/or inaccuracies of the modelled and/or implemented RMGC operations until the cause(s) for the unexpected measurements are identified. If necessary, the model is revised, the pilot runs are repeated and the expert validation of these runs is started again from the beginning. This validation process is repeated until no longer any unusual performance figures, errors and/or operational inaccuracies are found. Finally, the model resulting from the expert validation process is validated against both real-world performance figures of existing RMGC systems (e.g., HHLA CTA in Hamburg, Germany) and simulation results of other simulation models on RMGC systems (e.g., Dorndorf and Schneider 2010; Speer et al. 2011). It is found that the developed model is able to reproduce the results of these systems with only negligible differences in the compared figures (e.g., mean vehicle-waiting time in the handover area, crane productivities, container accessibility).

6.5 Concluding Remarks

In this chapter, the use of simulation as decision-support technique for planning problems of RMGC systems is addressed in detail. After introducing some basics on simulation analysis in general, a survey on simulation studies within the field of container-terminal planning and optimisation is provided, with special focus on simulation models for front-end-loading RMGC systems. Thereafter, several guiding principles for simulation modelling of RMGC systems are derived on the basis of both generally accepted modelling guidelines and the preceding literature overview on RMGC simulation. Finally, conceptual design, main features and assumptions as well as validation aspects of a new RMGC-simulation model, that is developed only for the purpose of this work, are addressed.

Numerous noteworthy advantages are offered by this simulation model compared to most known simulation models for RMGC systems. The most remarkable advantages of this simulation model are the extensive parametrisation options and the detailed reproduction of the highly dynamic, stochastic, real-time environment of an RMGC storage-yard system at a multi-berth container terminal, over a user-specified period of time. Most other simulation models that are described in the relevant literature name far fewer parametrisation options, make rather simplifying assumptions on the driving behaviour of the gantry cranes, take only berthing of a single vessel at a time into account and use comparably short simulation horizons (see Sect. 6.2). Considering all these advantages and the validity of the simulation model that has been confirmed by expert and statistical validation, the model appears to be very suitable for addressing the research objectives of this work. Hence, in the following chapter, it is used to investigate in how far the operational performance of container-storage yards is determined by decisions on the design of RMGC systems and to what extent these decisions are sensitive to changes of certain parameters—including, in particular, the choice of operational planning strategies.

Chapter 7
Simulation Study on RMGC-Design Planning

While the ground for answering the research questions of this work about the design and the operation of automated RMGC systems at seaport container terminals is prepared in the preceding chapters, this chapter is actually devoted to the numerical investigation of these questions. Within the framework of this numerical investigation, thousands of simulation experiments are conducted with the previously introduced RMGC-simulation model, statistically analysed, interpreted and discussed. Following the research objectives of this work (see Sect. 1.2), the simulation experiments are primarily targeted at the investigation of the RMGC-design-planning problem (see Chap. 4), but the effects of alternative operational strategies—that are introduced in Chap. 5—on the operational performance of RMGC systems are also compared. Firstly, the effects of decisions on the operating type of RMGC system and the yard-block layout on the operational performance of container-storage yards are investigated in great detail. Thereafter, it is investigated in how far the effects of the RMGC design on the operational performance are sensitive to changes of several factors, which include both parameters specifying the framework conditions of the regarded container terminal as well as the choice and the parametrisation of operational strategies for the container-stacking, crane-scheduling and crane-routing problems of RMGC systems.

This chapter is started with a detailed description of the experimental design of this simulation study in Sect. 7.1, including a specification of the conducted simulation experiments and the used parameter settings. Thereafter, the results of simulation experiments about the effects of RMGC-design decisions on the operational performance of the container-storage yard are presented and investigated using different statistical analysis techniques. The sensitivity analysis of the results on the terminal-design-planning problem are then presented in Sect. 7.3. In Sect. 7.4, all findings of this simulation study are discussed and summarised with respect to their practical implications. The chapter is closed with some concluding remarks.

N. Kemme, *Design and Operation of Automated Container Storage Systems*, Contributions to Management Science, DOI 10.1007/978-3-7908-2885-6_7,

7.1 Experimental Design

Complying with the typical steps in a sound simulation study, the experiments that are required in order to answer the research questions raised about RMGC systems need, first of all, to be specified before the simulation runs are actually conducted, analysed and interpreted (see Fig. 6.1). Here, the specification of the experimental design is composed of a description of the used experimental procedure, the general experimental setup and a definition of all parameter settings used for the simulation runs in order to make the obtained simulation results and findings transparent and traceable. Firstly, in Sect. 7.1.1, the experimental procedure of this simulation study is introduced, including the study objectives, the considered performance figures and the conducted simulation experiments. In Sect. 7.1.2, the general experimental setup that is used for all experiments throughout this simulation study is specified with regard to the length of each simulation run, the need for and the length of the warm-up period and the number of stochastically independent simulation runs for each experiment. Finally, a summarising overview on the default parameter settings of this simulation study is provided.

7.1.1 Experimental Procedure

Referring to the primary research objectives of this work (see Sect. 1.2), the aim is to quantify and explain the joint operational-performance effects of decisions on the operating type of RMGC system and the yard-block layout as well as to evaluate the influence of certain parameters on the operational performance and the design of RMGC systems within the framework of this simulation study.

In order to quantify the joint operational-performance effects of decisions on the operating type of RMGC system and the yard-block layout, different combinations of these terminal-design-planning variables need to be simulated and evaluated with respect to the resulting performance figures. In this study, 385 different yard-block layouts of reasonable size are each tested with the SRMGC, TRMGC, DRMGC and TriRMGC system. The number of different yard-block layouts results from combining eleven different block lengths, seven different block widths and five different stacking heights of typical order of magnitude for front-end-loading RMGC systems in every possible variation. In detail, the number of bays is varied in the interval from 28 to 48 in steps of two bays, the number of rows is changed from 6 to 12 and the number of tiers is varied in the interval from 2 to 6. In total, 1,540 simulation experiments (i.e., combinations of yard-block layouts and types of RMGC systems) are conducted for the purpose of quantifying the joint operational-performance effects of decisions on the operating type of RMGC system and the yard-block layout. Except for the changing yard-block layouts and crane systems, all other input parameters of the simulation model are set to the default settings (see Sect. 7.1.3) for these 1,540 experiments.

In order to evaluate the influence of certain parameters on the operational performance and the design of RMGC systems, some selected input parameters, that are supposed to have an effect on where RMGC-design decisions are advantageous (see Sect. 4.1.3), are investigated with respect to their operational-performance effects for varying settings within the framework of the following sensitivity analysis. The selected input parameters include the average filling rate of the yard block, the mean container-dwell time, the transshipment factor, the vessel-call pattern, the crane kinematics and the operational strategies for the container-stacking, crane-scheduling and crane-routing problems. Owing to the vast number of possible parametrisations for these input parameters, it is impossible to analyse the sensitivity of the findings about the RMGC-design-planning problem against all conceivable interdependencies between these input parameters. Instead, the sensitivity against each selected parameter is only analysed ceteris paribus. This is done by simulating the yard-block operations with different values departing from the default setting of the parameter under immediate analysis, while all other variables are held constant at their default values.

On the one hand, the selected input parameters need to be investigated for different yard-block layouts and types of RMGC systems in order to identify changes with respect to the previous findings on the operational-performance effects of the RMGC design. But on the other hand, conducting 1,540 experiments for each parameter setting of each investigated parameter would be far too time-consuming. Thus, as a trade-off between the analysis of different RMGC designs and the required simulation time, the investigated parameters are only tested for all combinations of nine representative yard-block layouts and all four types of RMGC systems. The yard-block layouts are selected with the aim to separately illustrate the operational-performance effects of an investigated parameter for the length, the width, the height and the stacking capacity of an RMGC yard block. Therefore, three different numbers of bays (28, 36, 44), rows (6, 8, 10) and tiers (2, 4, 6)—representing small, medium and large values of the corresponding block dimensions—are combined into nine different layouts in such a way that three layouts are available to study the operational-performance effects of each the block length, width, height and capacity. The nine representative yard-block layouts used to analyse the operational-performance effects of the investigated input parameters for each of these block dimensions are all in all specified in Table 7.1. For instance, for the block length, the performance effects of parameter changes are investigated by simulation experiments with the layouts "short", "medium" and "long". Altogether, 36 simulation experiments (that result from all combinations of nine layouts and four types of RMGC systems) are conducted for each parameter setting of each investigated parameter in order to analyse the effects of that parameter on decisions about the design of RMGC systems.

Due to otherwise exhaustive space requirements and only little additional insights provided, it is sensible not to display all collected figures of each simulation experiment in this work. Instead, the presentation of simulation results is mostly restricted to a subset of figures that are needed for differentiated analyses of the conducted experiments. These figures include most of all the resulting vehicle-waiting times

Table 7.1 Specification of yard-block layouts for the sensitivity analysis

Yard-block layout									
Name	Small	Low	Narrow	Short	Medium	Long	Wide	High	Big
Bays (n^x)	28	36	36	28	36	44	36	36	44
Rows (n^y)	6	8	6	8	8	8	10	8	10
Tiers (n^z)	2	2	4	4	4	4	4	6	6
$n^x \times n^y \times n^z$	336	576	864	896	1,152	1,408	1,440	1,728	2,640
Represented block dimension									
Length				√	√	√			
Width			√		√		√		
Height		√			√			√	
Capacity	√				√				√

in the handover areas of the yard block, which are identified as the most important performance figures of RMGC systems with regard to the operational performance of seaport container terminals as a whole (see Sect. 3.2). In addition to these KPIs, some explanatory figures (see Sect. 6.3)—indicating different reasons for vehicle-waiting times—are displayed and used to interpret the simulation results of this study in depth. Altogether, the simulation results of all conducted experiments are evaluated with respect to the mean vehicle-waiting time per job in the handover areas ($\overline{\omega}^{\mathrm{hr+}}_{\mathrm{total}}$, $\overline{\overline{\omega}}^{\mathrm{hr+}}_{\mathrm{total}}$), the mean XT-waiting time per job in the landside handover area ($\overline{\omega}^{\mathrm{hr+}}_{\mathrm{ls}}$, $\overline{\overline{\omega}}^{\mathrm{hr+}}_{\mathrm{ls}}$), the mean AGV/SC-waiting time per job in the waterside handover area ($\overline{\omega}^{\mathrm{hr+}}_{\mathrm{ws}}$, $\overline{\overline{\omega}}^{\mathrm{hr+}}_{\mathrm{ws}}$), the mean AGV/SC-waiting time per waterside retrieval job ($\overline{\omega}^{\mathrm{hr+}}_{\mathrm{wsout}}$,$\overline{\overline{\omega}}^{\mathrm{hr+}}_{\mathrm{wsout}}$), the 95% confidence interval of the mean AGV/SC-waiting time per waterside retrieval job (95% CI of $\overline{\omega}^{\mathrm{hr+}}_{\mathrm{wsout}}$, 95% CI of $\overline{\overline{\omega}}^{\mathrm{hr+}}_{\mathrm{wsout}}$), the mean crane-waiting time per job in the handover areas ($\overline{\omega}^{\mathrm{hr-}}_{\mathrm{total}}$, $\overline{\overline{\omega}}^{\mathrm{hr-}}_{\mathrm{total}}$), the mean crane-empty-movement time per job ($\overline{m}^{\mathrm{xye}}_{\mathrm{total}}$, $\overline{\overline{m}}^{\mathrm{xye}}_{\mathrm{total}}$), the mean crane-interference time per job ($\overline{m}^{\mathrm{cit}}_{\mathrm{total}}$, $\overline{\overline{m}}^{\mathrm{cit}}_{\mathrm{total}}$), the crane workload during the simulation horizon in terms of performed jobs ($|J|$, $\overline{|J|}$) and the container accessibility in terms of the mean number of shuffle moves per retrieval job ($\overline{\psi}$, $\overline{\overline{\psi}}$), where the resulting performance figures of a single simulation run and the averaged performance figures of a multi-run simulation experiment are denoted by the first and second tag in the brackets, respectively.

7.1.2 General Experimental Setup

For simulation models with great uncertainties involved as used for the RMGC model in this study, the outputs of only a single simulation run of somewhat arbitrary length are usually inappropriate to derive conclusions for the underlying real system, as the performance figures yielded are just estimates of their steady-state means which are based on particular realisations of random variables with probably large variances. Hence, decisions may be made on the basis of unrepresentative figures, considerably over- or underestimating the real performance of a system. As a consequence, experiments with stochastic simulation models have to be designed in such a way that the resulting estimates of steady-state means of performance figures are sufficiently reliable to make credible inferences about the modelled system. This is usually the case for unbiased steady-state means with small confidence intervals. A whole lot of techniques to improve a steady-state mean are described by Law and Kelton (2000, pp. 518–538). Usually, a steady-state mean is the more convincing, the more stochastically independent, representative data is used for its computation (i.e., the more and the longer independent simulation runs are conducted). However, not only the estimation quality of steady-state means have to be considered when defining the general experimental setup of a simulation study in terms of run length (T) and replications (n^{run}), but also the resulting simulation costs have to be taken into account. Altogether, the general experimental setup of a simulation study should be made with regard to both the simulation costs and the estimation quality of steady-state means required for the purpose of that study (Law and Kelton 2000, pp. 209–210).

In this study, the replication/deletion approach is applied to estimate the steady-state mean of the operational performance of RMGC systems. Hence, the simulation results are based on averaged values of multiple simulation runs which only use observations beyond the warm-up period for estimating the steady-state means in order to overcome the cold-start problem (Law and Kelton 2000, pp. 525–527). Owing to the fact that the modelled yard block is initially empty, it firstly needs to be filled up with containers and mixed thoroughly in order to collect representative data for estimating unbiased steady-state means of performance figures. Otherwise, the vehicle-waiting-time figures may be biased low. Based on the application of the graphical procedure of Welch (1981) to several pilot runs for estimating the steady-state mean of the mean vehicle-waiting time per waterside retrieval job ($\overline{\omega}^{\text{hr+}}_{\text{wsout}}$), the length of the warm-up period is set to $T^{\text{warm}} = 14\,\text{days}$.

By means of further pilot runs, the length T of each simulation run and the number n^{run} of independent replications are determined. It is found that no significant gain in the reliability of the simulation results is involved with very long simulation runs and exhaustive numbers of replications, as the steady-state mean estimates of the vehicle-waiting-time figures remain nearly unchanged and the corresponding confidence intervals do not improve either. Here, as a trade-off between additional reliability and simulation costs in terms of CPU runtime, the simulation length is set to $T = 42\,\text{days}$, and $n^{\text{run}} = 10$ stochastically independent replications with different seed-initialised random numbers are conducted for each experiment. The experiments are carried out in the Windows XP environment on a 2.2 GHz Pentium Dual Core 2 machine with 4 GB of RAM. The CPU runtime of the conducted experiments varies between 5 min and 7 days depending on the parameter settings used.

7.1.3 Default Parameter Settings

A detailed listing of all default parameter settings—as used throughout this simulation study—is provided in Appendix A.2. Here, only the most important parameter settings are briefly summarised, because of the huge number of possible parametrisations (see Sect. 6.4.2). The default settings of most parameters are based upon the author's professional experience, discussions with terminal staff and a number of papers on seaport container terminals (e.g., Hartmann 2004; Koch 2004; Steenken et al. 2004; Saanen and Valkengoed 2005).

The modelled yard block is embedded into a terminal with an annual throughput of $\pi^{\text{through}} = 1,250,000$ containers and a quay wall of $1,400$ m length. Its weekly repeated vessel-call pattern is depicted in Fig. 7.1. Nine deep-sea vessels arrive a week, whereof four vessels are of type 1 (1, 2, 3, 4) and five vessels are of type 2 (5, 6, 7, 8, 9). While vessels of type 1 randomly make between 2,400 and 3,600 moves per call, need 380 m berth length (including mooring) and have a maximum berthing window of 26 h each, vessels of type 2 make between 1,000 and 2,200 moves per call, need 340 m berth length and have a maximum berthing window of 16 h each. Of course, the exact arrival times and berthing windows of individual vessels vary randomly from week to week and depend on the random number of moves per call for the relevant vessel. In order to minimise driving times for the SCs, that are selected as the transport machines between the QCs and the yard blocks, it is assumed that only vessels of the first half of the quay are connected with the modelled yard block. Hence, only proportional fractions of containers that arrive or depart by vessels 1, 3, 5, 7 and 9 are stored in the block being analysed. The remaining quay-wall capacity is partly needed for arrivals of feeder vessels, which are either 210 m or 160 m long and randomly make between 100 and 180 or 40 and 100 moves per call, respectively.

The mean container-dwell time is set to $\overline{\delta} = \overline{\delta}^{\text{ts}} = \overline{\delta}^{\text{ie}} = 5$ days and the fraction of transshipment containers that are handled by the QCs is set to $\pi^{\text{ts}} = 30\%$. The TEU-factor is set to $\pi^{\text{teu}} = 1.6$. Furthermore, container arrivals are generated that yield an average filling rate of $\pi^{\text{fillavg}} = 75\%$ for the modelled yard block and a maximum block-filling rate of $\pi^{\text{fillmax}} = 80\%$ is allowed. A handover-area capacity of 10 containers is defined for the waterside handover area, while the capacity of the landside handover area is set to 6 XTs. The average residence time of XTs and SCs in the landside and waterside handover areas after loading or unloading a container is set to 90 s and 30 s, respectively. The triangular-distributed look-ahead times for vehicle arrivals in the waterside and landside handover areas are parametrised with $m_j^{\text{lat}} = (180, 300, 1320)$ s and $m_j^{\text{lat}} = (0, 60, 120)$ s, respectively.

The maximum speed of the crane portal is set to $4.0\,{}^{\text{m}}/_{\text{s}}$ for the inner small crane and to $3.5\,{}^{\text{m}}/_{\text{s}}$ for the outer large crane. Acceleration as well as deceleration of both portals are set to $0.8\,{}^{\text{m}}/_{\text{s}^2}$ and $1.0\,{}^{\text{m}}/_{\text{s}^2}$ for laden and unladen driving, respectively. For all trolleys, the maximum speed is assumed to be $1.0\,{}^{\text{m}}/_{\text{s}}$, independently of whether they are laden or not. The maximum lifting speed of the spreader is $0.8\,{}^{\text{m}}/_{\text{s}}$ if laden and $1.0\,{}^{\text{m}}/_{\text{s}}$ if empty. Acceleration and deceleration of all trolleys

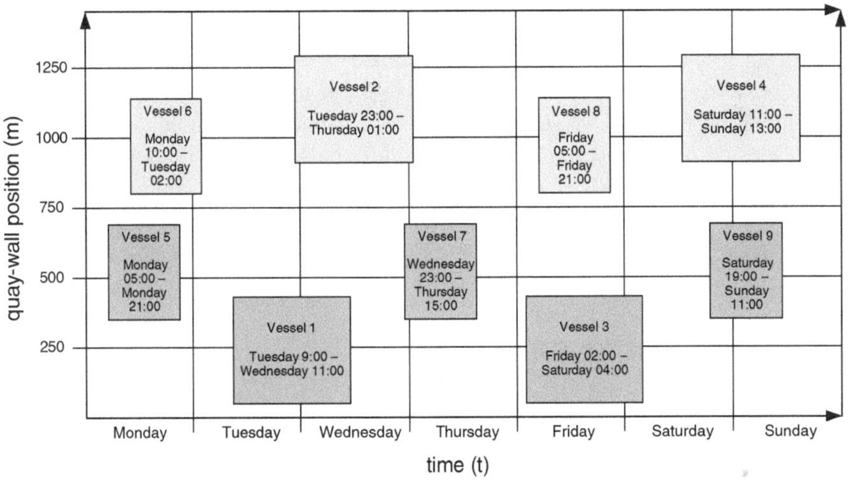

Fig. 7.1 Schematic illustration of weekly repeated vessel-call pattern VCP1

and spreaders are set to $0.4\,{}^{\mathrm{m}}\!/_{\mathrm{s}^2}$ and $0.5\,{}^{\mathrm{m}}\!/_{\mathrm{s}^2}$ for laden and empty movements, respectively. The gamma-distributed final-handover times of the spreader are parametrised with $h^{\mathrm{ws}} = (\mu = 10.00, \sigma = 4.47)$ s for the waterside handover area, $h^{\mathrm{ls}} = (40.00, 20.00)$ s for the landside handover area and $h^{\mathrm{b}} = (6.00, 2.68)$ s for inside the yard block.

Stacking positions for containers are determined in real-time by applying the CCFS container-positioning method (see Sect. 5.2.4). The cost function of that container-positioning method is parametrised such that containers departing by deep-sea vessel are stacked similarly as with the category-stacking strategy, while containers departing by feeder vessel or XT are stacked somehow randomly, but not intermingled with containers departing by other modes of transportation. Workload-smoothing objectives are only used as a tie breaker and retrieval-time aspects are completely neglected for the default parametrisation of the CCFS method. Likewise, the possibility for workload smoothing by use of the HHS method (see Sect. 5.2.5) is initially not used.

In the related simulation study of Kemme (2011a), it is argued that the resulting performance figures in terms of vehicle-waiting times suffer from the application of the simple EDD priority rule. Therefore, longer vehicle-waiting times than observed for relevant real-world systems are yielded in that simulation study. Here, based on several pilot experiments with different crane-scheduling strategies, a more elaborated scheduling strategy is defined as default that is able to produce more realistic performance figures in similarly short simulation times. As in Kemme (2011a), assigning job j with $\tau(j)$ to crane c is not restricted by any preselection method. But contrary to Kemme (2011a), PRIO2 is applied as the solution method here. Based on several preliminary experiments, the cost factors of the underlying cost function of PRIO2 are set to $\lambda^{\mathrm{edt}}_{\tau(j),g} = 7$, $\lambda^{\mathrm{late}}_{\tau(j),g} = -1$ and $\lambda^{\mathrm{early}}_{\tau(j),g} = 9$ for all $(\tau(j), g) \notin \{(\text{wsout}, 1); (\text{wsout}, 3)\}$ and to $\lambda^{\text{edt}}_{\tau(j),g} = 0.07$, $\lambda^{\text{late}}_{\tau(j),g} = -100$ and $\lambda^{\text{early}}_{\tau(j),g} = 0.09$ for $(\tau(j), g) \in \{(\text{wsout}, 1); (\text{wsout}, 3)\}$, thus resulting in a prioritised assignment of waterside retrieval jobs due to being most important for the operational performance of seaport container terminals as a whole (see Sect. 3.2). The cranes are routed according to the claiming-based routing rules introduced in Sect. 5.4.3. For the DRMGC and TriRMGC systems, CCP4 is applied in order to reduce the trolley-movement times of the outer large cranes required for crossing manoeuvres as much as possible, but the HAC mechanism is by default not used.

7.2 Results of RMGC-Design Study

In this section, the simulation results of all 1,540 experiments on the operational-performance effects of RMGC-design decisions, that are conducted with the previously introduced experimental setup and default parameter settings, are presented, analysed and discussed in great detail. Owing to the great number of conducted simulation experiments and collected performance figures, it is not sensible to explicitly display all simulation results here. Instead, only the most important performance figures of all RMGC designs with the nine example yard-block layouts (see Table 7.1) are actually shown in this section. These results are used as a starting point and motivation for a following, more detailed statistical analysis that is based on the results of all 1,540 simulation experiments and all 15,400 simulation runs.

In Sect. 7.2.1, the example simulation results are presented and discussed with respect to first observations on the dependencies of the presented performance figures and the operational-performance effects of RMGC-design alternatives. Based on this discussion of the example results and the deliberations in the preceding chapters, a number of research hypotheses are derived, which are then extensively investigated and validated in Sect. 7.2.2 by applying a variety of statistical analysis technology to all simulation results. Finally, the basic findings of this section about the joint effects of the yard-block layout and the operating type of RMGC system on the operational performance of container-storage yards are summarised in Sect. 7.2.3.

7.2.1 *First Observations and Formulation of Research Hypotheses*

A summarising impression on the simulation results of the whole simulation study on RMGC-design planning is given by the example results displayed in the Tables 7.2 and 7.3. The first table shows the most important performance figures for the nine representative yard-block layouts with both the SRMGC and TRMGC systems, while selected figures of DRMGC and TriRMGC systems for each of these layouts are shown in the second table. On close examination of these example results, a number of observations can be made on the mutual dependencies of these

Table 7.2 Performance figures for selected layouts of SRMGC and TRMGC systems

RMGC type	RMGC design: Block layout Name	n^x	n^y	n^z	Capacity	Vehicle-waiting-time figures: $\overline{\overline{\omega}}^{hr+}_{total}$ (s)	$\overline{\overline{\omega}}^{hr+}_{ls}$ (s)	$\overline{\overline{\omega}}^{hr+}_{ws}$ (s)	$\overline{\overline{\omega}}^{hr+}_{wsout}$ (s)	95% CI of $\overline{\overline{\omega}}^{hr+}_{wsout}$ (s)	Explanatory figures: $\overline{\overline{\omega}}^{hr-}_{total}$ (s)	$\overline{\overline{m}}^{xye}_{total}$ (s)	$\overline{\overline{m}}^{cit}_{total}$ (s)	$\overline{\lvert J\rvert}$ (jobs)	$\overline{\overline{\psi}}$ (jobs)
SRMGC	Small	28	6	2	336	28.26	65.90	1.69	3.24	(1.98;4.50)	124.38	26.05	0.00	1,871.8	0.322
	Low	36	8	2	576	41.28	95.41	2.86	5.52	(4.25;6.79)	94.92	31.87	0.00	3,208.8	0.300
	Narrow	36	6	4	864	117.06	226.61	40.46	78.00	(69.34;86.66)	63.84	26.97	0.00	6,596.5	1.135
	Short	28	8	4	896	100.44	204.03	28.71	56.04	(48.36;63.72)	67.26	23.22	0.00	6,792.8	1.120
	Medium	36	8	4	1,152	198.96	336.25	102.93	198.72	(182.82;214.62)	41.52	26.63	0.00	8,683.4	1.103
	Long	44	8	4	1,408	561.06	772.82	410.23	789.12	(739.00;839.24)	22.86	29.48	0.00	10,466.3	1.083
	Wide	36	10	4	1,440	484.56	675.77	350.05	671.58	(605.34;737.82)	25.80	26.57	0.00	10,776.3	1.083
	High	36	8	6	1,728	1,861.32	2,244.74	1,597.83	3,180.30	(3,050.94;3,309.66)	14.64	23.73	0.00	13,369.4	1.606
	Big	44	10	6	2,640	3,269.94	3,903.45	2,837.74	4,959.72	(4,798.04;5,121.40)	7.08	27.72	0.00	13,711.1	1.144
TRMGC	Small	28	6	2	336	8.82	19.48	1.19	2.28	(1.18;3.38)	135.84	23.34	2.22	1,903.5	0.324
	Low	36	8	2	576	13.44	29.13	2.14	4.14	(3.00;5.28)	112.32	28.35	2.10	3,224.1	0.296
	Narrow	36	6	4	864	38.16	82.08	7.79	15.06	(13.56;16.56)	87.84	33.76	11.92	6,592.4	1.127
	Short	28	8	4	896	35.58	77.19	6.74	13.20	(12.05;14.35)	91.26	30.25	12.42	6,857.8	1.130
	Medium	36	8	4	1,152	48.30	98.58	13.31	25.80	(23.23;28.37)	67.86	34.07	12.16	8,784.5	1.130
	Long	44	8	4	1,408	67.44	126.78	25.15	48.48	(41.71;55.25)	50.28	38.12	11.92	10,615.3	1.097
	Wide	36	10	4	1,440	61.98	118.96	21.79	42.12	(36.99;47.25)	53.40	34.64	12.14	10,900.6	1.090
	High	36	8	6	1,728	304.08	387.72	247.50	486.30	(452.65;519.95)	38.58	37.21	19.43	15,170.8	1.762
	Big	44	10	6	2,640	1,567.38	1,540.04	1,586.02	3,019.80	(2,787.82;3,251.78)	10.56	40.77	20.71	21,104.9	1.675

$\overline{\overline{\omega}}^{hr+}_{total}$: mean vehicle-waiting time per job in the handover areas, $\overline{\overline{\omega}}^{hr+}_{ls}$: mean XT-waiting time per job in the landside handover area, $\overline{\overline{\omega}}^{hr+}_{ws}$: mean SC-waiting time per job in the waterside handover area, $\overline{\overline{\omega}}^{hr+}_{wsout}$: mean SC-waiting time per waterside retrieval job, 95% CI of $\overline{\overline{\omega}}^{hr+}_{wsout}$: 95% confidence interval of mean SC-waiting time per waterside retrieval job, $\overline{\overline{\omega}}^{hr-}_{total}$: mean crane-waiting time per job in the handover areas, $\overline{\overline{m}}^{xye}_{total}$: mean crane-empty-movement time per job, $\overline{\overline{m}}^{cit}_{total}$: mean crane-interference time per job, $\overline{\lvert J\rvert}$: average crane workload during simulation horizon, $\overline{\overline{\psi}}$: mean number of shuffle moves per retrieval job

Table 7.3 Performance figures for selected layouts of DRMGC and TriRMGC systems

	RMGC design					Vehicle-waiting time-figures					Explanatory figures				
RMGC type	Block layout Name	n^x	n^y	n^z	Capacity	$\overline{\overline{\omega}}^{hr+}_{total}$ (s)	$\overline{\overline{\omega}}^{hr+}_{ls}$ (s)	$\overline{\overline{\omega}}^{hr+}_{ws}$ (s)	$\overline{\overline{\omega}}^{hr+}_{wsout}$ (s)	95% CI of $\overline{\overline{\omega}}^{hr+}_{wsout}$ (s)	$\overline{\overline{\omega}}^{hr-}_{total}$ (s)	$\overline{\overline{m}}^{xye}_{total}$ (s)	$\overline{\overline{m}}^{cit}_{total}$ (s)	$\overline{\lvert J \rvert}$ (jobs)	$\overline{\overline{\psi}}$ (jobs)
DRMGC	Small	28	6	2	336	13.86	31.48	1.44	2.76	(1.87;3.65)	139.32	55.77	31.09	1,901.9	0.320
	Low	36	8	2	576	23.58	52.60	2.76	5.34	(3.95;6.73)	117.48	69.14	38.13	3,222.4	0.297
	Narrow	36	6	4	864	53.82	116.45	10.37	20.10	(17.76;22.44)	95.28	62.73	35.30	6,623.5	1.137
	Short	28	8	4	896	54.36	118.90	9.57	18.72	(16.09;21.35)	95.46	62.89	39.74	6,834.0	1.118
	Medium	36	8	4	1,152	69.24	146.10	15.89	30.78	(28.28;33.28)	75.18	62.78	35.31	8,713.7	1.107
	Long	44	8	4	1,408	88.86	179.24	24.57	47.46	(44.41;50.51)	57.24	61.85	29.73	10,605.3	1.093
	Wide	36	10	4	1,440	88.86	181.10	23.92	46.26	(42.21;50.31)	57.66	60.88	32.78	10,893.6	1.087
	High	36	8	6	1,728	360.18	509.39	259.60	510.54	(474.32;546.76)	44.52	52.25	28.21	15,175.5	1.753
	Big	44	10	6	2,640	1,607.82	1,907.61	1,401.64	2,758.62	(2,599.69;2,917.55)	12.60	45.15	20.21	21,213.5	1.673
TriRMGC	Small	28	6	2	336	8.82	19.56	1.16	2.22	(1.65;2.79)	140.40	51.55	31.02	1,907.0	0.325
	Low	36	8	2	576	12.48	26.47	2.76	5.34	(4.31;6.37)	121.98	65.81	40.31	3,249.5	0.298
	Narrow	36	6	4	864	31.26	66.99	6.61	12.90	(11.33;14.47)	103.44	69.11	48.66	6,614.4	1.122
	Short	28	8	4	896	31.86	68.47	6.48	12.54	(10.08;15.00)	101.10	68.63	53.32	6,831.8	1.123
	Medium	36	8	4	1,152	37.98	80.43	8.44	16.32	(14.91;17.73)	84.00	70.12	49.18	8,732.5	1.113
	Long	44	8	4	1,408	46.86	98.14	10.23	19.68	(17.70;21.66)	68.22	70.81	44.71	10,583.9	1.092
	Wide	36	10	4	1,440	46.86	98.35	10.85	20.94	(19.44;22.44)	68.64	70.15	47.95	10,895.8	1.090
	High	36	8	6	1,728	117.54	208.77	56.00	109.68	(102.38;116.98)	58.38	66.70	49.43	15,192.1	1.763
	Big	44	10	6	2,640	574.98	754.71	451.96	883.26	(805.91;960.61)	23.88	60.22	41.62	23,097.9	1.758

$\overline{\overline{\omega}}^{hr+}_{total}$: mean vehicle-waiting time per job in the handover areas, $\overline{\overline{\omega}}^{hr+}_{ls}$: mean XT-waiting time per job in the landside handover area, $\overline{\overline{\omega}}^{hr+}_{ws}$: mean SC-waiting time per job in the waterside handover area, $\overline{\overline{\omega}}^{hr+}_{wsout}$: mean SC-waiting time per waterside retrieval job, 95% CI of $\overline{\overline{\omega}}^{hr+}_{wsout}$: 95% confidence interval of mean SC-waiting time per waterside retrieval job, $\overline{\overline{\omega}}^{hr-}_{total}$: mean crane-waiting time per job in the handover areas, $\overline{\overline{m}}^{xye}_{total}$: mean crane-empty-movement time per job, $\overline{\overline{m}}^{cit}_{total}$: mean crane-interference time per job, $\overline{\lvert J \rvert}$: average crane workload during simulation horizon, $\overline{\overline{\psi}}$: mean number of shuffle moves per retrieval job figures and on the operational-performance effects of the yard-block capacity, the yard-block dimensions and the operating type the of RMGC system—which mostly agree with causal relations that are qualitatively discussed in the preceding chapters.

7.2.1.1 Interdependencies of Performance Figures

With regard to the vehicle-waiting-time figures, it can be observed from the example simulation results that changes in the RMGC design have similar effects on all displayed waiting-time figures. The longer (shorter) $\overline{\overline{\omega}}_{\text{total}}^{\text{hr+}}$, the longer (shorter) are also $\overline{\overline{\omega}}_{\text{ls}}^{\text{hr+}}$, $\overline{\overline{\omega}}_{\text{ws}}^{\text{hr+}}$ and $\overline{\overline{\omega}}_{\text{wsout}}^{\text{hr+}}$. However, this can mostly be explained by trivial mathematical connections between these figures, instead of causal effects of the RMGC design. The mean vehicle-waiting time per job in both handover areas ($\overline{\overline{\omega}}_{\text{total}}^{\text{hr+}}$) is computed as the weighted average of landside ($\overline{\overline{\omega}}_{\text{ls}}^{\text{hr+}}$) and waterside mean vehicle-waiting times ($\overline{\overline{\omega}}_{\text{ws}}^{\text{hr+}}$). Owing to the share of transshipment containers, a greater number of vehicles need to be served at the waterside end of the yard block, and therefore $\overline{\overline{\omega}}_{\text{total}}^{\text{hr+}}$ is more affected by $\overline{\overline{\omega}}_{\text{ws}}^{\text{hr+}}$ than by $\overline{\overline{\omega}}_{\text{ls}}^{\text{hr+}}$. Similarly, the waterside mean vehicle-waiting time ($\overline{\overline{\omega}}_{\text{ws}}^{\text{hr+}}$) is defined by the weighted average of mean vehicle-waiting times for waterside storage and retrieval jobs. Due to the fact that SCs never need to wait in the handover areas when delivering containers, no vehicle-waiting time is induced for waterside storage jobs, but only for waterside retrieval jobs. Further considering the assumption on identical numbers of imported and exported containers throughout the simulation horizon (see Sect. 6.4.3), $\overline{\overline{\omega}}_{\text{ws}}^{\text{hr+}}$ is expected to be roughly half as long as $\overline{\overline{\omega}}_{\text{wsout}}^{\text{hr+}}$, just as it is observed for the example results. In contrast, the figures for vehicle-waiting times in the landside ($\overline{\overline{\omega}}_{\text{ls}}^{\text{hr+}}$) and waterside handover areas ($\overline{\overline{\omega}}_{\text{ws}}^{\text{hr+}}$, $\overline{\overline{\omega}}_{\text{wsout}}^{\text{hr+}}$) are not directly mathematically related to each other. But because most stored containers (i.e., all import and export containers) induce crane workload at both block ends and this crane workload is handled by the same (scarce) crane resources, changes in the RMGC design in terms of yard-block layout and operating type of RMGC system can be expected to have similar causal effects on the crane workload and the available crane resources for both handover areas. This leads to similar effects on the vehicle-waiting times in both handover areas (see Sect. 4.1.3).

In addition, it can be observed from the example results, that the mean XT-waiting time per job in the landside handover area ($\overline{\overline{\omega}}_{\text{ls}}^{\text{hr+}}$) is much longer than the mean SC-waiting time per job in the waterside handover area ($\overline{\overline{\omega}}_{\text{ws}}^{\text{hr+}}$), which can be simply explained as XTs need to wait for unloading and loading (i.e., storage and retrieval jobs) while SCs only need to wait for container supply (i.e., retrieval jobs). Thus, there is no risk for vehicle-waiting times for approximately half of the waterside crane jobs, while vehicle-waiting times can occur for all landside crane jobs. But for most of the example experiments the mean XT-waiting time per job in the landside handover area ($\overline{\overline{\omega}}_{\text{ls}}^{\text{hr+}}$) is even longer than the mean

SC-waiting time per waterside retrieval job ($\overline{\overline{\omega}}_{\text{wsout}}^{\text{hr+}}$), even though SC-waiting times can be connected with each waterside retrieval. This may be explained by both on average shorter look-ahead times for XT arrivals than for SC arrivals and greater numbers of shuffle moves required for landside retrieval jobs than for waterside retrieval jobs due to the use of the simple random-based container-positioning method for landside-departing containers compared to the shuffle-move-minimising category-stacking-based method applied to most waterside-departing containers (see Sect. 7.1.3). Based on all these observations and particular examples for the dependencies and differences of landside and waterside vehicle-waiting times, Research hypotheses 1.1.1 and 1.1.2 are formulated:

Research Hypothesis 1.1.1. All considered mean vehicle-waiting-time figures are significantly positively correlated with each other.

Research Hypothesis 1.1.2. The mean XT-waiting time per job in the landside handover area ($\overline{\omega}_{\text{ls}}^{\text{hr+}}$, $\overline{\overline{\omega}}_{\text{ls}}^{\text{hr+}}$) is significantly longer than both the mean SC-waiting time per job in the waterside handover area ($\overline{\omega}_{\text{ws}}^{\text{hr+}}$, $\overline{\overline{\omega}}_{\text{ws}}^{\text{hr+}}$) and the mean SC-waiting time per waterside retrieval job ($\overline{\omega}_{\text{wsout}}^{\text{hr+}}$, $\overline{\overline{\omega}}_{\text{wsout}}^{\text{hr+}}$).

Only little, intuitively expected observations on generally valid causal dependencies between the vehicle-waiting times in the handover areas and the named explanatory figures are made by a closer examination of the example results. For the shown design alternatives, longer mean vehicle-waiting times are accompanied with both increases and decreases of the mean crane-empty-movement time per job ($\overline{\overline{m}}_{\text{total}}^{\text{xye}}$), the mean crane-interference time per job ($\overline{\overline{m}}_{\text{total}}^{\text{cit}}$) and the mean number of shuffle moves per retrieval job ($\overline{\overline{\psi}}$). Thus, it may be concluded, that the vehicle-waiting times cannot be solely explained by one of these explanatory figures. Moreover, the yard-block layout and other explanatory figures have to be considered for evaluating the waiting-time effects of $\overline{\overline{m}}_{\text{total}}^{\text{xye}}$, $\overline{\overline{m}}_{\text{total}}^{\text{cit}}$ and $\overline{\overline{\psi}}$. In contrast, the vehicle-waiting times in the handover areas can be observed to increase with the average crane workload during the simulation horizon ($\overline{|J|}$) independently of the RMGC design, thus indicating a significant importance of the crane workload for the resulting vehicle-waiting times of all yard-block layouts and types of RMGC systems. This can be explained by the greater risk for and extent of jobs that need to be performed at about the same time with increasing workload, which in turn leads to an increasing risk for and extent of jobs being performed too late, thus increasing the mean vehicle-waiting times (see Sect. 4.1.3). In addition, the vehicle-waiting times are observed to increase with decreasing mean crane-waiting time per job in the handover areas ($\overline{\overline{\omega}}_{\text{total}}^{\text{hr}-}$), although it is argued in Sect. 5.3.1, that the vehicle-waiting times are expected to decrease with decreasing crane-waiting times. However, this is only true ceteris paribus, but not for different crane workloads like in this design study. Instead, increasing crane workloads reduce the possibility for and the extent of early crane arrivals in the handover areas, thus reducing the mean crane-waiting times, while increasing the mean vehicle-waiting times. Altogether, it can be logically explained and observed from the example simulation results that the crane workload is of great importance for several performance figures of all types of RMGC systems, which is summarised by Research hypotheses 1.1.3 and 1.1.4:

Research Hypothesis 1.1.3. The crane workload during the simulation horizon ($|J|$, $\overline{|J|}$) is significantly positively correlated with the mean vehicle-waiting times in the handover areas.

Research Hypothesis 1.1.4. The crane workload during the simulation horizon ($|J|$, $\overline{|J|}$) is significantly negatively correlated with the mean crane-waiting time in the handover areas ($\overline{\omega}^{hr-}_{total}$, $\overline{\overline{\omega}}^{hr-}_{total}$).

7.2.1.2 Effects of Yard-Block Capacity

Owing to the assumed constant filling rate of the yard block, the crane workload during the simulation horizon is mostly defined by the stacking capacity of the yard block (see Sect. 6.4.2). Therefore, it is observed from the example simulation results that both the crane workload during the simulation horizon and the mean vehicle-waiting times in the handover areas steadily increase with growing stacking capacity for each type of RMGC system. In addition, it can be seen from the example results, that the mean vehicle-waiting time for waterside retrieval jobs are mostly smaller than for landside jobs. Only for yard-block layouts with comparably large storage capacities, like "big", "high" and/or "long" this relation is reversed. Thus, it may be supposed that the mean vehicle-waiting time for waterside retrieval jobs ($\overline{\overline{\omega}}^{hr+}_{wsout}$) is more sensitive to changes in the yard-block capacity (i.e., growing faster with increasing capacity) than the mean vehicle-waiting time for landside jobs ($\overline{\overline{\omega}}^{hr+}_{ls}$). This may be explained by two causal factors: Firstly, the waterside handover area capacities are greater than the landside capacities. Secondly, discontinuous vessel arrivals may cause greater peak workloads at the waterside block end than the more continuous XT-arrivals at the landside block end. As a consequence, a potentially greater number of and a greater risk for simultaneously waiting vehicles may be involved with the waterside handover area than with the landside end of the block, thus possibly leading to a greater risk for and extent of vehicle-waiting times with increasing storage capacity for waterside retrieval jobs than for landside jobs. Based on these observations and causal explanations, Research hypotheses 1.2.1 and 1.2.2 are formulated on the operational-performance effects of the yard-block capacity for the total simulation results:

Research Hypothesis 1.2.1. The capacity of RMGC yard blocks ($n^x \times n^y \times n^z$) has significantly positive effects on the mean vehicle-waiting times in the handover areas.

Research Hypothesis 1.2.2. The capacity of RMGC yard blocks ($n^x \times n^y \times n^z$) has significantly greater effects on the mean vehicle-waiting time per waterside retrieval job ($\overline{\omega}^{\text{hr+}}_{\text{wsout}}$, $\overline{\overline{\omega}}^{\text{hr+}}_{\text{wsout}}$) than on the mean vehicle-waiting time in the landside handover area ($\overline{\omega}^{\text{hr+}}_{\text{ls}}$, $\overline{\overline{\omega}}^{\text{hr+}}_{\text{ls}}$).

7.2.1.3 Effects of Yard-Block Dimensions

The stacking capacity of a yard block is in turn defined by the multiplication of its dimensions. Therefore, longer vehicle-waiting times can be expected with increasing length, width and height of the yard block. In fact, it can be observed for the example layouts of each type of RMGC system that the vehicle-waiting times increase with growing block length (see layouts "short", "medium" and "long"), width (see layouts "narrow", " medium" and "wide") and height (see layouts "low", "medium" and "high"). However, a closer examination of the example simulation results, leads to the conjecture that increases in the vehicle-waiting times with growing block dimensions are not only caused by capacity-based increases of the crane workload, but also by other, intuitively expected side effects.

From the example layouts "low", "medium" and "high", it can be observed that the mean number of shuffle moves per retrieval job ($\overline{\overline{\psi}}$) increases with each additional tier for all types of RMGC systems. As a consequence, compared to increases of the block length and width, not only additional storage and retrieval jobs (i.e., productive crane workload) need to be performed with growing stacking height, but also overproportionally large numbers of shuffle jobs (i.e., unproductive crane workload) are additionally induced, which tie up valuable crane resources and thus, further increase the risk for and the extent of delayed executions for main jobs.

In addition, it is observed from the example layouts "short", "medium" and "long" that the mean crane-empty-movement time per job ($\overline{\overline{m}}^{\text{xye}}_{\text{total}}$) increases with the length of the block, which can be explained by prolonged crane-driving distances for longer yard blocks. As a consequence, the crane resources are, on average, tied up longer for the processing of a crane job, thus leading to an increased risk for and extent of delayed unloading and loading of vehicles in the handover areas. However, from the example results it can be seen that the mean empty-movement time only increases by very few seconds with growing block lengths, while the execution of each additional shuffle move that is induced by increases of the stacking height may take up to a few minutes. Thus, increases in the stacking height can be expected to tie up more crane resources and to induce longer vehicle-waiting times than increases in the length of the yard block. For increases of the block width, no further vehicle-waiting-time-prolonging side effects are observed in addition to the capacity-based increase of the crane workload. Based on these observations on the operational-performance effects of the yard-block dimensions, Research hypotheses 1.3.1–1.3.3 are formulated:

Research Hypothesis 1.3.1. The height (n^{z}), length (n^{x}) and width (n^{y}) of the yard block have significantly positive effects on the mean vehicle-waiting times in the handover areas.

Research Hypothesis 1.3.2. The height of the yard block (n^z) has significantly greater effects on the mean vehicle-waiting times in the handover areas than the length (n^x) and width of the block (n^y).

Research Hypothesis 1.3.3. The length of the yard block (n^x) has significantly greater effects on the mean vehicle-waiting times in the handover areas than the width of the block (n^y).

7.2.1.4 Effects of Crane Systems

Finally, several observations on the operational-performance effects of the operating type of the RMGC system can be made from the example simulation results. It can be seen that the vehicle-waiting times of each representative yard-block layout are the shorter, the more cranes are used by the relevant type of RMGC system. As a consequence, the TriRMGC system is observed to yield the shortest vehicle-waiting times, while the longest waiting times are induced by the SRMGC system. The resulting vehicle-waiting times with the TRMGC and DRMGC systems seem to be comparable and somewhere in between the SRMGC and TriRMGC systems, but with slight advantages for the TRMGC system. These observations can be explained through additionally available crane resources for the same amount of workload for each yard-block layout with increasing numbers of cranes deployed per yard block, thus reducing the risk for and the extent of vehicle-waiting times in the handover areas. But at the same time, it can be observed from the example results, that the mean crane-interference time per job ($\overline{\overline{m}}^{cit}_{total}$) increases with the number of cranes deployed per yard block. For the DRMGC system, more interference time is observed than for the TRMGC system, which may be a causal explanation for the slightly longer vehicle-waiting times as compared to the TRMGC system. This is surprising at first glance because of the greater operational flexibility that is involved with the DRMGC system. As a consequence of these observations on the operational-performance effects of the operating type of RMGC system, Research hypotheses 1.4.1 and 1.4.2 are formulated:

Research Hypothesis 1.4.1. The number of cranes deployed per block has significantly negative effects on the mean vehicle-waiting times in the handover areas.

Research Hypothesis 1.4.2. Significantly shorter mean vehicle-waiting times in the handover areas are obtained by the TRMGC system than by the DRMGC system.

7.2.2 In-Depth Analysis of Simulation Results

All observations and research hypotheses on dependencies of RMGC-performance figures and operational-performance effects of RMGC-design alternatives, that have so far been made on the basis of the example simulation results shown in the

Tables 7.2 and 7.3, are statistically investigated in this subsection using the results of all 1,540 simulation experiments and/or 15,400 simulation runs of this RMGC-design study. It is started with the investigation of interdependencies between the considered RMGC-performance figures and the validation of Research hypotheses 1.1.1–1.1.4, which is followed by an analysis of the operational-performance effects of the yard-block capacity, with particular focus on the validation of Research hypotheses 1.2.1 and 1.2.2. Thereafter, the operational-performance effects of all three yard-block dimensions are investigated and Research hypotheses 1.3.1–1.3.3 are tested as well as statistically validated. Finally, the investigation and validation of Research hypotheses 1.4.1 and 1.4.2 on the operational-performance effects of the type of RMGC system are addressed.

7.2.2.1 Interdependencies of Performance Figures

Regardless of any RMGC-design effects, several interdependencies between the most important performance figures of RMGC systems are identified and discussed in the previous subsection. Statistical tests with the collected data of all 15,400 simulation runs for normal distribution reveal that none of the regarded performance figures is normally distributed, which may be explained by biasing effects of the RMGC design. As a consequence, the widely used Pearson product-moment correlation coefficient is unsuited to evaluate the strength and significance of linear dependencies between the regarded performance figures (Stigler 1989). Instead, the Kendall-rank-correlation coefficient and the non-parametric tau hypothesis test are used to measure the strength and significance of associations between the performance figures, due to being particularly suited for non-normally distributed variables (Kendall 1938). The pairwise Kendall-rank-correlation coefficients between all considered performance figures in terms of Kendall-tau-b are shown in Table 7.4. The correlations postulated by Research hypotheses 1.1.1–1.1.4 are indicated in bold.

Most observations on causal connections between the RMGC-performance figures are confirmed by comparably high correlation coefficients. Here, in the context of analysing and interpreting simulation results, only strong and very strong correlations, that are indicated by absolute values of correlation coefficients in the interval $[0.6, 0.8)$ and $[0.8, 1.0)$, respectively (Brosius 1998, p. 503), are regarded as sufficiently convincing to derive and/or confirm general causal connections between RMGC-performance figures. Correlations indicated by coefficients with only absolute values in the range from 0.0 to 0.6 (i.e., very weak to mid-level correlations) are either regarded as unsubstantiated or expected to be influenced by the RMGC design.

However, even a high correlation coefficient does not necessarily indicate that there actually is a statistical connection between two variables, as the computed coefficients may possibly be resulting from contingencies in the collected data. A connection between variables is called to be significant if it is very unlikely caused by contingencies. In order to confirm a significant statistical connection between two variables, the hypothesis on this connection needs to be validated by a

Table 7.4 Kendall-rank-correlation coefficients (Kendall-tau-b) between performance figures

	$\overline{\omega}^{\text{hr+}}_{\text{total}}$	$\overline{\omega}^{\text{hr+}}_{\text{ls}}$	$\overline{\omega}^{\text{hr+}}_{\text{ws}}$	$\overline{\omega}^{\text{hr+}}_{\text{wsout}}$	$\overline{\omega}^{\text{hr}-}_{\text{total}}$	$\overline{m}^{\text{xye}}_{\text{total}}$	$\overline{m}^{\text{cit}}_{\text{total}}$	$\lvert J \rvert$	$\overline{\psi}$
$\overline{\omega}^{\text{hr+}}_{\text{total}}$	1.000	**0.967**	**0.873**	**0.875**	−0.795	−0.267	−0.219	**0.654**	0.498
$\overline{\omega}^{\text{hr+}}_{\text{ls}}$	**0.967**	1.000	**0.838**	**0.840**	−0.784	−0.272	−0.229	**0.632**	0.482
$\overline{\omega}^{\text{hr+}}_{\text{ws}}$	**0.873**	**0.838**	1.000	**0.994**	−0.779	−0.234	−0.154	**0.708**	0.537
$\overline{\omega}^{\text{hr+}}_{\text{wsout}}$	**0.875**	**0.840**	**0.994**	1.000	−0.780	−0.234	−0.153	**0.711**	0.541
$\overline{\omega}^{\text{hr}-}_{\text{total}}$	−0.795	−0.784	−0.779	−0.780	1.000	0.253	0.242	**−0.683**	−0.393
$\overline{m}^{\text{xye}}_{\text{total}}$	−0.267	−0.272	−0.234	−0.234	0.253	1.000	0.762	−0.032	−0.071
$\overline{m}^{\text{cit}}_{\text{total}}$	−0.219	−0.229	−0.154	−0.153	0.242	0.762	1.000	0.052	0.092
$\lvert J \rvert$	**0.654**	**0.632**	**0.708**	**0.711**	**−0.683**	−0.032	0.052	1.000	0.584
$\overline{\psi}$	0.498	0.482	0.537	0.541	−0.393	−0.071	0.092	0.584	1.000

statistical hypothesis test on a certain significance level α, denoting the probability of error when rejecting the so-called null hypothesis of the test (van den Honert 1999, p. 100). The smaller the significance level α, the smaller the risk of making an error when rejecting the null hypothesis. Depending on the research-specific framework conditions, usually significance levels of $\alpha = 0.01$, $\alpha = 0.05$ or $\alpha = 0.10$ are recommended (Cohen 1992). On the basis of the significance level α, a certain range is determined for the test statistic (i.e., a figure based on the collected data) that is incompatible with the null hypothesis. If the test statistic is outside the computed range, the null hypothesis is rejected on the specified significance level α. As a consequence, rejecting the null hypothesis is either the right decision or it is falsely done with only a small predefined probability (Ahrholdt 2010, p. 151).

A null hypothesis can only be rejected or not rejected, but cannot be accepted by the same test. Thus, the null hypothesis on a connection between two variables needs to be formulated contrary to the originally intended research hypothesis (i.e., on the existence of a connection), stating that there is no statistical connection between the considered variables. Hence, it can be concluded from the rejection of a hypothesis, that the collected data significantly plead for the correctness of the originally intended and/or formulated research hypothesis (Schlittgen 2008, p. 343). With regard to the correlation analyses of the most important RMGC-performance figures, it is stated by the null hypothesis for each pair of figures that there is no correlation between these figures (i.e., indicated by a correlation coefficient of zero), although the contrary is originally hypothesised (see Research hypotheses 1.1.1–1.1.4). Based on the collected data of all 15,400 simulation runs, all these null hypotheses on the correlations between the regarded figures are rejected by means of two-sided tau-hypothesis tests at a significance level of $\alpha = 0.01$. Hence, the correlations between all these figures and the correlation coefficients shown in Table 7.4—in particular those concerning the statistical connections postulated by Research hypotheses 1.1.1–1.1.4—are confirmed as being highly significant.

The postulated causal connections between the mean vehicle-waiting-time figures are confirmed by the computed correlation coefficients. Very strong correlations between all mean vehicle-waiting-time figures are indicated by the computed Kendall-rank-correlation coefficients in the range from 0.838 ($\overline{\omega}^{\text{hr+}}_{\text{ls}}$ with $\overline{\omega}^{\text{hr+}}_{\text{ws}}$)

Table 7.5 Descriptive statistics of $\overline{\omega}_{\mathrm{total}}^{\mathrm{hr+}}$, $\overline{\omega}_{\mathrm{ls}}^{\mathrm{hr+}}$, $\overline{\omega}_{\mathrm{ws}}^{\mathrm{hr+}}$ and $\overline{\omega}_{\mathrm{wsout}}^{\mathrm{hr+}}$ for all 15,400 simulation runs

	Mean	Standard deviation	Quantiles 0.25	0.50	0.75
$\overline{\omega}_{\mathrm{total}}^{\mathrm{hr+}}$	375.82	686.37	34.80	72.60	296.40
$\overline{\omega}_{\mathrm{ls}}^{\mathrm{hr+}}$	483.02	796.22	75.76	148.15	421.14
$\overline{\omega}_{\mathrm{ws}}^{\mathrm{hr+}}$	301.83	619.80	5.26	19.22	209.10
$\overline{\omega}_{\mathrm{wsout}}^{\mathrm{hr+}}$	570.41	1,143.46	10.20	37.20	406.80

to 0.994 ($\overline{\omega}_{\mathrm{ws}}^{\mathrm{hr+}}$ with $\overline{\omega}_{\mathrm{wsout}}^{\mathrm{hr+}}$). In particular, the hypothesised correlations of $\overline{\omega}_{\mathrm{ls}}^{\mathrm{hr+}}$ with $\overline{\omega}_{\mathrm{ws}}^{\mathrm{hr+}}$ and $\overline{\omega}_{\mathrm{wsout}}^{\mathrm{hr+}}$ (see Research hypothesis 1.1.1) are confirmed by correlation coefficients of 0.838 and 0.840, respectively. Thus, it would be possible to focus on a certain vehicle-waiting-time figure for analysing the operational-performance effects of the RMGC design without greatly compromising the validity of the findings for other waiting-time figures. However, the vehicle-waiting-time figures are not perfectly correlated, thus leaving room for the existence of design-dependent differences in the vehicle-waiting-time effects of decisions on the operating type of RMGC system and the yard-block layout. Therefore, in order to be able to identify even slight differences in the operational-performance effects of design decisions, in particular between the waterside and landside handover areas, it is rejected to focus on a certain vehicle-waiting-time figure for the subsequent analysis of the operational-performance effects of the RMGC design, but to mostly consider all introduced waiting-time figures.

In order to give a statistically more descriptive impression of the differences between the vehicle-waiting-time figures, than by the example results, some descriptive statistics of $\overline{\omega}_{\mathrm{total}}^{\mathrm{hr+}}$, $\overline{\omega}_{\mathrm{ls}}^{\mathrm{hr+}}$, $\overline{\omega}_{\mathrm{ws}}^{\mathrm{hr+}}$ and $\overline{\omega}_{\mathrm{wsout}}^{\mathrm{hr+}}$ for all 15,400 simulation runs are shown in Table 7.5. At first sight, contrasting findings are made with regard to the differences between the vehicle-waiting times for waterside and landside jobs. Contradicting Research hypothesis 1.1.2, the averaged vehicle-waiting times are longer for waterside retrieval jobs than for landside jobs, whereas, confirming Research hypothesis 1.1.2, the 0.25, 0.50 and 0.75 quantiles of the vehicle-waiting times are greater for landside jobs than for waterside (retrieval) jobs. A possible explanation for this phenomenon can be differences in the growth of waterside and landside vehicle-waiting times with the yard-block capacity (see Research hypothesis 1.2.2), leading to a great number of simulation runs (11,696) with slightly longer vehicle-waiting times for landside jobs and a small number of simulation runs (3,704) with much longer vehicle-waiting times for waterside retrieval jobs. However, by means of a two-sided Paired-Sample Wilcoxon Signed-Rank Test and a Paired-Sample Sign Test, both at a significance level of $\alpha = 0.01$, the vehicle-waiting times for waterside jobs as well as waterside retrieval jobs are confirmed to be significantly shorter than for landside jobs. Hence, both Research hypotheses 1.1.1 and 1.1.2 on the causal connections of the vehicle-waiting-time figures are both confirmed by the total sample of simulation results.

Similarly, Research hypotheses 1.1.3 and 1.1.4 are likewise confirmed by the computed correlation coefficients that are shown in Table 7.4. Firstly, the hypothesised causal connections between the crane workload over the simulation horizon and all mean vehicle-waiting times figures (see Research hypothesis 1.1.3) are confirmed by strong positive correlations in the range from 0.632 ($|J|$ with $\overline{\omega}_{\mathrm{ls}}^{\mathrm{hr+}}$) to 0.711 ($|J|$ with $\overline{\omega}_{\mathrm{wsout}}^{\mathrm{hr+}}$). Secondly, a strong negative correlation between the crane workload over the simulation horizon and the mean crane-waiting time in the handover areas, as postulated by Research hypothesis 1.1.4, is confirmed by a Kendall-rank-correlation coefficient of −0.683.

Altogether, with respect to the hypothesised causal connections between the RMGC-performance figures, it can be concluded from the analysis of all 15,400 simulation runs on the RMGC-design-planning problem that:

- Research hypothesis 1.1.1 is confirmed.
- Research hypothesis 1.1.2 is confirmed.
- Research hypothesis 1.1.3 is confirmed.
- Research hypothesis 1.1.4 is confirmed.

Except for the confirmed hypotheses, no other strong or very strong correlations between the regarded RMGC-performance figures are identified on the basis of the computed Kendall-rank-correlation coefficients, thus indicating the absence of further straight causal connections between these figures.

7.2.2.2 Effects of Yard-Block Capacity

After the design-independent causal connections between RMGC-performance figures are investigated in the previous subsection, the investigation of the operational-performance effects of the RMGC design is started here with the analysis of the vehicle-waiting-time effects of the yard-block capacity. In particular, presence, type and extent of the causal connections between the yard-block capacity and the mean vehicle-waiting times in the handover areas are separately investigated for each type of RMGC system by means of curve-fitting and/or regression analysis techniques in order to validate Research hypotheses 1.2.1 and 1.2.2.

The operational-performance effects of different yard-block capacities, in terms of vehicle-waiting times in the landside and waterside handover areas, are depicted in Figs. 7.2 and 7.3, respectively, for each type of RMGC system. The capacities, resulting from 385 different yard-block layouts, are noted on the abscissa and the corresponding performances, measured as averaged XT and SC-waiting time figures of 10 stochastically independent simulation runs (i.e., $\overline{\overline{\omega}}_{\mathrm{ls}}^{\mathrm{hr+}}$ and $\overline{\overline{\omega}}_{\mathrm{ws}}^{\mathrm{hr+}}$), are shown on the ordinate. Similar to the findings of Kemme (2011a) on the dependencies of the yard-block capacity and the mean SC-waiting time for waterside retrieval jobs ($\overline{\overline{\omega}}_{\mathrm{wsout}}^{\mathrm{hr+}}$), it can be observed from the figures that both $\overline{\overline{\omega}}_{\mathrm{ls}}^{\mathrm{hr+}}$ and $\overline{\overline{\omega}}_{\mathrm{ws}}^{\mathrm{hr+}}$ increase with growing yard-block capacity. More precisely, at first even the growth rates of $\overline{\overline{\omega}}_{\mathrm{ls}}^{\mathrm{hr+}}$ and $\overline{\overline{\omega}}_{\mathrm{ws}}^{\mathrm{hr+}}$ are observed to increase with the yard-block capacity for all types of RMGC systems, but for some types of RMGC systems the growth rates of $\overline{\overline{\omega}}_{\mathrm{ls}}^{\mathrm{hr+}}$ and

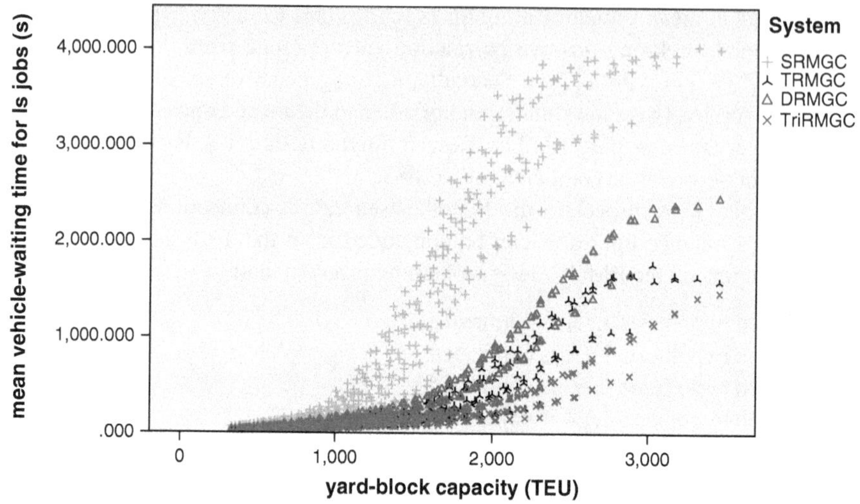

Fig. 7.2 RMGC-type-dependent XT-waiting-time effects of the yard-block capacity

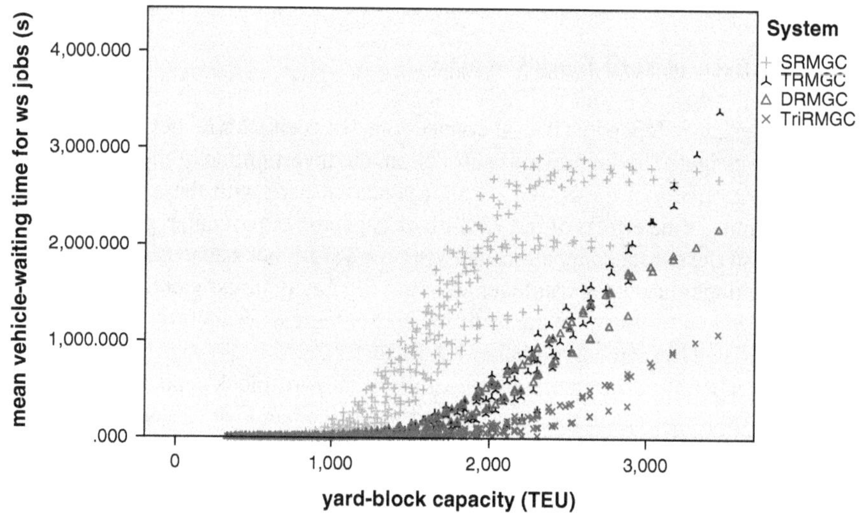

Fig. 7.3 RMGC-type-dependent SC-waiting-time effects of the yard-block capacity

$\overline{\overline{\omega}}^{\text{hr+}}_{\text{ws}}$ are also observed to decline with the capacity of the yard block after certain capacities are exceeded—in particular for the SRMGC system and $\overline{\overline{\omega}}^{\text{hr+}}_{\text{ls}}$.

For most capacities, $\overline{\overline{\omega}}^{\text{hr+}}_{\text{ls}}$ and $\overline{\overline{\omega}}^{\text{hr+}}_{\text{ws}}$ are by far the greatest for the SRMGC system and the smallest for the TriRMGC system. The performances of the DRMGC and TRMGC systems are comparable and somewhere in between those of the SRMGC and TriRMGC systems. For layouts with rather small capacities, the vehicle-waiting times are nearly comparable for all types of RMGC systems, while for larger yard blocks significant performance differences are observed between most types of RMGC systems. For instance, for the "small" example layout, the mean vehicle-waiting times for waterside retrieval jobs ($\overline{\overline{\omega}}^{\text{hr+}}_{\text{wsout}}$) only differ a few seconds between the SRMGC and TriRMGC systems and the corresponding 95% confidence intervals even overlap, whereas for the "big" example layout, a significant difference of more than one hour is observed between these types of RMGC systems (see Tables 7.2 and 7.3).

As anticipated by Research hypothesis 1.2.1, inspection of Figs. 7.2 and 7.3 suggests a functional relation between the yard-block capacity and the resulting vehicle-waiting times in the handover areas, which is also confirmed by highly significant, strong correlations between these variables. Based on all 15,400 simulation runs, significantly positive Kendall-rank-correlation coefficients (at a significance level of $\alpha = 0.01$) of 0.659, 0.639, 0.706 and 0.707 are computed for the correlations between the yard-block capacity and $\overline{\omega}^{\text{hr+}}_{\text{total}}$, $\overline{\omega}^{\text{hr+}}_{\text{ls}}$, $\overline{\omega}^{\text{hr+}}_{\text{ws}}$ and $\overline{\omega}^{\text{hr+}}_{\text{wsout}}$, respectively. To find out the function type that best explains the vehicle-waiting times by the yard-block capacity and to identify differences in the functional relation with respect to waiting-time figures and types of RMGC systems, separate curve-fitting analyses are carried out for all four types of RMGC systems and all considered vehicle-waiting-time figures, using the results of all individual simulation runs. Here, based on the point distributions shown in Figs. 7.2 and 7.3, quadratic ($\overline{\omega}^{\text{hr+}} = \beta_0 + \beta_1 \text{capacity} + \beta_2 \text{capacity}^2 + \epsilon$), cubic ($\overline{\omega}^{\text{hr+}} = \beta_0 + \beta_1 \text{capacity} + \beta_2 \text{capacity}^2 + \beta_3 \text{capacity}^3 + \epsilon$), power ($\overline{\omega}^{\text{hr+}} = \beta_0 \text{capacity}^{\beta_1} \times \epsilon$) and exponential functions ($\overline{\omega}^{\text{hr+}} = \beta_0 \; e^{\beta_1 \times \text{capacity}} + \epsilon$) are considered as reasonable function types to explain the vehicle-waiting times by the yard-block capacity, where $\beta_0, \ldots, \beta_3$ are the regression parameters and ϵ denotes the error term of the corresponding regression function. A typical linear regression function ($\overline{\omega}^{\text{hr+}} = \beta_0 + \beta_1 \; \text{capacity} + \epsilon$) can only, if at all, act as a benchmark. The curve-fitting results, in terms of regression parameters and coefficients of determination (R^2), for linear, quadratic and cubic regressions are shown in Table 7.6, while the results for power and exponential regressions are displayed in Table 7.7.

All regression models themselves as well as the influences of all regression parameters are qualified as being highly significant at a significance level of $\alpha = 0.01$ by means of F- and t-tests, respectively. The resulting coefficients of determination reveal that the spread of all kinds of mean vehicle-waiting-time figures for all types of RMGC systems can largely be explained by quadratic, cubic, power and exponential functions. Even a linear regression yields mostly acceptable coefficients of determination in the range from 0.523 to 0.859. However, for almost all types of RMGC systems and vehicle-waiting-time figures, the highest coefficients of determination are yielded with the cubic function, since this function type is the most adaptable one among all considered types of regression functions—in particular with regard to changes in the curvature.

For yard-block capacities of relevant size, the observations, made on the basis of Figs. 7.2 and 7.3 on the functional relations of vehicle-waiting times and yard-block

Table 7.6 Results for curve-fitting analysis of yard-block capacity (1) (for linear, quadratic and cubic regression functions)

			SRMGC	TRMGC	DRMGC	TriRMGC
Linear	β_0	$\overline{\omega}^{hr+}_{total}$	$-1,190.483$	-540.864	-540.694	-197.517
		$\overline{\omega}^{hr+}_{ls}$	$-1,344.912$	-441.687	-582.338	-232.003
		$\overline{\omega}^{hr+}_{ws}$	$-1,086.870$	-612.134	-512.829	-174.164
		$\overline{\omega}^{hr+}_{wsout}$	$-1,912.801$	$-1,136.420$	-988.292	-338.252
	β_1	$\overline{\omega}^{hr+}_{total}$	1.519	0.570	0.594	0.221
		$\overline{\omega}^{hr+}_{ls}$	17.769	0.521	0.700	0.290
		$\overline{\omega}^{hr+}_{ws}$	1.325	0.607	0.522	0.173
		$\overline{\omega}^{hr+}_{wsout}$	2.389	1.133	1.008	0.336
	R^2	$\overline{\omega}^{hr+}_{total}$	0.840	0.671	0.713	0.609
		$\overline{\omega}^{hr+}_{ls}$	0.859	0.728	0.750	0.687
		$\overline{\omega}^{hr+}_{ws}$	0.817	0.611	0.675	0.523
		$\overline{\omega}^{hr+}_{wsout}$	0.798	0.628	0.679	0.525
Quadratic	β_0	$\overline{\omega}^{hr+}_{total}$	-766.824	408.027	331.483	207.564
		$\overline{\omega}^{hr+}_{ls}$	-839.461	198.657	319.598	210.285
		$\overline{\omega}^{hr+}_{ws}$	-715.898	558.016	339.440	205.462
		$\overline{\omega}^{hr+}_{wsout}$	$-1,590.335$	960.416	615.640	395.047
	β_1	$\overline{\omega}^{hr+}_{total}$	0.873	-0.878	-0.737	-0.398
		$\overline{\omega}^{hr+}_{ls}$	1.032	-0.457	-0.676	-0.385
		$\overline{\omega}^{hr+}_{ws}$	0.759	-1.179	-0.779	-0.406
		$\overline{\omega}^{hr+}_{wsout}$	1.897	-2.067	-1.439	-0.783
	β_2	$\overline{\omega}^{hr+}_{total}$	2.029×10^{-4}	4.545×10^{-4}	4.178×10^{-4}	1.940×10^{-4}
		$\overline{\omega}^{hr+}_{ls}$	2.421×10^{-4}	3.067×10^{-4}	4.320×10^{-4}	2.119×10^{-4}
		$\overline{\omega}^{hr+}_{ws}$	1.777×10^{-4}	5.605×10^{-4}	4.082×10^{-4}	1.818×10^{-4}
		$\overline{\omega}^{hr+}_{wsout}$	1.544×10^{-4}	1.004×10^{-3}	7.683×10^{-4}	3.512×10^{-4}
	R^2	$\overline{\omega}^{hr+}_{total}$	0.849	0.929	0.927	0.895
		$\overline{\omega}^{hr+}_{ls}$	0.868	0.881	0.923	0.909
		$\overline{\omega}^{hr+}_{ws}$	0.826	0.927	0.926	0.874
		$\overline{\omega}^{hr+}_{wsout}$	0.800	0.927	0.918	0.873
Cubic	β_0	$\overline{\omega}^{hr+}_{total}$	1,327.929	207.813	355.330	-58.149
		$\overline{\omega}^{hr+}_{ls}$	1,479.832	376.127	415.042	-52.675
		$\overline{\omega}^{hr+}_{ws}$	1,225.621	83.369	314.192	-62.019
		$\overline{\omega}^{hr+}_{wsout}$	2,222.091	315.578	692.895	-109.433
	β_1	$\overline{\omega}^{hr+}_{total}$	-4.086	-0.404	-0.793	0.231
		$\overline{\omega}^{hr+}_{ls}$	-4.459	-0.877	-0.902	0.238
		$\overline{\omega}^{hr+}_{ws}$	-3.837	-0.055	-0.719	0.227
		$\overline{\omega}^{hr+}_{wsout}$	-7.128	-0.540	-1.622	0.411
	β_2	$\overline{\omega}^{hr+}_{total}$	35.050×10^{-4}	1.389×10^{-4}	4.554×10^{-4}	-2.248×10^{-4}
		$\overline{\omega}^{hr+}_{ls}$	38.981×10^{-4}	5.865×10^{-4}	5.825×10^{-4}	-2.027×10^{-4}
		$\overline{\omega}^{hr+}_{ws}$	32.382×10^{-4}	-1.877×10^{-4}	3.684×10^{-4}	-2.398×10^{-4}
		$\overline{\omega}^{hr+}_{wsout}$	61.641×10^{-4}	-1.210×10^{-5}	8.901×10^{-4}	-4.440×10^{-4}
	β_3	$\overline{\omega}^{hr+}_{total}$	-6.415×10^{-7}	6.131×10^{-8}	-7.303×10^{-9}	8.137×10^{-8}
		$\overline{\omega}^{hr+}_{ls}$	-7.102×10^{-7}	-5.435×10^{-8}	-2.923×10^{-8}	8.053×10^{-8}
		$\overline{\omega}^{hr+}_{ws}$	-5.946×10^{-7}	1.454×10^{-7}	7.732×10^{-9}	8.191×10^{-8}
		$\overline{\omega}^{hr+}_{wsout}$	-1.167×10^{-6}	1.975×10^{-7}	-2.366×10^{-8}	1.545×10^{-7}
	R^2	$\overline{\omega}^{hr+}_{total}$	0.909	0.932	0.927	0.929
		$\overline{\omega}^{hr+}_{ls}$	0.921	0.884	0.923	0.930
		$\overline{\omega}^{hr+}_{ws}$	0.892	0.941	0.926	0.920
		$\overline{\omega}^{hr+}_{wsout}$	0.876	0.935	0.918	0.917

Table 7.7 Results for curve-fitting analysis of yard-block capacity (2) (for power and exponential regression functions)

			SRMGC	TRMGC	DRMGC	TriRMGC
Power	β_0	$\overline{\omega}^{hr+}_{total}$	1.175×10^{-7}	2.796×10^{-7}	2.969×10^{-6}	2.023×10^{-5}
		$\overline{\omega}^{hr+}_{ls}$	6.904×10^{-6}	1.809×10^{-5}	9.490×10^{-5}	2.025×10^{-4}
		$\overline{\omega}^{hr+}_{ws}$	8.281×10^{-14}	9.777×10^{-12}	2.953×10^{-11}	1.764×10^{-8}
		$\overline{\omega}^{hr+}_{wsout}$	2.020×10^{-13}	1.931×10^{-11}	5.328×10^{-11}	3.248×10^{-8}
	β_1	$\overline{\omega}^{hr+}_{total}$	3.056	2.732	2.449	2.072
		$\overline{\omega}^{hr+}_{ls}$	2.553	2.221	2.048	1.841
		$\overline{\omega}^{hr+}_{ws}$	4.900	4.027	3.892	2.887
		$\overline{\omega}^{hr+}_{wsout}$	4.865	4.024	3.902	2.895
	R^2	$\overline{\omega}^{hr+}_{total}$	0.872	0.842	0.861	0.846
		$\overline{\omega}^{hr+}_{ls}$	0.885	0.860	0.880	0.870
		$\overline{\omega}^{hr+}_{ws}$	0.860	0.828	0.849	0.803
		$\overline{\omega}^{hr+}_{wsout}$	0.855	0.828	0.847	0.802
Exponential	β_0	$\overline{\omega}^{hr+}_{total}$	13.919	3.927	7.636	5.323
		$\overline{\omega}^{hr+}_{ls}$	37.742	12.115	22.126	13.634
		$\overline{\omega}^{hr+}_{ws}$	0.845	0.346	0.483	0.618
		$\overline{\omega}^{hr+}_{wsout}$	1.697	0.676	0.930	1.191
	β_1	$\overline{\omega}^{hr+}_{total}$	22.980×10^{-4}	21.695×10^{-4}	19.413×10^{-4}	16.452×10^{-4}
		$\overline{\omega}^{hr+}_{ls}$	19.290×10^{-4}	17.391×10^{-4}	16.110×10^{-4}	14.412×10^{-4}
		$\overline{\omega}^{hr+}_{ws}$	35.716×10^{-4}	31.761×10^{-4}	30.368×10^{-4}	23.101×10^{-4}
		$\overline{\omega}^{hr+}_{wsout}$	35.359×10^{-4}	31.702×10^{-4}	30.426×10^{-4}	23.150×10^{-4}
	R^2	$\overline{\omega}^{hr+}_{total}$	0.846	0.913	0.929	0.917
		$\overline{\omega}^{hr+}_{ls}$	0.868	0.906	0.936	0.917
		$\overline{\omega}^{hr+}_{ws}$	0.785	0.885	0.888	0.883
		$\overline{\omega}^{hr+}_{wsout}$	0.775	0.882	0.884	0.881

capacity, are mostly confirmed by the computed regression parameters. Confirming Research hypothesis 1.2.1, all types of regression functions are parametrised in such a way that all mean vehicle-waiting-time figures of all types of RMGC systems steadily increase with the yard-block capacity (in the domain of reasonable yard-block capacities). This can be explained by the positive waiting-time effects of increasing crane workloads, which are by definition connected with increasing yard-block capacities. More precisely, all quadratic, power and exponential functions as well as all cubic functions for multi-crane systems are parametrised such that the growth rates of the vehicle-waiting times steadily increase with growing yard-block capacity, whereas the parametrisations of the cubic functions for the single crane system lead to inflexion points in the domain of tested yard block capacities. For capacities to the left of the inflexion point, the slopes of the waiting time figures increase with the yard-block capacity, but decrease for capacities beyond the inflexions point. However, decreasing vehicle-waiting-time slopes are only observed and/or computed for yard-block layouts with comparably large capacities, which usually induce far too long vehicle-waiting times for practical terminal operations. In fact, from the parametrisation of the cubic regression functions, it can be concluded that decreasing growth rates of the vehicle-waiting times cannot be expected before yard-block capacities of about 1,750 TEUs and/or 25 min of mean vehicle-waiting time, which is—without a doubt—far away from practical suitability when considering the consequences for the total terminal operations (see Sect. 3.2). Thus, it can be concluded that the growth rates of the mean vehicle-waiting times at least increase steadily with yard-block capacities that are in the range of reasonable yard-block sizes with still acceptable vehicle-waiting times in the handover areas.

Increasing and decreasing growth rates of mean vehicle-waiting-time figures can be explained by two counteracted effects of increasing yard-block capacities. Firstly, with increasing capacities and crane workloads, the average number of simultaneously waiting vehicles in the handover areas increases as well. Considering that each possible delay arising in the execution of a main job does not only have waiting-time effects for the corresponding vehicle, but also for all other vehicles waiting in the handover areas, a linear growth of mean vehicle-waiting times can be expected with an increasing average number of simultaneously waiting vehicles, as long as the average execution time for main jobs remains unchanged with growing yard-block capacities. However, owing to increasing crane-driving distances and/or numbers of shuffle moves induced by increasing yard-block dimensions, the average execution time for main jobs—and thus the average crane delay induced by each main job—is expected to increase as well with the yard-block capacity. As a consequence, the effects of growing average numbers of simultaneously waiting vehicles in the handover areas and increasing average execution times for main jobs jointly lead to increasing growth rates of the mean vehicle-waiting times with the yard-block capacity.

Declining growth rates of the mean vehicle-waiting times with the yard-block capacities are to be explained by the effects of only limitedly available handover area capacities. Once the handover areas are fully occupied by containers or XTs, arriving vehicles to deliver a certain container are redirected to other yard blocks (see Sect. 6.4.3), thus undermining the previously described positive waiting-time effects of increasing numbers of simultaneously waiting vehicles in the handover areas and inducing reductions in the growth rates of mean vehicle-waiting-time figures with increasing yard-block capacities. Moreover, the mean vehicle-waiting times are indirectly even reduced by the redirection of arriving laden vehicles, as fewer containers will be stored in the block, and therefore fewer shuffle and retrieval jobs need to be performed in the future. Hence, the actually occurring crane workload during the simulation horizon is reduced by the redirection of arriving laden vehicles compared to the originally intended workload that is implicitly specified by the average filling rate of the yard block (see Sect. 6.4.2). For example, with the SRMGC (TRMGC, DRMGC, TriRMGC) system and the "big" example layout, on average, 3,667.1 (1,497.0, 1,385.5, 457.4) vehicles are redirected, leading to an actually realised average yard-block-filling rate of only 51.1% (63.3%, 63.3%, 65.2%), compared to the originally specified filling rate of 75%. As a consequence, more crane resources will be available for performing the remaining crane jobs, thus reducing the risk for and the extent of vehicle-waiting times involved with these jobs.

The more often the handover area capacities are fully occupied, the more the positive waiting-time effects of increasing numbers of simultaneously waiting vehicles and increasing average job-execution times are compensated by workload reductions induced by the redirection of arriving laden vehicles. Due to increasing numbers of vehicle arrivals with growing yard-block capacities, but unchanged handover area capacities, the number of redirections is expected to increase with the block capacity, which is also confirmed by a strongly positive correlation between these variables, that is significant at a significance level of $\alpha = 0.01$. For example, with the SRMGC (TRMGC, DRMGC, TriRMGC) system and the "small" example layout, on average, only 102.6 (90.2, 89.6, 90.9) vehicles are redirected to other yard blocks, while, as mentioned above, much more vehicles are redirected in the "big" layout. As a consequence, the effects of vehicle redirections become more pronounced with increasing yard-block capacities, thus explaining changes in the rate of change of the growth rates for some vehicle-waiting-time figures with increasing yard-block capacities—just as observed from Figs. 7.2 and 7.3 and indicated by the computed regression parameters for the cubic functions (see Table 7.6).

When comparing the vehicle-waiting-time effects of increasing yard-block capacities for landside jobs with those for waterside (retrieval) jobs, it has to be taken into account that the extent of the previously described effects, which are responsible for increasing and decreasing vehicle-waiting-time slopes, differ between the waterside and landside block ends depending on the yard-block capacity, thus leading to ambiguous findings with respect to Research hypothesis 1.2.2. At first, when only few vehicles are redirected due to fully occupied handover areas, increasing yard-block capacities mostly lead to increasing vehicle-waiting times and increasing vehicle-waiting-time growth rates at both ends of the block. Moreover, owing to the prioritised execution of waterside retrieval jobs (see Sect. 7.1.3), increasing yard-block capacities are found to have greater positive effects on the landside mean vehicle-waiting times ($\overline{\omega}_{\text{ls}}^{\text{hr+}}$) than on the mean vehicle-waiting times for waterside retrieval jobs ($\overline{\omega}_{\text{wsout}}^{\text{hr+}}$), as long as the effects causing declining vehicle-waiting-time growth rates do not become too pronounced for the landside handover area. In fact, by comparing the first derivatives of all parametrised quadratic, cubic, power and exponential regression functions for small- to medium-sized yard-block layouts, greater vehicle-waiting-time growth rates for landside jobs than for waterside retrieval jobs are mostly found, thus indicating more positive vehicle-waiting-time effects of increasing yard-block capacities for landside jobs than for waterside retrieval jobs and falsifying Research hypothesis 1.2.2. However, at the same time the mean vehicle-waiting time for landside jobs ($\overline{\omega}_{\text{ls}}^{\text{hr+}}$) is more affected by the crane-workload-reducing effects of vehicle redirections with increasing yard-block capacities than the waiting time for waterside retrieval jobs ($\overline{\omega}_{\text{wsout}}^{\text{hr+}}$), since the landside handover area is expected to be more often fully occupied than the waterside handover area with increasing yard-block capacity, because of smaller handover capacities at the landside block end compared to the waterside block end (see Sect. 7.1.3). In this way, it can be explained that the shapes of the scatter plots for the landside vehicle-waiting times are more kinking than for the waterside vehicle-waiting times (see Figs. 7.2 and 7.3). As a consequence, the vehicle-waiting-time growth with the yard-block capacity is slowed down for landside jobs as compared to waterside retrieval jobs, such that the gap in the vehicle-waiting-time growth rates between landside and waterside jobs is closed with increasing yard-block capacity, until, at certain yard-block capacities, the growth rates for waterside retrieval jobs exceed those for landside jobs. By analysing the first derivatives of all parametrised quadratic, cubic, power and exponential regression functions, greater vehicle-waiting-time growth rates for waterside retrieval jobs than for landside jobs are mostly found for yard-block layouts with large to very large capacities. This confirms the greater waiting-time effects of capacity increases for waterside retrieval jobs than for landside jobs, as postulated by Research hypothesis 1.2.2. In total, however, this research hypothesis cannot be confirmed due to the firstly higher growth rates for landside vehicle-waiting times.

The observed effects of the operating type of RMGC system on the functional relation of yard-block capacities and mean vehicle-waiting-time figures are mostly confirmed by the computed regression parameters. All regression functions are parametrised such that the vehicle-waiting times increase most with the yard-block capacity when using the SRMGC system, while they increase least when using the TriRMGC system. The regression functions for the TRMGC and DRMGC systems are parametrised such that mostly intermediate vehicle-waiting-times figures are yielded. In addition, it is found on the basis of the regression parameters for the cubic functions that the extent of drops in the slope of vehicle-waiting-time regression functions is dependent on the available crane resources. The fewer cranes are used, the greater is the risk for simultaneously waiting vehicles and fully occupied handover areas, thus increasing the number of vehicle redirections to other yard blocks and decreasing the slope of the vehicle-waiting-time growth rates. This is illustrated by the pronounced and comparably early kinking shapes of the scatter plots for the SRMGC system compared to steadily increasing shapes of the scatter plots with the TriRMGC system (see Figs. 7.2 and 7.3) and confirmed by the computed regression parameters of the cubic functions, that yield inflexion points for all types of waiting-time figures for the SRMGC system, while inducing no inflexion points for the TriRMGC system. In this way, it can also be explained that the waterside mean vehicle-waiting time for the TRMGC system is even greater than for the SRMGC system for very large yard blocks, as shown in Fig. 7.3. An in-depth analysis of the operational-performance effects of the used type of RMGC system is provided in Sect. 7.2.2.4.

In summary, the yard-block capacity is found to have steadily positive effects on the mean vehicle-waiting times in the handover areas. But due to contrasting effects of increasing yard-block capacities, the functional relation varies with the considered waiting-time figure and type of RMGC system. While for small- to medium-sized yard blocks the block capacity is found to have greater vehicle-waiting-time effects for landside jobs than for waterside retrieval jobs, this relation is reversed for large to very large yard blocks. As a consequence:

- Research hypothesis 1.2.1 is confirmed, while
- Research hypothesis 1.2.2 is not confirmed

for the considered experimental setup of this RMGC-design study.

7.2.2.3 Effects of Yard-Block Dimensions

After significantly positive vehicle-waiting-time effects of the yard-block capacity are confirmed in the previous subsection, the operational-performance effects of the yard-block layout are investigated in even more detail in this subsection by analysing the vehicle-waiting-time effects of the capacity-defining yard-block dimensions in much the same way as in Kemme (2011a). In order to validate Research hypotheses 1.3.1–1.3.3, the vehicle-waiting-time effects of length, width and height of the yard block are separately quantified and compared for each type of RMGC system by means of multiple regression analysis techniques.

The operational-performance effects of different numbers of bays, rows and tiers of a yard block are illustrated in Figs. 7.4–7.6, respectively, for each type of RMGC system. All considered block lengths, widths and heights of this design study, in terms of the numbers of bays, rows and tiers, respectively, are noted on the abscissa of the relevant figure. The corresponding operational performances, measured as averaged mean vehicle-waiting times ($\overline{\overline{\omega}}^{\text{hr+}}_{\text{total}}$) of all experiments with the relevant length, width or height, are shown on the ordinate. It can be seen from the figures that the mean vehicle-waiting times in the handover areas increase with the length, width and height of the yard block, just as postulated by Research hypothesis 1.3.1. By comparing the shapes of the scatter plots, it is additionally observed that the greatest growth of the vehicle-waiting time appears to be induced by increases of the stacking height, while increasing block length and width appear to be connected with similar vehicle-waiting-time growth. More precisely, it might be concluded from the figures that the vehicle-waiting times increase linearly with both growing block length and width, while they increase progressively with growing stacking height. Similar to the effects of the yard-block capacity (see Figs. 7.2 and 7.3), it is observed for increases of all three yard-block dimensions that the averaged mean vehicle-waiting times increase most with the SRMGC system, while increasing least with the TriRMGC system. The waiting-time increases of the DRMGC and TRMGC systems are comparable and somewhere in between those of the SRMGC and TriRMGC systems.

To quantify the vehicle-waiting-time effects of all three yard-block dimensions with respect to the operating type of RMGC system, once again separate regression analyses are conducted for all four types of RMGC systems and all considered vehicle-waiting-time figures based on the corresponding 3,850 individual observations of $\overline{\omega}^{\text{hr+}}_{\text{total}}$, $\overline{\omega}^{\text{hr+}}_{\text{ls}}$, $\overline{\omega}^{\text{hr+}}_{\text{ws}}$ and $\overline{\omega}^{\text{hr+}}_{\text{wsout}}$. For this purpose, a regression model is needed that has to fulfil three important properties: Firstly, the previously found functional relation between the yard-block capacity and the resulting mean vehicle-waiting times should be utilised in some way. Secondly, the numbers of bays (n^{x}), rows (n^{y}) and tiers (n^{z}) should explicitly be contained in the model to grasp their individual performance effects. Thirdly, the model should be easily interpretable and amenable to statistical significance testing of the model itself as well as its parameters. All these properties are fulfilled by the multiplicative regression model of Kemme (2011a)

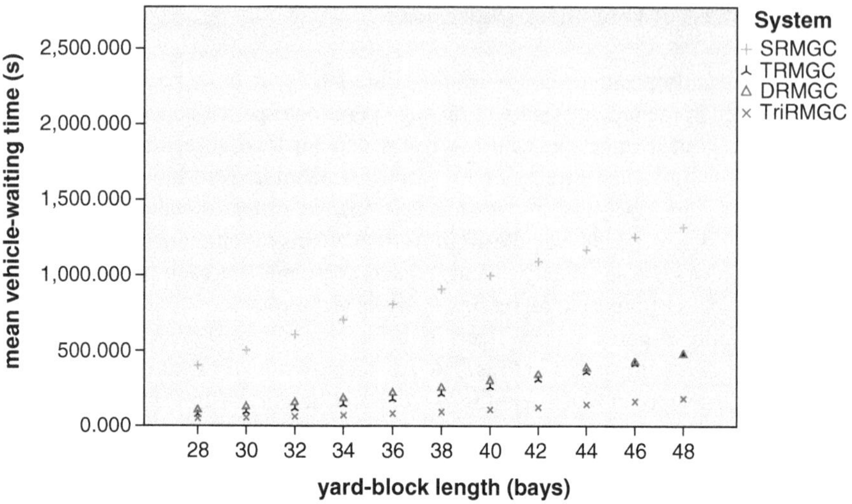

Fig. 7.4 RMGC-type-dependent vehicle-waiting-time effects of the yard-block length

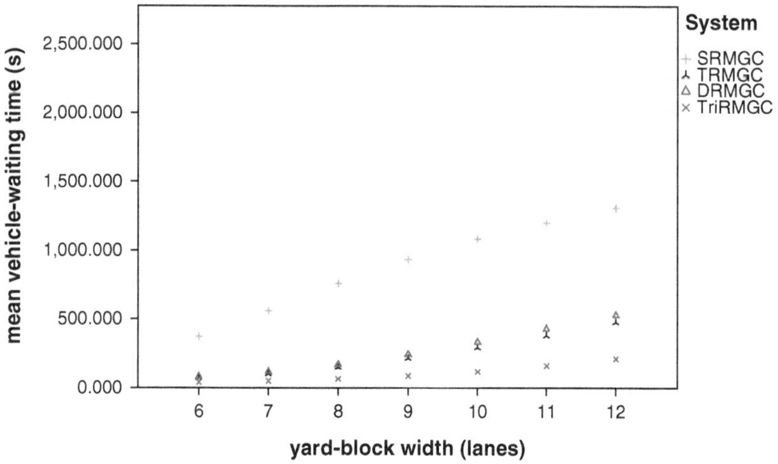

Fig. 7.5 RMGC-type-dependent vehicle-waiting-time effects of the yard-block width

$$\overline{\omega}^{\text{hr+}} = \beta_0 \times (n^{\text{x}})^{\beta_1} \times (n^{\text{y}})^{\beta_2} \times (n^{\text{z}})^{\beta_3} \times \epsilon \tag{7.1}$$

that can be used to estimate all considered kinds of mean vehicle-waiting-time figures ($\overline{\omega}^{\text{hr+}}_{\text{total}}$, $\overline{\omega}^{\text{hr+}}_{\text{ls}}$, $\overline{\omega}^{\text{hr+}}_{\text{ws}}$ and $\overline{\omega}^{\text{hr+}}_{\text{wsout}}$) for certain yard-block layouts. The first and second property are simultaneously fulfilled by replacing the capacity by its product $n^{\text{x}} \times n^{\text{y}} \times n^{\text{z}}$ in a function type that previously yielded promising coefficients of determination—the power function. Thus, n^{x}, n^{y} and n^{z} are explicitly built in and their individual performance effects can then be grasped by the exponential

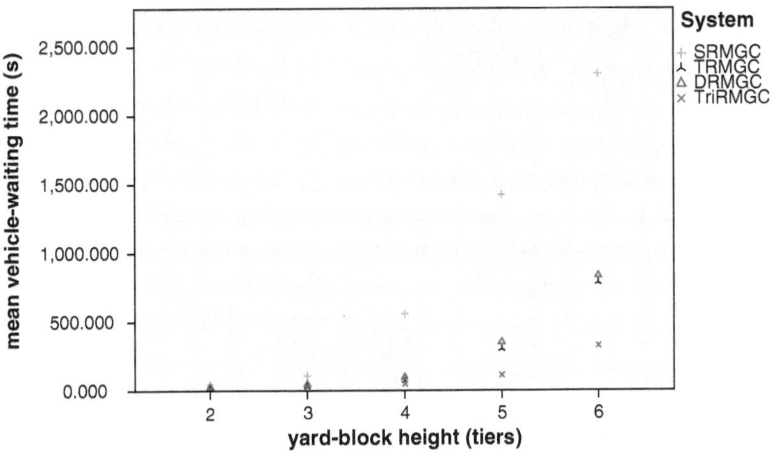

Fig. 7.6 RMGC-type-dependent vehicle-waiting-time effects of the yard-block height

regression parameters β_1, β_2 and $\beta 3$, respectively. The greater one of these parameter values is compared to the other ones, the more vehicle-waiting times in the handover areas are induced by the corresponding block dimension for the type of RMGC system being examined. The power function type is particularly well suited for the purpose of this regression analysis, as the yard-block dimensions can easily be integrated into the model without relinquishing the great explanatory power of the yard-block capacity for the spread of mean vehicle-waiting-time figures. Finally, property three is fulfilled as well, since the non-linear function (7.1) can be linearised by taking the (natural) logarithm. The estimation of the regression parameters β_1, β_2 and β_3 as well as the testing of the linearised model

$$\ln \overline{\omega}^{\text{hr+}} = \ln \beta_0 + \beta_1 \times \ln n^{\text{x}} + \beta_2 \times \ln n^{\text{y}} + \beta_2 \times \ln n^{\text{z}} + \ln \epsilon \qquad (7.2)$$

and its regression parameters for statistical significance is then straight forward (Backhaus et al. 2008, pp. 63–78).

The regression analyses are not only performed for one data set including all 15,400 simulation runs, but also for data sets which only include the runs yielding values of less than or equal to 600 s for the relevant mean waiting-time figure, because more meaningful regression results may be expected for data sets with limited vehicle-waiting times. This is to be explained the way that RMGC designs yielding long mean vehicle-waiting times, which exceed 600 s, cannot be expected to have any relevance for real-life applications (see Sect. 3.2). In addition, the used power function type is particularly well-suited to represent the progressive growth of the vehicle-waiting time for small- to medium-sized yard blocks, but unable to reflect sign changes in the increase of the vehicle-waiting-time growth rates, which may occur for very large-sized yard blocks that induce vehicle-waiting times possibly far beyond 600 s (see Sect. 7.2.2.2).

An overview on the computational results with regression model (7.2) for $\overline{\omega}_{\text{total}}^{\text{hr+}}$, $\overline{\omega}_{\text{ls}}^{\text{hr+}}$, $\overline{\omega}_{\text{ws}}^{\text{hr+}}$ and $\overline{\omega}_{\text{wsout}}^{\text{hr+}}$ in terms of regression parameters and coefficients of determination is provided in Table 7.8 for both data sets and all types of RMGC systems. The results for the complete and the filtered dates sets are labelled (A) and (B), respectively, and the corresponding regression parameters for standardised variables of regression function (7.2)—the so called beta values (Schroeder et al. 1986, pp. 31–32)—are noted in brackets. More detailed information on the regression results, including confidence intervals of the regression parameters as well as significance test results for the model itself and the parameters, are given in Appendix A.3.

Before the resulting regression parameters are compared and interpreted in detail, it is shortly checked to what extent the (linearised) model and its parameters are suitable to explain the simulation results. First of all, it is found, that all classical assumptions of linear regression analysis are fulfilled by regression model (7.2) and the underlying data sets, such that the computed regression parameters are BLUE (best linear unbiased estimators) (Backhaus et al. 2008, pp. 78–80). More precisely, the explanatory variables (n^{x}, n^{y}, n^{z}) are found to be linearly independent and the logarithmic error terms ($\ln \epsilon$) are found to be uncorrelated with each other as well as with the explanatory variables and to have a constant variance across observations (homoscedasticity) and an expected value of zero. In addition, the error terms ϵ are found to be log-normally distributed, and therefore the logarithmic error terms $\ln \epsilon$ follow a normal distribution, thus facilitating significance testing of the explanatory variables and the linearised regression model (7.2) by means t- and F-tests, respectively. It is found, that all regression parameters and models are highly significant at a significance level of $\alpha = 0.001$. For all vehicle-waiting-time figures, all types of RMGC systems and both data sets, the resulting coefficients of determination in the range from 0.765 to 0.954 confirm that the spread of vehicle-waiting times is very well explained by the suggested regression model. In particular, the spread of landside vehicle-waiting times and the spread of vehicle-waiting times with the SRMGC system are extraordinarily well explained by the model. Altogether, the regression model and its parameters are very suitable to explain the mean vehicle-waiting times in the handover areas of RMGC yard blocks.

The results of the regression analyses are structurally mostly identical, yielding parameters β_0, β_1, β_2, $\beta_3 > 0$ for all mean vehicle-waiting-time figures, types of RMGC systems and data sets. Hence, the block length, width and height are found to have significantly positive effects on the mean vehicle-waiting times in the handover areas, thus confirming Research hypothesis 1.3.1. To be specific: even a progressive growth of the mean vehicle-waiting-time figures with all three yard-block dimensions is indicated, as—apart from a few rare exceptions—parameters β_1, β_2, $\beta_3 > 1$ are mostly computed. This can be explained in much the same way as the progressive vehicle-waiting-time growth with the yard-block capacity (see Sect. 7.2.2.2).

At first glance, the β_0 values may be surprisingly small. But they are reasonable when considering the huge values for the product $(n^{\text{x}})^{\beta_1} \times (n^{\text{y}})^{\beta_2} \times (n^{\text{z}})^{\beta_3}$ that result from the relatively high values of n^{x}, n^{y} and n^{z} as well as their exponents β_1, β_2

Table 7.8 Results for regression analyses of yard-block dimensions

		All layouts			
(A)		SRMGC	TRMGC	DRMGC	TriRMGC
$\overline{\omega}^{hr+}_{total}$	β_0	9.531×10^{-6}	7.261×10^{-6}	4.758×10^{-5}	4.960×10^{-4}
	β_1	2.388 (0.257)	2.290 (0.271)	1.932 (0.258)	1.432 (0.224)
	β_2	1.803 (0.263)	1.697 (0.272)	1.846 (0.334)	1.461 (0.310)
	β_3	3.626 (0.892)	3.181 (0.860)	2.761 (0.842)	2.409 (0.861)
	R^2	0.930	0.888	0.886	0.888
$\overline{\omega}^{hr+}_{ls}$	β_0	1.588×10^{-4}	3.591×10^{-4}	8.744×10^{-4}	4.258×10^{-3}
	β_1	2.111 (0.274)	1.796 (0.264)	1.641 (0.265)	1.243 (0.222)
	β_2	1.590 (0.280)	1.311 (0.261)	1.552 (0.340)	1.238 (0.300)
	β_3	2.977 (0.883)	2.623 (0.881)	2.301 (0.848)	2.168 (0.884)
	R^2	0.933	0.915	0.905	0.920
$\overline{\omega}^{hr+}_{ws}$	β_0	1.342×10^{-9}	1.806×10^{-9}	7.654×10^{-9}	1.214×10^{-6}
	β_1	3.270 (0.218)	3.273 (0.260)	2.816 (0.227)	2.001 (0.219)
	β_2	2.441 (0.221)	2.460 (0.266)	2.706 (0.296)	2.160 (0.320)
	β_3	6.077 (0.926)	4.723 (0.859)	4.579 (0.844)	3.313 (0.827)
	R^2	0.954	0.877	0.851	0.835
$\overline{\omega}^{hr+}_{wsout}$	β_0	4.105×10^{-9}	4.048×10^{-9}	1.529×10^{-8}	2.415×10^{-6}
	β_1	3.185 (0.213)	3.242 (0.258)	2.806 (0.225)	1.993 (0.217)
	β_2	2.375 (0.215)	2.438 (0.263)	2.698 (0.293)	2.152 (0.318)
	β_3	6.064 (0.927)	4.732 (0.861)	4.600 (0.843)	3.329 (0.829)
	R^2	0.952	0.877	0.848	0.835
		Layouts with $\overline{\omega}^{hr+} \leq 600$ s			
(B)		SRMGC	TRMGC	DRMGC	TriRMGC
$\overline{\omega}^{hr+}_{total}$	β_0	2.316×10^{-3}	5.162×10^{-4}	2.547×10^{-3}	2.229×10^{-3}
	β_1	1.573 (0.334)	1.586 (0.252)	1.331 (0.254)	1.183 (0.209)
	β_2	1.075 (0.311)	1.120 (0.242)	1.238 (0.320)	1.249 (0.297)
	β_3	2.528 (1.008)	2.705 (0.953)	2.261 (0.950)	2.268 (0.907)
	R^2	0.876	0.903	0.905	0.907
$\overline{\omega}^{hr+}_{ls}$	β_0	4.564×10^{-2}	8.844×10^{-3}	3.115×10^{-2}	2.034×10^{-2}
	β_1	1.272 (0.393)	1.286 (0.257)	1.113 (0.278)	0.989 (0.206)
	β_2	0.833 (0.351)	0.862 (0.234)	1.001 (0.339)	1.014 (0.285)
	β_3	1.849 (1.030)	2.228 (0.981)	1.820 (0.981)	2.009 (0.943)
	R^2	0.916	0.946	0.951	0.948
$\overline{\omega}^{hr+}_{ws}$	β_0	1.277×10^{-8}	2.378×10^{-7}	3.415×10^{-7}	5.477×10^{-6}
	β_1	2.962 (0.280)	2.456 (0.243)	2.230 (0.217)	1.746 (0.206)
	β_2	2.084 (0.270)	1.807 (0.242)	2.134 (0.280)	1.952 (0.311)
	β_3	5.611 (1.030)	4.201 (0.924)	4.132 (0.891)	3.182 (0.854)
	R^2	0.913	0.853	0.800	0.834
$\overline{\omega}^{hr+}_{wsout}$	β_0	1.527×10^{-7}	3.057×10^{-6}	3.545×10^{-6}	4.725×10^{-5}
	β_1	2.689 (0.295)	2.198 (0.246)	2.007 (0.217)	1.523 (0.198)
	β_2	1.846 (0.276)	1.504 (0.228)	1.859 (0.272)	1.712 (0.300)
	β_3	5.219 (1.025)	3.880 (0.939)	3.834 (0.891)	3.015 (0.881)
	R^2	0.905	0.846	0.765	0.837

In brackets: regression parameters based on standardised variables—beta values and β_3. For instance, employing the regression results of the data set (A) for the SRMGC system with the "wide" layout yields an estimation of the mean vehicle-waiting time of

$$\overline{\omega}^{\text{hr+}}_{\text{total}} = 9.531 \times 10^{-6} \times 36^{2.388} \times 10^{1.803} \times 4^{3.626} = 480.46\,\text{s},$$

which differs only 0.85% from the actually observed waiting time (see Table 7.2).

The regression parameters β_1, β_2 and β_3 are of special importance for the analysis of the layout effects, as they indicate the influence of the corresponding block dimension on the operational performance of RMGC systems. To derive a sound ranking on the relative importance of the yard-block dimensions for the mean vehicle-waiting times in the handover areas, which is free of any unintended bias due to different scales of dimensions, the corresponding beta values of β_1, β_2 and β_3 have to be regarded. Similar to Kemme (2011a), the first finding is that the beta values of β_3 are always significantly greater than the beta values of β_1 and β_2—regardless of the considered type of RMGC system, waiting-time figure and data set. Hence, as postulated by Research hypothesis 1.3.2, of all three yard-block dimensions, the number of tiers is found to have the greatest influence on the mean vehicle-waiting times in the handover areas, which means most vehicle-waiting time is induced by the number of tiers. Besides its obvious effect on the yard-block capacity—which is to a great amount responsible for the positive vehicle-waiting-time effects—the number of tiers also influences the number of required shuffle moves. In fact, significantly positive Kendall-rank-correlation coefficients (at a significance level of $\alpha = 0.01$) of 0.798, 0.888, 0.889 and 0.895 are computed for the SRMGC, TRMGC, DRMGC and TriRMGC systems, respectively, between the mean number of shuffle moves per retrieval job ($\overline{\psi}$) and the number of tiers (n^z), thus confirming highly significant and fairly strong positive correlations between the container accessibility and the stacking height. Figure 7.7 shows the shuffle-move effects for all considered stacking heights and types of RMGC systems in terms of the averaged number of, on average, required shuffle moves per retrieval job of all simulation runs with the relevant number of tiers. It can roughly be observed that about 0.4 additional shuffle moves per retrieval job are induced by each increase of the stacking height of one tier. The slight decline in the growth of the averaged number of shuffle moves, that is observed from Fig. 7.7 for very high-stacked yard blocks, is to be explained by the workload-reducing effects of increasing number of vehicle redirections for very large-sized yard blocks, like high-stacked yard blocks (see Sect. 7.2.2.2). As a consequence of increasing numbers of shuffle moves with increasing stacking height, more unproductive shuffle jobs need to be performed by the same number of cranes within the same period of time, thus reducing the available crane resources for main jobs and increasing the risk for and the extent of vehicle-waiting times. Altogether, it can be concluded with regard to the effects of the stacking height, that longer crane-movement times for yard blocks with longer and wider layouts than a comparably sized yard block with more tiers do not compensate the effects of additional shuffle moves. Thus, it is advisable to stack in wide and long blocks instead of high piles if sufficient space is available.

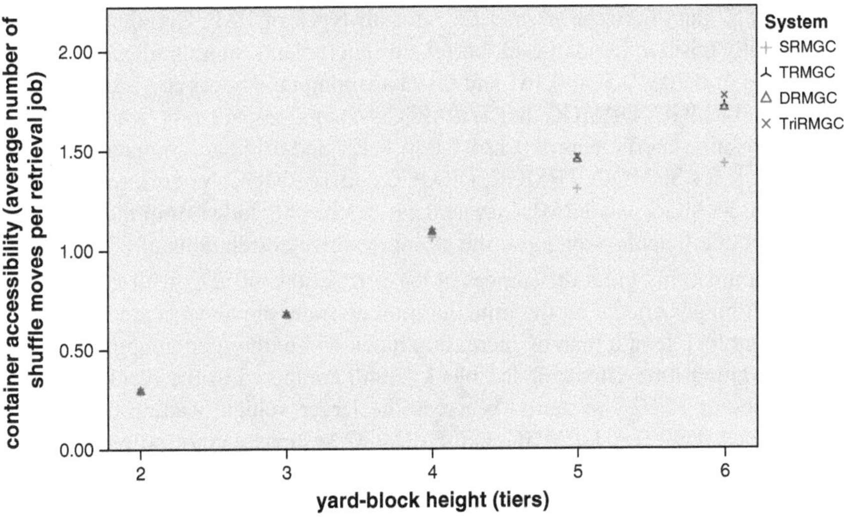

Fig. 7.7 RMGC-type-dependent shuffle-move effects of the yard-block height

The second finding is that the differences between the beta values of β_1 and β_2 are mostly rather small. For nearly half of the conducted regressions, even no significant differences between both regression parameters are found. Thus, no universal findings on the comparative importance of the block length and width for the operational performance of RMGC systems can be derived from the computed regression parameters, that are equally valid for all considered types of RMGC systems, vehicle-waiting-time figures and data sets.

With regard to data set (B), which is more relevant for practical terminal applications, it is observed for all kinds of vehicle-waiting-time figures that the beta value of β_1 is always greater than the beta value of β_2 for the SRMGC and TRMGC systems, while this relation is reversed for the DRMGC and TriRMGC systems. Therefore, it may be concluded that for SRMGC and TRMGC systems more mean vehicle-waiting time in the handover areas is induced by the number of bays than by the number of rows, while for DRMGC and TriRMGC systems more vehicle-waiting time is induced by the number of rows. This can be explained by two different effects. Firstly, the total time durations for empty and laden crane movements in the block (i.e., m_{jg}^{xye} and m_{jg}^{xyf}) are restricted by the maximum of portal and trolley-movement time (see (5.1) and (5.2)). Even though the portal is much faster than the trolley, the portal-movement time is clearly longer for most jobs since yard blocks are usually much longer than wide. Therefore, the total time duration of crane movements is mostly defined by the portal-movement time as compared to the trolley-movement time. As a consequence, increases of the block length can be expected to have greater effects on the time duration of crane movements than increases of the block width. This is also confirmed by bivariate correlation analyses between n^x, n^y and $\overline{m}_{jg}^{xye}$, which indicate stronger positive correlations between

n^{x} and $\overline{m}_{jg}^{\mathrm{xye}}$ than between n^{y} and $\overline{m}_{jg}^{\mathrm{xye}}$ for all types of RMGC systems. In fact, significantly positive Kendall-rank-correlation coefficients (at a significance level of $\alpha = 0.01$) of 0.702, 0.524, 0.161 and 0.193 are computed between n^{x} and $\overline{m}_{jg}^{\mathrm{xye}}$ for SRMGC, TRMGC, DRMGC and TriRMGC systems, respectively, while Kendall-rank-correlation coefficients of 0.124, 0.026, 0.127 and 0.143 are computed between n^{y} and $\overline{m}_{jg}^{\mathrm{xye}}$ for SRMGC, TRMGC, DRMGC and TriRMGC systems, respectively.

For the SRMGC and TRMGC systems, it can be concluded from the computed regression coefficients—owing to the strong positive correlations of n^{x} with $\overline{m}_{jg}^{\mathrm{xye}}$ and the comparably great differences in the correlations of $\overline{m}_{jg}^{\mathrm{xye}}$ with n^{x} and n^{y}—that much bigger effects on the time duration of crane movements are induced by increasing block length than by increasing block width, thus explaining the greater vehicle-waiting-time effects of the block length compared to the block width for these types of RMGC systems. Whereas the larger vehicle-waiting-time effects of the block width for DRMGC and TriRMGC systems cannot be explained by the effects of increasing block length and width for the time duration of crane movements, since only weak correlations with little differences in the correlation coefficients are computed for these types of RMGC systems. Moreover, the bigger vehicle-waiting-time effects of the block width can be explained by another effect which is connected with the crossing capabilities of the DRMGC and TriRMGC systems. For both types of RMGC systems, an increase in the mean crane-interference time is observed with increasing number of rows, which is indicated by significantly positive Kendall-rank-correlation coefficients (at a significance level of $\alpha = 0.01$) between n^{y} and $\overline{m}_{\mathrm{total}}^{\mathrm{cit}}$ of 0.248 and 0.242 for DRMGC and TriRMGC systems, respectively. This can be explained by prolonged trolley-movement times to the crossing position of the outer large crane, which cause prolonged crane-crossing manoeuvres. As a consequence, the inner small crane(s) can be expected to wait more often and longer for the trolley of the outer larger crane to be moved to the crossing position within wider blocks. Hence, for DRMGC and TriRMGC systems, the effects of increasing duration times of crane movements with the block length seem to be dominated by the effects of increasing crane-interference times with the block width, thus explaining the bigger vehicle-waiting-time effects of the block width as compared to the block length for these types of RMGC systems. Altogether, SRMGC and TRMGC systems should be operated in wider blocks rather than in longer ones for the investigated experimental setting, whereas it is advisable for DRMGC and TriRMGC systems to stack in longer blocks rather than in wider ones. Thus, Research hypothesis 1.3.3 cannot be confirmed as a whole, because it is only confirmed for SRMGC and TRMGC systems but not confirmed for DRMGC and TriRMGC systems.

In summary, all yard dimensions are found to have significantly positive effects on the mean vehicle-waiting times in the handover areas. For all considered types of RMGC systems, waiting-time figures and data sets, by far the greatest vehicle-waiting-time effects of all yard-block dimensions are induced by the stacking height. The ranking of the vehicle-waiting-time effects of the block length and width is found to depend on the operating type of RMGC system. While for SRMGC and

TRMGC systems, slightly more vehicle-waiting time is induced by increasing the number of bays than the number of rows, this relation is reversed for DRMGC and TriRMGC systems. As a consequence:

- Research hypothesis 1.3.1 is confirmed.
- Research hypothesis 1.3.2 is confirmed.
- Research hypothesis 1.3.3 is confirmed for SRMGC and TRMGC systems, but is not confirmed for DRMGC and TriRMGC systems

for the considered experimental setup of this RMGC-design study.

7.2.2.4 Effects of Crane Systems

In the preceding subsections on the operational-performance effects of the yard-block capacities and dimensions, it is already observed that substantial performance effects are induced by the operating type of RMGC system and the associated crane resources. In addition, the operating type of RMGC systems is found to have significant influence on the operational-performance effects of the yard-block capacity and the yard-block dimensions. In particular, the number of vehicle redirections that lead to drops in the vehicle-waiting-time growth rates with the yard-block capacity (see Sect. 7.2.2.2) and the ranking of the vehicle-waiting-time effects of the block length and width are found to depend on the operating type of RMGC system (see Sect. 7.2.2.3). In this subsection, the operational-performance effects of the operating type of RMGC system and the influences of the yard-block layout for the performance effects of the types of RMGC systems are investigated in detail. In particular, the operational-performance effects of the deployed number of yard cranes per yard block and the performance ranking of the considered types of RMGC systems are investigated—with special focus on the comparative performances of the TRMGC and DRMGC systems—in order to validate Research hypotheses 1.4.1 and 1.4.2.

The operational-performance effects of all four types of RMGC systems, in terms of mean vehicle-waiting times in the landside and waterside handover areas, are illustrated in Figs. 7.8 and 7.9, respectively. In these figures, the cumulative frequencies of layouts with certain maximum vehicle-waiting times—that results from ten stochastically independent simulation runs with that layout (i.e., $\overline{\overline{\omega}}_{\mathrm{ls}}^{\mathrm{hr+}}$ and $\overline{\overline{\omega}}_{\mathrm{ws}}^{\mathrm{hr+}}$)—are plotted against the corresponding vehicle-waiting time. In order to allow a better visualisation and interpretation, the mean vehicle-waiting times are given on the abscissa in a logarithmic scale. Mean XT-waiting times of $\overline{\overline{\omega}}_{\mathrm{ls}}^{\mathrm{hr+}} \leq 600$ s are, for example, yielded for only 210 (54.5%) yard-block layouts with the SRMGC system, 334 (86.8%) layouts with the TRMGC system, 317 (82.3%) layouts with the DRMGC system and 364 (94.5%) layouts with the TriRMGC system, while 235 (61.0%) layouts with the SRMGC systems, 339 (88.1%) layouts with the TRMGC system, 340 (88.3%) layouts with the DRMGC system and 376 (97.7%) layouts with the TriRMGC systems exhibit SC-waiting times of $\overline{\overline{\omega}}_{\mathrm{ws}}^{\mathrm{hr+}} \leq 600$ s.

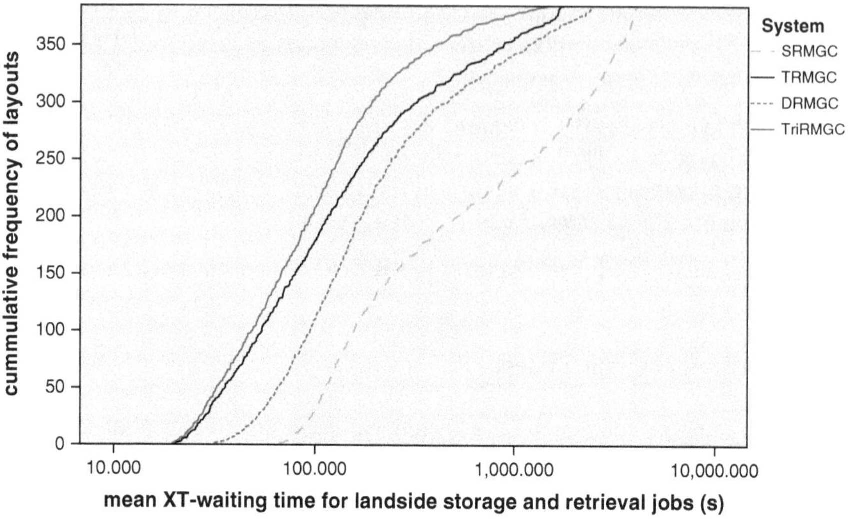

Fig. 7.8 Cumulative frequency histogram of mean XT-waiting time

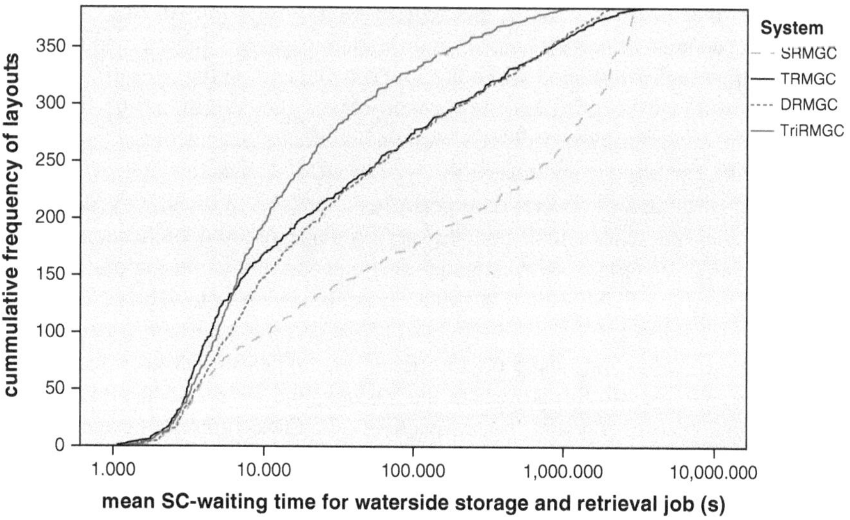

Fig. 7.9 Cumulative frequency histogram of mean SC-waiting time

The cumulative frequencies of layouts having a certain maximum vehicle-waiting time for a type of RMGC system, allow to draw conclusions about the maximum possible yard-block capacity and the flexibility in the layout planning offered by that type of RMGC system. The greater the cumulative frequency with a certain type of RMGC system, the better, as greater yard-block capacities and thus higher yard densities and/or lower costs per storage and retrieval jobs can be realised with that system without exceeding planning restrictions on the maximum permitted vehicle-waiting time (see Sect. 4.1.2). This gives more flexibility in the layout planning of the yard blocks. It can be seen from Figs. 7.8 and 7.9, that for most waterside and landside mean vehicle-waiting times the greatest cumulative frequencies of yard-block layouts are obtained by the TriRMGC system, while the smallest frequencies are given by the SRMGC system. This is in line with the findings of the previous subsections, which reveal that the vehicle-waiting times in the handover areas of SRMGC systems are most sensitive to changes of the yard-block capacities and dimensions, while being least sensitive to layout changes for the TriRMGC system (see Sect. 7.2.2.2 and 7.2.2.3). In a similar way, the previously found intermediate sensitivities to layout changes of the TRMGC and DRMGC are confirmed by comparable frequencies of layouts for these types of RMGC systems, that are in between those of the other types for most vehicle-waiting times, but with slight advantages for the TRMGC system—in particular for the XT-waiting times in the landside handover area.

By means of correlation analyses with the collected data of all 15,400 simulation runs, it is found—as expected by Research hypothesis 1.4.1—that the differences in the operational performance between the types of RMGC system can—to a great extent—be explained by the amount of crane resources that are associated with each type of RMGC system. Here, in order to avoid biased correlation results by the performance effects of the yard-block dimensions, partial correlation analyses are conducted with n^{x}, n^{y} and n^{z} being the control variables. Highly significantly negative correlation coefficients (at a significance level of $\alpha = 0.01$) of -0.513, -0.539, -0.479 and -0.486 are computed for the correlation of the number of deployed yard cranes with $\overline{\omega}^{\text{hr+}}_{\text{total}}$, $\overline{\omega}^{\text{hr+}}_{\text{ls}}$, $\overline{\omega}^{\text{hr+}}_{\text{ws}}$ and $\overline{\omega}^{\text{hr+}}_{\text{wsout}}$, respectively, thus confirming a strong causal connection between the available crane resources in a yard block and the mean vehicle-waiting times in its handover areas.

To allow a more profound and differentiated ranking of the operational performance of the SRMGC, TRMGC, DRMGC and TriRMGC systems—in particular with respect to the only slightly differing two-crane systems—the mean vehicle-waiting times in the landside and waterside handover areas of all types of RMGC systems are compared pairwise for all 385 considered yard-block layouts. The number of yard-block layouts, for which each type of RMGC system performs better than each other type are displayed in Table 7.9. There, the numbers of layouts with significantly shorter mean vehicle-waiting times—at a significance level of $\alpha = 0.05$—are noted in brackets. Owing to above mentioned reasons, mostly that type of RMGC system is found to perform (significantly) better, that deploys more cranes per yard block. Nevertheless, for very few yard-block layouts—mostly rather small-sized ones—types of RMGC systems with fewer crane resources are found to perform (significantly) better than types of RMGC systems that deploy more cranes per yard block. This can be explained the way that types of RMGC systems with a lot of crane resources do not pay off for a certain yard-block layout as long as even types of RMGC systems with fewer crane resources are able to perform the crane workload that is induced by that layout with only very few seconds of mean vehicle-waiting times. Usually, this is only possible for small-sized yard-block

Table 7.9 Pairwise performance comparison between types of RMGC systems with respect to $\overline{\overline{\omega}}_{\mathrm{ls}}^{\mathrm{hr+}}$ and $\overline{\overline{\omega}}_{\mathrm{ws}}^{\mathrm{hr+}}$

		Numbers of layouts							
		SRMGC		TRMGC		DRMGC		TriRMGC	
Compared to		leads to (significantly) shorter vehicle-waiting times							
SRMGC	$\overline{\overline{\omega}}_{\mathrm{ls}}^{\mathrm{hr+}}$	–	–	385	(385)	385	(385)	385	(385)
	$\overline{\overline{\omega}}_{\mathrm{ws}}^{\mathrm{hr+}}$	–	–	370	(308)	349	(308)	355	(311)
TRMGC	$\overline{\overline{\omega}}_{\mathrm{ls}}^{\mathrm{hr+}}$	0	(0)	–	–	0	(0)	366	(344)
	$\overline{\overline{\omega}}_{\mathrm{ws}}^{\mathrm{hr+}}$	15	(1)	–	–	100	(16)	287	(222)
DRMGC	$\overline{\overline{\omega}}_{\mathrm{ls}}^{\mathrm{hr+}}$	0	(0)	385	(385)	–	–	385	(385)
	$\overline{\overline{\omega}}_{\mathrm{ws}}^{\mathrm{hr+}}$	36	(3)	285	(117)	–	–	358	(271)
TriRMGC	$\overline{\overline{\omega}}_{\mathrm{ls}}^{\mathrm{hr+}}$	0	(0)	19	(3)	0	(0)	–	–
	$\overline{\overline{\omega}}_{\mathrm{ws}}^{\mathrm{hr+}}$	30	(0)	98	(11)	27	(0)	–	–

Numbers of layouts in which shorter vehicle-waiting times are yielded with one type of RMGC systems compared to another type; the number of layouts with significant differences is denoted in brackets

layouts. For such layouts, no (significant) performance advantage is induced by a greater number of cranes per yard block. Moreover, additional cranes increase the risk for and the extent of crane interferences, which leads to prolonged average job-execution times. As a consequence, the originally supposed performance advantage of additional crane resources may even turn into a drawback if they are not really required anyhow.

With regard to the performance comparison between the two-crane systems, the previously observed slight advantage of the TRMGC system versus the DRMGC systems is confirmed by the results of the pairwise performance comparison of all 385 layouts in Table 7.9. It can be seen that the TRMGC system leads to significantly shorter XT-waiting times than the DRMGC system for all considered yard-block layouts and to significantly shorter SC-waiting times for 117 layouts. The DRMGC system only leads to significantly shorter SC-waiting times than the TRMGC system for 16 layouts. No significant SC-waiting time differences are observed for 252 layouts. Hence, Research hypothesis 1.4.2 is principally confirmed by the results of this simulation study—in particular with regard to the landside vehicle-waiting times—but cannot be confirmed in total due to several yard-block layouts without significant performance advantage of the TRMGC system over the DRMGC system with regard to the mean SC-waiting time in the waterside handover area.

At first glance, it might be surprising that the TRMGC system leads to better operational performances than the DRMGC system at all, since one would expect that more flexibility in the crane operations—which is offered by the crossing capability of the DRMGC system—is always connected with shorter vehicle-waiting times due to inducing fewer and/or shorter crane interferences and allowing more freedom of choice for crane-scheduling decisions. However, upon closer examination of the simulation results, two sources for the performance advantage of the TRMGC system over the DRMGC system can be identified: the time duration for crane movements and the duration of crane-interference times. In fact, for most yard-block layouts, both the average time durations for crane movements along the x-axis and the mean crane-interference times are observed to be significantly longer—at a significance level of $\alpha = 0.05$—for the DRMGC system than for the TRMGC system, thus explaining longer job-execution and vehicle-waiting times for the DRMGC system as compared to the TRMGC system. Longer average time durations for crane movements along the x-axis of the DRMGC system can be explained since the portal of an outer large crane is assumed to have a slower maximum speed than the portal of an inner small crane (see Sect. 7.1.3). Longer crane-interference times for the DRMGC system may be explained by the comparably simple default strategies for crane scheduling and routing (see Sect. 7.1.3), which can be expected to induce more adverse planning decisions with regard to the interference times for the DRMGC system than for the TRMGC system. Despite of the crossing capability, basically, a greater risk for crane interferences is connected with the DRMGC system than with the TRMGC system, as the working areas of both cranes are more likely overlapping due to the fact that both cranes of the DRMGC system are allowed to serve both handover areas, while each crane of the TRMGC system can only serve one handover area. Therefore, disregarding possible crane interferences for decisions on crane scheduling—as done by the applied PRIO2 method (see Sect. 5.3.5)—can be expected to induce more and/or longer crane interferences for the DRMGC system. Additionally considering the fact that the HAC mechanism (see Sect. 5.4.3) is by default not applied for routing the cranes of the DRMGC systems, the handover areas are expected to be unnecessarily often blocked for operations of other cranes, thus inducing further crane-interference times for the DRMGC system as compared to the TRMGC system. In total, it may be concluded that, for most layouts, the flexibility of the DRMGC system does not compensate for the longer crane-interference times and the slower velocity of its cranes compared to the TRMGC system under the applied default parametrisation. In how far increases of the portal velocity of the outer large crane and/or the use of crane-interference-time-reducing crane-scheduling and routing strategies for the DRMGC system may lead to a reduction or even to a reversal of the performance differences between the DRMGC and TRMGC systems is in detail investigated in Sects. 7.3.5, 7.3.7 and 7.3.8.

It can be seen from the results of the pairwise performance comparison of RMGC systems in Table 7.9 and by comparing Figs. 7.8 and 7.9 that the performance advantages of the TRMGC system over the DRMGC system are more pronounced for the mean XT-waiting times in the landside handover area than for the mean SC-waiting times in the waterside handover area. This can be explained by workload imbalances between the waterside and landside handover areas and differences in the crane-scheduling strategies between TRMGC and DRMGC systems. Due to assuming a significant share of transshipment containers in this simulation study (see Sect. 7.1.3), more crane workload is induced for the waterside handover area than for the landside handover area. While the DRMGC system is able to flexibly react to these workload imbalances by allocating handling capacities of both cranes to the waterside handover area, the TRMGC system is far less flexible, as the waterside and landside handover areas can only be served by the respective cranes. As a consequence, the available crane resources for the landside handover area are reduced in the DRMGC system, while kept constant in the TRMGC system. Hence, more crane resources are available in the TRMGC system for performing the same workload than in the DRMGC system, thus reducing the risk for and the extent of XT-waiting times for the TRMGC system as compared to the DRMGC system.

Finally, it is illustrated by Figs. 7.2–7.6 that the extent of the performance differences between the types of RMGC systems appears to depend on the underlying yard-block layout. Firstly, it can be seen from Figs. 7.2 and 7.3 that the performance differences between the types of RMGC systems become more pronounced with increasing yard-block capacities. This can be explained by increasing risk for and increasing numbers of simultaneously waiting vehicles in the handover areas with growing yard-block capacities, as explained in Sect. 7.2.2.2. Similarly, for the reasons discussed in Sect. 7.2.2.3, the performance differences between all types of RMGC systems increase with the stacking height and width of the yard block (see Figs. 7.5 and 7.6). In contrast, the performance differences between the TRMGC and DRMGC system can be observed to decrease with increasing block length (see Fig. 7.4), which is to be explained by the more positive effects of the block length for the vehicle-waiting times of the TRMGC system than for the vehicle-waiting times of the DRMGC system (see Sect. 7.2.2.3).

In summary, the number of deployed cranes per yard block is found to have significantly negative effects on the mean vehicle-waiting times in the handover areas. Therefore, the TriRMGC system is found to perform best for most considered yard-block layouts, while the SRMGC system is mostly performing worst. With regard to the comparative performance ranking of the two-crane systems, it is found that the TRMGC system is mostly performing better than the DRMGC—in particular with respect to the landside vehicle-waiting times—but for some yard-block layouts also the opposite is observed. As a consequence,

- Research hypothesis 1.4.1 is confirmed, while
- Research hypothesis 1.4.2 is confirmed for the landside handover area, but is not confirmed for the waterside handover area

based on the simulation results of this terminal-design study.

7.2.3 Summary of the RMGC-Design Study

Within the framework of this section, it is confirmed by means of extensive simulation analyses that the operational performance of RMGC systems at seaport container terminals, in terms of the vehicle-waiting times in the handover areas of the yard blocks, is greatly determined by the design of these systems. Basically, the vehicle-waiting times in the handover areas are found to increase with the dimensions of the yard block and to decrease with the number of yard cranes deployed per yard block.

In more detail, with regard to the operational-performance effects of the yard-block layout, it is found that the vehicle-waiting times neither increase linearly with the yard-block capacity nor with one of the three yard-block dimensions. Moreover, in the range of practically relevant yard-block sizes, the vehicle-waiting times are found to increase progressively with the capacity (see Sect. 7.2.2.2) and the dimensions of the yard block (see Sect. 7.2.2.3), thus not allowing to determine constant rates of substitution between the vehicle-waiting-time effects of the yard-block dimensions. However, by means of regression analyses with a (linearised) power function, some important findings on the relative performance effects of the yard-block dimensions are revealed (see Sect. 7.2.2.3). The block height is found to induce the greatest vehicle-waiting-time effects of all three yard-block dimensions for all types of RMGC systems, whereas the relative importance of the block width and length for the resulting vehicle-waiting times is found to depend on the operating type of RMGC system. While for SRMGC and TRMGC systems, the block length is found to induce slightly bigger effects on the vehicle-waiting times in the handover areas than the block width, this relation is reversed for DRMGC and TriRMGC systems.

Considering the negative vehicle-waiting-time effects of the number of deployed cranes per yard block, the TriRMGC system is found to yield the shortest vehicle-waiting times of all analysed types of RMGC systems, while the SRMGC system is found to induce the longest vehicle-waiting times for almost all yard-block layouts of relevant size (see Sect. 7.2.2.4). Both types of two-crane systems are found to yield rather similar vehicle-waiting times in between those of the other types of RMGC systems. But different than expected, upon closer examination, the TRMGC system is found to perform slightly better than the DRMGC system, as for all considered yard-block layouts significantly shorter XT-waiting times and for most considered yard-block layouts even slightly shorter SC-waiting times are yielded with the TRMGC system. The performance differences between the different types of RMGC systems are found to increase with the yard-block capacities and dimensions, of which the block width is found to have particularly positive effects on the performance gap between the TRMGC and DRMGC systems (see Sect. 7.2.2.3).

7.3 Sensitivity Analysis of RMGC-Design Study

In this section, the previously made basic findings on the operational-performance effects of RMGC-design decisions are investigated by means of sensitivity analysis on a ceteris paribus basis in order to evaluate their robustness against changes of selected input factors that are supposed to have notable effects on the operational performance and the optimal design of RMGC systems. The investigated input factors include parameters specifying the amount and the distribution of the crane workload as well as the amount and the use of the available crane resources (see Sect. 4.1.3). The way the sensitivity against each of these input parameters is investigated is principally identical for all considered parameters: Firstly, research hypotheses on the expected effects of the investigated parameter on the operational performance and the optimal design of RMGC systems are formulated. Thereafter, the experimental setup used to analyse the effects of the investigated input parameter is specified. Finally, the simulation results of the specified experiments are presented, analysed and discussed—in particular with respect to the formulated research hypotheses.

In Sect. 7.3.1, the sensitivity analysis is started with investigating the effects of the average yard-block-filling rate on the operational performance and the design of RMGC systems, which is followed by analysing the influence of the mean container-dwell time in Sect. 7.3.2. Thereafter, the performance and design-planning effects of different transshipment factors and vessel-call patterns are studied in Sects. 7.3.3 and 7.3.4, respectively. The effects of changes in the crane kinematics on the performance and the design of RMGC systems are investigated in Sect. 7.3.5. The performance and design-planning effects of the applied strategies for the operational planning problems of RMGC systems are addressed in Sects. 7.3.6–7.3.8. Firstly, the effects of the applied container-stacking strategy are investigated. Thereafter, the effects of the used crane-scheduling strategy are analysed. Finally, the effects of varying crane-routing strategies are investigated. This section is closed with a summarising overview on the influence of the investigated input parameters on the operational performance and the design of RMGC systems.

7.3.1 Influence of the Filling Rate

The number of containers that are, on average, stored in a yard block is by definition not only determined by its stacking capacity, which is previously found to be of great importance for the operational performance of RMGC systems (see Sect. 7.2.2.2), but also by its average filling rate. Therefore, in Sect. 4.1.3, the average filling rate of the yard block is qualitatively expected to have notable effects on the vehicle-waiting times in the handover areas, thus, in a reverse conclusion, possibly influencing decisions on the design of RMGC systems. In this subsection, it is quantitatively investigated to what extent the operational performance of container-storage yards is actually affected by and in how far the previous findings on the RMGC-design-planning problem are sensitive to changes of the average yard-block-filling rate.

7.3.1.1 Research Hypotheses

Referring to Sect. 4.1.3.1, the average filling rate of the yard block π^{fillavg} can be expected to have significantly positive effects on the mean vehicle-waiting times in the handover areas of each RMGC yard block by implicitly defining the corresponding crane workload. The higher the average filling rate π^{fillavg}, the more containers need, ceteris paribus, to be stored, to be retrieved and to be shuffled by the same amount of crane resources, thus increasing the risk for and the extent of vehicle-waiting times in the handover areas. In particular, the number of shuffle moves required to retrieve a container can be expected to increase with the average yard-block-filling rate for two reasons: Firstly, the actually realised stacking height, which is previously found to have significantly positive effects on the risk for shuffle moves (see Sect. 7.2.2.3), increases with the average filling rate of the yard block, as more containers need to be stacked on the same number of ground slots. In addition, the number of allowed stacking positions (i.e., non-full piles and ground positions) can be expected to decrease with the filling rate (see Sect. 5.2.1). As a consequence, it becomes more likely that only stacking positions with a greater risk for shuffle moves are available for newly arriving and to-be-shuffled containers compared to situations with greater numbers of alternative stacking positions available.

Considering the fact that decisions on the design of RMGC systems are greatly affected by the operational performance of that system (see Sect. 4.1.2), the average yard-block-filling rate of a seaport container terminal can be expected to have notable effects for decisions on the right type of RMGC system and/or yard-block layout. While increasing yard-block-filling rates require smaller yard-block layouts and/or additional crane resources in order to avoid increasing vehicle-waiting times, decreasing filling rates allow to design larger yard blocks and/or to deploy fewer crane resources without impairing the operational performance of the container-storage yard. However, decisions on the design of RMGC systems are multi-objective planning problems that are not only made with respect to the operational-performance effects, but also with respect to the cost and area-performance effects (see Sect. 4.1.2). Therefore, the exact effects of changes in the average yard-block-filling rate on the design of RMGC systems cannot be anticipated only on the basis of the resulting vehicle-waiting times, but also need to consider the effects on the yard density, the unit cost of container-storage and retrieval operations and possible interdependencies between these performance indicators, which is beyond the scope of this work. However, due to the fact that all types of RMGC systems and yard-block layouts are equally affected by changes of the yard-block-filling rate, this parameter cannot be expected to structurally change the basic findings on the operational-performance effects of the yard-block layout and the type of RMGC (see Sect. 7.2.3). Based on this analysis, Research hypotheses 2.1.1 and 2.1.2 are formulated:

Research Hypothesis 2.1.1. The average filling rate of the yard block π^{fillavg} has significantly positive effects on the mean vehicle-waiting times in the handover areas.

Research Hypothesis 2.1.2. The basic findings on the operational-performance effects of the RMGC design are not structurally affected by changes of the average yard-block-filling rate π^{fillavg}.

7.3.1.2 Experimental Setup

To test the influence of the average yard-block-filling rate on the RMGC-design-planning problem, 324 simulation experiments are conducted. Each RMGC design, that results from all combinations of the four considered types of RMGC systems and the nine representative yard-block layouts (see Table 7.1), is simulated with nine different settings of the yard-block-filling rate around the default value of $\pi^{\text{fillavg}} = 75\%$. The average filling rate of the yard block is varied in the interval from $\pi^{\text{fillavg}} = 55\%$ to $\pi^{\text{fillavg}} = 95\%$ in steps of 5%. In addition, it needs to be ensured that the maximum allowed yard-block-filling rate is always greater than the average filling rate in order to enable the realisation of the average filling rate and to preserve some flexibility for fluctuations in the capacity utilisation. Here, in accordance with the default parameter settings, the maximum allowed filling rate π^{fillmax} is adapted in such a way that the maximum allowed filling rate is 5% greater than the average filling rate for all experiments with average yard-block-filling rates exceeding $\pi^{\text{fillavg}} = 75\%$. For experiments with average yard-block-filling rates below 75%, the maximum allowed filling rate is always left at the default value of $\pi^{\text{fillmax}} = 80\%$. Apart from the maximum allowed and average yard-block-filling rates, all other input parameters of the simulation model are set to the default settings as specified in Sect. 7.1.3.

7.3.1.3 Results and Discussion

The results of all simulation experiments on the influence of the average yard-block-filling rate are shown in Tables 7.10 and 7.11. In the first two columns of these tables, the average and maximum allowed yard-block-filling rates are noted, respectively, while the resulting performance figures for different RMGC designs are displayed in the following columns. For reasons of space, only the resulting mean XT and SC-waiting times in the handover areas are displayed in Tables 7.10 and 7.11, respectively, as only these figures are absolutely necessary to identify possible differences in the operational-performance effects of changing filling rates between the landside and waterside handover areas. The results of other important performance figures (see Sect. 7.1.1) are given in Appendix A.5.1. The default settings of the average and maximum allowed yard-block-filling rates and the resulting performance figures are highlighted in bold.

It can be seen from Tables 7.10 and 7.11 that both $\overline{\overline{\omega}}_{\text{ls}}^{\text{hr+}}$ and $\overline{\overline{\omega}}_{\text{ws}}^{\text{hr+}}$ increase with the average yard-block-filling rate for most considered yard-block layouts and types of RMGC systems, just as postulated by Research hypothesis 2.1.1. In fact, by means of correlation analyses, the average filling rate of the yard block π^{fillavg} is found to be strongly positively correlated with $\overline{\overline{\omega}}_{\text{ws}}^{\text{hr+}}$—at a significance level of $\alpha = 0.05$—for all considered layouts and RMGC systems, which can be explained by an increase in the crane workload with the average yard-block-filling rate (see Sect. 7.3.1.1). As conjectured, increases in the number of shuffle moves

Table 7.10 Influence of the average yard-block-filling rate (π^{fillavg}) on the mean XT-waiting time ($\overline{\overline{\omega}}^{\text{hr+}}_{\text{ls}}$) for selected yard-block layouts and all types of RMGC systems

Filling rate		Yard-block layout								
π^{fillavg}	π^{fillmax}	Small	Low	Narrow	Short	Medium	Long	Wide	High	Big
Resulting $\overline{\overline{\omega}}^{\text{hr+}}_{\text{ls}}$ with the SRMGC system (s)										
55%	80%	59.66	91.79	177.42	168.57	207.54	295.49	273.72	1,341.50	2,699.36
60%	80%	61.60	93.41	193.25	175.72	239.70	367.06	322.57	1,740.82	3,031.24
65%	80%	63.22	95.69	210.17	194.22	269.32	517.21	449.49	2,071.24	3,398.25
70%	80%	68.62	97.12	216.68	204.65	312.77	648.83	554.89	2,197.74	3,514.20
75%	**80%**	**65.90**	**95.41**	**226.61**	**204.03**	**336.25**	**772.82**	**675.77**	**2,244.74**	**3,903.45**
80%	85%	65.68	98.42	227.56	209.30	420.76	900.58	825.50	2,253.20	3,960.64
85%	90%	64.93	98.93	235.60	222.77	429.30	1,024.88	899.71	2,257.94	4,069.21
90%	95%	71.13	106.64	237.84	212.98	450.23	1,083.54	1,019.36	2,322.12	4,310.94
95%	100%	69.22	102.12	237.81	224.29	527.12	1,204.88	1,055.88	2,389.33	4,501.19
Resulting $\overline{\overline{\omega}}^{\text{hr+}}_{\text{ls}}$ with the TRMGC system (s)										
55%	80%	19.74	28.00	73.28	71.74	84.08	101.20	95.67	230.03	568.68
60%	80%	20.35	28.40	78.69	73.71	90.11	109.26	103.29	290.32	835.78
65%	80%	20.46	28.53	82.25	75.98	94.72	120.38	113.03	354.67	1,164.57
70%	80%	20.14	28.84	82.70	77.07	97.34	122.86	117.24	372.54	1,404.13
75%	**80%**	**19.48**	**29.13**	**82.08**	**77.19**	**98.58**	**126.78**	**118.96**	**387.72**	**1,540.04**
80%	85%	20.39	28.95	80.23	75.74	99.60	136.36	126.93	402.24	1,585.48
85%	90%	19.81	29.01	80.28	73.60	97.83	136.15	128.49	417.22	1,650.71
90%	95%	19.92	29.35	78.32	71.85	98.16	136.64	126.12	440.91	1,679.26
95%	100%	19.82	29.13	77.95	72.27	95.58	134.87	130.67	433.00	1,667.68
Resulting $\overline{\overline{\omega}}^{\text{hr+}}_{\text{ls}}$ with the DRMGC system (s)										
55%	80%	29.68	45.71	102.40	106.40	127.89	153.64	150.63	298.92	778.28
60%	80%	31.89	50.44	111.26	108.89	135.42	163.97	161.89	378.86	1,119.97
65%	80%	30.01	50.01	115.80	117.24	142.18	172.17	174.70	445.99	1,523.02
70%	80%	31.86	53.16	117.26	117.86	143.82	179.84	177.70	481.34	1,753.67
75%	**80%**	**31.48**	**52.60**	**116.45**	**118.90**	**146.10**	**179.24**	**181.10**	**509.36**	**1,907.61**
80%	85%	32.38	52.10	115.29	118.89	148.75	195.29	192.39	522.38	1,999.89
85%	90%	33.64	55.33	118.02	116.80	149.34	195.79	202.25	543.27	2,002.29
90%	95%	31.66	55.54	112.40	113.31	146.52	196.39	203.08	594.42	2,027.47
95%	100%	31.51	55.31	113.68	114.72	147.11	201.21	210.56	612.89	2,042.47
Resulting $\overline{\overline{\omega}}^{\text{hr+}}_{\text{ls}}$ with the TriRMGC system (s)										
55%	80%	20.65	28.39	63.16	66.12	75.91	85.44	88.83	172.11	304.27
60%	80%	20.84	27.93	66.16	69.51	77.35	89.54	91.43	190.54	414.34
65%	80%	20.02	26.81	67.53	70.69	81.02	93.00	98.02	211.59	594.07
70%	80%	19.42	26.77	69.09	71.17	81.41	97.19	97.23	213.51	688.43
75%	**80%**	**19.56**	**26.47**	**66.99**	**68.47**	**80.43**	**98.14**	**98.35**	**208.77**	**754.71**
80%	85%	19.34	26.38	65.04	67.38	82.28	100.85	98.75	210.84	801.73
85%	90%	19.50	26.53	65.86	67.26	81.11	99.01	100.34	220.20	818.07
90%	95%	19.00	26.25	64.16	63.60	77.01	97.91	99.99	231.89	859.74
95%	100%	18.68	25.83	61.21	64.14	78.07	97.42	102.42	239.53	879.70

Table 7.11 Influence of the average yard-block-filling rate (π^{fillavg}) on the mean SC-waiting time ($\overline{\overline{\omega}}_{\text{ws}}^{\text{hr+}}$) for selected yard-block layouts and all types of RMGC systems

Filling rate		Yard-block layout								
π^{fillavg}	π^{fillmax}	Small	Low	Narrow	Short	Medium	Long	Wide	High	Big
Resulting $\overline{\overline{\omega}}_{\text{ws}}^{\text{hr+}}$ with the SRMGC system (s)										
55%	80%	1.29	2.21	10.32	8.91	16.36	38.64	29.47	809.35	1,542.06
60%	80%	1.59	2.57	18.42	13.04	30.46	77.76	58.81	1,123.13	1,880.10
65%	80%	1.60	2.93	23.67	20.14	49.69	187.00	138.51	1,443.73	2,239.10
70%	80%	1.85	2.72	30.28	29.04	77.62	302.38	250.97	1,535.93	2,455.56
75%	**80%**	**1.69**	**2.86**	**40.46**	**28.71**	**102.93**	**410.23**	**350.05**	**1,597.83**	**2,837.74**
80%	85%	1.45	3.74	39.04	35.57	167.86	556.99	467.66	1,677.39	3,079.32
85%	90%	1.65	3.75	49.73	44.98	178.04	696.67	572.16	1,669.30	3,302.70
90%	95%	3.13	4.11	50.78	40.58	197.52	740.57	687.39	1,712.36	3,501.20
95%	100%	2.40	4.25	56.82	48.93	253.93	872.63	722.98	1,824.84	3,880.23
Resulting $\overline{\overline{\omega}}_{\text{ws}}^{\text{hr+}}$ with the TRMGC system (s)										
55%	80%	1.83	2.52	4.35	4.07	5.33	7.33	7.09	57.22	422.63
60%	80%	1.67	2.35	5.18	4.33	6.41	10.94	8.47	126.09	744.73
65%	80%	1.42	2.96	6.59	6.08	9.93	14.31	11.25	188.92	1,157.09
70%	80%	1.58	2.65	6.86	5.96	10.26	16.39	16.37	209.39	1,387.00
75%	**80%**	**1.19**	**2.14**	**7.79**	**6.74**	**13.31**	**25.15**	**21.79**	**247.50**	**1,586.02**
80%	85%	1.58	2.47	9.16	6.87	14.36	31.42	26.72	265.64	1,706.16
85%	90%	1.43	2.40	8.84	7.90	15.80	37.60	31.24	296.16	1,774.98
90%	95%	1.99	2.96	9.69	7.65	16.70	47.56	32.34	306.72	1,989.16
95%	100%	2.22	3.19	10.37	9.09	17.91	48.82	44.06	324.52	1,958.82
Resulting $\overline{\overline{\omega}}_{\text{ws}}^{\text{hr+}}$ with the DRMGC system (s)										
55%	80%	1.44	2.16	5.35	5.99	8.29	9.99	9.88	63.86	374.08
60%	80%	1.85	2.05	6.35	6.90	9.50	14.14	13.88	135.58	657.15
65%	80%	1.09	2.48	7.28	7.17	12.06	17.41	17.28	196.97	1,012.43
70%	80%	1.59	2.56	9.12	8.33	13.64	21.04	22.88	221.89	1,212.78
75%	**80%**	**1.44**	**2.76**	**10.37**	**9.57**	**15.89**	**24.57**	**23.92**	**259.60**	**1,401.64**
80%	85%	1.77	2.84	10.79	11.38	17.79	34.68	33.97	268.28	1,477.75
85%	90%	1.65	3.05	12.62	11.38	18.82	37.98	43.56	304.22	1,486.92
90%	95%	1.77	3.55	11.59	11.81	20.39	42.02	42.95	355.29	1,616.55
95%	100%	1.79	3.69	12.11	12.95	22.88	45.23	53.78	361.35	1,682.74
Resulting $\overline{\overline{\omega}}_{\text{ws}}^{\text{hr+}}$ with the TriRMGC system (s)										
55%	80%	1.22	1.77	3.93	4.31	5.61	6.96	7.38	22.26	67.31
60%	80%	1.49	2.56	5.09	4.45	6.54	7.61	7.67	33.18	141.53
65%	80%	1.39	2.70	5.40	5.16	6.97	8.45	9.24	49.28	291.45
70%	80%	1.83	2.93	5.24	6.51	7.53	9.41	10.50	53.44	373.74
75%	**80%**	**1.16**	**2.76**	**6.61**	**6.48**	**8.44**	**10.23**	**10.85**	**56.00**	**451.96**
80%	85%	1.49	2.59	6.62	6.74	9.18	12.81	12.56	59.94	512.28
85%	90%	1.99	2.83	7.04	7.24	9.07	12.77	13.99	68.79	527.00
90%	95%	1.89	2.72	6.55	6.97	9.88	14.39	13.75	83.42	587.75
95%	100%	1.63	3.44	8.21	7.29	10.25	15.24	16.50	85.90	610.69

are found to be particularly responsible for the workload increases, since highly significantly positive correlations are computed between the average yard-block-filling rate and the mean number of shuffle moves per retrieval job ($\overline{\overline{\psi}}$) for most considered RMGC designs. The observed differences in the extent of the vehicle-waiting-time increases with the filling rate between different RMGC designs can be explained by system-dependent differences in the available crane resources and layout-dependent differences in the absolute increase of the crane workload with increasing average filling rates. While in absolute terms only little additional crane workload is induced by filling-rate increases for small-sized yard blocks, increases in the filling rate lead to great additional amounts of workload for large-sized layouts. As explained in Sect. 7.2, greater increases of the workload can be expected to have bigger effects on the mean vehicle-waiting times in the handover areas than smaller increases—in particular for RMGC systems with only few crane resources.

Compared to $\overline{\overline{\omega}}_{\text{ws}}^{\text{hr+}}$, $\overline{\overline{\omega}}_{\text{ls}}^{\text{hr+}}$ is found to be less strongly correlated with the average yard-block-filling rate for certain yard-block layouts and types of RMGC systems—in particular for small-sized yard blocks like "small", "short", "narrow" and "low". This can also be seen from Table 7.10 by the drop in $\overline{\overline{\omega}}_{\text{ls}}^{\text{hr+}}$ for these layouts with comparably high filling rates. This counterintuitive observation can basically be explained as increasing average yard-block-filling rates lead to a shortage in the number of allowed stacking positions for newly arriving and to-be-shuffled containers, thus, in turn leading to more peaks in the block filling rate, where even no allowed stacking positions are available at all (i.e., $\Phi_c^{\text{allowed}} = \{\}$). By means of correlation analyses, the average yard-block-filling rate is confirmed to have highly significantly positive effects on the fraction of calls of the container-positioning method where no allowed stacking position is available, independently of the considered yard-block layout and the operating type of the RMGC system. But due to the fact that small-sized yard blocks inherently have fewer stacking options (i.e., piles and ground positions) than large-sized ones, the average yard-block-filling rate is found to have greater effects on the fraction of calls of the container-positioning method where no allowed stacking position is available for small-sized yard-block layouts. Within the framework of the CCFS container-positioning method (see Sect. 5.2.4), newly arriving and to-be-shuffled containers are redirected and relocated to other yard blocks, respectively, if no allowed stacking positions are available, thus reducing the crane workload for the considered yard block compared to the workload originally intended by the specified average filling rate π^{fillavg}. Owing to the fact that landside-departing containers can usually be expected to cause more shuffle moves than waterside-departing containers (see Sect. 5.2), the crane workload of the landside handover area is more reduced by the absence of allowed stacking positions with increasing average yard-block-filling rate. In total, increases in the average yard-block-filling rate may even lead to counterintuitive net reductions in the landside crane workload for small-sized yard-block layouts, as the originally supposed workload increases with growing average yard-block-filling rate are overcompensated by workload reductions due to increasing container relocations to other yard blocks for landside-departing containers. As a consequence, the risk for and the extent of XT-waiting times may even be reduced with very high average yard-block-filling rates, which may explain the partly counterintuitive results of Table 7.10.

Finally, it can be observed from Tables 7.10 and 7.11 that for all considered average yard-block-filling rates increasing yard-block capacities and dimensions lead to increasing mean vehicle-waiting times in the handover areas, just as observed, discussed and explained in Sect. 7.2. Similarly, it can be seen that independently of the considered filling rate the SRMGC system performs worst, the TriRMGC system performs best and the DRMGC and TRMGC systems lead to intermediate vehicle-waiting times, but with slight performance advantages for the TRMGC system, in particular with respect to $\overline{\overline{\omega}}_{\text{ls}}^{\text{hr+}}$. Thus, it can be concluded that the findings on the operational-performance effects of the yard-block layout and the type of RMGC system are structurally unaffected by changes in the average yard-block-filling rate, just as postulated by Research hypothesis 2.1.2.

Altogether, the average yard-block-filling rate is found to have significantly positive effects on the mean vehicle-waiting times in the handover areas, but the basic findings on the operational-performance effects of the RMGC design appear to be rather insensitive to changes in the filling rate. As a consequence,

- Research hypothesis 2.1.1 is confirmed and
- Research hypothesis 2.1.2 is confirmed

for the considered experimental setup of this simulation-based sensitivity analysis.

7.3.2 *Influence of the Container-Dwell Time*

The total workload for the cranes of a yard block, which is previously found to be of great importance for the operational performance of RMGC systems, is not only determined by the average number of stored containers, but also by their velocity of circulation, which is, by definition, inversely related to the time a container stays in the yard block. Therefore, by defining the average velocity of container circulation for yard blocks, the mean container-dwell time is likewise expected to be another vehicle-waiting time and RMGC-design-influencing input parameter (see Sect. 4.1.3). In this subsection, it is investigated to what extent the vehicle-waiting times in the handover areas are influenced by and in how far the operational-performance effects of the RMGC design are sensitive to changes of the mean container-dwell time.

7.3.2.1 Research Hypotheses

In contrast to the average yard-block-filling rate, the mean container-dwell time $\overline{\delta}$ can be expected to have significantly negative effects on the mean vehicle-waiting times in the handover areas, as the crane workload of a yard block increases with decreasing values of $\overline{\delta}$ (see Sect. 4.1.3.1). The shorter the mean container-dwell time $\overline{\delta}$, the more stack visits can be realised for a given storage capacity within the same period of time, thus, ceteris paribus, increasing the number of storage, retrieval and shuffle jobs that need to be performed in that period of time. But unlike for increases of the yard-block-filling rate, no overproportional increase of the, on average, required number of shuffle moves per retrieval job ($\overline{\overline{\psi}}$) is expected with decreasing mean container-dwell time $\overline{\delta}$, as the actually realised stacking heights and the number of allowed stacking positions are unaffected by increasing the velocity of container circulation for a yard block.

In practice, it can often be observed that the velocities of circulation differ between import/export containers and transshipment containers (Saanen 2004, pp. 42–43). Usually, transshipment containers are observed to stay shorter at the terminal than import/export containers, thus leading to shorter mean dwell times for transshipment terminals (see Sect. 2.3.1). In this work, the dwell-time distributions of both container flows are, by default, identically parametrised (see Sect. 7.1.3), although it is possible to specify different mean container-dwell times for import/export ($\overline{\delta}^{ie}$) and transshipment containers ($\overline{\delta}^{ts}$) in the used simulation model (see Sect. 6.4.2). However, as long as the mean container-dwell time over all handled containers ($\overline{\delta}$) remains unchanged, increasing differences between $\overline{\delta}^{ts}$ and $\overline{\delta}^{ie}$ are not expected to induce either positive nor negative effects on the vehicle-waiting times in the handover areas, as hardly any effects for the crane workload are induced by these differences. In fact, the difference in the mean dwell times of transshipment and import/export containers cannot be expected to have any influence on the total amount of crane workload, on the distribution of the crane workload between the waterside and landside handover areas as well as on the number and the extent of peak workloads at both block ends. Therefore, the operational performance of RMGC systems is only expected to depend on the overall mean container-dwell time $\overline{\delta}$, but not on the underlying differences between $\overline{\delta}^{ts}$ and $\overline{\delta}^{ie}$.

Owing to the expected influence of the mean container-dwell time $\overline{\delta}$ on the vehicle-waiting times in the handover areas, the decisions on the right type of RMGC system and yard-block layout are likewise expected to be influenced by this input parameter. While decreases of the mean container-dwell time require smaller yard-block layouts and/or additional crane resources in order to avoid longer vehicle-waiting times, increasing dwell times allow for the design of larger yard blocks and/or to deploy fewer crane resources without causing longer vehicle-waiting timcs. This allows to improve the area and/or cost performance of the container-storage yard without impairing its operational performance. However, similar to the effects of the average yard-block-filling rate for decisions on the design of RMGC systems, the mean container-dwell time can likewise not be expected to change the basic findings on the RMGC-design-planning problem structurally, as all types of RMGC systems and yard-block layouts are equally affected by changes in the mean container-dwell time. In summary, Research hypotheses 2.2.1–2.2.3 are formulated:

Research Hypothesis 2.2.1. The mean container-dwell time $\overline{\delta}$ has significantly negative effects on the mean vehicle-waiting times in the handover areas.

Research Hypothesis 2.2.2. The difference between the mean dwell time of transshipment containers ($\overline{\delta}^{ts}$) and the mean dwell time of import/export containers ($\overline{\delta}^{ie}$) does not have a significant effect on the mean vehicle-waiting times in the handover areas.

Research Hypothesis 2.2.3. The basic findings on the operational-performance effects of the RMGC design are not structurally affected by changes of the mean container-dwell time $\overline{\delta}$.

7.3.2.2 Experimental Setup

To investigate the influence of the container-dwell time on the operational performance and the design of RMGC systems, two experimental studies are conducted. Firstly, each combination of the four considered types of RMGC systems and the nine representative yard-block layouts is tested with different values for the mean container-dwell times $\overline{\delta}$, while still assuming $\overline{\delta} = \overline{\delta}^{ts} = \overline{\delta}^{ie}$, in order to analyse the effects of the mean container-dwell time $\overline{\delta}$ on the operational performance and the design of RMGC systems as well as to validate Research hypotheses 2.2.1 and 2.2.3. The mean container-dwell time $\overline{\delta}$ is varied in steps of 0.5 days in the interval of reasonable dwell times from $\overline{\delta} = 3$ to $\overline{\delta} = 8$ days (see Sect. 2.2.1), thus leading to eleven different settings for the mean container-dwell time and 396 simulation experiments in total. Secondly, each example RMGC design is simulated with different values for the mean dwell time of import/export containers ($\overline{\delta}^{ie}$) and the mean dwell time of transshipment containers ($\overline{\delta}^{ts}$), while the overall mean container-dwell time is held constant at the default value of $\overline{\delta} = 5$ days, in order to analyse the performance and design effects of differences between $\overline{\delta}^{ie}$ and $\overline{\delta}^{ts}$ as well as to investigate Research hypothesis 2.2.2. Here, the parametrisation of $\overline{\delta}^{ie}$ is varied in steps of 0.1 days in the interval from $\overline{\delta}^{ie} = 4.6$ to $\overline{\delta}^{ie} = 5.4$ days, while the setting of $\overline{\delta}^{ts}$ is always adjusted (i.e., it varies in the interval from $\overline{\delta}^{ts} = 7.27$ to $\overline{\delta}^{ts} = 2.73$ days) in such a way that an overall mean container-dwell time of $\overline{\delta} = 5$ days is ensured (see Sect. 6.4.2), thus leading to nine different settings for $\overline{\delta}^{ie}$ and $\overline{\delta}^{ts}$ and 324 simulation experiments in total. Apart from these variations of the mean container-dwell time parameters $\overline{\delta}$, $\overline{\delta}^{ie}$ and $\overline{\delta}^{ts}$, all other input parameters of the simulation model are set to the default settings for these experiments (see Sect. 7.1.3). In particular, the structure of the container-dwell-time-specifying probability density function (6.1) is left unchanged for all experiments.

7.3.2.3 Results and Discussion

The simulation results of both experimental studies on the influence of the mean container-dwell times on the operational performance and the design of RMGC systems are shown in Tables 7.12–7.15 in a similar way as the results on the effects of the yard-block-filling rate in the preceding subsection. While the mean vehicle-waiting times in the landside and waterside handover areas of experiments with different mean container-dwell times ($\overline{\delta}$) are displayed in Tables 7.12 and 7.13, respectively, the mean XT and SC-waiting times of experiments with varying differences between the mean dwell times of import/export and transshipment containers ($\overline{\delta}^{ie}, \overline{\delta}^{ts}$) are shown in Tables 7.14 and 7.15, respectively. In all four tables, the experimental settings for the mean container-dwell time parameters are noted in the leftmost column(s), while the corresponding vehicle-waiting times for different RMGC designs are shown in the following columns. The results of other important performance figures of both experimental studies are provided in Appendix A.5.2.

It can be observed from Tables 7.12 and 7.13 that the mean vehicle-waiting times in the landside and waterside handover areas decrease more or less steadily with increasing mean container-dwell time for all considered yard-block layouts and types of RMGC systems, just as expected by Research hypothesis 2.2.1. This observation is additionally confirmed by means of correlation analyses, which compute the mean container-dwell time to be strongly negatively correlated with $\overline{\overline{\omega}}_{ls}^{hr+}$ and $\overline{\overline{\omega}}_{ws}^{hr+}$—at a significance level of $\alpha = 0.05$—for most considered RMGC designs. Only for the "big" layout in combination with the SRMGC system, no further increases of $\overline{\overline{\omega}}_{ls}^{hr+}$ and $\overline{\overline{\omega}}_{ws}^{hr+}$ are observed by decreasing the mean container-dwell time below $\overline{\delta} = 5$ days. This can be explained as the effects of increasing vehicle redirections with increasing crane workloads due to limited handover-area capacities are particularly pronounced for the SRMGC system (see Sect. 7.2.2.2). Similarly to the effects of increasing filling rates, the observed differences between the considered RMGC designs in the extent of vehicle-waiting-time increases with decreasing mean container-dwell times can likewise be explained by system-dependent differences in the available crane resources and layout-dependent differences in the absolute increase of the crane workload with decreasing mean container-dwell times.

From the results of the second experimental study on the performance and design effects of the mean container-dwell times, that are shown in Tables 7.14 and 7.15, it can be observed that the mean XT and SC-waiting times neither increase nor decrease with increases of the difference between $\overline{\delta}^{ie}$ and $\overline{\delta}^{ts}$. Thus, neither positive nor negative effects on the operational performance of RMGC systems are induced by the difference between the mean dwell times of transshipment and import/export containers, as long as the mean container-dwell time over all handled containers ($\overline{\delta}$) remains unchanged, just as expected by Research hypothesis 2.2.2. Moreover, only slight, unsystematically appearing variations of the mean vehicle-waiting times are observed that may just be caused by random differences in the generated scenarios with different settings of $\overline{\delta}^{ie}$ and $\overline{\delta}^{ts}$, but not by causal effects of the difference between the mean dwell times of transshipment and import/export containers.

Table 7.12 Influence of the mean container-dwell time ($\overline{\delta}$) on the mean XT-waiting time ($\overline{\overline{\omega}}_{\mathrm{ls}}^{\mathrm{hr+}}$) for selected yard-block layouts and all types of RMGC systems

	Yard-block layout								
$\overline{\delta}$	Small	Low	Narrow	Short	Medium	Long	Wide	High	Big
Resulting $\overline{\overline{\omega}}_{\mathrm{ls}}^{\mathrm{hr+}}$ with the SRMGC system (s)									
3.0	77.91	116.65	495.87	424.94	1,184.60	2,011.21	1,846.75	3,538.33	3,845.12
3.5	77.55	111.39	344.59	308.13	805.87	1,714.17	1,561.41	3,301.61	3,802.71
4.0	73.25	104.33	277.01	247.71	557.87	1,337.59	1,198.44	3,020.60	3,783.34
4.5	64.72	102.24	245.07	225.51	412.88	991.12	865.80	2,670.17	3,836.15
5.0	**65.90**	**95.41**	**226.61**	**204.03**	**336.25**	**772.82**	**675.77**	**2,244.74**	**3,903.45**
5.5	61.51	91.12	206.97	185.41	293.67	562.22	485.24	1,870.68	3,762.09
6.0	55.98	90.29	194.28	178.68	257.05	435.58	390.44	1,594.95	3,712.17
6.5	56.57	87.53	185.21	165.87	234.93	376.93	337.37	1,331.55	3,646.73
7.0	56.67	82.25	172.50	167.29	227.43	326.96	284.62	1,114.76	3,628.31
7.5	54.53	79.29	163.16	158.32	208.86	296.13	269.71	909.09	3,330.17
8.0	50.04	80.31	162.64	150.15	200.06	272.98	248.11	819.70	2,912.09
Resulting $\overline{\overline{\omega}}_{\mathrm{ls}}^{\mathrm{hr+}}$ with the TRMGC system (s)									
3.0	22.13	34.31	104.98	98.35	138.20	216.06	193.23	1,202.21	1,366.14
3.5	21.65	32.07	95.36	89.39	122.86	174.57	160.68	916.53	1,485.59
4.0	21.12	31.32	92.23	83.38	111.30	150.98	142.51	659.86	1,547.95
4.5	19.64	29.48	87.00	80.00	102.14	138.49	126.60	518.49	1,633.63
5.0	**19.48**	**29.13**	**82.08**	**77.19**	**98.58**	**126.78**	**118.96**	**387.72**	**1,540.04**
5.5	19.28	28.07	80.43	74.40	95.80	119.68	110.29	309.73	1,313.41
6.0	19.00	26.46	76.68	73.01	89.70	114.29	103.60	265.68	1,103.09
6.5	19.46	25.65	75.19	69.26	86.68	108.72	100.44	238.89	949.88
7.0	19.46	25.62	71.39	66.70	85.75	103.37	96.11	215.71	765.09
7.5	18.94	25.98	72.28	65.54	80.27	100.26	92.73	200.87	599.48
8.0	18.45	25.91	70.42	65.09	77.88	96.65	89.54	193.27	508.95
Resulting $\overline{\overline{\omega}}_{\mathrm{ls}}^{\mathrm{hr+}}$ with the DRMGC system (s)									
3.0	41.72	71.66	148.13	154.05	207.84	309.05	309.56	1,469.90	2,292.57
3.5	37.97	64.63	139.97	138.17	176.98	248.13	261.25	1,099.84	2,314.90
4.0	35.62	58.22	133.17	129.72	167.20	216.68	212.40	828.98	2,188.20
4.5	32.20	54.01	121.21	123.67	152.72	195.12	187.05	645.89	2,119.54
5.0	**31.48**	**52.60**	**116.45**	**118.90**	**146.10**	**179.24**	**181.10**	**509.39**	**1,907.61**
5.5	29.33	48.55	112.94	112.45	140.37	174.78	169.26	414.94	1,610.58
6.0	27.53	45.29	106.09	108.43	136.03	164.04	160.46	338.74	1,363.71
6.5	27.07	42.04	101.16	101.21	126.86	155.30	153.89	301.50	1,164.23
7.0	26.65	42.27	96.39	98.51	124.41	149.59	145.92	276.34	949.06
7.5	26.53	40.65	95.49	97.93	114.93	142.73	144.77	256.89	772.26
8.0	25.44	41.14	92.26	91.79	112.11	135.59	137.83	247.03	671.96
Resulting $\overline{\overline{\omega}}_{\mathrm{ls}}^{\mathrm{hr+}}$ with the TriRMGC system (s)									
3.0	21.42	30.70	80.54	82.79	102.89	128.40	131.65	606.38	1,430.51
3.5	20.28	28.73	74.67	77.01	93.53	116.51	119.34	422.47	1,333.18
4.0	20.60	27.82	72.71	75.34	88.67	108.51	109.86	326.09	1,126.69
4.5	18.44	26.55	68.84	71.50	83.13	101.76	101.16	255.52	930.09
5.0	**19.56**	**26.47**	**66.99**	**68.47**	**80.43**	**98.14**	**98.35**	**208.77**	**754.71**
5.5	18.44	25.83	64.82	67.80	77.28	92.49	92.53	192.34	589.53
6.0	17.90	26.13	62.98	66.53	75.18	89.65	89.47	175.10	474.93
6.5	19.13	24.53	62.68	62.71	73.53	86.21	86.24	162.05	397.86
7.0	18.38	25.00	60.03	63.95	70.93	82.39	83.54	159.94	338.03
7.5	18.90	24.67	59.62	61.83	70.00	81.73	81.64	151.04	292.92
8.0	17.27	24.02	60.26	60.05	68.56	80.32	79.20	142.43	262.97

Table 7.13 Influence of the mean container-dwell time ($\bar{\delta}$) on the mean SC-waiting time ($\bar{\bar{\omega}}_{ws}^{hr+}$) for selected yard-block layouts and all types of RMGC systems

	Yard-block layout								
$\bar{\delta}$	Small	Low	Narrow	Short	Medium	Long	Wide	High	Big
Resulting $\bar{\bar{\omega}}_{ws}^{hr+}$ with the SRMGC system (s)									
3.0	2.45	4.31	229.64	182.06	766.39	1,386.06	1,208.84	2,789.02	2,689.34
3.5	3.07	3.40	115.91	86.11	474.25	1,142.71	1,041.12	2,584.73	2,604.24
4.0	2.10	2.94	70.69	54.32	254.56	869.40	769.15	2,301.91	2,705.70
4.5	1.63	3.21	43.95	41.86	164.13	605.64	490.10	1,942.05	2,763.77
5.0	**1.69**	**2.86**	**40.46**	**28.71**	**102.93**	**410.23**	**350.05**	**1,597.83**	**2,837.74**
5.5	1.34	2.75	32.18	22.32	76.62	263.46	205.27	1,353.21	2,830.10
6.0	2.05	2.27	24.24	20.35	50.02	170.56	136.70	1,111.04	2,696.84
6.5	1.29	2.28	22.43	16.95	38.73	123.37	99.97	882.73	2,643.75
7.0	1.36	1.54	18.52	14.98	36.37	89.28	65.95	732.97	2,645.85
7.5	1.15	1.63	15.36	12.33	30.31	66.41	57.38	578.21	2,356.43
8.0	0.79	1.70	13.36	13.23	24.78	54.72	46.21	500.69	2,116.33
Resulting $\bar{\bar{\omega}}_{ws}^{hr+}$ with the TRMGC system (s)									
3.0	2.30	4.00	18.09	14.32	37.99	175.09	118.41	1,327.32	4,909.88
3.5	2.09	3.35	12.73	10.17	20.85	71.91	59.31	885.36	3,434.29
4.0	1.74	3.27	10.64	8.95	16.37	42.53	38.10	554.35	2,518.01
4.5	1.25	2.70	8.87	8.06	13.62	30.86	23.52	358.69	1,934.27
5.0	**1.19**	**2.14**	**7.79**	**6.74**	**13.31**	**25.15**	**21.79**	**247.50**	**1,586.02**
5.5	1.78	2.56	6.27	6.01	10.36	20.33	14.63	163.48	1,166.14
6.0	1.22	2.94	6.37	5.97	9.20	16.17	15.25	124.87	947.86
6.5	1.37	2.44	5.83	5.93	8.92	13.76	12.66	107.93	774.62
7.0	1.13	2.33	5.27	5.61	8.42	11.43	10.73	76.95	613.79
7.5	0.76	1.72	4.89	4.11	6.96	10.92	9.34	66.79	441.64
8.0	0.83	1.84	4.87	4.56	6.60	10.34	8.26	60.47	340.67
Resulting $\bar{\bar{\omega}}_{ws}^{hr+}$ with the DRMGC system (s)									
3.0	2.08	5.16	18.24	20.66	41.88	117.04	120.45	1,124.11	2,684.48
3.5	2.09	3.91	15.24	14.05	25.43	64.49	74.16	781.08	2,144.03
4.0	1.33	3.27	12.66	12.23	20.43	41.42	44.71	539.33	1,730.91
4.5	1.54	3.17	10.58	10.96	16.02	30.87	30.07	361.75	1,577.40
5.0	**1.44**	**2.76**	**10.37**	**9.57**	**15.89**	**24.57**	**23.92**	**259.60**	**1,401.64**
5.5	1.28	2.65	8.61	10.14	13.67	21.80	19.90	183.11	1,152.58
6.0	1.25	1.94	8.27	7.23	13.52	18.35	18.81	137.00	949.35
6.5	0.85	1.92	7.98	7.48	11.23	15.51	16.75	98.44	767.68
7.0	1.22	2.49	6.55	7.31	9.44	15.74	14.00	84.16	612.33
7.5	0.76	2.06	6.02	6.24	9.48	14.14	13.39	70.91	464.61
8.0	0.76	1.54	5.68	6.04	8.22	12.20	13.39	64.01	364.48
Resulting $\bar{\bar{\omega}}_{ws}^{hr+}$ with the TriRMGC system (s)									
3.0	2.45	4.33	8.11	9.35	12.78	17.99	18.76	359.78	1,159.50
3.5	1.74	4.53	8.32	8.29	10.91	13.55	15.68	203.78	1,012.94
4.0	1.58	3.37	7.52	7.94	9.21	13.30	13.66	135.11	766.90
4.5	1.20	3.26	7.11	7.33	8.53	12.05	11.36	85.99	603.18
5.0	**1.16**	**2.76**	**6.61**	**6.48**	**8.44**	**10.23**	**10.85**	**56.00**	**451.96**
5.5	1.44	2.77	5.42	5.51	7.28	9.23	9.43	49.83	315.08
6.0	1.24	2.65	5.44	5.50	7.46	9.73	8.96	39.95	230.51
6.5	1.31	1.89	4.88	5.55	6.74	7.74	8.96	33.69	169.09
7.0	0.92	2.12	4.04	5.00	6.51	8.60	8.23	33.22	140.53
7.5	1.10	1.37	4.24	4.87	5.73	7.01	7.27	29.39	99.65
8.0	0.79	1.33	4.51	4.39	5.46	6.84	7.33	25.31	81.51

Table 7.14 Influence of differences between the mean container-dwell times of import/export and transshipment containers on the mean XT-waiting time ($\overline{\overline{\omega}}_{ls}^{hr+}$) for selected yard-block layouts and all types of RMGC systems

$\bar{\delta} = 5$		Yard-block layout								
$\bar{\delta}^{ie}$	$\bar{\delta}^{ts}$	Small	Low	Narrow	Short	Medium	Long	Wide	High	Big
Resulting $\overline{\overline{\omega}}_{ls}^{hr+}$ with the SRMGC system (s)										
4.60	7.27	61.41	94.21	215.59	201.64	326.23	747.08	651.09	2,124.35	3,854.60
4.70	6.70	59.97	94.05	221.34	200.74	323.82	755.45	651.37	2,189.08	3,742.98
4.80	6.13	58.78	94.67	219.93	203.35	323.70	757.49	621.77	2,190.13	3,956.72
4.90	5.57	63.38	98.69	225.01	205.02	329.04	736.91	633.13	2,212.62	3,875.62
5.00	**5.00**	**65.90**	**95.41**	**226.61**	**204.03**	**336.25**	**772.82**	**675.77**	**2,244.74**	**3,903.45**
5.10	4.43	65.24	95.60	220.54	207.27	330.38	760.69	661.36	2,234.21	3,774.34
5.20	3.87	62.42	92.85	224.25	205.80	333.71	742.16	641.75	2,320.32	3,853.04
5.30	3.30	60.89	97.87	222.88	205.93	327.35	786.63	673.02	2,318.59	3,729.00
5.40	2.73	66.77	97.96	222.48	206.04	331.86	758.76	628.78	2,339.18	3,698.00
Resulting $\overline{\overline{\omega}}_{ls}^{hr+}$ with the TRMGC system (s)										
4.60	7.27	19.44	28.66	80.33	74.04	97.35	126.63	117.64	388.76	1,542.51
4.70	6.70	19.45	27.56	82.37	77.04	96.31	125.91	117.93	404.79	1,534.44
4.80	6.13	19.53	28.50	81.92	77.38	96.52	128.30	116.91	385.35	1,497.78
4.90	5.57	19.96	28.38	82.38	76.80	96.38	128.28	117.84	388.17	1,541.91
5.00	**5.00**	**19.48**	**29.13**	**82.08**	**77.19**	**98.58**	**126.78**	**118.96**	**387.72**	**1,540.04**
5.10	4.43	19.48	28.60	82.29	77.44	97.61	130.33	118.73	381.86	1,517.55
5.20	3.87	19.90	29.35	83.05	77.60	99.05	126.96	121.07	385.60	1,579.25
5.30	3.30	20.80	29.87	80.61	78.77	99.28	128.64	122.98	384.44	1,513.12
5.40	2.73	19.79	29.14	84.94	77.93	98.88	129.24	120.13	389.59	1,538.24
Resulting $\overline{\overline{\omega}}_{ls}^{hr+}$ with the DRMGC system (s)										
4.60	7.27	31.03	51.49	115.10	114.28	144.49	180.34	179.86	492.13	1,875.84
4.70	6.70	29.57	52.33	115.57	119.91	144.55	180.52	180.05	518.62	1,875.23
4.80	6.13	30.15	51.33	117.55	116.00	148.28	175.46	181.34	476.82	1,910.20
4.90	5.57	31.89	53.10	119.71	119.08	142.74	179.03	180.31	497.90	1,958.59
5.00	**5.00**	**31.48**	**52.60**	**116.45**	**118.90**	**146.10**	**179.24**	**181.10**	**509.36**	**1,907.61**
5.10	4.43	29.42	51.64	117.98	119.99	146.37	183.71	180.85	493.55	1,914.82
5.20	3.87	30.31	54.51	117.47	119.30	146.82	179.23	183.74	518.57	1,960.31
5.30	3.30	30.44	53.40	117.60	118.92	149.58	185.40	183.72	507.11	1,919.60
5.40	2.73	30.06	53.15	118.15	120.78	151.02	183.75	182.69	503.61	1,909.67
Resulting $\overline{\overline{\omega}}_{ls}^{hr+}$ with the TriRMGC system (s)										
4.60	7.27	18.84	25.59	67.88	68.23	79.75	94.72	96.23	213.79	751.58
4.70	6.70	18.82	26.35	68.14	69.28	81.77	97.15	95.72	214.29	749.99
4.80	6.13	18.88	26.56	65.82	68.86	80.07	95.14	97.31	216.45	769.29
4.90	5.57	18.82	25.99	66.56	67.66	80.05	95.45	98.20	213.75	763.35
5.00	**5.00**	**19.56**	**26.47**	**66.99**	**68.47**	**80.43**	**98.14**	**98.35**	**208.77**	**754.71**
5.10	4.43	18.81	25.59	67.92	68.67	79.97	97.07	97.58	214.83	762.21
5.20	3.87	19.12	26.31	67.92	70.73	80.76	97.74	99.99	218.65	782.00
5.30	3.30	18.79	26.64	68.56	70.13	82.80	97.44	98.74	220.38	768.34
5.40	2.73	19.38	27.16	68.30	69.42	81.68	97.57	98.65	223.21	785.39

Table 7.15 Influence of differences between the mean container-dwell times of import/export and transshipment containers on the mean SC-waiting time ($\overline{\overline{\omega}}_{ws}^{hr+}$) for selected yard-block layouts and all types of RMGC systems

$\overline{\delta} = 5$		Yard-block layout								
$\overline{\delta}^{ie}$	$\overline{\delta}^{ts}$	Small	Low	Narrow	Short	Medium	Long	Wide	High	Big
Resulting $\overline{\overline{\omega}}_{ws}^{hr+}$ with the SRMGC system (s)										
4.60	7.27	1.47	2.83	35.42	29.73	96.95	416.72	324.79	1,525.48	2,907.64
4.70	6.70	1.81	2.59	39.85	29.89	100.59	403.99	333.10	1,608.70	2,868.99
4.80	6.13	0.94	2.52	40.28	29.53	94.27	410.50	306.83	1,561.73	2,934.66
4.90	5.57	1.88	2.91	38.95	28.98	98.50	412.25	307.79	1,558.40	2,896.35
5.00	**5.00**	**1.69**	**2.86**	**40.46**	**28.71**	**102.93**	**410.23**	**350.05**	**1,597.83**	**2,837.74**
5.10	4.43	1.09	3.51	39.56	30.38	100.46	399.30	326.32	1,545.76	2,778.54
5.20	3.87	1.41	2.62	40.44	31.10	100.31	391.80	312.97	1,649.12	2,780.52
5.30	3.30	1.35	2.95	36.94	30.74	94.88	423.70	331.52	1,647.94	2,691.26
5.40	2.73	2.05	2.86	36.16	27.74	91.21	392.75	298.49	1,654.84	2,627.30
Resulting $\overline{\overline{\omega}}_{ws}^{hr+}$ with the TRMGC system (s)										
4.60	7.27	1.40	2.37	8.47	6.97	13.46	26.23	20.29	240.53	1,614.08
4.70	6.70	1.97	1.95	8.08	7.20	12.60	24.75	20.77	256.35	1,532.38
4.80	6.13	1.52	2.83	8.91	7.07	13.86	24.15	18.58	244.30	1,547.75
4.90	5.57	1.33	2.36	8.38	6.28	11.68	24.44	18.82	247.90	1,597.36
5.00	**5.00**	**1.19**	**2.14**	**7.79**	**6.74**	**13.31**	**25.15**	**21.79**	**247.50**	**1,586.02**
5.10	4.43	1.68	2.73	8.93	7.39	12.48	22.85	19.44	235.75	1,536.02
5.20	3.87	1.28	2.28	8.85	7.40	12.01	23.54	19.91	234.11	1,534.98
5.30	3.30	1.44	2.64	8.24	7.32	12.48	21.53	16.53	242.40	1,540.64
5.40	2.73	2.12	2.47	8.30	7.15	11.14	21.42	18.19	236.96	1,551.40
Resulting $\overline{\overline{\omega}}_{ws}^{hr+}$ with the DRMGC system (s)										
4.60	7.27	1.78	2.87	10.45	10.10	16.47	25.55	25.59	247.08	1,400.78
4.70	6.70	1.53	2.64	9.85	10.59	15.59	26.88	27.17	265.75	1,394.68
4.80	6.13	1.08	2.68	9.68	10.94	15.38	22.23	24.26	236.78	1,405.24
4.90	5.57	1.70	2.73	9.45	9.47	15.49	24.36	25.69	252.81	1,451.26
5.00	**5.00**	**1.44**	**2.76**	**10.37**	**9.57**	**15.89**	**24.57**	**23.92**	**259.60**	**1,401.64**
5.10	4.43	1.43	3.33	9.05	10.55	15.33	24.12	24.97	239.98	1,386.39
5.20	3.87	1.34	3.38	10.33	9.27	13.06	24.14	26.59	261.93	1,426.46
5.30	3.30	1.53	2.54	9.82	9.84	15.24	27.01	23.58	246.89	1,394.53
5.40	2.73	2.02	2.99	10.47	10.04	14.97	25.95	24.26	244.49	1,385.31
Resulting $\overline{\overline{\omega}}_{ws}^{hr+}$ with the TriRMGC system (s)										
4.60	7.27	1.35	2.67	6.51	6.77	9.42	9.78	10.60	59.96	471.05
4.70	6.70	1.78	2.64	6.56	6.59	8.41	10.96	10.37	60.38	476.30
4.80	6.13	1.52	2.46	6.35	6.57	8.58	10.12	10.67	63.73	466.11
4.90	5.57	1.81	3.11	6.90	6.72	9.11	10.88	10.51	59.82	482.43
5.00	**5.00**	**1.16**	**2.76**	**6.61**	**6.48**	**8.44**	**10.23**	**10.85**	**56.00**	**451.96**
5.10	4.43	1.03	2.30	7.14	6.72	8.81	10.42	10.60	60.68	458.07
5.20	3.87	1.47	2.82	6.22	6.22	8.33	9.80	10.81	57.14	497.80
5.30	3.30	1.60	2.76	6.27	6.50	8.62	9.99	10.88	63.02	467.80
5.40	2.73	1.50	3.13	6.69	6.45	9.34	9.63	10.65	62.97	478.84

With regard to the RMGC-design-planning problem, it can be concluded on the basis of the results shown in Tables 7.12 and 7.13 that the basic findings on the operational-performance effects of the yard-block layout and the type of RMGC system (see Sect. 7.2) are structurally unaffected by changes in the mean container-dwell time—just as postulated by Research hypothesis 2.2.3. It can be seen from Tables 7.12 and 7.13 that, independently of the mean container-dwell time, increases of the yard-block capacities and dimensions induce longer mean vehicle-waiting times in the handover areas as well as that the SRMGC and TriRMGC systems are the worst and best-performing types of RMGC systems, respectively, for most considered dwell times, while the DRMGC and TRMGC systems lead to intermediate performances.

In summary, the mean container-dwell time is found to have significantly negative effects on the mean vehicle-waiting times in the handover areas, while the difference between the mean dwell times of transshipment and import–export containers is not found to have systematic effects on the operational performance of RMGC systems. Likewise, also the basic findings on the operational-performance effects of the RMGC design are not found to be sensitive to changes in the mean container-dwell time. In view of these findings,

- Research hypothesis 2.2.1 is confirmed,
- Research hypothesis 2.2.2 is confirmed and
- Research hypothesis 2.2.3 is confirmed

for the considered experimental setup of this simulation-based sensitivity analysis.

7.3.3 *Influence of the Transshipment Factor*

In contrast to the previously investigated input parameters, the transshipment factor of a seaport container terminal has, by definition, no effects on the total amount of workload the cranes of a yard block are faced with, but for the spatial distribution of the crane workload between the waterside and landside handover areas (see Sect. 2.3.1). Therefore, the transshipment factor is also expected to have notable effects on the operational performance and the design of RMGC systems (see Sect. 4.1.3). Subsequently, it is analysed in how far the vehicle-waiting times in the handover areas are affected by and to what extent the RMGC design is influenced by the transshipment factor.

7.3.3.1 Research Hypotheses

Referring to Sect. 4.1.3.1, increases of the transshipment factor π^{ts} can be expected to have significantly positive effects on the crane workload at the waterside block end, while having significantly negative effects on the crane workload in the landside handover area. On the one hand, the higher the transshipment factor π^{ts}, the more containers need, ceteris paribus, to be transshipped from vessel to vessel, thus inducing more storage and retrievals jobs at the waterside block end, while, on the other hand, fewer containers have to be transferred between XT and vessel, thus inducing fewer storage and retrieval jobs in the landside handover area. Thus, the risk for and the extent of vehicle-waiting times in the waterside handover area can be expected to increase with the transshipment factor π^{ts}, while the mean vehicle-waiting time in the landside handover area can be expected to decrease with an increasing transshipment factor π^{ts}.

Considering that types of RMGC systems with crossing capabilities are able to respond flexibly to workload imbalances between the waterside and landside handover areas by providing different amounts of crane resources at the block ends, the operational performance of these types of RMGC systems can be expected to improve with increasing transshipment factor π^{ts} compared to types of RMGC without crossing capabilities. Therefore, the previously found performance advantage of the TRMGC system over the DRMGC system can be expected to decrease with an increasing transshipment factor π^{ts}. In particular, the mean vehicle-waiting time in the waterside handover area ($\overline{\overline{\omega}}_{\text{ws}}^{\text{hr+}}$) can be expected to increase more with the transshipment factor π^{ts} for the TRMGC system than for the DRMGC system, thus possibly even leading to a reversal of the performance advantage of the TRMGC system over the DRMGC system at the waterside block end with increasing transshipment factor π^{ts}. Altogether, Research hypotheses 2.3.1–2.3.3 are formulated:

Research Hypothesis 2.3.1. The transshipment factor π^{ts} has significantly positive effects on the mean vehicle-waiting time in the waterside handover area ($\overline{\overline{\omega}}_{\text{ws}}^{\text{hr+}}$).

Research Hypothesis 2.3.2. The transshipment factor π^{ts} has significantly negative effects on the mean vehicle-waiting time in the landside handover area ($\overline{\overline{\omega}}_{\text{ls}}^{\text{hr+}}$).

Research Hypothesis 2.3.3. The transshipment factor π^{ts} has significantly negative effects on the performance advantage of the TRMGC system over the DRMGC system with respect to the mean vehicle-waiting times in the waterside handover area ($\overline{\overline{\omega}}_{\text{ws}}^{\text{hr+}}$).

7.3.3.2 Experimental Setup

To test the influence of the transshipment factor π^{ts} on the operational performance and the design of RMGC systems, each combination of the four considered types of RMGC systems and the nine representative yard-block layouts is simulated with different transshipment factors, representing import–export terminals, transshipment terminals and hybrid terminals (see Sect. 2.3.1). To be precise: the transshipment factor π^{ts} is varied in the interval from $\pi^{\text{ts}} = 0\%$—representing a pure import–export terminal—to $\pi^{\text{ts}} = 100\%$—representing a pure transshipment terminal—in steps of 10%. Thus, eleven different transshipment factors are tested, leading to 396 simulation experiments in total. Except for the transshipment factor π^{ts}, all other input parameters of the simulation model are set to the default settings for these experiments, as specified in Sect. 7.1.3.

7.3.3.3 Results and Discussion

The simulation results of all experiments conducted on the influence of the transshipment factor π^{ts} on the operational performance and the design of RMGC systems are summarised by the performance figures shown in Tables 7.16 and 7.17. There, the resulting mean vehicle-waiting times in the landside (see Table 7.16) and waterside handover areas (see Table 7.17) are noted for each combination of the considered transshipment factors and RMGC designs. The simulation results with respect to other important performance figures are given in Appendix A.5.3.

As expected by Research hypothesis 2.3.1, it can be seen from Table 7.17 that for all considered yard-block layouts and types of RMGC systems the mean vehicle-waiting time in the waterside handover area increases more or less steadily with the transshipment factor π^{ts}. This observation is additionally confirmed by correlation analyses, which compute the mean SC-waiting time to be strongly positively correlated with the transshipment factor π^{ts}—at a significance level of $\alpha = 0.05$—for all considered RMGC designs. In contrast, the effects of the transshipment factor π^{ts} for the mean XT-waiting time differ with respect to the type of RMGC system. While it can be seen from Table 7.16 that the mean XT-waiting times of TRMGC and TriRMGC systems slightly decrease with increasing transshipment factor for most considered yard-block layouts, just as postulated by Research hypothesis 2.3.2, the mean XT-waiting times of SRMGC and DRMGC systems are observed to increase with an increasing transshipment factor up to $\pi^{ts} = 90\%$. However, for all types of RMGC systems, no XT-waiting time is induced at all for a transshipment factor of $\pi^{ts} = 100\%$, as, by definition, no XTs are served at pure transshipment terminals. The observations on the XT-waiting-time effects of the transshipment factor π^{ts} are likewise confirmed by correlation analyses. The XT-waiting times of the TRMGC and TriRMGC systems are found to be strongly negatively correlated with the transshipment factor π^{ts}—at a significance level of $\alpha = 0.05$—for all considered yard-block layouts, whereas for all RMGC designs with the SRMGC and DRMGC systems, strong positive correlations are computed between $\overline{\overline{\omega}}_{ls}^{hr+}$ and π^{ts}, when $\pi^{ts} = 100\%$ is excluded from the analysis.

The type-dependent differences in the XT-waiting-time effects of the transshipment factor π^{ts} can basically be explained by differences between the considered types of RMGC systems with respect to the technical feasibility of the cranes for performing jobs of both handover areas, in combination with efficiency losses in the use of the crane resources with increasing transshipment factor π^{ts}. Considering that the triangular-distributed look-ahead times for vehicle arrivals in the landside and waterside handover areas are parametrised such that waterside jobs are more likely to be known far more in advance of the actual handover-area due date than

Table 7.16 Influence of the transshipment factor (π^{ts}) on the mean XT-waiting time ($\overline{\overline{\omega}}_{ls}^{hr+}$) for selected yard-block layouts and all types of RMGC systems

	Yard-block layout								
π^{ts}	Small	Low	Narrow	Short	Medium	Long	Wide	High	Big
Resulting $\overline{\overline{\omega}}_{ls}^{hr+}$ with the SRMGC system (s)									
0%	61.55	87.67	203.00	191.58	295.74	666.58	571.08	2,247.07	3,657.60
10%	55.90	87.25	212.82	188.43	328.73	701.56	582.37	2,350.49	3,816.75
20%	58.34	93.70	216.22	199.02	338.66	752.89	670.40	2,249.19	3,821.53
30%	**65.90**	**95.41**	**226.61**	**204.03**	**336.25**	**772.82**	**675.77**	**2,244.74**	**3,903.45**
40%	67.61	99.78	222.81	202.30	340.97	724.31	636.61	2,145.44	3,749.27
50%	68.08	97.70	221.58	211.22	353.49	788.62	681.38	2,366.77	4,023.35
60%	73.22	101.56	238.24	226.28	402.48	988.70	815.54	2,597.17	4,193.24
70%	77.18	110.68	260.65	227.09	491.28	1,070.05	869.51	2,528.25	4,363.40
80%	77.86	113.72	285.29	259.45	519.00	1,150.94	969.59	2,510.25	4,373.68
90%	77.17	117.32	299.39	268.01	601.61	1,365.56	1,134.88	2,684.11	4,706.76
100%	0.00	0.00	0.00	0.00	0.00	0.00	0.00	0.00	0.00
Resulting $\overline{\overline{\omega}}_{ls}^{hr+}$ with the TRMGC system (s)									
0%	21.12	31.22	88.64	82.66	107.90	144.34	134.82	417.04	1,790.41
10%	19.99	29.68	85.50	79.64	105.88	136.82	125.63	412.28	1,734.34
20%	20.32	29.45	85.91	76.31	101.23	135.44	125.39	393.65	1,701.80
30%	**19.48**	**29.13**	**82.08**	**77.19**	**98.58**	**126.78**	**118.96**	**387.72**	**1,540.04**
40%	18.55	27.67	76.50	73.97	93.53	118.74	110.97	378.95	1,372.68
50%	17.60	25.13	75.33	72.23	89.73	116.64	107.40	392.89	1,196.84
60%	17.65	24.12	71.76	68.10	87.56	111.64	100.97	426.88	1,028.99
70%	17.24	22.53	73.47	69.23	83.86	106.37	98.70	393.88	667.33
80%	15.78	20.78	69.95	64.36	77.17	100.88	91.91	358.64	435.55
90%	14.53	19.79	65.60	61.17	75.46	97.21	88.39	331.47	247.88
100%	0.00	0.00	0.00	0.00	0.00	0.00	0.00	0.00	0.00
Resulting $\overline{\overline{\omega}}_{ls}^{hr+}$ with the DRMGC system (s)									
0%	29.03	47.41	113.75	112.04	143.95	178.30	173.66	485.67	1,965.44
10%	28.96	48.61	114.64	113.98	142.86	180.92	176.81	510.27	1,971.85
20%	30.24	51.05	118.93	116.19	146.61	182.58	180.54	501.94	1,924.53
30%	**31.48**	**52.60**	**116.45**	**118.90**	**146.10**	**179.24**	**181.10**	**509.39**	**1,907.61**
40%	29.95	52.07	119.98	119.04	148.81	183.69	180.89	528.48	1,949.17
50%	31.04	54.20	113.30	118.99	146.98	181.62	184.79	572.10	2,102.50
60%	31.81	53.20	119.98	120.92	153.60	191.97	185.83	653.48	2,159.60
70%	34.97	57.60	126.52	127.54	156.69	204.10	197.41	670.86	2,222.56
80%	32.83	60.66	127.93	130.05	156.56	213.39	214.25	707.64	2,247.00
90%	35.67	64.67	128.29	127.09	168.40	221.96	235.39	825.80	2,292.48
100%	0.00	0.00	0.00	0.00	0.00	0.00	0.00	0.00	0.00
Resulting $\overline{\overline{\omega}}_{ls}^{hr+}$ with the TriRMGC system (s)									
0%	19.96	27.51	68.06	70.91	84.67	101.42	101.92	225.61	767.41
10%	19.00	27.44	68.43	71.46	84.61	98.82	99.51	223.96	785.22
20%	18.89	27.14	69.22	70.16	83.15	99.45	101.74	224.32	780.94
30%	**19.56**	**26.47**	**66.99**	**68.47**	**80.43**	**98.14**	**98.35**	**208.77**	**754.71**
40%	17.98	25.36	66.58	68.16	78.24	93.34	95.99	203.86	672.56
50%	18.22	24.95	63.40	66.08	75.87	92.66	91.45	195.08	586.25
60%	18.09	24.85	63.45	66.27	76.15	91.27	89.70	198.15	505.51
70%	17.23	24.19	64.24	64.84	74.89	89.48	90.17	182.50	427.38
80%	17.61	24.43	60.31	63.34	72.40	85.38	83.78	165.10	312.14
90%	15.27	23.33	60.65	60.39	69.77	83.88	82.90	152.37	187.66
100%	0.00	0.00	0.00	0.00	0.00	0.00	0.00	0.00	0.00

Table 7.17 Influence of the transshipment factor (π^{ts}) on the mean SC-waiting time ($\overline{\overline{\omega}}_{ws}^{hr+}$) for selected yard-block layouts and all types of RMGC systems

	Yard-block layout								
π^{ts}	Small	Low	Narrow	Short	Medium	Long	Wide	High	Big
Resulting $\overline{\overline{\omega}}_{ws}^{hr+}$ with the SRMGC system (s)									
0%	0.03	0.29	23.58	20.39	62.05	267.04	225.27	1,389.87	2,048.11
10%	0.42	1.29	28.72	21.46	90.67	331.12	236.77	1,486.83	2,360.47
20%	1.23	1.47	31.07	25.35	97.98	393.29	336.58	1,494.91	2,559.52
30%	**1.69**	**2.86**	**40.46**	**28.71**	**102.93**	**410.23**	**350.05**	**1,597.83**	**2,837.74**
40%	1.66	3.66	42.35	33.66	115.20	416.12	355.92	1,667.86	2,986.08
50%	2.84	4.98	41.28	38.58	127.96	466.60	404.19	1,823.44	3,108.03
60%	3.65	6.23	52.56	46.87	164.20	623.30	508.94	1,808.72	3,136.49
70%	4.70	6.39	66.40	52.76	256.31	757.93	574.32	1,845.75	3,196.41
80%	5.30	7.32	86.07	76.15	278.24	829.20	712.82	1,854.94	3,175.67
90%	6.63	9.21	89.57	78.89	364.03	1,017.18	831.71	1,904.40	3,073.77
100%	5.40	9.98	127.46	104.06	432.35	1,014.15	895.70	1,909.25	2,764.67
Resulting $\overline{\overline{\omega}}_{ws}^{hr+}$ with the TRMGC system (s)									
0%	0.09	0.22	4.08	2.97	6.64	12.97	9.91	173.73	1,016.82
10%	0.57	1.04	4.75	4.27	8.68	15.46	13.02	195.44	1,138.92
20%	0.75	2.02	5.98	5.11	10.38	21.88	18.59	200.88	1,345.99
30%	**1.19**	**2.14**	**7.79**	**6.74**	**13.31**	**25.15**	**21.79**	**247.50**	**1,586.02**
40%	2.21	3.32	8.60	8.37	14.06	29.15	22.21	319.87	1,875.26
50%	2.67	5.26	10.33	9.10	16.33	33.15	30.57	349.99	2,269.40
60%	3.78	5.47	12.41	11.79	19.61	50.98	35.91	482.05	2,498.23
70%	3.49	5.74	14.12	14.72	26.61	74.86	57.49	615.88	2,721.24
80%	4.39	7.37	16.41	14.68	31.85	108.48	81.15	734.84	2,857.07
90%	5.18	7.64	19.13	17.02	49.11	182.46	143.95	920.40	2,573.53
100%	5.23	8.98	26.29	22.33	54.85	304.74	201.48	1,067.25	2,418.63
Resulting $\overline{\overline{\omega}}_{ws}^{hr+}$ with the DRMGC system (s)									
0%	0.03	0.03	3.73	3.72	7.35	14.59	13.99	197.16	1,131.90
10%	0.38	0.94	5.76	5.85	10.60	19.45	17.92	227.77	1,239.66
20%	0.59	1.52	7.40	7.58	12.83	22.94	23.44	235.77	1,284.22
30%	**1.44**	**2.76**	**10.37**	**9.57**	**15.89**	**24.57**	**23.92**	**259.60**	**1,401.64**
40%	2.02	3.60	10.96	13.36	20.12	31.50	28.34	307.57	1,534.91
50%	3.64	4.71	14.73	14.59	21.57	31.34	36.91	368.25	1,672.57
60%	3.84	6.18	16.21	17.99	25.71	43.50	41.88	441.14	1,824.72
70%	3.89	6.72	20.13	22.02	31.84	55.84	60.91	507.75	2,034.96
80%	4.61	8.68	21.95	23.91	36.04	74.23	76.97	578.90	2,178.19
90%	6.15	10.60	24.81	26.42	48.04	94.05	108.54	711.34	2,331.78
100%	5.67	13.16	31.18	34.81	53.01	146.61	141.83	855.70	2,337.49
Resulting $\overline{\overline{\omega}}_{ws}^{hr+}$ with the TriRMGC system (s)									
0%	0.13	0.13	1.57	1.83	2.36	3.81	3.97	46.23	351.21
10%	0.48	0.75	2.93	2.89	4.73	5.99	6.24	53.50	402.18
20%	0.75	1.86	4.03	4.36	6.58	8.27	8.68	57.68	429.13
30%	**1.16**	**2.76**	**6.61**	**6.48**	**8.44**	**10.23**	**10.85**	**56.00**	**451.96**
40%	1.76	3.57	8.23	7.37	10.40	12.34	12.38	69.45	495.42
50%	2.96	4.71	9.56	10.01	12.35	14.94	16.82	84.10	580.83
60%	2.40	6.06	10.73	10.85	13.45	18.49	17.14	108.63	673.56
70%	4.46	6.51	13.48	13.81	16.42	21.17	22.55	133.84	812.61
80%	3.95	7.92	14.90	15.66	19.15	24.82	25.50	165.92	843.73
90%	5.26	10.78	15.32	17.42	22.96	30.65	30.10	199.96	916.38
100%	6.36	10.71	19.13	19.67	23.59	34.43	36.94	276.66	858.35

landside jobs (see Sect. 7.1.3), there is a far greater probability for inefficient crane-waiting times due to early crane arrivals ($\omega \text{total}^{\text{hr}-}$) in the waterside handover area than in the landside handover area. As a consequence, it can be expected that the risk for and the extent of inefficient crane-waiting times increases with the transshipment factor π^{ts}, as more waterside and fewer landside jobs need to be handled. In fact, upon closer examination of the simulation results, the mean crane-waiting times in the handover areas ($\overline{\overline{\omega}}_{\text{total}}^{\text{hr}-}$) are found to be strongly positively correlated with the transshipment factor π^{ts}—at a significance level of $\alpha = 0.05$—for all considered RMGC designs. Usually, increasing crane-waiting times in the handover areas reduce the actually available crane resources and thus increase the risk for and the extent of vehicle-waiting times in the handover areas. However, not all cranes of all four types of RMGC systems are equally affected by longer crane-waiting times in the waterside handover area. Considering the fact that the landside cranes of the TRMGC and TriRMGC systems cannot serve the waterside handover area, these cranes are not affected by increasing crane-waiting times in the waterside handover area with increasing transshipment factor π^{ts}. Moreover, apart from shuffle jobs, these cranes are exclusively responsible for the decreasing landside crane workload. Therefore, a lower landside crane workload needs to be performed by nearly unchanged crane resources. This yields mean XT-waiting times which decrease with the transshipment factor π^{ts} for the TRMGC and TriRMGC systems, just as expected by Research hypothesis 2.3.2. In contrast, all crane resources of the SRMGC and DRMGC systems can be flexibly allocated to workload of both handover areas, thus being equally affected by increases of the crane-waiting times with the transshipment factor π^{ts}. Additionally, considering that the actually available crane resources are allocated to the waterside and landside handover areas in proportion to the workload distribution between these handover areas, that is induced by the transshipment factor π^{ts}, also the workload of both handover areas is equally affected by reductions in the actually available crane resources due to longer crane-waiting times in the waterside handover areas with increasing transshipment factor π^{ts}. As a consequence, the actually available crane resources allocated to the landside handover area are declining faster with the transshipment factor π^{ts} than the workload related to that handover area, thus explaining slightly increasing mean XT-waiting times with the transshipment factor π^{ts} for the SRMGC and DRMGC systems against the expectations of Research hypothesis 2.3.2.

With regard to the performance advantage of the TRMGC system over the DRMGC system, inconsistent simulation results are observed. It can be seen from Table 7.17 that the differences between the mean SC-waiting times of DRMGC and TRMGC systems decrease with the transshipment factor π^{ts} for the medium- to large-sized yard-block layouts "medium", "long", "wide", "high" and "big", resulting even in shorter SC-waiting times for the DRMGC system than for the TRMGC system for transshipment factors above certain layout-dependent thresholds, just as expected by Research hypothesis 2.3.3. In contrast, no such effects can be observed for the small-sized layouts "short", "narrow", "low" and "small". This can mainly be explained by only small absolute increases of the waterside workload with the transshipment factor π^{ts} for small-sized yard blocks, compared to much greater absolute workload increases at the waterside block end for medium- to large-sized yard blocks. Thus, the option of the DRMGC system to deploy both cranes for performing waterside jobs does not pay off for small-sized yard-block layouts, as the waterside crane of the TRMGC system is principally able to handle small absolute increases of the crane workload without inducing great increases of the mean SC-waiting time. In addition, upon closer examination of the simulation results for the DRMGC system the mean crane-interference time $\overline{\overline{m}}^{cit}_{total}$ is observed to increase significantly with the transshipment factor π^{ts}, as the cranes of the DRMGC system are increasingly often deployed in nearby regions of the yard block with increasing transshipment factor π^{ts} (i.e., near the waterside handover area). In contrast, the mean interference times of the TRMGC system are found to be unaffected by the transshipment factor. Hence, for small-sized yard blocks, even slightly greater increases of the mean SC-waiting times with the transshipment factor π^{ts} can be explained for the DRMGC system than for TRMGC system. However, for medium- to large-sized yard blocks, comparably greater absolute increases of the waterside workload are induced by a growth in the transshipment factor π^{ts}, so that a more frequent use of both DRMGC cranes for waterside jobs does pay off despite causing more crane-interferences.

Altogether, the transshipment factor π^{ts} is found to have significantly positive effects on the mean SC-waiting times of all types of RMGC systems and the mean XT-waiting times of the SRMGC and DRMGC systems, while having significantly negative effects on the mean XT-waiting times of the TRMGC and TriRMGC systems. With regard to the performance comparison between the TRMGC and DRMGC systems, the transshipment factor π^{ts} is found to diminish the performance advantage of the TRMGC system over the DRMGC system with respect to the mean vehicle-waiting times in the waterside handover area of medium- to large-sized yard blocks, but not for very small ones. Owing to these findings,

- Research hypothesis 2.3.1 is confirmed,
- Research hypothesis 2.3.2 is confirmed for the TRMGC and TriRMGC systems, but is not confirmed for the SRMGC and DRMGC systems, and
- Research hypothesis 2.3.3 is confirmed for medium- to large-sized yard blocks, but is not confirmed for small-sized yard blocks

for the used setup of the conducted simulation experiments.

7.3.4 Influence of the Vessel-Call Pattern

Similar to the transshipment factor, the vessel-call pattern of a seaport container terminal has, ceteris paribus, also no effects on the total workload the cranes of a yard block are faced with. In contrast, by defining the berthing windows of deep-sea vessels, the distribution of container arrivals and collections over time in the waterside handover areas is determined by the vessel-call pattern, thus implicitly specifying the distribution of the crane workload at the waterside block end over time. Therefore, in Sect. 4.1.3, the vessel-call pattern is also qualitatively expected to have considerable effects on the operational performance and the design of RMGC systems. This subsection is aimed at verifying and quantifying the effects of the vessel-call pattern on the operational performance and the design of RMGC systems.

7.3.4.1 Research Hypotheses

Referring to Sect. 4.1.3.1, an uneven distribution of vehicle arrivals over time at the yard block can be expected to induce very pronounced peak workloads for the RMGC systems, which increase the risk for and the extent of vehicle-waiting times, whereas fewer and/or less pronounced peak workloads are induced by more uniformly distributed vehicle arrivals. Thus, due to the fact that the distribution of vehicle arrivals at the waterside block end is directly defined by the distribution of vessel arrivals at the quay over time, which is mostly—in particular for deep-sea vessels—determined by the vessel-call pattern, the mean vehicle-waiting time in the waterside handover area ($\overline{\overline{\omega}}_{ws}^{hr+}$) can be expected to increase with increasing unevenness of the vessel-call pattern.

Here, the unevenness of a vessel-call pattern is measured as the VCP-overlapping time, which is the sum of time that the berthing window of each deep-sea vessel, that is planned to deliver and collect containers to/from the yard block under analysis, overlaps with the berthing window of any of the other deep-sea vessels that are likewise planned to deliver and collect containers to/from that yard block. Owing to the fact that the vessel-call pattern is planned on an hourly basis, the VCP-overlapping time is measured in hours as well. For example, in the default vessel-call pattern VCP1, which is shown in Fig. 7.1, the berthing windows of vessels 1, 3, 5, 7 and 9, that are all planned to deliver and collect containers to/from the yard block under investigation, do not overlap at all. This results in the least overlapping distribution of berthing windows with a VCP-overlapping time of 0 h. In contrast, in the alternative vessel-call pattern VCP2, which is shown in Appendix A.4, the berthing windows of vessels 7 and 9, that both deliver and collect containers to/from the investigated yard block, are planned to overlap in the time interval from Friday, 3 pm to 9 pm, thus leading to a VCP-overlapping time of 12 h, as both vessel 7 and vessel 9 overlap with the berthing window of the other vessel for 6 h each. Referring to the previously expected vehicle-waiting-time effects of the unevenness of a vessel-call pattern, the vehicle-waiting times in the waterside handover area of the considered yard block can be expected to increase with increasing VCP-overlapping time.

Considering the fact that the workload and the available crane resources for the waterside and landside handover areas of a yard block are strongly interrelated, changes in the distribution of the waterside crane workload over time cannot only be expected to have effects on the vehicle-waiting times in the waterside handover area, but also for the landside vehicle-waiting times. In fact, it can be expected that fewer crane resources are available to serve landside storage and retrieval jobs during peak workload in the waterside handover area, as more crane resources are needed at the waterside block end, thus increasing the risk for and the extent of XT-waiting times during peak waterside workloads. In addition, it can also be expected that XT-waiting-time-causing peak workloads in the landside handover area are implicitly induced by peak waterside workloads, as each waterside-arriving (departing) import (export) container also needs to be to handled in the landside handover area at a later (earlier) point in time. In spite of individual container-dwell times and random XT-arrival times, most import (export) containers that are planned to arrive (depart) with a certain deep-sea vessel depart (arrive) a few days after (before) the calling vessel. This may lead to peak XT-arrival times in advance of and subsequent to arrivals of deep-sea vessels. Hence, increasingly overlapping berthing windows of deep-sea vessels can be expected to induce more pronounced peak workloads in the landside handover area as well. As a consequence, the vehicle-waiting times in the landside handover area ($\overline{\overline{\omega}}_{ls}^{hr+}$) can likewise be expected to increase with the VCP-overlapping time.

Owing to the fact that types of RMGC systems with crossing capabilities can flexibly respond to peak workloads at the waterside block end by allocating additional crane resources, these systems are more able to deal with overlapping vessel-call patterns than types of RMGC systems without crossing capabilities. Thus, similarly to the effects of the transshipment factor π^{ts}, the unevenness of the vessel-call pattern is expected to have smaller positive effects on the vehicle-waiting times in the waterside handover area for RMGC systems with crossing capabilities than for systems without crossing capabilities. As a consequence, the previously found differences in the mean SC-waiting times between the DRMGC and TRMGC systems can be expected to decrease with increasing VCP-overlapping time, thus reducing and/or possibly reversing the performance advantage of the TRMGC system over the DRMGC system with respect to the mean vehicle-waiting times in the waterside handover area ($\overline{\overline{\omega}}_{ws}^{hr+}$). In summary, Research hypotheses 2.4.1–2.4.3 are formulated:

Research Hypothesis 2.4.1. The unevenness of the vessel-call pattern in terms of the VCP-overlapping time has significantly positive effects on the mean vehicle-waiting time in the waterside handover area ($\overline{\overline{\omega}}_{ws}^{hr+}$).

Research Hypothesis 2.4.2. The unevenness of the vessel-call pattern in terms of the VCP-overlapping time has significantly positive effects on the mean vehicle-waiting time in the landside handover area ($\overline{\overline{\omega}}_{ls}^{hr+}$).

Research Hypothesis 2.4.3. The unevenness of the vessel-call pattern in terms of the VCP-overlapping time has significantly negative effects on the performance advantage of the TRMGC system over the DRMGC system with respect to the mean vehicle-waiting times in the waterside handover area ($\overline{\overline{\omega}}_{ws}^{hr+}$).

7.3.4.2 Experimental Setup

To analyse the influence of the unevenness of the vessel-call pattern on the operational performance and the design of RMGC systems, each combination of the four considered types of RMGC systems and the nine example yard-block layouts is tested with ten different vessel-call patterns, including in addition to the default vessel-call pattern VCP1 (see Fig. 7.1) nine newly created vessel-call patterns for the purpose of this sensitivity analysis that are displayed in Appendix A.4. All generated vessel-call patterns only differ with respect to the berthing windows of the calling deep-sea vessels, thus inducing different VCP-overlapping times, while being identical with respect to the number and the structure of the calling vessels. As described above for the default vessel-call pattern (see Sect. 7.1.3), nine deep-sea vessels are assumed to arrive per week, whereof four vessels (1, 2, 3, 4) are of the larger type 1 and five vessels (5, 6, 7, 8, 9) are of the smaller type 2, but only two vessels of type 1 (1, 3) and three vessels of type 2 (5, 7, 9) are assumed to deliver and/or collect containers to/from the yard block investigated. In summary, each of the 36 considered example RMGC designs is simulated with ten different vessel-call patterns, that induce VCP-overlapping times in the range from 0 to 148 h, thus leading to 360 simulation experiments for this sensitivity analysis. Apart from changes in the vessel-call pattern, all other input parameters of the simulation model are set to the default settings of this simulation study, as specified in Sect. 7.1.3.

7.3.4.3 Results and Discussion

The simulation results of all 360 experiments conducted on the effects of the unevenness of the vessel-call pattern on the operational performance and the design of RMGC systems are shown in Tables 7.18 and 7.19 in terms of mean vehicle-waiting times in the landside and waterside handover areas, respectively. There, the name of the vessel-call pattern and the corresponding VCP-overlapping time are noted in the two leftmost columns, while the resulting vehicle-waiting-time figures for all considered RMGC designs are displayed in the following columns. The simulation results of other important performance figures are provided in Appendix A.5.4.

It can be seen from Table 7.19, that the mean vehicle-waiting times in the waterside handover area increase more or less steadily with the VCP-overlapping time for all combinations of considered yard-block layouts and types of RMGC systems. Upon closer examination of the simulation results, the VCP-overlapping time is even found to be strongly positively correlated with the mean vehicle-waiting time in the waterside handover area—at a significance level of $\alpha = 0.05$—for all considered RMGC designs, thus confirming the positive SC-waiting-time effects of the unevenness of the vessel-call pattern, just as expected by Research hypothesis 2.4.1.

In contrast, differently than expected by Research hypothesis 2.4.2, the unevenness of the vessel-call pattern cannot be confirmed, on the basis of Table 7.18,

Table 7.18 Influence of the unevenness of the vessel-call pattern, in terms of the VCP-overlapping time (h), on the mean XT-waiting time ($\overline{\overline{\omega}}_{ls}^{hr+}$) for selected yard-block layouts and all types of RMGC systems

VCP		Yard-block layout								
Name	Overlap (h)	Small	Low	Narrow	Short	Medium	Long	Wide	High	Big
Resulting $\overline{\overline{\omega}}_{ls}^{hr+}$ with the SRMGC system (s)										
VCP1	**0**	**65.90**	**95.41**	**226.61**	**204.03**	**336.25**	**772.82**	**675.77**	**2,244.74**	**3,903.45**
VCP2	12	55.72	93.53	201.70	189.01	313.10	683.39	583.95	2,028.30	3,336.81
VCP3	24	60.57	96.81	228.82	203.61	410.47	934.03	814.27	2,154.39	3,706.27
VCP4	32	59.07	89.69	228.80	205.22	410.98	977.71	830.85	2,431.37	3,658.70
VCP5	52	60.92	87.84	217.92	200.61	423.99	1,025.88	886.66	2,353.47	3,397.65
VCP6	64	54.37	87.38	226.17	205.16	412.96	1,022.64	862.12	2,369.51	3,433.07
VCP7	84	54.14	84.22	231.84	209.01	535.79	1,117.81	1,006.10	2,267.42	3,309.02
VCP8	116	51.74	72.27	223.34	188.79	542.97	1,184.48	1,073.57	2,385.27	3,230.03
VCP9	138	46.84	76.05	222.83	196.46	498.25	1,102.88	1,035.13	2,239.36	2,888.07
VCP10	148	48.23	72.59	268.05	238.56	649.59	1,187.81	1,095.57	2,168.06	2,831.29
Resulting $\overline{\overline{\omega}}_{ls}^{hr+}$ with the TRMGC system (s)										
VCP1	**0**	**19.48**	**29.13**	**82.08**	**77.19**	**98.58**	**126.78**	**118.96**	**387.72**	**1,540.04**
VCP2	12	19.60	29.70	81.99	74.60	94.15	128.34	118.14	398.59	1,466.88
VCP3	24	19.95	28.62	82.73	77.33	98.57	133.44	126.61	387.56	1,143.35
VCP4	32	19.20	28.12	78.07	73.09	92.87	122.24	115.97	462.25	1,385.71
VCP5	52	17.98	26.39	74.34	68.69	88.66	112.62	106.84	511.08	957.89
VCP6	64	18.18	28.22	77.42	69.86	92.33	125.02	112.50	423.88	937.30
VCP7	84	17.89	26.34	74.04	68.30	87.22	111.50	104.66	501.07	766.74
VCP8	116	16.51	25.51	68.15	62.60	80.58	105.57	97.93	444.66	662.93
VCP9	138	16.01	25.80	69.38	63.74	83.83	107.00	101.75	355.42	394.73
VCP10	148	15.91	25.83	72.36	64.65	83.93	104.85	98.68	410.70	492.22
Resulting $\overline{\overline{\omega}}_{ls}^{hr+}$ with the DRMGC system (s)										
VCP1	**0**	**31.48**	**52.60**	**116.45**	**118.90**	**146.10**	**179.24**	**181.10**	**509.36**	**1,907.61**
VCP2	12	30.18	51.96	112.99	112.15	139.52	177.04	176.08	521.38	1,885.59
VCP3	24	30.02	50.77	115.73	119.83	146.90	198.23	193.65	589.19	1,753.19
VCP4	32	29.28	50.65	110.65	112.85	137.60	174.32	180.93	607.50	1,976.38
VCP5	52	30.26	47.32	108.43	107.05	132.08	164.11	172.52	718.18	1,835.16
VCP6	64	29.70	50.12	111.19	108.35	134.89	186.06	173.17	582.40	1,810.58
VCP7	84	28.88	49.15	103.39	103.57	132.43	170.09	172.44	754.02	1,819.10
VCP8	116	27.02	43.20	94.85	94.42	115.76	162.21	157.66	781.29	1,834.32
VCP9	138	27.47	42.82	93.50	98.01	121.30	166.36	166.45	625.61	1,656.23
VCP10	148	27.10	44.93	96.18	93.47	127.69	202.05	190.20	862.78	1,724.12
Resulting $\overline{\overline{\omega}}_{ls}^{hr+}$ with the TriRMGC system (s)										
VCP1	**0**	**19.56**	**26.47**	**66.99**	**68.47**	**80.43**	**98.14**	**98.35**	**208.77**	**754.71**
VCP2	12	18.82	26.09	66.21	66.54	78.63	95.66	95.35	223.58	784.48
VCP3	24	19.02	26.63	66.70	69.30	80.16	99.47	101.04	230.95	724.36
VCP4	32	18.44	25.89	64.37	65.74	76.97	93.61	94.07	242.91	879.39
VCP5	52	17.36	24.44	61.88	63.71	72.72	86.94	88.30	249.86	915.30
VCP6	64	17.44	25.02	62.52	65.14	76.60	92.35	93.18	232.14	780.66
VCP7	84	16.65	23.93	60.72	61.21	70.74	86.73	88.50	271.58	933.54
VCP8	116	15.86	23.73	55.95	56.07	65.92	77.43	81.99	263.25	891.56
VCP9	138	15.41	23.10	57.27	57.89	67.32	80.88	82.88	224.71	767.89
VCP10	148	16.16	24.25	57.45	59.60	65.95	83.70	84.86	324.01	863.66

Table 7.19 Influence of the unevenness of the vessel-call pattern, in terms of the VCP-overlapping time (h), on the mean SC-waiting time ($\overline{\overline{\omega}}^{hr+}_{ws}$) for selected yard-block layouts and all types of RMGC systems

VCP		Yard-block layout								
Name	Overlap (h)	Small	Low	Narrow	Short	Medium	Long	Wide	High	Big
Resulting $\overline{\overline{\omega}}^{hr+}_{ws}$ with the SRMGC system (s)										
VCP1	**0**	**1.69**	**2.86**	**40.46**	**28.71**	**102.94**	**410.23**	**350.05**	**1,597.83**	**2,837.74**
VCP2	12	2.71	4.09	41.68	28.50	110.47	402.43	335.71	1,623.97	2,838.05
VCP3	24	4.77	6.92	56.27	42.64	192.72	585.38	521.77	1,891.12	3,473.54
VCP4	32	2.51	3.15	54.82	42.01	200.78	712.96	567.88	2,163.97	3,403.60
VCP5	52	1.92	3.05	66.77	52.30	263.20	926.34	722.99	2,517.69	4,024.52
VCP6	64	2.69	5.79	66.25	59.67	256.73	920.65	731.39	2,890.73	4,060.20
VCP7	84	2.77	4.76	111.07	92.83	487.86	1,301.51	1,070.24	3,250.10	5,192.63
VCP8	116	3.08	4.56	129.29	90.17	611.76	1,590.98	1,310.17	3,648.72	6,139.22
VCP9	138	6.32	9.39	141.85	120.11	580.16	1,506.29	1,377.78	4,053.22	6,304.56
VCP10	148	3.99	6.97	304.57	247.91	1,014.33	2,073.12	1,843.55	4,697.00	8,133.99
Resulting $\overline{\overline{\omega}}^{hr+}_{ws}$ with the TRMGC system (s)										
VCP1	**0**	**1.19**	**2.14**	**7.79**	**6.74**	**13.31**	**25.15**	**21.79**	**247.50**	**1,586.02**
VCP2	12	2.61	5.12	9.78	8.23	14.78	30.80	27.64	284.41	1,808.74
VCP3	24	4.42	6.73	13.45	11.86	21.98	44.05	38.59	303.94	2,489.13
VCP4	32	1.50	3.21	9.67	8.25	14.06	34.77	28.34	453.73	2,565.21
VCP5	52	1.63	3.09	10.58	8.64	20.32	60.69	36.46	746.28	4,207.88
VCP6	64	2.37	4.79	12.11	9.89	18.82	58.06	38.53	528.45	3,897.93
VCP7	84	2.29	3.76	15.33	11.48	30.29	104.52	82.52	1,168.43	6,267.68
VCP8	116	2.90	3.90	16.28	11.28	44.18	190.21	136.58	1,774.34	8,233.00
VCP9	138	4.49	7.65	18.79	16.46	44.18	152.13	137.10	1,450.76	9,318.95
VCP10	148	3.53	3.94	30.25	25.24	99.21	479.77	359.49	3,042.97	10,837.76
Resulting $\overline{\overline{\omega}}^{hr+}_{ws}$ with the DRMGC system (s)										
VCP1	**0**	**1.44**	**2.76**	**10.37**	**9.57**	**15.89**	**24.57**	**23.92**	**259.60**	**1,401.64**
VCP2	12	2.52	5.18	13.71	14.05	19.06	31.59	36.01	298.08	1,483.18
VCP3	24	4.16	8.21	20.65	22.30	30.91	52.72	50.25	379.75	1,793.93
VCP4	32	1.69	3.66	13.11	12.95	18.07	35.80	37.30	421.99	1,976.49
VCP5	52	1.92	3.15	12.33	12.93	23.74	36.40	39.00	656.36	2,674.99
VCP6	64	3.14	5.05	16.66	15.66	23.44	52.60	42.97	476.89	2,468.87
VCP7	84	2.66	5.57	16.59	16.37	32.84	67.14	69.83	888.80	3,649.78
VCP8	116	2.51	5.07	19.10	19.16	32.41	85.77	85.79	1,147.50	4,805.02
VCP9	138	4.97	11.67	25.79	27.83	52.26	110.78	119.79	874.33	4,935.69
VCP10	148	5.03	6.25	26.58	26.56	70.18	257.04	236.66	1,784.10	6,099.13
Resulting $\overline{\overline{\omega}}^{hr+}_{ws}$ with the TriRMGC system (s)										
VCP1	**0**	**1.16**	**2.76**	**6.61**	**6.48**	**8.44**	**10.23**	**10.85**	**56.00**	**451.96**
VCP2	12	2.69	5.07	8.46	9.21	10.57	12.66	14.77	74.31	517.21
VCP3	24	5.23	7.34	14.70	14.46	17.13	19.35	20.26	84.95	559.41
VCP4	32	1.47	3.58	6.87	7.62	9.32	12.30	13.26	95.25	713.29
VCP5	52	1.58	3.62	8.02	7.74	10.21	11.95	12.79	132.46	956.52
VCP6	64	1.70	5.19	10.79	10.50	13.88	14.73	16.06	100.84	721.05
VCP7	84	3.02	5.60	8.79	10.10	13.87	15.76	16.57	197.04	1,262.58
VCP8	116	2.69	4.80	10.57	10.72	12.63	16.35	16.71	228.63	1,598.20
VCP9	138	5.59	9.85	16.71	17.50	18.41	23.47	25.23	186.28	1,553.61
VCP10	148	3.50	6.69	10.95	14.00	18.52	33.13	39.85	475.53	2,480.20

to have likewise strong positive effects on the mean vehicle-waiting time in the landside handover area. Moreover, the VCP-overlapping time can be observed to have slightly negative effects on the mean XT-waiting times of most considered RMGC designs—in particular for those with multi-crane systems. This can be explained by a workload-reducing effect of increasing VCP-overlapping time for the landside handover area, which is not considered in the formulation of Research hypothesis 2.4.2. As previously explained (see Sect. 7.2.2.2), laden arriving vehicles are redirected to other yard blocks if the relevant handover area capacities of the considered yard block are fully occupied. Considering the fact that the risk for fully occupied waterside handover areas increases with the waterside crane workload, more SC redirections are to be expected during peak workloads at the waterside block end, thus increasing the number of SC redirections with increasing VCP-overlapping time. As a consequence, fewer (import) containers need to be stored in the yard block and thus fewer shuffle and landside retrieval jobs have to be performed in the future. Hence, crane resources are saved for a more timely execution of other landside storage and retrieval jobs. Based on the simulation results, it can be concluded that for most considered RMGC designs, the previously supposed positive effects of the VCP-overlapping time on the mean vehicle-waiting time in the landside handover area (i.e., reduced crane resources and implicitly caused peak landside workloads) are predominated by these negative effects of the VCP-overlapping time on the mean XT-waiting time (i.e., SC redirections).

Finally, increases of the VCP-overlapping time are observed to have very similar effects on the performance advantage of the TRMGC system over the DRMGC system as increases of the transshipment factor π^{ts} (see Sect. 7.3.3). For medium- to large-sized yard-block layouts, the differences between the mean SC-waiting times of the DRMGC and TRMGC systems are observed to decrease with increases of the VCP-overlapping time, leading even to a reversal of the performance advantage of the TRMGC system over the DRMGC system at the waterside block end, just as expected by Research hypothesis 2.4.3. In contrast, no such effects are observed for small-sized yard blocks. Similar to the inconsistent effects of increases in the transshipment factor π^{ts}, this can be explained by capacity-dependent differences in the absolute extent of peak workloads. While for small-sized yard blocks only small absolute increases in the peak waterside workloads are induced by increasing VCP-overlapping times, much greater absolute increases in the peak workloads are induced for medium- to large-sized yard blocks. As a consequence, the possibility of the DRMGC system to provide additional crane resources for performing waterside jobs does only pay off for medium- to large-sized yard blocks, but not for small-sized ones.

In summary, the unevenness of the vessel-call pattern is found to have significantly positive effects on the mean SC-waiting times in the waterside handover areas of all considered RMGC designs, while having slightly negative effects on the mean XT-waiting times in the landside handover areas of most considered RMGC designs. Furthermore, the unevenness of the vessel-call pattern is found to have negative effects on the performance advantage of the TRMGC system over the DRMGC system for medium- to large-sized yard-block layouts only, while no such effects are found for small-sized yard blocks. As a consequence,

- Research hypothesis 2.4.1 is confirmed,
- Research hypothesis 2.4.2 is not confirmed and
- Research hypothesis 2.4.3 is confirmed for medium- to large-sized yard-block layouts, but is not confirmed for small-sized yard blocks

on basis of the simulation results yielded with the experimental setup of this simulation study.

7.3.5 Influence of the Crane Kinematics

In contrast to the previously investigated input parameters, the crane kinematics have no effects on the crane workload and its distribution in space and time. Instead, the duration of crane movements and the job-execution times are greatly determined by velocity, acceleration and deceleration of portal, trolley and spreader (see Sect. 5.1), thus having notable effects on the actually available crane resources. For this reason, in Sect. 4.1.3, also the crane kinematics are supposed to have a considerable influence on the operational performance and the design of RMGC systems. Subsequently, it is analysed in what way the operational performance and the design of RMGC systems are actually affected by changes in the crane kinematics. Thereby particular attention is given to the question, in how far the performance advantage of the TRMGC system over the DRMGC system is determined by the higher portal velocity of the inner small crane compared to that of the outer large crane.

7.3.5.1 Research Hypotheses

Referring to Sect. 4.1.3.2, the crane kinematics can be expected to have significantly negative effects on the mean vehicle-waiting times in the landside and waterside handover areas of each yard block by influencing the amount of crane resources available to perform certain crane workloads. The faster a crane is able to move, accelerate and/or decelerate, the shorter is the duration of crane movements and the execution times of most jobs. Hence, the cranes are occupied for a shorter period of time and released more quickly for performing the next job, thus increasing the actually available amount of crane resources and decreasing the risk for and the extent of vehicle-waiting times in the handover areas for the forthcoming jobs.

Considering identical percentage changes in the kinematics of portal, trolley and spreader of all cranes, no structural changes of the basic findings on the operational-performance effects of the RMGC design are to be expected by increases and/or decreases of the crane kinematics, as all types of RMGC systems and yard-block layouts are equally affected. Whereas disproportional changes in the kinematics of portal, trolley and spreader can be expected to make longer, wider and higher yard blocks more attractive, respectively. However, for similar reasons as described in Sect. 7.3.1, even proportional changes in the crane kinematics may lead to changing decisions on the RMGC design. Considering that increasing crane kinematics are supposed to have negative effects on the mean vehicle-waiting times in the handover areas, faster cranes can be expected to allow the design of RMGC systems with greater yard blocks and/or fewer cranes per yard block without impairing the operational performance of the container-storage yard.

In Sect. 7.2.2.4, it is argued that the surprisingly bad operational performance of the DRMGC system compared to the TRMGC system may to some extent be explained by the comparably slow portal velocity of the outer large crane in the DRMGC system, which only moves at 3.5 m/s, while all inner small cranes move at 4.0 m/s. Therefore, increases of the portal velocity of the outer large crane can be expected to have negative effects on both the mean vehicle waiting times in the handover areas of the DRMGC system and the operational performance advantage of the TRMGC system over the DRMGC system. In summary, Research hypotheses 2.5.1 and 2.5.2 are formulated:

Research Hypothesis 2.5.1. The crane kinematics have significantly negative effects on the mean vehicle-waiting times in the handover areas.

Research Hypothesis 2.5.2. The portal velocity for the outer large crane of the DRMGC system (v_2^{xe}, v_2^{xf}) has significantly negative effects on the performance advantage of the TRMGC systems over the DRMGC system.

7.3.5.2 Experimental Setup

To investigate the influence of the crane kinematics on the operational performance and the design of RMGC systems—in particular with respect to Research hypotheses 2.5.1 and 2.5.2—two experimental studies are conducted. Firstly, each combination of the four considered types of RMGC systems and the nine representative yard-block layouts is tested with several percentage changes of the default settings of all crane-kinematic-defining parameters in order to analyse the general effects of the crane kinematics on the operational performance of RMGC systems and to validate Research hypothesis 2.5.1. All parameters defining the crane kinematics are varied in steps of 5% of the default settings in the interval from −25% to +25% around the default crane kinematics (which are represented by 0%), thus leading to 11 different parameter settings for the crane kinematics and 396 simulation experiments in total. On top of that, the DRMGC system is tested with different portal velocities of the outer large crane for all considered yard-block layouts in order to investigate the effects of the portal velocity of the outer large crane on the performance advantage of the TRMGC system over the DRMGC system and to validate Research hypothesis 2.5.2. Both the empty and laden portal velocities of the outer large crane (v_2^{xe}, v_2^{xf}) are varied in the interval from 3.5 m/s to 4.0 m/s in steps of 0.05 m/s, thus leading to 11 different settings for the portal velocity of the outer large crane and 99 experiments in total. Except for the aforementioned changes of the parameter settings specifying the crane kinematics, all other input parameters are set to the default settings (see Sect. 7.1.3).

7.3.5.3 Results and Discussion

The simulation results of both experimental studies on the influence of the crane kinematics on the operational performance and the design of RMGC systems are shown in Tables 7.20–7.23. The vehicle-waiting times in the landside and waterside handover areas resulting from experiments with different percentage changes of all crane-kinematic-defining parameters are displayed in Tables 7.20 and 7.21, respectively. There, the percentage changes for all crane kinematic parameters are noted in the first column, while the resulting vehicle-waiting-time figures for different RMGC designs are shown in the following columns. The mean XT and SC-waiting times with different portal velocities for the outer large crane of the DRMGC system are displayed in Tables 7.22 and 7.23, respectively. The portal velocities for the outer large crane are noted in the first column, while the corresponding vehicle-waiting times are shown in the following columns. Other important performance figures of both experimental studies are provided in Appendix A.5.5.

It can be seen from Tables 7.20 and 7.21 that for almost all considered combinations of yard-block layouts and types of RMGC systems both $\overline{\overline{\omega}}_{\mathrm{ls}}^{\mathrm{hr+}}$ and $\overline{\overline{\omega}}_{\mathrm{ws}}^{\mathrm{hr+}}$ decrease with increasing velocity, acceleration and deceleration values of portal, trolley and spreader, just as expected by Research hypothesis 2.5.1. This observation is additionally confirmed by means of correlation analyses, which compute the crane kinematics to be strongly negatively correlated with $\overline{\overline{\omega}}_{\mathrm{ls}}^{\mathrm{hr+}}$ and $\overline{\overline{\omega}}_{\mathrm{ws}}^{\mathrm{hr+}}$—at a significance level of $\alpha = 0.05$—for almost all considered RMGC designs. Only for RMGC designs with the "small" layout no strong negative correlations are found between the crane kinematics and the mean vehicle-waiting time in the waterside handover area. This can be explained by the fact that even comparable slow cranes are able to perform the small workload that is induced by the storage capacity of the "small" layout with only very few seconds mean SC-waiting time. Thus, similarly to the operational-performance effects of the number of cranes per yard block (see Sect. 7.2.2.4), additional crane resources induced by faster cranes do not provide any significant performance advantage for very small-sized yard blocks.

Based on Tables 7.22 and 7.23, it can be seen that, differently than expected by Research hypothesis 2.5.2, the operational performance of the DRMGC system does not really improve with increasing portal velocity of the outer large crane. Neither the mean XT nor the mean SC-waiting time of the DRMGC system decreases significantly with increasing portal velocity for any of the example yard-block layouts. Thus, the operational performance disadvantage of the DRMGC system versus the TRMGC system cannot be explained by the slower portal velocity of the outer large crane alone. Hence, referring to the discussion on the performance differences between the different types of RMGC systems in Sect. 7.2.2.4, the performance advantage of the TRMGC system over the DRMGC systems is most

Table 7.20 Influence of percentage changes in the crane kinematics compared to the default settings on the mean XT-waiting time ($\overline{\overline{\omega}}_{ls}^{hr+}$) for selected yard-block layouts and all types of RMGC systems

	Yard-block layout								
Kinematic change	Small	Low	Narrow	Short	Medium	Long	Wide	High	Big
Resulting $\overline{\overline{\omega}}_{ls}^{hr+}$ with the SRMGC system (s)									
−25%	80.18	122.66	359.53	312.24	675.26	1,772.92	1,562.05	3,855.34	5,006.21
−20%	72.93	114.91	314.20	287.51	564.70	1,511.90	1,275.73	3,404.18	4,787.00
−15%	69.37	110.63	280.55	243.79	494.30	1,254.06	1,090.51	3,052.46	4,478.89
−10%	67.42	103.97	263.07	233.07	412.04	1,072.12	910.27	2,739.65	4,295.13
−5%	63.73	101.30	239.10	220.96	357.92	887.70	749.95	2,466.68	4,060.35
0%	**65.90**	**95.41**	**226.61**	**204.03**	**336.25**	**772.82**	**675.77**	**2,244.74**	**3,903.45**
+5%	62.52	92.50	211.56	191.60	297.70	657.30	568.32	1,989.12	3,636.82
+10%	58.79	90.35	200.73	183.49	261.68	577.58	506.96	1,828.11	3,494.88
+15%	59.24	90.08	190.41	179.29	253.99	519.93	440.12	1,638.65	3,330.80
+20%	56.37	89.28	180.04	173.13	235.02	468.78	399.83	1,532.26	3,218.84
+25%	55.64	86.69	172.37	165.52	223.70	408.63	373.09	1,428.26	3,146.67
Resulting $\overline{\overline{\omega}}_{ls}^{hr+}$ with the TRMGC system (s)									
−25%	29.57	43.61	120.56	111.72	146.64	203.21	185.29	818.21	2,132.48
−20%	26.12	39.34	108.94	99.88	131.61	181.75	165.97	698.33	2,016.17
−15%	24.59	35.69	101.46	93.73	120.66	164.72	151.28	590.60	1,912.44
−10%	22.25	33.31	93.44	86.76	112.12	151.03	137.45	503.21	1,743.96
−5%	20.84	30.72	86.27	83.21	104.00	137.49	128.91	440.53	1,635.01
0%	**19.48**	**29.13**	**82.08**	**77.19**	**98.58**	**126.78**	**118.96**	**387.72**	**1,540.04**
+5%	18.51	27.30	78.23	72.31	91.48	119.34	110.56	342.32	1,398.98
+10%	17.18	25.35	73.44	67.94	87.22	111.61	103.97	310.97	1,278.09
+15%	16.31	24.06	70.48	65.23	82.45	105.03	97.21	281.60	1,179.76
+20%	15.89	22.55	67.79	62.87	78.08	101.04	93.51	255.08	1,050.86
+25%	14.86	21.42	63.96	60.54	76.00	95.31	87.46	232.09	990.30
Resulting $\overline{\overline{\omega}}_{ls}^{hr+}$ with the DRMGC system (s)									
−25%	42.70	69.72	156.35	156.23	197.45	276.17	271.44	1,028.96	3,028.60
−20%	41.75	65.16	146.69	147.65	186.35	246.68	243.37	859.01	2,723.44
−15%	37.66	59.90	136.68	138.80	176.39	223.05	221.97	774.36	2,514.88
−10%	35.14	56.08	134.17	129.01	161.37	203.90	206.28	652.33	2,257.47
−5%	32.75	55.49	123.71	123.87	154.78	194.75	191.95	582.41	2,109.32
0%	**31.48**	**52.60**	**116.45**	**118.90**	**146.10**	**179.24**	**181.10**	**509.39**	**1,907.61**
+5%	30.63	50.01	111.45	113.69	138.55	171.09	172.31	457.08	1,766.30
+10%	28.60	47.51	108.13	109.34	138.10	162.84	165.07	393.94	1,567.47
+15%	26.49	45.15	103.29	105.93	129.82	155.13	155.45	359.58	1,456.93
+20%	25.42	43.55	101.10	101.23	124.98	148.50	148.61	336.87	1,324.00
+25%	24.43	42.50	96.18	98.91	121.70	142.27	144.48	308.56	1,232.03
Resulting $\overline{\overline{\omega}}_{ls}^{hr+}$ with the TriRMGC system (s)									
−25%	28.34	40.71	96.75	95.61	116.70	143.98	143.49	390.75	1,484.89
−20%	26.11	36.28	88.71	89.51	106.27	131.31	131.94	353.68	1,289.00
−15%	23.38	32.92	81.73	83.65	99.98	119.94	119.19	306.47	1,145.57
−10%	22.04	31.19	76.71	78.69	91.19	112.68	113.97	266.38	978.87
−5%	20.48	28.66	72.63	72.76	87.00	105.22	104.40	234.71	868.42
0%	**19.56**	**26.47**	**66.99**	**68.47**	**80.43**	**98.14**	**98.35**	**208.77**	**754.71**
+5%	17.41	24.49	63.44	65.34	77.26	91.96	91.95	202.11	666.10
+10%	16.66	23.26	61.64	63.73	71.22	86.58	86.65	190.23	575.91
+15%	15.70	21.42	58.10	58.66	68.17	80.22	81.85	172.36	517.99
+20%	14.58	20.35	54.88	57.38	65.60	76.90	79.26	158.92	471.36
+25%	13.79	19.58	54.23	53.43	61.99	73.90	74.28	150.84	431.02

Table 7.21 Influence of percentage changes in the crane kinematics compared to the default settings on the mean SC-waiting time ($\overline{\overline{\omega}}_{ws}^{hr+}$) for selected yard-block layouts and all types of RMGC systems

	Yard-block layout								
Kinematic change	Small	Low	Narrow	Short	Medium	Long	Wide	High	Big
Resulting $\overline{\overline{\omega}}_{ws}^{hr+}$ with the SRMGC system (s)									
−25%	1.51	4.61	116.17	80.72	347.03	1,145.31	1,025.24	2,752.45	3,407.34
−20%	2.39	3.23	90.48	69.76	267.49	982.03	811.63	2,450.36	3,308.61
−15%	1.85	3.74	69.16	46.70	212.45	789.46	663.48	2,205.73	3,153.85
−10%	2.07	3.30	56.99	45.55	144.10	633.10	536.57	1,969.69	3,110.31
−5%	1.79	3.39	44.33	35.82	116.03	497.96	395.79	1,765.60	2,989.58
0%	**1.69**	**2.86**	**40.46**	**28.71**	**102.93**	**410.23**	**350.05**	**1,597.83**	**2,837.74**
+5%	1.66	2.96	32.59	25.10	82.61	325.63	259.88	1,434.56	2,678.48
+10%	2.17	2.74	31.98	23.46	59.46	253.31	223.84	1,311.57	2,606.19
+15%	2.17	3.14	25.48	19.58	51.96	221.91	160.94	1,160.96	2,522.82
+20%	1.73	2.21	23.98	17.48	42.84	187.36	143.18	1,075.68	2,420.47
+25%	1.51	2.80	19.67	15.88	39.52	145.43	123.36	994.14	2,433.19
Resulting $\overline{\overline{\omega}}_{ws}^{hr+}$ with the TRMGC system (s)									
−25%	1.35	2.91	19.38	14.18	31.06	75.25	61.81	647.89	2,960.88
−20%	1.22	2.82	15.95	12.64	24.76	59.12	47.45	545.69	2,579.28
−15%	1.19	1.92	13.51	10.72	20.50	47.27	35.91	444.75	2,338.59
−10%	1.38	2.32	11.74	9.19	17.36	35.40	29.03	353.17	2,036.39
−5%	1.60	2.51	9.72	7.35	15.16	29.64	23.00	298.08	1,807.33
0%	**1.19**	**2.14**	**7.79**	**6.74**	**13.31**	**25.15**	**21.79**	**247.50**	**1,586.02**
+5%	1.25	2.26	8.18	6.53	11.88	19.66	14.75	200.44	1,427.61
+10%	0.91	2.20	7.04	5.37	9.42	17.21	13.67	162.63	1,220.66
+15%	1.28	1.70	6.16	5.67	8.89	12.96	11.88	136.76	1,090.44
+20%	1.19	2.29	6.24	5.76	6.84	12.52	9.47	114.95	969.70
+25%	1.03	2.41	5.58	4.45	7.34	9.55	9.04	97.74	899.55
Resulting $\overline{\overline{\omega}}_{ws}^{hr+}$ with the DRMGC system (s)									
−25%	1.97	3.47	20.01	19.09	33.79	74.29	72.09	654.89	2,283.10
−20%	1.81	2.66	16.98	15.40	28.73	56.92	54.74	530.05	2,065.03
−15%	1.53	2.76	15.23	13.95	24.26	44.38	42.02	469.05	1,900.72
−10%	1.44	2.79	12.66	12.34	20.08	34.71	37.66	376.03	1,651.55
−5%	1.47	2.82	12.83	10.64	18.67	32.01	29.26	316.44	1,566.29
0%	**1.44**	**2.76**	**10.37**	**9.57**	**15.89**	**24.57**	**23.92**	**259.60**	**1,401.64**
+5%	1.34	2.39	9.33	9.36	13.94	20.81	22.44	216.50	1,275.65
+10%	1.40	2.63	8.95	7.62	14.69	19.44	19.28	173.61	1,134.91
+15%	1.44	2.26	8.19	8.29	12.27	18.18	16.37	142.85	1,057.87
+20%	1.22	2.48	7.67	6.87	11.43	14.51	14.60	129.80	945.44
+25%	1.31	2.38	7.20	6.65	10.72	13.68	14.04	107.72	864.27
Resulting $\overline{\overline{\omega}}_{ws}^{hr+}$ with the TriRMGC system (s)									
−25%	1.57	2.92	11.66	11.03	17.16	20.70	22.56	171.87	1,046.78
−20%	1.51	2.89	9.12	9.46	12.86	17.50	18.19	148.80	881.89
−15%	1.45	2.49	8.49	8.54	11.62	14.81	15.07	116.39	770.08
−10%	1.57	2.76	7.35	8.15	10.49	13.27	14.01	93.05	654.86
−5%	1.70	3.17	6.81	6.34	9.75	11.03	11.81	71.54	567.19
0%	**1.16**	**2.76**	**6.61**	**6.48**	**8.44**	**10.23**	**10.85**	**56.00**	**451.96**
+5%	1.82	2.30	6.34	5.77	8.18	9.88	9.18	54.40	401.48
+10%	1.19	2.40	6.18	5.82	8.19	9.06	8.76	47.38	325.48
+15%	1.16	2.51	5.48	5.73	7.64	8.06	8.33	37.76	275.70
+20%	1.48	2.30	5.16	5.06	7.36	7.63	7.64	31.77	241.78
+25%	1.60	2.39	4.91	5.44	6.28	7.29	7.28	27.95	213.66

Table 7.22 Influence of the portal velocity of the outer large crane of the DRMGC system (v_2^{xe}, v_2^{xf}) on the mean XT-waiting time ($\overline{\overline{\omega}}_{ls}^{hr+}$) for selected yard-block layouts

	Yard-block layout								
v_2^{xe}, v_2^{xf}	Small	Low	Narrow	Short	Medium	Long	Wide	High	Big
Resulting $\overline{\overline{\omega}}_{ls}^{hr+}$ with the SRMGC system (s)									
	65.90	**95.41**	**226.61**	**204.03**	**336.25**	**772.82**	**675.77**	**2,244.74**	**3,903.45**
Resulting $\overline{\overline{\omega}}_{ls}^{hr+}$ with the TRMGC system (s)									
	19.48	**29.13**	**82.08**	**77.19**	**98.58**	**126.78**	**118.96**	**387.72**	**1,540.04**
Resulting $\overline{\overline{\omega}}_{ls}^{hr+}$ with the DRMGC system (s)									
3.50	**31.48**	**52.60**	**116.45**	**118.90**	**146.10**	**179.24**	**181.10**	**509.39**	**1,907.61**
3.55	31.54	52.07	115.73	119.25	148.53	181.38	180.87	488.35	1,901.50
3.60	31.17	53.05	116.74	116.68	146.94	178.91	181.39	502.28	1,892.68
3.65	31.24	52.21	117.53	117.88	145.55	181.07	178.17	488.21	1,868.08
3.70	31.71	51.03	117.08	116.80	145.80	175.95	179.89	508.09	1,889.45
3.75	29.82	50.62	114.22	114.88	145.80	178.38	178.87	471.90	1,866.96
3.80	29.88	50.93	115.99	114.93	143.10	177.50	178.79	485.21	1,850.55
3.85	30.48	49.79	114.07	116.81	146.15	178.85	178.11	506.62	1,868.52
3.90	30.80	49.75	115.89	116.14	143.29	177.35	175.73	481.29	1,859.25
3.95	30.37	51.35	116.33	115.77	143.61	178.39	177.91	478.11	1,851.59
4.00	30.34	50.59	117.89	118.07	144.48	176.51	177.12	477.51	1,800.29
Resulting $\overline{\overline{\omega}}_{ls}^{hr+}$ with the TriRMGC system (s)									
	19.56	**26.47**	**66.99**	**68.47**	**80.43**	**98.14**	**98.35**	**208.77**	**754.71**

Table 7.23 Influence of the portal velocity of the outer large crane of the DRMGC system (v_2^{xe}, v_2^{xf}) on the mean SC-waiting time ($\overline{\overline{\omega}}_{ws}^{hr+}$) for selected yard-block layouts

	Yard-block layout								
v_2^{xe}, v_2^{xf}	Small	Low	Narrow	Short	Medium	Long	Wide	High	Big
Resulting $\overline{\overline{\omega}}_{ws}^{hr+}$ with the SRMGC system (s)									
	1.69	**2.86**	**40.46**	**28.71**	**102.93**	**410.23**	**350.05**	**1,597.83**	**2,837.74**
Resulting $\overline{\overline{\omega}}_{ws}^{hr+}$ with the TRMGC system (s)									
	1.19	**2.14**	**7.79**	**6.74**	**13.31**	**25.15**	**21.79**	**247.50**	**1,586.02**
Resulting $\overline{\overline{\omega}}_{ws}^{hr+}$ with the DRMGC system (s)									
3.50	**1.44**	**2.76**	**10.37**	**9.57**	**15.89**	**24.57**	**23.92**	**259.60**	**1,401.64**
3.55	1.56	2.66	10.35	9.89	16.03	24.64	24.81	245.25	1,402.95
3.60	1.66	2.26	9.37	9.69	16.02	25.03	24.43	251.97	1,389.76
3.65	1.78	2.63	10.15	10.42	16.79	27.65	24.65	237.47	1,381.64
3.70	1.72	2.66	10.52	9.94	15.55	24.06	26.78	259.51	1,382.90
3.75	1.22	2.57	9.79	9.68	15.49	27.05	24.04	228.12	1,364.48
3.80	1.22	2.57	9.27	9.14	13.98	25.14	25.22	251.19	1,357.75
3.85	1.37	2.60	9.77	9.29	14.95	25.49	24.39	263.51	1,398.95
3.90	1.44	2.23	10.35	10.90	16.08	25.98	22.53	246.48	1,380.45
3.95	1.13	2.60	9.98	9.34	16.23	25.07	25.23	229.97	1,360.36
4.00	1.19	2.36	10.12	10.18	15.04	25.01	24.04	246.60	1,324.99
Resulting $\overline{\overline{\omega}}_{ws}^{hr+}$ with the TriRMGC system (s)									
	1.16	**2.76**	**6.61**	**6.48**	**8.44**	**10.23**	**10.85**	**56.00**	**451.96**

probably due to significantly longer crane-interference times for the DRMGC system than for the TRMGC system. In how far crane-interference-time-minimising crane-scheduling and routing strategies are actually able to close the performance gap between the TRMGC and DRMGC systems is analysed in Sects. 7.3.7 and 7.3.8, respectively.

Altogether, the crane kinematics are found to have significantly negative effects on the mean vehicle-waiting times in the landside and waterside handover areas. Whereas the portal velocity of the outer large crane is not found to have significantly negative effects on the performance advantage of the TRMGC system over the DRMGC system. As a consequence of these findings,

- Research hypothesis 2.5.1 is confirmed and
- Research hypothesis 2.5.2 is not confirmed

for the experimental setup of this simulation study.

7.3.6 *Influence of the Container-Stacking Strategy*

While the basically available amount of crane resources per yard block is determined by the number of cranes and their kinematics, the efficient use of these crane resources depends on the applied operational strategies. Therefore, in Sect. 4.1.3, both the selection and the parametrisation of operational strategies are discussed to be of considerable importance for the operational performance and the design of RMGC systems. In particular, the container-stacking strategy is supposed to have notable performance effects, as the number of required shuffle moves, which usually make up a large part of inefficient crane usage, is greatly determined by the way containers are stacked (see Sect. 5.2.1). In this subsection, it is verified and analysed in how far the vehicle-waiting times in the handover areas are affected by and to what extent the RMGC design is sensitive to changes of the operating container-stacking strategy and its parametrisation.

7.3.6.1 Research Hypotheses

Basically, a stacking strategy is the more efficient with respect to the operational performance of the container-storage yard, the fewer shuffle moves are induced and the more the crane workload is smoothed over time by stacking decisions resulting from that strategy (see Sect. 5.2.1). Thus, referring to the classification of reported stacking strategies in Sect. 5.2.3, CaS, RTS and PoS are identified as reasonable container-positioning methods that can be combined in different ways, whereas RaS and LeS should only be used as benchmarks. While CaS and RTS are useful approaches to reduce the number of shuffle moves, PoS can be applied in a way that is helpful to smooth the crane workload over time. However, none of these container-positioning methods is directly considered in this simulation study. Apart from RaS, which is used as benchmark method here, only the cost-function-based CCFS container-positioning method is considered for a goal-directed container stacking in this work (see Sect. 5.2.4). But due to extensive parametrisation possibilities, the CCFS method can be parametrised in such a way that the properties of CaS, PoS and RTS are combined to different degrees. Throughout this simulation study, a certain parametrisation of the CCFS method is used as default container-positioning method (see Sect. 7.1.3) that is almost exclusively based on CaS, while no properties of RTS and hardly any properties of PoS are considered. Thus, only containers departing by deep-sea vessel are stacked, by default, in a shuffle-move-minimising way. However, considering the fact that the RaS method is neither based on shuffle-move-minimisation nor workload-smoothing objectives for any container, the default parametrisation of the CCFS method can nevertheless be expected to yield significantly shorter mean vehicle-waiting times in the handover areas than applying the RaS method.

Because the CCFS method is by default parametrised in such a way that it only aims to minimise the number of shuffle moves for containers departing by deep-sea vessel, while all other containers are stacked somehow randomly, significant vehicle-waiting-time reductions can be expected by additionally considering shuffle-move-minimisation aspects for containers departing by XT and feeder vessel. In this work, it is proposed to consider the shuffle-move-minimisation objective for these containers by an RTS-related cost component in the CCFS method, which is based on individual container-delivery times (t_c^{in}) and the mean container-dwell time ($\overline{\delta}$) to anticipate container-retrieval sequences of certain stacks (see Sect. 5.2.4). By increasing the cost factor $\lambda_{\tau(j)}^{\text{rts}}$ for these retrieval-time-based shuffle-move costs, more attention is given to the shuffle-move-minimisation objective for containers that are planned to depart by XT and feeder vessel. Thus, the number of shuffle moves for these containers and thus also the mean vehicle-waiting times in the handover areas are expected to decrease by setting the retrieval-time cost factors $\lambda_{\tau(j)}^{\text{rts}} > 0$.

In Sect. 5.2.3.2, the PoS method is qualified as being a reasonable endorsement for the CaS method in order to additionally consider workload-smoothing aspects for determining container-stacking positions and thus to reduce the mean vehicle-waiting times in the handover areas. Hence, it may be advisable to increase the workload-smoothing cost factors ($\lambda_{\tau(j)}^{\text{dist}}$) of the CCFS method, thus paying more attention to the distribution of inbound and outbound crane-driving distances that result from certain stacking positions, in order to improve the performance of the CCFS method. However, it needs to be considered that increasing the workload-smoothing cost factors does not only lead to the selection of workload-smoothing stacking positions, but from a certain point onwards also to stacking positions that induce additional shuffle moves, since the PoS-related workload-smoothing costs become greater than the CaS-related shuffle-move costs. Therefore, increases of the workload-smoothing costs can only be expected to have negative effects on the vehicle-waiting times in the handover areas, as long as the vehicle-waiting-time-reducing effects of a more smoothed crane workload are not outweighed by the vehicle-waiting-time-increasing effects of additional shuffle moves. However, the inclusion of the workload-smoothing costs in the CCFS method (i.e., $\lambda^{\text{dist}}_{\tau(j)} > 0$) can be expected to have negative effects on the vehicle-waiting times compared to not considering any workload-smoothing aspects at all (i.e., $\lambda^{\text{dist}}_{\tau(j)} = 0$).

A further smoothing of the crane workload over time can be reached by applying the housekeeping concept which is based on the idea to relocate containers during times of low workload in such a way that future shuffle jobs and crane-driving distances to the outgoing handover areas are reduced. In this work, the HHS method is proposed to determine the time of relocation, the relocation container and the new stacking position for the relocation container (see Sect. 5.2.5). Provided that the underlying cost function of the HHS method is reasonably parametrised—considering CaS, RTS and/or PoS aspects as explained before—the crane workload is expected to be smoothed over time by applying the HHS method. Thus, the mean vehicle-waiting times in the handover areas can, ceteris paribus, be expected to decrease with the additional application of the HHS method compared to solely deploying a certain (parametrisation of a) container-positioning method.

Considering the fact that the risk for shuffle moves basically increases with the stacking height of a yard block (see Sect. 7.2.2.3), the differences in the resulting number of shuffle moves between different (parametrisations of) container-stacking strategies can be expected to become more pronounced with increasing stacking height than with increasing block length or width. As a consequence, the stacking height can also be expected to have larger positive effects on the differences in the resulting vehicle-waiting times between different (parametrisations of) container-stacking strategies than the block length or width. This means that the quality of the container-positioning method with respect to the shuffle-move-minimisation objective is expected to be of increasing importance with increasing stacking height. Altogether, Research hypotheses 2.6.1–2.6.5 are formulated:

Research Hypothesis 2.6.1. The inclusion of retrieval-time-based shuffle-move costs in the CCFS method (i.e., $\lambda^{\text{rts}}_{\tau(j)} > 0$) has significantly negative effects on the mean vehicle-waiting times in the handover areas.

Research Hypothesis 2.6.2. The inclusion of workload-smoothing costs in the CCFS method (i.e., $\lambda^{\text{dist}}_{\tau(j)} > 0$) has significantly negative effects on the mean vehicle-waiting times in the handover areas.

Research Hypothesis 2.6.3. The RaS method is significantly outperformed by reasonable parametrisations of the CCFS method.

Research Hypothesis 2.6.4. The additional application of the HHS method has significantly negative effects on the mean vehicle-waiting times in the handover areas.

Research Hypothesis 2.6.5. The container-stacking strategy is of increasing importance for the operational performance of RMGC systems with increasing stacking height of the yard block.

7.3.6.2 Experimental Setup

To investigate the influence of the container-stacking strategy on the operational performance and the design of RMGC systems—especially with regard to Research hypotheses 2.6.1–2.6.5—three experimental studies are conducted. Firstly, each combination of the four considered types of RMGC systems and the nine representative yard-block layouts is tested with different cost factors for the retrieval-time-based shuffle-move costs of the CCFS method ($\lambda^{\text{rts}}_{\tau(j)}$), while all other parameters of the CCFS method are kept unchanged compared to the default parametrisation (see Sect. 7.1.3), in order to analyse the pure performance effects of the RTS concept and to validate Research hypothesis 2.6.1. The cost factors for the retrieval-time-based shuffle-move costs of all types of jobs are varied in eleven steps between $\lambda^{\text{rts}}_{\tau(j)} = 0$ and $\lambda^{\text{rts}}_{\tau(j)} = 100$, thus leading to 396 simulation experiments for the first experimental study. Secondly, each example RMGC design is simulated with different cost factors for the workload-smoothing costs of the CCFS method ($\lambda^{\text{dist}}_{\tau(j)}$), while all other cost factors of this container-positioning method are set to the default settings, in order to investigate the pure performance effects of the PoS concept and to validate Research hypothesis 2.6.2. For this experimental study, the cost factors for the workload-smoothing costs of all types of jobs are varied in eleven steps between $\lambda^{\text{dist}}_{\tau(j)} = 0$ and $\lambda^{\text{dist}}_{\tau(j)} = 20$, thus likewise resulting in 396 simulation experiments.

Finally, all considered RMGC designs are tested with the RaS container-positioning method and four reasonable parametrisations of the CCFS method, both with and without additionally applying the HHS concept, in order to examine the operational-performance effects of the housekeeping concept and to validate Research hypotheses 2.6.3–2.6.5. The four different CCFS parametrisations, that are based on preliminary considerations and simulation experiments, are designed to represent the application of (1) a pure CaS concept, (2) a combination of the CaS and RTS concepts, (3) a combination of the CaS and PoS concepts as well as (4) a combination of the CaS, RTS and PoS concepts. The CaS parametrisation of the CCFS method is simply equivalent to the standardly applied parametrisation of that method (see Sect. 7.1.3). For the second CCFS parametrisation, the cost factors of the retrieval-time-based shuffle-move costs are set to $\lambda^{\text{rts}}_{\tau(j)} = 25.0$, while all other cost factors are kept unchanged compared to the default settings. Similarly, the cost factors of the workload-smoothing costs are set to $\lambda^{\text{dist}}_{\tau(j)} = 0.5$ for the third parametrisation of the CCFS method, while again all other cost factors are kept unchanged. For the fourth CCFS parametrisation, representing the combined application of the CaS, RTS and PoS concepts, the cost factors of the retrieval-time-based shuffle-move costs and the workload-smoothing costs are set to $\lambda^{\text{rts}}_{\tau(j)} = 25.0$ and $\lambda^{\text{dist}}_{\tau(j)} = 0.5$, respectively. For the HHS method, the acceptance levels for minimum possible and minimum realisable cost improvement are set to $\kappa^{\text{al}}_{\text{hhs}} = \kappa^{\text{mci}}_{\text{hhs}} = 0.5$.

Apart from the aforementioned experimental studies on the effects of the container-stacking strategy, that are based on default settings for all none-stacking related parameters, no further simulation experiments on container stacking are conducted. In particular, no simulation experiments on fine tuning of parameter settings for the CCFS container-positioning method are conducted, although slight performance improvements may be yielded by changing certain parameter settings. But considering the huge number of parametrisation possibilities of the CCFS method and the possibility for RMGC-design-dependent differences in the operational-performance effects of CCFS parametrisations, identifying the best parameter setting of the CCFS method for each RMGC design must be a very time-consuming process that is beyond the scope of this work. Instead, it is aimed at identifying general effects of selected stacking concepts on the operational performance and the design of RMGC systems in this subsection.

7.3.6.3 Results and Discussion

The simulation results of all three experimental studies on the influence of the container-stacking strategy on the operational performance and the design of RMGC systems are shown in Tables 7.24–7.29. The mean vehicle-waiting times in the landside and waterside handover areas that are yielded with different cost factors for the retrieval-time-based shuffle-move costs of the CCFS method ($\lambda^{\text{rts}}_{\tau(j)}$) are displayed in Tables 7.24 and 7.25, respectively, while Tables 7.26 and 7.27 show the resulting XT and SC-waiting times of simulation experiments with different cost factors for the workload-smoothing costs of the CCFS method ($\lambda^{\text{dist}}_{\tau(j)}$). In these tables, different values for the considered cost factor are noted in the first column, while the resulting vehicle-waiting-time figures for different RMGC designs are shown in the following columns. The mean vehicle-waiting times in the landside and waterside handover areas that result from applying different (parametrisations of) container-positioning methods with and without the additional use of the HHS concept are presented in Tables 7.28 and 7.29, respectively. There, the used container-positioning method is noted in the first column, the use of the HHS concept is indicated by a check in the second column and the resulting vehicle-waiting-time figures for different RMGC designs are displayed in the following columns. Further simulation results of all three experimental studies with respect to other important performance figures are shown in Appendix A.5.6.

It can be seen from Tables 7.24 and 7.25 that for almost all considered RMGC designs, the resulting XT and SC-waiting times in the handover areas decrease by including retrieval-time-based shuffle-moves costs (i.e., $\lambda^{\text{rts}}_{\tau(j)} > 0$) for deciding on stacking positions with the CCFS method, just as expected by Research hypothesis 2.6.1. It is even observed that both $\overline{\overline{\omega}}^{\text{hr+}}_{\text{ls}}$ and $\overline{\overline{\omega}}^{\text{hr+}}_{\text{ws}}$ decrease more or less steadily with increases of the cost factors for the retrieval-time-based shuffle-move costs ($\lambda^{\text{rts}}_{\tau(j)}$) in the investigated range. These observations are also mostly confirmed by means of correlation analyses, which compute $\lambda^{\text{rts}}_{\tau(j)}$ to be negatively correlated with $\overline{\overline{\omega}}^{\text{hr+}}_{\text{ls}}$ and $\overline{\overline{\omega}}^{\text{hr+}}_{\text{ws}}$ for almost all considered RMGC designs. While $\overline{\overline{\omega}}^{\text{hr+}}_{\text{ls}}$ is found to be very strongly and highly significantly correlated with $\lambda^{\text{rts}}_{\tau(j)}$ for almost all considered RMGC designs, less strong and/or less significant correlations between $\overline{\overline{\omega}}^{\text{hr+}}_{\text{ws}}$ and $\lambda^{\text{rts}}_{\tau(j)}$ are computed for most RMGC designs, thus

Table 7.24 Influence of the RTS concept (in terms of the cost factor $\lambda^{\text{rts}}_{\tau(j)}$) on the mean XT-waiting time ($\overline{\overline{\omega}}^{\text{hr+}}_{\text{ls}}$) for selected yard-block layouts and all types of RMGC systems

	Yard-block layout								
$\lambda^{\text{rts}}_{\tau(j)}$	Small	Low	Narrow	Short	Medium	Long	Wide	High	Big
Resulting $\overline{\overline{\omega}}^{\text{hr+}}_{\text{ls}}$ with the SRMGC system (s)									
0.00	**65.90**	**95.41**	**226.61**	**204.03**	**336.25**	**772.82**	**675.77**	**2,244.74**	**3,903.45**
0.01	62.39	96.06	225.56	205.50	326.60	765.28	665.35	2,205.08	3,841.33
0.10	63.22	96.80	216.88	201.64	311.63	752.15	644.06	2,057.09	3,852.88
0.50	63.25	96.93	209.94	198.11	305.55	757.49	639.71	1,767.84	3,885.83
1.00	60.21	97.57	204.99	188.93	303.59	716.02	622.85	1,797.21	3,907.82
2.00	62.25	96.48	202.39	186.72	310.09	710.03	599.14	1,751.25	3,976.51
5.00	62.51	97.60	204.55	188.48	301.67	694.38	604.50	1,677.17	3,920.76
10.00	66.56	95.51	204.62	189.66	294.86	716.42	580.36	1,690.59	3,909.83
25.00	63.65	97.86	199.74	188.37	296.44	666.36	565.19	1,626.54	3,995.37
50.00	62.69	93.55	205.26	185.23	291.70	710.97	556.40	1,662.36	3,968.73
100.00	60.35	95.10	194.68	183.05	295.59	703.22	578.91	1,569.47	4,069.75
Resulting $\overline{\overline{\omega}}^{\text{hr+}}_{\text{ls}}$ with the TRMGC system (s)									
0.00	**19.48**	**29.13**	**82.08**	**77.19**	**98.58**	**126.78**	**118.96**	**387.72**	**1,540.04**
0.01	19.67	29.11	81.89	77.10	97.50	128.39	117.48	385.44	1,533.76
0.10	19.39	28.34	81.09	75.94	97.63	128.31	115.80	348.51	1,445.82
0.50	18.77	27.79	74.89	69.89	92.91	121.48	112.42	284.58	1,315.15
1.00	19.10	27.73	73.52	66.57	87.02	118.63	109.15	260.53	1,216.44
2.00	19.82	27.95	72.82	66.65	87.87	119.24	106.98	254.85	1,128.18
5.00	19.36	28.16	73.63	66.68	88.25	116.61	106.84	250.07	1,138.17
10.00	19.94	28.54	72.18	67.41	86.83	116.45	106.20	243.31	1,149.30
25.00	19.60	28.27	71.60	65.25	84.35	117.17	105.11	239.48	1,108.60
50.00	19.14	28.42	71.09	64.81	85.77	114.34	106.03	237.34	1,158.64
100.00	19.29	27.51	70.30	63.03	83.86	114.37	105.69	243.35	1,118.17
Resulting $\overline{\overline{\omega}}^{\text{hr+}}_{\text{ls}}$ with the DRMGC system (s)									
0.00	**31.48**	**52.60**	**116.45**	**118.90**	**146.10**	**179.24**	**181.10**	**509.39**	**1,907.61**
0.01	32.41	52.08	116.80	118.91	147.88	181.85	180.39	511.38	1,903.22
0.10	30.70	50.31	115.34	118.12	145.65	180.35	179.34	456.85	1,833.61
0.50	30.19	50.11	108.54	107.79	135.90	171.74	174.12	367.79	1,589.64
1.00	30.02	49.02	105.69	101.65	130.60	168.65	166.56	341.19	1,496.66
2.00	28.51	49.25	102.41	103.08	130.67	163.57	162.10	326.62	1,456.93
5.00	29.63	49.13	100.60	97.78	125.65	165.44	161.37	303.25	1,386.09
10.00	29.42	50.16	99.47	98.53	125.86	164.80	161.65	303.81	1,376.00
25.00	28.53	50.22	100.07	99.53	127.04	158.90	158.91	309.22	1,383.80
50.00	28.74	49.43	97.24	98.95	125.61	160.87	160.22	310.04	1,349.74
100.00	27.64	49.05	97.94	97.63	125.48	159.37	159.15	310.58	1,367.00
Resulting $\overline{\overline{\omega}}^{\text{hr+}}_{\text{ls}}$ with the TriRMGC system (s)									
0.00	**19.56**	**26.47**	**66.99**	**68.47**	**80.43**	**98.14**	**98.35**	**208.77**	**754.71**
0.01	19.06	26.11	68.12	69.50	79.91	96.18	97.73	213.40	745.05
0.10	18.72	26.49	67.13	69.39	79.47	97.44	97.57	204.14	732.18
0.50	18.38	24.72	59.94	60.95	74.44	90.60	91.60	161.00	589.77
1.00	17.72	24.19	58.23	58.83	70.09	89.11	85.08	146.92	545.22
2.00	18.13	24.42	57.99	56.99	67.85	85.13	85.24	146.77	515.03
5.00	18.01	24.76	57.84	56.77	68.76	85.15	83.14	139.50	488.89
10.00	17.63	24.42	58.18	56.77	68.58	84.70	81.98	144.59	493.64
25.00	17.16	24.81	55.38	56.68	68.19	83.93	84.42	144.07	460.80
50.00	16.99	24.48	56.20	58.46	66.09	85.18	82.24	137.69	489.86
100.00	16.79	24.08	53.84	55.15	66.43	81.46	82.11	141.07	479.48

Table 7.25 Influence of the RTS concept (in terms of the cost factor $\lambda^{\text{rts}}_{\tau(j)}$) on the mean SC-waiting time ($\overline{\overline{\omega}}^{\text{hr+}}_{\text{ws}}$) for selected yard-block layouts and all types of RMGC systems

	Yard-block layout								
$\lambda^{\text{rts}}_{\tau(j)}$	Small	Low	Narrow	Short	Medium	Long	Wide	High	Big
Resulting $\overline{\overline{\omega}}^{\text{hr+}}_{\text{ws}}$ with the SRMGC system (s)									
0.00	**1.69**	**2.86**	**40.46**	**28.71**	**102.93**	**410.23**	**350.05**	**1,597.83**	**2,837.74**
0.01	1.72	3.11	39.70	32.15	98.70	400.72	334.91	1,597.26	2,900.41
0.10	1.19	3.55	35.53	26.93	87.79	383.53	327.24	1,416.12	2,911.23
0.50	1.22	3.51	33.41	24.53	81.23	401.53	317.23	1,189.23	2,933.23
1.00	2.17	3.17	35.35	22.80	82.02	367.32	315.11	1,237.03	2,962.22
2.00	1.60	3.27	34.65	26.61	88.37	366.02	293.55	1,201.38	3,000.01
5.00	1.32	3.21	30.65	24.96	81.70	336.46	309.29	1,156.44	3,016.92
10.00	1.60	2.24	32.06	23.80	82.61	360.43	288.54	1,183.62	3,043.92
25.00	2.10	2.93	33.98	25.21	78.03	331.90	268.11	1,105.25	3,106.92
50.00	1.83	3.02	33.31	24.20	76.56	358.16	259.11	1,133.72	3,073.49
100.00	1.85	3.76	30.84	23.91	81.42	368.29	280.90	1,066.02	3,230.01
Resulting $\overline{\overline{\omega}}^{\text{hr+}}_{\text{ws}}$ with the TRMGC system (s)									
0.00	**1.19**	**2.14**	**7.79**	**6.74**	**13.31**	**25.15**	**21.79**	**247.50**	**1,586.02**
0.01	0.87	2.04	8.69	7.54	11.65	24.22	17.50	241.81	1,571.06
0.10	1.38	2.70	8.15	6.37	12.42	22.53	18.17	206.91	1,496.41
0.50	1.22	2.23	8.21	6.83	12.28	22.81	19.96	169.83	1,316.39
1.00	1.16	2.33	8.13	7.18	10.55	22.58	19.07	150.78	1,218.17
2.00	1.16	1.74	7.94	6.27	11.68	20.54	19.72	148.83	1,178.81
5.00	1.31	2.60	8.18	6.19	12.02	22.12	16.76	135.90	1,165.52
10.00	1.38	2.39	8.64	5.67	10.74	24.43	16.85	135.01	1,204.35
25.00	1.19	2.45	7.87	7.07	10.76	23.51	17.05	131.67	1,106.11
50.00	1.63	1.95	7.45	6.86	10.90	22.34	18.72	138.52	1,174.94
100.00	0.78	2.26	8.60	6.07	10.77	24.83	19.99	140.72	1,118.59
Resulting $\overline{\overline{\omega}}^{\text{hr+}}_{\text{ws}}$ with the DRMGC system (s)									
0.00	**1.44**	**2.76**	**10.37**	**9.57**	**15.89**	**24.57**	**23.92**	**259.60**	**1,401.64**
0.01	1.78	2.72	9.94	9.48	15.48	24.56	23.81	267.26	1,420.79
0.10	1.44	2.51	10.34	9.58	16.33	24.02	22.51	216.37	1,327.69
0.50	1.37	2.94	9.50	7.97	13.96	23.49	24.38	160.30	1,160.62
1.00	1.53	2.48	9.58	8.78	15.39	23.07	23.53	148.27	1,088.35
2.00	1.57	2.69	9.44	8.95	14.33	23.32	22.35	142.12	1,052.48
5.00	1.03	2.88	9.57	8.44	14.07	24.68	22.60	122.99	1,022.40
10.00	1.47	2.82	9.79	8.18	14.38	24.12	24.29	124.61	1,013.46
25.00	1.28	2.48	9.04	8.05	13.51	23.05	24.14	124.01	1,024.14
50.00	1.50	2.70	8.76	9.36	13.50	24.14	23.63	132.01	1,004.27
100.00	1.00	2.35	9.10	7.74	13.09	23.24	23.54	128.11	1,023.11
Resulting $\overline{\overline{\omega}}^{\text{hr+}}_{\text{ws}}$ with the TriRMGC system (s)									
0.00	**1.16**	**2.76**	**6.61**	**6.48**	**8.44**	**10.23**	**10.85**	**56.00**	**451.96**
0.01	1.32	3.10	6.28	6.85	8.51	10.04	10.61	58.05	465.21
0.10	1.48	2.61	6.56	5.86	8.91	10.43	10.49	52.69	443.43
0.50	0.88	3.20	6.02	5.88	8.99	10.00	11.18	41.19	350.76
1.00	1.32	2.71	6.13	5.73	8.28	10.16	10.24	37.80	319.61
2.00	1.35	2.61	6.51	6.15	8.77	10.23	10.28	39.51	288.40
5.00	1.44	2.45	5.88	6.23	8.83	9.59	10.54	36.54	280.41
10.00	0.78	2.80	6.43	5.96	8.30	10.63	9.93	39.38	291.66
25.00	0.94	2.86	6.37	5.27	8.58	10.41	10.45	39.15	261.45
50.00	1.13	2.21	5.41	5.77	8.72	9.57	10.68	37.62	281.38
100.00	1.22	2.58	6.16	5.60	8.19	9.81	9.74	37.27	269.12

Table 7.26 Influence of the PoS concept (in terms of the cost factor $\lambda^{\text{dist}}_{\tau(j)}$) on the mean XT-waiting time ($\overline{\overline{\omega}}^{\text{hr+}}_{\text{ls}}$) for selected yard-block layouts and all types of RMGC systems

	Yard-block layout								
$\lambda^{\text{dist}}_{\tau(j)}$	Small	Low	Narrow	Short	Medium	Long	Wide	High	Big
Resulting $\overline{\overline{\omega}}^{\text{hr+}}_{\text{ls}}$ with the SRMGC system (s)									
0.00	71.08	113.73	252.62	226.95	380.69	963.60	766.84	2,609.75	4,383.60
0.01	**65.90**	**95.41**	**226.61**	**204.03**	**336.25**	**772.82**	**675.77**	**2,244.74**	**3,903.45**
0.10	63.42	97.45	215.25	206.38	328.26	749.79	660.09	2,387.31	3,793.74
0.50	59.80	99.63	206.85	196.26	300.46	636.30	564.13	2,502.53	3,765.41
1.00	63.52	99.14	204.37	192.39	290.40	618.62	563.58	2,506.64	3,739.98
1.50	62.47	97.70	204.73	190.90	288.00	610.06	547.65	2,498.02	3,843.95
2.50	62.82	95.90	201.39	192.65	289.55	602.44	581.26	2,481.96	3,914.22
5.00	64.50	99.88	204.07	189.51	287.61	620.62	570.79	2,431.88	3,808.57
7.50	66.51	98.65	203.28	197.42	310.10	633.98	592.70	2,487.29	4,077.81
10.00	64.88	101.14	205.72	200.40	305.75	638.06	600.82	2,463.68	4,078.16
20.00	65.08	99.83	209.02	202.59	303.39	667.86	630.24	2, 548.79	4,117.45
Resulting $\overline{\overline{\omega}}^{\text{hr+}}_{\text{ls}}$ with the TRMGC system (s)									
0.00	26.34	38.40	99.02	87.18	113.98	151.54	135.88	550.75	1,854.01
0.01	**19.48**	**29.13**	**82.08**	**77.19**	**98.58**	**126.78**	**118.96**	**387.72**	**1,540.04**
0.10	18.86	28.26	81.06	75.70	97.33	130.88	117.68	372.37	1,511.89
0.50	18.99	29.22	83.71	76.90	98.19	126.24	118.72	413.81	1,464.99
1.00	20.40	30.25	81.16	77.56	97.61	127.52	118.91	423.70	1,410.67
1.50	20.45	30.48	81.44	78.71	98.64	127.27	120.21	422.63	1,374.04
2.50	20.41	31.15	83.85	79.01	99.66	131.07	122.62	421.19	1,498.34
5.00	20.70	31.54	82.24	78.20	98.62	126.77	119.01	417.08	1,418.92
7.50	21.12	30.92	85.92	81.51	103.28	135.55	128.53	445.94	1,648.02
10.00	20.96	30.84	83.64	81.69	102.94	136.65	129.45	463.27	1,680.38
20.00	20.69	30.32	83.73	83.04	103.30	136.22	130.25	504.31	1,761.27
Resulting $\overline{\overline{\omega}}^{\text{hr+}}_{\text{ls}}$ with the DRMGC system (s)									
0.00	35.56	57.88	126.65	124.89	156.21	197.55	191.74	633.52	2,219.98
0.01	**31.48**	**52.60**	**116.45**	**118.90**	**146.10**	**179.24**	**181.10**	**509.39**	**1,907.61**
0.10	31.96	52.51	118.25	118.75	147.02	186.93	182.80	502.76	2,002.27
0.50	31.75	53.14	120.13	121.36	144.62	178.09	179.60	582.04	1,913.59
1.00	33.40	54.79	121.12	122.87	146.61	182.67	183.59	587.32	1,852.77
1.50	33.35	55.54	124.63	124.38	149.51	184.79	187.91	606.67	1,926.38
2.50	35.30	55.78	121.29	128.14	155.92	195.07	196.84	626.73	1,991.29
5.00	34.66	53.57	123.94	124.95	151.26	187.72	187.77	596.32	1,989.30
7.50	34.37	56.09	124.32	130.56	159.34	199.06	209.12	715.94	2,246.48
10.00	34.00	54.43	124.71	132.55	159.80	202.78	210.10	724.42	2,304.90
20.00	33.16	54.99	126.88	132.80	163.40	207.13	214.40	748.65	2,371.75
Resulting $\overline{\overline{\omega}}^{\text{hr+}}_{\text{ls}}$ with the TriRMGC system (s)									
0.00	23.78	34.33	77.74	76.46	90.09	108.87	105.54	245.01	907.96
0.01	**19.56**	**26.47**	**66.99**	**68.47**	**80.43**	**98.14**	**98.35**	**208.77**	**754.71**
0.10	19.86	26.03	69.10	71.54	81.33	97.95	98.72	222.35	777.13
0.50	20.38	28.08	69.10	73.16	82.96	97.47	98.98	233.33	796.96
1.00	20.79	29.06	71.43	73.44	83.57	100.41	101.88	246.74	785.91
1.50	21.49	28.12	73.62	73.98	84.87	101.85	104.25	253.28	799.19
2.50	21.49	29.19	74.49	77.67	87.76	105.42	110.07	267.63	828.22
5.00	21.41	29.28	73.54	76.17	86.82	102.70	105.48	251.57	771.38
7.50	21.34	29.45	77.29	79.27	91.92	109.09	115.23	296.90	1,007.11
10.00	21.34	29.34	77.00	80.11	91.53	109.90	114.21	305.62	1,071.19
20.00	20.70	28.69	76.17	81.24	93.26	111.08	115.86	317.40	1,109.86

Table 7.27 Influence of the PoS concept (in terms of the cost factor $\lambda^{\text{dist}}_{\tau(j)}$) on the mean SC-waiting time ($\overline{\overline{\omega}}^{\text{hr+}}_{\text{ws}}$) for selected yard-block layouts and all types of RMGC systems

	Yard-block layout								
$\lambda^{\text{dist}}_{\tau(j)}$	Small	Low	Narrow	Short	Medium	Long	Wide	High	Big
Resulting $\overline{\overline{\omega}}^{\text{hr+}}_{\text{ws}}$ with the SRMGC system (s)									
0.00	1.63	3.92	52.22	39.79	135.14	527.54	393.86	1,841.50	2,701.71
0.01	**1.69**	**2.86**	**40.46**	**28.71**	**102.93**	**410.23**	**350.05**	**1,597.83**	**2,837.74**
0.10	0.79	3.05	36.89	30.52	95.90	385.58	330.39	1,837.69	3,171.58
0.50	2.23	2.83	30.53	23.10	70.10	279.99	255.81	2,050.83	3,399.10
1.00	1.29	2.80	24.69	21.55	60.42	278.18	263.85	2,072.34	3,563.10
1.50	1.29	3.58	20.95	18.83	56.87	274.42	242.34	2,098.92	3,721.70
2.50	1.69	2.71	23.53	20.75	61.54	277.40	273.49	2,110.31	3,891.56
5.00	1.16	2.80	23.19	18.92	64.55	294.07	287.92	2,043.77	3,747.92
7.50	1.22	3.11	23.75	23.59	73.36	312.82	308.27	2,175.25	4,133.94
10.00	2.29	3.14	22.50	21.44	70.30	316.51	321.68	2,149.61	4,175.65
20.00	1.82	3.17	27.10	25.53	72.92	358.97	350.34	2,229.16	4,210.52
Resulting $\overline{\overline{\omega}}^{\text{hr+}}_{\text{ws}}$ with the TRMGC system (s)									
0.00	1.78	2.66	11.18	7.79	16.77	30.71	27.19	369.41	1,754.33
0.01	**1.19**	**2.14**	**7.79**	**6.74**	**13.31**	**25.15**	**21.79**	**247.50**	**1,586.02**
0.10	1.19	2.51	7.72	6.09	13.18	25.72	18.99	226.98	1,593.96
0.50	1.60	2.04	8.23	6.20	9.15	18.02	15.41	268.55	1,776.50
1.00	1.69	2.36	5.94	5.48	9.35	19.26	15.66	293.11	1,941.41
1.50	1.56	1.74	6.23	4.90	8.11	17.80	15.92	306.17	2,074.98
2.50	1.56	2.23	5.51	4.83	10.56	20.32	20.99	348.24	2,182.48
5.00	1.25	1.95	6.26	6.16	9.67	23.62	20.09	407.87	2,464.86
7.50	1.84	1.80	7.58	6.44	11.49	23.77	24.92	417.11	2,313.87
10.00	1.03	1.98	7.46	6.28	12.63	24.84	27.14	431.33	2,316.88
20.00	1.37	2.04	7.64	8.27	13.04	25.17	30.08	486.60	2,307.85
Resulting $\overline{\overline{\omega}}^{\text{hr+}}_{\text{ws}}$ with the DRMGC system (s)									
0.00	1.69	2.73	10.94	10.81	18.10	29.96	28.65	366.62	1,587.58
0.01	**1.44**	**2.76**	**10.37**	**9.57**	**15.89**	**24.57**	**23.92**	**259.60**	**1,401.64**
0.10	1.06	2.57	10.03	9.38	16.28	26.69	27.93	252.97	1,510.48
0.50	1.50	2.29	9.94	8.59	12.60	19.67	21.37	327.00	1,517.79
1.00	1.44	2.38	8.70	8.78	13.00	19.27	22.16	333.03	1,480.90
1.50	0.88	2.82	9.36	8.89	13.50	21.76	22.68	345.42	1,582.80
2.50	1.78	2.98	9.27	9.11	14.98	26.13	28.40	359.08	1,619.11
5.00	0.88	2.91	9.95	9.26	15.14	24.04	26.46	350.87	1,617.14
7.50	1.22	2.51	10.41	12.34	18.79	29.81	37.29	455.71	1,860.78
10.00	1.63	2.88	10.55	13.24	19.23	32.51	41.08	472.50	1,898.73
20.00	1.53	3.22	11.82	14.13	21.29	36.95	48.01	506.73	1,988.11
Resulting $\overline{\overline{\omega}}^{\text{hr+}}_{\text{ws}}$ with the TriRMGC system (s)									
0.00	1.76	3.48	7.30	6.61	9.40	10.98	11.68	77.37	583.71
0.01	**1.16**	**2.76**	**6.61**	**6.48**	**8.44**	**10.23**	**10.85**	**56.00**	**451.96**
0.10	0.91	2.70	5.73	6.42	9.96	10.63	11.15	62.23	492.31
0.50	1.48	2.89	6.20	6.34	9.57	9.47	9.48	67.05	539.72
1.00	1.07	2.80	6.14	6.07	8.21	9.13	10.02	72.46	532.66
1.50	1.47	2.58	6.81	7.32	8.86	9.54	10.22	72.77	553.38
2.50	1.60	2.85	5.32	6.35	9.05	11.38	13.04	91.68	594.57
5.00	1.22	2.58	6.13	6.32	9.11	10.38	11.78	90.84	586.58
7.50	1.51	2.24	7.39	7.94	11.16	13.41	16.99	123.40	801.72
10.00	1.00	2.33	7.52	8.37	11.66	14.50	17.36	133.49	858.82
20.00	1.41	2.70	8.46	10.25	12.08	14.78	18.55	152.17	921.64

Table 7.28 Influence of the used container-stacking strategy on the mean XT-waiting time ($\overline{\overline{\omega}}_{\text{ls}}^{\text{hr+}}$) for selected yard-block layouts and all types of RMGC systems

Stacking strategy		Yard-block layout								
Positioning	HHS	Small	Low	Narrow	Short	Medium	Long	Wide	High	Big
Resulting $\overline{\overline{\omega}}_{\text{ls}}^{\text{hr+}}$ with the SRMGC system (s)										
RaS	–	70.39	110.12	273.47	236.80	469.08	1,228.50	1,036.52	2,919.60	5,205.95
CCFS[a]	**–**	**65.90**	**95.41**	**226.61**	**204.03**	**336.25**	**772.82**	**675.77**	**2,244.74**	**3,903.45**
CCFS[b]	–	63.65	97.86	199.74	188.37	296.44	666.36	565.19	1,626.54	3,995.37
CCFS[c]	–	59.80	99.63	206.85	196.26	300.46	636.30	564.13	2,502.53	3,765.41
CCFS[d]	–	62.10	94.40	204.78	191.95	289.91	661.83	588.39	2,177.01	3,819.55
CCFS[a]	√	62.75	93.75	199.08	191.97	290.09	617.22	521.88	2,077.20	3,514.96
CCFS[b]	√	61.05	90.33	174.50	164.10	251.83	552.20	492.82	1,306.57	3,591.26
CCFS[c]	√	59.46	96.34	199.18	186.53	269.17	559.45	505.62	2,344.01	3,647.10
CCFS[d]	√	60.16	91.35	193.30	180.66	271.78	581.67	512.26	2,158.91	3,632.83
Resulting $\overline{\overline{\omega}}_{\text{ls}}^{\text{hr+}}$ with the TRMGC system (s)										
RaS	–	25.00	37.76	96.04	88.49	116.42	169.39	151.53	715.31	2,216.23
CCFS[a]	**–**	**19.48**	**29.13**	**82.08**	**77.19**	**98.58**	**126.78**	**118.96**	**387.72**	**1, 540.04**
CCFS[b]	–	19.60	28.27	71.60	65.25	84.35	117.17	105.11	239.48	1,108.60
CCFS[c]	–	18.99	29.22	83.71	76.90	98.19	126.24	118.72	413.81	1,464.99
CCFS[d]	–	18.60	26.95	73.73	68.55	89.32	117.71	108.84	284.31	1,451.59
CCFS[a]	√	19.06	27.96	77.55	72.86	92.99	116.21	109.82	361.67	1,166.97
CCFS[b]	√	17.23	24.56	60.62	56.58	74.77	99.68	93.02	189.15	889.12
CCFS[c]	√	19.63	28.75	77.67	77.09	91.71	119.08	113.12	365.89	1,141.35
CCFS[d]	√	18.08	26.34	69.96	65.93	85.27	112.11	104.83	271.85	1,274.51
Resulting $\overline{\overline{\omega}}_{\text{ls}}^{\text{hr+}}$ with the DRMGC system (s)										
RaS	–	35.22	57.07	126.23	121.84	163.46	221.60	211.93	841.63	2,509.24
CCFS[a]	**–**	**31.48**	**52.60**	**116.45**	**118.90**	**146.10**	**179.24**	**181.10**	**509.36**	**1, 907.61**
CCFS[b]	–	28.53	50.22	100.07	99.53	127.04	158.90	158.91	309.22	1,383.80
CCFS[c]	–	31.75	53.14	120.13	121.36	144.62	178.09	179.60	582.04	1,913.59
CCFS[d]	–	31.13	49.54	106.58	106.11	135.41	167.80	166.68	410.23	1,852.52
CCFS[a]	√	30.84	52.49	115.56	118.80	141.25	167.82	172.55	496.95	1,749.84
CCFS[b]	√	29.32	45.99	90.71	88.96	117.96	147.25	147.74	263.62	1,189.80
CCFS[c]	√	32.86	52.05	117.33	121.56	144.68	170.12	177.00	533.06	1,572.86
CCFS[d]	√	28.46	48.66	103.39	102.51	130.25	159.84	162.94	388.33	1,736.27
Resulting $\overline{\overline{\omega}}_{\text{ls}}^{\text{hr+}}$ with the TriRMGC system (s)										
RaS	–	23.63	33.09	78.02	75.61	89.77	116.13	113.71	312.65	1,151.01
CCFS[a]	**–**	**19.56**	**26.47**	**66.99**	**68.47**	**80.43**	**98.14**	**98.35**	**208.77**	**754.71**
CCFS[b]	–	17.16	24.81	55.38	56.68	68.19	83.93	84.42	144.07	460.80
CCFS[c]	–	20.38	28.08	69.10	73.16	82.96	97.47	98.98	233.33	796.96
CCFS[d]	–	17.27	24.79	57.76	58.50	70.06	88.61	85.62	171.63	666.81
CCFS[a]	√	19.84	27.71	71.27	74.50	84.37	97.44	101.67	224.13	727.06
CCFS[b]	√	16.96	24.00	51.53	54.12	64.75	80.45	78.78	131.68	431.34
CCFS[c]	√	19.96	27.74	71.48	75.64	85.05	99.41	103.92	247.06	672.34
CCFS[d]	√	17.38	23.88	58.38	62.29	71.33	87.94	89.07	175.08	662.99

[a]CaS parametrisation, [b]CaS-RTS parametrisation, [c]CaS-PoS parametrisation, [d]CaS-RTS-PoS parametrisation

Table 7.29 Influence of the used container-stacking strategy on the mean SC-waiting time ($\overline{\overline{\omega}}_{ws}^{hr+}$) for selected yard-block layouts and all types of RMGC systems

Stacking strategy: Positioning	HHS	Small	Low	Narrow	Short	Medium	Long	Wide	High	Big
Resulting $\overline{\overline{\omega}}_{ws}^{hr+}$ with the SRMGC system (s)										
RaS	–	2.04	4.14	96.54	60.59	281.58	1,049.47	878.56	2,724.15	5,236.32
CCFS[a]	–	**1.69**	**2.86**	**40.46**	**28.71**	**102.93**	**410.23**	**350.05**	**1,597.83**	**2,837.74**
CCFS[b]	–	2.10	2.93	33.98	25.21	78.03	331.90	268.11	1,105.25	3,106.92
CCFS[c]	–	2.23	2.83	30.53	23.10	70.10	279.99	255.81	2,050.83	3,399.10
CCFS[d]	–	2.13	2.71	31.96	24.63	73.56	331.90	293.39	1,740.23	3,549.54
CCFS[a]	√	2.10	3.61	30.96	23.78	68.42	243.07	190.53	1,400.41	2,329.76
CCFS[b]	√	1.82	2.71	24.81	18.52	49.88	221.03	187.45	822.28	2,739.03
CCFS[c]	√	1.26	2.65	27.64	22.23	53.24	217.92	193.66	1,935.18	3,581.66
CCFS[d]	√	1.95	2.33	29.29	24.79	61.44	253.88	225.96	1,732.17	3,604.67
Resulting $\overline{\overline{\omega}}_{ws}^{hr+}$ with the TRMGC system (s)										
RaS	–	1.41	2.70	13.28	11.07	21.52	59.57	47.51	595.70	2,245.64
CCFS[a]	–	**1.19**	**2.14**	**7.79**	**6.74**	**13.31**	**25.15**	**21.79**	**247.50**	**1,586.02**
CCFS[b]	–	1.19	2.45	7.87	7.07	10.76	23.51	17.05	131.67	1,106.11
CCFS[c]	–	1.60	2.04	8.23	6.20	9.15	18.02	15.41	268.55	1,776.50
CCFS[d]	–	1.25	2.23	7.56	7.26	9.86	18.02	17.30	172.11	1,575.82
CCFS[a]	√	1.22	2.42	7.89	5.78	9.48	14.86	13.59	188.41	1,090.50
CCFS[b]	√	1.00	2.29	6.39	5.16	9.49	16.59	13.83	92.72	814.24
CCFS[c]	√	1.28	2.48	6.04	5.88	9.55	14.65	11.37	206.52	1,152.11
CCFS[d]	√	1.53	1.95	6.63	6.18	10.23	17.11	13.95	154.72	1,264.68
Resulting $\overline{\overline{\omega}}_{ws}^{hr+}$ with the DRMGC system (s)										
RaS	–	1.53	3.04	15.10	12.87	28.19	60.34	58.40	674.33	2,357.04
CCFS[a]	–	**1.44**	**2.76**	**10.37**	**9.57**	**15.89**	**24.57**	**23.92**	**259.60**	**1,401.64**
CCFS[b]	–	1.28	2.48	9.04	8.05	13.51	23.05	24.14	124.01	1,024.14
CCFS[c]	–	1.50	2.29	9.94	8.59	12.60	19.67	21.37	327.00	1,517.79
CCFS[d]	–	1.06	2.79	9.24	8.70	15.43	21.63	24.14	207.52	1,472.42
CCFS[a]	√	1.00	2.17	8.95	8.43	13.24	18.96	19.45	231.06	1,221.44
CCFS[b]	√	1.16	2.29	7.79	7.86	12.16	17.70	17.26	90.63	799.60
CCFS[c]	√	1.09	2.45	9.10	8.46	12.16	17.05	19.76	268.47	1,201.56
CCFS[d]	√	0.91	2.69	8.05	8.15	13.49	20.01	21.17	177.91	1,376.84
Resulting $\overline{\overline{\omega}}_{ws}^{hr+}$ with the TriRMGC system (s)										
RaS	–	1.60	3.39	7.66	7.29	12.26	17.54	16.20	163.86	1,049.19
CCFS[a]	–	**1.16**	**2.76**	**6.61**	**6.48**	**8.44**	**10.23**	**10.85**	**56.00**	**451.96**
CCFS[b]	–	0.94	2.86	6.37	5.27	8.58	10.41	10.45	39.15	261.45
CCFS[c]	–	1.48	2.89	6.20	6.34	9.57	9.47	9.48	67.05	539.72
CCFS[d]	–	1.60	2.67	6.43	6.22	8.54	11.22	10.13	48.56	458.64
CCFS[a]	√	1.13	2.24	5.88	6.33	8.46	8.82	9.38	52.05	391.16
CCFS[b]	√	1.19	2.46	6.00	5.87	8.39	9.06	9.77	33.26	224.48
CCFS[c]	√	1.54	2.21	5.47	5.62	7.18	9.33	8.87	64.53	392.51
CCFS[d]	√	1.41	2.61	6.24	6.26	8.41	7.98	9.74	50.34	430.04

[a]CaS parametrisation, [b]CaS-RTS parametrisation, [c]CaS-PoS parametrisation, [d]CaS-RTS-PoS parametrisation

indicating negative, but (in absolute values) smaller vehicle-waiting-time effects of an increasing inclusion of the RTS concept (i.e., increasing $\lambda^{\text{rts}}_{\tau(j)}$) for SCs than for XTs. This can be explained by the fact that all landside-departing containers may benefit from fewer numbers of shuffle moves induced by increases in the inclusion of the RTS concept for stacking decisions, whereas only a small fraction of all waterside-departing containers—those departing by feeder vessel—may benefit from shuffle-move reductions induced by increases of $\lambda^{\text{rts}}_{\tau(j)}$. Therefore, increases of $\lambda^{\text{rts}}_{\tau(j)}$ lead to much more significant improvements of the container accessibility for landside-departing containers than for waterside-departing containers, thus having (in absolute values) larger negative effects on the mean vehicle-waiting times in the landside handover area than in the waterside handover area. In fact, upon closer examination of the simulation results, total decreases of the mean number of shuffle moves per retrieval job ($\overline{\overline{\psi}}$) of up to 25% are observed with increasing cost factors for the retrieval-time-based shuffle-move costs ($\lambda^{\text{rts}}_{\tau(j)}$), but more than two thirds of these shuffle-move reductions arise from smaller quantities of shuffle moves for landside-departing containers. However, indirectly also the waterside vehicle-waiting times are negatively affected by fewer shuffle moves for landside-departing containers, as the crane resources released by these workload reductions can also be used for a more timely execution of waterside jobs.

Similar to the retrieval-time-based shuffle-move costs, it can be observed from Tables 7.26 and 7.27 that both $\overline{\overline{\omega}}^{\text{hr+}}_{\text{ls}}$ and $\overline{\overline{\omega}}^{\text{hr+}}_{\text{ws}}$ are significantly smaller with cost factors $\lambda^{\text{dist}}_{\tau(j)} > 0$ than with $\lambda^{\text{dist}}_{\tau(j)} = 0$ for almost all considered RMGC designs, thus confirming negative vehicle-waiting-time effects of including workload-smoothing aspects for deciding on container-stacking positions, just as expected by Research hypothesis 2.6.2. But contrary to the retrieval-time-based shuffle-move costs, the vehicle-waiting times do not steadily decrease with increases of $\lambda^{\text{dist}}_{\tau(j)}$. Instead, only vehicle-waiting-time decreases up to certain design-specific points are observed with increasing $\lambda^{\text{dist}}_{\tau(j)}$, and increases of $\lambda^{\text{dist}}_{\tau(j)}$ beyond these points are observed to induce even longer vehicle-waiting times than including no workload-smoothing costs at all. As previously discussed, this can be explained by the fact that increases of $\lambda^{\text{dist}}_{\tau(j)}$ do not only lead to an increasing importance of the workload-smoothing objective for stacking decisions, but, on the other hand, also to a reduced relative importance of the shuffle-move-minimisation objective, thus increasing the risk for shuffle moves. In fact, upon closer investigation of the simulation results, $\lambda^{\text{dist}}_{\tau(j)}$ is found to be strongly positively correlated with $\overline{\overline{\psi}}$—at a significance level of $\alpha = 0.05$—for almost all considered RMGC designs. Therefore, the workload-smoothing aspect should not be overemphasised for stacking decisions. Instead, only comparably low weights should be given to the workload-smoothing objective. Here, it may be concluded from the simulation results of Tables 7.26 and 7.27 that cost factors of up to $\lambda^{\text{dist}}_{\tau(j)} \leq 1$ are mostly reasonable weightings of the workload-smoothing costs—provided that all other cost factors are set to their default settings—in order to actually yield vehicle-waiting-time reductions by including the workload-smoothing aspect for stacking decisions.

Several further findings on the operational-performance effects of the container-stacking strategy can be made on basis of Tables 7.28 and 7.29. First of all, it can be seen from these tables that significantly longer mean vehicle-waiting times in both handover areas are yielded with the RaS method than with all considered parametrisations of the CCFS method, thus confirming that the RaS method is significantly outperformed by any reasonable parametrisation of the CCFS method, just as expected by Research hypothesis 2.6.3. In addition, by pairwise comparisons of the vehicle-waiting times with and without applying the HHS concept for each evaluated parametrisation of the CCFS method, it is found that for almost all considered RMGC designs and CCFS parametrisations significantly shorter vehicle-waiting times are yielded by the additional use of the HHS method. Hence, the relocation of containers to shuffle-move-avoiding and outbound-driving-distance-reducing stacking positions during times of low crane workloads is confirmed to be beneficial for the operational performance of RMGC systems, just as expected by Research hypothesis 2.6.4.

Finally, it can be seen from Tables 7.28 and 7.29 that the basic findings on the operational-performance effects of the yard-block layout and the type of RMGC system (see Sect. 7.2.3) are mostly unaffected by changes of the container-stacking strategy. It is observed that the mean vehicle-waiting times increase with the yard-block capacities and dimensions and that the performance ranking of the considered types of RMGC systems is not affected by changes of the container-stacking strategy. Nevertheless, the optimal RMGC design may be influenced by the applied stacking strategy in so far as better-performing stacking strategies allow larger-sized yard blocks and/or fewer cranes per yard block without impairing the operational performance. For instance, it can be seen from the simulation results that for all types of RMGC systems elaborated stacking strategies are able to yield comparable and/or even shorter vehicle-waiting times for the layouts "long" and "wide" than the random strategy for the smaller-sized "medium" layout. In addition, by comparing the example yard-block layouts with respect to the (relative) differences in the vehicle-waiting times of the evaluated (parametrisations of) container-stacking strategies, it is found that the relative performance differences between the stacking strategies increase significantly more with the stacking height than with the block length or width. As a consequence, it can be concluded that the quality of the container-stacking strategy is more important for higher yard blocks than for wider and/or longer ones of similar size, just as expected by research hypothesis 2.6.5.

Altogether, the simple RaS method is found to be clearly outperformed by reasonable parametrisations of the CCFS method, which is proven to perform significantly better when retrieval-time-based shuffle-move costs and workload-smoothing costs are adequately taken into account and the possibility to relocate containers during times of low crane workloads is additionally included. The basic findings on the operational-performance effects of the RMGC design are found to be structurally unaffected by the applied container-stacking strategy, but its quality is found to be more important for high-stacking yard blocks. Based on these findings,

- Research hypothesis 2.6.1 is confirmed,
- Research hypothesis 2.6.2 is confirmed,
- Research hypothesis 2.6.3 is confirmed,
- Research hypothesis 2.6.4 is confirmed and
- Research hypothesis 2.6.5 is confirmed

for the considered experimental setup of this simulation-based sensitivity analysis.

7.3.7 Influence of the Crane-Scheduling Strategy

Considering the fact that inefficiencies in the use of the basically available crane resources per yard block are not only caused by shuffle moves, but also by crane-empty-movement times, crane-interference times and crane-waiting times in the handover areas, next to stacking decisions also deciding on crane assignment and sequencing of crane-transport jobs can be expected to have notable effects on the vehicle-waiting times in the handover areas. On top of that, the vehicle-waiting times are also directly affected by crane-scheduling decisions, as the start time of each job and thus also the corresponding arrival time in the handover area are determined by assignment and sequencing decisions. Based on this preliminary analysis, the selection and the parametrisation of crane-scheduling strategies are conjectured in Sect. 4.1.3 to have notable effects on the operational performance and the design of RMGC systems. In this subsection, it is investigated to what extent the operational performance of the container-storage yard is affected by and in how far the basic findings on the RMGC-design-planning problem are sensitive to changes of the operational crane-scheduling strategy with respect to the applied online policy and solution method (see Sect. 5.6). The performance and design effects of changes in the used preselection method are not investigated in this simulation study.

7.3.7.1 Research Hypotheses

Usually, a crane-scheduling strategy is the better with respect to the resulting mean vehicle-waiting times in the handover areas, the more crane-transport jobs are scheduled in such a way that late crane arrivals in the handover areas are minimised, which can either be directly operationalised or implicitly aimed for by minimising empty-movement times, crane-interference times and/or crane-waiting times in the handover areas due to early arrivals (see Sect. 5.3.1). Based on the online policies and solution methods introduced for the crane-scheduling problem in Sect. 5.3 (see Table 5.7), nine reasonable crane-scheduling strategies are investigated in this simulation study, that include one or even more of the aforementioned crane-scheduling objectives. The considered scheduling strategies range from single-objective priority rules (FIFO, EDD, NN) over multi-objective priority rules (PRIO1, PRIO2) to near optimal planning approaches that schedule sequences of jobs for each crane of a yard block in the style of the replan or ignore policy (GAM-ignore, GAM-replan, SFE-ignore, SFE-replan).

In Sect. 5.3.5, it is argued that including only one of several possible scheduling objectives in a greedy style, as is the case for single-objective priority rules, may lead to rather extreme and myopic scheduling decisions, that are reasonable with respect to the pursued objective in the short term, but may be adverse with respect to the operational performance of the container-storage yard in the long run. However, rather extreme and shortsighted scheduling decisions with respect to the operational performance, that result from the greedy nature of priority rules, can be counterbalanced by basing crane-assignment and job-sequencing decisions on a balanced trade-off between different scheduling objectives, as it is the case for the proposed multi-objective priority rules (PRIO1, PRIO2). Therefore, single-objective priority rules cannot be expected to perform as good as reasonably parametrised multi-objective priority rules.

For solution methods that do not greedily decide on the next job for a calling crane, but create (near) optimal sequences of jobs for all cranes of a yard block with respect to the pursued objective(s), there is no need to include other scheduling objectives than minimising the crane lateness in the handover areas, as an efficient usage of crane resources is a necessary prerequisite that has to be implicitly fulfilled to achieve this objective. Hence, for offline planning problems, (near) optimal solution methods that aim to minimise the crane lateness can undoubtedly be expected to perform better than all types and parametrisations of priority rules. But the situation is different for online-planning problems like the crane-scheduling problem, for which the performance advantage of (near) optimal solution methods over priority rules is less clear and may depend on the applied online policy (see Sect. 2.4.3.1). By applying the replan online policy to the crane-scheduling problem, all information on newly arrived and/or prospectively arriving vehicles are immediately incorporated into the job sequences of the cranes, in an (near) optimal way with respect to the vehicle-waiting-time objective. Therefore, (near) optimal replan strategies like GAM-replan and SFE-replan can be expected to perform at least as good as well-balanced multi-objective priority rules. In contrast, advantageous insertion options of new jobs are neglected during the execution of a once made schedule when applying the ignore policy, thus possibly leading to adverse scheduling decisions for ignored jobs in terms of unnecessarily late arrivals in the handover area and/or avoidably long empty-movement times. As a consequence, despite generating (near) optimal schedules for the initially considered jobs, (near) optimal ignore strategies like GAM-ignore and SFE-ignore cannot necessarily be expected to perform better than well-balanced multi-objective priority rules. Altogether, (near) optimal replan strategies can be expected to perform better than their ignoring counterparts as well as priority rules.

Apart from the parametrisation of the cost factors, which is not investigated for any solution method in this study, the performance of the SFE method is expected to be greatly determined by the maximum number $\kappa_{\text{sfe}}^{\text{jobs}}$ of plannable jobs for the full enumeration. Although it is argued in Sect. 5.3.7.2 that considering only subsets of all plannable jobs is not necessarily disadvantageous for the resulting mean vehicle-waiting times, as the $\kappa_{\mathrm{sfe}}^{\mathrm{jobs}}$ most important jobs are considered, increasing the maximum number $\kappa_{\mathrm{sfe}}^{\mathrm{jobs}}$ of plannable jobs can in turn not be expected to be harmful for the operational performance of the container-storage yard. Moreover, for comparably great maximum numbers of plannable jobs, the currently plannable jobs can be expected to be more foresightedly dispatched and/or sequenced with respect to the long run performance, whereas small maximum numbers of plannable jobs lead to a more myopic nature of the SFE method, which is previously argued to be harmful for the operational performance of the container-storage yard. For $\kappa_{\mathrm{sfe}}^{\mathrm{jobs}} = 1$, the SFE method can even be expected to perform similar to the EDD priority rule. Thus, the mean vehicle-waiting times in the handover areas can be expected to decrease with increasing maximum number $\kappa_{\mathrm{sfe}}^{\mathrm{jobs}}$ of plannable jobs for the SFE method.

Finally, the advantageousness of certain crane-scheduling strategies is not expected to be influenced by the yard-block dimensions and/or the operating type of RMGC system, as the functionality of all considered combinations of solution methods and online policies is not affected by the underlying yard-block layout and/or RMGC system. In a reverse conclusion, that means the basic findings on the operational-performance effects of the yard-block dimensions and the type of RMGC system are not expected to be structurally affected by the selected crane-scheduling strategy. However, owing to the expected operational-performance effects of the applied crane-scheduling strategy, improvements of its quality may induce changes of the planned RMGC design. The better performing a strategy is to be expected, the greater the yard block can be dimensioned and/or the fewer cranes may be needed per yard block, thus allowing improvements of the area and/or cost performance of the container-storage yard without impairing its operational performance. Altogether, Research hypotheses 2.7.1–2.7.4 are formulated:

Research Hypothesis 2.7.1. Single-objective priority rules like FIFO, EDD and NN induce significantly longer mean vehicle-waiting times in the handover areas ($\overline{\overline{\omega}}_{\mathrm{total}}^{\mathrm{hr+}}$) than reasonably parametrised multi-objective priority rules like PRIO1 and PRIO2.

Research Hypothesis 2.7.2. Heuristic replan crane-scheduling strategies like GAM-replan and SFE-replan yield significantly shorter mean vehicle-waiting times in the handover areas ($\overline{\overline{\omega}}_{\mathrm{total}}^{\mathrm{hr+}}$) than priority rules and heuristic ignore scheduling strategies like GAM-ignore and SFE-ignore.

Research Hypothesis 2.7.3. The maximum number $\kappa_{\mathrm{sfe}}^{\mathrm{jobs}}$ of plannable jobs for the SFE solution method has significantly negative effects on the mean vehicle-waiting time in the handover areas ($\overline{\overline{\omega}}_{\mathrm{total}}^{\mathrm{hr+}}$).

Research Hypothesis 2.7.4. The basic findings on the operational-performance effects of the RMGC design are not structurally affected by changes of the applied crane-scheduling strategy.

7.3.7.2 Experimental Setup

To analyse the influence of the crane-scheduling strategy on the operational performance and the design of RMGC systems—especially with regard to Research hypotheses 2.7.1–2.7.4—two experimental studies are conducted. Firstly, each combination of the four considered types of RMGC systems and the nine representative yard-block layouts is tested with a reasonable parametrisation of FIFO, EDD, NN, PRIO1, PRIO2, SFE-ignore, GAM-ignore, SFE-replan and GAM-replan in order to investigate the operational-performance effects of different scheduling strategies and to validate Research hypotheses 2.7.1, 2.7.2 and 2.7.4. Secondly, for all considered types of RMGC systems the "medium" yard-block layout is tested with seven different maximum numbers of plannable jobs for SFE-ignore and SFE-replan in the range from $\kappa_{\text{sfe}}^{\text{jobs}} = 1$ to $\kappa_{\text{sfe}}^{\text{jobs}} = 7$ in order to get an impression on the influence of this parameter on the operational performance of the SFE method and to validate Research hypothesis 2.7.3.

The parametrisations of all tested solution methods, that are used throughout this sensitivity analysis, are based on preliminary investigations and simulation experiments. Similar to the investigation of the container-stacking strategies, no simulation experiments on fine tuning of parameters for the solution methods are presented in this work, as determining the SC and XT-waiting-time-minimising parameterisations of all solution methods for each RMGC design would be a very time-consuming process that is expected to provide only little additional insights into the operational-performance effects of scheduling strategies for RMGC systems. Here, apart from the single-objective priority rules, all considered solution methods are parametrised in such a way that the execution of waterside retrieval jobs is prioritised, since these jobs are usually regarded as being most important for the operational performance of seaport container terminals as a whole (see Sect. 3.2). For PRIO1, the cost factors of assigning job j to crane g are set to $\lambda_{\tau(j),g}^{\text{edt}} = \lambda_{\tau(j),g}^{\text{dd}} = 1 \ \forall \ (\tau(j), g) \notin \{(\text{wsout}, 1)\,; (\text{wsout}, 3)\}$ and to $\lambda_{\text{wsout},1}^{\text{edt}} = \lambda_{\text{wsout},1}^{\text{dd}} = \lambda_{\text{wsout},3}^{\text{edt}} = \lambda_{\text{wsout},3}^{\text{dd}} = 0.2$. The cost factors of PRIO2 are set to the default settings (see Sect. 7.1.3). For the underlying cost function (5.66) of the SFE and GAM methods, the cost factors are set to $\lambda_{\tau(j),g}^{\text{late}} = 1 \ \forall \ (\tau(j), g) \notin \{(\text{wsout}, 1)\,; (\text{wsout}, 3)\}$ and to $\lambda_{\text{wsout},1}^{\text{late}} = \lambda_{\text{wsout},3}^{\text{late}} = 5$. In addition, the maximum number $\kappa_{\text{sfe}}^{\text{jobs}}$ of plannable jobs for SFE-ignore and SFE-replan is set to $\kappa_{\text{sfe}}^{\text{jobs}} = 5$ for the first experimental study. The detailed settings for the parameters $\kappa_{\text{gam}}^{\text{itinit}}$, $\kappa_{\text{gam}}^{\text{noinit}}$, $\kappa_{\text{gam}}^{\text{mut}}$, $\kappa_{\text{gam}}^{\max\Upsilon}$, $\kappa_{\text{gam}}^{\text{maxit}}$ and $\kappa_{\text{gam}}^{\text{al}}$ of the GAM solution method are provided in Appendix A.2. Except for the aforementioned changes of parameter settings defining the crane-scheduling strategy, all other input parameters of the simulation model are parametrised according to the default settings (see Sect. 7.1.3).

7.3.7.3 Results and Discussion

In contrast to the previous sensitivity analyses, the simulation results on the influence of the crane-scheduling strategy on the operational performance and the design of RMGC systems are not analysed on the basis of the mean vehicle-waiting times in the landside and waterside handover areas ($\overline{\overline{\omega}}_{\text{ls}}^{\text{hr+}}$, $\overline{\overline{\omega}}_{\text{ws}}^{\text{hr+}}$), but only based on the resulting mean total vehicle-waiting time in the handover areas ($\overline{\overline{\omega}}_{\text{total}}^{\text{hr+}}$). The main reason is that, apart from single-objective priority rules, the mean vehicle-waiting times in the waterside and landside handover areas do not only depend on the applied online policy and/or solution method, but also on the parameter settings for the cost factors that may lead to a biased distribution of vehicle-waiting times between both handover areas. Here, the cost factors of the underlying cost functions are parametrised in such a way that the waterside handover area is prioritised, thus inducing shorter SC and longer XT-waiting times. As a consequence, an analysis of the resulting waterside and/or landside vehicle-waiting times cannot reliably answer to what extent certain XT and/or SC-waiting-time reductions are induced by improved scheduling approaches and/or by prioritisation of the waterside handover area. Hence, considering that the total vehicle-waiting time is mostly unaffected by the distribution of XT and SC-waiting times, the operational-performance effects of the scheduling strategies themselves, and not of user-specified prioritisation, can best be evaluated on the basis of the resulting mean total vehicle-waiting time in the handover areas ($\overline{\overline{\omega}}_{\text{total}}^{\text{hr+}}$).

Tables 7.30 and 7.31 show the resulting mean total vehicle-waiting-time figures ($\overline{\overline{\omega}}_{\text{total}}^{\text{hr+}}$) of both experimental studies on the effects of the crane-scheduling strategy on the operational performance and the design of RMGC systems. The vehicle-waiting times in the handover areas ($\overline{\overline{\omega}}_{\text{total}}^{\text{hr+}}$) that result from different crane-scheduling strategies are shown in Table 7.30, while the resulting mean vehicle-waiting-time figures that result from different maximum numbers of plannable jobs for the SFE method are displayed in Table 7.31. The corresponding landside and waterside vehicle-waiting-time figures of both experimental studies are provided in Appendix A.5.7 together with other important performance figures.

At first glance, it can be seen from Table 7.30 that the mean vehicle-waiting times in the handover areas of the analysed RMGC designs differ considerably between the applied crane-scheduling strategies—at least in relative terms—thus indicating significant performance effects of the crane-scheduling strategy. Upon closer examination of the simulation results it can additionally be observed that the mean XT-waiting times differ only slightly between the investigated crane-scheduling strategies, while the differences in the mean SC-waiting times are very much larger (see Appendix A.5.7). These differences in the operational-performance effects of the crane-scheduling strategy can be explained by the prioritised assignment of waterside retrieval jobs by multi-objective priority rules and (near) optimal solution methods, just as conjectured before.

Table 7.30 Influence of the crane-scheduling strategy on the mean vehicle-waiting time in the handover areas ($\overline{\overline{\omega}}^{hr+}_{total}$) for selected yard-block layouts and all types of RMGC systems

	Yard-block layout								
Scheduling strategy	Small	Low	Narrow	Short	Medium	Long	Wide	High	Big
Resulting $\overline{\overline{\omega}}^{hr+}_{total}$ with the SRMGC system (s)									
FIFO	32.04	55.80	153.36	142.44	281.46	907.74	715.68	2,393.52	4,829.16
EDD	27.78	42.84	139.62	115.80	269.28	952.86	728.58	2,609.76	5,114.94
NN	29.28	46.02	151.26	132.48	270.24	672.36	600.66	2,236.86	4,174.98
PRIO1	26.94	42.48	118.50	103.50	219.54	694.38	568.98	2,235.48	4,325.28
PRIO2	**28.26**	**41.28**	**117.06**	**100.44**	**198.96**	**561.06**	**484.56**	**1,861.32**	**3,269.94**
SFE-ignore	28.08	46.56	132.48	116.64	241.50	743.34	623.10	2,293.62	4,482.36
GAM-ignore	27.72	47.10	136.62	118.62	235.32	693.42	589.20	2,335.32	4,141.80
SFE-replan	27.12	41.64	125.16	109.26	210.54	548.46	469.68	1,976.88	2,601.36
GAM-replan	27.42	41.10	125.16	107.88	221.88	598.86	523.38	2,001.30	2,673.06
Resulting $\overline{\overline{\omega}}^{hr+}_{total}$ with the TRMGC system (s)									
FIFO	9.12	13.98	43.08	38.46	55.32	78.96	71.64	387.12	1,938.66
EDD	8.94	13.50	43.02	38.16	55.02	88.08	75.54	461.46	2,029.26
NN	9.12	13.86	43.14	39.42	57.00	85.02	79.20	396.60	2,108.16
PRIO1	8.88	13.08	40.14	35.76	48.96	69.90	63.24	346.14	1,845.60
PRIO2	**8.82**	**13.44**	**38.16**	**35.58**	**48.30**	**67.44**	**61.98**	**304.08**	**1,567.38**
SFE-ignore	8.58	12.84	37.38	33.66	46.50	66.24	59.40	348.72	1,729.62
GAM-ignore	8.46	13.14	37.86	35.52	48.36	68.52	61.26	322.02	1,610.22
SFE-replan	8.58	13.02	36.18	32.70	44.52	60.36	54.06	277.86	1,532.46
GAM-replan	8.58	12.54	37.26	32.94	43.86	61.86	56.22	285.48	1,456.02
Resulting $\overline{\overline{\omega}}^{hr+}_{total}$ with the DRMGC system (s)									
FIFO	14.70	26.94	63.90	65.70	93.90	145.08	136.86	620.22	2,618.58
EDD	13.92	24.00	56.58	55.86	74.94	110.76	111.66	620.94	2,547.30
NN	14.70	23.64	61.32	61.02	84.54	120.12	120.54	487.32	2,285.70
PRIO1	13.56	23.58	54.48	54.60	70.68	94.38	95.58	446.16	2,046.06
PRIO2	**13.86**	**23.58**	**53.82**	**54.36**	**69.24**	**88.86**	**88.86**	**360.18**	**1,607.82**
SFE-ignore	12.06	19.62	48.66	48.66	66.60	88.56	88.92	410.70	1,949.94
GAM-ignore	12.54	21.18	53.88	53.16	72.66	99.48	98.34	440.22	2,057.82
SFE-replan	11.88	18.84	44.88	45.42	57.48	77.82	76.14	317.04	1,636.80
GAM-replan	12.06	20.58	48.24	47.94	61.56	82.14	82.44	378.60	1,838.04
Resulting $\overline{\overline{\omega}}^{hr+}_{total}$ with the TriRMGC system (s)									
FIFO	8.88	12.36	32.28	32.94	41.34	51.36	51.96	158.88	987.90
EDD	8.70	12.36	31.08	31.80	39.96	49.50	49.50	179.34	998.82
NN	8.70	11.94	33.12	32.70	41.28	51.00	52.98	156.36	867.42
PRIO1	8.82	12.90	31.68	32.82	39.36	46.26	46.32	142.26	763.08
PRIO2	**8.82**	**12.48**	**31.26**	**31.86**	**37.98**	**46.86**	**46.86**	**117.54**	**574.98**
SFE-ignore	8.10	12.00	30.06	30.54	36.48	44.34	44.70	134.94	713.88
GAM-ignore	8.22	12.84	31.80	33.54	39.90	47.46	46.50	126.00	612.18
SFE-replan	8.28	11.76	29.22	30.00	34.74	42.96	42.00	121.32	621.96
GAM-replan	8.40	12.06	30.96	32.04	37.44	44.76	45.30	118.56	565.56

Table 7.31 Influence of the maximum number κ_{sfe}^{jobs} of plannable jobs by the SFE method on the mean vehicle-waiting time in the handover areas ($\overline{\overline{\omega}}_{total}^{hr+}$) for different types of RMGC systems and online policies

	Ignore				Replan			
κ_{sfe}^{jobs}	SRMGC	TRMGC	DRMGC	TriRMGC	SRMGC	TRMGC	DRMGC	TriRMGC
1	269.28	55.02	74.94	39.96	269.28	55.02	74.94	39.96
2	253.02	47.34	65.64	37.14	212.88	47.88	62.40	36.54
3	250.50	46.80	66.06	36.36	220.02	44.64	59.22	35.46
4	241.68	46.86	65.58	36.00	219.72	44.46	58.68	35.40
5	241.50	46.50	66.60	36.48	210.54	44.52	57.48	34.74
6	238.62	45.60	64.80	36.54	209.34	43.62	58.14	36.24
7	237.60	45.24	66.24	36.84	217.20	43.86	57.12	35.58

By comparing the resulting vehicle-waiting times of single- and multi-objective priority rules, both PRIO1 and PRIO2 are found to perform significantly better than FIFO, EDD and NN for almost all considered RMGC designs, thus confirming Research hypothesis 2.7.1. Upon closer analysis, PRIO2 is even observed to yield (significantly) shorter mean vehicle-waiting times than PRIO1 for almost all investigated RMGC designs, which can be explained by the number of included scheduling objectives. While PRIO1 only aims to minimise the crane lateness and the empty-movement times, PRIO2 additionally incorporates the minimisation of the crane-waiting times in the handover areas due to early arrivals. Hence, greater possibilities to counterbalance the myopic nature of priority rules are offered by PRIO2, which is previously argued to be beneficial for the operational performance of RMGC systems (see Sect. 5.3.5).

Likewise, also (near) optimal solution methods are found to perform mostly better than single-objective priority rules. It can be seen from Table 7.30, that for almost all considered RMGC designs not only SFE-replan and GAM-replan lead to significantly shorter mean vehicle-waiting times in the handover areas than FIFO, EDD and NN, just as expected by Research hypothesis 2.7.2, but also their ignoring counterparts yield shorter vehicle-waiting times than single-objective priority rules for most RMGC designs. Upon closer examination of the vehicle-waiting-time figures obtained with the (near) optimal solution methods, SFE-replan and GAM-replan are observed to induce significantly shorter mean vehicle-waiting times for most investigated RMGC designs than SFE-ignore and GAM-ignore, respectively. Hence, as postulated by Research hypothesis 2.7.2, incorporating newly known jobs immediately is favourable in comparison to completely carrying out a once made schedule for the highly dynamic online environment of RMGC systems at seaport container terminals. In addition, it can be seen from Table 7.30 that SFE-replan and SFE-ignore mostly yield significantly shorter vehicle-waiting times than GAM-replan and GAM-ignore, respectively. Thus, it can be concluded that finding the optimal schedule for only subsets of plannable jobs is more beneficial with regard to the operational performance of RMGC systems than finding only near optimal schedules for all plannable jobs of the crane-scheduling problem.

By comparing the resulting vehicle-waiting times of multi-objective priority rules and (near) optimal solution methods, both SFE-replan and GAM-replan are found to perform (significantly) better than PRIO1 and PRIO2 for most considered RMGC designs, just as expected by Research hypothesis 2.7.2. In contrast, mostly similar vehicle-waiting times are yielded by applying (near) optimal ignore strategies and multi-objective priority rules. For some RMGC designs, SFE-ignore and/or GAM-ignore are found to perform better, while for other RMGC designs shorter vehicle-waiting times are induced by PRIO1 and/or PRIO2. Thus, as previously conjectured, the greater computational effort of (near) optimal solution methods does not pay off against much more simple multi-objective priority rules, when being applied in the style of the ignore online policy. Overall, SFE-replan is found to perform best among all nine investigated crane-scheduling strategies for RMGC systems. For two thirds of the analysed RMGC designs, the shortest vehicle-waiting times are obtained by SFE-replan, and for 95% of the investigated RMGC designs, SFE-replan is even found to be among the three best-performing strategies.

As expected by Research hypothesis 2.7.3, it can be seen from Table 7.31 that the mean vehicle-waiting times in the handover areas of all considered RMGC designs decrease with increasing maximum number $\kappa_{\text{sfe}}^{\text{jobs}}$ of plannable jobs by SFE-replan and SFE-ignore. This observation is also confirmed by means of correlation analyses, which compute $\kappa_{\text{sfe}}^{\text{jobs}}$ to be strongly negatively correlated with $\overline{\overline{\omega}}_{\text{total}}^{\text{hr+}}$—at a significance level of $\alpha = 0.05$—for all types of RMGC systems. Upon closer examination of the simulation results, it can also be observed that increasing the maximum number of plannable jobs has comparably great negative vehicle-waiting-time effects for small values of $\kappa_{\text{sfe}}^{\text{jobs}}$, while having smaller and smaller negative effects on the mean vehicle-waiting time with increases of $\kappa_{\text{sfe}}^{\text{jobs}}$. The mean vehicle-waiting times even seem to converge towards a lower bound with increasing maximum number $\kappa_{\text{sfe}}^{\text{jobs}}$ of plannable jobs. Thus, due to the factorial growth of the computational effort for the SFE method with increasing the maximum number of plannable jobs, only little additional performance at the expense of high computation time is obtained by increasing $\kappa_{\text{sfe}}^{\text{jobs}}$. A value of $\kappa_{\text{sfe}}^{\text{jobs}} = 5$, as used for the simulation results of Table 7.30, appears to be a reasonable trade-off for this simulation study that yields (near) optimal schedules for RMGC systems in a satisfactorily short amount of time.

Finally, it can be seen from Table 7.30 that the vehicle-waiting times increase with the yard-block capacities and dimensions, just as observed, discussed and explained in Sect. 7.2, independently of the applied crane-scheduling strategy. Likewise, for all considered scheduling strategies, the TriRMGC and SRMGC systems are found to perform best and worst, respectively, while the TRMGC system is found to perform slightly better than the DRMGC system. Therefore, it can be concluded that the basic findings on the operational-performance effects of the yard-block dimensions and the type of RMGC system (see Sect. 7.2) are not structurally affected by the applied crane-scheduling strategy, just as postulated by Research hypothesis 2.7.4. This is also confirmed by comparing the regression results on the operational-performance effects of the yard-block dimensions presented in this work (see Sect. 7.2.2.3) with those provided by Kemme (2011a), which are both based on the same regression model, but differ with respect to the applied crane-scheduling strategies for generating the underlying simulation results. It is found that the regression coefficients computed here, using the quite well performing PRIO2 method, are slightly smaller than the coefficients yielded in Kemme (2011a), that are based on the much worse performing EDD priority rule. Hence, as it could be expected from the results of Table 7.30, longer vehicle-waiting times are induced by each block dimension when applying the EDD rule instead of PRIO2. However, the ranking of the corresponding beta values is nearly identical for both regression analyses, thus indicating that the basic findings on the relative importance of the block dimensions for the operational performance of RMGC systems are not structurally affected by using either PRIO2 or EDD.

Altogether, well-balanced multi-objective priority rules like PRIO1 and PRIO2 are found to perform significantly better than single-objective priority rules like FIFO, EDD and NN, but (near) optimal replan strategies like SFE-replan and GAM-replan are found to perform even better than these multi-objective priority rules. In addition, the operational performance of the enumerative SFE method is found to depend on the maximum number of plannable jobs, whereas the basic findings on the operational-performance effects of the RMGC design are found not to be structurally affected by the applied crane-scheduling strategy. As a consequence,

- Research hypothesis 2.7.1 is confirmed,
- Research hypothesis 2.7.2 is confirmed,
- Research hypothesis 2.7.3 is confirmed and
- Research hypothesis 2.7.4 is confirmed

by the simulation results obtained with the experimental setup of this sensitivity analysis.

7.3.8 Influence of the Crane-Routing Strategy

In addition to decisions on container stacking and crane scheduling, the efficient use of the basically available crane resources of a yard block is also influenced by crane-routing decisions, as the amount of crane-interference times and the duration of crane movements are to a great extent determined by the way in which the cranes of a yard block are routed. Thus, despite having received much less attention so far in the OR and logistics literature than container-stacking and crane-scheduling strategies, the crane-routing strategy is also conjectured to have notable effects on the operational performance and the design of RMGC systems in Sect. 4.1.3. In particular, multi-crane systems with crossing capabilities offer various options for alternative crane-routing strategies—especially with regard to the way crane-crossing manoeuvres are conducted. Some of them are introduced in Sect. 5.4.3. Here, it is investigated to what extent the XT and SC-waiting times in the handover areas are influenced by and in how far the basic findings on the operational-performance effects of the RMGC design are sensitive to changes in the crane-routing strategies for multi-crane systems with crossing capabilities.

7.3.8.1 Research Hypotheses

In order to ensure a collision-free crane routing and to take advantage of the additional flexibility in the crane deployment, that is induced by the crossing capabilities of the DRMGC and TriRMGC systems, the trolley of the outer large crane needs to be moved to the crossing position. However, owing to the time required to move the trolley to its crossing position, such trolley movements can be expected to cause prolonged execution times for jobs performed by the outer large crane, which reduces the available crane resources and increases the risk for and the extent of vehicle-waiting times in the handover areas. Hence, in order to deploy the outer large crane as efficiently as possible, without interfering the movements of the inner small crane(s), the crane-crossing processes should be organised in such a way that as little job-execution time as possible is induced by trolley movements to the crossing position only. As a consequence, crane-routing strategies that minimise the number of trolley movements to the crossing position and/or use the trolley-movement time as efficiently as possible (e.g., by performing simultaneous portal movements) can be expected to yield significantly shorter mean vehicle-waiting times in the handover areas than routing strategies that always require the trolley of the outer large crane to be moved to the crossing position before starting portal movements. Therefore, referring to the crane-crossing processes introduced in Sect. 5.4.3, the CCP2 process, that allows simultaneous portal and trolley movements of the outer large crane, can be expected to yield shorter mean vehicle-waiting times than CCP1, which does not allow such crane movements. Furthermore, even shorter mean vehicle-waiting times than with CCP2 can be expected by applying either CCP3 or CCP4, as these crossing processes additionally avoid trolley movements to the crossing position if possible and beneficial.

Considering that, regardless of the way crane-crossing manoeuvres are conducted, further inefficiencies in the use of the crane resources of DRMGC and TriRMGC systems may be caused by unnecessary blockings of the handover areas due to early arriving cranes compared to the relevant due dates, the mean vehicle-waiting times in the handover areas are expected to be reduced by avoiding such handover-area blockings (see Sect. 5.4.1). In this work the HAC mechanism is introduced that prevents a crane from entering a handover area if being expected to block that zone for operations of other cranes (see Sect. 5.4.3). Hence, the additional application of the HAC mechanism to the routing of multi-crane systems with crossing capabilities can be expected to reduce the crane-interference times for these systems, which also reduces the mean vehicle-waiting times in their handover areas. Further considering the fact that the HAC mechanism is by default not applied for all previously conducted simulation experiments (see Sect. 7.1.3), the additional use of this mechanism can be expected to induce a reduction or even a reversal of the found performance advantage of the TRMGC system over the DRMGC system. Based on this, Research hypotheses 2.8.1 and 2.8.2 are formulated:

Research Hypothesis 2.8.1. The crane-crossing process CCP2 induces significantly shorter mean vehicle-waiting times in the handover areas of DRMGC and TriRMGC systems than CCP1, and even shorter vehicle-waiting times are obtained with CCP3 and CCP4.

Research Hypothesis 2.8.2. The additional application of the HAC mechanism has significantly negative effects on the mean vehicle-waiting times in the handover areas of DRMGC and TriRMGC systems and thus on the performance advantage of the TRMGC system over the DRMGC system.

7.3.8.2 Experimental Setup

To examine the influence of crane-routing strategies for multi-crane systems with crossing capabilities on the operational performance and the design of RMGC systems, the types of RMGC systems having crossing capabilities are tested with eight different claiming-based crane-routing strategies that differ with respect to the crane-crossing processes and the use of the HAC mechanism. To be precise: all RMGC designs, that result from combining the DRMGC system and the TriRMGC system with the nine example yard-block layouts in every possible way, are simulated with the crane-crossing processes CCP1, CCP2, CCP3 and CCP4, both with and without additionally applying the HAC mechanism, thus leading to 144 simulation experiments in total. Except for the crane-crossing process and the use of the HAC mechanism, no other parameters of the crane-routing strategy are varied in these experiments. In particular, the claiming concept is applied as specified in Sect. 5.4.3. All other input parameters of the simulation model are set to the default parameter settings of this simulation study (see Sect. 7.1.3).

7.3.8.3 Results and Discussion

The simulation results of all experiments on the influence of the crane-routing strategy for multi-crane systems with crossing capabilities on the operational performance and the design planning of RMGC systems are summarised in Tables 7.32 and 7.33 that show the resulting mean vehicle-waiting times in the landside and waterside handover areas, respectively. There, the applied crane-crossing process is noted in the first column, the use of the HAC mechanism is indicated by a check in the second column and the resulting vehicle-waiting-time figures for different RMGC designs are displayed in the following columns. In order to allow a direct performance comparison between all types of RMGC systems, not only the resulting vehicle-waiting times of the DRMGC and TriRMGC systems in combination with different routing strategies are displayed in Tables 7.32 and 7.33, but also the simulation results of the SRMGC and TRMGC systems with the default settings are shown.

It can be seen from Tables 7.32 and 7.33 that, regardless of whether applying the HAC mechanism or not, significantly shorter XT and SC-waiting times in the handover areas of the DRMGC and TriRMGC systems are obtained with the crane-crossing process CCP2 than with CCP1—at a significance level of $\alpha = 0.05$—for

Table 7.32 Influence of the crane-routing strategy on the mean XT-waiting time ($\overline{\overline{\omega}}_{ls}^{hr+}$) for selected yard-block layouts with the DRMGC and TriRMGC systems

		Yard-block layout								
CCP	HAC	Small	Low	Narrow	Short	Medium	Long	Wide	High	Big
Resulting $\overline{\overline{\omega}}_{ls}^{hr+}$ with the SRMGC system (s)										
		65.90	**95.41**	**226.61**	**204.03**	**336.25**	**772.82**	**675.77**	**2,244.74**	**3,903.45**
Resulting $\overline{\overline{\omega}}_{ls}^{hr+}$ with the TRMGC system (s)										
		19.48	**29.13**	**82.08**	**77.19**	**98.58**	**126.78**	**118.96**	**387.72**	**1,540.04**
Resulting $\overline{\overline{\omega}}_{ls}^{hr+}$ with the DRMGC system (s)										
1	–	42.56	70.91	143.36	146.13	187.95	250.66	256.46	839.31	2,683.60
2	–	36.08	57.18	125.68	131.39	160.07	203.11	206.26	622.66	2,277.15
3	–	31.56	52.40	115.12	118.00	144.69	180.17	184.80	499.06	1,887.70
4	**–**	**31.48**	**52.60**	**116.45**	**118.90**	**146.10**	**179.24**	**181.10**	**509.36**	**1,907.61**
1	√	40.49	63.93	136.31	138.26	180.02	239.99	242.50	859.86	2,725.45
2	√	32.96	52.40	119.04	124.40	149.85	193.24	196.23	635.23	2,236.24
3	√	29.65	47.73	108.01	109.95	137.09	172.47	171.45	493.90	1,903.83
4	√	28.37	47.20	109.95	109.36	136.34	172.73	171.34	509.73	1,861.66
Resulting $\overline{\overline{\omega}}_{ls}^{hr+}$ with the TriRMGC system (s)										
1	–	24.30	34.09	77.62	77.94	91.42	111.38	115.90	254.63	961.71
2	–	21.26	28.86	70.75	72.76	83.69	100.52	103.20	238.38	819.16
3	–	19.88	26.98	68.57	68.86	81.18	97.96	98.02	212.46	763.77
4	**–**	**19.56**	**26.47**	**66.99**	**68.47**	**80.43**	**98.14**	**98.35**	**208.77**	**754.71**
1	√	24.18	33.39	77.01	77.69	92.87	109.44	112.14	249.66	922.31
2	√	20.35	28.92	71.37	72.40	83.79	100.76	103.08	252.29	813.51
3	√	17.85	26.17	67.21	68.09	79.01	96.53	96.83	216.37	748.14
4	√	17.93	25.71	66.54	68.26	79.93	96.30	97.13	219.98	744.91

almost all considered yard-block layouts. Hence, it is confirmed that allowing simultaneous portal and trolley movements of the outer large crane is beneficial for the operational performance of RMGC systems, just as expected by Research hypothesis 2.8.1. In addition, both CCP3 and CCP4 are found to induce significantly shorter vehicle-waiting times in the handover areas of most yard-block layouts than CCP2 does, thus also confirming the advantageousness of direct trolley movements to the next destination without prior movements to the crossing position, as expected by Research hypothesis 2.8.1. The mean vehicle-waiting times in the handover areas resulting from CCP3 and CCP4 are found to differ only slightly and not significantly for most considered RMGC designs. Thus, it may be concluded that it is not necessarily beneficial for the operational performance of RMGC systems to move a conflicting inner small crane out of the way in order to enable direct or simultaneous trolley movements of the outer large crane, as aimed at by CCP4 compared to CCP3, whenever the conflicting crane is idle. This can be explained by two contrasting effects: On the one hand, the outer large crane is able to reach its destination more quickly if the conflicting crane is moved out of the way, thus decreasing the risk for and the extent of vehicle-waiting times for jobs of the outer large crane. But on the other hand, moving the inner small crane out of the way may induce other crane interferences and/or delayed start times for jobs arriving during the evasive manoeuvre, thus increasing the risk for and the extent of vehicle-waiting

Table 7.33 Influence of the crane-routing strategy on the mean SC-waiting time ($\overline{\overline{\omega}}_{ws}^{hr+}$) for selected yard-block layouts with the DRMGC and TriRMGC systems

		Yard-block layout								
CCP	HAC	Small	Low	Narrow	Short	Medium	Long	Wide	High	Big
Resulting $\overline{\overline{\omega}}_{ws}^{hr+}$ with the SRMGC system (s)										
		1.69	**2.86**	**40.46**	**28.71**	**102.93**	**410.23**	**350.05**	**1,597.83**	**2,837.74**
Resulting $\overline{\overline{\omega}}_{ws}^{hr+}$ with the TRMGC system (s)										
		1.19	**2.14**	**7.79**	**6.74**	**13.31**	**25.15**	**21.79**	**247.50**	**1,586.02**
Resulting $\overline{\overline{\omega}}_{ws}^{hr+}$ with the DRMGC system (s)										
1	–	1.56	3.35	14.47	15.12	27.32	52.16	56.89	494.24	1,895.96
2	–	1.69	2.29	12.44	11.47	18.99	33.60	35.55	338.83	1,646.38
3	–	1.09	2.73	10.00	9.40	15.89	22.51	24.10	245.92	1,394.30
4	**–**	**1.44**	**2.76**	**10.37**	**9.57**	**15.89**	**24.57**	**23.92**	**259.60**	**1,401.64**
1	√	0.31	1.15	12.06	10.65	22.11	48.32	47.43	516.19	1,932.91
2	√	0.50	1.08	8.32	8.79	16.09	30.32	29.54	359.90	1,593.74
3	√	0.78	1.05	6.38	6.12	11.51	22.49	22.35	253.65	1,402.66
4	√	0.59	1.61	6.97	5.36	11.60	21.59	21.52	258.85	1,367.33
Resulting $\overline{\overline{\omega}}_{ws}^{hr+}$ with the TriRMGC system (s)										
1	–	1.19	3.29	7.31	7.82	11.26	13.19	14.41	82.90	668.56
2	–	1.07	2.36	6.84	7.10	9.25	11.51	12.97	74.43	517.54
3	–	1.19	2.64	6.89	6.49	9.05	11.34	11.23	57.52	474.70
4	**–**	**1.16**	**2.76**	**6.61**	**6.48**	**8.44**	**10.23**	**10.85**	**56.00**	**451.96**
1	√	0.72	0.93	4.24	5.09	6.81	9.90	9.56	76.84	627.19
2	√	0.38	0.99	3.63	3.81	5.43	7.54	8.74	77.76	511.09
3	√	0.25	0.96	3.26	3.69	5.65	7.00	6.25	56.82	460.03
4	√	0.41	1.06	3.14	3.47	5.12	6.79	7.81	60.77	459.94

times for jobs of the inner small crane(s). From the simulation results it may be concluded that both effects roughly compensate each other.

By pairwise comparisons of the vehicle-waiting-time figures with and without applying the HAC mechanism for each considered crane-crossing process, it is found that for almost all considered RMGC designs and crossing processes significantly shorter vehicle-waiting times are yielded by the additional use of the HAC mechanism, just as expected by Research hypothesis 2.8.2. In particular, the SC-waiting times in the waterside handover areas of small- to medium-sized yard blocks are found to be much shorter when applying the HAC mechanism, whereas only small reductions of the XT-waiting times in the landside handover areas of large-sized yard blocks are induced by the HAC mechanism. Considering the fact that the risk for early crane arrivals in the handover areas and thus the need for the HAC mechanism is the greater, the longer the corresponding vehicle arrivals are known in advance of the actual arrival times and the smaller the crane workload the cranes of a yard block are faced with, these differences in the effects of the HAC mechanism can be explained by handover-area-dependent differences in the look-ahead times for vehicle arrivals and layout-dependent differences in the crane workload. In fact, the crane workload is previously found to increase with the stacking capacity (see Sect. 7.2.2.2) and the look-ahead times for vehicle arrivals is defined to be, on average, longer for waterside arrivals than for landside arrivals (see

Sect. 7.1.3). As a consequence, there is a greater risk for early crane arrivals in the handover areas and thus a greater benefit of the HAC mechanism for the waterside handover areas of smaller-sized yard blocks than for the landside handover areas of larger-sized yard blocks.

As a consequence of the negative vehicle-waiting-time effects of the HAC mechanism, the performance advantage of the TRMGC system over the DRMGC system is found to be significantly reduced by the additional use of the HAC mechanism, just as expected by Research hypothesis 2.8.2. Owing to the great effectiveness of the HAC mechanism for the waterside handover area, it can even be observed from Table 7.33 that the additional use of the HAC mechanism leads to a reversal of the previously found performance advantage of the TRMGC system over the DRMGC system with regard to the waterside vehicle-waiting times for almost all investigated yard-block layouts (see Sect. 7.2.2.4). In fact, the DRMGC system is found to induce (significantly) shorter mean SC-waiting times than the TRMGC system for eight (seven) of nine example yard-block layouts when applying CCP4 in combination with the HAC mechanism, whereas the TRMGC system is observed to yield (significantly) shorter mean SC-waiting times than the DRMGC system for seven (six) of nine yard-block layouts when deploying CCP4 without the HAC mechanism. In further simulation experiments, where the portal of the outer larger crane is additionally specified to move with identical velocity as the inner small crane (i.e., $v_2^{xe} = v_2^{xf} = 4\,{}^{m}/_{s}$), the DRMGC system is even observed to induce significantly shorter mean SC-waiting times than the TRMGC system for all nine investigated yard-block layouts when applying CCP4 in combination with the HAC mechanism. In contrast, no reversal of the performance advantage of the TRMGC system over the DRMGC system with regard to the landside vehicle-waiting times is induced by the HAC mechanism (see Table 7.32), as there are system-dependent differences in the allocation of the crane resources between both handover areas that favour shorter XT-waiting times for the TRMGC system than for the DRMGC system (see Sect. 7.2.2.4). However, in view of these findings, it can be concluded that the previously found, surprisingly bad operational performance of the DRMGC system compared to the TRMGC system is mainly to be explained by the default settings for crane routing of multi-crane systems with crossing capabilities, that do not consider unnecessary blockings of the handover areas due to early crane arrivals.

Altogether, the operational performance of multi-crane systems with crossing capabilities is found to be the better, the more the cranes are routed in such a way that handover-area blockings due to early crane arrivals are avoided and that trolley movements to the crossing position are reduced and/or used as efficiently as possible. Thus, the vehicle-waiting times in the handover areas of the DRMGC and TriRMGC system and, as a consequence also the performance advantage of the TRMGC system over the DRMGC system, are found to decrease in the order of CCP1 $>$ CCP2 $>$ CCP3 $\approx$ CCP4. The additional application of the HAC mechanism is even found to reverse the performance advantage of the TRMGC system over the DRMGC system with regard to the mean vehicle-waiting time in the waterside handover area. As a consequence,

- Research hypothesis 2.8.1 is confirmed and
- Research hypothesis 2.8.2 is confirmed

by the simulation results obtained with the experimental setup of this sensitivity analysis.

7.3.9 Summary of the Sensitivity Analysis

Within the framework of this sensitivity analysis of the basic findings on the operational-performance effects of the RMGC design, several input parameters of the RMGC-design-planning problem, that define the terminal-framework conditions and the operational planning strategies, are investigated with respect to their effects on the operational performance and the design of RMGC systems. Basically, almost all investigated parameters are found to have significant effects on the operational performance of RMGC systems. Thus, they also influence decisions on the appropriate size of the yard block and the most suited type of RMGC system. However, the basic findings on the operational-performance effects of the RMGC design (see Sect. 7.2.3) are mostly found not to be structurally affected by changes of these input parameters.

Of the considered terminal-framework conditions, the mean container-dwell time and the crane kinematics are found to have significantly negative effects on the mean vehicle-waiting times in the waterside and landside handover areas (see Sects. 7.3.2 and 7.3.5), whereas the average yard-block-filling rate is found to have significantly positive effects on the mean vehicle-waiting times (see Sect. 7.3.1). For the operational-performance effects of the transshipment factor and the unevenness of the vessel-call pattern, it has to be distinguished between the handover areas and the types of RMGC systems. While the unevenness of the vessel-call pattern is found to have significantly positive effects on the mean vehicle-waiting time in the waterside handover area, slightly negative effects on the waiting time in the landside handover area are discovered (see Sect. 7.3.4). Similarly, also the transshipment factor is found to have significantly positive effects on the mean vehicle-waiting time in the waterside handover area, but negative effects on the landside vehicle-waiting time are only observed for the TRMGC and TriRMGC systems. In contrast, for the SRMGC and DRMGC systems, the transshipment factor is found to have positive effects on the mean vehicle-waiting time in the landside handover area (see Sect. 7.3.3).

Also the selection and the parametrisation of operational planning strategies for RMGC systems are found to have substantial effects on the operational performance of RMGC systems. With regard to the container-stacking strategy, both stacking of containers that are planned to depart by deep-sea vessel according to their categories and stacking of containers that are planned to depart by feeder vessel and XT according to their delivery times are found to have significantly negative effects on the mean vehicle-waiting times in both handover areas. In addition, for reasons of workload smoothing, also the inclusion of the resulting inbound and outbound crane-driving distances into the decisions on stacking positions and the option to relocate containers to better stacking positions whenever possible and beneficial are found to have significantly negative effects on the mean vehicle-waiting times (see Sect. 7.3.6). With regard to the crane-scheduling strategies, crane dispatching and job sequencing on the basis of well-balanced multi-objective priority rules as well as (near) optimal solution methods are found to have significantly negative vehicle-waiting-time effects compared to single-objective priority rules. Of all investigated scheduling strategies, the repeated generation of optimal jobs sequences for all cranes of a yard block, whenever a job is completed, is found to be the best-performing strategy (see Sect. 7.3.7). Finally, also the crane-routing strategies are found to have substantial effects on the operational performance of multi-crane systems with crossing capabilities. The use of routing strategies that avoid handover-area blockings due to early crane arrivals and that try to reduce trolley movements to the crossing position and/or use the trolley-movement times for simultaneous portal movements are found to have significantly negative effects on the mean vehicle-waiting times compared to simpler routing strategies (see Sect. 7.3.8).

In view of the highly significant operational-performance effects of most investigated input parameters of the RMGC-design-planning problem, planning assumptions on the terminal-framework conditions and the operational planning strategies are concluded to be of great importance for decisions on the design of RMGC systems. The larger the value of a terminal-framework-defining input parameter with negative vehicle-waiting-time effects, the larger the yard block can be dimensioned and/or the fewer cranes can be installed per yard block without inducing significantly longer mean vehicle-waiting times. As a consequence, the area and/or cost performance of the container-storage yard can be improved without impairing its operational performance. In contrast, for input parameters with positive vehicle-waiting-time effects, these relations are reversed. Similarly, assumptions on the future use of quite well-performing operational planning strategies for the RMGC system under design also allow to construct larger-sized yard blocks and/or to install fewer cranes per yard block than assuming the use of rather badly performing strategies without deteriorating the resulting operational performance. However, in how far changing assumptions on the terminal-framework conditions and/or the operational planning strategies actually lead to revised decisions on the yard-block layout and/or type of RMGC system is not only determined by the operational-performance effects of these parameters, but also by the effects of these parameters on the area and cost performance of the container-storage yard as well as by the terminal-specific importance of these design-planning objectives (see Sect. 4.1.2). However, due to the great importance of all investigated input parameters for the operational performance of container-storage yards, it is highly recommended to take realistic planning assumptions on the terminal-framework conditions and planning strategies into account when deciding on the design of RMGC systems in order to avoid the construction of RMGC systems, that turn out to be suboptimal for the terminal after having been put into operation. Otherwise, notably oversized or undersized yard-block dimensions and/or crane resources might be the result, which may be adverse, not just for the operational performance of the container-storage yard, but also for the operational performance, the area performance and/or the cost performance of the whole terminal system.

In spite of the great effects of all investigated input parameters on the operational performance of RMGC systems, the previously discovered basic findings on the operational-performance effects of the RMGC design (see Sect. 7.2.3) are found to be mainly insensitive to changes of the average yard-block-filling rate, the mean container-dwell time, the crane kinematics, the container-stacking strategy and the crane-scheduling strategy. Of all investigated input parameters, only certain parametrisations of the transshipment factor, the unevenness of the vessel-call pattern and the crane-routing strategy are found to induce some structural changes of the basic findings. Based on negative effects of these parameters on the differences in the mean SC-waiting times between the DRMGC and TRMGC systems, comparably high transshipment factors, uneven vessel-call patterns and routing strategies for the DRMGC system that avoid handover-area blockings are found to reverse the previously discovered performance advantage of the TRMGC system over the DRMGC system with regard to the vehicle-waiting times in the waterside handover area (see Sects. 7.3.3, 7.3.4 and 7.3.8).

7.4 Management Implications

After the results of this simulation study are presented, statistically analysed and qualitatively explained in the previous sections, subsequently the most important findings are discussed with respect to their practical implications for terminal planners, terminal operators and/or all kinds of decision makers at seaport container terminals. It is started with a summarising discussion on the validity and the practical relevance of the results and findings of this simulation study. Thereafter, the main findings of this simulation study are critically discussed with respect to their managerial insights for the RMGC-design-planning problem. Finally, the most important management implications of this simulation study for decisions on the design and the operation of RMGC systems are summarised in bullet point form.

The simulation study reveals that the operational performance of RMGC systems at seaport container terminals depends greatly on the planning decisions for the layout of the yard block and the operating type of RMGC system. It is found that high stacking has to be avoided and longer blocks are preferable for DRMGC and TriRMGC systems, while wider layouts are preferable for SRMGC and TRMGC systems. In addition, the TriRMGC system is found to perform best, the SRMGC system is found to perform worst and the DRMGC and TRMGC systems are found to yield intermediate performance figures. Of course, these findings specifically apply to the investigated experimental setting of this simulation study. However, the conducted sensitivity analyses indicate that the basic findings on the operational-performance effects of the RMGC design are structurally unaffected by most parameter changes. In addition, in view of the thoroughly verified and validated simulation model (see Sect. 6.4), the operational-performance figures can be expected to be close to reality. As a consequence, the findings of this simulation study and thus the insights gained into the operational-performance effects of the RMGC design can be expected to have practical relevance for terminal-design planning.

Owing to the fact that the vehicle-waiting times in the handover areas are found to increase with the yard-block dimensions and to decrease with the number of cranes deployed per yard block, it would be advisable to design very small-sized yard blocks that deploy two or even three cranes per yard block in order to optimise the operational performance of the container-storage yard. However, in practice, it is expected that decisions on the design of RMGC systems are not only based on the operational performance of RMGC-design alternatives, but on a trade-off between the operational performance, the cost performance and the area performance of alternative RMGC designs (see Sect. 4.1.2). Therefore, no decisions on the design of RMGC systems at seaport container terminals can be made based on the simulation results and findings of the preceding subsections alone. Instead, both the cost and area performance of RMGC designs need additionally to be determined and to be taken into account for decision-making. In order to illustrate in how far decisions on the optimal design of RMGC systems are influenced by the additional inclusion of area and cost-performance effects of RMGC designs, once again the 36 example RMGC designs are regarded, which are comprehensively investigated throughout the sensitivity analysis in Sect. 7.3. While the operational performance of these RMGC designs, in terms of the mean vehicle-waiting times in the waterside and landside handover areas, are already presented in the preceding sections (see Tables 7.2 and 7.3), the cost and area performance of these RMGC designs still need to be evaluated.

For computing the area performance of a certain RMGC design in terms of the yard density, only the on average used stacking capacity of a single yard block with that design needs to be divided by the space required for that yard block, which is composed of the actual container-storage area, the waterside and landside handover areas and the additional space requirements of the crane system for rail tracks and a service lane. The space requirements of other terminal subsystems do not need to be taken into account because they are not relevant to decisions on the design of RMGC systems. The size of the actual storage area of a yard block is computed by multiplying its length and width, which can be calculated based on the numbers of bays and rows and the length and width of an individual TEU groundslot. Based on the metrics of a TEU and some additional safety distance, a TEU groundslot is assumed to be 6.4 m long and 2.8 m wide in this work (see Sect. 3.3.3). The size of the handover areas can be computed by multiplying their lengths, which are each assumed to be 28 m long (Ranau 2011), with the width of the storage area. The additional space requirements of the crane system for rail tracks and a service lane are computed by multiplying the length of the yard block, including the storage area and both handover areas, with the width of the rail tracks and the service lane. Considering RMGC-type-dependent differences in the required numbers of rail tracks for each yard block and in the need for special service lanes beyond the profile(s) of the cranes, rail tracks and service lanes of crane systems with and without crossing capabilities are assumed to be 12 m and 5 m wide in total, respectively (see Sect. 3.4.1). Based on these assumptions and specifications, the yard density of the RMGC design with the DRMGC system and the "medium" yard-block layout can, for instance, be computed by

$$\begin{aligned}\underset{(36,\,8,\,4,\,\text{DRMGC})}{\text{Yard density}} &= \frac{\text{Stacking capacity}}{\text{Storage area} + \text{Handover area} + \text{Crane system area}} \qquad (7.3)\\ &= \frac{0.75\cdot 36\cdot 8\cdot 4\,\text{TEU}}{\frac{36\cdot 6.4\,\text{m}\cdot 8\cdot 2.8\,\text{m}}{10{,}000}+\frac{2\cdot 28\,\text{m}\cdot 8\cdot 2.8\,\text{m}}{10{,}000}+\frac{12\,\text{m}\cdot(36\cdot 6.4\,\text{m}+2\cdot 28\,\text{m})}{10{,}000}}\\ &= 876.97\,{}^{\text{TEU}}\!/_{\text{ha}}.\end{aligned}$$

For the computation of the cost performance in terms of the unit cost of container-storage and retrieval jobs, it is only focused on expenses that differ between the RMGC designs. Therefore, the investment costs for cranes, rail tracks and pavement of a single yard block as well as operating costs for unproductive terminal operations that are caused by the RMGC design are considered for computing the unit cost of container-storage and retrieval jobs. Whereas operating costs for storage and retrieval jobs themselves as well as investment costs for handover-area equipment and TOS additions for RMGC systems are neglected due to being mostly identical for different RMGC designs. As a consequence, the computed costs per storage and retrieval job do not reflect the real total costs of the RMGC designs, but only the decision-relevant costs. The investment costs for cranes, rail tracks and pavement are included in terms of linear depreciations over 20 years and imputed interest according to the average cost method with a calculatory interest rate of 8% (Saanen 2006; Mumm 2008, pp. 82–85). The investment costs for the cranes of a yard block are composed of a basic price and a size-dependent surcharge for each crane. Here, inner small and outer large cranes are assumed to have basic prices of € 1,800,000 and € 2,000,000, respectively, and for each tier of the yard block the purchasing prices of both cranes are assumed to increase by another € 50,000 (Saanen 2006). The investment costs for the rail tracks (including groundworks) are computed by multiplying the length of the considered yard block with an assumed cost rate of 750 €/m rail track. Similarly, the investment costs for the heavy pavement of the storage area are calculated by multiplying the area size with an assumed cost factor of 120 €/m^2 storage area (Saanen 2006). In order to evaluate the cost effects of RMGC-design decisions not only with regard to the investment costs, but also with regard to the consequential costs for the terminal operations, the operating costs for unproductive terminal operations that are caused by the RMGC design need to be taken into account for computing the decision-relevant unit cost of container-storage and retrieval operations. In particular, shuffle moves inside the yard block as well as vehicle redirections and container relocations to other yard blocks, due the absence of adequate stacking positions within the considered block, can be regarded as unproductive terminal operations that are affected by the design of the RMGC system (see Sect. 5.2.4). Thus, the decision-relevant operating costs incurred for each storage and retrieval job can be computed by multiplying the numbers of shuffle moves, redirections and relocations, that are observed within the simulation period analysed ($T - T^{\mathrm{warm}}$), with fixed cost rates for these operations and dividing the sum of these products by the number of storage and retrieval jobs in that period of time. Considering typical operating costs for energy, labour and M&R of RMGCs and SCs (Saanen 2006), the cost rates for shuffle moves, redirections and relocations can be assumed to be 7.50 €, 5.00 € and 20.00 €, respectively. Altogether, the costs per storage and retrieval operation of a certain RMGC design can then be computed by

$$\begin{aligned}\begin{array}{c}\text{Storage costs}\\ (n^{\mathrm{x}}, n^{\mathrm{y}}, n^{\mathrm{z}}, \text{RMGC type})\end{array} &= \frac{\text{Depreciation \& interest of crane investment}}{\text{Yearly number of storage and retrivals jobs}} \\ &+ \frac{\text{Depreciation \& interest of rail track investment}}{\text{Yearly number of storage and retrivals jobs}} \\ &+ \frac{\text{Depreciation \& interest of pavement investment}}{\text{Yearly number of storage and retrivals jobs}} \\ &+ \frac{\text{Operating costs for shuffling, redirecting \& relocating}}{\text{Number of storage and retrivals jobs}}\end{aligned} \tag{7.4}$$

if all relevant data is available. For instance, for the RMGC design with the DRMGC system and the "medium" yard-block layout, average numbers of 5,615.2 storage and retrieval jobs, 3,098.5 shuffle moves, 248.8 redirections and 48.5 relocations are observed in simulation experiments with the default settings. Based on these figures, decision-relevant unit cost of container-storage and retrieval operations of

$$\begin{aligned}\begin{array}{c}\text{Storage costs}\\ (36, 8, 4, \text{DRMGC})\end{array} &= \frac{(1,800,000\,€ + 2,000,000\,€ + 50,000\,€ \times 4 \times 2) \times \left(\frac{0.08}{2} + \frac{1}{20}\right)}{5,615.2\,\text{jobs} \times \frac{365}{28}} \\ &+ \frac{750\,€/\text{m} \times (36 \times 6.4\,\text{m} + 2 \times 28\,\text{m}) \times 4 \times \left(\frac{0.08}{2} + \frac{1}{20}\right)}{5,615.2\,\text{jobs} \times \frac{365}{28}} \\ &+ \frac{120\,€/\text{m}^2 \times (36 \times 6.4\,\text{m} + 2 \times 28\,\text{m}) \times 8 \times 2.8\,\text{m} \times \left(\frac{0.08}{2} + \frac{1}{20}\right)}{5,615.2\,\text{jobs} \times \frac{365}{28}} \\ &+ \frac{7.50\,€ \times 3,098.5 + 5.00\,€ \times 248.8 + 20.00\,€ \times 48.5}{5,615.2\,\text{jobs}} \\ &= 11.70\,€/\text{job}\end{aligned} \tag{7.5}$$

can be computed for that RMGC design. The resulting yard densities and unit costs of container-storage and retrieval operations of all 36 example RMGC designs are shown in Table 7.34 together with the corresponding mean vehicle-waiting times in the landside and waterside handover areas observed in the main simulation study (see Tables 7.2 and 7.3).

It can bee seen from the performance figures of Table 7.34 that, as argued before (see Sect. 4.1.2), the operational performance of RMGC designs is the better, the more cranes are used per yard block and/or the smaller the yard-block capacity. In contrast, the cost performance of RMGC designs is observed to be the better, the fewer cranes are used and the bigger the capacity of the yard block is, while the area performance is found to be the better, the fewer rail tracks are needed by the relevant type of RMGC system and the higher containers are stacked in the yard block. In fact, the RMGC design with the SRMGC system and the "big" layout is found to yield the highest yard density and the RMGC design with the SRMGC system and the "wide" layout is found to perform best with respect to the unit cost of container-storage and retrieval jobs. In contrast, the RMGC design with the TRMGC system and the "small" layout is found to induce the shortest mean vehicle-waiting time in the landside handover area, while the RMGC design with the TriRMGC system and the "small" layout is found to perform best with respect to the waterside mean vehicle-waiting time. However, in practice, none of these rather extreme RMGC designs is expected to be selected due to performing very badly with respect to other RMGC-design-planning objectives. Instead, based on a trade-off between the operational performance, the cost performance and the area performance, RMGC designs are expected to be selected that do not perform really badly for any of these design-planning objectives. Which RMGC design is actually selected for a certain seaport container terminal, depends on the terminal-specific framework conditions and the relative importance of the different design-planning objectives.

Although, RMGC-design planning has to be regarded as a multi-objective planning problem, that cannot be solved by considering the operational performance of alternative RMGC designs alone, the results and findings of this simulation study can nevertheless be regarded to be of particular importance for decision-making about the design of RMGC systems in practice. In fact, while cost and area performance of alternative RMGC designs are easy to calculate by decision makers, the operational performance cannot easily be computed and/or estimated in an analytical way because of the great degree of complexity and dynamics of RMGC systems (see Sect. 4.2). Therefore, the results and findings of this extensive RMGC-design study are expected to provide valuable insights into the effects of design-planning decisions on the operational performance of RMGC systems, that are also of practical relevance. In fact, several management implications for practical terminal-design-planning decisions can be deduced from the results and findings that are presented and analysed in Sects. 7.2 and 7.3. Basically, it is found to be advisable for the operational performance of RMGC systems:

- To design small-sized yard blocks rather than large-sized yard blocks for all types of RMGC systems (see Sect. 7.2.2.2).
- To design wider and/or longer yard blocks rather than higher yard blocks of the same size for all types of RMGC systems (see Sect. 7.2.2.3).

Table 7.34 Comparison of example RMGC designs with respect to the operational performance, the cost performance and the area performance

RMGC design		Operational performance				Cost performance		Area performance	
RMGC type	Block layout	$\overline{\overline{\omega}}_{\text{ls}}^{\text{hr+}}$ (s)	Rank	$\overline{\overline{\omega}}_{\text{ws}}^{\text{hr+}}$ (s)	Rank	Costs/main job (€/job)	Rank	Yard density (TEUs/ha)	Rank
SRMGC	Small	65.90	7	1.69	4	13.21	24	491.48	31
	Low	95.41	13	2.86	8	9.06	4	550.50	29
	Narrow	226.61	26	40.46	25	9.71	8	1,037.88	17
	Short	204.03	24	28.71	24	9.48	6	1,042.75	15
	Medium	336.25	27	102.93	27	8.45	3	1,101.01	13
	Long	772.82	32	410.23	31	7.84	2	1,141.59	11
	Wide	675.77	30	350.05	30	7.72	1	1,142.71	9
	High	2,244.74	35	1,597.83	35	10.44	11	1,651.51	3
	Big	3,903.45	36	2,837.74	36	9.33	5	1,777.25	1
TRMGC	Small	19.48	1	1.19	2	21.00	34	491.48	31
	Low	29.13	4	2.14	5	13.65	26	550.50	29
	Narrow	82.08	12	7.79	12	12.95	22	1,037.88	17
	Short	77.19	10	6.74	11	12.65	20	1,042.75	15
	Medium	98.58	16	13.31	18	10.97	14	1,101.01	13
	Long	126.78	20	25.15	23	9.85	9	1,141.59	11
	Wide	118.96	19	21.79	20	9.64	7	1,142.71	9
	High	387.72	28	247.50	28	12.72	21	1,651.51	3
	Big	1,540.04	33	1,586.02	34	10.69	13	1,777.25	1
DRMGC	Small	31.48	5	1.44	3	23.30	35	372.02	35
	Low	52.60	6	2.76	6	15.22	30	438.48	33
	Narrow	116.45	17	10.37	16	14.06	27	785.61	27
	Short	118.90	18	9.57	14	13.45	25	830.56	25
	Medium	146.10	21	15.89	19	11.70	16	876.97	23
	Long	179.24	22	24.57	22	10.57	12	909.29	21
	Wide	181.10	23	23.92	21	10.24	10	942.74	19
	High	509.39	29	259.60	29	13.14	23	1,315.45	7
	Big	1,907.61	34	1,401.64	33	11.09	15	1,466.23	5
TriRMGC	Small	19.56	2	1.16	1	31.31	36	372.02	35
	Low	26.47	3	2.76	7	19.75	33	438.48	33
	Narrow	66.99	8	6.61	10	17.18	32	785.61	27
	Short	68.47	9	6.48	9	16.56	31	830.56	25
	Medium	80.43	11	8.44	13	14.16	28	876.97	23
	Long	98.14	14	10.23	15	12.55	19	909.29	21
	Wide	98.35	15	10.85	17	12.22	17	942.74	19
	High	208.77	25	56.00	26	15.01	29	1,315.45	7
	Big	754.71	31	451.96	32	12.53	18	1,466.23	5

- To design wider yard blocks rather than longer yard blocks of the same size for SRMGC and TRMGC systems (see Sect. 7.2.2.3).
- To design longer yard blocks rather than wider yard blocks of the same size for DRMGC and TriRMGC systems (see Sect. 7.2.2.3).
- To deploy more cranes per block for each yard-block layout (see Sect. 7.2.2.4).
- To use the TRMGC system rather than the DRMGC system for all yard-block layouts if the landside vehicle-waiting times are of great importance (see Sect. 7.2.2.4).
- To avoid excessively filled yard blocks for each RMGC design (Sect. 7.3.1).
- To deploy more cranes per block and/or to design smaller yard blocks for each RMGC design if it is a terminal with a short mean container-dwell time (see Sect. 7.3.2).
- To use the TRMGC system rather than the DRMGC system for all yard-block layouts if it is an import–export terminal (see Sect. 7.3.3), a terminal with an evenly distributed vessel-call pattern (see Sect. 7.3.4) and/or a terminal using very simple routing strategies for the DRMGC system (see Sect. 7.3.8).
- To deploy the DRMGC system rather than the TRMGC system for all yard-block layouts if it is a transshipment terminal (see Sect. 7.3.3), a terminal with a very unevenly distributed vessel-call pattern (see Sect. 7.3.4) and/or a terminal using sophisticated routing strategies for the DRMGC system (see Sect. 7.3.8).
- To consider reasonable planning assumptions on the terminal-framework conditions when deciding on the RMGC design in order to avoid misjudgements of RMGC designs (see Sects. 7.3.1–7.3.5).
- To consider the use of sophisticated container-stacking, crane-scheduling and crane-routing strategies when deciding on the RMGC design in order to avoid misjudgements of RMGC designs (see Sects. 7.3.6–7.3.8).

On top of these findings on the design of RMGC systems, several insights into the operation of these systems are gained, that provide valuable implications for the selection and parametrisation of container-stacking, crane-scheduling and crane-routing strategies in practice, not only for RMGC systems under development, but also for systems that are already under operation. Basically, it is found to be advisable for the operation of RMGC systems:

- To stack containers departing by deep-sea vessel based on their categories (see Sect. 7.3.6).
- To stack containers departing by feeder vessel and XT based on their delivery times (see Sect. 7.3.6).
- To stack all containers in such a way that the workload is reduced and/or smoothed over time (see Sect. 7.3.6).
- To apply the housekeeping concept for reasons of workload smoothing (see Sect. 7.3.6).
- To deploy multi-objective priority rules rather than single-objective priority rules (see Sect. 7.3.7).
- To apply the replan online policy rather than the ignore policy (see Sect. 7.3.7).

- To create optimal crane schedules for few jobs rather than to create near optimal schedules for large numbers of jobs (see Sect. 7.3.7).
- To deploy crane-routing strategies for DRMGC and TriRMGC systems that avoid handover-area blockings and that try to reduce trolley movements to the crossing position and/or use the trolley-movement times for simultaneous portal movements (see Sect. 7.3.8).

7.5 Concluding Remarks

In this chapter, all research objectives and questions that are raised in Chap. 1 are addressed and/or answered by means of this extensive simulation study with the previously introduced RMGC-simulation model (see Sect. 6.4). After the experimental design of this simulation study is described in Sect. 7.1, the resulting performance figures are presented, statistically analysed, interpreted and discussed in the two following sections. Firstly, simulation experiments on the effects of RMGC-design decisions on the operational performance of the container-storage yard are addressed and thereafter, sensitivity analyses on selected parameters, which are supposed to have effects on the operational performance and the design of RMGC systems, are presented. Finally, the basic findings of these two sections are discussed and summarised with respect to their practical implications.

Throughout this simulation study, the analysis of the operational-performance effects of the RMGC design (see Sect. 7.2) as well as the analysis of operational-performance and design effects of selected input parameters (see Sect. 7.3) are guided by research hypotheses. Firstly, research hypotheses are formulated based on preliminary investigations. Thereafter, the simulation experiments required to validate these hypotheses are specified and conducted. Finally, the formulated research hypotheses are validated based on relevant performance figures from the results of the simulation experiments conducted. Altogether, 35 research hypotheses are formulated and validated within the framework of this chapter—ranging from hypotheses on logical connections between performance figures to research hypotheses on the advantageousness of operational planning strategies for RMGC systems. An informative impression on the scope and the depth of this simulation study can therefore best be provided by a summarising overview on these research hypotheses. This is given in Table 7.35, where a compact formulation of each research hypothesis is noted together with the outcome of its validation.

In this work, the validation of each individual research hypothesis is usually based on a broad data basis that is composed of the results of dozens of different simulation experiments, that comprise hundreds of individual simulation runs with several months of RMGC system operations at seaport container terminals (see Sect. 7.1). Altogether, more than 5,000 different simulation experiments and over 50,000 individual simulation runs are conducted within the framework of this simulation study on RMGC-design planning—not including pilot runs and

Table 7.35 Summarising overview on formulated and validated research hypotheses

No.	Compact formulation of research hypothesis	Status
1.1.1	Positive correlation between XT and SC-waiting times	√
1.1.2	XT greater than SC-waiting time	√
1.1.3	Positive correlation of crane workload and vehicle-waiting times	√
1.1.4	Negative correlation of crane workload and crane-waiting time	√
1.2.1	Positive vehicle-waiting-time effects of block capacity	√
1.2.2	Larger SC than XT-waiting-time effects of block capacity	x
1.3.1	Positive vehicle-waiting-time effects of block dimensions	√
1.3.2	Block height has larger vehicle-waiting-time effects than length and width	√
1.3.3	Block length has larger vehicle-waiting-time effects than width	(√)
1.4.1	Negative vehicle-waiting-time effects of the number of cranes per yard block	√
1.4.2	Shorter vehicle-waiting times with TRMGC than with DRMGC	(√)
2.1.1	Positive vehicle-waiting-time effects of the average block-filling rate	√
2.1.2	Average block-filling rate has no effects on basic RMGC-design findings	√
2.2.1	Negative vehicle-waiting-time effects of the mean container-dwell time	√
2.2.2	No vehicle-waiting-time effects of the difference between $\overline{\delta}^{ie}$ and $\overline{\delta}^{ts}$	√
2.2.3	Mean container-dwell time has no effects on basic RMGC-design findings	√
2.3.1	Positive SC-waiting-time effects of the transshipment factor	√
2.3.2	Negative XT-waiting-time effects of the transshipment factor	(√)
2.3.3	Negative effects of transshipment factor on TRMGC vs. DRMGC	(√)
2.4.1	Positive SC-waiting-time effects of the VCP unevenness	√
2.4.2	Positive XT-waiting-time effects of the VCP unevenness	x
2.4.3	Negative effects of VCP unevenness on TRMGC vs. DRMGC	(√)
2.5.1	Negative vehicle-waiting-time effects of the crane kinematics	√
2.5.2	Negative effects of large crane velocity on TRMGC vs. DRMGC	x
2.6.1	Negative vehicle-waiting-time effects of including RTS costs for stacking	√
2.6.2	Negative vehicle-waiting-time effects of including PoS costs for stacking	√
2.6.3	RaS strategy is outperformed by CCFS strategy	√
2.6.4	Negative vehicle-waiting-time effects of using HHS with CCFS	√
2.6.5	Quality of applied stacking strategy more important for higher blocks	√
2.7.1	FIFO, EDD & NN yield longer vehicle-waiting times than PRIO1 & PRIO2	√
2.7.2	GAM-replan and SFE-replan yield the shortest vehicle-waiting times	√
2.7.3	Negative vehicle-waiting-time effects of max. no. of plannable jobs by SFE	√
2.7.4	Crane-scheduling strategy has no effects on basic RMGC-design findings	√
2.8.1	CCP3 & CCP4 yield shorter vehicle-waiting times than CCP1 & CCP2	√
2.8.2	Negative vehicle-waiting-time effects of the HAC mechanism	√

preliminary investigations. Thus, neglecting the warm-up period, the presented simulation results are based on nearly 4,000 years of RMGC system operations at seaport container terminals within which more than half a billion individual crane-transport jobs are performed.

In spite of the broad scope of this simulation study and the great number of simulation experiments conducted, some questions on the design and the operation of RMGC systems remain unanswered, thus providing the motivation for future simulation experiments. In particular, although a great variety of input parameters is already regarded with respect to their influences on RMGC-design-planning decisions, the performance and design effects of even more input parameters are not investigated in this simulation analysis. Thus, future simulation experiments should be directed to explore the effects of the TEU-factor, the applied equipment type for the waterside horizontal transport (i.e., passive vs. active), the arrival-time distribution of XTs, the look-ahead times for vehicle arrivals and the final-handover times of the crane on the operational performance and the design of RMGC systems. In addition, it might be of interest to analyse the effects of some already investigated input parameters in some more detail, by conducting further simulation experiments with greater numbers of different RMGC designs and/or simultaneous changes of different input parameters in order to identify performance interdependencies between these factors.

Chapter 8
Summary and Outlook

8.1 Summary

Within the framework of the preceding chapters, the research objectives of this work are realised as follows: The first chapter is dedicated to a general introduction of this work and a synopsis of the subsequent chapters. Basic terms, facts, processes and problems of seaport container terminals are introduced in Chap. 2. It is started with a general introduction of the container-logistics sector. Thereafter, functions, operations and equipment types of seaport container terminals are introduced, which is followed by definitions of indicators to assess the design and the performance of container terminals. It is found, that the storage yard is of crucial importance for the performance of seaport container terminals. The chapter is closed with a summarising overview on all relevant planning problems of container terminals.

In Chap. 3, the container-storage yard is addressed in more detail. After characterising the container-storage yard as an open transshipment store, it is discussed in how far the performance of the total terminal system is influenced by its storage yard. It is found that the operational performance of seaport container terminals as a whole is greatly determined by the waiting times of horizontal-transport vehicles at the storage yard—in particular of internal ones for the horizontal transport between the quay and the stack. Thereafter, three predominantly used basic types of storage-yard systems are presented and discussed with respect to their advantages and disadvantages. Finally, the RMGC system, that is found to be a promising storage system for container terminals due to its great possibilities for automation, is introduced in great detail, including its design alternatives, processes and planning problems.

The problem of designing a functional, high-performing and competitive RMGC system for seaport container terminals is introduced in Chap. 4. It is started with an explication of this planning problem, including a classification of decisions to be made, a discussion on objectives to be aimed at and an overview on parameters that are supposed to affect the operational performance and the design of RMGC systems. Besides several externally given parameters, that define the framework

N. Kemme, *Design and Operation of Automated Container Storage Systems*, Contributions to Management Science, DOI 10.1007/978-3-7908-2885-6_8,

conditions of RMGC systems, among others, also the selection and parametrisation of operational planning strategies for the container-stacking, crane-scheduling and crane-routing problems are discussed to be of great importance for the operational performance and the design of RMGC systems. Thereafter, relevant literature on the RMGC-design-planning problem is presented and discussed. By analysing the presented literature and comparing alternative types of research approaches, simulation is found to be the best suited technique to investigate this planning problem.

In Chap. 5, the three operational planning problems of RMGC systems on container stacking, crane scheduling and crane routing are one by one addressed, after some common terms and notations for these problems are introduced. Firstly, it is dealt with the container-stacking problem. After introducing that planning problem and classifying known stacking strategies from the relevant literature, a new cost-based stacking strategy that combines different aspects of previously classified approaches and a yard-reorganisation strategy that aims at improving the stacking positions of containers if possible and beneficial are introduced. Thereafter, the crane-scheduling problem is addressed in a similar way. After that scheduling problem is introduced and a classifying overview on known solution approaches is provided, new scheduling strategies are presented, ranging from priority rules to optimal and heuristic solution procedures. In particular, a new IP formulation of the crane-scheduling problem is introduced for all types of RMGC systems that can be solved to optimality with commercial solver software. However, by means of numerical tests, the inapplicability of that approach for practical crane scheduling is revealed, due to not being real-time compliant. The chapter is closed with the crane-routing problem. After introducing that problem and reviewing known solution approaches, different claiming-based routing rules for each type of RMGC system are introduced. In particular, for RMGC systems with crossing capabilities several different routing strategies are presented that mainly differ in the way crane-crossing manoeuvres are conducted.

The sixth chapter is dedicated to the use of simulation for investigating the RMGC-design-planning problem. After providing a brief introduction to the field of simulation analysis and reviewing known simulation studies on container-terminal-planning problems, some basic principles for simulation modelling of RMGC systems at seaport container terminals are summarised. Based on these principles, a new RMGC-simulation model is developed for the special purpose of addressing the research objectives of this work. That simulation model is introduced in Sect. 6.4 by providing a summarising overview on its conceptual design, main features, limitations and assumptions. The model offers extensive parametrisation possibilities and is able to reproduce the highly dynamic, stochastic, real-time environment of an RMGC system at a multi-berth container terminal, over a user-specified period of time in a realistic way.

In Chap. 7, an extensive simulation study on the RMGC-design-planning problem is presented, that is based on the previously introduced simulation model. After the experimental design of the simulation study is introduced, the simulation results are presented, statistically analysed, interpreted and discussed. Firstly, it is dealt with the operational-performance effects of the RMGC design, and thereafter, the influence of selected input factors—including terminal-framework conditions and operational planning strategies—on the operational performance and the design of RMGC systems is addressed. Basically, it is found that the operational performance of RMGC systems is negatively affected by increases of the yard-block dimensions and decreases of the number of cranes deployed per yard block. But increases of the stacking height are found to have more negative effects on the operational performance than increases of the block width and length. While the SRMGC and TriRMGC systems are found to perform worst and best, respectively, the TRMGC system is found to perform slightly better than the DRMGC system, although more flexibility is provided by the latter type of RMGC system. But the performance advantage of the TRMGC system over the DRMGC system is found to decrease with increases of the transshipment factor and the unevenness of the vessel-call pattern, and found to be reversed by deploying more sophisticated routing strategies for the DRMGC system. In addition, the operational performance of RMGC systems is found to improve with increases of the container-dwell time and the crane kinematics as well as with decreases of the yard-block-filling rate. Finally, also the selection and parametrisation of operational planning strategies are found to have substantial effects on the operational performance and the design of RMGC systems. It is found that containers departing by deep-sea vessel should be stacked according to their categories, while containers departing by external truck and feeder vessel should be stacked according to their delivery times. In addition, for the purpose of workload smoothing, all containers should be stacked with respect to the resulting inbound and outbound crane-driving distances and be relocated to better stacking positions afterwards, whenever possible and beneficial. Among the investigated crane-scheduling strategies, well-balanced multi-criteria priority rules are found to perform much better than single-objective priority rules, but scheduling strategies that repeatedly generate (near) optimal sequences of jobs for all cranes, whenever a new vehicle arrives at the yard block, are found to perform even better. On top of that, it is found that cranes with crossing capabilities should be routed in a such way that handover-area blocking is avoided and that trolley movements to the crossing position are reduced and/or used as efficiently as possible.

8.2 Outlook

Considering the estimated positive growth of the worldwide container turnover in the coming years in combination with trends towards increasingly scarce land resources in international port areas, ever stricter legislative limits on noise and exhaust emissions, increasing demands for sustainable terminal designs and operations as well as rising cost pressure on seaport container terminals due to increasing competition among ports, it is expected that increasing numbers of storage systems will be installed at seaport container terminals all around the world, which are densely stacking, automatable and electrically powered at the same time (HPA 2010; Rijsenbrij and Wieschemann 2011). Thus, it can be expected that automated RMGC systems become an increasingly attractive storage system for international seaport container terminals in the coming years—in particular for those terminals that are located in grown industrial port areas of high-labour-cost countries with high environmental standards (Pirhonen 2011; Rijsenbrij and Wieschemann 2011).

Driven by the expected increase in the use of RMGC systems at seaport container terminals, it can be expected that planning problems on the design and the operation of these systems will remain on the research agenda for the foreseeable future. Indeed, despite or because of the findings of the underlying work, there are several options for further developments and investigations on the design and the operation of RMGC systems at seaport container terminals. First of all, several more computational tests can be conducted with the introduced simulation model. The sensitivity analysis may be extended to consider the operational-performance and design effects of further input parameter changes, like the TEU-factor, the distribution of XT arrivals, the applied equipment type for the waterside horizontal transport and the look-ahead times for vehicle arrivals. In addition, some already investigated input parameters may be analysed in some more detail, by testing the operational-performance effects of parameter changes for greater numbers of different RMGC designs and/or by simultaneously changing different input parameters in order to identify mutual interdependencies between these input parameters.

The simulation model can also be used to conduct detailed experiments on the fine tuning of parameter settings for certain operational planning strategies and RMGC designs. But of even greater interest may be the development of alternative planning strategies for the container-stacking, crane-scheduling and crane-routing problems. Future research in this field may be directed to develop container-stacking strategies that take into account uncertain information of truck-appointment systems on arrivals of external trucks, formulating alternative linear programmes of the crane-scheduling problem, developing further (meta) heuristically-based crane-scheduling strategies as well as an integrated optimisation of the container-stacking, crane-scheduling and crane-routing problems.

In this work, it is mainly focused on the influence of the RMGC design on the operational performance of container-storage yards and seaport container terminals as a whole, in terms of vehicle-waiting times in the handover areas of the RMGC yard blocks, whereas the effects of RMGC-design decisions on the cost and area performance are only addressed as a sideline. Thus, future research on the design of RMGC systems may be devoted to a more detailed investigation of the trade-off between the operational performance, the cost performance and the area performance of alternative RMGC designs. Of particular interest might be an empirical investigation on the relative importance and the substitution effects of these three design-planning objectives from the point of view of real-world decision makers at seaport container terminals in order to gain more insights into the RMGC-design-planning process and a deeper understanding of RMGC-design-planning decisions.

Finally, the introduced RMGC-simulation model, that is developed for the purpose of this work, may be modified and/or extended in several ways, thus allowing to address different research questions that are not investigated here. Firstly, the simulation model may be extended to the waterside horizontal-transport subsystem by explicitly modelling the movements and the operations of the waterside horizontal-transport equipment. This would allow to investigate interdependencies between the design and the operation of the waterside horizontal-transport subsystem and the storage subsystem as well as to consider an integrated optimisation of both terminal subsystems. In addition, the simulation model can be modified in such a way that the operations of other crane systems than considered here are modelled. Comparatively simple modifications would, for example, allow the simulation of RTGC systems at seaport container terminals or gantry-crane systems at rail hinterland terminals.

Altogether, the present work does not only provide a variety of insights on the design and the operation of RMGC systems at seaport container terminals, but also various starting points for further research in this area.

Appendix

A.1 Screenshots of Simulation Model

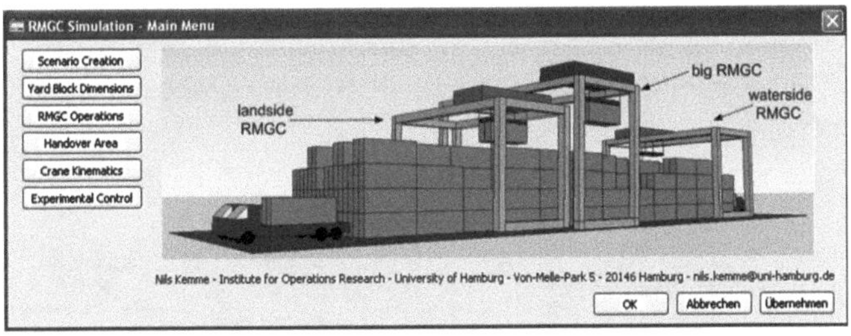

Fig. A.1 Screenshot of RMGC-simulation model—main menu (TriRMGC)

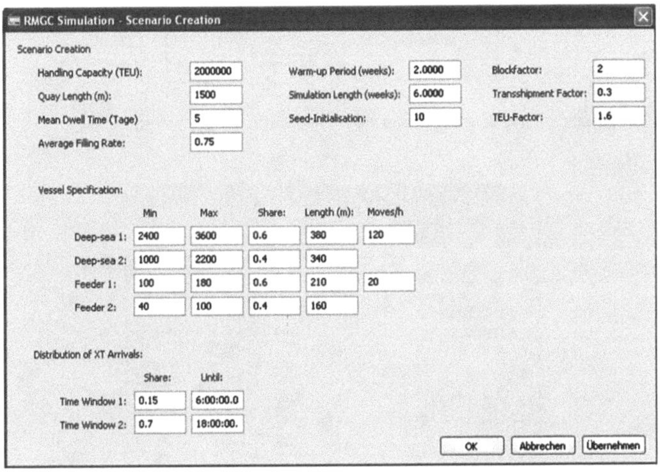

Fig. A.2 Screenshot of RMGC-simulation model—scenario-creation menu

N. Kemme, *Design and Operation of Automated Container Storage Systems*, Contributions to Management Science, DOI 10.1007/978-3-7908-2885-6,

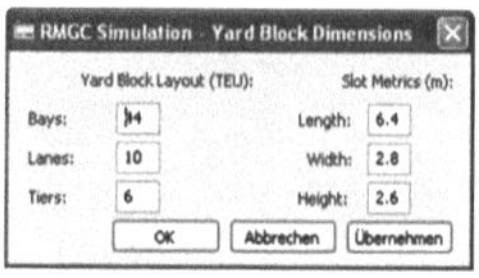

Fig. A.3 Screenshot of RMGC-simulation model—yard-block-dimensions menu

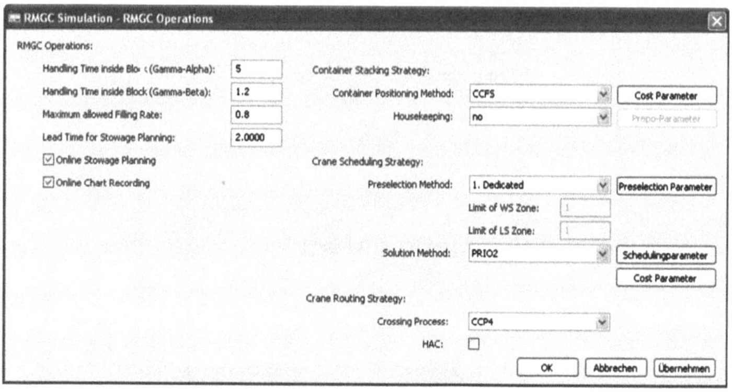

Fig. A.4 Screenshot of RMGC-simulation model—RMGC-operations menu (TriRMGC)

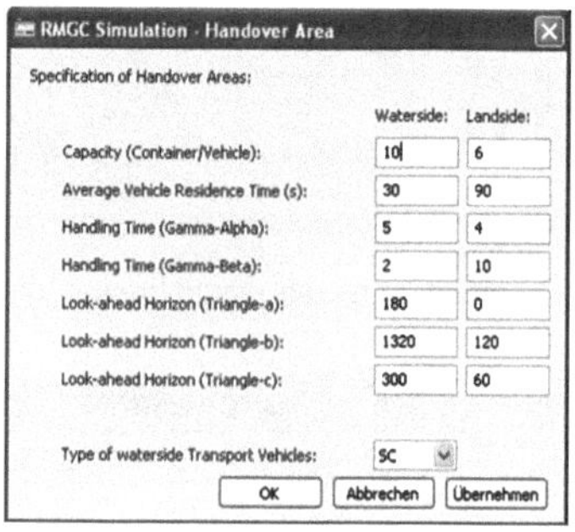

Fig. A.5 Screenshot of RMGC-simulation model—handover-area menu

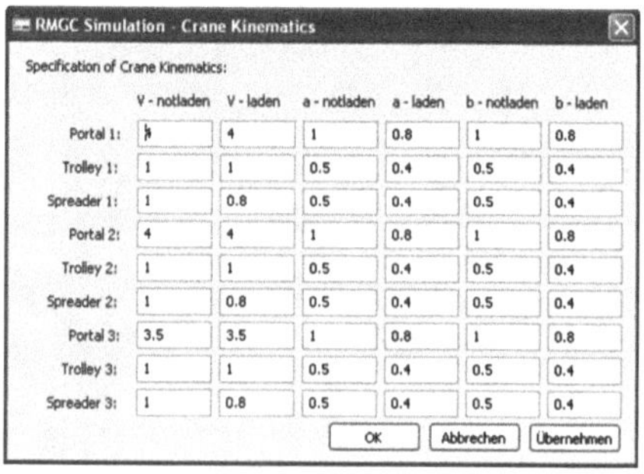

Fig. A.6 Screenshot of RMGC-simulation model—crane-kinematics menu (TriRMGC)

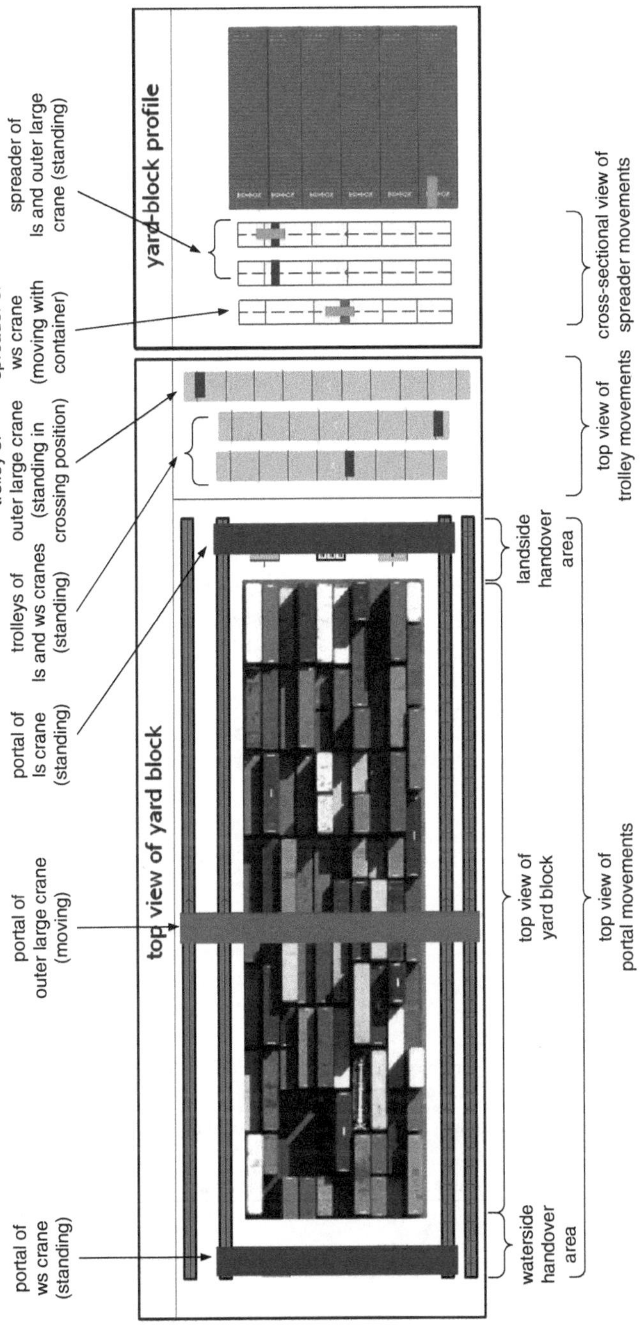

Fig. A.7 Screenshot of RMGC-simulation model—example visualisation of RMGC operations (TriRMGC)

A.2 Default Parameter Settings

Table A.1 Specification of default parameter settings for the simulation study

Parameter	Default setting
Length of simulation period:	$T = 42$ days
Length of warm-up period:	$T^{\text{warm}} = 14$ days
Number of simulation runs per experiment:	$n^{\text{run}} = 10$ runs
Annual terminal throughput:	$\pi^{\text{through}} = 1,250,000$ container
Quay-wall length:	$1,400$ m
Vessel-call pattern:	See Fig. 7.1
Length of deep-sea 1:	380 m
Length of deep-sea 2:	340 m
Moves per call of deep-sea 1:	Rectangular-dist. in $(2,400; 3,600)$
Moves per call of deep-sea 2:	Rectangular-dist. in $(1,000; 2,200)$
Total deep-sea GCR:	120 containers/h
Length of feeder 1:	210 m
Length of feeder 2:	160 m
Moves per call of feeder 1:	Rectangular-dist. in (100; 180)
Moves per call of feeder 2:	Rectangular-dist. in (40; 100)
Total feeder GCR (container/h):	120 containers/h
Share of feeder 1:	60%
Share of feeder 2:	40%
Number of time intervals for XT arrivals:	3
Share of XT arrivals in time interval 1:	15%
Share of XT arrivals in time interval 2:	70%
Share of XT arrivals in time interval 3:	15%
XT-arrival time in interval 1:	Rectangular-dist. in t_j^{hd} =(0:00; 6:00)
XT-arrival time in interval 2:	Rectangular-dist. in t_j^{hd} =(6:00; 18:00)
XT-arrival time in interval 3:	Rectangular-dist. in t_j^{hd} =(18:00; 24:00)
Mean dwell time (all):	Exponential-dist. with $\overline{\delta} = 5$ days
Mean dwell time (import/export):	Exponential-dist. with $\overline{\delta}^{\text{ie}} = 5$ days
Mean dwell time (transshipment):	Exponential-dist. with $\overline{\delta}^{\text{ts}} = 5$ days
Transshipment factor:	$\pi^{\text{ts}} = 30\%$
TEU-factor:	$\pi^{\text{teu}} = 1.6$ TEU
Average filling rate of yard block:	$\pi^{\text{fillavg}} = 75\%$
Maximum allowed filling rate of yard block:	$\pi^{\text{fillmax}} = 80\%$
Horizontal-transport equipment:	SC
Capacity of waterside handover area:	10 containers
Capacity of landside handover area:	6 XTs
SC-residence time in ws handover area:	Exponential-dist. with $\mu^{\text{rtws}} = 30$ s

(continued)

Table A.1 (continued)

Parameter	Default setting
XT-residence time in ls handover area:	Exponential-dist. with $\mu^{\text{rtls}} = 90$ s
Final-handover time at the waterside:	Gamma-dist. with $h^{\text{ws}} = (10.0; 4.47)$ s
Final-handover time at the landside:	Gamma-dist. with $h^{\text{ls}} = (40.0; 20.00)$ s
Final-handover time in the yard block:	Gamma-dist. with $h^{\text{b}} = (6.0; 2.68)$ s
Look-ahead time for ws vehicle arrivals:	Triangular-dist. with $m_j^{\text{lat}} = (180, 300, 1, 320)$ s
Look-ahead time for ls vehicle arrivals:	Triangular-dist. with $m_j^{\text{lat}} = (0, 60, 120)$ s
Length of a single TEU slot:	6.4 m
Width of a single TEU slot:	2.8 m
Height of a single TEU slot:	2.6 m
Applying online stowage planning:	True
Container-positioning method:	CCFS
Applying HHS:	False
Modality-intermingling cost factor:	$\lambda_{\tau(j)}^{\text{mod}} = 1,000.00$ for $\forall\ \tau(j)$
Category-based shuffle-move cost factor:	$\lambda_{\tau(j)}^{\text{cat}} = 100.00$ for $\forall\ \tau(j)$
Retrieval-time-based shuffle-move cost factor:	$\lambda_{\tau(j)}^{\text{rts}} = 0.00$ for $\forall\ \tau(j)$
Workload-smoothing cost factor:	$\lambda_{\tau(j)}^{\text{dist}} = 0.01$ for $\forall\ \tau(j)$
Ground-position cost factor:	$\lambda_{\tau(j)}^{\text{gs}} = 1.00$ for $\forall\ \tau(j)$
Preselection method:	None
Acceptance level for deserving relocation:	$\kappa_{\text{hhs}}^{\text{al}} = 0.5$
Acceptance level for initiating relocation:	$\kappa_{\text{hhs}}^{\text{mci}} = 0.5$
Solution method for crane scheduling:	PRIO2
EDT cost factor for wsin jobs:	$\lambda_{\text{wsin},g}^{\text{edt}} = 7.00$ for $\forall\ g \in G$
EDT cost factor for wsout jobs:	$\lambda_{\text{wsout},g}^{\text{edt}} = \begin{cases} 0.07 & \text{for } g \in \{1, 3\} \\ 7.00 & \text{for } g = 2 \end{cases}$
EDT cost factor for lsin jobs:	$\lambda_{\text{lsin},g}^{\text{edt}} = 7.00$ for $\forall\ g \in G$
EDT cost factor for lsout jobs:	$\lambda_{\text{lsout},g}^{\text{edt}} = 7.00$ for $\forall\ g \in G$
EDT cost factor for wsshu jobs:	$\lambda_{\text{wsshu},g}^{\text{edt}} = 7.00$ for $\forall\ g \in G$
EDT cost factor for lsshu jobs:	$\lambda_{\text{lsshu},g}^{\text{edt}} = 7.00$ for $\forall\ g \in G$
Lateness cost factor for wsin jobs:	$\lambda_{\text{wsin},g}^{\text{late}} = -1.00$ for $\forall\ g \in G$
Lateness cost factor for wsout jobs:	$\lambda_{\text{wsout},g}^{\text{late}} = \begin{cases} -100.00 & \text{for } g \in \{1, 3\} \\ -1.00 & \text{for } g = 2 \end{cases}$
Lateness cost factor for lsin jobs:	$\lambda_{\text{lsin},g}^{\text{late}} = -1.00$ for $\forall\ g \in G$
Lateness cost factor for lsout jobs:	$\lambda_{\text{lsout},g}^{\text{late}} = -1.00$ for $\forall\ g \in G$
Lateness cost factor for wsshu jobs:	$\lambda_{\text{wsshu},g}^{\text{late}} = -1.00$ for $\forall\ g \in G$
Lateness cost factor for lsshu jobs:	$\lambda_{\text{lsshu},g}^{\text{late}} = -1.00$ for $\forall\ g \in G$
Earliness cost factor for wsin jobs:	$\lambda_{\text{wsin},g}^{\text{early}} = 9.00$ for $\forall\ g \in G$
Earliness cost factor for wsout jobs:	$\lambda_{\text{wsout},g}^{\text{early}} = \begin{cases} 0.09 & \text{for } g \in \{1, 3\} \\ 9.00 & \text{for } g = 2 \end{cases}$
Earliness cost factor for lsin jobs:	$\lambda_{\text{lsin},g}^{\text{early}} = 9.00$ for $\forall\ g \in G$

(continued)

Table A.1 (continued)

Parameter	Default setting
Earliness cost factor for lsout jobs:	$\lambda^{\text{early}}_{\text{lsout},g} = 9.00$ for $\forall\ g \in G$
Earliness cost factor for wsshu jobs:	$\lambda^{\text{early}}_{\text{wsshu},g} = 9.00$ for $\forall\ g \in G$
Earliness cost factor for lsshu jobs:	$\lambda^{\text{early}}_{\text{lsshu},g} = 9.00$ for $\forall\ g \in G$
Maximum number of plannable jobs:	$\kappa^{\text{jobs}}_{\text{sfe}} = 5$
Max initially generated solutions:	$\kappa^{\text{itinit}}_{\text{gam}} = 100$
Max initially included solutions:	$\kappa^{\text{noinit}}_{\text{gam}} = 10$
Mutation probability:	$\kappa^{\text{mut}}_{\text{gam}} = 0.05$
Max allowed size of the population:	$\kappa^{\max \Upsilon}_{\text{gam}} = 50$
Max allowed repetitions of inheritance:	$\kappa^{\text{maxit}}_{\text{gam}} = 500$
Aspiration level	$\kappa^{\text{al}}_{\text{gam}} = 0.3$
Crane-routing strategy:	CCP4
Applying HAC:	False
Laden top speed of the crane portal:	$v^{\text{xf}}_g = \begin{cases} 4.0\,\text{m/s} & \text{for } g = 1 \\ 4.0\,\text{m/s} & \text{for } g = 2 \text{ in TriRMGC} \\ 3.5\,\text{m/s} & \text{for } g = 2 \text{ in DRMGC} \\ 3.5\,\text{m/s} & \text{for } g = 3 \text{ in TriRMGC} \end{cases}$
Laden top speed of the trolley:	$v^{\text{yf}}_g = 1.0$ for $\forall\ g \in G$
Laden top speed of the spreader:	$v^{\text{zf}}_g = 0.8$ for $\forall\ g \in G$
Empty top speed of the crane portal:	$v^{\text{xe}}_g = \begin{cases} 4.0\,\text{m/s} & \text{for } g = 1 \\ 4.0\,\text{m/s} & \text{for } g = 2 \text{ in TriRMGC} \\ 3.5\,\text{m/s} & \text{for } g = 2 \text{ in DRMGC} \\ 3.5\,\text{m/s} & \text{for } g = 3 \text{ in TriRMGC} \end{cases}$
Empty top speed of the trolley:	$v^{\text{ye}}_g = 1.0$ for $\forall\ g \in G$
Empty top speed of the spreader:	$v^{\text{ze}}_g = 1.0$ for $\forall\ g \in G$
Laden portal acceleration:	$a^{\text{xf}}_g = 0.8$ for $\forall\ g \in G$
Laden trolley acceleration:	$a^{\text{yf}}_g = 0.4$ for $\forall\ g \in G$
Laden spreader acceleration:	$a^{\text{zf}}_g = 0.4$ for $\forall\ g \in G$
Empty portal acceleration:	$a^{\text{xe}}_g = 1.0$ for $\forall\ g \in G$
Empty trolley acceleration:	$a^{\text{ye}}_g = 0.5$ for $\forall\ g \in G$
Empty spreader acceleration:	$a^{\text{ze}}_g = 0.5$ for $\forall\ g \in G$
Laden portal deceleration:	$b^{\text{xf}}_g = 0.8$ for $\forall\ g \in G$
Laden trolley deceleration:	$b^{\text{yf}}_g = 0.4$ for $\forall\ g \in G$
Laden spreader deceleration:	$b^{\text{zf}}_g = 0.4$ for $\forall\ g \in G$
Empty portal deceleration:	$b^{\text{xe}}_g = 1.0$ for $\forall\ g \in G$
Empty trolley deceleration:	$b^{\text{ye}}_g = 0.5$ for $\forall\ g \in G$
Empty spreader deceleration:	$b^{\text{ze}}_g = 0.5$ for $\forall\ g \in G$

A.3 Additional Regression Results of Yard-Block Dimensions

Table A.2 Results for yard-block-dimension regression of $\overline{\omega}_{\text{total}}^{\text{hr+}}$

(A)		All layouts SRMGC	TRMGC	DRMGC	TriRMGC
β_0	Ø	9.531×10^{-6}	7.261×10^{-6}	4.758×10^{-5}	4.960×10^{-4}
	CI min	6.976×10^{-6}	5.071×10^{-6}	3.455×10^{-5}	3.782×10^{-4}
	CI max	1.302×10^{-5}	1.040×10^{-5}	6.560×10^{-5}	6.503×10^{-4}
	Sig.	0.000	0.000	0.000	0.000
β_1	Ø	2.388	2.290	1.932	1.432
	CI min	2.310	2.201	1.852	1.364
	CI max	2.466	2.380	2.012	1.500
	Beta	0.257	0.271	0.258	0.224
	Sig.	0.000	0.000	0.000	0.000
β_2	Ø	1.803	1.697	1.846	1.461
	CI min	1.745	1.631	1.787	1.411
	CI max	1.860	1.763	1.905	1.511
	Beta	0.263	0.272	0.334	0.310
	Sig.	0.000	0.000	0.000	0.000
β_3	Ø	3.626	3.181	2.761	2.409
	CI min	3.592	3.142	2.726	2.379
	CI max	3.660	3.220	2.796	2.439
	Beta	0.892	0.860	0.842	0.861
	Sig.	0.000	0.000	0.000	0.000
R^2		0.930	0.888	0.886	0.888
Sig. model		0.000	0.000	0.000	0.000
(B)		Layouts with $\overline{\omega}_{\text{total}}^{\text{hr+}} \leq 600$ s			
β_0	Ø	2.316×10^{-3}	5.162×10^{-4}	2.547×10^{-3}	2.229×10^{-3}
	CI min	1.707×10^{-3}	3.898×10^{-4}	2.017×10^{-3}	1.775×10^{-3}
	CI max	3.139×10^{-3}	6.837×10^{-4}	3.215×10^{-3}	2.800×10^{-3}
	Sig.	0.000	0.000	0.000	0.000
β_1	Ø	1.573	1.586	1.331	1.183
	CI min	1.501	1.519	1.276	1.128
	CI max	1.644	1.653	1.387	1.239
	Beta	0.334	0.252	0.254	0.209
	Sig.	0.000	0.000	0.000	0.000
β_2	Ø	1.075	1.120	1.238	1.249
	CI min	1.022	1.070	1.197	1.207
	CI max	1.127	1.169	1.280	1.290
	Beta	0.311	0.242	0.320	0.297
	Sig.	0.000	0.000	0.000	0.000
β_3	Ø	2.528	2.705	2.261	2.268
	CI min	2.489	2.675	2.236	2.244
	CI max	2.568	2.736	2.287	2.293
	Beta	1.008	0.953	0.950	0.907
	Sig.	0.000	0.000	0.000	0.000
R^2		0.876	0.903	0.905	0.907
Sig. model		0.000	0.000	0.000	0.000

Ø: Values of the corresponding regression parameters, CI min/max: minimum and maximum levels of the confidence interval of the corresponding regression parameters on a 95% level, Sig.: significance level for which a t-test of the corresponding regression parameters still yields statistical significance, Beta: regression parameter based on standardised variables, R^2: coefficient of determination, Sig. Model: significance level for which an F-test of the regression model still yields statistical significance

Table A.3 Results for yard-block-dimension regression of $\overline{\omega}_{\mathrm{ls}}^{\mathrm{hr+}}$

		All layouts			
(A)		SRMGC	TRMGC	DRMGC	TriRMGC
β_0	Ø	1.588×10^{-4}	3.591×10^{-4}	8.744×10^{-4}	4.258×10^{-3}
	CI min	1.234×10^{-4}	2.791×10^{-4}	6.864×10^{-4}	3.483×10^{-3}
	CI max	2.045×10^{-4}	4.615×10^{-4}	1.114×10^{-3}	5.206×10^{-3}
	Sig.	0.000	0.000	0.000	0.000
β_1	Ø	2.111	1.796	1.641	1.243
	CI min	2.047	1.733	1.580	1.193
	CI max	2.174	1.859	1.701	1.293
	Beta	0.274	0.264	0.265	0.222
	Sig.	0.000	0.000	0.000	0.000
β_2	Ø	1.590	1.311	1.552	1.238
	CI min	1.544	1.265	1.507	1.201
	CI max	1.637	1.357	1.597	1.275
	Beta	0.280	0.261	0.340	0.300
	Sig.	0.000	0.000	0.000	0.000
β_3	Ø	2.977	2.623	2.301	2.168
	CI min	2.949	2.595	2.274	2.146
	CI max	3.004	2.650	2.327	2.189
	Beta	0.883	0.881	0.848	0.884
	Sig.	0.000	0.000	0.000	0.000
R^2		0.933	0.915	0.905	0.920
Sig. model		0.000	0.000	0.000	0.000
(B)		Layouts with $\overline{\omega}_{\mathrm{ls}}^{\mathrm{hr+}} \leq 600$ s			
β_0	Ø	4.564×10^{-2}	8.844×10^{-3}	3.115×10^{-2}	2.034×10^{-2}
	CI min	3.812×10^{-2}	7.484×10^{-3}	2.732×10^{-2}	1.758×10^{-2}
	CI max	5.464×10^{-2}	1.045×10^{-2}	3.547×10^{-2}	2.354×10^{-2}
	Sig.	0.000	0.000	0.000	0.000
β_1	Ø	1.272	1.286	1.113	0.989
	CI min	1.230	1.247	1.081	0.954
	CI max	1.314	1.326	1.144	1.025
	Beta	0.393	0.257	0.278	0.206
	Sig.	0.000	0.000	0.000	0.000
β_2	Ø	0.833	0.862	1.001	1.014
	CI min	0.802	0.833	0.978	0.987
	CI max	0.864	0.892	1.025	1.040
	Beta	0.351	0.234	0.339	0.285
	Sig.	0.000	0.000	0.000	0.000
β_3	Ø	1.849	2.228	1.820	2.009
	CI min	1.825	2.210	1.806	1.993
	CI max	1.874	2.247	1.835	2.025
	Beta	1.030	0.981	0.981	0.943
	Sig.	0.000	0.000	0.000	0.000
R^2		0.916	0.946	0.951	0.948
Sig. model		0.000	0.000	0.000	0.000

Ø: Values of the corresponding regression parameters, CI min/max: minimum and maximum levels of the confidence interval of the corresponding regression parameters on a 95% level, Sig.: significance level for which a t-test of the corresponding regression parameters still yields statistical significance, Beta: regression parameter based on standardised variables, R^2: coefficient of determination, Sig. Model: significance level for which an F-test of the regression model still yields statistical significance

Table A.4 Results for yard-block-dimension regression of $\overline{\omega}_{\text{ws}}^{\text{hr+}}$

(A)		All layouts: SRMGC	TRMGC	DRMGC	TriRMGC
β_0	Ø	1.342×10^{-9}	1.806×10^{-9}	7.654×10^{-9}	1.214×10^{-6}
	CI min	8.907×10^{-10}	1.033×10^{-9}	4.176×10^{-9}	7.577×10^{-7}
	CI max	2.020×10^{-9}	3.162×10^{-9}	1.403×10^{-8}	1.944×10^{-6}
	Sig.	0.000	0.000	0.000	0.000
β_1	Ø	3.270	3.273	2.816	2.001
	CI min	3.168	3.133	2.665	1.884
	CI max	3.372	3.412	2.967	2.119
	Beta	0.218	0.260	0.227	0.219
	Sig.	0.000	0.000	0.000	0.000
β_2	Ø	2.441	2.460	2.706	2.160
	CI min	2.366	2.357	2.595	2.073
	CI max	2.517	2.563	2.818	2.247
	Beta	0.221	0.266	0.296	0.320
	Sig.	0.000	0.000	0.000	0.000
β_3	Ø	6.077	4.723	4.579	3.313
	CI min	6.032	4.662	4.513	3.262
	CI max	6.122	4.784	4.645	3.365
	Beta	0.926	0.859	0.844	0.827
	Sig.	0.000	0.000	0.000	0.000
R^2		0.954	0.877	0.851	0.835
Sig. model		0.000	0.000	0.000	0.000
(B)		Layouts with $\overline{\omega}_{\text{ws}}^{\text{hr+}} \leq 600$ s			
β_0	Ø	1.277×10^{-8}	2.378×10^{-7}	3.415×10^{-7}	5.477×10^{-6}
	CI min	7.325×10^{-9}	1.368×10^{-7}	1.774×10^{-7}	3.485×10^{-6}
	CI max	2.227×10^{-8}	3.158×10^{-7}	6.567×10^{-7}	8.598×10^{-6}
	Sig.	0.000	0.000	0.000	0.000
β_1	Ø	2.962	2.456	2.230	1.746
	CI min	2.832	2.324	2.074	1.636
	CI max	3.092	2.588	2.386	1.857
	Beta	0.280	0.242	0.217	0.206
	Sig.	0.000	0.000	0.000	0.000
β_2	Ø	2.084	1.807	2.134	1.952
	CI min	1.988	1.710	2.018	1.870
	CI max	2.180	1.905	2.250	2.034
	Beta	0.270	0.242	0.280	0.311
	Sig.	0.000	0.000	0.000	0.000
β_3	Ø	5.611	4.201	4.132	3.182
	CI min	5.541	4.141	4.061	3.133
	CI max	5.681	4.261	4.203	3.230
	Beta	1.030	0.924	0.891	0.854
	Sig.	0.000	0.000	0.000	0.000
R^2		0.913	0.853	0.800	0.834
Sig. model		0.000	0.000	0.000	0.000

Ø: Values of the corresponding regression parameters, CI min/max: minimum and maximum levels of the confidence interval of the corresponding regression parameters on a 95% level, Sig.: significance level for which a t-test of the corresponding regression parameters still yields statistical significance, Beta: regression parameter based on standardised variables, R^2: coefficient of determination, Sig. Model: significance level for which an F-test of the regression model still yields statistical significance

Table A.5 Results for yard-block-dimension regression of $\overline{\omega}^{hr+}_{wsout}$

(A)		All layouts SRMGC	TRMGC	DRMGC	TriRMGC
β_0	Ø	4.105×10^{-9}	4.048×10^{-9}	1.529×10^{-8}	2.415×10^{-6}
	CI min	2.708×10^{-9}	2.319×10^{-9}	8.259×10^{-8}	1.506×10^{-6}
	CI max	6.217×10^{-9}	7.066×10^{-9}	2.828×10^{-8}	3.871×10^{-6}
	Sig.	0.000	0.000	0.000	0.000
β_1	Ø	3.185	3.242	2.806	1.993
	CI min	3.081	3.103	2.652	1.876
	CI max	3.289	3.381	2.959	2.111
	Beta	0.213	0.258	0.225	0.217
	Sig.	0.000	0.000	0.000	0.000
β_2	Ø	2.375	2.438	2.698	2.152
	CI min	2.298	2.336	2.585	2.065
	CI max	2.451	2.541	2.811	2.239
	Beta	0.215	0.263	0.293	0.318
	Sig.	0.000	0.000	0.000	0.000
β_3	Ø	6.064	4.732	4.600	3.329
	CI min	6.018	4.671	4.533	3.278
	CI max	6.109	4.793	4.667	3.381
	Beta	0.927	0.861	0.843	0.829
	Sig.	0.000	0.000	0.000	0.000
R^2		0.952	0.877	0.848	0.835
Sig. model		0.000	0.000	0.000	0.000
(B)		Layouts with $\overline{\omega}^{hr+}_{wsout} \leq 600$ s			
β_0	Ø	1.527×10^{-7}	3.057×10^{-6}	3.545×10^{-6}	4.725×10^{-5}
	CI min	8.986×10^{-8}	1.816×10^{-6}	1.818×10^{-6}	3.108×10^{-5}
	CI max	2.591×10^{-7}	5.153×10^{-6}	6.914×10^{-6}	7.177×10^{-5}
	Sig.	0.000	0.000	0.000	0.000
β_1	Ø	2.689	2.198	2.007	1.523
	CI min	2.565	2.074	1.848	1.421
	CI max	2.813	2.322	2.166	1.624
	Beta	0.295	0.246	0.217	0.198
	Sig.	0.000	0.000	0.000	0.000
β_2	Ø	1.846	1.504	1.859	1.712
	CI min	1.755	1.413	1.741	1.636
	CI max	1.937	1.596	1.978	1.787
	Beta	0.276	0.228	0.272	0.300
	Sig.	0.000	0.000	0.000	0.000
β_3	Ø	5.219	3.880	3.834	3.015
	CI min	5.147	3.822	3.758	2.970
	CI max	5.291	3.938	3.909	3.060
	Beta	1.025	(0.939)	0.891	0.881
	Sig.	0.000	0.000	0.000	0.000
R^2		0.905	0.846	0.765	0.837
Sig. model		0.000	0.000	0.000	0.000

Ø: Values of the corresponding regression parameters, CI min/max: minimum and maximum levels of the confidence interval of the corresponding regression parameters on a 95% level, Sig.: significance level for which a t-test of the corresponding regression parameters still yields statistical significance, Beta: regression parameter based on standardised variables, R^2: coefficient of determination, Sig. Model: significance level for which an F-test of the regression model still yields statistical significance

A.4 Additional Vessel-Call Patterns

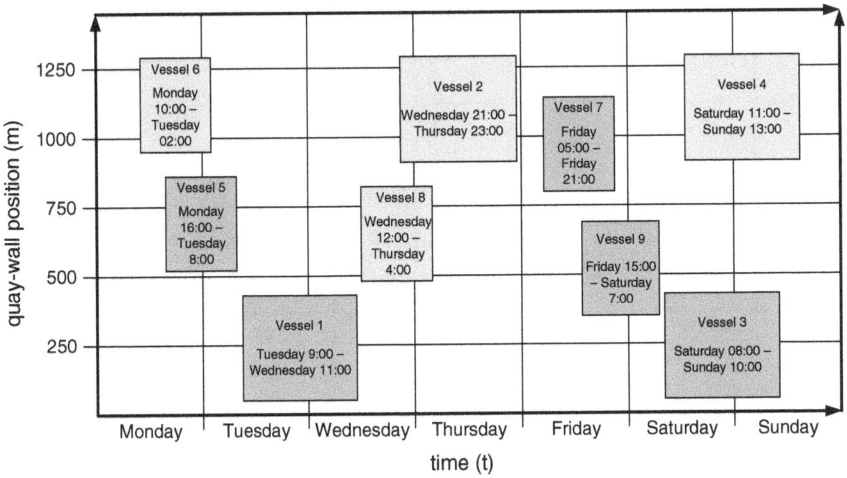

Fig. A.8 Schematic illustration of alternative vessel-call pattern VCP2 (with vessels 1,3,5,7 and 9 delivering and collecting containers to/from the yard block under scrutiny, resulting in a VCP-overlapping time of 12 h)

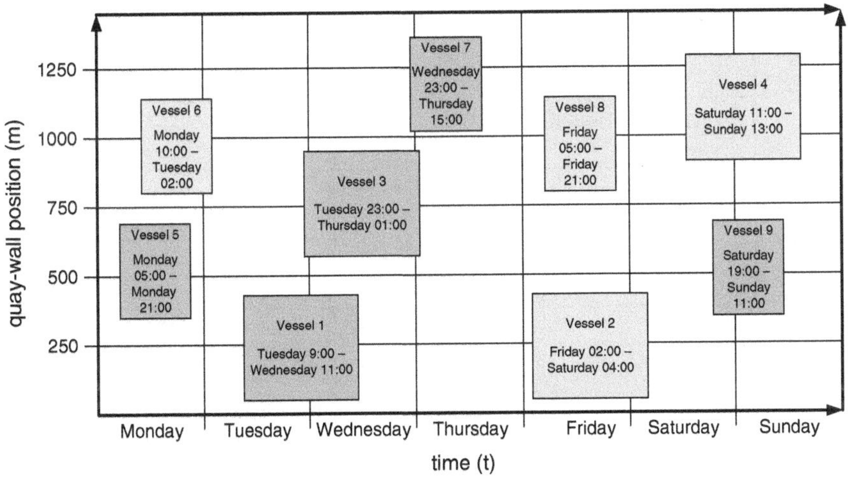

Fig. A.9 Schematic illustration of alternative vessel-call pattern VCP3 (with vessels 1,3,5,7 and 9 delivering and collecting containers to/from the yard block under scrutiny, resulting in a VCP-overlapping time of 24 h)

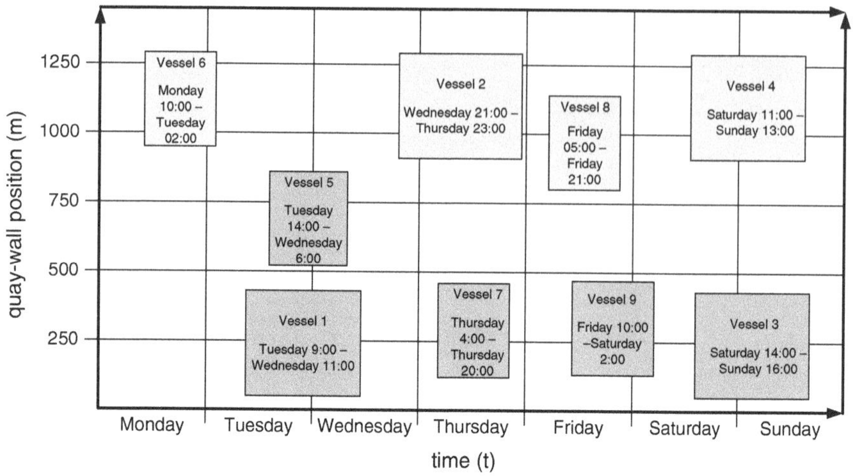

Fig. A.10 Schematic illustration of alternative vessel-call pattern VCP4 (with vessels 1,3,5,7 and 9 delivering and collecting containers to/from the yard block under scrutiny, resulting in a VCP-overlapping time of 32 h)

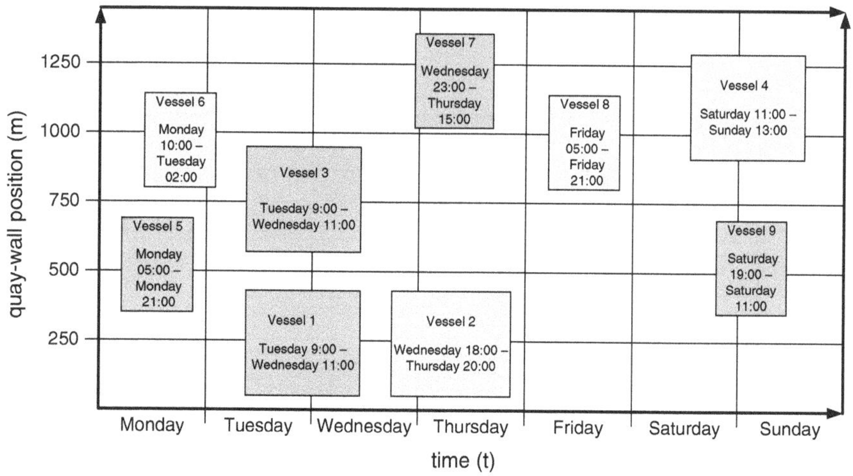

Fig. A.11 Schematic illustration of alternative vessel-call pattern VCP5 (with vessels 1,3,5,7 and 9 delivering and collecting containers to/from the yard block under scrutiny, resulting in a VCP-overlapping time of 52 h)

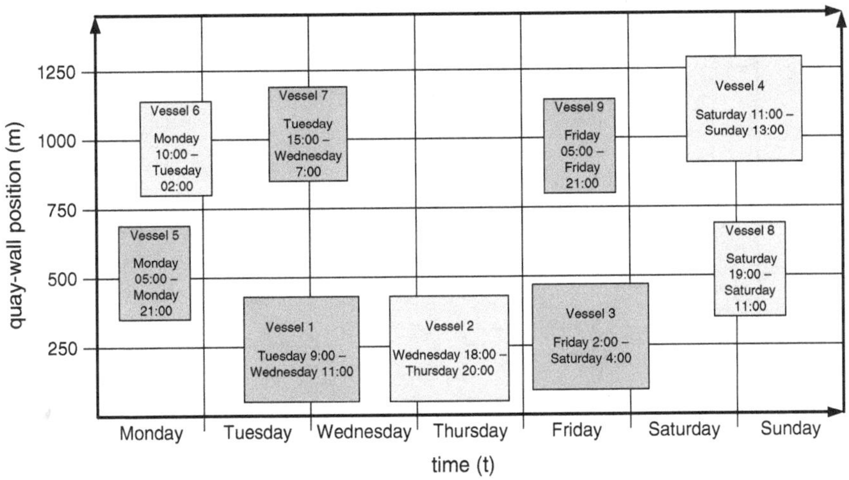

Fig. A.12 Schematic illustration of alternative vessel-call pattern VCP6 (with vessels 1,3,5,7 and 9 delivering and collecting containers to/from the yard block under scrutiny, resulting in a VCP-overlapping time of 64 h)

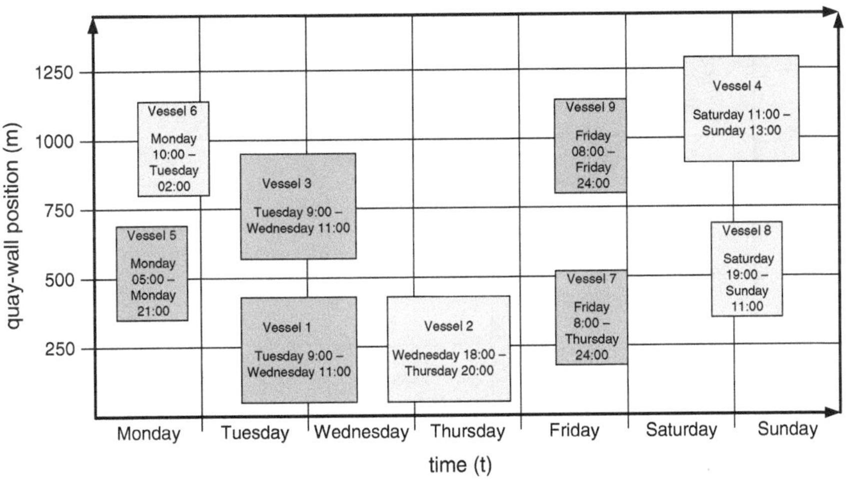

Fig. A.13 Schematic illustration of alternative vessel-call pattern VCP7 (with vessels 1,3,5,7 and 9 delivering and collecting containers to/from the yard block under scrutiny, resulting in a VCP-overlapping time of 84 h)

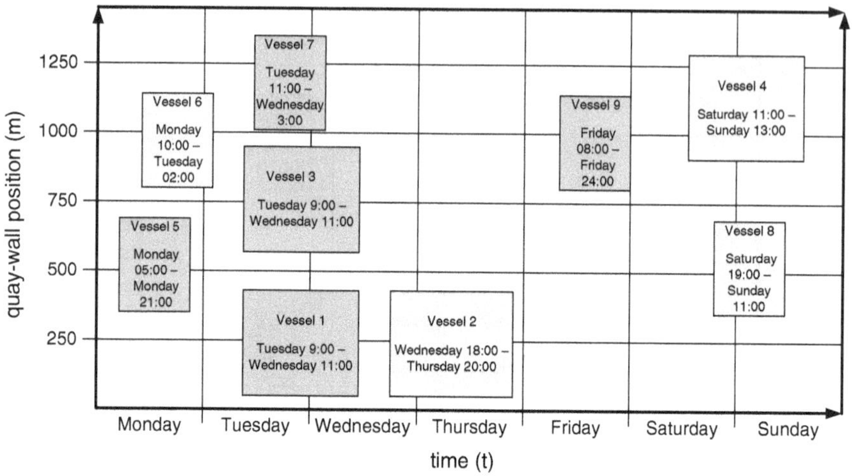

Fig. A.14 Schematic illustration of alternative vessel-call pattern VCP8 (with vessels 1,3,5,7 and 9 delivering and collecting containers to/from the yard block under scrutiny, resulting in a VCP-overlapping time of 116 h)

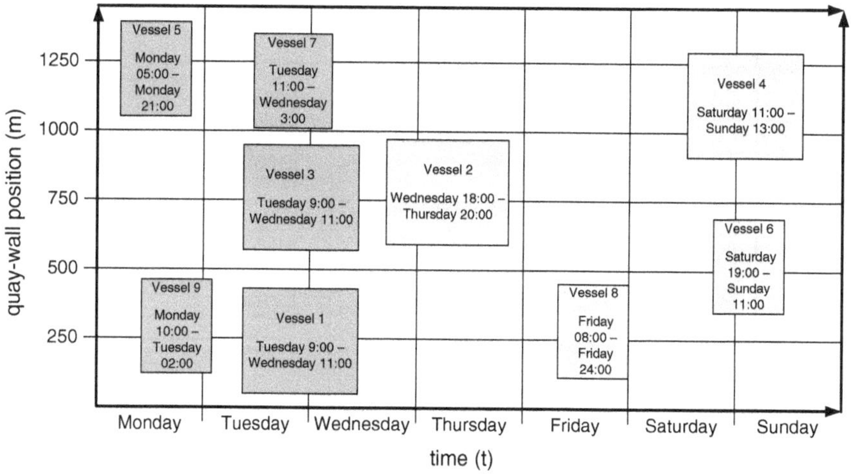

Fig. A.15 Schematic illustration of alternative vessel-call pattern VCP9 (with vessels 1,3,5,7 and 9 delivering and collecting containers to/from the yard block under scrutiny, resulting in a VCP-overlapping time of 138 h)

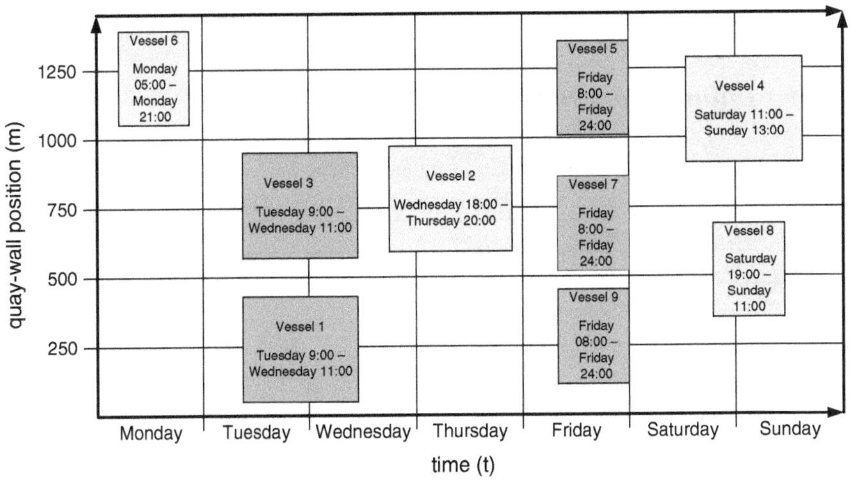

Fig. A.16 Schematic illustration of alternative vessel-call pattern VCP10 (with vessels 1,3,5,7 and 9 delivering and collecting containers to/from the yard block under scrutiny, resulting in a VCP-overlapping time of 148 h)

A.5 Additional Simulation Results of Sensitivity Analysis

A.5.1 Influence of the Filling Rate

Table A.6 Influence of the planned average yard-block-filling rate (π^{fillavg}) on the mean vehicle-waiting time ($\overline{\overline{\omega}}^{\text{hr+}}_{\text{total}}$) for selected yard-block layouts and all types of RMGC systems

Filling rate		Yard-block layout								
π^{fillavg}	π^{fillmax}	Small	Low	Narrow	Short	Medium	Long	Wide	High	Big
Resulting $\overline{\overline{\omega}}^{\text{hr+}}_{\text{total}}$ with the SRMGC system (s)										
55%	80%	25.32	39.18	79.14	74.82	94.98	144.24	129.78	1,027.26	2,016.78
60%	80%	26.46	40.08	90.12	79.86	116.88	196.98	167.16	1,375.74	2,350.44
65%	80%	27.18	41.34	100.44	91.62	139.98	323.64	266.64	1,699.86	2,706.84
70%	80%	29.46	41.82	106.92	101.22	174.24	445.80	376.44	1,806.72	2,887.02
75%	**80%**	**28.26**	**41.28**	**117.06**	**100.44**	**198.96**	**561.06**	**484.56**	**1,861.32**	**3,269.94**
80%	85%	28.08	43.14	116.52	106.50	271.32	698.10	614.70	1,913.70	3,436.08
85%	90%	27.84	42.96	125.34	117.36	281.04	831.00	706.14	1,911.00	3,613.20
90%	95%	31.32	46.20	126.90	110.88	300.54	880.44	821.94	1,962.42	3,826.02
95%	100%	29.94	44.40	130.74	120.18	365.70	1,007.82	858.66	2,055.72	4,132.14
Resulting $\overline{\overline{\omega}}^{\text{hr+}}_{\text{total}}$ with the TRMGC system (s)										
55%	80%	9.30	13.02	32.88	31.98	37.68	45.90	43.50	128.34	483.24
60%	80%	9.48	13.14	35.46	32.82	40.92	51.42	47.40	193.50	782.58
65%	80%	9.24	13.50	37.74	34.68	44.70	58.20	53.28	256.80	1,160.34
70%	80%	9.06	13.38	37.98	35.10	46.14	60.66	57.90	276.18	1,394.34
75%	**80%**	**8.82**	**13.44**	**38.16**	**35.58**	**48.30**	**67.44**	**61.98**	**304.08**	**1,567.38**
80%	85%	9.42	13.50	38.22	34.98	49.26	74.46	67.86	320.94	1,656.54
85%	90%	9.06	13.38	37.80	34.56	49.26	77.94	70.98	345.36	1,723.98
90%	95%	9.42	13.74	37.62	33.78	49.74	83.88	70.44	361.32	1,859.94
95%	100%	9.48	13.98	37.86	34.80	49.62	83.82	79.26	368.64	1,838.58
Resulting $\overline{\overline{\omega}}^{\text{hr+}}_{\text{total}}$ with the DRMGC system (s)										
55%	80%	13.14	20.28	45.42	47.40	57.48	69.06	67.74	160.68	541.26
60%	80%	14.34	21.90	49.38	48.72	61.32	75.78	74.58	235.32	847.20
65%	80%	13.14	22.26	52.08	52.32	65.52	81.30	82.14	298.80	1,219.38
70%	80%	14.04	23.46	53.46	53.10	67.20	86.88	86.88	328.02	1,434.96
75%	**80%**	**13.86**	**23.58**	**53.82**	**54.36**	**69.24**	**88.86**	**88.86**	**360.18**	**1,607.82**
80%	85%	14.64	23.28	53.52	55.14	71.40	100.62	98.82	371.16	1,689.72
85%	90%	14.94	24.78	55.56	54.24	72.24	102.42	108.30	401.52	1,697.52
90%	95%	14.10	24.72	52.50	53.04	71.64	105.06	107.94	452.10	1,783.50
95%	100%	14.04	25.02	53.34	54.36	73.38	108.66	117.54	463.86	1,830.42
Resulting $\overline{\overline{\omega}}^{\text{hr+}}_{\text{total}}$ with the TriRMGC system (s)										
55%	80%	9.36	12.78	28.32	29.82	34.44	39.30	40.92	83.94	165.24
60%	80%	9.60	13.08	30.18	31.02	35.70	41.34	42.06	97.80	254.04
65%	80%	9.30	12.72	31.02	32.16	37.38	43.44	45.84	115.62	414.72
70%	80%	9.06	12.78	31.44	33.06	37.92	45.72	46.38	118.80	502.62
75%	**80%**	**8.82**	**12.48**	**31.26**	**31.86**	**37.98**	**46.86**	**46.86**	**117.54**	**574.98**
80%	85%	9.06	12.48	30.48	31.38	39.06	48.96	47.82	120.78	629.58
85%	90%	9.30	12.54	31.08	31.56	38.52	47.82	49.32	130.38	644.88
90%	95%	9.00	12.42	29.94	30.06	37.26	48.54	48.72	143.52	697.56
95%	100%	8.58	12.66	29.58	30.42	37.86	48.72	51.48	148.14	719.52

Table A.7 Influence of the planned average yard-block-filling rate (π^{fillavg}) on the vehicle-waiting time per waterside retrieval job ($\overline{\overline{\omega}}^{\text{hr+}}_{\text{wsout}}$) for selected yard-block layouts and all types of RMGC systems

Filling rate		Yard-block layout								
π^{fillavg}	π^{fillmax}	Small	Low	Narrow	Short	Medium	Long	Wide	High	Big
Resulting $\overline{\overline{\omega}}^{\text{hr+}}_{\text{wsout}}$ with the SRMGC system (s)										
55%	80%	2.58	4.38	20.58	17.88	32.82	77.34	58.98	1,611.30	2,838.06
60%	80%	3.18	5.16	36.78	26.16	60.96	155.52	117.72	2,229.96	3,410.40
65%	80%	3.18	5.82	47.22	40.14	99.24	372.96	275.94	2,859.90	4,013.76
70%	80%	3.66	5.34	59.64	57.72	152.22	592.50	492.54	3,046.92	4,337.16
75%	**80%**	**3.24**	**5.52**	**78.00**	**56.04**	**198.72**	**789.12**	**671.58**	**3,180.30**	**4,959.72**
80%	85%	2.76	7.20	75.78	69.42	326.46	1,084.02	909.54	3,336.84	5,337.12
85%	90%	3.18	7.20	96.24	86.64	341.52	1,346.16	1,106.88	3,317.40	5,649.78
90%	95%	6.00	7.92	96.06	76.86	376.50	1,416.72	1,319.22	3,408.54	5,980.80
95%	100%	4.56	8.10	106.14	91.68	481.08	1,660.98	1,374.90	3,589.20	6,562.62
Resulting $\overline{\overline{\omega}}^{\text{hr+}}_{\text{wsout}}$ with the TRMGC system (s)										
55%	80%	3.66	5.04	8.70	8.16	10.68	14.70	14.16	114.60	833.94
60%	80%	3.36	4.68	10.38	8.70	12.84	21.90	16.98	252.30	1,450.32
65%	80%	2.82	5.88	13.20	12.12	19.80	28.62	22.44	376.26	2,230.80
70%	80%	3.12	5.22	13.50	11.76	20.22	32.22	32.16	414.96	2,655.24
75%	**80%**	**2.28**	**4.14**	**15.06**	**13.20**	**25.80**	**48.48**	**42.12**	**486.30**	**3,019.80**
80%	85%	3.06	4.74	17.82	13.38	28.02	61.20	52.14	515.76	3,229.62
85%	90%	2.76	4.62	17.10	15.30	30.42	72.72	60.54	574.32	3,362.70
90%	95%	3.84	5.70	18.48	14.58	31.98	90.48	61.74	584.34	3,734.16
95%	100%	4.26	6.12	19.56	17.22	33.72	92.04	83.04	615.12	3,671.40
Resulting $\overline{\overline{\omega}}^{\text{hr+}}_{\text{wsout}}$ with the DRMGC system (s)										
55%	80%	2.88	4.32	10.68	12.00	16.62	20.04	19.74	127.92	740.40
60%	80%	3.72	4.08	12.72	13.86	19.02	28.32	27.84	271.32	1,291.86
65%	80%	2.16	4.92	14.58	14.28	24.06	34.80	34.44	392.28	1,992.24
70%	80%	3.12	5.04	17.94	16.44	26.88	41.34	44.94	440.46	2,371.92
75%	**80%**	**2.76**	**5.34**	**20.10**	**18.72**	**30.78**	**47.46**	**46.26**	**510.54**	**2,758.62**
80%	85%	3.42	5.46	21.00	22.26	34.62	67.68	66.24	521.40	2,905.20
85%	90%	3.18	5.88	24.42	22.02	36.18	73.50	84.24	591.78	2,916.78
90%	95%	3.42	6.84	22.08	22.62	38.94	80.04	81.96	680.04	3,177.48
95%	100%	3.42	7.08	22.80	24.48	43.08	85.26	101.22	690.60	3,261.54
Resulting $\overline{\overline{\omega}}^{\text{hr+}}_{\text{wsout}}$ with the TriRMGC system (s)										
55%	80%	2.46	3.54	7.86	8.64	11.22	13.98	14.76	44.70	134.58
60%	80%	3.00	5.10	10.20	8.94	13.08	15.24	15.36	66.42	281.10
65%	80%	2.76	5.40	10.80	10.32	13.92	16.92	18.42	98.22	577.26
70%	80%	3.60	5.76	10.32	12.84	14.82	18.54	20.58	105.84	738.84
75%	**80%**	**2.22**	**5.34**	**12.90**	**12.54**	**16.32**	**19.68**	**20.94**	**109.68**	**883.26**
80%	85%	2.88	4.98	12.84	13.08	17.88	25.08	24.48	115.44	994.62
85%	90%	3.84	5.46	13.62	13.98	17.40	24.66	27.06	131.94	1,027.32
90%	95%	3.66	5.28	12.54	13.26	18.84	27.42	26.28	158.28	1,141.98
95%	100%	3.12	6.60	15.48	13.74	19.32	28.74	31.08	161.34	1,177.08

Table A.8 Influence of the planned average yard-block-filling rate (π^{fillavg}) on the mean crane-waiting time in the handover areas ($\overline{\overline{\omega}}_{\text{total}}^{\text{hr}-}$) for selected yard-block layouts and all types of RMGC systems

Filling rate		Yard-block layout								
π^{fillavg}	π^{fillmax}	Small	Low	Narrow	Short	Medium	Long	Wide	High	Big
Resulting $\overline{\overline{\omega}}_{\text{total}}^{\text{hr}-}$ with the SRMGC system (s)										
55%	80%	140.34	111.84	83.64	85.62	63.06	42.24	45.12	22.44	8.64
60%	80%	137.70	109.56	78.36	79.32	56.76	35.46	39.06	18.30	8.52
65%	80%	134.34	104.40	72.12	74.64	50.76	30.30	33.12	15.84	7.80
70%	80%	131.46	99.18	69.18	70.74	45.18	26.70	29.10	14.40	7.68
75%	**80%**	**124.38**	**94.92**	**63.84**	**67.26**	**41.52**	**22.86**	**25.80**	**14.64**	**7.08**
80%	85%	120.42	90.54	65.88	66.42	42.78	23.52	26.04	12.96	6.24
85%	90%	121.62	88.80	63.66	65.40	41.88	22.56	24.96	12.66	5.88
90%	95%	121.50	90.00	62.76	66.00	40.98	21.84	25.26	12.06	5.88
95%	100%	121.14	89.70	62.10	65.10	40.38	22.20	24.78	12.90	5.04
Resulting $\overline{\overline{\omega}}_{\text{total}}^{\text{hr}-}$ with the TRMGC system (s)										
55%	80%	151.86	128.76	104.88	106.44	88.44	70.44	72.30	51.06	17.76
60%	80%	146.76	124.02	101.46	102.84	83.10	64.32	67.20	44.40	14.76
65%	80%	144.30	120.78	96.60	98.46	77.58	59.58	61.56	40.38	12.72
70%	80%	142.20	116.58	92.34	95.22	71.88	54.60	57.24	38.52	11.64
75%	**80%**	**135.84**	**112.32**	**87.84**	**91.26**	**67.86**	**50.28**	**53.40**	**38.58**	**10.56**
80%	85%	133.74	109.56	89.94	89.64	69.06	50.46	52.44	36.96	11.04
85%	90%	134.58	106.02	87.48	89.16	68.10	49.26	50.88	36.18	10.02
90%	95%	133.14	108.30	85.38	87.30	66.66	48.66	52.26	36.42	10.50
95%	100%	134.52	106.62	84.36	87.18	66.00	48.78	50.82	37.20	10.26
Resulting $\overline{\overline{\omega}}_{\text{total}}^{\text{hr}-}$ with the DRMGC system (s)										
55%	80%	151.62	133.26	112.38	112.02	95.28	78.78	78.90	57.60	22.38
60%	80%	148.44	131.16	108.48	107.70	89.82	72.60	73.20	50.88	18.96
65%	80%	146.46	124.80	105.18	103.08	84.30	68.04	66.66	46.44	15.96
70%	80%	143.88	122.40	99.96	98.82	78.60	62.46	62.16	43.86	14.34
75%	**80%**	**139.32**	**117.48**	**95.28**	**95.46**	**75.18**	**57.24**	**57.66**	**44.52**	**12.60**
80%	85%	136.68	112.44	95.88	95.04	75.78	58.20	57.84	43.20	11.88
85%	90%	136.08	111.24	94.92	93.90	74.04	57.84	56.70	42.00	11.28
90%	95%	136.86	114.06	93.78	92.34	73.20	57.00	57.06	42.18	11.34
95%	100%	134.52	112.50	91.32	90.96	71.94	56.22	55.92	42.48	10.68
Resulting $\overline{\overline{\omega}}_{\text{total}}^{\text{hr}-}$ with the TriRMGC system (s)										
55%	80%	155.10	135.72	118.32	117.12	103.38	88.74	87.96	71.10	36.18
60%	80%	152.16	133.62	114.84	114.00	97.98	82.86	82.50	65.46	31.08
65%	80%	148.74	130.68	109.56	110.04	92.58	79.14	77.34	60.90	27.84
70%	80%	145.68	126.36	107.16	105.96	87.60	73.20	72.60	57.66	24.84
75%	**80%**	**140.40**	**121.98**	**103.44**	**101.10**	**84.00**	**68.22**	**68.64**	**58.38**	**23.88**
80%	85%	138.54	117.96	103.38	101.28	84.36	69.60	69.12	57.06	23.04
85%	90%	139.98	116.22	101.22	100.26	82.50	68.52	68.28	55.20	22.68
90%	95%	139.80	118.68	100.92	98.64	82.02	68.34	67.02	54.66	22.74
95%	100%	140.04	117.00	98.04	97.98	80.70	67.14	66.24	55.56	22.68

Table A.9 Influence of the planned average yard-block-filling rate (π^{fillavg}) on the mean crane-empty-movement time per job ($\overline{\overline{m}}^{\text{xye}}_{\text{total}}$) for selected yard-block layouts and all types of RMGC systems

Filling rate		Yard-block layout								
π^{fillavg}	π^{fillmax}	Small	Low	Narrow	Short	Medium	Long	Wide	High	Big
Resulting $\overline{\overline{m}}^{\text{xye}}_{\text{total}}$ with the SRMGC system (s)										
55%	80%	26.59	32.45	28.01	23.79	27.91	31.49	27.78	24.11	28.10
60%	80%	26.57	32.27	27.54	23.49	27.30	30.85	27.54	23.81	27.89
65%	80%	26.24	31.99	27.26	23.32	27.00	30.19	26.87	23.51	27.85
70%	80%	26.20	31.99	27.22	23.23	26.80	29.80	26.63	23.58	27.68
75%	**80%**	**26.05**	**31.87**	**26.97**	**23.22**	**26.63**	**29.48**	**26.57**	**23.73**	**27.72**
80%	85%	26.02	31.54	27.09	23.03	26.55	29.55	26.40	23.71	27.59
85%	90%	25.89	31.39	27.17	23.16	26.62	29.60	26.43	23.77	27.57
90%	95%	25.67	31.23	27.17	23.24	26.63	29.53	26.61	23.93	27.55
95%	100%	25.85	31.39	27.09	23.22	26.67	29.60	26.37	23.99	27.50
Resulting $\overline{\overline{m}}^{\text{xye}}_{\text{total}}$ with the TRMGC system (s)										
55%	80%	22.59	27.89	33.37	29.60	33.29	37.36	33.76	37.03	40.08
60%	80%	22.65	27.81	33.51	29.92	33.86	37.68	33.85	37.31	40.68
65%	80%	23.00	28.05	33.48	29.95	33.88	37.88	34.33	37.26	40.79
70%	80%	22.87	28.30	33.80	30.12	33.99	38.07	34.40	37.34	40.60
75%	**80%**	**23.34**	**28.35**	**33.76**	**30.25**	**34.07**	**38.12**	**34.64**	**37.21**	**40.77**
80%	85%	23.35	28.46	33.82	30.27	34.07	38.39	34.74	37.02	40.56
85%	90%	23.66	28.82	33.98	30.23	34.09	38.47	34.67	37.15	40.39
90%	95%	23.64	29.05	34.10	30.31	34.29	38.51	34.73	36.85	40.54
95%	100%	23.80	28.97	33.90	30.29	34.29	38.44	34.71	36.94	40.47
Resulting $\overline{\overline{m}}^{\text{xye}}_{\text{total}}$ with the DRMGC system (s)										
55%	80%	52.41	66.31	66.04	65.86	68.66	69.48	68.72	57.89	51.09
60%	80%	53.55	67.43	65.44	65.28	67.25	67.56	66.49	54.66	49.05
65%	80%	54.06	67.84	65.46	64.66	65.14	65.60	64.32	52.95	47.17
70%	80%	55.81	69.09	64.01	63.46	63.99	63.94	62.51	52.45	46.11
75%	**80%**	**55.77**	**69.14**	**62.73**	**62.89**	**62.78**	**61.85**	**60.88**	**52.25**	**45.15**
80%	85%	56.66	68.14	62.86	63.20	62.10	62.07	60.37	52.22	45.03
85%	90%	56.53	70.17	63.34	62.72	62.47	61.22	59.89	51.88	44.90
90%	95%	57.56	69.93	63.01	62.43	62.25	60.97	59.87	52.14	44.90
95%	100%	56.01	69.01	62.82	61.76	61.45	60.53	58.99	51.82	44.67
Resulting $\overline{\overline{m}}^{\text{xye}}_{\text{total}}$ with the TriRMGC system (s)										
55%	80%	48.20	61.44	68.96	68.81	73.14	74.97	74.22	70.81	66.38
60%	80%	50.08	63.58	69.78	69.06	72.06	73.98	73.65	69.47	63.92
65%	80%	49.89	63.80	69.39	69.45	71.72	73.41	73.07	67.57	61.53
70%	80%	50.75	65.47	69.33	69.22	71.18	72.21	71.55	66.56	60.68
75%	**80%**	**51.55**	**65.81**	**69.11**	**68.63**	**70.12**	**70.81**	**70.15**	**66.70**	**60.22**
80%	85%	53.51	66.37	68.34	69.03	70.68	70.99	69.97	66.74	60.30
85%	90%	53.45	66.18	68.70	68.82	69.89	70.70	69.88	66.26	60.16
90%	95%	52.99	67.09	68.55	68.01	70.02	70.82	69.75	66.11	60.00
95%	100%	52.84	66.03	67.92	67.78	69.04	70.20	68.99	65.70	60.15

Table A.10 Influence of the planned average yard-block-filling rate (π^{fillavg}) on the mean crane-interference time per job ($\overline{\overline{m}}^{\text{cit}}_{\text{total}}$) for selected yard-block layouts and all types of RMGC systems

Filling rate		Yard-block layout								
π^{fillavg}	π^{fillmax}	Small	Low	Narrow	Short	Medium	Long	Wide	High	Big
Resulting $\overline{\overline{m}}^{\text{cit}}_{\text{total}}$ with the SRMGC system (s)										
55%	80%	0.00	0.00	0.00	0.00	0.00	0.00	0.00	0.00	0.00
60%	80%	0.00	0.00	0.00	0.00	0.00	0.00	0.00	0.00	0.00
65%	80%	0.00	0.00	0.00	0.00	0.00	0.00	0.00	0.00	0.00
70%	80%	0.00	0.00	0.00	0.00	0.00	0.00	0.00	0.00	0.00
75%	**80%**	**0.00**	**0.00**	**0.00**	**0.00**	**0.00**	**0.00**	**0.00**	**0.00**	**0.00**
80%	85%	0.00	0.00	0.00	0.00	0.00	0.00	0.00	0.00	0.00
85%	90%	0.00	0.00	0.00	0.00	0.00	0.00	0.00	0.00	0.00
90%	95%	0.00	0.00	0.00	0.00	0.00	0.00	0.00	0.00	0.00
95%	100%	0.00	0.00	0.00	0.00	0.00	0.00	0.00	0.00	0.00
Resulting $\overline{\overline{m}}^{\text{cit}}_{\text{total}}$ with the TRMGC system (s)										
55%	80%	1.38	1.60	10.27	11.09	10.08	10.14	10.33	19.20	18.96
60%	80%	1.54	1.64	11.27	11.42	11.00	10.85	11.03	19.84	19.95
65%	80%	1.89	1.87	11.54	11.90	11.69	11.42	11.67	20.20	20.64
70%	80%	2.02	2.02	11.87	12.28	11.94	11.74	12.08	20.03	20.71
75%	**80%**	**2.22**	**2.10**	**11.92**	**12.42**	**12.16**	**11.92**	**12.14**	**19.43**	**20.71**
80%	85%	2.63	2.44	11.91	12.51	11.97	12.14	12.34	19.29	20.58
85%	90%	2.88	2.77	11.89	12.14	11.76	12.11	12.18	19.14	20.38
90%	95%	3.02	3.08	11.65	11.97	11.70	11.99	11.98	18.58	20.26
95%	100%	3.10	3.02	11.58	12.06	11.72	11.82	11.96	18.65	19.92
Resulting $\overline{\overline{m}}^{\text{cit}}_{\text{total}}$ with the DRMGC system (s)										
55%	80%	27.23	34.51	37.71	42.01	39.94	36.24	39.87	32.73	23.93
60%	80%	28.88	36.58	37.25	41.22	38.98	34.87	37.99	30.18	22.75
65%	80%	29.09	37.30	37.52	40.90	37.29	33.29	35.99	28.85	21.38
70%	80%	31.47	37.83	36.27	39.90	36.14	31.55	34.77	28.50	20.89
75%	**80%**	**31.09**	**38.13**	**35.30**	**39.74**	**35.31**	**29.73**	**32.78**	**28.21**	**20.21**
80%	85%	32.10	37.95	35.51	39.80	34.93	30.54	32.93	28.34	20.08
85%	90%	31.80	39.43	36.00	39.48	35.00	29.80	32.67	27.91	19.97
90%	95%	32.68	39.88	35.46	39.08	34.47	29.68	32.38	28.22	19.99
95%	100%	31.71	38.77	35.49	38.73	34.25	29.06	31.96	27.90	19.76
Resulting $\overline{\overline{m}}^{\text{cit}}_{\text{total}}$ with the TriRMGC system (s)										
55%	80%	26.88	35.57	46.91	51.02	50.71	48.34	51.65	52.88	44.94
60%	80%	29.49	37.97	48.79	51.93	50.52	47.75	51.47	51.90	43.69
65%	80%	28.77	38.76	48.34	52.55	50.13	47.25	50.68	50.72	42.21
70%	80%	30.45	40.17	48.52	53.10	49.95	45.87	49.73	49.75	41.80
75%	**80%**	**31.02**	**40.31**	**48.66**	**52.32**	**49.18**	**44.71**	**47.95**	**49.43**	**41.62**
80%	85%	33.42	41.20	47.83	52.83	50.03	45.23	48.26	49.61	41.38
85%	90%	34.10	41.17	48.45	52.74	48.60	44.85	48.55	49.03	41.06
90%	95%	33.16	42.39	47.84	52.01	48.75	44.91	47.91	48.79	41.22
95%	100%	33.30	41.26	47.55	51.56	47.98	44.42	47.73	48.74	40.96

Table A.11 Influence of the planned average yard-block-filling rate (π^{fillavg}) on the crane workload during the simulation horizon in terms of performed jobs ($\overline{|J|}$) for selected yard-block layouts and all types of RMGC systems

Filling rate		Yard-block layout								
π^{fillavg}	π^{fillmax}	Small	Low	Narrow	Short	Medium	Long	Wide	High	Big
Resulting $\overline{|J|}$ with the SRMGC system (jobs)										
55%	80%	1,487.0	2,541.8	4,922.2	5,141.9	6,529.4	7,911.8	8,125.2	11,608.8	12,580.4
60%	80%	1,624.6	2,772.4	5,573.2	5,716.8	7,328.8	8,834.7	8,984.9	12,492.2	13,038.9
65%	80%	1,754.6	3,009.2	6,128.5	6,320.7	8,087.6	9,687.7	9,942.6	13,129.6	13,313.3
70%	80%	1,817.5	3,147.2	6,430.8	6,686.8	8,446.6	10,240.0	10,477.6	13,259.0	13,483.3
75%	**80%**	**1,871.8**	**3,208.8**	**6,596.5**	**6,792.8**	**8,683.4**	**10,466.3**	**10,776.3**	**13,369.4**	**13,711.1**
80%	85%	2,044.3	3,473.8	6,831.3	7,120.2	9,194.4	11,017.6	11,314.7	13,406.7	13,928.2
85%	90%	2,203.3	3,722.2	6,941.6	7,328.5	9,325.5	11,242.1	11,513.9	13,505.3	14,048.9
90%	95%	2,309.7	4,016.3	6,999.0	7,263.0	9,434.7	11,350.4	11,713.4	13,532.1	14,251.4
95%	100%	2,351.7	4,096.4	7,082.2	7,437.2	9,598.3	11,530.7	11,926.1	13,638.2	14,467.0
Resulting $\overline{|J|}$ with the TRMGC system (jobs)										
55%	80%	1,479.9	2,532.2	4,912.1	5,161.8	6,496.0	7,913.9	8,125.4	12,185.3	17,422.2
60%	80%	1,616.2	2,783.8	5,572.0	5,710.6	7,303.8	8,851.0	9,030.8	13,790.1	18,906.3
65%	80%	1,752.1	3,005.4	6,125.7	6,306.6	8,102.6	9,796.0	10,037.5	14,732.7	20,045.4
70%	80%	1,839.1	3,158.9	6,409.9	6,602.8	8,499.1	10,291.1	10,564.0	14,982.2	20,648.4
75%	**80%**	**1,903.5**	**3,224.1**	**6,592.4**	**6,857.8**	**8,784.5**	**10,615.3**	**10,900.6**	**15,170.8**	**21,104.9**
80%	85%	2,049.1	3,477.2	6,829.8	7,182.1	9,364.2	11,397.7	11,693.7	15,286.5	21,340.9
85%	90%	2,213.6	3,750.2	7,066.9	7,249.7	9,413.0	11,628.1	11,926.1	15,420.9	21,498.0
90%	95%	2,327.9	3,981.4	7,074.1	7,310.4	9,581.4	11,678.0	12,055.4	15,391.4	21,699.4
95%	100%	2,392.4	4,089.5	7,184.6	7,461.1	9,613.8	11,906.9	12,282.0	15,540.8	21,707.3
Resulting $\overline{|J|}$ with the DRMGC system (jobs)										
55%	80%	1,483.9	2,533.2	4,931.6	5,136.4	6,505.7	7,921.1	8,085.9	12,168.3	17,308.1
60%	80%	1,615.4	2,781.1	5,577.2	5,701.1	7,271.7	8,891.7	9,029.9	13,740.7	18,802.9
65%	80%	1,747.6	3,003.1	6,072.7	6,292.3	8,053.6	9,761.4	9,996.9	14,599.7	20,093.6
70%	80%	1,836.1	3,167.1	6,407.6	6,632.8	8,497.7	10,275.8	10,528.5	14,967.3	20,721.0
75%	**80%**	**1,901.9**	**3,222.4**	**6,623.5**	**6,834.0**	**8,713.7**	**10,605.3**	**10,893.6**	**15,175.5**	**21,213.5**
80%	85%	2,044.8	3,467.9	6,877.5	7,188.9	9,322.2	11,333.9	11,621.5	15,135.7	21,550.4
85%	90%	2,215.9	3,742.2	7,021.5	7,242.4	9,396.9	11,609.7	11,830.0	15,325.5	21,540.0
90%	95%	2,337.5	3,975.9	7,070.8	7,341.0	9,590.0	11,602.0	12,067.5	15,440.1	21,614.3
95%	100%	2,365.7	4,114.8	7,180.9	7,490.5	9,660.4	11,978.2	12,264.3	15,674.4	21,805.9
Resulting $\overline{|J|}$ with the TriRMGC system (jobs)										
55%	80%	1,480.8	2,532.6	4,915.2	5,116.9	6,532.3	7,907.2	8,094.1	12,205.3	18,035.3
60%	80%	1,617.7	2,786.8	5,508.7	5,704.3	7,325.0	8,903.1	9,057.1	13,709.7	20,244.4
65%	80%	1,751.0	3,008.1	6,082.2	6,331.5	8,074.5	9,724.5	10,051.8	14,767.2	22,130.5
70%	80%	1,832.0	3,163.1	6,456.6	6,672.0	8,544.2	10,280.1	10,495.0	15,142.7	22,866.3
75%	**80%**	**1,907.0**	**3,249.5**	**6,614.4**	**6,831.8**	**8,732.5**	**10,583.9**	**10,895.8**	**15,192.1**	**23,097.9**
80%	85%	2,057.3	3,471.7	6,848.5	7,148.9	9,278.5	11,388.3	11,637.0	15,249.9	23,441.7
85%	90%	2,218.3	3,720.8	7,006.1	7,290.1	9,473.2	11,674.1	11,885.3	15,560.0	23,575.6
90%	95%	2,324.1	3,986.0	7,054.1	7,300.3	9,637.2	11,661.4	12,133.5	15,758.0	23,829.9
95%	100%	2,387.4	4,124.8	7,203.4	7,445.4	9,662.8	11,959.7	12,316.2	15,846.5	23,868.9

Table A.12 Influence of the planned average yard-block-filling rate (π^{fillavg}) on the container accessibility ($\overline{\overline{\psi}}$), in terms of the mean number of shuffle moves per retrieval job, for selected yard-block layouts and all types of RMGC systems

Filling rate		Yard-block layout								
π^{fillavg}	π^{fillmax}	Small	Low	Narrow	Short	Medium	Long	Wide	High	Big
Resulting $\overline{\overline{\psi}}$ with the SRMGC system (jobs)										
55%	80%	0.266	0.257	0.920	0.948	0.910	0.884	0.893	1.574	1.166
60%	80%	0.282	0.267	1.020	1.002	0.989	0.960	0.948	1.628	1.166
65%	80%	0.308	0.288	1.084	1.082	1.061	1.042	1.026	1.661	1.141
70%	80%	0.311	0.301	1.117	1.125	1.099	1.074	1.070	1.635	1.132
75%	**80%**	**0.322**	**0.300**	**1.135**	**1.120**	**1.103**	**1.083**	**1.083**	**1.606**	**1.144**
80%	85%	0.363	0.329	1.117	1.112	1.115	1.098	1.088	1.559	1.148
85%	90%	0.389	0.365	1.099	1.120	1.099	1.083	1.084	1.541	1.146
90%	95%	0.391	0.386	1.087	1.083	1.083	1.058	1.070	1.489	1.130
95%	100%	0.399	0.387	1.077	1.098	1.073	1.047	1.066	1.479	1.150
Resulting $\overline{\overline{\psi}}$ with the TRMGC system (jobs)										
55%	80%	0.259	0.261	0.917	0.954	0.893	0.889	0.884	1.631	1.512
60%	80%	0.275	0.269	1.034	1.007	0.985	0.953	0.962	1.780	1.585
65%	80%	0.305	0.280	1.095	1.083	1.071	1.045	1.045	1.826	1.642
70%	80%	0.322	0.292	1.121	1.099	1.102	1.079	1.080	1.812	1.671
75%	**80%**	**0.324**	**0.296**	**1.127**	**1.130**	**1.130**	**1.097**	**1.090**	**1.762**	**1.675**
80%	85%	0.368	0.334	1.116	1.134	1.134	1.131	1.127	1.743	1.667
85%	90%	0.388	0.376	1.123	1.102	1.109	1.112	1.111	1.718	1.659
90%	95%	0.389	0.386	1.096	1.091	1.099	1.094	1.087	1.662	1.636
95%	100%	0.403	0.384	1.090	1.091	1.076	1.077	1.082	1.650	1.598
Resulting $\overline{\overline{\psi}}$ with the DRMGC system (jobs)										
55%	80%	0.265	0.262	0.930	0.940	0.897	0.892	0.871	1.629	1.509
60%	80%	0.275	0.267	1.034	1.003	0.973	0.967	0.962	1.771	1.571
65%	80%	0.300	0.278	1.070	1.080	1.055	1.037	1.036	1.802	1.641
70%	80%	0.317	0.299	1.119	1.108	1.100	1.077	1.070	1.807	1.677
75%	**80%**	**0.320**	**0.297**	**1.137**	**1.118**	**1.107**	**1.093**	**1.087**	**1.753**	**1.673**
80%	85%	0.366	0.329	1.125	1.130	1.134	1.113	1.108	1.712	1.672
85%	90%	0.396	0.373	1.117	1.109	1.104	1.108	1.103	1.689	1.630
90%	95%	0.400	0.382	1.109	1.095	1.105	1.088	1.087	1.663	1.605
95%	100%	0.380	0.391	1.078	1.091	1.082	1.088	1.085	1.662	1.576
Resulting $\overline{\overline{\psi}}$ with the TriRMGC system (jobs)										
55%	80%	0.268	0.264	0.919	0.931	0.906	0.887	0.884	1.644	1.554
60%	80%	0.279	0.267	1.000	1.001	0.989	0.973	0.960	1.755	1.669
65%	80%	0.302	0.282	1.079	1.095	1.058	1.028	1.044	1.836	1.768
70%	80%	0.320	0.298	1.128	1.122	1.108	1.083	1.062	1.819	1.793
75%	**80%**	**0.325**	**0.298**	**1.122**	**1.123**	**1.113**	**1.092**	**1.090**	**1.763**	**1.758**
80%	85%	0.368	0.331	1.122	1.123	1.121	1.126	1.113	1.728	1.734
85%	90%	0.381	0.364	1.113	1.115	1.114	1.112	1.113	1.718	1.711
90%	95%	0.392	0.377	1.103	1.081	1.101	1.090	1.093	1.704	1.673
95%	100%	0.393	0.393	1.082	1.092	1.075	1.080	1.087	1.679	1.644

A.5.2 *Influence of the Container-Dwell Time*

Table A.13 Influence of the mean container-dwell time ($\bar{\delta}$) on the mean vehicle-waiting time ($\overline{\overline{\omega}}^{hr+}_{total}$) for selected yard-block layouts and all types of RMGC systems

	Yard-block layout								
$\bar{\delta}$	Small	Low	Narrow	Short	Medium	Long	Wide	High	Big
Resulting $\overline{\overline{\omega}}^{hr+}_{total}$ with the SRMGC system (s)									
3.0	33.54	50.58	339.78	282.24	938.16	1,642.38	1,471.26	3,092.70	3,159.48
3.5	33.78	47.76	209.58	177.72	611.16	1,378.02	1,256.40	2,877.00	3,092.76
4.0	31.74	44.70	155.34	134.04	379.68	1,061.52	945.12	2,595.78	3,142.56
4.5	27.78	44.16	126.30	117.24	267.18	764.52	645.06	2,239.50	3,200.16
5.0	**28.26**	**41.28**	**117.06**	**100.44**	**198.96**	**561.06**	**484.56**	**1,861.32**	**3,269.94**
5.5	26.28	39.36	104.10	89.64	166.62	387.18	321.00	1,565.46	3,207.66
6.0	24.42	38.34	94.26	85.50	135.00	280.08	241.44	1,308.06	3,108.84
6.5	24.24	37.20	88.98	78.06	119.52	228.48	197.52	1,066.68	3,049.56
7.0	24.30	35.16	81.78	77.58	114.66	186.66	156.00	888.30	3,043.62
7.5	23.10	33.78	76.44	71.88	103.44	160.68	144.66	712.38	2,751.18
8.0	21.06	34.02	74.52	69.36	96.36	144.36	129.30	629.64	2,440.56
Resulting $\overline{\overline{\omega}}^{hr+}_{total}$ with the TRMGC system (s)									
3.0	10.50	16.50	54.00	48.96	79.32	192.12	149.58	1,276.92	3,397.80
3.5	10.08	15.12	46.50	42.84	63.00	114.36	101.28	898.08	2,611.74
4.0	9.78	14.70	44.16	39.72	55.32	87.36	81.06	597.42	2,112.60
4.5	8.88	13.68	40.92	37.68	50.22	75.24	66.12	423.54	1,809.24
5.0	**8.82**	**13.44**	**38.16**	**35.58**	**48.30**	**67.44**	**61.98**	**304.08**	**1,567.38**
5.5	9.06	13.08	36.66	34.20	45.60	61.44	54.00	223.08	1,227.66
6.0	8.64	12.60	35.28	33.42	42.18	56.76	51.78	182.22	1,011.36
6.5	8.88	12.12	34.02	31.74	40.92	53.04	48.72	161.52	846.48
7.0	8.70	11.94	32.52	30.60	40.02	49.14	45.72	133.50	675.66
7.5	8.40	11.64	32.58	29.22	37.02	47.52	43.50	121.20	506.04
8.0	8.10	11.76	31.38	29.28	35.82	45.72	41.64	114.36	409.26
Resulting $\overline{\overline{\omega}}^{hr+}_{total}$ with the DRMGC system (s)									
3.0	18.42	32.46	71.82	75.84	110.40	196.32	198.66	1,264.86	2,525.46
3.5	16.80	28.92	66.30	65.16	88.20	140.28	151.44	910.68	2,214.72
4.0	15.48	25.98	62.28	60.66	80.88	113.76	113.82	657.00	1,917.90
4.5	14.22	24.06	55.98	57.30	72.54	98.64	94.80	477.24	1,798.68
5.0	**13.86**	**23.58**	**53.82**	**54.36**	**69.24**	**88.86**	**88.86**	**360.18**	**1,607.82**
5.5	12.90	21.60	51.48	52.14	65.94	84.90	81.54	277.50	1,339.56
6.0	12.24	19.86	48.54	48.60	63.78	78.54	77.40	218.82	1,118.16
6.5	11.64	18.54	45.90	45.72	58.80	73.20	73.02	181.38	929.52
7.0	11.70	19.02	43.50	44.76	56.34	70.56	68.16	162.24	749.76
7.5	11.46	17.88	42.78	43.74	52.68	66.60	67.32	146.52	590.10
8.0	10.80	17.82	40.86	41.10	50.70	62.70	64.56	138.36	489.66
Resulting $\overline{\overline{\omega}}^{hr+}_{total}$ with the TriRMGC system (s)									
3.0	10.20	15.12	38.10	39.66	50.04	63.60	65.40	460.08	1,270.56
3.5	9.36	14.40	35.58	36.84	45.18	56.04	58.68	292.14	1,143.84
4.0	9.48	13.38	34.32	35.70	41.94	52.56	53.22	212.58	913.14
4.5	8.46	12.84	32.40	33.60	39.54	48.96	48.54	154.62	737.40
5.0	**8.82**	**12.48**	**31.26**	**31.86**	**37.98**	**46.86**	**46.86**	**117.54**	**574.98**
5.5	8.40	12.30	29.88	31.08	36.18	43.74	43.68	107.76	426.66
6.0	8.22	12.36	29.04	30.48	35.40	42.78	42.30	94.86	330.06
6.5	8.70	11.34	28.62	28.92	34.26	40.08	40.68	85.92	262.68
7.0	8.04	11.64	27.18	29.28	32.82	39.00	38.94	84.84	221.10
7.5	8.52	10.98	27.06	28.20	32.04	37.56	37.74	78.78	178.38
8.0	7.50	10.74	27.48	27.36	31.38	36.96	36.84	72.60	155.64

Table A.14 Influence of the mean container-dwell time ($\overline{\delta}$) on the vehicle-waiting time per waterside retrieval job ($\overline{\omega}^{hr+}_{wsout}$) for selected yard-block layouts and all types of RMGC systems

	Yard-block layout								
$\overline{\delta}$	Small	Low	Narrow	Short	Medium	Long	Wide	High	Big
Resulting $\overline{\omega}^{hr+}_{wsout}$ with the SRMGC system (s)									
3.0	4.56	8.04	427.44	337.74	1,407.78	2,493.96	2,195.46	4,903.56	4,251.66
3.5	5.76	6.42	218.64	162.84	891.42	2,114.04	1,935.30	4,701.12	4,237.32
4.0	3.96	5.58	135.72	103.68	483.42	1,638.72	1,450.44	4,354.14	4,518.72
4.5	3.06	6.18	85.38	80.40	313.68	1,156.26	938.76	3,814.44	4,707.42
5.0	**3.24**	**5.52**	**78.00**	**56.04**	**198.72**	**789.12**	**671.58**	**3,180.30**	**4,959.72**
5.5	2.58	5.34	62.94	43.86	149.04	508.74	398.64	2,728.14	5,036.58
6.0	3.96	4.38	47.70	39.72	97.68	330.00	265.86	2,245.20	4,923.90
6.5	2.52	4.44	44.22	33.36	76.26	241.50	195.00	1,793.46	4,903.32
7.0	2.70	3.00	36.54	29.64	72.24	177.18	130.38	1,477.08	5,012.70
7.5	2.28	3.18	30.54	24.54	60.12	131.70	113.70	1,159.80	4,546.68
8.0	1.56	3.36	26.82	26.40	49.20	109.08	92.16	1,005.60	4,110.72
Resulting $\overline{\omega}^{hr+}_{wsout}$ with the TRMGC system (s)									
3.0	4.32	7.50	33.96	26.88	70.92	325.20	219.36	2,533.26	7,995.18
3.5	3.96	6.36	24.12	19.26	39.42	135.00	111.36	1,725.84	5,888.28
4.0	3.30	6.24	20.40	17.10	31.20	80.76	72.42	1,088.40	4,474.86
4.5	2.40	5.16	17.28	15.54	26.22	59.52	45.18	708.12	3,585.96
5.0	**2.28**	**4.14**	**15.06**	**13.20**	**25.80**	**48.48**	**42.12**	**486.30**	**3,019.80**
5.5	3.42	4.98	12.30	11.82	20.16	39.54	28.44	323.22	2,263.32
6.0	2.34	5.70	12.54	11.70	17.94	31.74	29.70	244.86	1,863.72
6.5	2.70	4.80	11.52	11.70	17.64	27.00	24.72	214.14	1,532.58
7.0	2.22	4.56	10.44	11.10	16.74	22.68	21.12	152.28	1,217.64
7.5	1.50	3.36	9.72	8.16	13.86	21.60	18.54	132.96	880.26
8.0	1.62	3.66	9.72	9.12	13.20	20.64	16.50	120.54	677.40
Resulting $\overline{\omega}^{hr+}_{wsout}$ with the DRMGC system (s)									
3.0	3.90	9.66	34.20	38.70	78.00	217.50	223.44	2,201.34	4,695.36
3.5	3.96	7.44	28.92	26.64	48.06	121.02	139.44	1,544.76	3,904.44
4.0	2.52	6.24	24.24	23.46	38.88	78.66	84.96	1,064.82	3,237.84
4.5	2.94	6.06	20.64	21.18	30.84	59.46	57.66	715.56	3,028.08
5.0	**2.76**	**5.34**	**20.10**	**18.72**	**30.78**	**47.46**	**46.26**	**510.54**	**2,758.62**
5.5	2.46	5.16	16.86	19.92	26.58	42.36	38.70	362.34	2,288.82
6.0	2.40	3.78	16.26	14.16	26.46	35.94	36.66	268.08	1,896.06
6.5	1.68	3.78	15.78	14.76	22.20	30.48	32.70	194.64	1,534.38
7.0	2.40	4.86	12.96	14.46	18.72	31.32	27.54	166.08	1,221.06
7.5	1.50	4.02	12.00	12.36	18.90	27.96	26.58	141.00	929.88
8.0	1.50	3.06	11.34	12.06	16.44	24.36	26.70	127.68	726.18
Resulting $\overline{\omega}^{hr+}_{wsout}$ with the TriRMGC system (s)									
3.0	4.62	8.10	15.24	17.46	23.88	33.48	34.92	695.10	2,100.18
3.5	3.30	8.58	15.78	15.66	20.58	25.50	29.52	396.36	1,904.58
4.0	3.00	6.42	14.40	15.24	17.58	25.32	25.98	262.74	1,478.52
4.5	2.28	6.24	13.86	14.16	16.38	23.22	21.78	168.96	1,177.74
5.0	**2.22**	**5.34**	**12.90**	**12.54**	**16.32**	**19.68**	**20.94**	**109.68**	**883.26**
5.5	2.76	5.40	10.56	10.74	14.10	18.00	18.24	97.98	618.30
6.0	2.40	5.16	10.68	10.80	14.52	18.96	17.52	78.24	455.04
6.5	2.58	3.72	9.66	10.92	13.32	15.18	17.52	66.36	332.70
7.0	1.80	4.14	7.98	9.96	12.90	17.04	16.26	65.40	277.26
7.5	2.16	2.70	8.40	9.72	11.40	13.92	14.46	58.56	198.42
8.0	1.56	2.64	9.06	8.82	10.92	13.68	14.58	50.10	162.24

Table A.15 Influence of the mean container-dwell time ($\overline{\delta}$) on the mean crane-waiting time in the handover areas ($\overline{\overline{\omega}}^{hr-}_{total}$) for selected yard-block layouts and all types of RMGC systems

	Yard-block layout								
$\overline{\delta}$	Small	Low	Narrow	Short	Medium	Long	Wide	High	Big
Resulting $\overline{\overline{\omega}}^{hr-}_{total}$ with the SRMGC system (s)									
3.0	99.48	62.82	28.38	30.60	15.12	9.90	10.26	7.26	4.62
3.5	107.58	72.54	38.34	40.80	20.04	11.70	11.52	7.20	5.46
4.0	114.24	80.82	47.82	49.32	27.54	14.64	16.32	8.82	5.88
4.5	117.30	88.74	56.88	58.44	34.68	17.82	19.32	10.50	6.66
5.0	**124.38**	**94.92**	**63.84**	**67.26**	**41.52**	**22.86**	**25.80**	**14.64**	**7.08**
5.5	128.82	100.26	71.76	73.32	47.22	29.34	32.34	15.96	7.26
6.0	131.88	104.52	77.16	78.72	54.36	34.68	37.92	20.34	7.68
6.5	136.26	111.12	83.70	85.98	61.20	40.32	43.62	25.68	7.98
7.0	141.06	112.68	88.32	88.32	66.66	45.84	50.28	30.84	8.40
7.5	144.42	116.94	93.90	95.28	72.36	51.36	55.02	35.22	9.78
8.0	144.06	119.64	98.82	99.18	76.20	56.88	59.52	39.12	10.74
Resulting $\overline{\overline{\omega}}^{hr-}_{total}$ with the TRMGC system (s)									
3.0	114.60	82.86	53.34	55.44	36.54	21.90	24.24	13.14	7.44
3.5	122.40	92.04	65.10	66.06	44.76	28.62	30.36	17.10	7.80
4.0	127.74	99.12	73.08	73.62	53.82	36.90	39.24	23.64	9.06
4.5	133.92	105.96	82.02	82.62	61.44	43.68	45.54	30.06	9.42
5.0	**135.84**	**112.32**	**87.84**	**91.26**	**67.86**	**50.28**	**53.40**	**38.58**	**10.56**
5.5	140.34	116.46	94.32	96.60	74.52	57.30	59.52	43.20	13.44
6.0	139.32	121.68	100.02	101.82	80.82	62.70	65.46	50.10	15.84
6.5	146.46	127.08	105.90	106.26	85.98	67.92	70.74	55.62	19.92
7.0	150.48	128.22	107.88	109.98	91.38	73.38	75.30	61.56	23.82
7.5	151.74	129.48	112.86	113.04	95.64	77.46	80.70	65.34	28.44
8.0	152.94	133.68	117.60	118.86	99.42	83.58	85.68	69.60	32.04
Resulting $\overline{\overline{\omega}}^{hr-}_{total}$ with the DRMGC system (s)									
3.0	118.62	89.40	60.00	59.22	40.92	27.24	26.82	14.82	6.06
3.5	125.46	98.46	72.12	69.90	50.28	34.92	33.78	20.82	6.66
4.0	129.30	106.38	80.10	79.68	59.34	43.62	43.02	28.74	8.16
4.5	134.28	111.72	89.16	86.82	67.38	50.76	50.22	35.70	9.90
5.0	**139.32**	**117.48**	**95.28**	**95.46**	**75.18**	**57.24**	**57.66**	**44.52**	**12.60**
5.5	140.28	121.26	102.18	102.00	80.58	65.22	63.90	49.74	16.38
6.0	143.22	124.62	106.86	105.60	87.66	70.80	70.62	56.94	19.44
6.5	149.58	131.16	112.50	112.02	92.88	75.72	76.44	62.46	24.96
7.0	149.64	132.18	114.42	114.54	97.08	82.74	81.42	67.56	29.58
7.5	152.64	134.40	119.82	117.24	103.20	86.34	86.46	71.94	34.56
8.0	153.60	137.64	122.58	122.64	106.14	91.86	91.08	75.96	38.04
Resulting $\overline{\overline{\omega}}^{hr-}_{total}$ with the TriRMGC system (s)									
3.0	123.90	95.28	70.32	69.24	53.28	39.78	39.30	26.04	9.18
3.5	129.72	104.40	80.64	79.02	61.32	48.06	46.62	34.32	10.68
4.0	133.14	111.66	88.32	87.54	69.72	56.34	55.26	42.72	14.40
4.5	137.76	116.10	97.86	94.74	76.80	62.28	61.50	49.56	18.60
5.0	**140.40**	**121.98**	**103.44**	**101.10**	**84.00**	**68.22**	**68.64**	**58.38**	**23.88**
5.5	144.54	126.06	106.38	106.26	88.62	75.48	74.52	63.24	29.28
6.0	146.58	128.70	112.86	112.32	94.08	79.74	80.10	68.82	34.08
6.5	150.36	135.36	117.42	115.98	100.14	84.90	85.92	75.42	39.72
7.0	153.48	134.64	120.60	118.92	104.94	90.84	90.90	78.06	44.64
7.5	156.84	136.98	122.70	123.06	108.72	94.56	95.40	82.62	49.62
8.0	157.68	141.90	127.80	127.02	112.92	100.38	98.94	87.48	52.32

Table A.16 Influence of the mean container-dwell time ($\overline{\delta}$) on the mean crane-empty-movement time per job ($\overline{\overline{m}}_{total}^{xye}$) for selected yard-block layouts and all types of RMGC systems

	Yard-block layout								
$\overline{\delta}$	Small	Low	Narrow	Short	Medium	Long	Wide	High	Big
Resulting $\overline{\overline{m}}_{total}^{xye}$ with the SRMGC system (s)									
3.0	26.11	31.90	25.81	22.38	25.52	28.92	25.94	23.73	29.28
3.5	26.12	31.95	26.03	22.63	25.74	28.71	25.93	23.43	28.80
4.0	26.23	32.08	26.55	22.72	26.15	29.04	26.11	23.36	28.41
4.5	26.18	31.94	26.82	22.94	26.49	29.22	26.33	23.37	27.99
5.0	**26.05**	**31.87**	**26.97**	**23.22**	**26.63**	**29.48**	**26.57**	**23.73**	**27.72**
5.5	25.90	32.02	27.30	23.33	26.88	30.11	26.82	23.72	27.39
6.0	26.23	32.10	27.63	23.46	27.07	30.28	27.06	24.08	27.29
6.5	26.29	32.05	27.63	23.55	27.28	30.79	27.32	24.27	27.23
7.0	26.27	31.92	27.80	23.61	27.50	31.03	27.58	24.52	27.02
7.5	26.32	32.06	27.88	23.80	27.79	31.27	27.69	24.70	27.16
8.0	26.50	32.04	28.06	23.74	28.11	31.77	28.07	24.88	27.20
Resulting $\overline{\overline{m}}_{total}^{xye}$ with the TRMGC system (s)									
3.0	23.40	29.09	33.57	29.84	33.62	37.84	34.21	36.59	40.53
3.5	23.32	28.93	33.67	30.15	33.82	37.79	34.30	36.71	40.81
4.0	23.20	28.57	33.81	30.39	34.04	38.02	34.36	36.82	40.81
4.5	23.15	28.53	33.61	29.98	34.02	38.17	34.56	36.91	40.76
5.0	**23.34**	**28.35**	**33.76**	**30.25**	**34.07**	**38.12**	**34.64**	**37.21**	**40.77**
5.5	23.05	28.23	33.96	30.28	34.25	38.30	34.57	37.45	40.54
6.0	22.94	27.98	33.97	30.19	34.41	38.29	34.59	37.68	40.55
6.5	22.96	27.87	33.96	30.41	34.21	38.50	34.75	38.03	41.13
7.0	23.00	27.83	33.94	30.42	34.43	38.37	34.81	37.78	41.04
7.5	22.68	28.00	33.74	30.32	34.39	38.55	34.73	38.11	41.23
8.0	22.97	27.94	34.09	30.44	34.29	38.50	34.72	38.32	41.38
Resulting $\overline{\overline{m}}_{total}^{xye}$ with the DRMGC system (s)									
3.0	61.94	70.30	57.45	56.41	53.54	51.08	50.66	42.07	43.73
3.5	60.24	70.97	60.38	59.39	56.71	54.43	53.42	44.84	43.63
4.0	58.25	70.80	61.73	61.48	59.28	57.29	56.18	47.49	43.77
4.5	56.77	69.61	62.68	62.23	61.69	60.16	59.19	49.73	44.13
5.0	**55.77**	**69.14**	**62.73**	**62.89**	**62.78**	**61.85**	**60.88**	**52.25**	**45.15**
5.5	53.59	68.40	63.90	63.63	64.29	64.15	62.89	54.21	46.95
6.0	53.01	66.05	64.24	63.02	65.52	65.32	64.36	56.02	48.14
6.5	51.99	64.64	63.28	63.40	65.31	66.60	65.48	57.24	49.94
7.0	51.13	64.93	63.70	64.10	65.95	68.09	66.89	58.29	51.97
7.5	50.39	64.73	63.57	62.75	66.48	68.04	67.58	59.36	53.30
8.0	49.24	64.11	63.63	63.48	66.49	68.73	67.92	60.40	54.75
Resulting $\overline{\overline{m}}_{total}^{xye}$ with the TriRMGC system (s)									
3.0	59.84	69.38	65.77	65.36	63.68	62.46	61.66	56.95	55.52
3.5	56.75	68.51	67.43	67.29	66.07	65.51	64.44	60.12	55.28
4.0	54.39	67.76	68.52	67.92	67.76	67.64	66.65	62.39	56.56
4.5	52.81	66.50	69.45	68.57	69.40	69.52	69.09	64.57	58.43
5.0	**51.55**	**65.81**	**69.11**	**68.63**	**70.12**	**70.81**	**70.15**	**66.70**	**60.22**
5.5	49.52	64.96	68.33	68.47	71.26	72.49	71.59	68.30	62.64
6.0	48.33	63.20	68.28	67.96	71.40	72.92	72.14	69.41	63.96
6.5	48.31	61.55	67.61	67.89	70.80	73.69	72.67	70.57	65.27
7.0	47.14	60.71	67.37	68.30	71.36	74.68	74.07	70.73	67.41
7.5	45.42	59.31	66.83	67.46	71.80	74.51	74.34	71.79	68.93
8.0	44.16	58.77	67.17	67.09	71.44	75.22	56.95	72.41	70.24

Table A.17 Influence of the mean container-dwell time ($\overline{\delta}$) on the mean crane-interference time per job ($\overline{\overline{m}}^{\text{cit}}_{\text{total}}$) for selected yard-block layouts and all types of RMGC systems

	Yard-block layout								
$\overline{\delta}$	Small	Low	Narrow	Short	Medium	Long	Wide	High	Big
Resulting $\overline{\overline{m}}^{\text{cit}}_{\text{total}}$ with the SRMGC system (s)									
3.0	0.00	0.00	0.00	0.00	0.00	0.00	0.00	0.00	0.00
3.5	0.00	0.00	0.00	0.00	0.00	0.00	0.00	0.00	0.00
4.0	0.00	0.00	0.00	0.00	0.00	0.00	0.00	0.00	0.00
4.5	0.00	0.00	0.00	0.00	0.00	0.00	0.00	0.00	0.00
5.0	**0.00**	**0.00**	**0.00**	**0.00**	**0.00**	**0.00**	**0.00**	**0.00**	**0.00**
5.5	0.00	0.00	0.00	0.00	0.00	0.00	0.00	0.00	0.00
6.0	0.00	0.00	0.00	0.00	0.00	0.00	0.00	0.00	0.00
6.5	0.00	0.00	0.00	0.00	0.00	0.00	0.00	0.00	0.00
7.0	0.00	0.00	0.00	0.00	0.00	0.00	0.00	0.00	0.00
7.5	0.00	0.00	0.00	0.00	0.00	0.00	0.00	0.00	0.00
8.0	0.00	0.00	0.00	0.00	0.00	0.00	0.00	0.00	0.00
Resulting $\overline{\overline{m}}^{\text{cit}}_{\text{total}}$ with the TRMGC system (s)									
3.0	2.03	2.35	11.57	11.90	11.66	11.97	11.80	19.73	18.25
3.5	2.12	2.24	11.75	12.17	11.71	11.85	11.92	19.75	19.39
4.0	2.10	2.16	11.91	12.49	11.82	11.96	12.02	19.64	20.26
4.5	2.07	2.17	11.83	12.23	11.83	12.21	12.05	19.73	20.65
5.0	**2.22**	**2.10**	**11.92**	**12.42**	**12.16**	**11.92**	**12.14**	**19.43**	**20.71**
5.5	2.15	2.10	12.07	12.57	12.29	12.00	12.21	19.82	20.60
6.0	2.11	2.03	12.04	12.60	12.16	11.98	12.15	19.78	20.49
6.5	2.03	2.05	12.28	12.65	12.03	12.10	12.34	20.14	20.36
7.0	2.13	2.00	12.02	12.59	12.06	11.86	12.10	19.95	20.43
7.5	2.06	2.00	11.98	12.48	12.14	12.14	12.18	19.98	20.29
8.0	2.13	1.92	11.95	12.62	11.87	11.86	11.98	20.17	20.21
Resulting $\overline{\overline{m}}^{\text{cit}}_{\text{total}}$ with the DRMGC system (s)									
3.0	37.47	40.13	30.91	34.08	27.49	21.65	24.80	20.94	19.57
3.5	35.72	40.48	33.39	36.62	29.99	24.25	27.06	22.68	19.53
4.0	33.46	40.21	34.66	38.51	32.01	26.43	29.18	24.79	19.51
4.5	31.59	39.05	35.26	39.09	34.12	28.62	31.47	26.30	19.66
5.0	**31.09**	**38.13**	**35.30**	**39.74**	**35.31**	**29.73**	**32.78**	**28.21**	**20.21**
5.5	28.67	37.43	36.11	40.17	36.44	31.56	34.68	29.69	21.29
6.0	27.89	35.37	36.16	38.95	37.39	32.74	36.02	31.01	22.09
6.5	26.91	34.06	34.87	39.54	37.21	33.59	36.73	31.98	23.26
7.0	26.38	33.77	35.59	39.91	37.58	35.13	38.29	32.73	24.51
7.5	24.76	33.41	34.89	38.32	37.61	34.97	38.58	33.61	25.52
8.0	23.78	32.67	34.98	39.16	37.79	35.17	38.95	34.45	26.48
Resulting $\overline{\overline{m}}^{\text{cit}}_{\text{total}}$ with the TriRMGC system (s)									
3.0	40.16	45.04	44.99	49.52	43.16	37.10	40.25	42.30	38.50
3.5	37.31	43.92	47.08	51.11	44.89	39.95	42.89	44.28	38.44
4.0	34.60	42.72	47.92	52.15	46.40	42.28	45.30	46.07	39.45
4.5	32.52	41.14	48.86	52.28	47.96	43.37	47.13	47.92	40.27
5.0	**31.02**	**40.31**	**48.66**	**52.32**	**49.18**	**44.71**	**47.95**	**49.43**	**41.62**
5.5	29.41	39.14	47.62	51.91	49.83	46.15	49.69	50.91	42.83
6.0	28.08	38.14	47.28	51.28	50.25	46.82	50.45	51.74	43.92
6.5	27.79	36.51	46.99	51.22	49.34	47.30	50.79	53.08	44.48
7.0	26.28	35.40	46.41	51.64	49.58	48.48	52.18	53.44	46.25
7.5	25.20	33.41	45.29	50.42	50.16	48.19	52.37	54.31	47.54
8.0	23.33	32.84	46.27	49.89	49.64	48.38	51.36	54.40	48.61

Table A.18 Influence of the mean container-dwell time ($\overline{\delta}$) on the crane workload during the simulation horizon in terms of performed jobs ($\overline{|J|}$) for selected yard-block layouts and all types of RMGC systems

	Yard-block layout								
$\overline{\delta}$	Small	Low	Narrow	Short	Medium	Long	Wide	High	Big
Resulting $\overline{\lvert J\rvert}$ with the SRMGC system (jobs)									
3.0	2,911.7	4,913.2	9,742.1	9,993.8	12,193.5	13,220.5	13,807.4	14,547.9	13,594.2
3.5	2,564.7	4,349.3	8,757.9	9,061.0	11,321.2	12,680.5	13,224.7	14,549.3	13,563.8
4.0	2,285.9	3,892.7	7,939.9	8,201.5	10,296.9	11,963.4	12,331.0	14,324.5	13,609.4
4.5	2,057.9	3,536.5	7,207.4	7,454.0	9,472.1	11,252.6	11,443.6	13,927.8	13,680.2
5.0	**1,871.8**	**3,208.8**	**6,596.5**	**6,792.8**	**8,683.4**	**10,466.3**	**10,776.3**	**13,369.4**	**13,711.1**
5.5	1,729.1	2,967.8	6,066.8	6,289.6	8,069.6	9,688.6	9,922.2	12,806.5	13,768.0
6.0	1,624.0	2,745.6	5,627.9	5,846.9	7,454.2	8,960.5	9,237.4	12,142.2	13,778.6
6.5	1,484.1	2,539.3	5,224.9	5,377.7	6,947.2	8,403.2	8,608.3	11,581.7	13,723.6
7.0	1,402.0	2,396.0	4,824.2	5,110.9	6,559.2	7,911.6	8,064.2	10,984.7	13,763.1
7.5	1,314.9	2,236.9	4,514.0	4,725.6	6,107.4	7,464.3	7,545.2	10,383.1	13,551.9
8.0	1,229.3	2,115.3	4,240.5	4,465.8	5,753.6	6,973.6	7,082.1	9,980.4	13,247.6
Resulting $\overline{\lvert J\rvert}$ with the TRMGC system (jobs)									
3.0	2,947.2	4,959.3	9,979.2	10,255.6	13,036.7	15,707.6	15,840.9	21,513.0	22,026.9
3.5	2,600.1	4,387.6	8,832.7	9,093.8	11,569.8	13,940.1	14,240.5	20,089.4	21,821.4
4.0	2,290.7	3,909.0	7,986.1	8,219.6	10,480.8	12,608.2	12,949.2	18,237.9	21,637.4
4.5	2,080.1	3,515.3	7,267.6	7,499.3	9,491.7	11,597.0	11,755.0	16,622.8	21,568.2
5.0	**1,903.5**	**3,224.1**	**6,592.4**	**6,857.8**	**8,784.5**	**10,615.3**	**10,900.6**	**15,170.8**	**21,104.9**
5.5	1,741.6	2,999.9	6,091.6	6,297.3	8,065.0	9,816.0	10,042.1	13,959.1	20,373.2
6.0	1,612.7	2,750.9	5,605.7	5,873.9	7,438.2	9,098.8	9,225.0	12,867.5	19,441.7
6.5	1,508.7	2,533.1	5,210.3	5,453.3	6,937.5	8,491.8	8,680.6	12,148.6	18,396.7
7.0	1,390.3	2,397.5	4,883.8	5,051.2	6,566.3	7,946.4	8,124.2	11,300.0	17,404.8
7.5	1,308.9	2,246.7	4,568.1	4,726.1	6,070.5	7,483.9	7,608.1	10,717.3	16,481.5
8.0	1,226.7	2,139.6	4,265.1	4,435.0	5,707.1	6,984.3	7,135.2	10,137.3	15,562.3
Resulting $\overline{\lvert J\rvert}$ with the DRMGC system (jobs)									
3.0	2,944.9	4,982.4	9,915.9	10,268.0	12,957.8	15,577.7	15,814.2	21,383.4	22,229.1
3.5	2,594.4	4,374.8	8,857.5	9,103.8	11,530.9	13,903.9	14,316.7	19,809.2	22,256.0
4.0	2,281.2	3,903.1	7,969.7	8,158.3	10,483.8	12,619.5	12,944.1	18,056.4	21,986.8
4.5	2,083.7	3,518.8	7,242.1	7,499.9	9,481.6	11,565.2	11,696.0	16,409.1	21,827.2
5.0	**1,901.9**	**3,222.4**	**6,623.5**	**6,834.0**	**8,713.7**	**10,605.3**	**10,893.6**	**15,175.5**	**21,213.5**
5.5	1,744.4	3,007.3	6,080.4	6,328.4	8,026.7	9,827.1	10,040.6	13,929.9	20,387.2
6.0	1,615.9	2,744.6	5,628.2	5,862.9	7,465.2	9,081.7	9,272.6	12,784.5	19,450.0
6.5	1,512.8	2,528.7	5,227.9	5,458.7	6,916.2	8,493.6	8,652.4	12,058.3	18,276.0
7.0	1,389.5	2,403.8	4,865.1	5,067.2	6,556.7	7,957.2	8,081.6	11,273.5	17,213.6
7.5	1,305.5	2,240.2	4,549.0	4,753.5	6,029.5	7,464.0	7,610.4	10,715.9	16,345.0
8.0	1,229.4	2,148.8	4,309.1	4,421.3	5,718.7	7,014.0	7,157.7	10,120.7	15,520.1
Resulting $\overline{\lvert J\rvert}$ with the TriRMGC system (jobs)									
3.0	2,928.9	4,963.2	9,882.5	10,214.1	12,926.1	15,572.3	15,903.1	23,085.1	27,763.2
3.5	2,588.4	4,367.4	8,870.1	9,085.5	11,456.9	13,875.5	14,227.7	20,702.8	27,464.9
4.0	2,292.9	3,911.8	7,948.0	8,278.2	10,459.0	12,505.5	12,968.9	18,613.9	26,349.0
4.5	2,084.7	3,515.3	7,278.4	7,466.0	9,506.8	11,502.6	11,700.3	16,910.9	24,796.1
5.0	**1,907.0**	**3,249.5**	**6,614.4**	**6,831.8**	**8,732.5**	**10,583.9**	**10,895.8**	**15,192.1**	**23,097.9**
5.5	1,748.4	3,005.9	6,036.9	6,264.9	8,004.8	9,829.5	10,016.2	14,025.2	21,587.6
6.0	1,607.0	2,758.1	5,612.4	5,869.8	7,456.9	9,067.0	9,294.0	12,903.4	20,108.3
6.5	1,512.8	2,535.5	5,226.6	5,424.5	6,923.0	8,470.0	8,684.0	11,947.1	18,769.3
7.0	1,391.5	2,397.5	4,861.5	5,069.2	6,507.0	7,900.6	8,116.4	11,498.2	17,622.1
7.5	1,313.8	2,264.0	4,566.9	4,729.7	6,074.3	7,495.4	7,565.9	10,729.6	16,604.2
8.0	1,213.0	2,125.5	4,307.8	4,454.1	5,728.5	7,012.8	7,144.7	10,065.1	15,802.9

Table A.19 Influence of the mean container-dwell time ($\overline{\delta}$) on the container accessibility ($\overline{\overline{\psi}}$), in terms of the mean number of shuffle moves per retrieval job, for selected yard-block layouts and all types of RMGC systems

	Yard-block layout								
$\overline{\delta}$	Small	Low	Narrow	Short	Medium	Long	Wide	High	Big
Resulting $\overline{\overline{\psi}}$ with the SRMGC system (jobs)									
3.0	0.298	0.270	1.021	1.001	0.934	0.806	0.819	1.091	0.630
3.5	0.311	0.281	1.068	1.059	1.018	0.918	0.928	1.275	0.761
4.0	0.312	0.286	1.112	1.100	1.054	0.993	0.992	1.418	0.904
4.5	0.320	0.297	1.103	1.115	1.098	1.054	1.041	1.530	1.024
5.0	**0.322**	**0.300**	**1.135**	**1.120**	**1.103**	**1.083**	**1.083**	**1.606**	**1.144**
5.5	0.321	0.308	1.133	1.129	1.126	1.103	1.093	1.671	1.250
6.0	0.329	0.309	1.145	1.146	1.132	1.104	1.110	1.709	1.350
6.5	0.326	0.313	1.142	1.128	1.146	1.128	1.107	1.750	1.446
7.0	0.326	0.311	1.132	1.149	1.145	1.120	1.116	1.778	1.540
7.5	0.316	0.315	1.133	1.129	1.133	1.116	1.106	1.783	1.597
8.0	0.322	0.311	1.140	1.143	1.136	1.117	1.097	1.818	1.645
Resulting $\overline{\overline{\psi}}$ with the TRMGC system (job)									
3.0	0.305	0.267	1.060	1.038	0.999	0.968	0.943	1.579	1.079
3.5	0.312	0.283	1.079	1.075	1.044	1.011	0.996	1.672	1.261
4.0	0.316	0.291	1.108	1.110	1.068	1.043	1.040	1.707	1.425
4.5	0.314	0.291	1.122	1.116	1.095	1.092	1.071	1.758	1.576
5.0	**0.324**	**0.296**	**1.127**	**1.130**	**1.130**	**1.097**	**1.090**	**1.762**	**1.675**
5.5	0.325	0.306	1.137	1.129	1.132	1.112	1.102	1.805	1.744
6.0	0.322	0.308	1.131	1.138	1.127	1.110	1.091	1.811	1.795
6.5	0.326	0.313	1.146	1.137	1.129	1.128	1.127	1.836	1.808
7.0	0.325	0.312	1.134	1.136	1.143	1.125	1.121	1.828	1.827
7.5	0.335	0.310	1.135	1.125	1.139	1.126	1.123	1.851	1.846
8.0	0.334	0.303	1.128	1.130	1.116	1.108	1.108	1.864	1.850
Resulting $\overline{\overline{\psi}}$ with the DRMGC system (jobs)									
3.0	0.306	0.276	1.049	1.047	0.993	0.944	0.941	1.542	1.082
3.5	0.311	0.275	1.085	1.077	1.038	1.007	1.007	1.638	1.274
4.0	0.314	0.284	1.101	1.084	1.077	1.048	1.041	1.681	1.432
4.5	0.318	0.291	1.113	1.109	1.093	1.087	1.058	1.723	1.584
5.0	**0.320**	**0.297**	**1.137**	**1.118**	**1.107**	**1.093**	**1.087**	**1.753**	**1.673**
5.5	0.332	0.311	1.141	1.142	1.124	1.119	1.100	1.798	1.731
6.0	0.324	0.301	1.144	1.134	1.129	1.114	1.105	1.787	1.785
6.5	0.334	0.310	1.149	1.144	1.122	1.126	1.119	1.823	1.797
7.0	0.327	0.319	1.127	1.139	1.139	1.127	1.110	1.820	1.800
7.5	0.326	0.302	1.127	1.155	1.116	1.120	1.127	1.850	1.838
8.0	0.340	0.314	1.141	1.130	1.116	1.116	1.117	1.865	1.843
Resulting $\overline{\overline{\psi}}$ with the TriRMGC system (jobs)									
3.0	0.306	0.272	1.037	1.030	0.991	0.944	0.943	1.625	1.340
3.5	0.312	0.278	1.082	1.069	1.024	0.997	0.991	1.692	1.544
4.0	0.323	0.290	1.093	1.103	1.073	1.029	1.038	1.746	1.648
4.5	0.306	0.291	1.124	1.114	1.097	1.069	1.058	1.773	1.726
5.0	**0.325**	**0.298**	**1.122**	**1.123**	**1.113**	**1.092**	**1.090**	**1.763**	**1.758**
5.5	0.323	0.307	1.128	1.126	1.122	1.104	1.097	1.805	1.786
6.0	0.329	0.311	1.135	1.144	1.134	1.128	1.105	1.810	1.810
6.5	0.335	0.306	1.148	1.137	1.130	1.135	1.126	1.811	1.830
7.0	0.329	0.312	1.140	1.144	1.138	1.107	1.119	1.854	1.844
7.5	0.335	0.307	1.133	1.135	1.137	1.129	1.113	1.844	1.857
8.0	0.321	0.297	1.140	1.133	1.127	1.121	1.117	1.862	1.860

Table A.20 Influence of differences between the mean container-dwell times of import/export and transshipment containers on the mean vehicle-waiting time ($\overline{\omega}^{hr+}_{total}$) for selected yard-block layouts and all types of RMGC systems

$\overline{\delta} = 5$		Yard-block layout								
$\overline{\delta}^{ie}$	$\overline{\delta}^{ts}$	Small	Low	Narrow	Short	Medium	Long	Wide	High	Big
Resulting $\overline{\omega}^{hr+}_{total}$ with the SRMGC system (s)										
4.60	7.27	26.46	40.74	109.44	100.08	191.58	553.98	459.30	1,770.30	3,291.30
4.70	6.70	25.98	40.50	114.42	99.90	192.60	550.08	464.64	1,845.66	3,223.20
4.80	6.13	24.90	40.56	113.82	100.62	188.64	554.40	436.44	1,819.02	3,347.40
4.90	5.57	27.24	42.66	115.02	100.98	193.56	547.02	442.38	1,827.18	3,293.70
5.00	**5.00**	**28.26**	**41.28**	**117.06**	**100.44**	**198.96**	**561.06**	**484.56**	**1,861.32**	**3,269.94**
5.10	4.43	27.60	41.94	113.70	102.54	195.24	548.46	464.88	1,824.90	3,182.22
5.20	3.87	26.64	40.02	115.74	102.66	196.62	536.94	448.26	1,922.94	3,214.98
5.30	3.30	26.10	42.36	113.28	102.48	190.80	574.14	472.74	1,921.44	3,112.80
5.40	2.73	28.80	42.24	112.50	100.92	190.14	544.56	434.70	1,933.38	3,061.80
Resulting $\overline{\omega}^{hr+}_{total}$ with the TRMGC system (s)										
4.60	7.27	8.88	13.32	37.98	34.44	48.12	67.98	60.66	300.54	1,584.72
4.70	6.70	9.12	12.60	38.64	35.82	47.04	66.78	60.72	316.38	1,533.72
4.80	6.13	9.00	13.50	38.88	35.82	47.88	67.38	59.22	301.38	1,526.64
4.90	5.57	9.12	13.14	38.94	35.16	46.26	67.44	59.76	304.56	1,574.34
5.00	**5.00**	**8.82**	**13.44**	**38.16**	**35.58**	**48.30**	**67.44**	**61.98**	**304.08**	**1,567.38**
5.10	4.43	9.00	13.56	39.00	36.00	47.58	67.32	60.54	294.84	1,528.08
5.20	3.87	9.06	13.50	39.36	36.06	47.70	66.42	61.74	295.38	1,552.74
5.30	3.30	9.60	13.98	37.98	36.60	48.18	65.94	60.54	299.64	1,529.34
5.40	2.73	9.36	13.62	39.78	36.18	47.16	66.12	60.36	298.56	1,545.90
Resulting $\overline{\omega}^{hr+}_{total}$ with the DRMGC system (s)										
4.60	7.27	13.98	23.16	53.46	52.80	69.30	89.76	89.22	346.08	1,594.20
4.70	6.70	13.20	23.22	53.22	55.38	68.64	90.72	90.24	367.98	1,589.88
4.80	6.13	13.26	22.86	54.00	53.82	70.08	85.74	89.04	333.54	1,610.58
4.90	5.57	14.16	23.64	54.84	54.30	67.68	88.32	89.46	351.60	1,656.72
5.00	**5.00**	**13.86**	**23.58**	**53.82**	**54.36**	**69.24**	**88.86**	**88.86**	**360.18**	**1,607.82**
5.10	4.43	12.96	23.40	53.58	55.26	69.18	90.12	89.28	342.12	1,601.46
5.20	3.87	13.50	24.66	54.00	54.42	67.92	88.50	91.38	365.70	1,643.22
5.30	3.30	13.50	23.76	54.00	54.48	70.44	92.70	89.82	351.72	1,608.30
5.40	2.73	13.68	23.76	54.66	55.44	70.80	91.50	89.82	349.08	1,598.82
Resulting $\overline{\omega}^{hr+}_{total}$ with the TriRMGC system (s)										
4.60	7.27	8.64	12.18	31.68	32.04	38.28	44.88	45.90	121.98	585.00
4.70	6.70	8.88	12.36	31.92	32.28	38.52	46.74	45.54	122.58	587.34
4.80	6.13	8.76	12.48	30.78	32.10	37.98	45.42	46.50	125.28	589.32
4.90	5.57	8.88	12.54	31.44	31.80	38.22	45.96	46.56	121.92	596.52
5.00	**5.00**	**8.82**	**12.48**	**31.26**	**31.86**	**37.98**	**46.86**	**46.86**	**117.54**	**574.98**
5.10	4.43	8.40	12.06	31.86	32.10	37.98	46.44	46.50	122.88	581.76
5.20	3.87	8.82	12.54	31.44	32.76	38.10	46.20	47.76	122.28	613.32
5.30	3.30	8.76	12.66	31.80	32.52	39.18	46.20	47.22	126.42	590.46
5.40	2.73	8.88	13.08	31.92	32.28	39.06	46.08	46.98	127.62	603.78

Table A.21 Influence of differences between the mean container-dwell times of import/export and transshipment containers on the vehicle-waiting time per waterside retrieval job ($\overline{\omega}^{hr+}_{wsout}$) for selected yard-block layouts and all types of RMGC systems

$\overline{\delta} = 5$		Yard-block layout								
$\overline{\delta}^{ie}$	$\overline{\delta}^{ts}$	Small	Low	Narrow	Short	Medium	Long	Wide	High	Big
Resulting $\overline{\omega}^{hr+}_{wsout}$ with the SRMGC system (s)										
4.60	7.27	2.82	5.46	68.58	57.90	187.86	798.78	622.80	3,066.06	5,098.02
4.70	6.70	3.48	4.98	77.58	58.50	193.80	775.86	636.66	3,221.34	5,000.28
4.80	6.13	1.80	4.86	77.88	57.36	181.92	788.88	588.60	3,135.72	5,125.50
4.90	5.57	3.60	5.64	75.78	56.34	189.24	791.22	592.68	3,117.18	5,062.44
5.00	**5.00**	**3.24**	**5.52**	**78.00**	**56.04**	**198.72**	**789.12**	**671.58**	**3,180.30**	**4,959.72**
5.10	4.43	2.10	6.84	76.20	59.10	193.98	769.44	629.70	3,097.74	4,836.00
5.20	3.87	2.70	5.04	78.72	60.84	194.28	755.52	602.52	3,284.88	4,854.66
5.30	3.30	2.58	5.70	71.58	59.76	182.82	814.98	640.26	3,278.28	4,697.04
5.40	2.73	3.96	5.58	70.02	54.12	176.10	757.44	577.08	3,290.58	4,586.76
Resulting $\overline{\omega}^{hr+}_{wsout}$ with the TRMGC system (s)										
4.60	7.27	2.70	4.56	16.44	13.56	26.10	50.40	39.12	473.58	3,069.18
4.70	6.70	3.78	3.78	15.72	14.04	24.48	47.58	39.96	506.10	2,917.56
4.80	6.13	2.94	5.46	17.28	13.80	26.94	46.44	35.76	478.62	2,941.80
4.90	5.57	2.58	4.56	16.38	12.30	22.62	47.10	36.24	487.92	3,043.44
5.00	**5.00**	**2.28**	**4.14**	**15.06**	**13.20**	**25.80**	**48.48**	**42.12**	**486.30**	**3,019.80**
5.10	4.43	3.24	5.28	17.34	14.46	24.24	44.04	37.50	463.26	2,917.08
5.20	3.87	2.46	4.44	17.16	14.40	23.28	45.36	38.40	462.24	2,909.16
5.30	3.30	2.76	5.10	16.02	14.22	24.30	41.52	32.10	477.24	2,929.74
5.40	2.73	4.08	4.80	16.20	13.98	21.54	41.40	35.22	467.46	2,942.28
Resulting $\overline{\omega}^{hr+}_{wsout}$ with the DRMGC system (s)										
4.60	7.27	3.42	5.52	20.28	19.62	31.92	49.08	49.26	486.36	2,750.70
4.70	6.70	2.94	5.10	19.20	20.70	30.18	51.60	52.32	525.96	2,751.72
4.80	6.13	2.10	5.16	18.78	21.36	29.88	42.72	46.68	463.98	2,757.60
4.90	5.57	3.30	5.28	18.48	18.54	29.94	46.98	49.56	497.82	2,850.60
5.00	**5.00**	**2.76**	**5.34**	**20.10**	**18.72**	**30.78**	**47.46**	**46.26**	**510.54**	**2,758.62**
5.10	4.43	2.76	6.42	17.58	20.64	29.76	46.68	48.24	473.82	2,726.10
5.20	3.87	2.58	6.60	20.04	18.06	25.32	46.50	51.24	517.98	2,797.44
5.30	3.30	2.94	4.92	19.08	19.14	29.64	52.02	45.78	484.44	2,729.64
5.40	2.73	3.90	5.82	20.34	19.62	29.04	50.16	47.04	481.68	2,709.84
Resulting $\overline{\omega}^{hr+}_{wsout}$ with the TriRMGC system (s)										
4.60	7.27	2.58	5.16	12.72	13.14	18.18	18.78	20.46	117.42	920.82
4.70	6.70	3.42	5.10	12.78	12.84	16.32	21.06	19.98	118.32	930.90
4.80	6.13	2.94	4.74	12.42	12.72	16.68	19.44	20.58	124.56	911.10
4.90	5.57	3.48	6.00	13.50	13.02	17.58	20.94	20.22	117.42	942.18
5.00	**5.00**	**2.22**	**5.34**	**12.90**	**12.54**	**16.32**	**19.68**	**20.94**	**109.68**	**883.26**
5.10	4.43	1.98	4.44	13.86	13.08	16.98	20.04	20.46	118.50	896.88
5.20	3.87	2.82	5.46	12.12	12.12	16.14	18.90	20.82	112.38	974.52
5.30	3.30	3.06	5.34	12.30	12.60	16.68	19.26	21.12	123.60	917.10
5.40	2.73	2.88	6.06	13.02	12.54	18.06	18.60	20.58	123.72	934.32

Table A.22 Influence of differences between the mean container-dwell times of import/export and transshipment containers on the mean crane-waiting time in the handover areas ($\overline{\overline{\omega}}^{hr-}_{total}$) for selected yard-block layouts and all types of RMGC systems

$\overline{\delta} = 5$		Yard-block layout								
$\overline{\delta}^{ie}$	$\overline{\delta}^{ts}$	Small	Low	Narrow	Short	Medium	Long	Wide	High	Big
Resulting $\overline{\overline{\omega}}^{hr-}_{total}$ with the SRMGC system (s)										
4.60	7.27	123.00	95.16	64.14	67.14	41.64	23.04	26.58	14.22	6.66
4.70	6.70	124.80	94.92	64.98	68.22	41.46	22.98	26.52	14.22	6.78
4.80	6.13	125.40	95.34	64.68	66.60	41.82	23.52	26.10	14.34	6.78
4.90	5.57	125.10	95.40	64.62	66.96	42.48	23.64	26.16	14.40	6.84
5.00	**5.00**	**124.38**	**94.92**	**63.84**	**67.26**	**41.52**	**22.86**	**25.80**	**14.64**	**7.08**
5.10	4.43	126.00	95.34	64.02	66.30	41.52	23.16	26.28	14.16	6.90
5.20	3.87	126.00	94.86	65.22	66.00	41.70	23.28	26.64	13.86	7.02
5.30	3.30	126.24	96.36	64.02	66.00	42.06	22.74	25.74	13.44	7.14
5.40	2.73	125.88	95.46	63.30	66.60	41.58	23.10	25.92	13.68	7.08
Resulting $\overline{\overline{\omega}}^{hr-}_{total}$ with the TRMGC system (s)										
4.60	7.27	138.54	110.70	88.14	90.96	68.82	50.64	53.04	38.70	10.56
4.70	6.70	136.86	112.26	88.50	89.70	69.60	50.40	53.28	38.16	10.98
4.80	6.13	136.26	111.42	88.38	91.68	68.10	50.40	52.86	38.46	10.68
4.90	5.57	137.64	111.48	88.08	90.36	68.34	50.10	52.92	38.88	10.44
5.00	**5.00**	**135.84**	**112.32**	**87.84**	**91.26**	**67.86**	**50.28**	**53.40**	**38.58**	**10.56**
5.10	4.43	136.02	112.50	87.72	91.14	68.70	49.98	53.40	39.06	10.68
5.20	3.87	136.02	112.02	88.20	90.60	68.88	50.52	52.80	38.10	10.44
5.30	3.30	135.96	111.78	88.20	89.64	68.40	50.58	52.68	38.70	10.80
5.40	2.73	137.22	112.74	88.20	91.02	67.50	49.80	53.16	37.92	10.44
Resulting $\overline{\overline{\omega}}^{hr-}_{total}$ with the DRMGC system (s)										
4.60	7.27	141.30	116.52	95.28	95.52	75.60	57.18	57.72	45.18	12.30
4.70	6.70	138.48	117.54	96.00	96.12	74.52	57.36	57.78	44.70	12.90
4.80	6.13	138.96	116.76	94.98	95.40	74.58	57.72	57.36	45.24	12.60
4.90	5.57	139.68	117.12	95.70	95.34	74.58	58.44	58.08	45.00	12.24
5.00	**5.00**	**139.32**	**117.48**	**95.28**	**95.46**	**75.18**	**57.24**	**57.66**	**44.52**	**12.60**
5.10	4.43	138.78	117.12	95.88	95.82	75.30	58.02	58.26	44.22	12.42
5.20	3.87	138.00	118.08	95.88	94.80	74.88	57.18	57.60	44.28	12.48
5.30	3.30	138.30	117.36	95.52	94.80	74.88	57.84	57.66	44.40	12.24
5.40	2.73	139.26	117.12	94.38	95.40	74.70	57.36	57.72	43.92	12.06
Resulting $\overline{\overline{\omega}}^{hr-}_{total}$ with the TriRMGC system (s)										
4.60	7.27	141.78	121.50	102.54	101.34	84.18	68.34	69.42	58.38	23.64
4.70	6.70	139.86	121.20	102.18	102.42	84.78	68.70	68.70	58.44	24.06
4.80	6.13	142.08	120.30	103.32	101.64	83.88	68.34	68.64	58.08	23.82
4.90	5.57	141.42	121.08	103.50	101.88	83.88	68.70	68.94	58.62	23.70
5.00	**5.00**	**140.40**	**121.98**	**103.44**	**101.10**	**84.00**	**68.22**	**68.64**	**58.38**	**23.88**
5.10	4.43	141.18	121.20	102.30	101.70	83.16	68.58	69.54	58.02	23.46
5.20	3.87	142.32	122.34	102.72	102.24	84.24	68.16	68.16	57.42	23.16
5.30	3.30	140.82	120.84	103.98	101.64	83.22	68.10	68.82	57.54	22.56
5.40	2.73	141.24	121.74	101.46	101.76	83.52	68.10	68.76	57.24	22.68

Table A.23 Influence of differences between the mean container-dwell times of import/export and transshipment containers on the mean crane-empty-movement time per job ($\overline{\overline{m}}^{xye}_{total}$) for selected yard-block layouts and all types of RMGC systems

$\overline{\delta} = 5$		Yard-block layout								
$\overline{\delta}^{ie}$	$\overline{\delta}^{ts}$	Small	Low	Narrow	Short	Medium	Long	Wide	High	Big
Resulting $\overline{\overline{m}}^{xye}_{total}$ with the SRMGC system (s)										
4.60	7.27	26.28	32.20	27.22	23.25	26.75	29.86	26.74	23.75	27.74
4.70	6.70	26.10	31.92	27.21	23.26	26.72	29.78	26.71	23.75	27.77
4.80	6.13	26.17	31.99	27.19	23.14	26.77	29.71	26.63	23.79	27.63
4.90	5.57	26.23	32.12	27.05	23.05	26.62	29.59	26.57	23.69	27.73
5.00	**5.00**	**26.05**	**31.87**	**26.97**	**23.22**	**26.63**	**29.48**	**26.57**	**23.73**	**27.72**
5.10	4.43	26.12	31.80	26.94	23.10	26.63	29.68	26.52	23.67	27.79
5.20	3.87	26.20	31.98	26.98	23.16	26.62	29.59	26.55	23.75	27.78
5.30	3.30	26.19	32.01	27.17	23.04	26.54	29.70	26.49	23.59	27.91
5.40	2.73	26.10	31.84	27.06	23.05	26.76	29.59	26.46	23.66	27.83
Resulting $\overline{\overline{m}}^{xye}_{total}$ with the TRMGC system (s)										
4.60	7.27	23.34	28.47	34.02	30.17	34.15	38.24	34.55	37.27	40.72
4.70	6.70	23.23	28.39	33.85	30.19	34.39	38.20	34.56	37.24	40.46
4.80	6.13	23.28	28.47	33.84	30.26	34.24	38.40	34.59	37.12	40.67
4.90	5.57	23.15	28.35	33.91	29.96	33.99	38.17	34.62	37.25	40.71
5.00	**5.00**	**23.34**	**28.35**	**33.76**	**30.25**	**34.07**	**38.12**	**34.64**	**37.21**	**40.77**
5.10	4.43	23.24	28.32	33.86	30.09	34.20	38.17	34.54	36.91	40.58
5.20	3.87	23.13	28.33	33.73	30.24	34.22	38.19	34.49	37.16	40.29
5.30	3.30	23.14	28.34	33.58	30.14	34.09	37.90	34.39	37.00	40.38
5.40	2.73	23.02	28.27	33.64	30.03	33.93	38.04	34.31	37.20	40.44
Resulting $\overline{\overline{m}}^{xye}_{total}$ with the DRMGC system (s)										
4.60	7.27	55.84	68.70	63.28	62.91	62.86	62.15	60.94	52.70	45.19
4.70	6.70	54.61	69.64	63.36	63.27	62.90	62.17	60.99	52.51	45.31
4.80	6.13	56.35	68.94	63.67	62.87	63.20	62.40	60.92	52.35	45.41
4.90	5.57	56.26	69.42	63.36	62.77	62.76	62.25	60.86	52.15	45.18
5.00	**5.00**	**55.77**	**69.14**	**62.73**	**62.89**	**62.78**	**61.85**	**60.88**	**52.25**	**45.15**
5.10	4.43	55.22	68.90	63.45	62.75	63.13	62.38	61.18	52.22	45.12
5.20	3.87	54.99	69.69	63.53	63.07	63.02	62.16	60.71	52.22	45.23
5.30	3.30	54.66	69.08	63.25	62.99	62.79	61.80	60.82	52.17	44.89
5.40	2.73	54.69	68.60	63.15	62.57	62.94	61.88	60.92	51.81	45.10
Resulting $\overline{\overline{m}}^{xye}_{total}$ with the TriRMGC system (s)										
4.60	7.27	50.96	65.21	68.32	68.61	69.84	70.78	70.35	66.67	60.39
4.70	6.70	50.78	64.91	68.24	68.40	70.56	70.99	70.08	66.81	60.70
4.80	6.13	51.01	65.27	68.68	69.12	70.68	70.89	70.04	66.96	60.39
4.90	5.57	50.74	65.28	68.74	68.42	70.45	71.14	70.22	66.74	60.08
5.00	**5.00**	**51.55**	**65.81**	**69.11**	**68.63**	**70.12**	**70.81**	**70.15**	**66.70**	**60.22**
5.10	4.43	51.17	65.50	68.94	68.53	69.79	70.91	69.96	66.58	60.07
5.20	3.87	50.96	65.54	68.76	68.96	70.89	70.79	69.90	66.73	59.83
5.30	3.30	51.22	65.41	68.72	68.76	70.13	70.95	69.90	66.79	59.72
5.40	2.73	51.48	65.59	68.84	68.67	70.13	70.61	69.99	66.78	59.68

Table A.24 Influence of differences between the mean container-dwell times of import/export and transshipment containers on the mean crane-interference time per job ($\overline{\overline{m}}^{cit}_{total}$) for selected yard-block layouts and all types of RMGC systems

$\overline{\delta} = 5$		Yard-block layout								
$\overline{\delta}^{ie}$	$\overline{\delta}^{ts}$	Small	Low	Narrow	Short	Medium	Long	Wide	High	Big
Resulting $\overline{\overline{m}}^{cit}_{total}$ with the SRMGC system (s)										
4.60	7.27	0.00	0.00	0.00	0.00	0.00	0.00	0.00	0.00	0.00
4.70	6.70	0.00	0.00	0.00	0.00	0.00	0.00	0.00	0.00	0.00
4.80	6.13	0.00	0.00	0.00	0.00	0.00	0.00	0.00	0.00	0.00
4.90	5.57	0.00	0.00	0.00	0.00	0.00	0.00	0.00	0.00	0.00
5.00	**5.00**	**0.00**	**0.00**	**0.00**	**0.00**	**0.00**	**0.00**	**0.00**	**0.00**	**0.00**
5.10	4.43	0.00	0.00	0.00	0.00	0.00	0.00	0.00	0.00	0.00
5.20	3.87	0.00	0.00	0.00	0.00	0.00	0.00	0.00	0.00	0.00
5.30	3.30	0.00	0.00	0.00	0.00	0.00	0.00	0.00	0.00	0.00
5.40	2.73	0.00	0.00	0.00	0.00	0.00	0.00	0.00	0.00	0.00
Resulting $\overline{\overline{m}}^{cit}_{total}$ with the TRMGC system (s)										
4.60	7.27	2.23	2.17	12.03	12.21	12.04	11.89	12.07	19.73	20.61
4.70	6.70	2.15	2.09	11.89	12.40	12.13	12.00	12.13	19.61	20.45
4.80	6.13	2.17	2.10	12.07	12.36	12.05	12.10	12.19	19.42	20.58
4.90	5.57	2.18	2.08	12.03	12.32	11.86	12.04	12.15	19.60	20.73
5.00	**5.00**	**2.22**	**2.10**	**11.92**	**12.42**	**12.16**	**11.92**	**12.14**	**19.43**	**20.71**
5.10	4.43	2.20	2.19	12.07	12.11	12.01	11.98	12.15	19.42	20.64
5.20	3.87	2.12	2.01	11.95	12.37	12.15	11.98	12.20	19.58	20.58
5.30	3.30	2.18	2.20	11.72	12.27	11.85	11.90	12.04	19.41	20.60
5.40	2.73	2.06	2.04	11.77	12.22	11.96	12.10	11.99	19.60	20.77
Resulting $\overline{\overline{m}}^{cit}_{total}$ with the DRMGC system (s)										
4.60	7.27	30.92	37.76	35.53	39.48	35.19	30.23	32.66	28.43	20.06
4.70	6.70	29.64	38.17	35.51	39.96	35.27	30.06	32.87	28.51	20.35
4.80	6.13	30.84	37.92	36.00	39.26	35.50	30.00	32.89	28.17	20.38
4.90	5.57	31.66	38.51	35.70	39.09	35.02	30.26	33.07	28.33	20.31
5.00	**5.00**	**31.09**	**38.13**	**35.30**	**39**.74	**35.31**	**29.73**	**32.78**	**28.21**	**20.21**
5.10	4.43	30.29	38.72	35.94	39.46	35.52	30.18	33.27	28.10	20.16
5.20	3.87	29.92	39.14	36.19	39.63	35.28	29.90	32.85	28.25	20.27
5.30	3.30	30.18	38.40	36.01	39.73	34.94	30.13	32.98	28.16	20.11
5.40	2.73	29.94	38.12	36.00	39.36	35.84	30.06	33.06	27.89	20.38
Resulting $\overline{\overline{m}}^{cit}_{total}$ with the TriRMGC system (s)										
4.60	7.27	30.34	39.96	47.75	52.17	49.26	44.57	48.36	49.48	41.25
4.70	6.70	30.52	39.55	47.87	52.36	49.54	44.77	47.93	49.75	41.54
4.80	6.13	30.60	39.94	48.09	52.88	49.47	44.69	48.06	49.82	41.29
4.90	5.57	30.77	40.58	48.13	52.10	49.15	44.93	48.20	49.40	41.35
5.00	**5.00**	**31.02**	**40.31**	**48.66**	**53**.32	**49.18**	**44.71**	**47.95**	**49.43**	**41.62**
5.10	4.43	30.96	40.09	48.53	52.54	48.90	44.75	48.15	49.53	41.45
5.20	3.87	31.14	40.60	48.37	52.90	49.95	44.88	48.14	49.73	41.31
5.30	3.30	31.28	40.02	48.59	52.65	49.13	44.86	48.27	49.57	41.33
5.40	2.73	31.31	40.79	48.12	52.40	49.33	44.81	48.36	49.48	40.93

Table A.25 Influence of differences between the mean container-dwell times of import/export and transshipment containers on the crane workload during the simulation horizon in terms of performed jobs ($\overline{|J|}$) for selected yard-block layouts and all types of RMGC systems

$\overline{\delta} = 5$		Yard-block layout								
$\overline{\delta}^{ie}$	$\overline{\delta}^{ts}$	Small	Low	Narrow	Short	Medium	Long	Wide	High	Big
Resulting $\overline{|J|}$ with the SRMGC system (s)										
4.60	7.27	1,850.6	3,207.7	6,534.5	6,798.0	8,712.1	10,394.1	10,610.5	13,377.0	13,740.0
4.70	6.70	1,865.0	3,207.2	6,535.7	6,771.3	8,638.2	10,392.8	10,627.5	13,341.8	13,667.3
4.80	6.13	1,879.4	3,216.2	6,543.1	6,777.3	8,611.4	10,415.4	10,664.3	13,323.3	13,800.8
4.90	5.57	1,875.9	3,201.1	6,615.6	6,797.8	8,587.0	10,447.1	10,697.7	13,344.1	13,765.1
5.00	**5.00**	**1,871.8**	**3,208.8**	**6,596.5**	**6,792.8**	**8,683.4**	**10,466.3**	**10,776.3**	**13,369.4**	**13,711.1**
5.10	4.43	1,904.5	3,241.4	6,611.9	6,826.5	8,739.8	10,497.3	10,788.8	13,409.8	13,677.0
5.20	3.87	1,890.9	3,214.5	6,623.6	6,827.5	8,741.0	10,546.7	10,681.1	13,514.5	13,653.5
5.30	3.30	1,884.5	3,225.0	6,581.8	6,833.0	8,641.6	10,489.7	10,817.1	13,528.2	13,594.6
5.40	2.73	1,904.3	3,266.0	6,621.3	6,855.1	8,678.9	10,495.0	10,790.5	13,516.1	13,621.2
Resulting $\overline{|J|}$ with the TRMGC system (s)										
4.60	7.27	1,899.7	3,207.4	6,586.5	6,775.4	8,739.7	10,518.0	10,800.9	15,189.8	21,178.5
4.70	6.70	1,871.6	3,229.1	6,579.0	6,872.3	8,725.0	10,544.4	10,842.6	15,300.2	21,019.0
4.80	6.13	1,900.0	3,218.4	6,607.0	6,847.1	8,739.6	10,540.5	10,858.4	15,260.8	21,008.6
4.90	5.57	1,899.1	3,204.7	6,666.1	6,858.9	8,708.7	10,587.4	10,857.6	15,133.8	21,177.2
5.00	**5.00**	**1,903.5**	**3,224.1**	**6,592.4**	**6,857.8**	**8,784.5**	**10,615.3**	**10,900.6**	**15,170.8**	**21,104.9**
5.10	4.43	1,905.6	3,257.5	6,661.2	6,837.8	8,724.7	10,655.1	10,866.7	15,252.6	21,076.8
5.20	3.87	1,894.8	3,265.4	6,628.0	6,834.3	8,803.1	10,564.6	10,871.1	15,328.5	21,242.0
5.30	3.30	1,900.4	3,250.1	6,634.8	6,898.3	8,779.5	10,666.7	11,003.8	15,212.4	21,106.6
5.40	2.73	1,897.2	3,240.3	6,696.2	6,870.6	8,750.9	10,625.1	10,920.3	15,318.3	21,152.3
Resulting $\overline{|J|}$ with the DRMGC system (s)										
4.60	7.27	1,899.8	3,195.8	6,572.2	6,768.5	8,716.5	10,545.3	10,741.4	15,034.3	21,136.8
4.70	6.70	1,874.1	3,220.3	6,577.0	6,855.5	8,675.4	10,527.0	10,836.7	15,158.1	21,089.8
4.80	6.13	1,898.3	3,207.0	6,597.7	6,834.5	8,716.1	10,481.5	10,842.4	15,047.5	21,064.5
4.90	5.57	1,898.6	3,215.1	6,661.6	6,895.5	8,663.7	10,526.1	10,804.5	15,008.9	21,284.7
5.00	**5.00**	**1,901.9**	**3,222.4**	**6,623.5**	**6,834.0**	**8,713.7**	**10,605.3**	**10,893.6**	**15,175.5**	**21,213.5**
5.10	4.43	1,907.6	3,233.9	6,622.5	6,857.7	8,759.2	10,633.4	10,863.9	15,222.4	21,153.3
5.20	3.87	1,896.0	3,266.0	6,584.2	6,822.6	8,743.1	10,547.5	10,855.5	15,276.0	21,165.9
5.30	3.30	1,886.5	3,244.9	6,634.6	6,896.1	8,789.8	10,638.0	10,987.3	15,142.3	21,205.3
5.40	2.73	1,896.1	3,256.9	6,656.2	6,871.9	8,784.7	10,647.6	10,891.2	15,276.3	21,255.3
Resulting $\overline{|J|}$ with the TriRMGC system (s)										
4.60	7.27	1,893.2	3,213.5	6,601.6	6,769.7	8,661.9	10,527.7	10,788.3	15,280.8	23,038.8
4.70	6.70	1,873.8	3,202.0	6,610.4	6,823.3	8,718.1	10,519.0	10,771.1	15,215.8	23,025.3
4.80	6.13	1,900.8	3,215.6	6,571.1	6,804.4	8,720.7	10,493.8	10,867.2	15,302.3	23,088.5
4.90	5.57	1,884.7	3,223.9	6,588.1	6,794.2	8,655.4	10,506.3	10,858.2	15,219.3	23,182.2
5.00	**5.00**	**1,907.0**	**3,249.5**	**6,614.4**	**6,831.8**	**8,732.5**	**10,583.9**	**10,895.8**	**15,192.1**	**23,097.9**
5.10	4.43	1,898.0	3,238.6	6,569.5	6,786.7	8,690.4	10,579.0	10,857.9	15,277.0	23,203.3
5.20	3.87	1,894.1	3,215.1	6,627.8	6,888.9	8,722.3	10,614.3	10,850.1	15,380.2	23,293.6
5.30	3.30	1,901.6	3,232.3	6,599.7	6,849.4	8,762.1	10,626.3	10,856.2	15,365.7	23,271.8
5.40	2.73	1,899.8	3,251.3	6,654.9	6,829.2	8,668.0	10,567.5	10,878.6	15,449.9	23,452.0

Table A.26 Influence of differences between the mean container-dwell times of import/export and transshipment containers on the container accessibility ($\overline{\overline{\psi}}$), in terms of the mean number of shuffle moves per retrieval job, for selected yard-block layouts and all types of RMGC systems

$\overline{\delta} = 5$		Yard-block layout								
$\overline{\delta}^{ie}$	$\overline{\delta}^{ts}$	Small	Low	Narrow	Short	Medium	Long	Wide	High	Big
Resulting $\overline{\overline{\psi}}$ with the SRMGC system (s)										
4.60	7.27	0.323	0.298	1.126	1.123	1.109	1.085	1.064	1.611	1.144
4.70	6.70	0.328	0.305	1.120	1.110	1.097	1.081	1.071	1.611	1.153
4.80	6.13	0.322	0.298	1.125	1.117	1.102	1.085	1.085	1.591	1.164
4.90	5.57	0.319	0.296	1.122	1.133	1.103	1.088	1.072	1.593	1.160
5.00	**5.00**	**0.322**	**0.300**	**1.135**	**1.120**	**1.103**	**1.083**	**1.083**	**1.606**	**1.144**
5.10	4.43	0.332	0.301	1.124	1.115	1.119	1.075	1.079	1.584	1.126
5.20	3.87	0.314	0.291	1.121	1.116	1.099	1.095	1.066	1.608	1.122
5.30	3.30	0.316	0.297	1.109	1.114	1.089	1.072	1.071	1.597	1.102
5.40	2.73	0.331	0.295	1.105	1.107	1.091	1.065	1.069	1.579	1.106
Resulting $\overline{\overline{\psi}}$ with the TRMGC system (s)										
4.60	7.27	0.329	0.303	1.127	1.110	1.124	1.090	1.096	1.775	1.682
4.70	6.70	0.325	0.300	1.124	1.145	1.122	1.103	1.101	1.784	1.683
4.80	6.13	0.325	0.300	1.138	1.126	1.120	1.099	1.092	1.777	1.665
4.90	5.57	0.339	0.298	1.137	1.122	1.108	1.103	1.091	1.773	1.684
5.00	**5.00**	**0.324**	**0.296**	**1.127**	**1.130**	**1.130**	**1.097**	**1.090**	**1.762**	**1.675**
5.10	4.43	0.324	0.307	1.128	1.116	1.104	1.104	1.093	1.774	1.669
5.20	3.87	0.326	0.299	1.129	1.117	1.120	1.081	1.094	1.777	1.684
5.30	3.30	0.329	0.299	1.120	1.117	1.097	1.091	1.087	1.745	1.672
5.40	2.73	0.320	0.294	1.116	1.109	1.093	1.071	1.074	1.749	1.659
Resulting $\overline{\overline{\psi}}$ with the DRMGC system (s)										
4.60	7.27	0.328	0.294	1.121	1.121	1.121	1.094	1.090	1.760	1.661
4.70	6.70	0.326	0.297	1.119	1.134	1.112	1.102	1.094	1.759	1.675
4.80	6.13	0.324	0.291	1.127	1.125	1.116	1.088	1.091	1.757	1.661
4.90	5.57	0.332	0.304	1.138	1.137	1.100	1.086	1.078	1.766	1.671
5.00	**5.00**	**0.320**	**0.297**	**1.137**	**1.118**	**1.107**	**1.093**	**1.087**	**1.753**	**1.673**
5.10	4.43	0.324	0.296	1.118	1.120	1.117	1.089	1.090	1.764	1.672
5.20	3.87	0.327	0.296	1.119	1.114	1.103	1.075	1.093	1.767	1.649
5.30	3.30	0.315	0.296	1.117	1.116	1.099	1.089	1.086	1.739	1.650
5.40	2.73	0.321	0.305	1.106	1.108	1.097	1.082	1.068	1.751	1.642
Resulting $\overline{\overline{\psi}}$ with the TriRMGC system (s)										
4.60	7.27	0.321	0.296	1.127	1.108	1.114	1.092	1.091	1.794	1.752
4.70	6.70	0.328	0.297	1.141	1.119	1.118	1.097	1.084	1.782	1.761
4.80	6.13	0.323	0.296	1.139	1.115	1.112	1.090	1.097	1.781	1.748
4.90	5.57	0.326	0.296	1.132	1.116	1.107	1.081	1.093	1.782	1.762
5.00	**5.00**	**0.325**	**0.298**	**1.122**	**1.123**	**1.113**	**1.092**	**1.090**	**1.763**	**1.758**
5.10	4.43	0.319	0.293	1.122	1.108	1.101	1.090	1.087	1.776	1.756
5.20	3.87	0.325	0.299	1.132	1.117	1.109	1.088	1.093	1.782	1.752
5.30	3.30	0.317	0.295	1.118	1.110	1.101	1.082	1.069	1.762	1.752
5.40	2.73	0.322	0.289	1.110	1.093	1.085	1.063	1.071	1.766	1.750

A.5.3 Influence of the Transshipment Factor

Table A.27 Influence of the transshipment factor (π^{ts}) on the mean vehicle-waiting time ($\overline{\omega}^{hr+}_{total}$) for selected yard-block layouts and all types of RMGC systems

	Yard-block layout								
π^{ts}	Small	Low	Narrow	Short	Medium	Long	Wide	High	Big
Resulting $\overline{\omega}^{hr+}_{total}$ with the SRMGC system (s)									
0%	30.72	44.04	113.04	105.60	178.80	466.86	398.10	1,813.26	2,843.64
10%	26.82	42.00	115.44	100.44	202.98	506.82	401.58	1,891.98	3,040.50
20%	26.76	42.60	112.98	101.76	205.20	553.20	484.80	1,829.34	3,109.74
30%	**28.26**	**41.28**	**117.06**	**100.44**	**198.96**	**561.06**	**484.56**	**1,861.32**	**3,269.94**
40%	26.46	39.84	109.92	96.90	200.04	532.38	461.46	1,845.90	3,270.54
50%	24.72	36.06	101.46	95.94	203.04	574.32	496.68	2,005.02	3,410.34
60%	23.94	33.90	105.96	98.58	233.04	729.12	598.50	2,033.40	3,440.16
70%	21.60	30.60	111.06	93.42	310.44	831.24	643.68	2,004.54	3,475.50
80%	17.52	24.90	119.52	106.80	318.48	884.10	756.48	1,970.22	3,392.16
90%	13.14	19.08	108.42	96.36	385.80	1,049.82	860.04	1,980.60	3,246.90
100%	5.34	9.90	127.50	104.16	432.42	1,014.48	895.74	1,909.44	2,764.80
Resulting $\overline{\omega}^{hr+}_{total}$ with the TRMGC system (s)									
0%	10.56	15.78	46.32	42.60	57.18	78.66	72.48	292.92	1,400.22
10%	9.72	14.58	42.72	39.96	54.42	72.96	66.60	296.64	1,418.58
20%	9.42	14.28	41.46	36.60	50.76	72.66	66.06	285.42	1,502.34
30%	**8.82**	**13.44**	**38.16**	**35.58**	**48.30**	**67.44**	**61.98**	**304.08**	**1,567.38**
40%	8.34	12.60	33.90	33.00	44.04	62.94	55.68	341.52	1,682.88
50%	7.62	11.94	31.98	30.12	40.80	61.32	56.28	364.02	1,898.76
60%	7.80	10.74	29.58	28.08	39.18	68.46	54.84	466.26	2,049.00
70%	6.72	9.60	27.84	27.36	39.78	82.26	67.02	564.18	2,194.80
80%	6.30	9.72	25.50	23.10	39.54	107.22	82.92	670.08	2,394.54
90%	6.00	8.76	23.46	21.06	51.54	174.66	138.84	862.80	2,317.02
100%	5.16	8.94	26.28	22.38	54.90	305.04	201.54	1,067.28	2,419.32
Resulting $\overline{\omega}^{hr+}_{total}$ with the DRMGC system (s)									
0%	14.46	23.82	58.50	57.54	75.60	96.48	93.96	338.58	1,544.70
10%	13.74	23.58	56.88	56.94	72.84	96.12	93.60	359.40	1,582.86
20%	13.92	23.76	56.76	55.56	72.24	94.20	93.18	352.68	1,565.04
30%	**13.86**	**23.58**	**53.82**	**54.36**	**69.24**	**88.86**	**88.86**	**360.18**	**1,607.82**
40%	12.54	21.78	51.84	53.04	68.40	88.98	85.80	388.98	1,688.76
50%	12.78	21.24	47.40	49.50	63.24	81.84	86.34	435.36	1,814.64
60%	12.06	19.68	46.20	47.58	62.70	86.46	83.52	501.30	1,920.60
70%	11.16	18.48	44.88	46.38	60.66	90.42	92.64	545.52	2,079.06
80%	9.36	17.52	39.78	41.88	56.34	97.92	100.32	600.42	2,190.18
90%	8.88	15.72	34.32	35.70	59.22	105.72	120.12	721.86	2,328.00
100%	5.64	13.14	31.26	34.80	53.04	146.70	141.84	855.66	2,337.96
Resulting $\overline{\omega}^{hr+}_{total}$ with the TriRMGC system (s)									
0%	9.96	13.80	34.80	36.18	43.50	52.68	52.98	134.04	556.14
10%	9.24	13.44	33.72	35.28	42.36	50.04	50.58	132.90	581.16
20%	8.76	13.08	33.00	33.48	40.74	49.02	50.16	130.50	582.60
30%	**8.82**	**12.48**	**31.26**	**31.86**	**37.98**	**46.86**	**46.86**	**117.54**	**574.98**
40%	7.92	11.76	30.00	30.30	36.00	42.90	43.92	122.22	593.76
50%	7.98	11.40	27.54	28.68	33.54	40.98	41.76	129.48	668.04
60%	6.90	11.52	25.80	26.82	31.44	39.48	37.92	143.88	741.66
70%	7.44	10.50	25.20	25.62	29.94	37.08	38.28	161.70	848.22
80%	6.24	10.74	22.50	23.58	28.26	34.86	35.40	180.66	862.74
90%	6.18	12.00	19.50	21.42	27.24	35.52	34.98	206.58	916.98
100%	6.36	10.74	19.20	19.74	23.58	34.32	37.02	276.72	858.60

Table A.28 Influence of the transshipment factor (π^{ts}) on the vehicle-waiting time per waterside retrieval job ($\overline{\overline{\omega}}^{hr+}_{wsout}$) for selected yard-block layouts and all types of RMGC systems

	Yard-block layout								
π^{ts}	Small	Low	Narrow	Short	Medium	Long	Wide	High	Big
Resulting $\overline{\overline{\omega}}^{hr+}_{wsout}$ with the SRMGC system (s)									
0%	0.06	0.54	45.00	39.00	118.14	508.62	429.24	2,801.64	3,613.74
10%	0.78	2.46	55.20	41.16	171.96	629.88	452.52	2,995.44	4,146.66
20%	2.34	2.82	60.60	49.20	189.42	757.44	644.10	3,020.28	4,522.62
30%	**3.24**	**5.52**	**78.00**	**56.04**	**198.72**	**789.12**	**671.58**	**3,180.30**	**4,959.72**
40%	3.18	7.08	81.72	64.86	222.42	796.92	680.58	3,319.08	5,210.52
50%	5.46	9.54	79.92	74.76	247.62	897.00	775.74	3,610.02	5,553.96
60%	7.08	12.06	102.24	91.20	319.38	1,198.50	981.36	3,617.70	5,650.38
70%	9.18	12.54	131.04	104.40	500.10	1,481.58	1,125.42	3,715.98	5,867.70
80%	10.38	14.40	170.40	151.08	548.64	1,630.08	1,399.14	3,725.40	5,893.02
90%	13.08	18.18	178.02	156.00	719.46	2,010.42	1,647.36	3,871.56	5,858.40
100%	10.80	19.98	255.06	208.56	865.20	2,028.48	1,788.36	3,928.02	5,519.16
Resulting $\overline{\overline{\omega}}^{hr+}_{wsout}$ with the TRMGC system (s)									
0%	0.18	0.42	7.80	5.64	12.66	24.72	18.84	335.46	2,005.74
10%	1.08	1.98	9.18	8.16	16.56	29.70	24.78	380.88	2,222.04
20%	1.44	3.90	11.64	9.90	20.04	42.18	35.76	396.72	2,601.24
30%	**2.28**	**4.14**	**15.06**	**13.20**	**25.80**	**48.48**	**42.12**	**486.30**	**3,019.80**
40%	4.26	6.42	16.68	16.26	27.18	55.98	42.72	627.42	3,520.14
50%	5.10	10.14	20.10	17.64	31.62	64.26	58.80	687.24	4,233.60
60%	7.32	10.62	24.18	22.92	38.04	98.94	69.72	957.96	4,644.00
70%	6.84	11.28	27.90	29.04	52.08	146.16	112.80	1,234.20	5,061.18
80%	8.58	14.46	32.46	29.22	62.64	213.60	159.90	1,470.78	5,352.66
90%	10.26	15.18	38.04	33.78	97.26	360.48	285.00	1,856.52	4,944.36
100%	10.50	17.94	52.50	44.70	109.50	606.72	402.42	2,164.38	4,818.54
Resulting $\overline{\overline{\omega}}^{hr+}_{wsout}$ with the DRMGC system (s)									
0%	0.06	0.06	7.14	7.08	14.04	27.84	26.64	383.46	2,248.92
10%	0.72	1.80	11.10	11.22	20.16	37.20	34.08	442.98	2,464.38
20%	1.14	2.94	14.46	14.64	24.78	44.28	45.12	466.20	2,540.40
30%	**2.76**	**5.34**	**20.10**	**18.72**	**30.78**	**47.46**	**46.26**	**510.54**	**2,758.62**
40%	3.90	6.96	21.30	25.98	38.88	60.48	54.48	605.34	2,997.90
50%	6.96	9.06	28.68	28.26	41.64	60.72	70.98	725.40	3,272.40
60%	7.44	12.00	31.50	34.98	49.92	84.42	81.36	882.12	3,564.00
70%	7.62	13.20	39.90	43.44	62.28	109.08	119.46	1,022.94	4,009.74
80%	9.00	17.04	43.50	47.58	70.80	146.34	151.92	1,167.78	4,284.24
90%	12.18	21.06	49.32	52.38	95.04	186.00	214.92	1,452.30	4,612.80
100%	11.40	26.28	62.22	69.78	105.84	291.96	283.38	1,767.00	4,668.78
Resulting $\overline{\overline{\omega}}^{hr+}_{wsout}$ with the TriRMGC system (s)									
0%	0.24	0.24	3.00	3.48	4.50	7.26	7.56	89.40	690.18
10%	0.90	1.44	5.64	5.52	9.00	11.46	11.88	103.32	791.34
20%	1.44	3.60	7.86	8.46	12.66	15.90	16.68	113.28	841.92
30%	**2.22**	**5.34**	**12.90**	**12.54**	**16.32**	**19.68**	**20.94**	**109.68**	**883.26**
40%	3.36	6.84	15.90	14.40	20.10	23.76	23.94	135.42	967.44
50%	5.70	9.12	18.54	19.38	23.82	28.80	32.28	164.58	1,132.50
60%	4.62	11.76	20.94	21.06	26.16	36.06	33.18	215.04	1,319.82
70%	8.70	12.72	26.64	27.12	32.28	41.46	44.34	267.36	1,600.26
80%	7.74	15.60	29.46	30.96	37.62	48.84	50.04	332.82	1,653.66
90%	10.44	21.36	30.30	34.62	45.60	60.78	59.58	403.80	1,812.36
100%	12.72	21.42	38.22	39.30	47.10	68.58	73.68	560.22	1,719.24

Table A.29 Influence of the transshipment factor (π^{ts}) on the mean crane-waiting time in the handover areas ($\overline{\omega}^{hr-}_{total}$) for selected yard-block layouts and all types of RMGC systems

	Yard-block layout								
π^{ts}	Small	Low	Narrow	Short	Medium	Long	Wide	High	Big
Resulting $\overline{\omega}^{hr-}_{total}$ with the SRMGC system (s)									
0%	107.04	80.28	54.24	56.64	34.56	17.76	20.34	9.60	2.34
10%	110.52	84.30	57.66	58.92	37.20	19.44	22.02	10.86	3.66
20%	118.50	88.32	61.20	63.42	38.88	20.58	23.40	11.52	5.28
30%	**124.38**	**94.92**	**63.84**	**67.26**	**41.52**	**22.86**	**25.80**	**14.64**	**7.08**
40%	131.64	99.48	68.40	69.36	45.12	26.58	29.58	16.86	9.30
50%	139.20	106.20	72.54	73.98	48.84	29.40	32.58	19.26	11.58
60%	150.54	115.32	78.24	79.14	53.22	32.82	34.74	22.32	13.80
70%	162.78	125.04	85.20	86.46	57.90	38.40	38.46	26.94	16.92
80%	175.74	136.26	90.36	91.56	64.14	44.16	45.60	32.10	20.58
90%	193.14	147.84	100.68	102.84	72.78	51.00	54.66	39.12	26.70
100%	216.90	164.40	115.44	114.84	81.66	63.18	63.24	48.30	34.74
Resulting $\overline{\omega}^{hr-}_{total}$ with the TRMGC system (s)									
0%	119.10	96.12	77.28	78.60	60.78	45.06	47.40	35.22	5.88
10%	123.78	101.22	82.38	81.42	62.88	47.16	48.90	35.16	7.38
20%	130.56	106.26	83.88	86.58	65.82	49.02	51.06	36.06	8.82
30%	**135.84**	**112.32**	**87.84**	**91.26**	**67.86**	**50.28**	**53.40**	**38.58**	**10.56**
40%	142.62	117.96	92.70	93.54	71.52	52.56	55.56	40.38	13.32
50%	151.68	122.34	96.90	94.92	73.98	54.48	57.60	40.38	17.16
60%	161.64	131.10	100.02	99.90	76.56	55.80	57.90	41.04	20.04
70%	172.74	140.64	106.44	105.60	80.94	59.16	59.64	44.58	24.42
80%	184.74	150.00	110.88	111.12	83.70	60.78	64.80	45.96	28.68
90%	202.56	160.02	117.48	118.56	88.38	64.74	67.20	49.38	33.78
100%	220.74	170.82	125.04	125.10	92.76	71.34	70.80	52.20	37.50
Resulting $\overline{\omega}^{hr-}_{total}$ with the DRMGC system (s)									
0%	120.36	102.30	83.10	82.02	66.18	50.82	50.40	39.72	9.72
10%	124.98	105.66	87.66	85.86	68.76	53.16	52.50	40.56	10.62
20%	132.84	110.16	90.42	89.82	71.16	55.44	55.38	41.58	11.34
30%	**139.32**	**117.48**	**95.28**	**95.46**	**75.18**	**57.24**	**57.66**	**44.52**	**12.60**
40%	145.68	124.02	100.08	99.12	78.96	60.42	61.14	46.74	13.92
50%	152.82	128.58	106.38	100.86	82.26	63.90	64.80	48.30	17.22
60%	165.66	138.30	111.36	108.78	86.34	67.62	66.60	49.62	19.80
70%	173.22	149.94	117.84	115.68	93.00	72.30	70.38	54.30	22.14
80%	188.64	158.34	124.26	122.04	98.04	76.92	78.00	57.30	26.34
90%	207.84	172.50	133.74	132.06	105.96	84.78	82.86	62.64	30.42
100%	231.36	187.86	145.50	142.08	116.04	93.78	89.88	66.96	37.86
Resulting $\overline{\omega}^{hr-}_{total}$ with the TriRMGC system (s)									
0%	124.08	106.26	90.18	89.04	74.34	61.32	60.78	52.20	21.06
10%	129.12	110.16	93.96	91.74	77.10	64.02	63.00	54.06	21.66
20%	135.90	115.74	97.44	97.68	79.14	65.94	65.52	54.90	22.80
30%	**140.40**	**121.98**	**103.44**	**101.10**	**84.00**	**68.22**	**68.64**	**58.38**	**23.88**
40%	148.38	127.32	106.98	104.88	87.48	70.98	71.40	61.08	26.28
50%	156.12	134.46	109.68	108.66	90.78	74.46	75.36	60.90	27.12
60%	165.48	141.90	118.44	114.84	94.86	78.12	77.40	63.42	29.46
70%	178.02	151.08	126.18	121.62	100.20	82.86	81.96	66.54	31.08
80%	191.04	160.86	130.74	127.62	105.60	87.66	85.20	69.24	33.42
90%	208.86	175.14	140.10	137.16	112.92	93.12	91.32	71.88	37.92
100%	231.48	190.02	149.76	147.96	118.08	98.16	96.42	75.12	43.86

Table A.30 Influence of the transshipment factor (π^{ts}) on the mean crane-empty-movement time per job ($\overline{\overline{m}}^{xye}_{total}$) for selected yard-block layouts and all types of RMGC systems

	Yard-block layout								
π^{ts}	Small	Low	Narrow	Short	Medium	Long	Wide	High	Big
Resulting $\overline{\overline{m}}^{xye}_{total}$ with the SRMGC system (s)									
0%	26.22	32.10	27.24	23.01	26.47	29.49	26.33	23.22	27.43
10%	26.00	32.21	27.07	23.08	26.51	29.54	26.44	23.40	27.61
20%	25.98	31.98	27.13	23.20	26.61	29.47	26.46	23.56	27.73
30%	**26.05**	**31.87**	**26.97**	**23.22**	**26.63**	**29.48**	**26.57**	**23.73**	**27.72**
40%	26.20	32.01	27.12	23.20	26.66	30.03	26.80	23.91	27.79
50%	26.01	31.94	26.98	23.08	26.73	29.94	26.71	23.83	27.89
60%	25.79	31.79	27.09	23.20	26.79	30.19	26.74	23.96	27.93
70%	25.46	31.36	27.01	22.92	26.61	30.10	26.73	24.27	28.23
80%	24.63	30.76	26.52	22.69	26.62	29.93	26.61	24.04	28.50
90%	23.78	29.64	26.31	22.18	25.95	29.82	26.22	24.05	28.32
100%	21.76	27.83	24.28	21.13	24.92	28.70	25.42	23.32	27.81
Resulting $\overline{\overline{m}}^{xye}_{total}$ with the TRMGC system (s)									
0%	23.83	29.34	34.29	30.95	34.81	38.68	35.02	36.81	38.53
10%	23.71	29.11	34.24	30.67	34.48	38.50	34.85	36.80	39.01
20%	23.18	28.68	34.01	30.55	34.45	38.49	34.77	37.10	39.69
30%	**23.34**	**28.35**	**33.76**	**30.25**	**34.07**	**38.12**	**34.64**	**37.21**	**40.77**
40%	22.86	28.08	33.54	30.04	33.77	38.04	34.43	37.61	41.56
50%	22.63	28.06	33.51	30.03	33.82	37.87	34.31	37.63	42.16
60%	22.58	27.72	33.36	29.82	33.92	38.18	34.47	37.97	43.00
70%	22.43	27.72	33.43	29.73	33.91	38.46	34.69	38.70	43.76
80%	22.25	27.90	33.52	29.79	34.13	38.68	35.02	39.43	44.21
90%	22.62	27.91	33.47	29.84	34.35	39.30	35.43	39.99	43.79
100%	23.17	29.02	33.63	29.95	34.77	40.10	36.07	40.61	43.98
Resulting $\overline{\overline{m}}^{xye}_{total}$ with the DRMGC system (s)									
0%	52.05	65.37	61.55	60.89	61.87	61.40	60.84	52.07	44.24
10%	52.64	67.01	62.54	61.70	62.20	61.79	60.76	51.67	44.54
20%	53.98	67.49	62.89	62.57	62.67	61.89	60.56	51.79	44.77
30%	**55.77**	**69.14**	**62.73**	**62.89**	**62.78**	**61.85**	**60.88**	**52.25**	**45.15**
40%	57.37	70.79	64.53	63.15	63.37	62.05	61.44	52.69	45.99
50%	58.80	72.06	65.36	63.89	64.14	62.94	61.81	52.81	46.98
60%	60.30	72.99	66.57	65.31	64.94	62.98	62.14	52.92	48.58
70%	61.78	76.18	67.51	66.43	65.45	63.73	62.97	54.11	50.05
80%	63.31	77.74	68.98	68.33	66.73	65.05	64.94	54.77	52.33
90%	67.18	80.67	71.42	69.85	68.14	67.00	66.10	56.95	54.67
100%	70.11	84.76	72.30	71.68	70.75	68.87	69.00	58.78	58.76
Resulting $\overline{\overline{m}}^{xye}_{total}$ with the TriRMGC system (s)									
0%	48.00	62.07	67.10	66.82	69.38	71.52	70.60	67.01	59.95
10%	48.57	63.14	68.53	67.01	69.83	71.67	70.04	66.69	59.63
20%	49.99	64.89	68.23	68.27	70.30	71.37	70.23	66.63	59.85
30%	**51.55**	**65.81**	**69.11**	**68.63**	**70.12**	**70.81**	**70.15**	**66.70**	**60.22**
40%	52.43	66.80	69.07	69.26	70.36	70.90	70.17	66.85	60.81
50%	54.06	68.92	70.66	69.74	71.00	70.98	70.40	66.62	60.90
60%	54.80	69.82	71.35	71.41	71.10	71.07	70.76	66.58	62.01
70%	58.63	71.94	72.83	72.23	72.35	72.30	71.50	67.60	63.15
80%	60.58	73.95	74.67	73.80	73.55	73.26	72.86	68.42	64.67
90%	64.17	77.47	75.94	76.13	75.93	75.62	75.03	70.27	68.19
100%	67.43	82.63	78.49	78.94	77.90	77.56	77.59	72.15	74.20

Table A.31 Influence of the transshipment factor (π^{ts}) on the mean crane-interference time per job ($\overline{\overline{m}}^{cit}_{total}$) for selected yard-block layouts and all types of RMGC systems

	Yard-block layout								
π^{ts}	Small	Low	Narrow	Short	Medium	Long	Wide	High	Big
Resulting $\overline{\overline{m}}^{cit}_{total}$ with the SRMGC system (s)									
0%	0.00	0.00	0.00	0.00	0.00	0.00	0.00	0.00	0.00
10%	0.00	0.00	0.00	0.00	0.00	0.00	0.00	0.00	0.00
20%	0.00	0.00	0.00	0.00	0.00	0.00	0.00	0.00	0.00
30%	**0.00**	**0.00**	**0.00**	**0.00**	**0.00**	**0.00**	**0.00**	**0.00**	**0.00**
40%	0.00	0.00	0.00	0.00	0.00	0.00	0.00	0.00	0.00
50%	0.00	0.00	0.00	0.00	0.00	0.00	0.00	0.00	0.00
60%	0.00	0.00	0.00	0.00	0.00	0.00	0.00	0.00	0.00
70%	0.00	0.00	0.00	0.00	0.00	0.00	0.00	0.00	0.00
80%	0.00	0.00	0.00	0.00	0.00	0.00	0.00	0.00	0.00
90%	0.00	0.00	0.00	0.00	0.00	0.00	0.00	0.00	0.00
100%	0.00	0.00	0.00	0.00	0.00	0.00	0.00	0.00	0.00
Resulting $\overline{\overline{m}}^{cit}_{total}$ with the TRMGC system (s)									
0%	2.19	2.30	12.36	13.09	12.60	12.72	12.81	20.13	20.97
10%	2.15	2.17	12.35	12.86	12.53	12.40	12.63	19.89	20.54
20%	2.14	2.12	12.33	12.58	12.15	12.43	12.50	19.97	20.70
30%	**2.22**	**2.10**	**11.92**	**12.42**	**12.16**	**11.92**	**12.14**	**19.43**	**20.71**
40%	2.07	2.01	11.54	12.15	11.61	11.62	11.78	19.38	20.54
50%	2.08	2.15	11.34	12.05	11.38	11.34	11.49	19.34	20.05
60%	2.11	2.11	11.33	11.77	11.53	11.52	11.42	19.39	20.14
70%	2.27	2.25	11.44	11.90	11.44	11.58	11.61	19.46	19.90
80%	2.43	2.57	11.35	11.67	11.24	11.49	11.51	19.90	19.37
90%	2.61	2.51	11.33	11.88	11.53	11.61	11.66	19.87	18.84
100%	2.80	2.97	11.36	11.81	11.64	12.00	11.95	20.55	18.65
Resulting $\overline{\overline{m}}^{cit}_{total}$ with the DRMGC system (s)									
0%	25.29	31.86	31.59	35.14	32.21	27.90	31.20	27.45	20.05
10%	26.12	34.19	33.09	36.37	33.26	28.68	31.62	27.43	20.01
20%	28.36	35.87	34.58	38.21	34.13	29.35	32.23	27.76	20.11
30%	**31.09**	**38.13**	**35.30**	**39.74**	**35.31**	**29.73**	**32.78**	**28.21**	**20.21**
40%	33.43	41.08	37.66	40.88	36.66	31.02	34.21	28.96	20.83
50%	36.47	43.57	39.85	42.45	38.12	32.30	35.45	29.41	21.45
60%	39.41	47.13	41.63	45.06	39.78	33.27	36.21	29.93	22.65
70%	42.13	51.97	44.27	48.11	41.69	34.88	38.17	31.08	23.74
80%	46.95	56.81	47.43	51.10	44.76	37.42	41.33	32.44	26.02
90%	53.39	64.46	52.17	55.13	47.76	41.67	44.62	35.94	28.70
100%	59.02	73.98	56.77	59.99	53.71	46.53	50.31	39.49	34.45
Resulting $\overline{\overline{m}}^{cit}_{total}$ with the TriRMGC system (s)									
0%	25.64	33.19	43.56	47.99	45.36	43.12	46.20	49.21	42.17
10%	26.51	35.13	45.76	49.00	47.23	43.87	46.57	49.06	41.39
20%	29.25	38.58	46.52	50.76	48.08	44.31	47.53	49.33	41.45
30%	**31.02**	**40.31**	**48.66**	**53.32**	**49.18**	**44.71**	**47.95**	**49.43**	**41.62**
40%	33.42	43.34	50.26	54.08	50.11	45.65	49.24	50.15	41.63
50%	36.22	46.48	51.71	55.56	51.63	46.76	50.80	50.49	41.64
60%	37.27	49.26	53.65	58.57	52.98	48.14	51.59	51.44	42.00
70%	44.17	54.01	57.27	61.11	56.14	50.39	53.54	52.33	43.67
80%	47.79	58.56	60.37	64.41	58.50	52.55	56.06	53.98	45.33
90%	53.42	66.28	63.58	68.88	63.40	56.54	60.21	57.03	49.06
100%	59.92	72.63	69.15	73.78	67.16	60.95	64.75	60.45	55.69

Table A.32 Influence of the transshipment factor (π^{ts}) on the crane workload during the simulation horizon in terms of performed jobs ($\overline{|J|}$) for selected yard-block layouts and all types of RMGC systems

π^{ts}	Yard-block layout								
	Small	Low	Narrow	Short	Medium	Long	Wide	High	Big
Resulting $\overline{\lvert J\rvert}$ with the SRMGC system (jobs)									
0%	1,881.6	3,225.9	6,578.9	6,879.7	8,739.8	10,492.2	10,756.2	13,748.6	13,889.6
10%	1,870.5	3,215.0	6,598.4	6,807.8	8,772.2	10,416.4	10,705.9	13,645.9	13,741.7
20%	1,859.6	3,253.6	6,610.4	6,889.3	8,793.6	10,615.9	10,816.1	13,479.0	13,722.2
30%	**1,871.8**	**3,208.8**	**6,596.5**	**6,792.8**	**8,683.4**	**10,466.3**	**10,776.3**	**13,369.4**	**13,711.1**
40%	1,868.1	3,222.5	6,449.5	6,699.7	8,605.3	10,190.9	10,505.8	13,152.0	13,440.6
50%	1,854.5	3,106.9	6,324.1	6,597.6	8,416.7	10,073.3	10,275.0	12,892.9	13,443.0
60%	1,857.1	3,113.7	6,362.5	6,609.0	8,416.7	10,058.2	10,302.9	12,684.9	13,222.0
70%	1,850.1	3,169.0	6,479.3	6,638.0	8,556.1	10,239.5	10,454.3	12,512.2	13,217.9
80%	1,816.2	3,119.6	6,431.9	6,717.3	8,377.7	9,978.1	10,238.3	12,226.4	12,905.4
90%	1,791.4	3,060.2	6,233.5	6,423.2	8,318.6	9,822.3	10,101.3	12,012.7	12,455.1
100%	1,768.7	3,006.5	6,264.2	6,461.3	8,297.9	9,656.4	9,990.4	11,791.9	12,100.7
Resulting $\overline{\lvert J\rvert}$ with the TRMGC system (jobs)									
0%	1,901.2	3,234.8	6,659.0	6,895.6	8,808.7	10,693.7	10,853.5	15,482.1	21,944.1
10%	1,879.5	3,238.0	6,640.0	6,836.1	8,826.1	10,675.3	10,780.4	15,450.5	21,706.6
20%	1,893.8	3,244.3	6,690.7	6,870.3	8,815.6	10,655.2	10,973.2	15,196.3	21,557.1
30%	**1,903.5**	**3,224.1**	**6,592.4**	**6,857.8**	**8,784.5**	**10,615.3**	**10,900.6**	**15,170.8**	**21,104.9**
40%	1,876.5	3,223.7	6,499.2	6,798.5	8,596.7	10,309.9	10,639.9	15,001.3	20,364.2
50%	1,836.4	3,163.7	6,370.2	6,589.8	8,423.6	10,263.0	10,467.2	14,761.8	19,608.3
60%	1,837.4	3,122.2	6,391.8	6,649.1	8,495.2	10,322.2	10,426.8	14,866.5	18,698.0
70%	1,886.5	3,203.9	6,473.9	6,777.4	8,613.7	10,455.6	10,650.1	14,727.3	17,824.4
80%	1,829.2	3,147.8	6,414.9	6,673.7	8,419.4	10,296.5	10,458.8	14,537.1	16,427.9
90%	1,822.4	3,061.5	6,264.9	6,498.1	8,419.2	10,092.1	10,361.3	14,094.2	14,901.7
100%	1,775.5	3,025.5	6,251.8	6,547.5	8,310.2	9,948.7	10,210.8	13,695.4	13,722.5
Resulting $\overline{\lvert J\rvert}$ with the DRMGC system (jobs)									
0%	1,903.8	3,223.1	6,650.1	6,874.2	8,821.5	10,696.2	10,826.5	15,293.5	21,528.5
10%	1,879.1	3,244.3	6,614.1	6,837.6	8,832.7	10,624.7	10,785.4	15,339.4	21,433.7
20%	1,897.3	3,238.2	6,645.3	6,859.3	8,832.3	10,653.3	10,975.9	15,204.9	21,406.7
30%	**1,901.9**	**3,222.4**	**6,623.5**	**6,834.0**	**8,713.7**	**10,605.3**	**10,893.6**	**15,175.5**	**21,213.5**
40%	1,872.1	3,218.4	6,524.6	6,766.5	8,604.7	10,288.2	10,637.7	15,052.1	20,799.1
50%	1,837.6	3,149.4	6,356.1	6,596.8	8,407.1	10,253.0	10,473.3	14,758.3	20,481.5
60%	1,839.2	3,127.7	6,350.7	6,651.0	8,436.9	10,283.0	10,435.7	14,818.2	19,901.7
70%	1,882.6	3,200.4	6,484.0	6,792.0	8,619.3	10,407.1	10,616.1	14,839.5	19,782.7
80%	1,821.8	3,134.1	6,419.0	6,696.4	8,385.9	10,307.8	10,486.9	14,641.4	19,088.7
90%	1,818.8	3,056.0	6,269.6	6,450.3	8,416.2	10,099.3	10,373.0	14,499.2	18,367.6
100%	1,773.5	3,025.9	6,279.4	6,566.9	8,270.0	10,050.5	10,262.9	14,524.7	17,514.3
Resulting $\overline{\lvert J\rvert}$ with the TriRMGC system (jobs)									
0%	1,903.1	3,230.9	6,633.7	6,863.7	8,800.2	10,647.8	10,827.4	15,550.1	23,524.7
10%	1,889.8	3,237.0	6,617.4	6,836.5	8,812.2	10,580.0	10,777.4	15,461.2	23,472.7
20%	1,892.0	3,241.6	6,687.0	6,907.8	8,778.7	10,636.5	10,950.4	15,366.2	23,413.4
30%	**1,907.0**	**3,249.5**	**6,614.4**	**6,831.8**	**8,732.5**	**10,583.9**	**10,895.8**	**15,192.1**	**23,097.9**
40%	1,870.5	3,201.8	6,468.1	6,725.8	8,584.5	10,367.8	10,698.4	15,114.2	22,727.5
50%	1,844.1	3,135.2	6,381.2	6,592.7	8,395.5	10,259.9	10,378.7	14,963.2	22,614.5
60%	1,813.7	3,144.7	6,418.4	6,629.2	8,504.3	10,308.3	10,381.3	15,012.6	22,330.6
70%	1,848.2	3,179.9	6,498.9	6,752.5	8,698.3	10,357.7	10,618.2	15,252.2	22,106.0
80%	1,830.0	3,156.0	6,395.3	6,697.2	8,444.9	10,257.8	10,390.1	15,055.2	21,302.1
90%	1,812.9	3,080.3	6,257.8	6,518.6	8,416.6	10,105.7	10,281.6	14,948.5	20,551.3
100%	1,777.0	3,031.7	6,262.4	6,500.7	8,368.5	10,113.8	10,209.4	14,906.3	18,562.8

Table A.33 Influence of the transshipment factor (π^{ts}) on the container accessibility ($\overline{\overline{\psi}}$), in terms of the mean number of shuffle moves per retrieval job, for selected yard-block layouts and all types of RMGC systems

	Yard-block layout								
π^{ts}	Small	Low	Narrow	Short	Medium	Long	Wide	High	Big
Resulting $\overline{\overline{\psi}}$ with the SRMGC system (jobs)									
0%	0.321	0.296	1.121	1.135	1.111	1.085	1.085	1.691	1.213
10%	0.315	0.296	1.128	1.137	1.114	1.082	1.079	1.655	1.178
20%	0.323	0.296	1.122	1.116	1.122	1.105	1.093	1.639	1.161
30%	**0.322**	**0.300**	**1.135**	**1.120**	**1.103**	**1.083**	**1.083**	**1.606**	**1.144**
40%	0.313	0.292	1.107	1.111	1.101	1.054	1.057	1.570	1.101
50%	0.305	0.281	1.092	1.090	1.078	1.040	1.039	1.532	1.102
60%	0.317	0.291	1.083	1.098	1.082	1.033	1.044	1.524	1.093
70%	0.317	0.302	1.118	1.101	1.093	1.057	1.064	1.486	1.101
80%	0.303	0.295	1.119	1.116	1.081	1.042	1.048	1.479	1.060
90%	0.307	0.281	1.069	1.085	1.076	1.023	1.029	1.445	1.046
100%	0.310	0.275	1.096	1.103	1.076	1.006	1.024	1.456	1.047
Resulting $\overline{\overline{\psi}}$ with the TRMGC system (jobs)									
0%	0.322	0.302	1.128	1.140	1.112	1.099	1.093	1.815	1.747
10%	0.314	0.296	1.129	1.137	1.122	1.104	1.087	1.787	1.731
20%	0.321	0.301	1.147	1.129	1.120	1.118	1.115	1.792	1.709
30%	**0.324**	**0.296**	**1.127**	**1.130**	**1.130**	**1.097**	**1.090**	**1.762**	**1.675**
40%	0.322	0.300	1.106	1.118	1.091	1.062	1.065	1.742	1.636
50%	0.315	0.295	1.093	1.096	1.080	1.055	1.049	1.728	1.576
60%	0.315	0.293	1.097	1.097	1.093	1.069	1.049	1.751	1.539
70%	0.327	0.295	1.119	1.127	1.095	1.089	1.084	1.758	1.492
80%	0.322	0.305	1.108	1.107	1.073	1.069	1.068	1.779	1.410
90%	0.322	0.286	1.083	1.098	1.092	1.050	1.048	1.744	1.316
100%	0.319	0.281	1.080	1.108	1.083	1.050	1.040	1.760	1.248
Resulting $\overline{\overline{\psi}}$ with the DRMGC system (jobs)									
0%	0.324	0.292	1.122	1.124	1.116	1.102	1.089	1.787	1.727
10%	0.317	0.302	1.119	1.130	1.123	1.103	1.088	1.785	1.699
20%	0.329	0.299	1.133	1.130	1.125	1.116	1.117	1.788	1.694
30%	**0.320**	**0.297**	**1.137**	**1.118**	**1.107**	**1.093**	**1.087**	**1.753**	**1.673**
40%	0.325	0.294	1.111	1.109	1.093	1.058	1.065	1.748	1.633
50%	0.312	0.288	1.089	1.099	1.082	1.053	1.059	1.718	1.614
60%	0.312	0.295	1.090	1.099	1.077	1.057	1.053	1.726	1.573
70%	0.322	0.296	1.115	1.126	1.098	1.078	1.080	1.736	1.569
80%	0.315	0.295	1.109	1.122	1.064	1.074	1.075	1.723	1.534
90%	0.319	0.284	1.084	1.085	1.094	1.030	1.045	1.702	1.490
100%	0.319	0.281	1.090	1.114	1.067	1.051	1.035	1.737	1.447
Resulting $\overline{\overline{\psi}}$ with the TriRMGC system (jobs)									
0%	0.323	0.298	1.124	1.119	1.110	1.091	1.086	1.806	1.791
10%	0.325	0.297	1.121	1.135	1.120	1.091	1.088	1.810	1.791
20%	0.320	0.300	1.147	1.132	1.117	1.112	1.114	1.816	1.777
30%	**0.325**	**0.298**	**1.122**	**1.123**	**1.113**	**1.092**	**1.090**	**1.763**	**1.758**
40%	0.327	0.296	1.106	1.103	1.082	1.070	1.074	1.755	1.749
50%	0.322	0.286	1.087	1.099	1.060	1.053	1.050	1.739	1.728
60%	0.314	0.291	1.102	1.109	1.079	1.066	1.038	1.755	1.706
70%	0.309	0.294	1.132	1.116	1.109	1.088	1.082	1.775	1.713
80%	0.321	0.293	1.104	1.109	1.073	1.064	1.053	1.778	1.699
90%	0.309	0.283	1.089	1.089	1.078	1.035	1.031	1.769	1.639
100%	0.308	0.276	1.101	1.089	1.070	1.041	1.025	1.783	1.558

A.5.4 *Influence of the Vessel-Call Pattern*

Table A.34 Influence of the unevenness of the vessel-call pattern, in terms of the VCP-overlapping time (h), on the mean vehicle-waiting time ($\overline{\omega}^{hr+}_{total}$) for selected yard-block layouts and all types of RMGC systems

VCP		Yard-block layout								
Name	Overlap (h)	Small	Low	Narrow	Short	Medium	Long	Wide	High	Big
Resulting $\overline{\omega}^{hr+}_{total}$ with the SRMGC system (s)										
VCP1	**0**	**28.26**	**41.28**	**117.06**	**100.44**	**198.96**	**561.06**	**484.56**	**1,861.32**	**3,269.94**
VCP2	12	24.72	41.22	107.34	94.20	193.74	519.06	438.30	1,790.28	3,042.24
VCP3	24	27.96	43.98	127.14	108.78	282.42	729.54	642.66	1,998.66	3,569.40
VCP4	32	26.10	38.94	126.54	108.96	287.28	822.42	676.26	2,272.08	3,508.02
VCP5	52	26.46	38.10	129.18	113.52	329.70	967.68	791.52	2,451.12	3,769.56
VCP6	64	24.18	39.54	132.24	119.34	321.66	962.70	785.40	2,678.04	3,803.94
VCP7	84	24.06	37.80	160.68	140.64	507.72	1,225.38	1,043.88	2,850.06	4,417.44
VCP8	116	23.28	32.88	168.12	131.04	584.52	1,422.24	1,212.24	3,133.32	4,937.16
VCP9	138	23.16	37.08	175.50	151.98	546.66	1,338.66	1,236.06	3,307.08	4,886.58
VCP10	148	22.38	34.08	289.50	244.14	864.90	1,706.34	1,533.36	3,664.68	5,941.92
Resulting $\overline{\omega}^{hr+}_{total}$ with the TRMGC system (s)										
VCP1	**0**	**8.82**	**13.44**	**38.16**	**35.58**	**48.30**	**67.44**	**61.98**	**304.08**	**1,567.38**
VCP2	12	9.66	15.18	39.48	35.40	47.34	71.28	64.92	330.96	1,667.04
VCP3	24	10.92	15.84	42.06	38.64	53.40	81.00	75.06	338.46	1,920.60
VCP4	32	8.88	13.56	37.74	34.74	46.50	70.98	64.56	457.26	2,074.80
VCP5	52	8.46	12.72	37.08	33.30	48.54	82.20	65.64	649.56	2,835.96
VCP6	64	8.94	14.52	38.88	34.56	49.26	85.92	69.24	485.04	2,645.76
VCP7	84	8.82	13.08	39.42	34.86	53.82	107.64	91.80	891.18	3,917.94
VCP8	116	8.52	12.84	37.62	32.46	59.22	155.22	120.72	1,223.04	4,996.68
VCP9	138	9.24	15.18	39.54	35.88	60.54	133.62	122.58	990.24	5,443.14
VCP10	148	8.64	12.90	47.76	41.58	93.06	322.56	251.76	1,941.42	6,385.44
Resulting $\overline{\omega}^{hr+}_{total}$ with the DRMGC system (s)										
VCP1	**0**	**13.86**	**23.58**	**53.82**	**54.36**	**69.24**	**88.86**	**88.86**	**360.18**	**1,607.82**
VCP2	12	14.04	24.48	54.48	54.18	68.46	91.98	93.78	389.16	1,647.06
VCP3	24	14.88	25.86	59.70	62.16	78.36	112.92	109.38	465.66	1,776.78
VCP4	32	13.26	23.22	53.22	54.00	67.26	93.06	96.66	498.00	1,976.46
VCP5	52	13.62	21.60	51.96	51.60	68.40	89.22	94.50	681.30	2,332.74
VCP6	64	14.28	23.70	55.56	53.82	69.60	107.82	96.96	519.66	2,201.04
VCP7	84	13.56	23.64	52.26	52.14	74.04	109.80	112.44	832.92	2,900.46
VCP8	116	12.84	20.94	50.52	50.28	66.78	117.66	115.62	997.56	3,585.90
VCP9	138	14.40	24.66	53.64	56.64	80.64	133.92	139.14	770.88	3,581.16
VCP10	148	14.22	22.38	55.38	54.24	93.96	233.70	217.50	1,407.78	4,303.62
Resulting $\overline{\omega}^{hr+}_{total}$ with the TriRMGC system (s)										
VCP1	**0**	**8.82**	**12.48**	**31.26**	**31.86**	**37.98**	**46.86**	**46.86**	**117.54**	**574.98**
VCP2	12	9.36	13.74	32.10	32.58	38.46	47.10	48.00	134.94	626.58
VCP3	24	11.04	15.42	36.12	36.96	43.02	52.62	53.64	144.66	627.72
VCP4	32	8.58	12.84	30.54	31.50	37.32	46.14	46.68	155.76	781.32
VCP5	52	8.16	12.18	30.24	30.72	36.06	43.14	44.16	180.06	939.54
VCP6	64	8.34	13.44	31.98	33.06	39.60	46.98	48.06	154.50	745.98
VCP7	84	8.64	13.20	30.24	31.14	37.32	45.18	46.44	227.46	1,127.58
VCP8	116	8.22	12.60	29.40	29.40	34.62	41.70	43.98	243.18	1,304.22
VCP9	138	9.66	15.36	33.30	34.14	38.52	47.28	49.14	202.26	1,227.00
VCP10	148	8.76	13.98	30.24	32.76	38.28	54.06	58.50	413.70	1,806.54

Table A.35 Influence of the unevenness of the vessel-call pattern, in terms of the VCP-overlapping time (h), on the mean vehicle-waiting time per waterside retrieval job ($\overline{\omega}_{\mathrm{wsout}}^{\mathrm{hr+}}$) for selected yard-block layouts and all types of RMGC systems

VCP		Yard-block layout								
Name	Overlap (h)	Small	Low	Narrow	Short	Medium	Long	Wide	High	Big
Resulting $\overline{\omega}_{\mathrm{wsout}}^{\mathrm{hr+}}$ with the SRMGC system (s)										
VCP1	**0**	**3.24**	**5.52**	**78.00**	**56.04**	**198.72**	**789.12**	**671.58**	**3,180.30**	**4,959.72**
VCP2	12	5.16	7.86	79.86	55.32	210.78	763.32	636.66	3,149.52	4,785.06
VCP3	24	9.18	13.26	109.98	83.64	372.36	1,112.10	989.04	3,558.18	5,567.76
VCP4	32	4.68	5.94	102.84	79.20	375.36	1,326.84	1,062.24	4,203.12	5,725.98
VCP5	52	3.48	5.52	120.36	95.76	473.58	1,664.52	1,312.98	4,644.60	6,377.64
VCP6	64	4.92	10.86	123.78	112.08	476.28	1,679.58	1,345.86	5,283.06	6,452.22
VCP7	84	4.98	8.64	202.26	169.32	876.18	2,293.50	1,908.60	5,745.60	7,926.24
VCP8	116	5.34	7.92	226.44	158.16	1,052.46	2,710.08	2,260.86	6,222.84	9,125.64
VCP9	138	10.92	16.50	258.06	218.16	1,022.22	2,535.18	2,341.08	6,518.28	8,825.16
VCP10	148	7.02	12.48	543.54	437.82	1,744.56	3,464.58	3,126.24	7,844.28	11,774.76
Resulting $\overline{\omega}_{\mathrm{wsout}}^{\mathrm{hr+}}$ with the TRMGC system (s)										
VCP1	**0**	**2.28**	**4.14**	**15.06**	**13.20**	**25.80**	**48.48**	**42.12**	**486.30**	**3,019.80**
VCP2	12	5.04	9.84	18.90	15.90	28.32	58.80	52.62	547.20	3,352.56
VCP3	24	8.46	12.90	26.28	23.10	42.60	84.72	73.86	580.80	4,227.06
VCP4	32	2.82	6.06	18.24	15.66	26.34	65.22	53.10	866.46	4,632.84
VCP5	52	2.94	5.64	19.32	15.78	36.66	109.56	66.36	1,400.76	7,198.50
VCP6	64	4.38	9.06	22.86	18.66	35.34	107.88	71.94	993.36	6,496.92
VCP7	84	4.14	6.84	27.90	21.00	54.72	188.64	150.00	2,144.34	10,128.36
VCP8	116	5.04	6.84	28.74	19.86	76.56	328.32	237.54	3,142.02	12,744.00
VCP9	138	7.74	13.62	34.20	29.94	78.54	267.18	242.10	2,438.52	13,132.80
VCP10	148	6.18	7.08	54.60	45.12	175.26	824.88	622.92	5,195.70	16,348.74
Resulting $\overline{\omega}_{\mathrm{wsout}}^{\mathrm{hr+}}$ with the DRMGC system (s)										
VCP1	**0**	**2.76**	**5.34**	**20.10**	**18.72**	**30.78**	**47.46**	**46.26**	**510.54**	**2,758.62**
VCP2	12	4.86	9.96	26.46	27.18	36.60	60.42	68.70	580.14	2,849.94
VCP3	24	7.98	15.72	40.20	43.74	60.00	102.12	96.48	749.16	3,299.22
VCP4	32	3.18	6.90	24.72	24.60	33.84	67.08	69.72	811.56	3,782.46
VCP5	52	3.48	5.76	22.44	23.70	42.90	65.76	70.98	1,242.66	4,868.58
VCP6	64	5.82	9.54	31.32	29.70	44.04	97.80	80.22	916.44	4,445.52
VCP7	84	4.80	10.14	30.24	29.88	59.28	121.68	127.14	1,681.62	6,416.34
VCP8	116	4.38	8.88	33.66	33.48	56.28	149.04	149.58	2,118.54	8,073.54
VCP9	138	8.58	20.76	46.86	50.22	93.48	197.46	213.78	1,624.50	7,773.66
VCP10	148	8.82	11.22	47.94	47.52	124.86	451.08	416.82	3,212.94	10,217.16
Resulting $\overline{\omega}_{\mathrm{wsout}}^{\mathrm{hr+}}$ with the TriRMGC system (s)										
VCP1	**0**	**2.22**	**5.34**	**12.90**	**12.54**	**16.32**	**19.68**	**20.94**	**109.68**	**883.26**
VCP2	12	5.16	9.72	16.32	17.70	20.22	24.18	28.08	144.54	996.60
VCP3	24	9.96	13.98	28.74	28.32	33.00	37.14	39.00	167.70	1,050.54
VCP4	32	2.76	6.72	12.96	14.28	17.46	23.10	24.90	182.34	1,362.42
VCP5	52	2.82	6.54	14.64	14.10	18.36	21.66	23.28	249.42	1,756.26
VCP6	64	3.12	9.72	20.40	19.86	25.98	27.48	29.94	193.38	1,330.44
VCP7	84	5.40	10.08	16.08	18.36	25.08	28.56	30.18	369.54	2,254.02
VCP8	116	4.62	8.40	18.66	18.72	22.02	28.50	29.22	420.48	2,744.64
VCP9	138	9.60	17.40	30.42	31.80	32.88	41.76	45.06	348.66	2,519.04
VCP10	148	6.18	12.00	19.74	25.14	32.94	58.56	70.74	850.86	4,176.54

Table A.36 Influence of the unevenness of the vessel-call pattern, in terms of the VCP-overlapping time (h), on the mean crane-waiting time in the handover areas ($\overline{\omega}^{hr-}_{total}$) for selected yard-block layouts and all types of RMGC systems

VCP		Yard-block layout								
Name	Overlap (h)	Small	Low	Narrow	Short	Medium	Long	Wide	High	Big
Resulting $\overline{\omega}^{hr-}_{total}$ with the SRMGC system (s)										
VCP1	**0**	**124.38**	**94.92**	**63.84**	**67.26**	**41.52**	**22.86**	**25.80**	**14.64**	**7.08**
VCP2	12	123.18	94.86	63.72	66.42	41.28	23.22	26.88	14.58	7.44
VCP3	24	126.24	94.98	62.28	65.28	40.02	23.76	26.34	17.16	10.68
VCP4	32	116.94	87.36	58.50	60.06	37.38	21.78	24.24	14.22	8.82
VCP5	52	109.92	81.54	52.80	55.20	35.10	21.90	24.48	16.08	11.70
VCP6	64	109.80	82.86	51.30	53.40	32.34	21.18	23.34	16.20	11.58
VCP7	84	102.24	73.62	45.48	46.98	28.80	21.60	22.92	17.16	12.84
VCP8	116	100.02	72.90	47.64	50.64	33.60	24.78	26.28	19.32	14.82
VCP9	138	98.70	74.22	42.90	46.32	30.42	24.06	25.80	22.50	17.82
VCP10	148	88.98	60.96	36.90	37.62	27.12	23.04	24.60	20.52	16.26
Resulting $\overline{\omega}^{hr-}_{total}$ with the TRMGC system (s)										
VCP1	**0**	**135.84**	**112.32**	**87.84**	**91.26**	**67.86**	**50.28**	**53.40**	**38.58**	**10.56**
VCP2	12	136.86	111.66	87.72	88.14	66.48	49.32	52.08	37.74	11.34
VCP3	24	136.14	112.26	85.26	86.16	64.50	46.08	48.36	36.12	14.88
VCP4	32	129.78	103.80	80.64	81.36	61.80	45.30	47.40	33.30	12.90
VCP5	52	121.56	97.98	74.34	76.38	57.24	42.72	45.00	31.14	14.64
VCP6	64	119.94	96.84	72.96	75.48	53.88	39.54	42.30	29.76	15.06
VCP7	84	113.46	88.80	65.22	67.26	47.46	35.64	37.98	28.32	16.56
VCP8	116	109.98	85.56	64.80	66.90	49.20	38.46	41.04	29.70	18.36
VCP9	138	109.32	85.32	61.32	62.88	44.58	33.18	35.94	29.88	22.08
VCP10	148	100.62	74.76	51.78	54.36	38.04	30.60	32.04	26.58	20.76
Resulting $\overline{\omega}^{hr-}_{total}$ with the DRMGC system (s)										
VCP1	**0**	**139.32**	**117.48**	**95.28**	**95.46**	**75.18**	**57.24**	**57.66**	**44.52**	**12.60**
VCP2	12	139.32	117.18	93.78	93.00	73.08	57.18	56.58	43.32	13.92
VCP3	24	138.30	116.16	93.36	93.24	71.70	53.94	53.10	41.04	16.38
VCP4	32	131.58	109.92	87.84	87.00	68.52	52.50	51.60	39.18	13.44
VCP5	52	124.62	102.54	80.88	81.72	63.12	48.90	49.26	36.00	13.98
VCP6	64	124.20	103.68	81.42	80.70	60.54	45.36	45.96	34.44	14.40
VCP7	84	117.30	96.00	73.50	72.48	53.16	41.22	42.06	32.52	14.58
VCP8	116	113.34	91.80	71.58	71.82	55.68	43.86	44.46	32.64	17.34
VCP9	138	109.92	93.18	69.30	68.04	50.64	38.76	39.96	30.54	20.22
VCP10	148	105.90	82.08	60.24	59.46	43.62	33.78	34.80	29.40	18.06
Resulting $\overline{\omega}^{hr-}_{total}$ with the TriRMGC system (s)										
VCP1	**0**	**140.40**	**121.98**	**103.44**	**101.10**	**84.00**	**68.22**	**68.64**	**58.38**	**23.88**
VCP2	12	141.60	120.30	101.34	100.38	81.96	67.68	67.38	56.16	24.48
VCP3	24	141.42	118.62	101.34	100.50	80.94	65.76	65.04	52.68	24.72
VCP4	32	134.04	113.94	94.74	92.34	76.62	62.52	62.52	50.94	22.62
VCP5	52	125.70	107.28	88.02	87.84	71.40	58.98	58.92	47.64	20.64
VCP6	64	126.54	107.52	89.16	86.64	69.18	55.68	56.58	45.66	20.64
VCP7	84	118.14	99.18	80.58	79.14	62.76	51.12	50.76	41.58	20.04
VCP8	116	113.52	94.50	76.98	76.80	62.70	52.38	51.48	41.52	23.34
VCP9	138	112.80	96.18	76.02	75.60	59.52	47.40	47.70	38.40	22.98
VCP10	148	109.38	85.26	66.24	66.60	51.00	41.82	41.82	34.44	22.08

Table A.37 Influence of the unevenness of the vessel-call pattern, in terms of the VCP-overlapping time (h), on the mean crane-empty-movement time per job ($\overline{\overline{m}}_{\text{total}}^{\text{xye}}$) for selected yard-block layouts and all types of RMGC systems

VCP		Yard-block layout								
Name	Overlap (h)	Small	Low	Narrow	Short	Medium	Long	Wide	High	Big
Resulting $\overline{\overline{m}}_{\text{total}}^{\text{xye}}$ with the SRMGC system (s)										
VCP1	**0**	**26.05**	**31.87**	**26.97**	**23.22**	**26.63**	**29.48**	**26.57**	**23.73**	**27.72**
VCP2	12	25.28	31.23	26.71	23.01	26.54	29.58	26.39	23.77	27.83
VCP3	24	25.20	30.70	26.30	22.51	25.60	29.05	26.13	23.83	29.15
VCP4	32	25.92	31.80	26.70	22.91	26.39	29.68	26.56	23.86	28.45
VCP5	52	25.75	31.53	26.82	23.08	26.47	30.10	26.76	24.12	29.12
VCP6	64	25.57	31.19	26.24	22.68	25.92	29.62	26.45	24.17	29.31
VCP7	84	25.46	31.29	26.30	22.63	26.17	29.90	26.74	24.51	30.11
VCP8	116	25.37	31.39	26.67	22.84	26.78	30.63	27.24	25.07	30.98
VCP9	138	24.50	29.89	25.89	22.19	25.81	29.94	26.68	25.41	32.42
VCP10	148	25.21	30.84	26.11	22.42	26.61	31.03	27.29	25.58	32.12
Resulting $\overline{\overline{m}}_{\text{total}}^{\text{xye}}$ with the TRMGC system (s)										
VCP1	**0**	**23.34**	**28.35**	**33.76**	**30.25**	**34.07**	**38.12**	**34.64**	**37.21**	**40.77**
VCP2	12	23.00	27.78	33.48	29.93	33.62	37.80	34.44	37.24	41.45
VCP3	24	22.39	27.31	32.69	29.24	32.97	37.11	33.70	36.78	43.29
VCP4	32	23.38	28.34	33.74	30.10	33.92	37.99	34.32	37.38	41.88
VCP5	52	23.03	28.19	33.70	30.07	34.08	38.13	34.27	38.25	42.88
VCP6	64	23.04	28.14	33.19	29.63	33.42	37.78	34.18	37.85	43.15
VCP7	84	23.19	28.50	33.60	29.80	34.05	38.15	34.55	39.15	44.02
VCP8	116	23.36	28.34	33.52	29.79	34.09	38.61	34.64	39.69	44.41
VCP9	138	22.78	27.46	32.72	29.36	33.59	37.90	34.56	39.66	45.22
VCP10	148	23.46	28.56	33.42	29.85	34.15	38.68	35.02	40.06	44.41
Resulting $\overline{\overline{m}}_{\text{total}}^{\text{xye}}$ with the DRMGC system (s)										
VCP1	**0**	**55.77**	**69.14**	**62.73**	**62.89**	**62.78**	**61.85**	**60.88**	**52.25**	**45.15**
VCP2	12	54.49	67.24	61.86	61.61	61.69	60.99	59.49	51.60	46.67
VCP3	24	52.51	64.91	60.00	59.00	58.70	57.62	56.52	50.23	47.69
VCP4	32	55.66	69.10	61.40	60.93	60.64	59.91	58.53	50.44	46.46
VCP5	52	55.52	65.69	59.85	59.26	58.76	58.05	56.72	49.12	46.98
VCP6	64	57.18	67.24	59.67	58.96	57.26	55.97	55.52	48.61	47.11
VCP7	84	58.39	66.43	57.75	56.76	55.17	54.40	53.80	48.70	48.55
VCP8	116	55.73	63.58	56.02	54.94	55.37	55.15	54.23	48.75	49.64
VCP9	138	52.65	60.99	54.05	52.62	51.61	52.03	51.39	47.30	50.84
VCP10	148	58.50	63.22	53.46	52.26	50.92	51.31	50.40	47.74	51.14
Resulting $\overline{\overline{m}}_{\text{total}}^{\text{xye}}$ with the TriRMGC system (s)										
VCP1	**0**	**51.55**	**65.81**	**69.11**	**68.63**	**70.12**	**70.81**	**70.15**	**66.70**	**60.22**
VCP2	12	50.04	64.03	67.30	66.85	68.83	69.52	68.82	65.57	60.72
VCP3	24	48.97	61.91	64.80	65.62	65.85	66.39	65.60	62.49	60.00
VCP4	32	52.36	64.92	66.84	66.28	67.43	68.53	67.39	63.90	60.02
VCP5	52	51.01	62.86	64.77	64.48	65.59	65.93	65.58	63.10	60.19
VCP6	64	52.66	63.92	64.27	64.66	64.13	64.44	63.90	62.17	59.65
VCP7	84	54.38	63.07	63.22	62.57	62.52	62.80	61.91	61.31	60.35
VCP8	116	49.82	60.02	60.85	60.00	61.09	62.38	61.76	61.18	62.13
VCP9	138	51.34	58.40	59.49	58.07	57.83	58.61	58.25	58.41	61.77
VCP10	148	56.51	61.97	59.07	58.21	57.50	57.89	57.55	59.18	63.04

Table A.38 Influence of the unevenness of the vessel-call pattern, in terms of the VCP-overlapping time (h), on the mean crane-interference time per job ($\overline{\overline{m}}^{\text{cit}}_{\text{total}}$) for selected yard-block layouts and all types of RMGC systems

VCP		Yard-block layout								
Name	Overlap (h)	Small	Low	Narrow	Short	Medium	Long	Wide	High	Big
Resulting $\overline{\overline{m}}^{\text{cit}}_{\text{total}}$ with the SRMGC system (s)										
VCP1	**0**	**0.00**	**0.00**	**0.00**	**0.00**	**0.00**	**0.00**	**0.00**	**0.00**	**0.00**
VCP2	12	0.00	0.00	0.00	0.00	0.00	0.00	0.00	0.00	0.00
VCP3	24	0.00	0.00	0.00	0.00	0.00	0.00	0.00	0.00	0.00
VCP4	32	0.00	0.00	0.00	0.00	0.00	0.00	0.00	0.00	0.00
VCP5	52	0.00	0.00	0.00	0.00	0.00	0.00	0.00	0.00	0.00
VCP6	64	0.00	0.00	0.00	0.00	0.00	0.00	0.00	0.00	0.00
VCP7	84	0.00	0.00	0.00	0.00	0.00	0.00	0.00	0.00	0.00
VCP8	116	0.00	0.00	0.00	0.00	0.00	0.00	0.00	0.00	0.00
VCP9	138	0.00	0.00	0.00	0.00	0.00	0.00	0.00	0.00	0.00
VCP10	148	0.00	0.00	0.00	0.00	0.00	0.00	0.00	0.00	0.00
Resulting $\overline{\overline{m}}^{\text{cit}}_{\text{total}}$ with the TRMGC system (s)										
VCP1	**0**	**2.22**	**2.10**	**11.92**	**12.42**	**12.16**	**11.92**	**12.14**	**19.43**	**20.71**
VCP2	12	2.30	2.06	12.04	12.18	11.77	11.96	12.14	19.72	20.60
VCP3	24	2.19	2.22	11.70	12.01	11.86	12.12	12.11	19.24	20.17
VCP4	32	2.15	2.00	11.74	12.12	11.83	11.68	11.69	19.37	20.21
VCP5	52	1.97	2.02	11.17	11.81	11.32	11.27	11.36	19.49	19.54
VCP6	64	2.01	1.93	11.62	11.97	11.73	11.87	11.91	19.70	19.65
VCP7	84	1.97	2.05	11.56	11.80	11.51	11.49	11.65	20.13	18.94
VCP8	116	1.89	2.00	11.13	11.40	11.16	11.26	11.16	19.43	18.23
VCP9	138	2.06	2.04	11.21	11.59	11.58	11.47	11.69	19.25	16.75
VCP10	148	1.85	2.01	11.31	11.77	11.37	11.03	11.33	19.08	16.89
Resulting $\overline{\overline{m}}^{\text{cit}}_{\text{total}}$ with the DRMGC system (s)										
VCP1	**0**	**31.09**	**38.13**	**35.30**	**39.74**	**35.31**	**29.73**	**32.78**	**28.21**	**20.21**
VCP2	12	31.32	39.58	35.84	39.67	34.98	29.96	32.50	27.89	21.18
VCP3	24	32.85	40.49	36.57	39.62	34.40	28.56	31.22	27.36	21.78
VCP4	32	30.84	39.33	34.68	38.21	33.48	28.63	30.95	27.04	20.85
VCP5	52	31.31	35.72	32.96	36.90	31.94	26.64	29.30	25.84	21.03
VCP6	64	33.93	39.41	33.93	37.02	30.97	25.60	28.76	25.33	21.10
VCP7	84	34.08	37.56	31.72	34.85	28.83	23.87	26.97	25.30	21.88
VCP8	116	32.27	34.67	30.24	33.27	29.03	24.56	27.29	25.18	22.18
VCP9	138	33.49	38.49	30.73	33.35	27.50	22.90	25.77	24.25	23.15
VCP10	148	36.37	35.51	28.19	30.95	25.25	21.34	23.96	24.14	23.15
Resulting $\overline{\overline{m}}^{\text{cit}}_{\text{total}}$ with the TriRMGC system (s)										
VCP1	**0**	**31.02**	**40.31**	**48.66**	**52.32**	**49.18**	**44.71**	**47.95**	**49.43**	**41.62**
VCP2	12	31.54	41.90	48.40	52.19	48.97	44.88	48.21	49.28	41.76
VCP3	24	34.32	43.21	49.18	53.81	49.05	44.07	47.23	47.65	41.30
VCP4	32	32.57	40.48	46.13	50.43	46.66	42.62	46.07	47.52	40.74
VCP5	52	31.39	38.77	44.62	48.58	44.69	40.17	43.53	46.07	40.30
VCP6	64	33.54	41.43	46.09	49.73	45.00	39.89	43.33	45.70	39.75
VCP7	84	35.18	39.85	43.54	47.11	42.56	37.67	40.59	44.52	39.78
VCP8	116	30.99	36.39	40.96	44.65	40.52	36.83	40.18	43.96	40.20
VCP9	138	36.44	40.65	42.98	46.30	40.04	35.73	38.83	42.95	40.19
VCP10	148	37.69	38.63	39.71	43.37	37.66	33.04	36.52	41.85	40.68

Table A.39 Influence of the unevenness of the vessel-call pattern, in terms of the VCP-overlapping time (h), on the crane workload during the simulation horizon in terms of performed jobs ($\overline{|J|}$) for selected yard-block layouts and all types of RMGC systems

VCP		Yard-block layout								
Name	Overlap (h)	Small	Low	Narrow	Short	Medium	Long	Wide	High	Big
Resulting $\overline{\lvert J\rvert}$ with the SRMGC system (jobs)										
VCP1	**0**	**1,871.8**	**3,208.8**	**6,596.5**	**6,792.8**	**8,683.4**	**10, 466.3**	**10, 776.3**	**13, 369.4**	**13, 711.1**
VCP2	12	1,874.0	3,163.1	6,449.4	6,638.6	8,508.4	10, 216.6	10, 524.4	13, 011.9	13, 145.6
VCP3	24	1,877.8	3,174.5	6,461.2	6,675.2	8,422.6	9, 875.8	10, 054.7	11, 844.5	11, 658.6
VCP4	32	1,816.9	3,137.3	6,309.4	6,462.0	8,327.2	9, 811.9	10, 171.7	12, 401.1	12, 655.9
VCP5	52	1,745.0	2,925.9	5,861.5	6,078.4	7,669.0	9, 040.5	9, 364.8	11, 314.0	11, 406.0
VCP6	64	1,773.4	3,065.1	6,177.7	6,338.6	8,054.5	9, 278.1	9, 616.4	11, 330.8	11, 309.8
VCP7	84	1,709.4	2,953.5	5,938.2	6,088.6	7,631.3	8, 770.9	9, 034.5	10, 576.8	10, 728.6
VCP8	116	1,640.0	2,721.8	5,395.6	5,633.2	6,987.7	8, 029.6	8, 363.5	9, 785.3	9, 951.5
VCP9	138	1,619.0	2,766.2	5,613.7	5,761.9	7,147.6	7, 853.9	8, 207.3	8, 942.1	8, 844.5
VCP10	148	1,658.9	2,857.4	5,589.3	5,691.9	6,866.5	7, 648.7	7, 991.8	9, 230.8	9, 529.4
Resulting $\overline{\lvert J\rvert}$ with the TRMGC system (jobs)										
VCP1	**0**	**1,903.5**	**3,224.1**	**6,592.4**	**6,857.8**	**8,784.5**	**10, 615.3**	**10, 900.6**	**15, 170.8**	**21, 104.9**
VCP2	12	1,884.7	3,185.0	6,541.2	6,737.0	8,550.7	10, 455.1	10, 724.2	14, 876.3	20, 235.7
VCP3	24	1,854.0	3,149.9	6,440.7	6,729.3	8,555.2	10, 389.5	10, 609.8	14, 031.6	17, 313.9
VCP4	32	1,841.9	3,118.9	6,312.8	6,555.2	8,359.5	10, 119.0	10, 360.4	14, 708.4	19, 031.9
VCP5	52	1,739.8	2,941.0	5,853.1	6,130.3	7,677.0	9, 359.6	9, 646.5	13, 990.1	17, 008.1
VCP6	64	1,766.8	3,054.2	6,229.5	6,413.9	8,191.2	9, 940.2	10, 158.9	14, 083.4	16, 857.2
VCP7	84	1,746.0	2,942.1	5,881.7	6,158.9	7,735.0	9, 317.0	9, 611.7	13, 364.9	15, 611.1
VCP8	116	1,641.7	2,761.7	5,482.7	5,688.2	7,155.5	8, 707.1	8, 888.9	12, 347.9	14, 571.1
VCP9	138	1,600.8	2,819.0	5,664.2	5,905.7	7,413.4	8, 905.2	9, 179.1	11, 474.1	12, 606.6
VCP10	148	1,658.1	2,855.8	5,724.9	5,858.3	7,294.9	8, 427.0	8, 792.7	11, 580.1	13, 329.3

(continued)

Table A.39 (continued)

VCP		Yard-block layout								
Name	Overlap (h)	Small	Low	Narrow	Short	Medium	Long	Wide	High	Big
Resulting $\overline{\lvert J \rvert}$ with the DRMGC system (jobs)										
VCP1	**0**	**1,901.9**	**3,222.4**	**6,623.5**	**6,834.0**	**8,713.7**	**10,605.3**	**10,893.6**	**15,175.5**	**21,213.5**
VCP2	12	1,894.2	3,189.7	6,514.2	6,703.7	8,561.1	10,457.1	10,741.7	14,871.4	20,326.7
VCP3	24	1,846.3	3,143.3	6,391.1	6,721.7	8,527.9	10,367.6	10,608.8	14,089.9	17,755.0
VCP4	32	1,840.7	3,117.5	6,298.3	6,563.0	8,320.3	10,089.9	10,391.8	14,598.1	19,555.9
VCP5	52	1,744.7	2,945.3	5,856.5	6,133.1	7,669.0	9,313.5	9,619.9	14,030.6	17,670.1
VCP6	64	1,775.9	3,051.9	6,198.4	6,436.4	8,157.3	9,902.7	10,133.2	14,079.8	17,730.5
VCP7	84	1,740.7	2,938.1	5,871.4	6,097.0	7,760.7	9,344.2	9,630.6	13,643.9	16,610.8
VCP8	116	1,640.7	2,757.4	5,467.3	5,640.4	7,142.9	8,759.4	8,870.4	12,621.6	15,363.7
VCP9	138	1,611.2	2,812.5	5,652.2	5,894.1	7,456.0	8,978.3	9,172.1	12,192.3	13,686.1
VCP10	148	1,665.8	2,852.4	5,684.6	5,838.7	7,296.6	8,738.6	8,932.7	12,128.1	14,624.3
Resulting $\overline{\lvert J \rvert}$ with the TriRMGC system (jobs)										
VCP1	**0**	**1,907.0**	**3,249.5**	**6,614.4**	**6,831.8**	**8,732.5**	**10,583.9**	**10,895.8**	**15,192.1**	**23,097.9**
VCP2	12	1,883.0	3,167.6	6,505.8	6,754.7	8,492.4	10,475.0	10,659.8	15,145.7	22,640.0
VCP3	24	1,861.2	3,168.1	6,440.3	6,694.8	8,547.9	10,376.8	10,672.2	14,860.2	20,492.7
VCP4	32	1,852.8	3,127.8	6,318.8	6,519.2	8,354.8	10,099.9	10,388.4	15,047.8	21,900.0
VCP5	52	1,730.3	2,919.6	5,867.1	6,139.5	7,685.5	9,350.1	9,589.3	14,472.2	20,183.3
VCP6	64	1,766.5	3,069.6	6,197.0	6,471.3	8,239.4	9,919.9	10,227.7	14,584.8	20,292.7
VCP7	84	1,735.5	2,930.5	5,920.9	6,118.6	7,748.2	9,339.6	9,634.8	14,197.6	19,039.1
VCP8	116	1,626.9	2,754.6	5,531.4	5,640.1	7,213.6	8,673.7	8,917.7	13,289.4	17,470.3
VCP9	138	1,613.1	2,783.3	5,689.7	5,903.0	7,456.3	8,994.6	9,221.7	13,011.0	16,256.7
VCP10	148	1,663.7	2,880.8	5,662.7	5,853.8	7,393.0	8,895.1	9,121.7	12,967.6	16,507.5

Table A.40 Influence of the unevenness of the vessel-call pattern, in terms of the VCP-overlapping time (h), on the container accessibility ($\overline{\overline{\psi}}$), in terms of the mean number of shuffle moves per retrieval job, for selected yard-block layouts and all types of RMGC systems

VCP		Yard-block layout								
Name	Overlap (h)	Small	Low	Narrow	Short	Medium	Long	Wide	High	Big
Resulting $\overline{\overline{\psi}}$ with the SRMGC system (jobs)										
VCP1	**0**	**0.322**	**0.300**	**1.135**	**1.120**	**1.103**	**1.083**	**1.083**	**1.606**	**1.144**
VCP2	12	0.319	0.292	1.107	1.094	1.090	1.045	1.065	1.568	1.064
VCP3	24	0.329	0.298	1.103	1.096	1.076	1.025	1.025	1.443	0.922
VCP4	32	0.309	0.290	1.096	1.074	1.052	1.019	1.024	1.490	1.008
VCP5	52	0.289	0.272	1.025	1.021	0.995	0.935	0.947	1.372	0.874
VCP6	64	0.299	0.273	1.078	1.059	1.036	0.944	0.958	1.356	0.865
VCP7	84	0.283	0.267	1.021	1.020	0.985	0.907	0.910	1.278	0.789
VCP8	116	0.282	0.251	0.953	0.970	0.897	0.827	0.840	1.166	0.694
VCP9	138	0.292	0.258	0.993	0.990	0.928	0.816	0.828	1.040	0.541
VCP10	148	0.291	0.264	0.978	0.959	0.872	0.759	0.789	1.072	0.628
Resulting $\overline{\overline{\psi}}$ with the TRMGC system (jobs)										
VCP1	**0**	**0.324**	**0.296**	**1.127**	**1.130**	**1.130**	**1.097**	**1.090**	**1.762**	**1.675**
VCP2	12	0.316	0.288	1.118	1.117	1.088	1.068	1.074	1.749	1.610
VCP3	24	0.326	0.298	1.110	1.116	1.102	1.096	1.085	1.683	1.426
VCP4	32	0.314	0.287	1.095	1.087	1.068	1.046	1.030	1.717	1.525
VCP5	52	0.294	0.272	1.009	1.031	0.987	0.974	0.981	1.659	1.363
VCP6	64	0.302	0.276	1.083	1.071	1.050	1.043	1.024	1.664	1.341
VCP7	84	0.298	0.273	1.036	1.037	0.996	0.966	0.976	1.625	1.233
VCP8	116	0.277	0.259	0.966	0.975	0.934	0.917	0.908	1.518	1.146
VCP9	138	0.284	0.263	1.010	1.014	1.000	0.956	0.976	1.436	0.956
VCP10	148	0.280	0.260	1.010	0.995	0.944	0.859	0.892	1.409	1.014
Resulting $\overline{\overline{\psi}}$ with the DRMGC system (jobs)										
VCP1	**0**	**0.320**	**0.297**	**1.137**	**1.118**	**1.107**	**1.093**	**1.087**	**1.753**	**1.673**
VCP2	12	0.331	0.291	1.111	1.112	1.088	1.067	1.078	1.729	1.597
VCP3	24	0.317	0.297	1.096	1.113	1.093	1.083	1.076	1.667	1.431
VCP4	32	0.313	0.286	1.086	1.090	1.056	1.043	1.044	1.692	1.541
VCP5	52	0.296	0.273	1.014	1.028	0.981	0.961	0.977	1.663	1.398
VCP6	64	0.305	0.275	1.074	1.071	1.037	1.025	1.019	1.644	1.398
VCP7	84	0.292	0.268	1.030	1.017	1.006	0.966	0.979	1.616	1.291
VCP8	116	0.275	0.258	0.963	0.968	0.927	0.926	0.898	1.514	1.205
VCP9	138	0.296	0.263	0.999	1.023	0.999	0.953	0.961	1.474	1.050
VCP10	148	0.289	0.263	0.993	0.991	0.928	0.899	0.898	1.423	1.136
Resulting $\overline{\overline{\psi}}$ with the TriRMGC system (jobs)										
VCP1	**0**	**0.325**	**0.298**	**1.122**	**1.123**	**1.113**	**1.092**	**1.090**	**1.763**	**1.758**
VCP2	12	0.324	0.290	1.108	1.107	1.079	1.070	1.070	1.777	1.739
VCP3	24	0.329	0.292	1.107	1.104	1.095	1.092	1.085	1.747	1.596
VCP4	32	0.319	0.281	1.094	1.088	1.064	1.052	1.038	1.745	1.681
VCP5	52	0.291	0.267	1.027	1.034	0.986	0.973	0.962	1.702	1.571
VCP6	64	0.305	0.280	1.075	1.078	1.063	1.033	1.034	1.707	1.569
VCP7	84	0.283	0.261	1.027	1.026	0.996	0.961	0.966	1.679	1.474
VCP8	116	0.283	0.255	0.991	0.967	0.939	0.904	0.905	1.590	1.377
VCP9	138	0.291	0.258	1.028	1.016	0.996	0.967	0.968	1.571	1.278
VCP10	148	0.289	0.261	0.999	1.002	0.956	0.919	0.920	1.510	1.293

A.5.5 Influence of the Crane Kinematics

Table A.41 Influence of percentage changes in the crane kinematics compared to the default settings on the mean vehicle-waiting time ($\overline{\omega}^{hr+}_{total}$) for selected yard-block layouts and all types of RMGC systems

Kinematic change	Yard-block layout								
	Small	Low	Narrow	Short	Medium	Long	Wide	High	Big
Resulting $\overline{\omega}^{hr+}_{total}$ with the SRMGC system (s)									
−25%	34.14	53.64	216.12	175.56	482.10	1,405.38	1,246.02	3,200.64	4,055.04
−20%	31.56	49.56	182.46	158.70	389.88	1,201.98	1,002.96	2,838.54	3,905.16
−15%	29.82	48.06	155.94	127.38	328.56	982.50	839.64	2,550.84	3,690.84
−10%	29.22	45.12	141.66	122.34	254.46	815.52	690.84	2,282.46	3,591.06
−5%	27.54	43.92	124.44	111.66	215.46	659.94	542.04	2,050.74	3,423.78
0%	**28.26**	**41.28**	**117.06**	**100.44**	**198.96**	**561.06**	**484.56**	**1,861.32**	**3,269.94**
+5%	26.94	40.20	106.08	93.36	171.18	463.68	387.06	1,660.08	3,068.52
+10%	25.56	39.18	101.34	88.92	142.68	388.20	340.50	1,521.84	2,967.78
+15%	25.80	39.24	93.42	84.78	135.24	345.78	276.24	1,355.28	2,852.22
+20%	24.30	38.34	88.08	81.06	122.10	304.38	249.12	1,261.74	2,745.42
+25%	23.88	37.68	82.32	77.22	115.32	255.06	226.62	1,170.66	2,723.40
Resulting $\overline{\omega}^{hr+}_{total}$ with the TRMGC system (s)									
−25%	12.96	19.86	60.84	54.00	78.48	128.34	112.80	716.76	2,615.76
−20%	11.58	18.00	54.18	48.30	68.52	110.10	96.30	607.08	2,345.04
−15%	10.92	15.90	49.38	44.88	61.68	95.94	83.58	503.64	2,161.56
−10%	9.96	15.18	45.24	40.80	56.28	83.40	73.86	413.88	1,915.56
−5%	9.66	14.28	41.10	38.52	51.60	74.52	66.78	355.68	1,736.28
0%	**8.82**	**13.44**	**38.16**	**35.58**	**48.30**	**67.44**	**61.98**	**304.08**	**1,567.38**
+5%	8.40	12.66	36.84	33.42	44.52	61.08	54.30	257.88	1,416.18
+10%	7.68	11.82	34.20	30.90	41.34	56.46	51.00	222.60	1,244.76
+15%	7.56	10.92	32.52	30.06	39.12	51.12	47.10	195.36	1,127.52
+20%	7.32	10.68	31.44	29.10	36.24	49.26	44.28	171.60	1,003.32
+25%	6.72	10.26	29.46	27.30	35.46	45.18	41.46	151.92	936.54
Resulting $\overline{\omega}^{hr+}_{total}$ with the DRMGC system (s)									
−25%	18.90	30.96	75.84	75.24	100.86	158.22	154.26	806.76	2,584.32
−20%	18.30	28.56	69.96	69.54	93.30	135.78	132.66	663.36	2,331.72
−15%	16.62	26.46	64.86	65.04	86.64	118.50	116.34	592.62	2,150.16
−10%	15.48	24.90	62.28	60.24	78.00	104.88	107.28	487.74	1,898.10
−5%	14.46	24.66	58.26	57.00	74.40	99.54	96.42	423.84	1,786.74
0%	**13.86**	**23.58**	**53.82**	**54.36**	**69.24**	**88.86**	**88.86**	**360.18**	**1,607.82**
+5%	13.50	22.08	51.00	52.14	65.10	83.10	84.36	313.50	1,475.52
+10%	12.72	21.30	49.50	49.02	65.28	79.02	79.62	262.32	1,310.94
+15%	11.82	20.10	47.16	48.24	60.42	75.06	73.86	230.34	1,219.98
+20%	11.34	19.56	45.90	45.42	58.02	70.32	69.96	213.42	1,099.50
+25%	10.92	18.96	43.62	44.28	56.28	67.02	67.98	188.64	1,013.52
Resulting $\overline{\omega}^{hr+}_{total}$ with the TriRMGC system (s)									
−25%	12.60	18.54	46.38	45.60	58.02	71.88	72.42	260.16	1,225.14
−20%	11.82	16.62	41.64	42.18	51.24	64.80	65.04	231.66	1,047.24
−15%	10.50	15.06	38.40	39.36	47.88	58.56	58.02	193.20	922.74
−10%	10.08	14.52	35.70	36.96	43.56	54.42	55.20	163.02	786.84
−5%	9.42	13.74	33.60	33.60	41.46	50.22	50.04	137.28	689.76
0%	**8.82**	**12.48**	**31.26**	**31.86**	**37.98**	**46.86**	**46.86**	**117.54**	**574.98**
+5%	8.28	11.40	29.58	30.24	36.54	43.98	43.26	113.94	508.80
+10%	7.56	11.04	28.80	29.52	33.90	41.22	40.92	105.12	427.20
+15%	7.26	10.26	26.82	27.42	32.46	37.98	38.64	92.04	374.22
+20%	6.84	9.84	25.38	26.52	31.32	36.48	37.26	82.98	334.98
+25%	6.78	9.48	25.02	25.02	29.16	34.86	34.92	77.64	301.80

Table A.42 Influence of percentage changes in the crane kinematics compared to the default settings on the mean vehicle-waiting time per waterside retrieval job ($\overline{\omega}^{hr+}_{wsout}$) for selected yard-block layouts and all types of RMGC systems

Kinematic change	Yard-block layout								
	Small	Low	Narrow	Short	Medium	Long	Wide	High	Big
Resulting $\overline{\omega}^{hr+}_{wsout}$ with the SRMGC system (s)									
−25%	2.88	8.88	224.28	157.86	672.60	2,198.76	1,968.84	5,264.16	5,754.00
−20%	4.56	6.24	174.96	136.44	518.34	1,889.28	1,557.12	4,726.56	5,617.44
−15%	3.54	7.20	133.56	91.32	410.70	1,522.32	1,275.48	4,291.74	5,397.96
−10%	3.96	6.36	110.04	88.98	278.52	1,219.62	1,029.48	3,878.88	5,371.32
−5%	3.42	6.54	85.56	69.84	224.40	958.50	758.40	3,505.08	5,193.54
0%	**3.24**	**5.52**	**78.00**	**56.04**	**198.72**	**789.12**	**671.58**	**3,180.30**	**4,959.72**
+5%	3.18	5.70	63.12	48.84	159.72	626.64	498.54	2,868.18	4,710.72
+10%	4.14	5.28	61.86	45.84	114.90	487.74	429.48	2,622.66	4,595.40
+15%	4.14	6.06	49.20	38.16	100.26	427.26	308.88	2,333.04	4,487.04
+20%	3.30	4.26	46.26	34.08	82.62	360.18	274.74	2,163.36	4,319.88
+25%	2.88	5.40	37.98	31.02	76.38	279.78	236.58	1,997.40	4,371.90
Resulting $\overline{\omega}^{hr+}_{wsout}$ with the TRMGC system (s)									
−25%	2.58	5.64	37.56	27.72	60.18	144.78	119.40	1,281.84	5,305.50
−20%	2.34	5.46	30.84	24.66	48.00	114.12	91.74	1,078.20	4,678.20
−15%	2.28	3.72	26.16	20.88	39.72	91.20	69.42	879.06	4,307.76
−10%	2.64	4.50	22.74	18.00	33.66	68.28	56.10	696.48	3,790.02
−5%	3.06	4.86	18.78	14.34	29.40	57.18	44.46	588.54	3,408.30
0%	**2.28**	**4.14**	**15.06**	**13.20**	**25.80**	**48.48**	**42.12**	**486.30**	**3,019.80**
+5%	2.40	4.38	15.84	12.78	23.04	37.86	28.56	394.02	2,738.28
+10%	1.74	4.26	13.62	10.50	18.24	33.12	26.40	319.32	2,353.20
+15%	2.46	3.30	11.94	11.10	17.22	24.96	22.98	268.86	2,103.66
+20%	2.28	4.44	12.06	11.28	13.26	24.12	18.30	226.32	1,881.78
+25%	1.98	4.68	10.80	8.70	14.22	18.42	17.46	191.82	1,746.36
Resulting $\overline{\omega}^{hr+}_{wsout}$ with the DRMGC system (s)									
−25%	3.78	6.72	38.82	37.38	65.58	143.28	139.32	1,312.08	4,302.18
−20%	3.48	5.16	32.94	30.12	55.68	109.74	105.84	1,053.24	3,952.02
−15%	2.94	5.34	29.46	27.30	46.98	85.56	81.18	932.34	3,664.80
−10%	2.76	5.40	24.60	24.06	38.88	66.90	72.78	742.98	3,207.36
−5%	2.82	5.46	24.78	20.76	36.18	61.74	56.58	624.18	3,052.32
0%	**2.76**	**5.34**	**20.10**	**18.72**	**30.78**	**47.46**	**46.26**	**510.54**	**2,758.62**
+5%	2.58	4.62	18.12	18.30	27.00	40.14	43.38	425.64	2,503.56
+10%	2.70	5.10	17.34	14.94	28.50	37.44	37.26	340.68	2,235.66
+15%	2.76	4.38	15.90	16.20	23.76	35.04	31.62	281.16	2,086.68
+20%	2.34	4.80	14.82	13.44	22.14	27.96	28.26	255.00	1,861.74
+25%	2.52	4.62	13.98	13.02	20.76	26.34	27.12	211.20	1,702.20
Resulting $\overline{\omega}^{hr+}_{wsout}$ with the TriRMGC system (s)									
−25%	3.00	5.64	22.74	21.36	33.12	39.90	43.50	336.72	2,046.54
−20%	2.88	5.58	17.76	18.36	24.84	33.72	35.04	292.50	1,727.04
−15%	2.76	4.80	16.56	16.50	22.44	28.50	29.04	228.18	1,509.36
−10%	3.00	5.34	14.34	15.78	20.28	25.56	27.06	182.34	1,284.84
−5%	3.24	6.12	13.26	12.30	18.84	21.24	22.80	140.58	1,110.60
0%	**2.22**	**5.34**	**12.90**	**12.54**	**16.32**	**19.68**	**20.94**	**109.68**	**883.26**
+5%	3.48	4.44	12.36	11.16	15.78	19.02	17.70	106.62	785.34
+10%	2.28	4.62	12.06	11.28	15.84	17.46	16.92	92.82	634.92
+15%	2.22	4.86	10.68	11.10	14.76	15.54	16.08	73.92	538.02
+20%	2.82	4.44	10.08	9.78	14.22	14.70	14.76	62.22	470.82
+25%	3.06	4.62	9.60	10.56	12.12	14.04	14.04	54.84	416.52

Table A.43 Influence of percentage changes in the crane kinematics compared to the default settings on the mean crane-waiting time in the handover areas ($\overline{\omega}^{hr-}_{total}$) for selected yard-block layouts and all types of RMGC systems

Kinematic change	Yard-block layout								
	Small	Low	Narrow	Short	Medium	Long	Wide	High	Big
Resulting $\overline{\omega}^{hr-}_{total}$ with the SRMGC system (s)									
−25%	117.42	86.52	51.42	55.50	29.10	13.68	15.96	9.06	5.64
−20%	120.24	88.26	53.64	58.44	31.92	15.24	18.12	10.08	6.06
−15%	119.70	90.42	57.36	61.62	34.98	17.52	20.22	10.92	6.36
−10%	121.62	92.10	59.82	63.96	37.20	19.38	21.84	12.00	6.42
−5%	123.06	94.14	62.70	64.56	39.78	21.00	24.24	13.38	6.72
0%	**124.38**	**94.92**	**63.84**	**67.26**	**41.52**	**22.86**	**25.80**	**14.64**	**7.08**
+5%	125.04	96.00	66.24	67.74	43.86	25.14	28.26	15.72	7.02
+10%	125.34	97.38	68.10	71.34	45.66	26.40	29.76	16.80	7.50
+15%	126.12	98.46	68.88	71.94	47.10	28.50	31.38	18.54	7.62
+20%	127.68	99.78	70.08	72.90	48.60	29.82	32.64	19.44	7.80
+25%	127.62	101.04	71.64	73.86	50.10	31.32	34.68	20.76	7.80
Resulting $\overline{\omega}^{hr-}_{total}$ with the TRMGC system (s)									
−25%	131.76	103.68	79.02	81.18	57.60	37.62	41.28	25.50	8.04
−20%	131.82	106.86	80.88	83.64	59.76	40.62	44.22	28.38	8.52
−15%	133.80	108.06	83.16	85.56	63.06	43.74	46.68	30.78	8.88
−10%	133.86	109.86	85.44	87.72	65.04	45.78	49.26	34.02	9.42
−5%	135.66	110.16	86.28	88.14	67.26	48.06	51.24	35.64	10.02
0%	**135.84**	**112.32**	**87.84**	**91.26**	**67.86**	**50.28**	**53.40**	**35.58**	**10.56**
+5%	136.68	112.68	89.46	91.98	70.38	51.42	54.66	40.02	11.28
+10%	138.00	114.42	90.78	92.34	71.58	53.16	55.92	42.06	12.06
+15%	139.02	114.00	92.46	94.02	72.78	55.20	57.96	44.04	13.14
+20%	140.22	116.82	92.82	94.56	73.92	56.46	58.44	45.72	14.28
+25%	139.62	116.40	93.78	96.00	74.76	57.54	60.18	47.34	15.48
Resulting $\overline{\omega}^{hr-}_{total}$ with the DRMGC system (s)									
−25%	133.74	112.38	88.32	87.84	66.36	46.38	47.46	31.38	7.68
−20%	134.94	113.28	89.58	89.16	67.62	49.38	49.86	34.86	8.34
−15%	136.74	112.80	90.90	91.62	69.78	51.78	51.24	36.84	9.12
−10%	137.70	115.02	93.72	92.58	71.82	53.82	53.94	40.08	10.08
−5%	138.60	116.64	93.78	93.84	73.68	55.20	55.98	42.00	11.34
0%	**139.32**	**117.48**	**95.28**	**95.46**	**75.18**	**57.24**	**57.66**	**44.52**	**12.60**
+5%	139.50	117.84	96.90	96.36	76.50	58.92	58.98	47.04	13.74
+10%	139.56	118.98	97.86	99.06	77.28	60.12	60.60	48.12	14.88
+15%	141.00	119.40	99.00	99.06	78.96	61.08	61.32	49.44	16.02
+20%	139.80	119.16	98.88	99.18	79.74	62.40	62.82	50.58	17.52
+25%	139.86	120.36	100.32	99.78	80.40	63.78	64.08	52.50	18.84
Resulting $\overline{\omega}^{hr-}_{total}$ with the TriRMGC system (s)									
−25%	136.62	115.68	96.54	95.70	77.10	59.46	60.06	47.58	13.68
−20%	136.74	117.84	98.28	97.38	78.18	61.38	62.10	48.66	15.36
−15%	139.44	118.98	99.66	96.96	80.58	63.48	64.32	51.54	17.76
−10%	138.84	120.00	100.98	99.60	81.72	65.52	65.64	54.30	19.62
−5%	139.98	121.08	101.46	100.20	82.92	66.72	67.68	56.76	21.72
0%	**140.40**	**121.98**	**103.44**	**101.10**	**84.00**	**68.22**	**68.64**	**58.38**	**23.88**
+5%	140.40	122.34	103.38	101.52	84.72	69.12	69.84	59.04	25.32
+10%	142.08	122.76	105.12	102.48	86.34	70.80	71.04	60.66	27.48
+15%	142.80	123.72	105.48	103.20	86.82	71.94	72.18	62.22	28.98
+20%	143.58	124.86	106.38	103.98	87.60	72.36	73.20	63.78	30.18
+25%	143.40	124.68	106.56	104.58	87.48	73.44	74.28	64.32	31.92

Table A.44 Influence of percentage changes in the crane kinematics compared to the default settings on the mean crane-empty-movement time per job ($\overline{\overline{m}}_{\text{total}}^{\text{xye}}$) for selected yard-block layouts and all types of RMGC systems

Kinematic change	Yard-block layout								
	Small	Low	Narrow	Short	Medium	Long	Wide	High	Big
Resulting $\overline{\overline{m}}_{\text{total}}^{\text{xye}}$ with the SRMGC system (s)									
−25%	33.64	41.13	34.27	29.36	33.57	37.53	33.64	30.14	36.64
−20%	31.82	38.84	32.43	27.85	32.01	35.45	31.94	28.59	34.48
−15%	30.04	36.81	30.91	26.57	30.43	33.77	30.27	27.06	32.49
−10%	28.58	35.01	29.47	25.20	29.01	32.18	28.79	25.90	30.73
−5%	27.21	33.32	28.15	24.18	27.69	30.97	27.65	24.76	29.00
0%	**26.05**	**31.87**	**26.97**	**23.22**	**26.63**	**29.48**	**26.57**	**23.73**	**27.72**
+5%	25.00	30.52	26.01	22.25	25.68	28.54	25.57	22.80	26.41
+10%	24.21	29.33	24.98	21.48	24.75	27.47	24.61	22.00	25.48
+15%	23.37	28.25	24.09	20.77	23.96	26.58	23.85	21.25	24.36
+20%	22.44	27.14	23.40	20.07	23.17	25.76	23.09	20.55	23.50
+25%	21.71	26.35	22.65	19.42	22.34	24.91	22.36	19.91	22.55
Resulting $\overline{\overline{m}}_{\text{total}}^{\text{xye}}$ with the TRMGC system (s)									
−25%	29.54	36.58	42.82	38.25	43.44	48.88	44.00	46.86	52.46
−20%	27.96	34.45	40.38	36.12	40.95	46.21	41.64	44.27	49.58
−15%	26.59	32.55	38.81	34.30	39.03	43.72	39.53	42.07	46.95
−10%	25.36	30.95	36.79	32.72	37.29	41.65	37.68	40.27	44.73
−5%	24.32	29.65	35.27	31.34	35.33	39.75	35.81	38.41	42.47
0%	**23.34**	**28.35**	**33.76**	**30.25**	**34.07**	**38.12**	**34.64**	**37.21**	**40.77**
+5%	22.37	27.19	32.63	29.04	32.69	36.71	33.13	35.63	39.19
+10%	21.57	25.97	31.30	28.05	31.45	35.14	31.97	34.55	37.41
+15%	20.80	25.07	30.22	27.20	30.33	33.99	30.76	33.28	36.24
+20%	20.03	24.24	29.47	26.30	29.53	33.03	29.88	32.11	34.92
+25%	19.56	23.41	28.45	25.56	28.64	31.97	28.93	31.25	34.06
Resulting $\overline{\overline{m}}_{\text{total}}^{\text{xye}}$ with the DRMGC system (s)									
−25%	64.11	79.14	71.70	71.51	71.07	69.81	68.74	59.02	55.49
−20%	62.51	76.76	69.79	69.24	69.34	68.02	66.65	57.12	52.94
−15%	60.93	74.12	67.87	67.56	66.98	66.14	64.76	55.74	50.21
−10%	58.19	71.97	66.62	65.31	65.30	64.54	63.48	54.37	48.45
−5%	57.31	70.72	64.44	64.62	64.14	63.38	62.40	53.01	46.60
0%	**55.77**	**69.14**	**62.73**	**62.89**	**62.78**	**61.85**	**60.88**	**52.25**	**45.15**
+5%	54.95	68.01	61.71	61.63	61.58	60.98	59.55	51.49	44.04
+10%	53.64	66.64	60.73	61.52	60.43	59.85	58.63	50.22	43.19
+15%	52.10	65.27	59.69	59.46	59.62	58.46	57.64	49.49	41.93
+20%	51.30	64.00	58.63	58.79	58.57	57.79	56.71	48.69	41.17
+25%	49.51	63.43	57.65	58.02	57.53	56.95	55.84	48.29	40.42
Resulting $\overline{\overline{m}}_{\text{total}}^{\text{xye}}$ with the TriRMGC system (s)									
−25%	57.97	74.63	79.16	78.77	80.80	81.65	80.38	76.80	70.39
−20%	56.17	72.64	76.43	76.32	78.11	78.92	77.68	73.89	67.60
−15%	54.79	70.60	74.30	73.54	75.57	76.51	75.26	72.34	65.48
−10%	53.57	68.05	72.13	71.50	73.74	74.63	73.63	70.29	63.23
−5%	52.31	66.96	70.13	70.38	71.79	72.43	71.60	68.46	61.56
0%	**51.55**	**65.81**	**69.11**	**68.63**	**70.12**	**70.81**	**70.15**	**66.70**	**60.22**
+5%	49.58	64.51	67.43	67.08	68.95	69.21	68.55	65.12	58.74
+10%	48.71	62.83	65.94	65.91	67.42	67.85	67.39	64.30	57.64
+15%	48.45	62.11	64.82	64.47	66.52	66.93	66.09	63.03	56.29
+20%	47.72	60.31	63.94	63.36	65.03	65.60	64.87	61.77	55.15
+25%	46.75	60.17	63.32	63.00	63.98	64.04	64.15	60.72	54.27

Table A.45 Influence of percentage changes in the crane kinematics compared to the default settings on the mean crane-interference time per job ($\overline{\overline{m}}^{cit}_{total}$) for selected yard-block layouts and all types of RMGC systems

Kinematic change	Yard-block layout								
	Small	Low	Narrow	Short	Medium	Long	Wide	High	Big
Resulting $\overline{\overline{m}}^{cit}_{total}$ with the SRMGC system (s)									
−25%	0.00	0.00	0.00	0.00	0.00	0.00	0.00	0.00	0.00
−20%	0.00	0.00	0.00	0.00	0.00	0.00	0.00	0.00	0.00
−15%	0.00	0.00	0.00	0.00	0.00	0.00	0.00	0.00	0.00
−10%	0.00	0.00	0.00	0.00	0.00	0.00	0.00	0.00	0.00
−5%	0.00	0.00	0.00	0.00	0.00	0.00	0.00	0.00	0.00
0%	**0.00**	**0.00**	**0.00**	**0.00**	**0.00**	**0.00**	**0.00**	**0.00**	**0.00**
+5%	0.00	0.00	0.00	0.00	0.00	0.00	0.00	0.00	0.00
+10%	0.00	0.00	0.00	0.00	0.00	0.00	0.00	0.00	0.00
+15%	0.00	0.00	0.00	0.00	0.00	0.00	0.00	0.00	0.00
+20%	0.00	0.00	0.00	0.00	0.00	0.00	0.00	0.00	0.00
+25%	0.00	0.00	0.00	0.00	0.00	0.00	0.00	0.00	0.00
Resulting $\overline{\overline{m}}^{cit}_{total}$ with the TRMGC system (s)									
−25%	2.69	2.70	14.74	15.13	14.99	15.12	15.13	24.06	25.08
−20%	2.48	2.59	13.94	14.40	14.06	14.39	14.45	22.99	24.20
−15%	2.42	2.40	13.48	13.75	13.55	13.69	13.70	21.98	23.39
−10%	2.35	2.35	12.78	13.09	12.97	12.85	13.07	20.83	22.43
−5%	2.27	2.16	12.26	12.71	12.41	12.41	12.59	20.16	21.51
0%	**2.22**	**2.10**	**11.92**	**12.42**	**12.16**	**11.92**	**12.14**	**19.43**	**20.71**
+5%	2.16	2.04	11.69	11.89	11.50	11.56	11.52	18.74	20.06
+10%	2.04	1.99	11.32	11.46	11.26	11.11	11.31	18.28	19.18
+15%	2.03	1.85	10.87	11.34	10.81	10.84	10.83	17.69	18.73
+20%	1.92	1.80	10.82	11.04	10.69	10.65	10.64	17.00	17.84
+25%	1.96	1.68	10.46	10.84	10.41	10.28	10.37	16.67	17.59
Resulting $\overline{\overline{m}}^{cit}_{total}$ with the DRMGC system (s)									
−25%	31.45	38.32	35.95	40.70	35.00	28.68	32.62	28.76	23.41
−20%	31.46	37.89	36.05	40.27	35.32	29.16	32.53	28.19	22.43
−15%	31.82	37.40	36.02	40.20	34.91	29.36	32.27	28.38	21.55
−10%	30.52	37.68	36.31	39.35	35.01	29.71	32.55	28.19	21.13
−5%	30.85	38.30	36.08	40.03	35.36	29.80	32.94	28.01	20.57
0%	**31.09**	**38.13**	**35.30**	**39.74**	**35.31**	**29.73**	**32.78**	**28.21**	**20.21**
+5%	31.22	38.34	35.59	39.52	35.35	30.18	32.95	28.33	20.13
+10%	30.81	38.39	35.75	39.91	35.46	30.63	33.03	27.98	20.01
+15%	30.41	38.19	35.90	39.20	35.57	30.38	32.77	28.24	19.64
+20%	30.35	38.31	35.56	38.91	35.68	30.83	33.02	28.02	19.60
+25%	29.29	38.57	35.61	38.99	35.39	30.90	33.10	28.20	19.55
Resulting $\overline{\overline{m}}^{cit}_{total}$ with the TriRMGC system (s)									
−25%	30.73	40.68	51.45	56.27	52.84	46.97	51.02	54.34	47.09
−20%	30.59	41.07	50.63	55.57	51.63	46.01	50.21	53.09	45.57
−15%	30.91	40.28	49.69	54.05	50.80	45.65	49.06	52.19	44.33
−10%	31.76	40.10	48.94	53.61	50.07	45.34	49.22	51.35	42.97
−5%	31.20	40.42	48.66	52.79	49.79	44.92	48.66	50.43	42.39
0%	**31.02**	**40.31**	**48.66**	**52.32**	**49.18**	**44.71**	**47.95**	**49.43**	**41.62**
+5%	30.29	40.41	48.22	51.67	48.63	44.74	47.66	48.62	40.60
+10%	30.63	40.23	47.63	51.20	48.62	44.10	47.44	48.62	40.02
+15%	30.59	40.24	47.58	50.73	48.73	44.13	47.40	48.04	39.52
+20%	30.97	39.63	47.16	50.46	48.25	43.88	46.95	47.45	39.03
+25%	30.12	40.32	47.48	50.51	47.72	43.33	46.71	47.10	38.61

Table A.46 Influence of percentage changes in the crane kinematics compared to the default settings on the crane workload during the simulation horizon in terms of performed jobs ($\overline{|J|}$) for selected yard-block layouts and all types of RMGC systems

Kinematic change	Yard-block layout								
	Small	Low	Narrow	Short	Medium	Long	Wide	High	Big
Resulting $\overline{|J|}$ with the SRMGC system (jobs)									
−25%	1,870.7	3,219.2	6,565.5	6,812.0	8,646.0	10,061.4	10,418.3	11,823.7	11,160.7
−20%	1,866.2	3,219.3	6,606.9	6,811.2	8,662.1	10,225.5	10,534.0	12,203.9	11,675.7
−15%	1,872.4	3,202.7	6,575.2	6,733.0	8,654.1	10,303.3	10,651.1	12,577.0	12,228.4
−10%	1,871.9	3,211.1	6,590.1	6,758.0	8,636.3	10,363.8	10,705.7	12,845.4	12,732.3
−5%	1,869.9	3,215.6	6,546.7	6,780.2	8,702.9	10,406.4	10,681.5	13,072.4	13,270.0
0%	**1,871.8**	**3,208.8**	**6,596.5**	**6,792.8**	**8,683.4**	**10,466.3**	**10,776.3**	**13,369.4**	**13,711.1**
+5%	1,871.3	3,211.5	6,599.2	6,765.9	8,683.4	10,476.7	10,770.5	13,568.1	14,153.1
+10%	1,864.0	3,214.1	6,617.9	6,778.8	8,660.7	10,522.0	10,803.6	13,726.9	14,561.7
+15%	1,862.7	3,214.3	6,603.8	6,780.8	8,664.1	10,478.5	10,783.5	13,829.8	15,027.0
+20%	1,870.8	3,209.4	6,591.6	6,766.2	8,672.1	10,492.3	10,805.4	14,004.5	15,406.2
+25%	1,873.9	3,210.8	6,589.2	6,815.1	8,673.0	10,506.9	10,786.6	14,193.0	15,911.2
Resulting $\overline{|J|}$ with the TRMGC system (jobs)									
−25%	1,903.1	3,227.5	6,631.5	6,877.3	8,747.2	10,575.9	10,843.1	14,907.1	17,856.4
−20%	1,896.8	3,234.4	6,619.9	6,843.5	8,704.2	10,621.4	10,880.3	15,018.0	18,587.9
−15%	1,904.6	3,229.2	6,608.8	6,835.9	8,755.8	10,617.0	10,893.4	15,132.7	19,340.8
−10%	1,901.4	3,241.8	6,600.3	6,853.2	8,759.5	10,602.8	10,865.4	15,084.2	19,947.3
−5%	1,897.1	3,230.6	6,598.7	6,849.1	8,745.7	10,608.4	10,893.7	15,313.3	20,541.2
0%	**1,903.5**	**3,224.1**	**6,592.4**	**6,857.8**	**8,784.5**	**10,615.3**	**10,900.6**	**15,170.8**	**21,104.9**
+5%	1,905.0	3,233.4	6,632.7	6,831.9	8,745.5	10,585.9	10,919.9	15,340.7	21,590.6
+10%	1,904.7	3,233.4	6,618.7	6,818.3	8,757.2	10,570.7	10,856.4	15,388.3	21,893.4
+15%	1,905.1	3,224.9	6,622.7	6,849.0	8,728.5	10,576.2	10,844.4	15,335.1	22,256.5
+20%	1,906.2	3,229.5	6,645.3	6,869.4	8,749.7	10,602.4	10,907.7	15,338.1	22,544.1
+25%	1,901.0	3,233.8	6,625.1	6,870.5	8,783.9	10,594.1	10,877.1	15,400.8	22,712.7
Resulting $\overline{|J|}$ with the DRMGC system (jobs)									
−25%	1,906.0	3,223.8	6,631.6	6,826.1	8,722.6	10,595.2	10,902.8	14,791.8	18,121.9
−20%	1,906.7	3,219.8	6,616.0	6,842.1	8,738.0	10,595.3	10,892.9	14,903.3	18,911.5
−15%	1,905.3	3,222.7	6,589.0	6,827.0	8,732.8	10,563.1	10,867.2	15,046.1	19,700.5
−10%	1,901.0	3,230.4	6,630.8	6,826.0	8,732.5	10,568.8	10,870.1	15,008.7	20,212.5
−5%	1,900.4	3,222.4	6,587.5	6,815.6	8,760.6	10,605.0	10,873.3	15,164.2	20,764.2
0%	**1,901.9**	**3,222.4**	**6,623.5**	**6,834.0**	**8,713.7**	**10,605.3**	**10,893.6**	**15,175.5**	**21,213.5**
+5%	1,905.8	3,232.6	6,593.8	6,852.3	8,732.0	10,571.6	10,862.4	15,072.1	21,530.0
+10%	1,905.9	3,233.1	6,607.0	6,838.5	8,774.0	10,558.5	10,872.8	15,128.6	21,790.7
+15%	1,900.0	3,231.7	6,634.8	6,873.3	8,721.0	10,588.2	10,882.1	15,266.7	22,206.3
+20%	1,902.7	3,233.8	6,605.8	6,848.3	8,722.3	10,582.4	10,877.6	15,372.8	22,335.5
+25%	1,900.7	3,229.2	6,630.0	6,832.8	8,741.7	10,544.5	10,844.8	15,227.9	22,626.8
Resulting $\overline{|J|}$ with the TriRMGC system (jobs)									
−25%	1,904.3	3,249.7	6,615.5	6,832.8	8,717.5	10,556.9	10,887.8	14,981.2	21,713.7
−20%	1,906.3	3,252.5	6,606.3	6,811.7	8,722.4	10,567.8	10,872.2	15,333.1	22,199.2
−15%	1,899.3	3,239.0	6,632.1	6,837.7	8,737.7	10,531.8	10,881.0	15,205.2	22,547.9
−10%	1,904.4	3,250.8	6,622.6	6,834.2	8,734.2	10,577.8	10,909.4	15,228.2	22,816.2
−5%	1,900.2	3,244.0	6,622.3	6,857.2	8,711.5	10,593.4	10,901.8	15,224.5	22,997.9
0%	**1,907.0**	**3,249.5**	**6,614.4**	**6,831.8**	**8,732.5**	**10,583.9**	**10,895.8**	**15,192.1**	**23,097.9**
+5%	1,905.6	3,246.2	6,618.4	6,813.3	8,712.2	10,600.6	10,878.9	15,370.9	23,362.9
+10%	1,910.9	3,246.7	6,648.2	6,867.4	8,730.2	10,579.6	10,889.9	15,376.4	23,287.7
+15%	1,910.4	3,238.0	6,613.0	6,820.6	8,735.0	10,542.6	10,869.7	15,420.4	23,331.7
+20%	1,911.0	3,251.6	6,594.9	6,857.7	8,742.8	10,564.8	10,865.4	15,352.0	23,526.4
+25%	1,917.8	3,245.4	6,610.6	6,851.9	8,751.0	10,575.0	10,854.4	15,433.9	23,581.3

Table A.47 Influence of percentage changes in the crane kinematics compared to the default settings on the container accessibility ($\overline{\overline{\psi}}$), in terms of the mean number of shuffle moves per retrieval job, for selected yard-block layouts and all types of RMGC systems

Kinematic change	Yard-block layout								
	Small	Low	Narrow	Short	Medium	Long	Wide	High	Big
Resulting $\overline{\overline{\psi}}$ with the SRMGC system (jobs)									
−25%	0.321	0.304	1.122	1.127	1.096	1.046	1.040	1.478	0.959
−20%	0.316	0.306	1.132	1.124	1.099	1.065	1.054	1.507	1.000
−15%	0.319	0.299	1.123	1.102	1.094	1.072	1.069	1.542	1.032
−10%	0.320	0.300	1.129	1.109	1.088	1.073	1.077	1.564	1.075
−5%	0.318	0.301	1.108	1.113	1.107	1.073	1.066	1.577	1.118
0%	**0.322**	**0.300**	**1.135**	**1.120**	**1.103**	**1.083**	**1.083**	**1.606**	**1.144**
+5%	0.321	0.304	1.127	1.117	1.101	1.083	1.080	1.615	1.172
+10%	0.313	0.304	1.134	1.115	1.098	1.092	1.085	1.628	1.202
+15%	0.309	0.300	1.135	1.115	1.094	1.080	1.076	1.636	1.238
+20%	0.318	0.302	1.127	1.115	1.098	1.079	1.080	1.651	1.265
+25%	0.320	0.298	1.125	1.122	1.096	1.083	1.075	1.662	1.306
Resulting $\overline{\overline{\psi}}$ with the TRMGC system (jobs)									
−25%	0.327	0.299	1.141	1.138	1.118	1.092	1.082	1.740	1.477
−20%	0.319	0.301	1.135	1.129	1.102	1.097	1.082	1.747	1.527
−15%	0.328	0.298	1.135	1.123	1.120	1.096	1.088	1.763	1.578
−10%	0.322	0.307	1.128	1.122	1.119	1.095	1.080	1.760	1.608
−5%	0.320	0.297	1.127	1.131	1.116	1.093	1.088	1.776	1.647
0%	**0.324**	**0.296**	**1.127**	**1.130**	**1.130**	**1.097**	**1.090**	**1.762**	**1.675**
+5%	0.323	0.301	1.140	1.121	1.115	1.090	1.089	1.774	1.707
+10%	0.325	0.301	1.135	1.110	1.121	1.090	1.080	1.784	1.722
+15%	0.325	0.295	1.133	1.124	1.107	1.087	1.073	1.781	1.736
+20%	0.327	0.299	1.144	1.132	1.117	1.096	1.089	1.782	1.743
+25%	0.320	0.300	1.139	1.131	1.132	1.091	1.087	1.792	1.752
Resulting $\overline{\overline{\psi}}$ with the DRMGC system (jobs)									
−25%	0.327	0.296	1.135	1.115	1.109	1.091	1.094	1.724	1.482
−20%	0.330	0.294	1.130	1.125	1.117	1.092	1.092	1.730	1.527
−15%	0.327	0.296	1.126	1.120	1.119	1.084	1.082	1.735	1.593
−10%	0.323	0.300	1.129	1.128	1.118	1.086	1.082	1.752	1.623
−5%	0.320	0.293	1.133	1.119	1.122	1.095	1.084	1.749	1.645
0%	**0.320**	**0.297**	**1.137**	**1.118**	**1.107**	**1.093**	**1.087**	**1.753**	**1.673**
+5%	0.325	0.302	1.123	1.127	1.120	1.086	1.081	1.744	1.690
+10%	0.327	0.298	1.127	1.117	1.126	1.085	1.084	1.754	1.697
+15%	0.321	0.300	1.132	1.134	1.109	1.089	1.085	1.767	1.722
+20%	0.325	0.300	1.128	1.127	1.106	1.088	1.085	1.776	1.724
+25%	0.322	0.297	1.129	1.119	1.116	1.079	1.077	1.759	1.736
Resulting $\overline{\overline{\psi}}$ with the TriRMGC system (jobs)									
−25%	0.325	0.298	1.130	1.123	1.112	1.082	1.091	1.736	1.701
−20%	0.329	0.300	1.126	1.111	1.110	1.091	1.086	1.776	1.719
−15%	0.324	0.291	1.133	1.127	1.118	1.081	1.087	1.760	1.741
−10%	0.330	0.296	1.126	1.118	1.114	1.090	1.090	1.773	1.748
−5%	0.324	0.296	1.127	1.123	1.110	1.093	1.086	1.768	1.760
0%	**0.325**	**0.298**	**1.122**	**1.123**	**1.113**	**1.092**	**1.090**	**1.763**	**1.758**
+5%	0.324	0.293	1.123	1.116	1.110	1.096	1.085	1.776	1.774
+10%	0.330	0.295	1.140	1.127	1.116	1.087	1.084	1.778	1.759
+15%	0.330	0.289	1.126	1.108	1.115	1.075	1.083	1.790	1.753
+20%	0.330	0.298	1.121	1.132	1.116	1.082	1.081	1.782	1.773
+25%	0.338	0.292	1.120	1.124	1.123	1.088	1.078	1.782	1.769

Table A.48 Influence of the portal velocity of the outer large crane of the DRMGC system (v_2^{xf}, v_2^{xe}) on the mean vehicle-waiting time ($\overline{\omega}_{total}^{hr+}$) for selected yard-block layouts

v_2^{xe}, v_2^{xf}	Yard-block layout Small	Low	Narrow	Short	Medium	Long	Wide	High	Big
Resulting $\overline{\omega}_{total}^{hr+}$ with the SRMGC system (s)									
	28.26	**41.28**	**117.06**	**100.44**	**198.96**	**561.06**	**484.56**	**1,861.32**	**3,269.94**
Resulting $\overline{\omega}_{total}^{hr+}$ with the TRMGC system (s)									
	8.82	**13.44**	**38.16**	**35.58**	**48.30**	**67.44**	**61.98**	**304.08**	**1,567.38**
Resulting $\overline{\omega}_{total}^{hr+}$ with the DRMGC system (s)									
3.50	**13.86**	**23.58**	**53.82**	**54.36**	**69.24**	**88.86**	**88.86**	**360.18**	**1,607.82**
3.55	13.98	23.22	53.58	54.66	70.32	89.70	89.28	343.38	1,605.30
3.60	13.92	23.34	53.34	53.46	69.66	88.92	89.22	352.92	1,593.72
3.65	14.04	23.16	54.06	54.42	69.66	91.32	88.08	338.76	1,579.26
3.70	14.16	22.74	54.12	53.64	69.00	87.12	90.00	360.00	1,588.08
3.75	13.08	22.62	52.44	52.68	69.00	89.88	88.08	326.58	1,569.00
3.80	13.14	22.56	52.92	52.32	66.96	88.38	88.56	345.78	1,558.08
3.85	13.44	22.20	52.50	53.28	68.88	89.16	87.90	361.74	1,589.28
3.90	13.56	21.90	53.64	54.00	68.34	88.74	85.86	341.28	1,575.12
3.95	13.26	22.80	53.40	52.80	68.40	88.68	88.26	330.18	1,560.00
4.00	13.32	22.32	54.12	54.30	68.16	87.84	87.18	339.78	1,518.00
Resulting $\overline{\omega}_{total}^{hr+}$ with the TriRMGC system (s)									
	8.82	**12.48**	**31.26**	**31.86**	**37.98**	**46.86**	**46.86**	**117.54**	**574.98**

Table A.49 Influence of the portal velocity of the outer large crane of the DRMGC system (v_2^{xf}, v_2^{xe}) on the mean vehicle-waiting time per waterside retrieval job ($\overline{\omega}_{wsout}^{hr+}$) for selected yard-block layouts

v_2^{xe}, v_2^{xf}	Yard-block layout Small	Low	Narrow	Short	Medium	Long	Wide	High	Big
Resulting $\overline{\omega}_{wsout}^{hr+}$ with the SRMGC system (s)									
	3.24	**5.52**	**78.00**	**56.04**	**198.72**	**789.12**	**671.58**	**3,180.30**	**4,959.72**
Resulting $\overline{\omega}_{wsout}^{hr+}$ with the TRMGC system (s)									
	2.28	**4.14**	**15.06**	**13.20**	**25.80**	**48.48**	**42.12**	**486.30**	**3,019.80**
Resulting $\overline{\omega}_{wsout}^{hr+}$ with the DRMGC system (s)									
3.50	**2.76**	**5.34**	**20.10**	**18.72**	**30.78**	**47.46**	**46.26**	**510.54**	**2,758.62**
3.55	3.00	5.16	20.10	19.32	31.02	47.46	48.00	483.12	2,755.14
3.60	3.18	4.38	18.18	18.96	31.08	48.30	47.22	497.40	2,718.54
3.65	3.42	5.10	19.68	20.34	32.46	53.28	47.64	466.44	2,719.32
3.70	3.30	5.16	20.40	19.44	30.12	46.32	51.78	511.86	2,723.88
3.75	2.34	4.98	18.96	18.96	30.00	52.08	46.44	449.82	2,671.98
3.80	2.34	4.98	18.00	17.88	27.12	48.54	48.72	495.60	2,660.76
3.85	2.64	5.04	18.90	18.18	28.98	49.08	47.16	518.76	2,748.78
3.90	2.76	4.32	20.04	21.30	31.14	50.04	43.50	484.32	2,705.94
3.95	2.16	5.04	19.32	18.24	31.50	48.36	48.78	451.80	2,673.66
4.00	2.28	4.56	19.62	19.86	29.10	48.18	46.44	485.52	2,601.12
Resulting $\overline{\omega}_{wsout}^{hr+}$ with the TriRMGC system (s)									
	2.22	**5.34**	**12.90**	**12.54**	**16.32**	**19.68**	**20.94**	**109.68**	**883.26**

Table A.50 Influence of the portal velocity of the outer large crane of the DRMGC system (v_2^{xf}, v_2^{xe}) on the mean crane-waiting time in the handover areas ($\overline{\overline{\omega}}^{hr-}_{total}$) for selected yard-block layouts

	Yard-block layout								
v_2^{xe}, v_2^{xf}	Small	Low	Narrow	Short	Medium	Long	Wide	High	Big
Resulting $\overline{\overline{\omega}}^{hr-}_{total}$ with the SRMGC system (s)									
	124.38	**94.92**	**63.84**	**67.26**	**41.52**	**22.86**	**25.80**	**14.64**	**7.08**
Resulting $\overline{\overline{\omega}}^{hr-}_{total}$ with the TRMGC system (s)									
	135.84	**112.32**	**87.84**	**91.26**	**67.86**	**50.28**	**53.40**	**35.58**	**10.56**
Resulting $\overline{\overline{\omega}}^{hr-}_{total}$ with the DRMGC system (s)									
3.50	**139.32**	**117.48**	**95.28**	**95.46**	**75.18**	**57.24**	**57.66**	**44.52**	**12.60**
3.55	139.92	116.52	95.94	96.18	74.70	57.48	57.30	44.70	12.36
3.60	140.22	117.72	96.66	96.06	74.82	57.48	57.42	44.46	13.02
3.65	140.46	117.60	96.12	95.04	75.30	57.72	57.78	45.48	12.84
3.70	139.98	118.38	95.94	96.84	75.96	57.78	58.14	44.46	12.54
3.75	139.38	118.02	95.94	96.12	75.24	57.72	57.78	45.06	12.48
3.80	138.96	117.96	96.12	96.30	74.88	58.14	58.14	45.42	12.90
3.85	138.96	118.68	95.88	96.48	75.78	57.90	58.38	44.82	13.08
3.90	139.86	118.08	95.88	95.76	75.66	57.60	58.38	45.30	12.90
3.95	139.02	117.66	95.94	95.34	75.54	58.56	58.62	45.36	13.02
4.00	139.14	117.96	96.48	96.00	75.96	58.08	58.14	45.30	13.26
Resulting $\overline{\overline{\omega}}^{hr-}_{total}$ with the TriRMGC system (s)									
	140.40	**121.98**	**103.44**	**101.10**	**84.00**	**68.22**	**68.64**	**58.38**	**23.88**

Table A.51 Influence of the portal velocity of the outer large crane of the DRMGC system (v_2^{xf}, v_2^{xe}) on the mean crane-empty-movement time per job ($\overline{\overline{m}}^{xye}_{total}$) for selected yard-block layouts

	Yard-block layout								
v_2^{xe}, v_2^{xf}	Small	Low	Narrow	Short	Medium	Long	Wide	High	Big
Resulting $\overline{\overline{m}}^{xye}_{total}$ with the SRMGC system (s)									
	26.05	**31.87**	**26.97**	**23.22**	**26.63**	**29.48**	**26.57**	**23.73**	**27.72**
Resulting $\overline{\overline{m}}^{xye}_{total}$ with the TRMGC system (s)									
	23.34	**28.35**	**33.76**	**30.25**	**34.07**	**38.12**	**34.64**	**37.21**	**40.77**
Resulting $\overline{\overline{m}}^{xye}_{total}$ with the DRMGC system (s)									
3.50	**55.77**	**69.14**	**62.73**	**62.89**	**62.78**	**61.85**	**60.88**	**52.25**	**45.15**
3.55	55.90	68.65	62.51	62.92	62.46	61.91	60.62	52.29	45.16
3.60	55.55	68.52	62.99	62.99	62.51	61.85	60.52	52.12	45.19
3.65	55.34	68.31	62.88	62.88	62.10	61.60	60.69	52.20	45.02
3.70	55.21	68.56	62.72	62.86	62.32	61.53	60.16	51.74	45.05
3.75	55.45	68.27	62.73	62.66	62.36	61.37	60.36	52.01	44.72
3.80	55.11	68.13	62.26	62.66	62.32	61.45	60.62	52.05	44.82
3.85	54.79	68.16	62.37	62.76	62.23	61.25	60.24	51.52	44.54
3.90	55.20	68.41	62.16	62.37	62.18	60.88	60.20	51.79	44.61
3.95	55.25	68.38	62.25	62.75	61.85	60.91	59.75	51.66	44.57
4.00	55.14	67.90	62.36	62.21	61.96	60.91	60.02	51.53	44.48
Resulting $\overline{\overline{m}}^{xye}_{total}$ with the TriRMGC system (s)									
	51.55	**65.81**	**69.11**	**68.63**	**70.12**	**70.81**	**70.15**	**66.70**	**60.22**

Table A.52 Influence of the portal velocity of the outer large crane of the DRMGC system (v_2^{xf}, v_2^{xe}) on the mean crane-interference time per job ($\overline{m}_{total}^{cit}$) for selected yard-block layouts

v_2^{xe}, v_2^{xf}	Yard-block layout Small	Low	Narrow	Short	Medium	Long	Wide	High	Big
Resulting $\overline{m}_{total}^{cit}$ with the SRMGC system (s)									
	0.00	**0.00**	**0.00**	**0.00**	**0.00**	**0.00**	**0.00**	**0.00**	**0.00**
Resulting $\overline{m}_{total}^{cit}$ with the TRMGC system (s)									
	2.22	**2.10**	**11.92**	**12.42**	**12.16**	**11.92**	**12.14**	**19.43**	**20.71**
Resulting $\overline{m}_{total}^{cit}$ with the DRMGC system (s)									
3.50	**31.09**	**38.13**	**35.30**	**39.74**	**35.31**	**29.73**	**32.78**	**28.21**	**20.21**
3.55	31.69	38.05	35.35	39.62	35.20	30.06	32.66	28.24	20.19
3.60	31.43	37.80	35.98	39.93	35.40	30.23	32.79	28.33	20.27
3.65	31.40	38.18	35.82	40.05	35.07	29.95	32.95	28.55	20.33
3.70	31.19	38.37	35.98	39.75	35.58	30.11	32.73	28.28	20.45
3.75	30.90	38.14	36.41	39.64	35.55	30.16	32.84	28.38	20.24
3.80	31.03	38.43	35.71	39.76	35.47	30.37	33.33	28.70	20.43
3.85	30.93	38.57	36.01	39.76	35.68	30.22	33.04	28.24	20.23
3.90	31.42	38.50	36.02	39.88	35.76	30.03	33.03	28.50	20.43
3.95	31.42	38.64	36.09	40.22	35.47	30.22	32.85	28.45	20.50
4.00	31.42	38.21	36.22	39.92	35.77	30.34	33.01	28.57	20.34
Resulting $\overline{m}_{total}^{cit}$ with the TriRMGC system (s)									
	31.02	**40.31**	**48.66**	**52.32**	**49.18**	**44.71**	**47.95**	**49.43**	**41.62**

Table A.53 Influence of the portal velocity of the outer large crane of the DRMGC system (v_2^{xf}, v_2^{xe}) on the crane workload during the simulation horizon in terms of performed jobs ($\overline{|J|}$) for selected yard-block layouts

v_2^{xe}, v_2^{xf}	Yard-block layout Small	Low	Narrow	Short	Medium	Long	Wide	High	Big
Resulting $\overline{|J|}$ with the SRMGC system (jobs)									
	1,871.8	**3,208.8**	**6,596.5**	**6,792.8**	**8,683.4**	**10,466.3**	**10,776.3**	**13,369.4**	**13,711.1**
Resulting $\overline{|J|}$ with the TRMGC system (jobs)									
	1,903.5	**3,224.1**	**6,592.4**	**6,857.8**	**8,784.5**	**10,615.3**	**10,900.6**	**15,170.8**	**21,104.9**
Resulting $\overline{|J|}$ with the DRMGC system (jobs)									
3.50	**1,901.9**	**3,222.4**	**6,623.5**	**6,834.0**	**8,713.7**	**10,605.3**	**10,893.6**	**15,175.5**	**21,213.5**
3.55	1,903.7	3,227.4	6,629.1	6,830.7	8,784.8	10,557.4	10,889.8	15,061.9	21,177.3
3.60	1,901.5	3,234.2	6,619.3	6,813.8	8,744.3	10,584.7	10,888.0	15,177.7	21,143.5
3.65	1,901.4	3,230.5	6,597.1	6,811.4	8,728.8	10,566.6	10,861.2	15,107.9	21,118.2
3.70	1,902.8	3,227.0	6,608.0	6,839.6	8,755.7	10,505.7	10,913.1	15,206.5	21,188.2
3.75	1,897.3	3,222.0	6,593.2	6,820.5	8,737.9	10,571.8	10,895.3	15,110.2	21,298.0
3.80	1,898.5	3,225.3	6,606.4	6,835.9	8,743.3	10,577.4	10,847.9	15,072.8	21,217.1
3.85	1,904.6	3,225.0	6,586.4	6,824.1	8,738.0	10,598.4	10,906.0	15,221.7	21,299.7
3.90	1,905.4	3,218.0	6,609.3	6,826.0	8,728.8	10,587.7	10,852.7	15,119.3	21,309.2
3.95	1,901.0	3,222.8	6,643.5	6,796.9	8,786.9	10,628.2	10,854.8	15,117.1	21,323.7
4.00	1,900.9	3,217.8	6,617.0	6,840.1	8,714.2	10,604.5	10,854.7	15,133.4	21,224.5
Resulting $\overline{|J|}$ with the TriRMGC system (jobs)									
	1,907.0	**3,249.5**	**6,614.4**	**6,831.8**	**8,732.5**	**10,583.9**	**10,895.8**	**15,192.1**	**23,097.9**

Table A.54 Influence of the portal velocity of the outer large crane of the DRMGC system (v_2^{xf}, v_2^{xe}) on the container accessibility ($\overline{\overline{\psi}}$), in terms of the mean number of shuffle moves per retrieval job, for selected yard-block layouts

	Yard-block layout								
v_2^{xe}, v_2^{xf}	Small	Low	Narrow	Short	Medium	Long	Wide	High	Big
Resulting $\overline{\overline{\psi}}$ with the SRMGC system (jobs)									
	0.322	**0.300**	**1.135**	**1.120**	**1.103**	**1.083**	**1.083**	**1.606**	**1.144**
Resulting $\overline{\overline{\psi}}$ with the TRMGC system (jobs)									
	0.324	**0.296**	**1.127**	**1.130**	**1.130**	**1.097**	**1.090**	**1.762**	**1.675**
Resulting $\overline{\overline{\psi}}$ with the DRMGC system (jobs)									
3.50	**0.320**	**0.297**	**1.137**	**1.118**	**1.107**	**1.093**	**1.087**	**1.753**	**1.673**
3.55	0.324	0.297	1.134	1.122	1.129	1.082	1.088	1.744	1.669
3.60	0.323	0.300	1.127	1.116	1.114	1.087	1.087	1.755	1.662
3.65	0.321	0.296	1.120	1.116	1.118	1.086	1.080	1.764	1.653
3.70	0.324	0.296	1.128	1.124	1.120	1.075	1.091	1.765	1.666
3.75	0.319	0.294	1.124	1.113	1.115	1.089	1.091	1.749	1.668
3.80	0.321	0.296	1.129	1.121	1.112	1.085	1.076	1.746	1.659
3.85	0.326	0.297	1.124	1.114	1.109	1.096	1.094	1.762	1.678
3.90	0.326	0.291	1.128	1.120	1.113	1.092	1.078	1.754	1.676
3.95	0.324	0.297	1.142	1.109	1.125	1.102	1.080	1.757	1.674
4.00	0.324	0.294	1.137	1.125	1.110	1.101	1.079	1.748	1.667
Resulting $\overline{\overline{\psi}}$ with the TriRMGC system (jobs)									
	0.325	**0.298**	**1.122**	**1.123**	**1.113**	**1.092**	**1.090**	**1.763**	**1.758**

A.5.6 *Influence of the Container-Stacking Strategy*

Table A.55 Influence of the RTS concept (in terms of the cost factor $\lambda^{rts}_{\tau(j)}$) on the mean vehicle-waiting time ($\overline{\omega}^{hr+}_{total}$) for selected yard-block layouts and all types of RMGC systems

	Yard-block layout								
$\lambda^{rts}_{\tau(j)}$	Small	Low	Narrow	Short	Medium	Long	Wide	High	Big
Resulting $\overline{\omega}^{hr+}_{total}$ with the SRMGC system (s)									
0.00	**28.26**	**41.28**	**117.06**	**100.44**	**198.96**	**561.06**	**486.56**	**1,861.32**	**3,269.94**
0.01	26.76	41.82	116.22	102.96	192.54	552.54	471.18	1,845.78	3,281.64
0.10	26.88	42.24	110.04	98.16	179.82	536.64	457.92	1,678.20	3,293.70
0.50	27.00	42.18	105.66	95.16	172.98	548.46	449.40	1,426.02	3,321.72
1.00	26.28	42.36	104.52	90.36	172.50	511.38	440.82	1,465.56	3,347.10
2.00	26.76	41.94	102.96	91.68	179.10	508.38	418.50	1,426.38	3,398.22
5.00	26.76	42.36	101.82	91.44	171.60	484.26	430.08	1,369.80	3,384.90
10.00	28.56	41.04	102.54	91.26	169.26	507.42	407.76	1,391.22	3,395.82
25.00	27.54	42.30	101.64	91.50	167.40	470.04	389.52	1,318.44	3,469.02
50.00	27.06	40.62	103.50	89.76	164.58	503.82	380.82	1,349.22	3,438.36
100.00	26.16	41.58	97.80	88.74	168.90	506.58	402.78	1,271.40	3,571.14
Resulting $\overline{\omega}^{hr+}_{total}$ with the TRMGC system (s)									
0.00	**8.82**	**13.44**	**38.16**	**35.58**	**48.30**	**67.44**	**61.98**	**304.08**	**1,567.38**
0.01	8.64	13.32	38.82	35.94	46.98	67.44	58.86	299.82	1,556.22
0.10	8.88	13.26	37.98	34.74	47.28	66.48	58.44	264.24	1,475.82
0.50	8.46	12.84	35.28	32.52	45.24	63.42	57.96	216.06	1,315.86
1.00	8.64	12.84	34.80	31.44	41.70	62.10	55.92	195.12	1,218.06
2.00	8.94	12.66	34.32	30.90	42.78	61.08	55.32	191.76	1,158.36
5.00	8.76	13.14	34.80	30.84	43.02	60.84	53.58	181.98	1,154.70
10.00	9.06	13.32	34.56	30.84	41.70	62.28	53.46	178.80	1,181.76
25.00	8.88	13.20	33.84	30.78	40.62	62.10	52.98	175.20	1,107.36
50.00	8.82	12.96	33.36	30.36	41.34	60.18	54.36	178.44	1,168.80
100.00	8.40	12.72	33.66	29.16	40.50	61.50	54.96	182.22	1,118.52
Resulting $\overline{\omega}^{hr+}_{total}$ with the DRMGC system (s)									
0.00	**13.86**	**23.58**	**53.82**	**54.36**	**69.24**	**88.86**	**88.86**	**360.18**	**1,607.82**
0.01	14.46	23.22	53.76	54.24	69.78	89.88	88.50	366.00	1,616.82
0.10	13.50	22.44	53.22	54.00	69.24	88.80	87.18	313.56	1,533.60
0.50	13.26	22.50	49.74	48.60	63.54	84.60	85.74	244.08	1,335.06
1.00	13.32	21.78	48.72	46.68	62.40	82.92	82.02	226.02	1,254.30
2.00	12.78	21.96	47.22	47.34	61.68	81.00	79.44	216.66	1,216.98
5.00	12.84	22.08	46.62	44.82	59.40	82.56	79.32	195.96	1,169.76
10.00	12.96	22.44	46.20	44.88	59.70	81.84	80.52	196.98	1,160.52
25.00	12.66	22.32	46.02	45.36	59.70	78.78	79.26	199.08	1,170.18
50.00	12.78	22.14	44.88	45.78	59.10	80.28	79.38	203.82	1,144.74
100.00	12.06	21.66	45.18	44.34	58.74	79.20	78.96	202.02	1,162.50
Resulting $\overline{\omega}^{hr+}_{total}$ with the TriRMGC system (s)									
0.00	**8.82**	**12.48**	**31.26**	**31.86**	**37.98**	**46.86**	**46.86**	**117.54**	**574.98**
0.01	8.64	12.54	31.56	32.52	37.92	45.84	46.50	120.72	578.76
0.10	8.76	12.48	31.26	31.92	37.80	46.56	46.26	113.58	560.64
0.50	8.16	12.06	27.84	28.26	35.58	43.20	44.10	89.40	447.48
1.00	8.22	11.58	27.24	27.30	33.36	42.60	40.74	81.60	410.82
2.00	8.28	11.64	27.30	26.76	32.88	41.04	40.86	82.80	380.16
5.00	8.28	11.70	26.88	26.76	33.24	40.62	40.14	78.12	364.86
10.00	7.68	11.64	27.30	26.58	32.76	41.04	39.36	81.90	373.50
25.00	7.74	11.88	26.10	26.16	32.70	40.56	40.50	81.54	342.12
50.00	7.74	11.34	25.98	27.18	32.04	40.56	39.90	78.18	365.70
100.00	7.80	11.46	25.32	25.86	31.74	39.18	39.24	79.20	354.24

Table A.56 Influence of the RTS concept (in terms of the cost factor $\lambda^{\text{rts}}_{\tau(j)}$) on the mean vehicle-waiting time per waterside retrieval job ($\overline{\overline{\omega}}^{\text{hr+}}_{\text{wsout}}$) for selected yard-block layouts and all types of RMGC systems

	Yard-block layout								
$\lambda^{\text{rts}}_{\tau(j)}$	Small	Low	Narrow	Short	Medium	Long	Wide	High	Big
Resulting $\overline{\overline{\omega}}^{\text{hr+}}_{\text{wsout}}$ with the SRMGC system (s)									
0.00	**3.24**	**5.52**	**78.00**	**56.04**	**198.72**	**789.12**	**671.58**	**3,180.30**	**4,959.72**
0.01	3.30	6.00	76.68	62.70	190.86	770.34	642.96	3,183.06	5,064.96
0.10	2.28	6.84	68.82	52.62	170.46	740.40	628.80	2,833.74	5,086.86
0.50	2.34	6.78	64.92	48.12	158.16	782.64	618.30	2,396.94	5,146.20
1.00	4.14	6.12	68.70	44.52	159.60	715.86	614.52	2,504.22	5,195.64
2.00	3.06	6.30	67.02	51.90	171.72	714.18	571.20	2,427.00	5,276.28
5.00	2.52	6.18	59.34	48.60	158.40	654.18	601.08	2,328.48	5,308.08
10.00	3.06	4.32	61.92	46.32	160.20	701.10	560.34	2,380.20	5,343.06
25.00	4.02	5.64	65.58	49.14	151.08	642.54	519.00	2,232.18	5,467.32
50.00	3.48	5.82	64.26	47.16	148.56	695.70	502.92	2,283.78	5,404.14
100.00	3.54	7.26	59.52	46.50	157.86	714.78	545.04	2,153.52	5,679.72
Resulting $\overline{\overline{\omega}}^{\text{hr+}}_{\text{wsout}}$ with the TRMGC system (s)									
0.00	**2.28**	**4.14**	**15.06**	**13.20**	**25.80**	**48.48**	**42.12**	**486.30**	**3,019.80**
0.01	1.68	3.96	16.80	14.76	22.56	46.74	33.78	474.90	2,986.02
0.10	2.64	5.22	15.84	12.48	24.12	43.62	35.16	406.44	2,849.04
0.50	2.34	4.32	15.96	13.38	24.00	44.52	39.00	329.76	2,534.64
1.00	2.22	4.50	15.78	14.04	20.58	43.98	37.20	292.44	2,356.14
2.00	2.22	3.36	15.36	12.24	22.74	39.90	38.40	287.58	2,279.58
5.00	2.52	5.04	15.84	12.06	23.34	42.96	32.58	261.18	2,255.28
10.00	2.64	4.62	16.68	11.04	20.88	47.28	32.70	258.36	2,331.36
25.00	2.28	4.74	15.24	13.74	20.88	45.60	33.12	253.44	2,133.72
50.00	3.12	3.78	14.40	13.32	21.12	43.26	36.36	266.82	2,265.30
100.00	1.50	4.38	16.62	11.82	20.82	47.94	38.82	270.36	2,166.30
Resulting $\overline{\overline{\omega}}^{\text{hr+}}_{\text{wsout}}$ with the DRMGC system (s)									
0.00	**2.76**	**5.34**	**20.10**	**18.72**	**30.78**	**47.46**	**46.26**	**510.54**	**2,758.62**
0.01	3.42	5.28	19.26	18.54	30.00	47.28	46.02	525.42	2,779.44
0.10	2.76	4.86	20.16	18.78	31.74	46.38	43.56	424.32	2,614.92
0.50	2.64	5.70	18.48	15.60	27.30	45.84	47.64	312.00	2,302.26
1.00	2.94	4.80	18.60	17.10	29.94	44.88	46.02	286.08	2,161.44
2.00	3.00	5.22	18.30	17.46	27.84	45.36	43.50	274.50	2,086.32
5.00	1.98	5.58	18.48	16.44	27.24	47.88	43.98	235.62	2,024.64
10.00	2.82	5.46	18.96	15.90	27.90	46.80	47.22	239.88	2,016.54
25.00	2.46	4.80	17.40	15.66	26.16	44.52	46.86	238.80	2,030.94
50.00	2.88	5.22	16.92	18.24	26.10	46.74	45.84	253.56	1,989.54
100.00	1.92	4.56	17.58	15.06	25.38	45.00	45.78	246.42	2,035.86
Resulting $\overline{\overline{\omega}}^{\text{hr+}}_{\text{wsout}}$ with the TriRMGC system (s)									
0.00	**2.22**	**5.34**	**12.90**	**12.54**	**16.32**	**19.68**	**20.94**	**109.68**	**883.26**
0.01	2.52	6.00	12.24	13.26	16.44	19.32	20.46	113.76	908.76
0.10	2.82	5.04	12.84	11.40	17.28	20.10	20.28	102.60	866.46
0.50	1.68	6.18	11.76	11.40	17.52	19.50	21.84	79.50	680.76
1.00	2.52	5.22	11.94	11.10	16.02	19.74	19.92	72.84	619.98
2.00	2.58	5.04	12.72	11.88	16.92	19.86	19.98	75.84	556.44
5.00	2.76	4.74	11.40	12.06	17.04	18.60	20.40	69.90	538.26
10.00	1.50	5.40	12.48	11.52	16.02	20.58	19.26	75.60	559.86
25.00	1.80	5.52	12.36	10.20	16.56	20.16	20.28	74.76	501.42
50.00	2.16	4.26	10.50	11.16	16.80	18.54	20.70	72.12	540.72
100.00	2.34	4.98	11.94	10.80	15.78	18.96	18.84	71.34	517.74

Table A.57 Influence of the RTS concept (in terms of the cost factor $\lambda^{rts}_{\tau(j)}$) on the mean crane-waiting time in the handover areas ($\overline{\overline{\omega}}^{hr-}_{total}$) for selected yard-block layouts and all types of RMGC systems

	Yard-block layout								
$\lambda^{rts}_{\tau(j)}$	Small	Low	Narrow	Short	Medium	Long	Wide	High	Big
Resulting $\overline{\overline{\omega}}^{hr-}_{total}$ with the SRMGC system (s)									
0.00	**124.38**	**94.92**	**63.84**	**67.26**	**41.52**	**22.86**	**25.80**	**14.64**	**7.08**
0.01	123.54	95.70	63.78	67.38	41.94	22.86	26.22	14.58	6.90
0.10	123.48	95.70	64.62	67.74	42.72	23.46	26.64	15.30	7.02
0.50	123.90	95.46	68.52	72.72	46.68	26.28	30.12	17.70	6.78
1.00	123.78	96.12	70.44	72.84	48.54	27.36	31.02	17.76	6.96
2.00	124.14	95.28	70.80	73.50	48.30	27.66	31.44	18.36	6.66
5.00	124.08	95.04	70.44	74.04	49.08	28.62	31.80	19.32	6.66
10.00	124.38	94.68	71.94	73.44	49.20	27.90	32.04	19.32	6.72
25.00	123.18	95.16	71.28	74.22	49.20	28.74	33.30	19.80	6.78
50.00	123.84	95.16	72.18	74.16	48.60	28.56	32.88	19.56	7.08
100.00	123.18	95.46	72.30	74.28	49.56	28.86	32.34	20.46	6.72
Resulting $\overline{\overline{\omega}}^{hr-}_{total}$ with the TRMGC system (s)									
0.00	**135.84**	**112.32**	**87.84**	**91.26**	**67.86**	**50.28**	**53.40**	**38.58**	**10.56**
0.01	133.86	112.14	87.96	91.08	67.92	50.04	52.98	38.58	10.56
0.10	134.88	111.00	89.46	91.20	68.82	50.70	52.92	39.42	11.04
0.50	136.26	113.34	92.88	95.04	72.84	54.30	56.64	45.48	12.84
1.00	136.56	112.74	92.76	96.96	74.46	55.08	58.02	47.28	13.68
2.00	136.56	112.56	93.54	95.82	75.06	56.22	59.58	48.00	14.64
5.00	135.72	112.38	93.78	96.42	75.78	56.40	59.64	49.14	14.76
10.00	135.18	112.50	94.32	95.88	75.36	57.00	59.82	49.74	15.06
25.00	134.94	112.56	94.86	97.80	75.90	56.94	59.88	49.74	15.18
50.00	135.60	112.20	95.04	97.50	75.72	56.76	59.88	50.16	15.48
100.00	136.26	113.22	94.68	97.56	76.32	57.90	59.94	49.38	15.54
Resulting $\overline{\overline{\omega}}^{hr-}_{total}$ with the DRMGC system (s)									
0.00	**139.32**	**117.48**	**95.28**	**95.46**	**75.18**	**57.24**	**57.66**	**44.52**	**12.60**
0.01	138.66	116.82	95.76	95.04	75.48	56.70	58.02	44.88	12.72
0.10	140.10	117.06	97.26	95.82	76.02	57.72	57.90	46.62	13.14
0.50	136.68	118.44	99.48	99.72	79.62	61.74	62.04	52.02	15.60
1.00	137.10	117.18	100.74	101.10	81.66	63.66	63.78	54.60	17.04
2.00	139.44	117.48	100.68	101.28	82.02	64.20	64.86	55.26	17.58
5.00	139.02	117.60	100.80	101.64	82.62	64.50	65.22	57.66	18.12
10.00	137.76	117.72	102.24	102.48	82.20	64.74	65.52	56.76	18.60
25.00	139.20	117.66	101.94	102.54	82.98	65.64	65.94	57.18	19.50
50.00	139.62	117.72	102.36	102.72	83.94	65.82	66.06	57.90	19.44
100.00	137.64	118.50	101.94	102.18	82.74	65.52	65.64	56.82	18.78
Resulting $\overline{\overline{\omega}}^{hr-}_{total}$ with the TriRMGC system (s)									
0.00	**140.40**	**121.98**	**103.44**	**101.10**	**84.00**	**68.22**	**68.64**	**58.38**	**23.88**
0.01	141.00	121.38	102.84	100.80	84.18	67.98	68.76	58.44	23.94
0.10	141.66	121.26	104.16	102.48	85.26	68.58	69.06	60.30	24.96
0.50	140.88	122.04	106.92	106.92	88.32	72.60	72.66	65.46	29.46
1.00	141.42	121.68	107.46	105.66	89.28	73.20	74.34	66.30	31.08
2.00	141.66	121.14	107.70	106.68	90.48	74.46	74.28	67.32	32.82
5.00	140.64	121.68	106.50	106.68	90.78	74.22	75.30	68.10	33.66
10.00	141.42	122.70	108.30	106.98	90.24	75.72	75.12	68.28	33.90
25.00	141.24	121.68	107.94	106.68	90.60	75.54	75.54	68.70	34.26
50.00	142.62	121.62	106.92	106.50	90.84	75.42	75.66	68.88	34.56
100.00	141.06	122.28	108.72	107.52	91.62	75.60	75.66	68.58	34.50

Table A.58 Influence of the RTS concept (in terms of the cost factor $\lambda^{\text{rts}}_{\tau(j)}$) on the mean crane-empty-movement time per job ($\overline{\overline{m}}^{\text{xye}}_{\text{total}}$) for selected yard-block layouts and all types of RMGC systems

	Yard-block layout								
$\lambda^{\text{rts}}_{\tau(j)}$	Small	Low	Narrow	Short	Medium	Long	Wide	High	Big
Resulting $\overline{\overline{m}}^{\text{xye}}_{\text{total}}$ with the SRMGC system (s)									
0.00	**26.05**	**31.87**	**26.97**	**23.22**	**26.63**	**29.48**	**26.57**	**23.73**	**27.72**
0.01	26.24	31.89	27.08	23.23	26.67	29.53	26.53	23.53	27.80
0.10	26.24	31.97	27.01	23.18	26.66	29.58	26.50	23.83	27.62
0.50	26.34	31.89	27.64	23.63	27.14	30.00	26.96	24.55	27.96
1.00	26.27	32.08	27.90	23.83	27.59	30.45	27.16	24.73	28.13
2.00	26.27	32.24	28.29	24.11	27.69	30.72	27.32	25.06	28.21
5.00	26.36	32.16	28.31	24.17	27.93	30.96	27.53	25.20	28.44
10.00	26.30	32.20	28.38	24.09	27.78	30.90	27.54	25.29	28.50
25.00	26.20	32.16	28.46	24.18	27.89	31.20	27.59	25.37	28.43
50.00	26.20	32.19	28.45	24.22	27.82	31.12	27.57	25.21	28.57
100.00	26.42	32.13	28.52	24.33	27.86	31.16	27.63	25.52	28.54
Resulting $\overline{\overline{m}}^{\text{xye}}_{\text{total}}$ with the TRMGC system (s)									
0.00	**23.34**	**28.35**	**33.76**	**30.25**	**34.07**	**38.12**	**34.64**	**37.21**	**40.77**
0.01	23.17	28.34	33.70	30.08	34.05	38.04	34.58	37.06	40.52
0.10	23.06	28.13	33.65	30.07	33.99	38.17	34.36	37.08	40.60
0.50	22.95	28.35	33.63	30.06	33.92	38.21	34.49	37.30	40.83
1.00	23.10	28.47	33.59	29.85	33.99	38.48	34.54	36.96	40.87
2.00	23.12	28.38	33.71	29.85	34.12	38.58	34.66	37.34	41.25
5.00	23.30	28.52	33.87	29.92	34.27	38.80	34.77	37.41	41.44
10.00	23.23	28.61	33.67	30.00	34.02	38.61	34.86	37.38	41.45
25.00	23.21	28.64	33.64	29.96	34.16	38.68	34.78	37.66	41.33
50.00	23.33	28.60	33.65	30.03	34.04	38.72	34.91	37.65	41.60
100.00	23.27	28.46	33.57	30.01	34.13	38.90	34.98	37.69	41.47
Resulting $\overline{\overline{m}}^{\text{xye}}_{\text{total}}$ with the DRMGC system (s)									
0.00	**55.77**	**69.14**	**62.73**	**62.89**	**62.78**	**61.85**	**60.88**	**52.25**	**45.15**
0.01	55.97	69.45	62.86	63.00	62.88	62.07	61.33	52.30	45.25
0.10	55.57	68.79	63.48	63.23	63.31	62.01	60.95	52.98	45.56
0.50	54.75	68.78	63.67	63.65	63.82	63.38	61.86	55.22	46.63
1.00	54.31	69.03	64.04	63.76	63.81	63.73	62.19	55.95	47.01
2.00	54.03	68.29	63.77	63.70	63.98	63.68	62.36	56.16	47.36
5.00	54.70	68.59	63.51	63.60	64.46	63.69	62.42	56.73	47.62
10.00	54.81	68.68	63.85	63.68	64.27	64.12	62.69	56.65	47.77
25.00	54.67	69.04	63.81	63.96	64.88	64.58	62.71	56.61	48.34
50.00	53.65	68.69	63.76	63.84	64.61	64.28	62.69	56.89	48.08
100.00	53.53	67.86	63.93	63.72	64.58	64.40	63.06	56.51	47.88
Resulting $\overline{\overline{m}}^{\text{xye}}_{\text{total}}$ with the TriRMGC system (s)									
0.00	**51.55**	**65.81**	**69.11**	**68.63**	**70.12**	**70.81**	**70.15**	**66.70**	**60.22**
0.01	51.78	65.30	68.74	68.41	69.73	70.76	69.96	66.64	60.31
0.10	50.82	65.28	69.10	68.33	70.45	71.09	69.95	67.63	60.87
0.50	50.69	65.18	68.57	68.39	70.93	71.85	70.81	69.13	62.71
1.00	50.28	64.83	68.65	68.12	70.40	71.92	71.11	69.22	63.41
2.00	51.39	64.98	68.75	68.13	70.79	72.28	71.33	69.55	63.24
5.00	50.51	65.48	68.42	67.95	70.70	72.05	71.01	69.13	64.03
10.00	49.92	65.33	68.34	67.72	70.97	72.33	71.01	69.67	64.21
25.00	49.95	65.64	68.32	68.28	70.79	72.25	71.26	69.36	63.77
50.00	49.61	65.07	68.59	68.33	70.51	72.19	71.02	69.48	64.37
100.00	50.51	65.53	68.12	68.08	70.66	72.12	71.44	69.68	64.26

Table A.59 Influence of the RTS concept (in terms of the cost factor $\lambda^{\mathrm{rts}}_{\tau(j)}$) on the mean crane-interference time per job ($\overline{\overline{m}}^{\mathrm{cit}}_{\mathrm{total}}$) for selected yard-block layouts and all types of RMGC systems

	Yard-block layout								
$\lambda^{\mathrm{rts}}_{\tau(j)}$	Small	Low	Narrow	Short	Medium	Long	Wide	High	Big
Resulting $\overline{\overline{m}}^{\mathrm{cit}}_{\mathrm{total}}$ with the SRMGC system (s)									
0.00	**0.00**	**0.00**	**0.00**	**0.00**	**0.00**	**0.00**	**0.00**	**0.00**	**0.00**
0.01	0.00	0.00	0.00	0.00	0.00	0.00	0.00	0.00	0.00
0.10	0.00	0.00	0.00	0.00	0.00	0.00	0.00	0.00	0.00
0.50	0.00	0.00	0.00	0.00	0.00	0.00	0.00	0.00	0.00
1.00	0.00	0.00	0.00	0.00	0.00	0.00	0.00	0.00	0.00
2.00	0.00	0.00	0.00	0.00	0.00	0.00	0.00	0.00	0.00
5.00	0.00	0.00	0.00	0.00	0.00	0.00	0.00	0.00	0.00
10.00	0.00	0.00	0.00	0.00	0.00	0.00	0.00	0.00	0.00
25.00	0.00	0.00	0.00	0.00	0.00	0.00	0.00	0.00	0.00
50.00	0.00	0.00	0.00	0.00	0.00	0.00	0.00	0.00	0.00
100.00	0.00	0.00	0.00	0.00	0.00	0.00	0.00	0.00	0.00
Resulting $\overline{\overline{m}}^{\mathrm{cit}}_{\mathrm{total}}$ with the TRMGC system (s)									
0.00	**2.22**	**2.10**	**11.92**	**12.42**	**12.16**	**11.92**	**12.14**	**19.43**	**20.71**
0.01	2.16	2.12	12.10	12.06	11.89	12.00	12.07	19.54	20.68
0.10	2.01	2.01	11.90	12.25	11.85	11.96	11.82	19.21	20.56
0.50	1.86	2.09	11.32	11.71	11.47	11.60	11.66	18.04	19.84
1.00	2.00	2.14	11.12	11.52	11.24	11.50	11.51	17.69	19.38
2.00	2.12	2.04	11.02	11.40	11.10	11.41	11.38	17.95	19.19
5.00	2.22	2.07	11.22	11.36	11.23	11.41	11.36	17.59	19.09
10.00	2.15	2.16	11.02	11.51	11.13	11.29	11.47	17.56	19.06
25.00	2.21	2.21	10.91	11.53	11.00	11.30	11.30	17.48	18.88
50.00	2.20	2.16	10.83	11.51	10.99	11.27	11.34	17.53	19.19
100.00	2.19	2.12	10.80	11.29	10.91	11.35	11.39	17.72	18.90
Resulting $\overline{\overline{m}}^{\mathrm{cit}}_{\mathrm{total}}$ with the DRMGC system (s)									
0.00	**31.09**	**38.13**	**35.30**	**39.74**	**35.31**	**29.73**	**32.78**	**28.21**	**20.21**
0.01	31.18	38.66	35.49	39.40	35.53	30.02	33.25	28.41	20.47
0.10	30.55	37.94	36.39	40.18	35.94	30.19	33.02	29.05	20.55
0.50	29.97	38.74	36.55	40.51	36.28	31.14	33.97	30.40	20.91
1.00	29.89	38.66	36.67	40.66	36.65	31.40	34.41	30.90	20.97
2.00	30.01	38.04	36.71	40.98	36.63	31.30	34.38	30.91	21.12
5.00	30.22	38.53	36.32	40.39	37.01	31.31	34.50	31.72	21.18
10.00	30.54	38.25	36.64	40.50	36.98	31.52	34.80	31.39	21.24
25.00	30.05	38.69	36.48	40.63	37.07	31.96	34.65	31.58	21.68
50.00	29.54	38.59	36.35	40.90	37.21	31.95	34.96	31.72	21.62
100.00	29.44	37.94	36.44	40.61	37.13	31.61	34.79	31.28	21.28
Resulting $\overline{\overline{m}}^{\mathrm{cit}}_{\mathrm{total}}$ with the TriRMGC system (s)									
0.00	**31.02**	**40.31**	**48.66**	**52.32**	**49.18**	**44.71**	**47.95**	**49.43**	**41.62**
0.01	31.14	40.20	48.21	52.53	49.08	44.61	48.15	49.54	41.20
0.10	30.40	40.02	49.15	51.85	49.54	45.11	48.06	50.56	42.09
0.50	30.35	40.81	48.20	52.70	50.45	45.82	49.16	51.49	42.44
1.00	30.65	39.75	48.58	52.43	49.89	45.95	49.37	51.45	42.73
2.00	31.93	40.19	48.59	52.74	50.20	46.16	49.77	51.53	42.36
5.00	31.44	41.03	48.45	52.56	50.51	45.84	49.50	51.02	42.96
10.00	29.66	40.80	48.70	52.15	50.58	46.54	49.17	51.53	42.77
25.00	30.74	41.34	48.23	52.17	50.22	46.29	50.02	51.57	42.58
50.00	30.01	40.50	48.29	52.91	50.17	46.40	49.61	51.33	43.16
100.00	31.64	41.73	48.02	52.53	50.32	46.29	50.09	51.80	43.24

Table A.60 Influence of the RTS concept (in terms of the cost factor $\lambda^{rts}_{\tau(j)}$) on the crane workload during the simulation horizon in terms of performed jobs ($\overline{|J|}$) for selected yard-block layouts and all types of RMGC systems

	Yard-block layout								
$\lambda^{rts}_{\tau(j)}$	Small	Low	Narrow	Short	Medium	Long	Wide	High	Big
Resulting $\overline{\lvert J\rvert}$ with the SRMGC system (jobs)									
0.00	**1,871.8**	**3,208.8**	**6,596.5**	**6,792.8**	**8,683.4**	**10,466.3**	**10,776.3**	**13,369.4**	**13,711.1**
0.01	1,867.4	3,211.6	6,570.5	6,744.1	8,651.6	10,431.5	10,738.7	13,362.6	13,697.2
0.10	1,868.3	3,202.9	6,557.9	6,720.0	8,647.0	10,419.3	10,701.2	13,011.6	13,632.0
0.50	1,847.5	3,177.0	6,255.1	6,435.4	8,367.2	10,269.1	10,451.0	12,261.3	13,430.6
1.00	1,843.7	3,164.4	6,139.5	6,327.8	8,159.0	10,085.9	10,332.9	12,183.5	13,329.1
2.00	1,845.1	3,164.8	6,012.1	6,200.7	8,151.4	9,954.2	10,238.7	11,955.1	13,385.0
5.00	1,838.0	3,156.6	6,037.8	6,177.7	8,042.9	9,812.8	10,179.6	11,825.4	13,308.5
10.00	1,842.1	3,151.1	5,967.9	6,216.4	8,042.2	9,895.7	10,119.1	11,821.1	13,279.0
25.00	1,843.2	3,145.5	5,937.0	6,173.2	8,031.1	9,742.4	9,976.7	11,725.9	13,318.8
50.00	1,842.6	3,134.7	5,960.5	6,122.7	8,053.7	9,785.0	10,016.5	11,771.4	13,226.0
100.00	1,832.6	3,136.7	5,888.8	6,093.8	8,000.0	9,770.7	10,034.5	11,578.1	13,311.0
Resulting $\overline{\lvert J\rvert}$ with the TRMGC system (jobs)									
0.00	**1,903.5**	**3,224.1**	**6,592.4**	**6,857.8**	**8,784.5**	**10,615.3**	**10,900.6**	**15,170.8**	**21,104.9**
0.01	1,905.6	3,233.7	6,619.2	6,826.0	8,747.1	10,612.8	10,843.2	15,177.4	21,119.0
0.10	1,901.7	3,224.4	6,595.5	6,775.4	8,691.5	10,584.0	10,796.0	14,791.9	20,849.8
0.50	1,875.2	3,188.2	6,278.2	6,447.8	8,411.0	10,327.8	10,634.0	13,157.3	19,812.9
1.00	1,876.3	3,167.4	6,118.4	6,219.0	8,126.4	10,118.4	10,442.4	12,766.1	19,345.0
2.00	1,881.2	3,171.5	6,019.9	6,210.6	8,049.9	9,945.4	10,200.9	12,516.6	18,987.9
5.00	1,876.6	3,166.0	5,977.6	6,153.4	8,033.7	9,837.2	10,120.5	12,253.2	18,859.7
10.00	1,874.0	3,175.9	5,980.6	6,170.9	8,016.8	9,762.5	10,107.6	12,199.2	18,802.5
25.00	1,876.3	3,161.5	5,921.0	6,062.3	7,878.5	9,799.8	10,041.5	12,185.3	18,716.5
50.00	1,867.6	3,166.9	5,859.0	6,079.8	7,862.5	9,743.4	10,049.2	12,083.9	18,676.8
100.00	1,872.6	3,162.7	5,866.4	5,999.2	7,788.4	9,624.3	10,060.5	12,261.8	18,613.9
Resulting $\overline{\lvert J\rvert}$ with the DRMGC system (jobs)									
0.00	**1,901.9**	**3,222.4**	**6,623.5**	**6,834.0**	**8,713.7**	**10,605.3**	**10,893.6**	**15,175.5**	**21,213.5**
0.01	1,899.8	3,229.0	6,614.7	6,855.0	8,742.4	10,540.1	10,853.1	15,194.4	21,097.4
0.10	1,894.1	3,215.3	6,569.2	6,793.4	8,685.6	10,553.3	10,827.7	14,581.4	20,897.9
0.50	1,881.4	3,196.5	6,259.8	6,420.8	8,393.2	10,303.5	10,614.6	13,198.2	19,850.7
1.00	1,883.6	3,182.7	6,146.8	6,244.9	8,146.5	10,040.0	10,384.5	12,700.7	19,383.4
2.00	1,873.5	3,171.1	6,065.5	6,196.1	8,076.7	9,958.6	10,218.6	12,541.2	19,163.6
5.00	1,876.2	3,172.1	5,973.2	6,104.7	7,938.9	9,891.7	10,128.6	12,084.3	18,891.2
10.00	1,878.6	3,164.1	5,949.8	6,071.8	7,906.9	9,847.4	10,120.7	12,187.1	18,730.5
25.00	1,876.5	3,163.5	5,891.3	6,083.3	7,869.3	9,677.1	10,023.1	12,113.2	18,578.1
50.00	1,867.8	3,156.1	5,868.8	6,072.0	7,842.5	9,702.7	10,038.5	12,050.4	18,675.0
100.00	1,862.1	3,163.5	5,886.2	6,026.3	7,864.3	9,682.3	9,993.3	12,147.3	18,686.7
Resulting $\overline{\lvert J\rvert}$ with the TriRMGC system (jobs)									
0.00	**1,907.0**	**3,249.5**	**6,614.4**	**6,831.8**	**8,732.5**	**10,583.9**	**10,895.8**	**15,192.1**	**23,097.9**
0.01	1,905.3	3,238.7	6,608.0	6,825.7	8,737.6	10,511.1	10,877.7	15,245.1	23,074.6
0.10	1,905.7	3,240.2	6,583.2	6,800.1	8,669.3	10,541.6	10,862.7	14,667.8	22,589.2
0.50	1,880.4	3,211.4	6,206.2	6,379.2	8,361.0	10,319.9	10,619.3	13,084.5	20,772.6
1.00	1,881.2	3,196.3	6,071.2	6,297.2	8,166.4	10,128.8	10,309.2	12,635.4	20,080.9
2.00	1,880.4	3,190.1	6,014.4	6,221.3	8,000.1	9,932.8	10,218.0	12,421.4	19,645.1
5.00	1,875.5	3,191.8	5,978.5	6,165.8	7,964.4	9,889.1	10,076.6	12,132.4	19,290.9
10.00	1,876.3	3,184.1	5,957.4	6,128.6	7,930.2	9,769.4	10,125.0	12,259.8	19,194.2
25.00	1,875.2	3,194.3	5,894.2	6,151.2	7,942.3	9,731.2	10,126.6	12,079.8	19,010.8
50.00	1,875.6	3,186.1	5,968.9	6,130.5	7,861.5	9,773.1	10,001.6	12,019.9	19,077.6
100.00	1,871.7	3,195.5	5,817.1	6,083.3	7,790.8	9,645.7	10,000.8	12,071.2	18,962.0

Table A.61 Influence of the RTS concept (in terms of the cost factor $\lambda^{\mathrm{rts}}_{\tau(j)}$) on the container accessibility ($\overline{\overline{\psi}}$), in terms of the mean number of shuffle moves per retrieval job, for selected yard-block layouts and all types of RMGC systems

	Yard-block layout								
$\lambda^{\mathrm{rts}}_{\tau(j)}$	Small	Low	Narrow	Short	Medium	Long	Wide	High	Big
Resulting $\overline{\overline{\psi}}$ with the SRMGC system (jobs)									
0.00	**0.322**	**0.300**	**1.135**	**1.120**	**1.103**	**1.083**	**1.083**	**1.606**	**1.144**
0.01	0.316	0.300	1.118	1.105	1.084	1.078	1.074	1.589	1.145
0.10	0.315	0.296	1.106	1.087	1.084	1.067	1.060	1.539	1.118
0.50	0.290	0.276	1.006	0.998	1.002	1.012	0.985	1.397	1.060
1.00	0.281	0.265	0.980	0.975	0.961	0.980	0.960	1.371	1.031
2.00	0.283	0.264	0.943	0.946	0.956	0.948	0.948	1.334	1.044
5.00	0.280	0.262	0.958	0.944	0.939	0.937	0.941	1.312	1.032
10.00	0.282	0.258	0.937	0.943	0.945	0.951	0.935	1.318	1.026
25.00	0.286	0.256	0.934	0.946	0.944	0.925	0.918	1.302	1.034
50.00	0.284	0.249	0.939	0.927	0.943	0.933	0.920	1.310	1.015
100.00	0.270	0.248	0.920	0.922	0.935	0.935	0.926	1.286	1.041
Resulting $\overline{\overline{\psi}}$ with the TRMGC system (jobs)									
0.00	**0.324**	**0.296**	**1.127**	**1.130**	**1.130**	**1.097**	**1.090**	**1.762**	**1.675**
0.01	0.325	0.301	1.136	1.112	1.115	1.098	1.081	1.761	1.681
0.10	0.322	0.296	1.115	1.093	1.099	1.084	1.058	1.702	1.646
0.50	0.290	0.272	1.017	1.004	1.012	1.007	0.999	1.470	1.515
1.00	0.291	0.258	0.967	0.948	0.961	0.965	0.968	1.410	1.463
2.00	0.298	0.258	0.951	0.944	0.946	0.947	0.938	1.396	1.418
5.00	0.291	0.254	0.939	0.936	0.938	0.926	0.926	1.354	1.404
10.00	0.285	0.259	0.941	0.936	0.942	0.924	0.929	1.354	1.406
25.00	0.291	0.251	0.923	0.913	0.915	0.928	0.915	1.345	1.400
50.00	0.280	0.253	0.916	0.921	0.915	0.920	0.914	1.348	1.401
100.00	0.285	0.251	0.920	0.901	0.901	0.908	0.923	1.362	1.387
Resulting $\overline{\overline{\psi}}$ with the DRMGC system (jobs)									
0.00	**0.320**	**0.297**	**1.137**	**1.118**	**1.107**	**1.093**	**1.087**	**1.753**	**1.673**
0.01	0.319	0.298	1.135	1.125	1.116	1.079	1.078	1.766	1.650
0.10	0.311	0.291	1.104	1.101	1.095	1.077	1.068	1.672	1.625
0.50	0.295	0.273	1.011	0.993	1.006	1.001	1.002	1.471	1.492
1.00	0.296	0.263	0.980	0.956	0.962	0.966	0.958	1.418	1.448
2.00	0.292	0.257	0.956	0.939	0.955	0.948	0.943	1.387	1.425
5.00	0.292	0.259	0.946	0.927	0.929	0.938	0.925	1.344	1.395
10.00	0.295	0.251	0.933	0.913	0.921	0.934	0.926	1.350	1.385
25.00	0.291	0.252	0.922	0.919	0.924	0.917	0.914	1.337	1.371
50.00	0.283	0.248	0.919	0.918	0.919	0.913	0.915	1.335	1.372
100.00	0.278	0.248	0.918	0.903	0.916	0.911	0.906	1.345	1.382
Resulting $\overline{\overline{\psi}}$ with the TriRMGC system (jobs)									
0.00	**0.325**	**0.298**	**1.122**	**1.123**	**1.113**	**1.092**	**1.090**	**1.763**	**1.758**
0.01	0.322	0.291	1.127	1.114	1.118	1.074	1.084	1.771	1.752
0.10	0.329	0.291	1.112	1.099	1.091	1.077	1.074	1.680	1.700
0.50	0.296	0.270	0.996	0.988	1.001	1.002	0.995	1.464	1.521
1.00	0.295	0.265	0.965	0.962	0.965	0.975	0.948	1.398	1.451
2.00	0.295	0.256	0.956	0.944	0.940	0.944	0.935	1.378	1.418
5.00	0.291	0.258	0.945	0.935	0.933	0.936	0.924	1.344	1.389
10.00	0.291	0.252	0.947	0.927	0.927	0.920	0.927	1.356	1.379
25.00	0.286	0.261	0.928	0.938	0.926	0.913	0.926	1.343	1.366
50.00	0.287	0.255	0.942	0.925	0.912	0.920	0.908	1.330	1.381
100.00	0.284	0.257	0.910	0.912	0.908	0.907	0.911	1.344	1.374

Table A.62 Influence of the PoS concept (in terms of the cost factor $\lambda^{\text{dist}}_{\text{type}(j)}$) on the mean vehicle-waiting time ($\overline{\varpi}^{\text{hr+}}_{\text{total}}$) for selected yard-block layouts and all types of RMGC systems

	Yard-block layout								
$\lambda^{\text{dist}}_{\tau(j)}$	Small	Low	Narrow	Short	Medium	Long	Wide	High	Big
Resulting $\overline{\varpi}^{\text{hr+}}_{\text{total}}$ with the SRMGC system (s)									
0.00	30.36	49.44	134.82	116.46	236.64	708.84	547.62	2, 153.46	3, 379.02
0.01	**28.26**	**41.28**	**117.06**	**100.44**	**198.96**	**561.06**	**486.56**	**1, 861.32**	**3, 269.94**
0.10	26.82	42.24	109.98	102.30	191.10	536.82	466.38	2, 061.42	3, 425.94
0.50	26.10	43.02	103.38	94.08	165.06	428.22	383.28	2, 235.60	3, 548.04
1.00	27.18	42.66	98.88	91.68	155.40	419.70	387.78	2, 249.46	3, 635.40
1.50	26.58	42.60	96.84	89.58	152.28	414.12	368.58	2, 261.52	3, 771.30
2.50	27.00	41.40	97.02	91.38	155.70	412.74	400.56	2, 261.58	3, 900.36
5.00	27.42	43.02	97.86	89.04	156.66	430.02	404.76	2, 201.82	3, 772.50
7.50	28.20	42.66	97.80	95.16	171.12	446.52	425.94	2, 301.72	4, 111.32
10.00	28.26	43.86	98.22	95.04	167.58	450.42	436.80	2, 277.24	4, 136.04
20.00	27.96	43.32	102.30	98.34	168.00	487.50	465.96	2, 359.02	4, 172.64
Resulting $\overline{\varpi}^{\text{hr+}}_{\text{total}}$ with the TRMGC system (s)									
0.00	11.94	17.46	47.34	40.56	56.70	81.00	72.18	442.92	1, 795.38
0.01	**8.82**	**13.44**	**38.16**	**35.58**	**48.30**	**67.44**	**61.98**	**304.08**	**1, 567.38**
0.10	8.58	13.26	37.74	34.56	47.70	69.30	59.82	285.84	1, 560.54
0.50	8.88	13.32	39.30	35.28	45.84	63.00	58.14	327.24	1, 647.72
1.00	9.54	13.86	36.96	35.22	45.72	64.26	58.26	346.26	1, 720.98
1.50	9.42	13.62	37.08	35.22	45.42	63.24	58.98	353.82	1, 784.52
2.50	9.30	14.28	37.68	35.34	47.28	66.30	63.12	378.12	1, 899.42
5.00	9.36	14.22	37.56	35.82	46.20	66.54	60.96	411.78	2, 029.92
7.50	9.84	13.98	39.78	37.32	49.38	70.26	67.68	428.64	2, 038.44
10.00	9.24	13.86	38.70	37.38	49.80	71.34	69.42	444.48	2, 054.28
20.00	9.36	13.80	39.00	39.06	50.28	71.34	71.52	493.80	2, 082.30
Resulting $\overline{\varpi}^{\text{hr+}}_{\text{total}}$ with the DRMGC system (s)									
0.00	15.78	25.50	58.44	57.72	75.00	99.60	95.94	474.72	1, 843.98
0.01	**13.86**	**23.58**	**53.82**	**54.36**	**69.24**	**88.86**	**88.86**	**360.18**	**1, 607.82**
0.10	13.80	23.28	54.24	53.94	69.78	93.06	91.80	353.76	1, 710.66
0.50	14.04	23.34	55.32	54.96	66.96	85.50	86.64	430.44	1, 679.04
1.00	14.64	24.18	54.96	55.74	68.04	87.12	88.86	436.80	1, 632.48
1.50	14.28	24.72	56.76	56.52	69.48	89.52	90.96	452.70	1, 722.78
2.50	15.72	24.84	55.38	58.08	72.96	96.30	97.98	469.38	1, 770.84
5.00	14.88	23.94	56.82	56.88	71.10	92.16	93.12	451.86	1, 768.98
7.50	14.94	24.78	57.36	61.02	76.62	100.14	108.36	562.44	2, 017.26
10.00	15.00	24.24	57.60	62.40	76.98	103.26	110.82	576.06	2, 063.40
20.00	14.64	24.60	59.22	63.06	79.80	107.76	116.76	605.88	2, 143.74
Resulting $\overline{\varpi}^{\text{hr+}}_{\text{total}}$ with the TriRMGC system (s)									
0.00	10.92	16.14	36.18	35.34	42.60	51.78	50.28	145.26	716.10
0.01	**8.82**	**12.48**	**31.26**	**31.86**	**37.98**	**46.86**	**46.86**	**117.54**	**574.98**
0.10	8.76	12.36	31.50	33.00	39.12	46.86	47.10	126.78	608.40
0.50	9.24	13.38	31.92	33.84	39.66	45.96	46.38	134.22	645.00
1.00	9.18	13.56	32.82	33.78	39.18	47.10	47.88	143.70	636.72
1.50	9.84	13.08	34.14	34.74	40.08	47.88	48.96	146.82	654.60
2.50	9.78	13.74	33.66	35.82	41.40	50.52	52.98	164.04	690.84
5.00	9.54	13.56	33.78	34.98	41.10	48.66	50.40	156.90	662.52
7.50	9.72	13.38	36.00	37.32	44.34	53.16	57.48	194.76	886.14
10.00	9.42	13.50	35.94	37.80	44.46	54.30	57.18	204.42	945.96
20.00	9.48	13.44	36.12	39.48	45.48	54.72	58.68	220.14	998.70

Table A.63 Influence of the PoS concept (in terms of the cost factor $\lambda_{\tau(j)}^{dist}$) on the mean vehicle-waiting time per waterside retrieval job ($\overline{\omega}_{wsout}^{hr+}$) for selected yard-block layouts and all types of RMGC systems

	Yard-block layout								
$\lambda_{\tau(j)}^{dist}$	Small	Low	Narrow	Short	Medium	Long	Wide	High	Big
Resulting $\overline{\omega}_{wsout}^{hr+}$ with the SRMGC system (s)									
0.00	3.12	7.56	100.14	77.22	259.80	1,014.36	755.10	3,688.44	4,828.20
0.01	**3.24**	**5.52**	**78.00**	**56.04**	**198.72**	**789.12**	**671.58**	**3,180.30**	**4,959.72**
0.10	1.50	5.88	71.40	59.64	186.30	741.24	633.48	3,619.56	5,500.98
0.50	4.26	5.46	58.38	44.82	134.82	536.88	489.30	3,982.08	5,887.56
1.00	2.46	5.40	47.16	41.64	116.16	532.62	504.78	3,973.14	6,181.38
1.50	2.46	6.90	39.96	36.36	109.20	525.42	463.68	4,015.86	6,475.50
2.50	3.24	5.22	44.94	40.08	118.20	531.54	523.32	4,028.58	6,786.24
5.00	2.22	5.40	44.28	36.48	123.90	564.48	551.88	3,915.78	6,545.22
7.50	2.34	6.00	45.42	45.54	141.06	599.52	589.74	4,143.96	7,232.10
10.00	4.38	6.06	42.96	41.40	134.94	606.36	615.18	4,097.28	7,302.72
20.00	3.48	6.12	51.78	49.26	139.98	688.08	670.74	4,257.42	7,387.14
Resulting $\overline{\omega}_{wsout}^{hr+}$ with the TRMGC system (s)									
0.00	3.42	5.16	21.48	15.12	32.34	59.10	52.50	732.48	3,390.72
0.01	**2.28**	**4.14**	**15.06**	**13.20**	**25.80**	**48.48**	**42.12**	**486.30**	**3,019.80**
0.10	2.28	4.86	15.00	11.94	25.68	49.68	36.78	446.40	2,991.00
0.50	3.06	3.96	15.84	12.06	17.64	34.68	29.76	528.42	3,293.52
1.00	3.24	4.56	11.40	10.62	18.06	37.08	30.24	572.94	3,585.18
1.50	3.00	3.36	11.94	9.48	15.66	34.26	30.72	592.32	3,816.24
2.50	3.00	4.32	10.56	9.36	20.40	39.12	40.56	668.22	4,020.06
5.00	2.40	3.78	12.00	11.94	18.66	45.48	38.82	790.98	4,573.20
7.50	3.54	3.48	14.52	12.48	22.14	45.72	48.12	800.04	4,274.34
10.00	1.98	3.84	14.28	12.18	24.36	47.82	52.44	826.50	4,285.32
20.00	2.64	3.96	14.64	16.02	25.14	48.48	58.14	934.68	4,271.70
Resulting $\overline{\omega}_{wsout}^{hr+}$ with the DRMGC system (s)									
0.00	3.24	5.28	21.06	20.94	34.92	57.60	55.32	727.02	3,121.50
0.01	**2.76**	**5.34**	**20.10**	**18.72**	**30.78**	**47.46**	**46.26**	**510.54**	**2,758.62**
0.10	2.04	4.98	19.50	18.42	31.68	51.54	54.18	498.72	2,931.66
0.50	2.88	4.44	19.08	16.68	24.30	37.86	41.28	644.70	2,917.14
1.00	2.76	4.62	16.68	16.98	25.08	37.08	42.78	651.54	2,835.78
1.50	1.68	5.46	17.94	17.22	26.04	41.88	43.80	667.74	3,032.40
2.50	3.42	5.76	17.76	17.64	28.86	50.28	54.84	690.06	3,111.96
5.00	1.68	5.64	19.08	17.94	29.16	46.26	51.06	677.34	3,116.88
7.50	2.34	4.86	19.98	23.88	36.24	57.30	72.00	877.14	3,612.72
10.00	3.12	5.58	20.22	25.62	37.08	62.58	79.32	908.34	3,681.36
20.00	2.94	6.24	22.68	27.36	41.04	71.16	92.64	974.82	3,859.20
Resulting $\overline{\omega}_{wsout}^{hr+}$ with the TriRMGC system (s)									
0.00	3.36	6.72	14.16	12.72	18.06	21.12	22.50	152.46	1,140.78
0.01	**2.22**	**5.34**	**12.90**	**12.54**	**16.32**	**19.68**	**20.94**	**109.68**	**883.26**
0.10	1.74	5.22	11.22	12.48	19.32	20.52	21.54	122.16	960.96
0.50	2.82	5.58	12.00	12.18	18.42	18.24	18.30	132.48	1,041.48
1.00	2.04	5.40	11.82	11.64	15.78	17.58	19.32	141.48	1,016.40
1.50	2.82	4.98	13.14	14.04	17.04	18.36	19.68	140.94	1,057.26
2.50	3.06	5.52	10.26	12.18	17.40	21.90	25.14	176.10	1,134.30
5.00	2.34	4.98	11.82	12.12	17.52	19.98	22.68	175.20	1,121.34
7.50	2.88	4.32	14.28	15.24	21.48	25.80	32.76	237.00	1,537.50
10.00	1.92	4.50	14.52	16.08	22.44	27.90	33.48	255.96	1,648.38
20.00	2.70	5.22	16.32	19.68	23.22	28.44	35.76	292.02	1,773.72

Table A.64 Influence of the PoS concept (in terms of the cost factor $\lambda^{\text{dist}}_{\tau(j)}$) on the mean crane-waiting time in the handover areas ($\overline{\overline{\omega}}^{\text{hr}-}_{\text{total}}$) for selected yard-block layouts and all types of RMGC systems

	Yard-block layout								
$\lambda^{\text{dist}}_{\tau(j)}$	Small	Low	Narrow	Short	Medium	Long	Wide	High	Big
Resulting $\overline{\overline{\omega}}^{\text{hr}-}_{\text{total}}$ with the SRMGC system (s)									
0.00	124.68	97.20	62.76	66.24	40.92	23.58	26.58	13.86	6.30
0.01	**124.38**	**94.92**	**63.84**	**67.26**	**41.52**	**22.86**	**25.80**	**14.64**	**7.08**
0.10	123.36	95.70	64.56	68.52	43.02	22.50	26.04	12.84	6.78
0.50	123.60	94.32	61.26	64.50	40.56	21.84	25.38	12.06	6.90
1.00	121.86	94.62	61.20	64.08	39.90	22.38	25.08	11.88	6.84
1.50	123.78	95.04	60.78	63.72	39.90	21.96	24.90	12.12	6.78
2.50	122.70	93.66	60.66	64.32	39.96	22.14	25.08	12.12	6.54
5.00	124.32	95.04	62.22	64.98	42.00	24.12	26.70	11.82	6.48
7.50	122.70	94.32	61.62	63.84	40.50	22.20	24.96	11.76	6.60
10.00	124.62	95.76	61.44	64.38	40.20	22.32	24.78	11.94	6.54
20.00	123.60	95.70	60.84	64.32	40.74	21.96	24.66	12.00	6.54
Resulting $\overline{\overline{\omega}}^{\text{hr}-}_{\text{total}}$ with the TRMGC system (s)									
0.00	138.24	114.54	88.56	90.06	69.54	51.18	54.96	37.50	10.44
0.01	**135.84**	**112.32**	**87.84**	**91.26**	**67.86**	**50.28**	**53.40**	**38.58**	**10.56**
0.10	136.26	113.04	88.68	91.92	69.84	50.46	53.16	36.84	10.20
0.50	135.48	111.06	84.96	88.32	66.00	48.18	51.66	33.60	9.90
1.00	135.60	111.06	84.18	87.48	65.70	48.00	51.18	31.56	9.84
1.50	136.02	111.12	84.24	87.00	66.00	48.12	51.48	30.66	9.96
2.50	133.86	112.02	83.10	86.52	65.58	48.18	51.48	29.04	9.84
5.00	136.92	111.96	85.62	88.02	67.14	50.04	53.16	31.92	9.54
7.50	135.18	110.82	83.16	86.16	65.76	48.30	51.60	28.50	9.72
10.00	134.10	111.30	83.22	85.62	65.58	47.82	51.30	28.38	9.72
20.00	134.70	110.52	83.88	86.46	65.28	47.94	51.12	27.84	9.66
Resulting $\overline{\overline{\omega}}^{\text{hr}-}_{\text{total}}$ with the DRMGC system (s)									
0.00	140.94	118.20	94.62	93.84	74.22	57.18	57.30	41.34	12.30
0.01	**139.32**	**117.48**	**95.28**	**95.46**	**75.18**	**57.24**	**57.66**	**44.52**	**12.60**
0.10	137.82	117.18	96.36	97.32	76.32	57.66	57.90	43.80	11.52
0.50	137.94	115.86	93.36	92.82	73.32	55.74	56.46	38.88	11.10
1.00	137.76	116.70	92.52	92.94	73.50	56.04	56.58	36.60	10.80
1.50	138.00	117.18	91.62	91.86	72.72	56.34	55.92	34.86	11.10
2.50	138.96	117.54	91.32	92.04	73.14	55.92	56.34	34.20	10.92
5.00	136.92	117.18	92.58	92.88	73.92	56.76	56.64	35.52	11.10
7.50	138.18	117.24	91.80	92.04	72.42	55.74	55.74	34.20	10.44
10.00	137.76	116.04	91.44	92.04	72.72	55.80	55.92	34.32	10.50
20.00	136.92	115.92	91.44	91.92	72.84	55.02	55.80	34.14	10.56
Resulting $\overline{\overline{\omega}}^{\text{hr}-}_{\text{total}}$ with the TriRMGC system (s)									
0.00	141.72	123.66	102.54	100.38	83.76	68.34	69.06	56.16	21.66
0.01	**140.40**	**121.98**	**103.44**	**101.10**	**84.00**	**68.22**	**68.64**	**58.38**	**23.88**
0.10	141.78	120.84	103.50	102.42	85.62	68.40	69.12	57.54	21.84
0.50	141.36	120.42	100.26	99.30	82.92	67.14	67.80	54.18	19.32
1.00	140.52	120.78	100.32	99.00	81.84	66.90	67.86	51.00	18.60
1.50	139.44	121.02	100.32	97.98	82.50	66.54	67.20	49.32	18.54
2.50	139.74	121.02	99.54	97.98	82.02	66.84	67.14	48.00	18.18
5.00	140.34	121.50	99.42	98.22	82.74	67.44	68.04	50.10	18.96
7.50	140.76	120.60	99.00	98.40	82.08	66.90	67.14	47.70	17.64
10.00	140.22	121.26	99.60	97.86	81.48	66.66	66.96	47.46	17.88
20.00	140.82	120.54	99.72	97.98	81.36	66.48	66.60	47.04	17.58

Table A.65 Influence of the PoS concept (in terms of the cost factor $\lambda^{\text{dist}}_{\tau(j)}$) on the mean crane-empty-movement time per job ($\overline{\overline{m}}^{\text{xye}}_{\text{total}}$) for selected yard-block layouts and all types of RMGC systems

$\lambda^{\text{dist}}_{\tau(j)}$	Yard-block layout Small	Low	Narrow	Short	Medium	Long	Wide	High	Big
Resulting $\overline{\overline{m}}^{\text{xye}}_{\text{total}}$ with the SRMGC system (s)									
0.00	26.56	32.44	28.15	23.97	27.81	31.18	27.70	24.92	29.33
0.01	**26.05**	**31.87**	**26.97**	**23.22**	**26.63**	**29.48**	**26.57**	**23.73**	**27.72**
0.10	26.03	31.67	26.96	23.11	26.63	29.68	26.64	23.53	27.98
0.50	25.85	31.29	26.52	22.95	26.28	29.18	26.33	22.82	26.59
1.00	25.29	30.59	25.82	22.44	25.71	28.44	25.85	22.21	25.51
1.50	24.92	30.21	25.36	22.17	25.40	28.07	25.65	21.96	24.97
2.50	24.74	29.99	24.67	21.78	24.98	27.59	25.11	21.36	24.21
5.00	24.97	30.24	25.21	22.03	25.08	27.73	25.23	21.45	24.58
7.50	24.68	29.97	24.06	21.19	24.23	26.76	24.54	20.78	23.38
10.00	24.64	29.84	23.94	21.04	24.18	26.69	24.44	20.60	23.20
20.00	24.52	29.84	23.72	21.00	24.01	26.44	24.18	20.41	23.15
Resulting $\overline{\overline{m}}^{\text{xye}}_{\text{total}}$ with the TRMGC system (s)									
0.00	24.37	29.78	34.27	30.32	34.74	39.26	35.32	37.61	40.88
0.01	**23.34**	**28.35**	**33.76**	**30.25**	**34.07**	**38.12**	**34.64**	**37.21**	**40.77**
0.10	22.95	28.34	34.21	30.91	34.86	38.71	35.04	37.58	41.17
0.50	22.99	28.26	34.60	31.15	34.69	38.71	35.04	37.57	41.79
1.00	22.59	28.11	34.53	31.25	34.83	38.66	35.51	37.86	42.44
1.50	22.71	28.06	34.42	31.89	35.00	38.75	35.63	37.97	42.75
2.50	22.42	28.09	34.97	32.31	35.28	38.91	35.93	38.82	43.32
5.00	22.57	27.81	33.59	30.71	34.81	38.34	35.43	38.71	43.75
7.50	22.49	28.18	35.53	33.09	35.66	38.97	36.47	39.58	43.61
10.00	22.62	28.14	35.48	33.16	35.74	39.09	36.59	39.57	43.50
20.00	22.65	28.23	35.49	33.41	36.02	38.97	36.74	39.82	43.08
Resulting $\overline{\overline{m}}^{\text{xye}}_{\text{total}}$ with the DRMGC system (s)									
0.00	55.10	67.86	62.20	61.61	62.09	61.85	60.14	50.47	45.24
0.01	**55.77**	**69.14**	**62.73**	**62.89**	**62.78**	**61.85**	**60.88**	**52.25**	**45.15**
0.10	55.92	69.13	63.50	63.76	63.51	62.19	61.03	52.62	45.39
0.50	55.61	69.12	63.64	63.62	63.44	62.54	61.50	50.85	45.02
1.00	56.38	69.43	64.30	64.12	63.68	62.62	61.61	50.07	44.84
1.50	55.52	69.73	64.09	64.26	63.29	62.17	61.78	50.32	45.25
2.50	57.43	69.22	64.05	65.06	63.95	62.21	61.54	50.03	45.53
5.00	55.90	68.78	64.57	64.81	63.88	62.52	61.92	50.06	45.48
7.50	57.27	69.68	63.96	65.04	63.81	61.87	61.85	50.95	45.36
10.00	56.53	69.63	64.03	65.18	63.67	61.58	61.59	50.90	45.65
20.00	57.02	69.09	63.66	65.10	63.36	61.33	61.35	51.04	45.61
Resulting $\overline{\overline{m}}^{\text{xye}}_{\text{total}}$ with the TriRMGC system (s)									
0.00	50.79	66.25	68.71	68.79	69.97	71.48	70.18	65.47	58.62
0.01	**51.55**	**65.81**	**69.11**	**68.63**	**70.12**	**70.81**	**70.15**	**66.70**	**60.22**
0.10	51.33	66.12	69.16	69.39	70.86	71.16	70.47	67.46	60.02
0.50	51.01	65.35	68.72	69.12	70.82	71.72	70.95	66.57	59.47
1.00	51.98	65.53	69.47	69.65	71.13	71.51	71.30	65.90	59.60
1.50	51.58	64.85	69.87	69.90	71.47	71.60	70.84	65.81	60.26
2.50	52.19	65.61	69.75	71.11	71.87	71.80	71.79	66.41	61.15
5.00	51.76	65.94	70.06	70.30	72.11	72.05	71.52	66.57	60.79
7.50	52.39	65.24	70.99	71.39	72.50	72.15	72.27	67.29	61.49
10.00	51.87	65.24	70.97	72.04	72.30	72.20	72.58	67.75	62.08
20.00	51.88	65.33	70.51	71.64	72.02	72.08	72.61	67.77	62.07

Table A.66 Influence of the PoS concept (in terms of the cost factor $\lambda_{\tau(j)}^{dist}$) on the mean crane-interference time per job ($\overline{\overline{m}}_{total}^{cit}$) for selected yard-block layouts and all types of RMGC systems

$\lambda_{\tau(j)}^{dist}$	Yard-block layout Small	Low	Narrow	Short	Medium	Long	Wide	High	Big
Resulting $\overline{\overline{m}}_{total}^{cit}$ with the SRMGC system (s)									
0.00	0.00	0.00	0.00	0.00	0.00	0.00	0.00	0.00	0.00
0.01	**0.00**	**0.00**	**0.00**	**0.00**	**0.00**	**0.00**	**0.00**	**0.00**	**0.00**
0.10	0.00	0.00	0.00	0.00	0.00	0.00	0.00	0.00	0.00
0.50	0.00	0.00	0.00	0.00	0.00	0.00	0.00	0.00	0.00
1.00	0.00	0.00	0.00	0.00	0.00	0.00	0.00	0.00	0.00
1.50	0.00	0.00	0.00	0.00	0.00	0.00	0.00	0.00	0.00
2.50	0.00	0.00	0.00	0.00	0.00	0.00	0.00	0.00	0.00
5.00	0.00	0.00	0.00	0.00	0.00	0.00	0.00	0.00	0.00
7.50	0.00	0.00	0.00	0.00	0.00	0.00	0.00	0.00	0.00
10.00	0.00	0.00	0.00	0.00	0.00	0.00	0.00	0.00	0.00
20.00	0.00	0.00	0.00	0.00	0.00	0.00	0.00	0.00	0.00
Resulting $\overline{\overline{m}}_{total}^{cit}$ with the TRMGC system (s)									
0.00	2.92	2.85	12.60	12.89	12.55	12.61	12.42	20.69	20.54
0.01	**2.22**	**2.10**	**11.92**	**12.42**	**12.16**	**11.92**	**12.14**	**19.43**	**20.71**
0.10	2.03	2.05	12.14	12.63	12.36	12.38	12.35	20.04	21.45
0.50	2.01	2.25	12.51	12.75	12.34	12.41	12.47	20.49	22.45
1.00	2.13	2.82	12.67	13.02	12.78	12.93	12.95	21.14	23.39
1.50	2.47	3.04	12.99	13.63	13.15	13.33	13.44	21.27	24.08
2.50	2.52	3.40	13.63	14.26	13.88	14.12	14.10	22.70	25.40
5.00	2.47	3.17	13.24	13.47	13.31	13.36	13.55	21.77	24.95
7.50	2.82	3.72	15.21	15.66	15.18	14.96	15.50	24.66	26.52
10.00	3.00	3.66	15.07	15.90	15.28	15.20	15.84	24.73	26.72
20.00	3.12	3.72	15.28	16.29	15.58	15.36	15.91	25.33	26.65
Resulting $\overline{\overline{m}}_{total}^{cit}$ with the DRMGC system (s)									
0.00	30.90	37.52	34.22	37.84	33.95	28.88	31.63	25.67	18.76
0.01	**31.09**	**38.13**	**35.30**	**39.74**	**35.31**	**29.73**	**32.78**	**28.21**	**20.21**
0.10	30.96	38.34	36.63	40.79	36.35	30.64	33.65	29.15	21.09
0.50	30.78	38.48	37.14	40.84	36.89	31.23	34.17	28.53	21.58
1.00	31.18	39.10	38.39	41.93	37.59	32.22	34.80	28.27	22.16
1.50	30.77	39.23	38.76	42.30	37.52	32.23	35.41	29.14	23.00
2.50	32.94	38.98	38.99	43.34	38.81	32.82	35.91	29.51	23.70
5.00	31.08	38.71	39.33	43.40	38.43	32.78	35.74	29.35	23.66
7.50	32.23	39.12	39.60	44.12	39.10	33.16	36.67	31.40	24.58
10.00	31.86	39.44	39.56	44.40	38.99	33.27	36.56	31.71	24.82
20.00	32.02	38.84	39.29	44.16	38.96	32.71	36.50	32.05	25.00
Resulting $\overline{\overline{m}}_{total}^{cit}$ with the TriRMGC system (s)									
0.00	31.65	42.12	49.12	53.38	49.90	45.20	48.71	49.28	40.07
0.01	**31.02**	**40.31**	**48.66**	**52.32**	**49.18**	**44.71**	**47.95**	**49.43**	**41.62**
0.10	31.37	40.52	48.97	53.30	50.18	45.15	48.52	50.48	41.88
0.50	31.06	40.99	48.34	52.86	49.90	45.42	48.85	49.74	41.60
1.00	31.90	41.54	49.37	53.03	50.53	46.07	49.59	49.80	42.52
1.50	31.50	40.87	50.39	53.42	51.66	46.64	49.85	49.83	43.43
2.50	31.85	41.24	50.33	55.19	52.31	47.48	51.69	51.26	45.01
5.00	31.64	41.25	50.29	53.66	52.18	47.20	50.77	50.71	43.16
7.50	32.27	40.86	52.45	55.91	53.47	48.63	52.56	53.39	46.47
10.00	31.39	40.72	52.37	56.46	53.29	48.61	52.93	53.82	47.24
20.00	32.03	40.95	52.01	56.37	52.71	48.57	52.94	53.82	47.55

Table A.67 Influence of the PoS concept (in terms of the cost factor $\lambda^{\text{dist}}_{\tau(j)}$) on the crane workload during the simulation horizon in terms of performed jobs ($\overline{|J|}$) for selected yard-block layouts and all types of RMGC systems

	Yard-block layout								
$\lambda^{\text{dist}}_{\tau(j)}$	Small	Low	Narrow	Short	Medium	Long	Wide	High	Big
Resulting $\overline{\lvert J\rvert}$ with the SRMGC system (jobs)									
0.00	1,875.1	3,194.8	6,554.7	6,760.1	8,572.2	10,210.0	10,499.9	13,312.6	13,424.1
0.01	**1,871.8**	**3,208.8**	**6,596.5**	**6,792.8**	**8,683.4**	**10,466.3**	**10,776.3**	**13,369.4**	**13,711.1**
0.10	1,880.6	3,220.8	6,590.2	6,768.5	8,699.0	10,492.5	10,781.9	13,726.2	13,811.6
0.50	1,882.0	3,251.4	6,554.1	6,750.4	8,704.5	10,526.0	10,789.5	14,118.4	14,233.5
1.00	1,921.9	3,332.0	6,599.4	6,816.5	8,781.5	10,618.1	10,909.6	14,265.8	14,592.7
1.50	1,946.5	3,367.3	6,623.9	6,828.7	8,850.6	10,727.7	10,941.7	14,353.1	14,840.3
2.50	1,968.3	3,403.3	6,784.8	6,891.5	8,916.1	10,835.3	11,112.9	14,530.5	15,225.7
5.00	1,949.6	3,369.3	6,664.7	6,814.1	8,860.6	10,801.6	11,065.7	14,537.9	15,092.2
7.50	1,992.2	3,426.7	6,922.6	7,109.6	9,196.0	11,110.0	11,381.8	14,783.6	15,745.1
10.00	1,994.9	3,434.7	6,936.0	7,192.8	9,203.7	11,153.6	11,440.7	14,902.6	15,903.7
20.00	1,996.8	3,441.2	7,055.4	7,221.3	9,299.1	11,297.0	11,592.2	15,093.6	15,971.0
Resulting $\overline{\lvert J\rvert}$ with the TRMGC system (jobs)									
0.00	1,893.0	3,204.7	6,598.2	6,815.6	8,667.2	10,405.0	10,691.4	15,814.3	21,108.0
0.01	**1,903.5**	**3,224.1**	**6,592.4**	**6,857.8**	**8,784.5**	**10,615.3**	**10,900.6**	**15,170.8**	**21,104.9**
0.10	1,908.7	3,238.0	6,617.5	6,823.9	8,760.9	10,682.8	10,943.2	15,412.8	21,190.5
0.50	1,911.6	3,272.2	6,627.5	6,858.1	8,727.9	10,647.6	10,941.8	16,154.9	21,266.9
1.00	1,949.8	3,370.9	6,616.6	6,841.5	8,788.3	10,779.5	10,987.5	16,463.0	21,295.8
1.50	1,971.4	3,406.8	6,639.2	6,868.0	8,856.0	10,880.1	11,078.5	16,483.6	21,329.1
2.50	2,010.9	3,447.3	6,759.2	6,962.2	9,008.0	11,066.6	11,268.5	16,601.6	21,627.0
5.00	1,976.3	3,408.4	6,693.4	6,902.1	8,892.7	10,897.9	11,182.9	16,610.6	21,802.4
7.50	2,022.7	3,465.2	7,015.7	7,199.4	9,267.5	11,371.2	11,624.3	16,961.1	22,195.6
10.00	2,026.2	3,472.0	7,006.4	7,263.8	9,341.3	11,420.1	11,708.4	17,071.6	22,311.4
20.00	2,030.1	3,457.2	7,061.5	7,329.2	9,409.0	11,573.7	11,812.7	17,474.2	22,595.2
Resulting $\overline{\lvert J\rvert}$ with the DRMGC system (jobs)									
0.00	1,896.4	3,204.4	6,578.3	6,787.2	8,659.6	10,378.9	10,681.0	15,731.5	20,884.0
0.01	**1,901.9**	**3,222.4**	**6,623.5**	**6,834.0**	**8,713.7**	**10,605.3**	**10,893.6**	**15,175.5**	**21,213.5**
0.10	1,901.7	3,237.5	6,606.8	6,803.9	8,783.0	10,638.7	10,942.8	15,238.2	21,529.4
0.50	1,915.9	3,276.5	6,596.0	6,822.2	8,693.0	10,606.1	10,831.9	16,142.4	21,660.0
1.00	1,942.7	3,367.4	6,607.3	6,809.7	8,788.5	10,741.0	10,941.9	16,464.8	21,759.2
1.50	1,980.4	3,410.2	6,674.0	6,859.5	8,847.5	10,869.0	11,089.8	16,447.5	21,839.7
2.50	2,005.1	3,440.2	6,742.9	6,930.9	9,008.6	11,071.4	11,269.2	16,560.4	22,074.9
5.00	1,981.3	3,413.3	6,706.4	6,867.6	8,864.8	10,924.9	11,118.6	16,509.0	22,012.5
7.50	2,018.4	3,466.7	6,992.2	7,246.9	9,265.5	11,310.9	11,646.1	16,887.6	22,759.5
10.00	2,025.8	3,460.9	7,010.8	7,231.5	9,346.6	11,405.1	11,692.9	16,928.0	22,765.9
20.00	2,027.9	3,471.8	7,072.9	7,355.4	9,409.7	11,561.6	11,790.7	17,118.6	22,938.5
Resulting $\overline{\lvert J\rvert}$ with the TriRMGC system (jobs)									
0.00	1,896.7	3,243.5	6,603.7	6,771.4	8,628.2	10,417.4	10,698.7	15,835.6	23,376.8
0.01	**1,907.0**	**3,249.5**	**6,614.4**	**6,831.8**	**8,732.5**	**10,583.9**	**10,895.8**	**15,192.1**	**23,097.9**
0.10	1,914.5	3,254.6	6,636.4	6,832.5	8,745.9	10,615.9	10,904.4	15,421.9	23,594.0
0.50	1,911.9	3,274.8	6,610.4	6,845.8	8,693.9	10,606.0	10,844.5	16,166.0	24,096.6
1.00	1,943.5	3,385.8	6,597.0	6,776.8	8,714.2	10,733.9	10,954.9	16,551.6	24,199.0
1.50	1,978.5	3,419.3	6,691.1	6,851.0	8,788.9	10,844.0	11,069.9	16,649.5	24,319.6
2.50	2,014.0	3,483.2	6,813.3	6,953.0	8,971.8	11,096.4	11,381.6	16,681.8	24,389.2
5.00	1,982.8	3,445.4	6,711.7	6,891.8	8,879.7	10,889.7	11,149.7	16,663.2	24,345.9
7.50	2,023.3	3,494.2	7,052.3	7,236.3	9,313.0	11,432.7	11,762.9	17,163.4	25,053.6
10.00	2,026.7	3,495.8	7,046.4	7,285.8	9,382.5	11,507.6	11,786.8	17,293.0	25,130.6
20.00	2,029.3	3,497.8	7,140.0	7,399.1	9,448.5	11,560.8	11,893.1	17,520.4	25,355.8

Table A.68 Influence of the PoS concept (in terms of the cost factor $\lambda_{\tau(j)}^{\text{dist}}$) on the container accessibility ($\overline{\overline{\psi}}$), in terms of the mean number of shuffle moves per retrieval job, for selected yard-block layouts and all types of RMGC systems

	Yard-block layout								
$\lambda_{\tau(j)}^{\text{dist}}$	Small	Low	Narrow	Short	Medium	Long	Wide	High	Big
Resulting $\overline{\overline{\psi}}$ with the SRMGC system (jobs)									
0.00	0.319	0.290	1.122	1.107	1.073	1.021	1.016	1.565	1.097
0.01	**0.322**	**0.300**	**1.135**	**1.120**	**1.103**	**1.083**	**1.083**	**1.606**	**1.144**
0.10	0.332	0.306	1.131	1.115	1.106	1.094	1.086	1.656	1.192
0.50	0.335	0.330	1.127	1.110	1.118	1.102	1.092	1.702	1.293
1.00	0.379	0.390	1.147	1.142	1.144	1.133	1.125	1.725	1.373
1.50	0.412	0.415	1.162	1.151	1.167	1.164	1.132	1.733	1.428
2.50	0.437	0.439	1.233	1.177	1.192	1.193	1.181	1.776	1.530
5.00	0.416	0.418	1.179	1.147	1.176	1.178	1.159	1.760	1.482
7.50	0.468	0.456	1.299	1.285	1.290	1.273	1.258	1.849	1.681
10.00	0.469	0.461	1.309	1.316	1.298	1.288	1.276	1.874	1.711
20.00	0.473	0.467	1.362	1.333	1.335	1.329	1.322	1.931	1.745
Resulting $\overline{\overline{\psi}}$ with the TRMGC system (jobs)									
0.00	0.313	0.281	1.134	1.117	1.091	1.038	1.033	1.807	1.634
0.01	**0.324**	**0.296**	**1.127**	**1.130**	**1.130**	**1.097**	**1.090**	**1.762**	**1.675**
0.10	0.330	0.305	1.128	1.115	1.122	1.109	1.098	1.790	1.697
0.50	0.338	0.328	1.144	1.134	1.120	1.108	1.101	1.870	1.706
1.00	0.383	0.400	1.149	1.134	1.134	1.147	1.116	1.915	1.712
1.50	0.407	0.425	1.162	1.149	1.159	1.176	1.146	1.930	1.735
2.50	0.453	0.456	1.208	1.191	1.213	1.229	1.194	1.966	1.806
5.00	0.416	0.427	1.184	1.162	1.174	1.184	1.172	1.954	1.784
7.50	0.467	0.468	1.334	1.295	1.313	1.324	1.303	2.056	1.957
10.00	0.473	0.473	1.337	1.323	1.331	1.335	1.317	2.091	1.978
20.00	0.476	0.463	1.359	1.351	1.364	1.376	1.348	2.177	2.047
Resulting $\overline{\overline{\psi}}$ with the DRMGC system (jobs)									
0.00	0.315	0.283	1.125	1.110	1.088	1.035	1.034	1.783	1.604
0.01	**0.320**	**0.297**	**1.137**	**1.118**	**1.107**	**1.093**	**1.087**	**1.753**	**1.673**
0.10	0.326	0.303	1.129	1.112	1.119	1.098	1.098	1.767	1.709
0.50	0.342	0.334	1.141	1.120	1.103	1.097	1.075	1.857	1.714
1.00	0.374	0.396	1.139	1.125	1.139	1.136	1.106	1.917	1.726
1.50	0.418	0.429	1.177	1.149	1.161	1.176	1.148	1.940	1.759
2.50	0.446	0.450	1.211	1.177	1.217	1.238	1.197	1.964	1.807
5.00	0.417	0.429	1.191	1.147	1.172	1.193	1.160	1.948	1.774
7.50	0.464	0.468	1.323	1.324	1.313	1.312	1.303	2.058	1.953
10.00	0.469	0.468	1.339	1.315	1.339	1.333	1.325	2.066	1.970
20.00	0.475	0.472	1.364	1.372	1.361	1.376	1.353	2.118	2.021
Resulting $\overline{\overline{\psi}}$ with the TriRMGC system (jobs)									
0.00	0.315	0.291	1.122	1.100	1.086	1.045	1.036	1.811	1.752
0.01	**0.325**	**0.298**	**1.122**	**1.123**	**1.113**	**1.092**	**1.090**	**1.763**	**1.758**
0.10	0.333	0.300	1.130	1.121	1.111	1.096	1.086	1.795	1.796
0.50	0.334	0.317	1.130	1.132	1.109	1.097	1.071	1.861	1.854
1.00	0.372	0.395	1.144	1.112	1.122	1.134	1.107	1.921	1.881
1.50	0.413	0.419	1.179	1.144	1.148	1.172	1.138	1.954	1.897
2.50	0.459	0.462	1.232	1.193	1.209	1.242	1.225	1.981	1.920
5.00	0.418	0.435	1.185	1.159	1.176	1.180	1.164	1.965	1.904
7.50	0.468	0.475	1.345	1.315	1.329	1.343	1.333	2.092	2.060
10.00	0.471	0.474	1.345	1.339	1.353	1.363	1.342	2.137	2.083
20.00	0.475	0.472	1.387	1.390	1.380	1.381	1.372	2.187	2.134

Table A.69 Influence of the used container-stacking strategy on the mean vehicle-waiting time ($\overline{\omega}_{\text{total}}^{\text{hr+}}$) for selected yard-block layouts and all types of RMGC systems

Stacking strategy		Yard-block layout								
Positioning	HHS	Small	Low	Narrow	Short	Medium	Long	Wide	High	Big
Resulting $\overline{\omega}_{\text{total}}^{\text{hr+}}$ with the SRMGC system (s)										
RaS	–	30.42	48.18	169.62	133.02	358.80	1,123.74	943.44	2,802.96	5,224.02
CCFS[a]	**–**	**28.26**	**41.28**	**117.06**	**100.44**	**198.96**	**561.06**	**486.48**	**1,861.32**	**3,269.94**
CCFS[b]	–	27.54	42.30	101.64	91.50	167.40	470.04	389.52	1,318.44	3,469.02
CCFS[c]	–	26.10	43.02	103.38	94.08	165.06	428.22	383.28	2,235.60	3,548.04
CCFS[d]	–	27.00	40.68	102.66	92.88	162.18	468.66	414.54	1,920.24	3,660.12
CCFS[a]	✓	27.12	41.10	100.38	92.70	159.84	398.82	327.36	1,677.00	2,810.76
CCFS[b]	✓	26.40	39.06	85.92	77.70	132.30	357.30	312.24	1,019.46	3,086.34
CCFS[c]	✓	25.38	41.52	98.58	89.76	142.44	360.06	322.74	2,102.40	3,608.70
CCFS[d]	✓	26.04	39.30	96.60	88.38	147.96	390.18	344.40	1,908.12	3,616.50
Resulting $\overline{\omega}_{\text{total}}^{\text{hr+}}$ with the TRMGC system (s)										
RaS	–	11.16	17.16	47.52	42.90	60.54	105.24	90.54	644.58	2,233.56
CCFS[a]	**–**	**8.82**	**13.44**	**38.16**	**35.58**	**48.30**	**67.44**	**61.98**	**304.08**	**1,567.38**
CCFS[b]	–	8.88	13.20	33.84	30.78	40.62	62.10	52.98	175.20	1,107.36
CCFS[c]	–	8.88	13.32	39.30	35.28	45.84	63.00	58.14	327.24	1,647.72
CCFS[d]	–	8.46	12.42	34.44	32.22	42.12	59.10	54.78	217.32	1,525.62
CCFS[a]	✓	8.58	12.96	36.48	33.30	43.86	57.06	53.46	258.78	1,122.06
CCFS[b]	✓	7.68	11.64	28.32	26.04	36.12	50.58	46.14	131.70	845.04
CCFS[c]	✓	8.82	13.32	35.58	35.22	43.44	58.02	53.34	271.62	1,148.04
CCFS[d]	✓	8.34	12.12	32.52	30.42	40.98	56.40	51.48	201.96	1,268.94
Resulting $\overline{\omega}_{\text{total}}^{\text{hr+}}$ with the DRMGC system (s)										
RaS	–	15.42	25.44	60.78	57.72	83.94	127.32	121.92	742.74	2,418.30
CCFS[a]	**–**	**13.86**	**23.58**	**53.82**	**54.36**	**69.24**	**88.86**	**88.86**	**360.18**	**1,607.82**
CCFS[b]	–	12.66	22.32	46.02	45.36	59.70	78.78	79.26	199.08	1,170.18
CCFS[c]	–	14.04	23.34	55.32	54.96	66.96	85.50	86.64	430.44	1,679.04
CCFS[d]	–	13.50	22.20	48.96	48.36	64.32	82.02	82.62	289.44	1,627.62
CCFS[a]	✓	13.38	23.10	52.74	53.76	65.82	80.70	82.68	338.88	1,436.76
CCFS[b]	✓	12.84	20.46	41.46	40.68	55.26	70.80	70.44	160.38	958.26
CCFS[c]	✓	14.28	23.10	53.70	55.02	66.72	80.58	84.78	377.04	1,353.18
CCFS[d]	✓	12.30	21.78	47.04	46.62	61.14	77.88	79.50	262.98	1,523.64
Resulting $\overline{\omega}_{\text{total}}^{\text{hr+}}$ with the TriRMGC system (s)										
RaS	–	10.74	15.60	36.60	35.40	44.16	58.50	56.46	225.06	1,090.62
CCFS[a]	**–**	**8.82**	**12.48**	**31.26**	**31.86**	**37.98**	**46.86**	**46.86**	**117.54**	**574.98**
CCFS[b]	–	7.74	11.88	26.10	26.16	32.70	40.56	40.50	81.54	342.12
CCFS[c]	–	9.24	13.38	31.92	33.84	39.66	45.96	46.38	134.22	645.00
CCFS[d]	–	8.16	11.94	27.30	27.54	33.54	43.14	40.92	98.04	543.18
CCFS[a]	✓	8.94	12.78	32.70	34.32	39.66	45.72	47.46	121.80	528.30
CCFS[b]	✓	7.80	11.34	24.48	25.32	31.32	38.22	37.80	72.84	308.04
CCFS[c]	✓	9.18	12.78	32.52	34.38	39.18	46.80	48.00	139.20	507.72
CCFS[d]	✓	8.10	11.40	27.48	29.04	34.02	41.04	42.30	100.62	524.76

[a]CaS parametrisation, [b]CaS-RTS parametrisation, [c]CaS-PoS parametrisation, [d]CaS-RTS-PoS parametrisation

Table A.70 Influence of the used container-stacking strategy on the mean vehicle-waiting time per waterside retrieval job ($\overline{\overline{\omega}}^{hr+}_{wsout}$) for selected yard-block layouts and all types of RMGC systems

Stacking strategy		Yard-block layout								
Positioning	HHS	Small	Low	Narrow	Short	Medium	Long	Wide	High	Big
Resulting $\overline{\overline{\omega}}^{hr+}_{wsout}$ with the SRMGC system (s)										
RaS	–	3.90	7.98	186.60	118.86	545.64	2,040.00	1,704.66	5,520.06	9,524.40
CCFS[a]	**–**	**3.24**	**5.52**	**78.00**	**56.04**	**198.72**	**789.12**	**671.58**	**3,180.30**	**4,959.72**
CCFS[b]	–	4.02	5.64	65.58	49.14	151.08	642.54	519.00	2,232.18	5,467.32
CCFS[c]	–	4.26	5.46	58.38	44.82	134.82	536.88	489.30	3,982.08	5,887.56
CCFS[d]	–	4.08	5.22	62.28	48.30	143.64	645.36	568.08	3,452.58	6,209.28
CCFS[a]	✓	4.02	6.96	59.40	46.38	131.64	465.48	364.56	2,756.22	4,010.34
CCFS[b]	✓	3.48	5.22	47.88	35.94	96.36	427.68	363.36	1,626.96	4,745.88
CCFS[c]	✓	2.40	5.10	52.80	42.96	102.42	416.46	369.84	3,682.26	6,170.28
CCFS[d]	✓	3.72	4.50	56.70	48.60	119.22	487.80	433.68	3,384.12	6,254.10
Resulting $\overline{\overline{\omega}}^{hr+}_{wsout}$ with the TRMGC system (s)										
RaS	–	2.70	5.22	25.74	21.72	41.88	115.56	92.34	1,196.58	4,458.90
CCFS[a]	**–**	**2.28**	**4.14**	**15.06**	**13.20**	**25.80**	**48.48**	**42.12**	**486.30**	**3,019.80**
CCFS[b]	–	2.28	4.74	15.24	13.74	20.88	45.60	33.12	253.44	2,133.72
CCFS[c]	–	3.06	3.96	15.84	12.06	17.64	34.68	29.76	528.42	3,293.52
CCFS[d]	–	2.40	4.32	14.70	14.28	19.26	35.22	33.90	336.06	2,994.18
CCFS[a]	✓	2.34	4.68	15.18	11.22	18.30	28.62	26.28	371.16	2,001.24
CCFS[b]	✓	1.92	4.44	12.36	10.02	18.42	32.10	26.82	177.78	1,523.70
CCFS[c]	✓	2.46	4.80	11.58	11.40	18.42	28.20	21.96	401.52	2,089.86
CCFS[d]	✓	2.94	3.78	12.90	12.18	19.92	33.18	27.12	302.82	2,359.56
Resulting $\overline{\overline{\omega}}^{hr+}_{wsout}$ with the DRMGC system (s)										
RaS	–	2.94	5.88	29.28	25.20	54.78	116.64	113.46	1,349.16	4,745.40
CCFS[a]	**–**	**2.76**	**5.34**	**20.10**	**18.72**	**30.78**	**47.46**	**46.26**	**510.54**	**2,758.62**
CCFS[b]	–	2.46	4.80	17.40	15.66	26.16	44.52	46.86	238.80	2,030.94
CCFS[c]	–	2.88	4.44	19.08	16.68	24.30	37.86	41.28	644.70	2,917.14
CCFS[d]	–	2.04	5.40	18.06	17.10	30.18	42.18	47.04	408.54	2,895.72
CCFS[a]	✓	1.92	4.20	17.22	16.38	25.56	36.48	37.56	456.30	2,358.06
CCFS[b]	✓	2.22	4.44	15.06	15.36	23.64	34.32	33.54	173.58	1,569.60
CCFS[c]	✓	2.10	4.74	17.46	16.38	23.46	32.82	38.16	518.88	2,265.36
CCFS[d]	✓	1.74	5.22	15.66	16.02	26.34	38.82	41.16	350.70	2,675.28
Resulting $\overline{\overline{\omega}}^{hr+}_{wsout}$ with the TriRMGC system (s)										
RaS	–	3.06	6.54	14.94	14.16	23.70	34.02	31.50	327.36	2,092.44
CCFS[a]	**–**	**2.22**	**5.34**	**12.90**	**12.54**	**16.32**	**19.68**	**20.94**	**109.68**	**883.26**
CCFS[b]	–	1.80	5.52	12.36	10.20	16.56	20.16	20.28	74.76	501.42
CCFS[c]	–	2.82	5.58	12.00	12.18	18.42	18.24	18.30	132.48	1,041.48
CCFS[d]	–	3.06	5.16	12.60	12.12	16.62	21.84	19.80	94.62	895.74
CCFS[a]	✓	2.16	4.32	11.40	12.18	16.26	16.98	18.06	102.36	754.56
CCFS[b]	✓	2.28	4.74	11.64	11.34	16.20	17.58	18.90	63.54	426.42
CCFS[c]	✓	2.94	4.26	10.56	10.80	13.80	17.94	17.10	125.22	743.34
CCFS[d]	✓	2.70	5.04	12.24	12.24	16.38	15.48	18.96	98.40	838.74

[a]CaS parametrisation, [b]CaS-RTS parametrisation, [c]CaS-PoS parametrisation, [d]CaS-RTS-PoS parametrisation

Table A.71 Influence of the used container-stacking strategy on the mean crane-waiting time in the handover areas ($\overline{\omega}^{hr-}_{total}$) for selected yard-block layouts and all types of RMGC systems

Stacking strategy		Yard-block layout								
Positioning	HHS	Small	Low	Narrow	Short	Medium	Long	Wide	High	Big
Resulting $\overline{\omega}^{hr-}_{total}$ with the SRMGC system (s)										
RaS	–	125.28	97.44	62.64	66.48	41.46	23.58	26.52	13.14	5.88
CCFS[a]	**–**	**124.38**	**94.92**	**63.84**	**67.26**	**41.52**	**22.86**	**25.80**	**14.64**	**7.08**
CCFS[b]	–	123.18	95.16	71.28	74.22	49.20	28.74	33.30	19.80	6.78
CCFS[c]	–	123.60	94.32	61.26	64.50	40.56	21.84	25.38	12.06	6.90
CCFS[d]	–	122.46	94.92	66.60	70.38	44.16	23.88	27.72	13.56	6.72
CCFS[a]	√	122.76	93.78	60.84	65.04	39.54	22.14	25.08	12.96	6.72
CCFS[b]	√	125.40	94.50	71.52	74.70	49.02	27.54	31.44	20.76	6.72
CCFS[c]	√	122.46	94.68	59.82	63.18	38.82	21.48	24.00	11.16	6.30
CCFS[d]	√	123.24	95.04	64.20	67.14	41.76	21.72	24.96	12.24	6.54
Resulting $\overline{\omega}^{hr-}_{total}$ with the TRMGC system (s)										
RaS	–	137.34	115.14	89.34	91.08	69.54	51.54	54.18	34.74	10.50
CCFS[a]	**–**	**135.84**	**112.32**	**87.84**	**91.26**	**67.86**	**50.28**	**53.40**	**38.58**	**10.56**
CCFS[b]	–	134.94	112.56	94.86	97.80	75.90	56.94	59.88	49.74	15.18
CCFS[c]	–	135.48	111.06	84.96	88.32	66.00	48.18	51.66	33.60	9.90
CCFS[d]	–	136.32	111.48	90.48	93.90	71.46	52.26	56.10	42.24	10.56
CCFS[a]	√	134.64	110.94	83.28	87.00	64.26	45.42	49.08	31.38	9.42
CCFS[b]	√	136.02	110.82	91.62	94.56	72.30	53.40	57.06	48.00	13.98
CCFS[c]	√	135.54	110.52	83.58	85.44	64.92	45.66	49.50	29.16	9.60
CCFS[d]	√	134.40	111.90	86.88	92.16	66.36	47.70	51.12	39.54	9.72
Resulting $\overline{\omega}^{hr-}_{total}$ with the DRMGC system (s)										
RaS	–	139.14	118.44	95.82	95.70	74.94	57.60	57.90	38.82	12.60
CCFS[a]	**–**	**139.32**	**117.48**	**95.28**	**95.46**	**75.18**	**57.24**	**57.66**	**44.52**	**12.60**
CCFS[b]	–	139.20	117.66	101.94	102.54	82.98	65.64	65.94	57.18	19.50
CCFS[c]	–	137.94	115.86	93.36	92.82	73.32	55.74	56.46	38.88	11.10
CCFS[d]	–	138.12	116.40	98.58	98.82	78.72	59.34	60.84	48.30	12.54
CCFS[a]	√	139.14	115.68	92.58	92.88	73.38	55.62	55.74	39.36	10.98
CCFS[b]	√	139.08	116.88	100.86	101.76	81.54	63.78	64.50	57.54	18.36
CCFS[c]	√	137.58	116.22	92.46	91.92	72.36	55.68	55.74	35.16	10.44
CCFS[d]	√	139.26	116.70	96.66	98.28	77.52	57.54	58.62	46.14	11.16
Resulting $\overline{\omega}^{hr-}_{total}$ with the TriRMGC system (s)										
RaS	–	142.26	123.24	102.42	100.98	84.06	69.30	69.48	53.70	21.60
CCFS[a]	**–**	**140.40**	**121.98**	**103.44**	**101.10**	**84.00**	**68.22**	**68.64**	**58.38**	**23.88**
CCFS[b]	–	141.24	121.68	107.94	106.68	90.60	75.54	75.54	68.70	34.26
CCFS[c]	–	141.36	120.42	100.26	99.30	82.92	67.14	67.80	54.18	19.32
CCFS[d]	–	141.12	121.26	106.50	105.66	86.94	70.44	72.42	62.16	25.68
CCFS[a]	√	141.36	119.76	100.50	98.40	81.78	66.18	66.12	52.32	18.96
CCFS[b]	√	141.48	120.96	107.22	106.14	89.40	73.14	74.22	67.50	33.12
CCFS[c]	√	140.64	120.00	99.24	98.58	81.78	66.48	67.02	48.72	17.22
CCFS[d]	√	141.06	120.90	104.46	103.68	84.84	68.28	70.02	60.06	23.40

[a]CaS parametrisation, [b]CaS-RTS parametrisation, [c]CaS-PoS parametrisation, [d]CaS-RTS-PoS parametrisation

Table A.72 Influence of the used container-stacking strategy on the mean crane-empty-movement time per job ($\overline{\overline{m}}^{xye}_{total}$) for selected yard-block layouts and all types of RMGC systems

Stacking strategy		Yard-block layout								
Positioning	HHS	Small	Low	Narrow	Short	Medium	Long	Wide	High	Big
Resulting $\overline{\overline{m}}^{xye}_{total}$ with the SRMGC system (s)										
RaS	–	26.22	31.70	27.40	23.43	26.73	29.86	26.76	24.09	27.77
CCFS[a]	**–**	**26.05**	**31.87**	**26.97**	**23.22**	**26.63**	**29.48**	**26.57**	**23.73**	**27.72**
CCFS[b]	–	26.20	32.16	28.46	24.18	27.89	31.20	27.59	25.37	28.43
CCFS[c]	–	25.85	31.29	26.52	22.95	26.28	29.18	26.33	22.82	26.59
CCFS[d]	–	25.81	31.52	27.27	23.61	26.89	29.67	26.56	23.64	27.12
CCFS[a]	✓	25.17	31.05	26.51	22.72	26.20	29.68	26.57	23.80	28.31
CCFS[b]	✓	24.88	30.75	27.56	23.49	27.32	30.84	27.37	25.56	28.60
CCFS[c]	✓	25.12	30.56	26.03	22.56	26.10	29.24	26.46	23.15	26.83
CCFS[d]	✓	24.99	30.57	26.61	22.95	26.39	29.49	26.43	23.63	27.54
Resulting $\overline{\overline{m}}^{xye}_{total}$ with the TRMGC system (s)										
RaS	–	24.67	30.14	33.76	30.13	34.45	38.80	34.97	35.42	38.83
CCFS[a]	**–**	**23.34**	**28.35**	**33.76**	**30.25**	**34.07**	**38.12**	**34.64**	**37.21**	**40.77**
CCFS[b]	–	23.21	28.64	33.64	29.96	34.16	38.68	34.78	37.66	41.33
CCFS[c]	–	22.99	28.26	34.60	31.15	34.69	38.71	35.04	37.57	41.79
CCFS[d]	–	22.93	28.25	33.44	30.13	33.92	38.00	34.54	37.09	40.88
CCFS[a]	✓	22.99	28.10	33.19	29.84	33.34	37.28	33.64	35.57	38.70
CCFS[b]	✓	23.07	28.19	32.93	29.41	33.27	37.75	34.01	36.04	39.74
CCFS[c]	✓	22.78	28.16	33.85	30.78	34.17	38.26	34.71	36.77	40.45
CCFS[d]	✓	22.65	28.03	33.42	30.07	33.62	37.33	34.01	36.42	39.38
Resulting $\overline{\overline{m}}^{xye}_{total}$ with the DRMGC system (s)										
RaS	–	54.64	66.73	61.12	60.83	60.66	59.23	57.89	47.94	43.39
CCFS[a]	**–**	**55.77**	**69.14**	**62.73**	**62.89**	**62.78**	**61.85**	**60.88**	**52.25**	**45.15**
CCFS[b]	–	54.67	69.04	63.81	63.96	64.88	64.58	62.71	56.61	48.34
CCFS[c]	–	55.61	69.12	63.64	63.62	63.44	62.54	61.50	50.85	45.02
CCFS[d]	–	55.21	68.43	64.08	63.67	63.66	62.10	61.53	53.68	44.88
CCFS[a]	✓	52.18	65.04	58.53	58.70	58.67	58.56	57.81	49.37	45.01
CCFS[b]	✓	51.09	63.12	58.39	57.91	59.56	59.65	58.56	53.98	47.52
CCFS[c]	✓	52.45	65.57	59.70	59.56	60.14	59.57	58.89	49.19	45.82
CCFS[d]	✓	51.61	64.54	59.81	59.46	59.46	58.88	58.03	51.66	44.81
Resulting $\overline{\overline{m}}^{xye}_{total}$ with the TriRMGC system (s)										
RaS	–	50.61	64.87	68.02	67.95	69.25	70.15	69.18	62.86	55.92
CCFS[a]	**–**	**51.55**	**65.81**	**69.11**	**68.63**	**70.12**	**70.81**	**70.15**	**66.70**	**60.22**
CCFS[b]	–	49.95	65.64	68.32	68.28	70.79	72.25	71.26	69.36	63.77
CCFS[c]	–	51.01	65.35	68.72	69.12	70.82	71.72	70.95	66.57	59.47
CCFS[d]	–	50.39	65.07	69.65	68.75	70.90	71.50	70.98	68.22	61.15
CCFS[a]	✓	50.54	63.01	65.11	64.79	66.23	67.02	66.65	63.13	58.07
CCFS[b]	✓	49.91	62.24	64.66	64.38	66.33	67.79	67.00	66.07	62.02
CCFS[c]	✓	50.52	63.25	66.42	66.52	67.99	68.38	68.18	63.47	58.79
CCFS[d]	✓	50.26	62.75	65.98	66.25	67.72	68.00	67.69	65.79	59.97

[a]CaS parametrisation, [b]CaS-RTS parametrisation, [c]CaS-PoS parametrisation, [d]CaS-RTS-PoS parametrisation

Table A.73 Influence of the used container-stacking strategy on the mean crane-interference time per job ($\overline{\overline{m}}^{\text{cit}}_{\text{total}}$) for selected yard-block layouts and all types of RMGC systems

Stacking strategy		Yard-block layout								
Positioning	HHS	Small	Low	Narrow	Short	Medium	Long	Wide	High	Big
Resulting $\overline{\overline{m}}^{\text{cit}}_{\text{total}}$ with the SRMGC system (s)										
RaS	–	0.00	0.00	0.00	0.00	0.00	0.00	0.00	0.00	0.00
CCFS[a]	**–**	**0.00**	**0.00**	**0.00**	**0.00**	**0.00**	**0.00**	**0.00**	**0.00**	**0.00**
CCFS[b]	–	0.00	0.00	0.00	0.00	0.00	0.00	0.00	0.00	0.00
CCFS[c]	–	0.00	0.00	0.00	0.00	0.00	0.00	0.00	0.00	0.00
CCFS[d]	–	0.00	0.00	0.00	0.00	0.00	0.00	0.00	0.00	0.00
CCFS[a]	√	0.00	0.00	0.00	0.00	0.00	0.00	0.00	0.00	0.00
CCFS[b]	√	0.00	0.00	0.00	0.00	0.00	0.00	0.00	0.00	0.00
CCFS[c]	√	0.00	0.00	0.00	0.00	0.00	0.00	0.00	0.00	0.00
CCFS[d]	√	0.00	0.00	0.00	0.00	0.00	0.00	0.00	0.00	0.00
Resulting $\overline{\overline{m}}^{\text{cit}}_{\text{total}}$ with the TRMGC system (s)										
RaS	–	4.06	4.20	13.39	13.67	13.60	14.01	13.91	20.87	21.00
CCFS[a]	**–**	**2.22**	**2.10**	**11.92**	**12.42**	**12.16**	**11.92**	**12.14**	**19.43**	**20.71**
CCFS[b]	–	2.21	2.21	10.91	11.53	11.00	11.30	11.30	17.48	18.88
CCFS[c]	–	2.01	2.25	12.51	12.75	12.34	12.41	12.47	20.49	22.45
CCFS[d]	–	2.00	2.13	11.35	11.88	11.54	11.57	11.69	18.31	20.79
CCFS[a]	√	2.60	2.78	12.21	12.47	12.21	12.21	12.02	19.66	19.82
CCFS[b]	√	2.66	2.77	11.05	11.38	11.25	11.55	11.65	17.13	18.77
CCFS[c]	√	2.32	2.71	12.51	13.06	12.53	12.91	12.80	20.30	21.59
CCFS[d]	√	2.27	2.65	11.89	12.08	12.01	12.06	12.14	18.26	20.20
Resulting $\overline{\overline{m}}^{\text{cit}}_{\text{total}}$ with the DRMGC system (s)										
RaS	–	30.21	36.77	33.16	36.73	32.70	27.33	29.89	24.06	17.99
CCFS[a]	**–**	**31.09**	**38.13**	**35.30**	**39.74**	**35.31**	**29.73**	**32.78**	**28.21**	**20.21**
CCFS[b]	–	30.05	38.69	36.48	40.63	37.07	31.96	34.65	31.58	21.68
CCFS[c]	–	30.78	38.48	37.14	40.84	36.89	31.23	34.17	28.53	21.58
CCFS[d]	–	30.89	38.47	37.11	41.09	37.11	30.74	34.09	29.91	20.75
CCFS[a]	√	27.52	34.68	31.73	35.69	31.36	26.86	30.05	25.65	19.92
CCFS[b]	√	28.19	33.93	31.67	35.48	32.54	27.67	31.07	29.04	20.84
CCFS[c]	√	28.08	35.14	33.45	37.17	33.54	28.36	31.87	26.65	21.29
CCFS[d]	√	27.51	35.09	33.05	36.88	33.00	27.89	30.87	28.05	20.23
Resulting $\overline{\overline{m}}^{\text{cit}}_{\text{total}}$ with the TriRMGC system (s)										
RaS	–	31.74	40.65	48.33	52.99	49.40	44.95	48.57	48.22	39.28
CCFS[a]	**–**	**31.02**	**40.31**	**48.66**	**52.32**	**49.18**	**44.71**	**47.95**	**49.43**	**41.62**
CCFS[b]	–	30.74	41.34	48.23	52.17	50.22	46.29	50.02	51.57	42.58
CCFS[c]	–	31.06	40.99	48.34	52.86	49.90	45.42	48.85	49.74	41.60
CCFS[d]	–	31.04	41.12	49.61	52.87	50.31	45.73	49.34	51.06	42.13
CCFS[a]	√	32.20	39.09	46.35	50.57	47.40	42.32	46.32	47.79	41.45
CCFS[b]	√	32.97	39.76	46.38	50.76	48.05	43.78	47.59	49.91	42.60
CCFS[c]	√	31.84	39.33	46.76	51.00	48.10	43.56	47.35	48.37	41.81
CCFS[d]	√	31.80	39.95	46.83	52.04	48.34	43.51	47.59	49.86	42.07

[a]CaS parametrisation, [b]CaS-RTS parametrisation, [c]CaS-PoS parametrisation, [d]CaS-RTS-PoS parametrisation

Table A.74 Influence of the used container-stacking strategy on the crane workload during the simulation horizon in terms of performed jobs ($\overline{|J|}$) for selected yard-block layouts and all types of RMGC systems

Stacking strategy		Yard-block layout								
Positioning	HHS	Small	Low	Narrow	Short	Medium	Long	Wide	High	Big
Resulting $\overline{|J|}$ with the SRMGC system (s)										
RaS	–	1, 979.2	3, 394.6	6, 931.6	7, 146.1	9, 145.4	10, 930.9	11, 293.4	13, 833.3	14, 285.8
CCFS[a]	**–**	**1, 871.8**	**3, 208.8**	**6, 596.5**	**6, 792.8**	**8, 683.4**	**10, 466.3**	**10, 776.3**	**13, 369.4**	**13, 711.1**
CCFS[b]	–	1, 843.2	3, 145.5	5, 937.0	6, 173.2	8, 031.1	9, 742.4	9, 976.7	11, 725.9	13, 318.8
CCFS[c]	–	1, 882.0	3, 251.4	6, 554.1	6, 750.4	8, 704.5	10, 526.0	10, 789.5	14, 118.4	14, 233.5
CCFS[d]	–	1, 862.8	3, 188.4	6, 379.1	6, 473.5	8, 477.6	10, 379.7	10, 618.2	13, 304.9	13, 721.1
CCFS[a]	✓	2, 098.0	3, 553.8	7, 332.2	7, 608.2	9, 556.8	11, 306.9	11, 572.2	14, 333.9	14, 275.6
CCFS[b]	✓	2, 086.0	3, 562.9	6, 661.8	6, 809.4	8, 770.0	10, 658.8	10, 996.3	12, 345.1	14, 036.6
CCFS[c]	✓	2, 083.6	3, 594.4	7, 304.6	7, 444.3	9, 501.0	11, 457.3	11, 710.4	15, 049.1	15, 650.1
CCFS[d]	✓	2, 023.3	3, 479.4	7, 050.4	7, 298.4	9, 294.8	11, 073.2	11, 456.7	14, 321.7	14, 641.0
Resulting $\overline{|J|}$ with the TRMGC system (jobs)										
RaS	–	1, 997.5	3, 440.1	6, 942.0	7, 205.9	9, 234.6	11, 305.9	11, 658.2	16, 699.8	21, 809.7
CCFS[a]	**–**	**1, 903.5**	**3, 224.1**	**6, 592.4**	**6, 857.8**	**8, 784.5**	**10, 615.3**	**10, 900.6**	**15, 170.8**	**21, 104.9**
CCFS[b]	–	1, 876.3	3, 161.5	5, 921.0	6, 062.3	7, 878.5	9, 799.8	10, 041.5	12, 185.3	18, 716.5
CCFS[c]	–	1, 911.6	3, 272.2	6, 627.5	6, 858.1	8, 727.9	10, 647.6	10, 941.8	16, 154.9	21, 266.9
CCFS[d]	–	1, 886.2	3, 215.9	6, 364.5	6, 506.9	8, 423.2	10, 401.9	10, 623.2	13, 672.3	20, 788.8
CCFS[a]	✓	2, 145.9	3, 613.1	7, 576.8	7, 807.6	9, 941.3	11, 894.1	12, 208.2	17, 593.7	22, 693.3
CCFS[b]	✓	2, 103.5	3, 561.0	6, 873.1	6, 951.4	9, 108.0	11, 206.2	11, 513.2	13, 410.9	20, 256.7
CCFS[c]	✓	2, 104.7	3, 562.4	7, 385.0	7, 697.8	9, 776.4	11, 906.4	12, 099.1	17, 776.8	22, 929.7
CCFS[d]	✓	2, 034.5	3, 461.7	7, 306.4	7, 425.1	9, 605.0	11, 699.4	11, 994.7	15, 218.9	22, 255.6

Table A.74 (continued)

Stacking strategy		Yard-block layout								
Positioning	HHS	Small	Low	Narrow	Short	Medium	Long	Wide	High	Big
Resulting $\overline{\|J\|}$ with the DRMGC system (jobs)										
RaS	–	1, 993.4	3, 440.4	6, 916.8	7, 150.7	9, 251.7	11, 275.4	11, 619.2	16, 728.8	21, 597.4
CCFS[a]	**–**	**1, 901.9**	**3, 222.4**	**6, 623.5**	**6, 834.0**	**8, 713.7**	**10, 605.3**	**10, 893.6**	**15, 175.5**	**21, 213.5**
CCFS[b]	–	1, 876.5	3, 163.5	5, 891.3	6, 083.3	7, 869.3	9, 677.1	10, 023.1	12, 113.2	18, 578.1
CCFS[c]	–	1, 915.9	3, 276.5	6, 596.0	6, 822.2	8, 693.0	10, 606.1	10, 831.9	16, 142.4	21, 660.0
CCFS[d]	–	1, 882.4	3, 209.7	6, 346.2	6, 511.7	8, 490.6	10, 440.7	10, 623.9	13, 964.4	21, 055.8
CCFS[a]	✓	2, 139.2	3, 619.5	7, 504.3	7, 809.5	9, 890.3	11, 789.7	12, 114.7	17, 310.5	22, 666.2
CCFS[b]	✓	2, 106.6	3, 559.5	6, 872.7	7, 050.7	9, 128.5	11, 221.3	11, 409.1	13, 227.8	20, 228.2
CCFS[c]	✓	2, 128.4	3, 567.9	7, 407.8	7, 648.6	9, 707.7	11, 738.6	12, 075.0	17, 515.4	23, 027.1
CCFS[d]	✓	2, 057.1	3, 480.4	7, 217.2	7, 352.9	9, 551.2	11, 600.5	11, 937.2	15, 395.4	22, 468.6
Resulting $\overline{\|J\|}$ with the TriRMGC system (jobs)										
RaS	–	2, 003.4	3, 449.0	6, 950.5	7, 212.7	9, 244.8	11, 304.3	11, 647.1	17, 061.3	24, 351.4
CCFS[a]	**–**	**1, 907.0**	**3, 249.5**	**6, 614.4**	**6, 831.8**	**8, 732.5**	**10, 583.9**	**10, 895.8**	**15, 192.1**	**23, 097.9**
CCFS[b]	–	1, 875.2	3, 194.3	5, 894.2	6, 151.2	7, 942.3	9, 731.2	10, 126.6	12, 079.8	19, 010.8
CCFS[c]	–	1, 911.9	3, 274.8	6, 610.4	6, 845.8	8, 693.9	10, 606.0	10, 844.5	16, 166.0	24, 096.6
CCFS[d]	–	1, 884.6	3, 238.6	6, 321.4	6, 461.8	8, 392.4	10, 430.3	10, 658.8	13, 799.4	22, 121.0
CCFS[a]	✓	2, 081.5	3, 556.0	7, 385.5	7, 677.3	9, 682.6	11, 726.7	11, 981.3	17, 569.2	25, 461.9
CCFS[b]	✓	2, 067.7	3, 510.0	6, 592.1	6, 854.5	8, 880.8	11, 111.8	11, 255.4	13, 266.4	20, 487.9
CCFS[c]	✓	2, 048.7	3, 517.7	7, 199.0	7, 459.6	9, 458.6	11, 577.9	11, 858.2	17, 758.1	25, 316.4
CCFS[d]	✓	2, 002.2	3, 445.0	7, 006.1	7, 269.8	9, 314.3	11, 485.1	11, 763.9	15, 159.6	23, 572.7

[a]CaS parametrisation, [b]CaS-RTS parametrisation, [c]CaS-PoS parametrisation, [d]CaS-RTS-PoS parametrisation

Table A.75 Influence of the used container-stacking strategy on the container accessibility ($\overline{\overline{\psi}}$), in terms of the mean number of shuffle moves per retrieval job, for selected yard-block layouts and all types of RMGC systems

Stacking strategy		Yard-block layout								
Positioning	HHS	Small	Low	Narrow	Short	Medium	Long	Wide	High	Big
Resulting $\overline{\overline{\psi}}$ with the SRMGC system (s)										
RaS	–	0.450	0.434	1.290	1.281	1.276	1.257	1.249	1.790	1.483
CCFS[a]	**–**	**0.322**	**0.300**	**1.135**	**1.120**	**1.103**	**1.083**	**1.083**	**1.606**	**1.144**
CCFS[b]	–	0.286	0.256	0.934	0.946	0.944	0.925	0.918	1.302	1.034
CCFS[c]	–	0.335	0.330	1.127	1.110	1.118	1.102	1.092	1.702	1.293
CCFS[d]	–	0.309	0.287	1.029	0.994	1.022	1.035	1.016	1.533	1.122
CCFS[a]	✓	0.320	0.287	1.092	1.095	1.069	1.026	1.011	1.591	1.097
CCFS[b]	✓	0.286	0.251	0.883	0.872	0.867	0.882	0.874	1.211	0.990
CCFS[c]	✓	0.345	0.360	1.130	1.089	1.084	1.097	1.071	1.674	1.381
CCFS[d]	✓	0.310	0.297	1.011	1.004	1.015	1.001	1.010	1.533	1.124
Resulting $\overline{\overline{\psi}}$ with the TRMGC system (jobs)										
RaS	–	0.438	0.449	1.289	1.285	1.285	1.293	1.296	2.019	1.873
CCFS[a]	**–**	**0.324**	**0.296**	**1.127**	**1.130**	**1.130**	**1.097**	**1.090**	**1.762**	**1.675**
CCFS[b]	–	0.291	0.251	0.923	0.913	0.915	0.928	0.915	1.345	1.400
CCFS[c]	–	0.338	0.328	1.144	1.134	1.120	1.108	1.101	1.870	1.706
CCFS[d]	–	0.306	0.286	1.016	1.002	1.009	1.012	0.995	1.517	1.597
CCFS[a]	✓	0.331	0.306	1.118	1.107	1.090	1.043	1.040	1.796	1.600
CCFS[b]	✓	0.286	0.250	0.882	0.864	0.884	0.877	0.882	1.256	1.324
CCFS[c]	✓	0.349	0.352	1.109	1.112	1.086	1.092	1.058	1.865	1.665
CCFS[d]	✓	0.312	0.301	1.031	0.998	1.015	1.017	1.005	1.511	1.565
Resulting $\overline{\overline{\psi}}$ with the DRMGC system (jobs)										
RaS	–	0.435	0.448	1.279	1.274	1.288	1.289	1.287	1.038	1.852
CCFS[a]	**–**	**0.320**	**0.297**	**1.137**	**1.118**	**1.107**	**1.093**	**1.087**	**1.753**	**1.673**
CCFS[b]	–	0.291	0.252	0.922	0.919	0.924	0.917	0.914	1.337	1.371
CCFS[c]	–	0.342	0.334	1.141	1.120	1.103	1.097	1.075	1.857	1.714
CCFS[d]	–	0.300	0.284	1.004	0.997	1.019	1.019	1.001	1.548	1.609
CCFS[a]	✓	0.333	0.306	1.113	1.118	1.091	1.042	1.039	1.799	1.649
CCFS[b]	✓	0.286	0.255	0.895	0.873	0.890	0.893	0.882	1.258	1.345
CCFS[c]	✓	0.352	0.349	1.126	1.104	1.089	1.070	1.068	1.858	1.674
CCFS[d]	✓	0.305	0.298	1.022	0.985	1.001	1.007	1.006	1.545	1.591
Resulting $\overline{\overline{\psi}}$ with the TriRMGC system (jobs)										
RaS	–	0.443	0.437	1.292	1.290	1.296	1.293	1.291	2.065	1.996
CCFS[a]	**–**	**0.325**	**0.298**	**1.122**	**1.123**	**1.113**	**1.092**	**1.090**	**1.763**	**1.758**
CCFS[b]	–	0.286	0.261	0.928	0.938	0.926	0.913	0.926	1.343	1.366
CCFS[c]	–	0.334	0.317	1.130	1.132	1.109	1.097	1.071	1.861	1.854
CCFS[d]	–	0.300	0.291	1.016	0.992	1.000	1.023	0.999	1.528	1.631
CCFS[a]	✓	0.336	0.302	1.115	1.116	1.085	1.049	1.041	1.804	1.754
CCFS[b]	✓	0.288	0.257	0.876	0.888	0.885	0.889	0.874	1.258	1.296
CCFS[c]	✓	0.343	0.338	1.122	1.111	1.087	1.078	1.055	1.878	1.796
CCFS[d]	✓	0.307	0.295	1.002	0.999	0.998	1.014	0.999	1.514	1.606

[a]CaS parametrisation, [b]CaS-RTS parametrisation, [c]CaS-PoS parametrisation, [d]CaS-RTS-PoS parametrisation

A.5.7 *Influence of the Crane-Scheduling Strategy*

Table A.76 Influence of the crane-scheduling strategy on the mean XT-waiting time ($\overline{\overline{\omega}}_{ls}^{hr+}$) for selected yard-block layouts and all types of RMGC systems

Scheduling strategy	Yard-block layout								
	Small	Low	Narrow	Short	Medium	Long	Wide	High	Big
Resulting $\overline{\overline{\omega}}_{ls}^{hr+}$ with the SRMGC system (s)									
FIFO	74.06	127.42	280.91	269.13	428.55	996.28	825.07	2,372.32	4,077.05
EDD	63.87	95.59	202.80	184.77	304.54	885.36	678.19	2,329.64	4,065.97
NN	68.12	104.38	263.74	244.04	430.03	930.11	848.63	2,507.79	4,137.41
PRIO1	62.27	98.02	217.65	198.35	322.68	790.02	642.13	2,293.39	3,922.64
PRIO2	**65.90**	**95.41**	**226.61**	**204.03**	**336.25**	**772.82**	**675.77**	**2,244.74**	**3,903.45**
SFE-ignore	65.76	107.22	256.94	237.99	394.74	910.74	764.98	2,355.21	3,909.55
GAM-ignore	65.08	108.74	262.91	242.32	405.83	977.72	845.79	2,676.45	4,052.55
SFE-replan	62.75	96.55	269.19	241.35	444.10	1,150.81	992.44	3,621.07	4,249.39
GAM-replan	63.40	95.35	254.75	231.35	421.45	1,124.51	1,006.32	3,474.28	4,612.25
Resulting $\overline{\overline{\omega}}_{ls}^{hr+}$ with the TRMGC system (s)									
FIFO	19.63	29.09	84.00	78.41	103.09	135.18	124.02	424.83	1,723.28
EDD	19.37	29.15	82.51	75.86	98.45	130.69	118.41	406.24	1,673.15
NN	19.48	29.14	81.88	76.75	99.38	128.39	120.28	381.72	1,262.84
PRIO1	19.42	28.52	83.44	76.08	98.95	127.79	118.90	384.26	1,657.98
PRIO2	**19.48**	**29.13**	**82.08**	**77.19**	**98.58**	**126.78**	**118.96**	**387.72**	**1,540.04**
SFE-ignore	18.98	26.99	79.70	72.93	94.97	129.41	116.58	433.98	1,677.31
GAM-ignore	18.76	27.76	80.96	77.11	100.86	132.47	121.56	460.37	1,780.05
SFE-replan	19.08	27.78	77.93	72.47	94.28	121.91	112.67	421.58	1,627.92
GAM-replan	18.63	27.66	80.48	72.18	94.11	125.20	114.99	440.41	1,748.18
Resulting $\overline{\overline{\omega}}_{ls}^{hr+}$ with the DRMGC system (s)									
FIFO	33.42	60.43	137.08	142.78	191.62	272.20	267.98	756.44	2,700.40
EDD	31.58	52.77	115.52	116.67	142.71	185.55	183.99	631.67	2,394.52
NN	33.12	52.87	128.57	130.22	168.21	224.29	223.06	718.43	2,561.77
PRIO1	30.72	52.61	117.06	117.57	146.70	183.30	183.43	534.64	2,148.54
PRIO2	**31.48**	**52.60**	**116.45**	**118.90**	**146.10**	**179.24**	**181.10**	**509.36**	**1,907.61**
SFE-ignore	27.83	44.10	107.82	109.79	142.04	181.38	183.47	536.66	1,998.47
GAM-ignore	28.90	47.65	115.61	116.19	151.25	197.43	197.22	609.27	2,355.56
SFE-replan	27.49	42.49	98.85	101.48	123.65	160.02	157.48	473.89	1,834.19
GAM-replan	27.45	45.67	104.31	105.00	128.53	162.33	164.74	527.63	2,201.05
Resulting $\overline{\overline{\omega}}_{ls}^{hr+}$ with the TriRMGC system (s)									
FIFO	18.86	26.21	67.83	68.95	81.98	99.75	101.59	242.18	1,011.31
EDD	18.75	26.04	65.94	66.88	79.69	95.08	94.61	215.37	897.01
NN	18.44	25.54	69.42	68.23	80.65	95.78	97.35	228.35	879.45
PRIO1	19.26	26.94	66.98	70.29	81.14	95.93	96.25	222.04	812.13
PRIO2	**19.56**	**26.47**	**66.99**	**68.47**	**80.43**	**98.14**	**98.35**	**208.77**	**754.71**
SFE-ignore	18.06	25.93	66.94	68.08	79.56	95.77	96.42	229.48	814.67
GAM-ignore	18.44	27.01	69.40	72.20	83.79	98.94	98.36	219.68	813.98
SFE-replan	18.42	26.12	66.11	66.44	77.24	93.87	92.64	226.88	832.49
GAM-replan	18.74	26.35	67.52	69.57	79.17	95.72	96.85	209.81	795.34

Table A.77 Influence of the crane-scheduling strategy on the mean SC-waiting time ($\overline{\overline{\omega}}_{ws}^{hr+}$) for selected yard-block layouts and all types of RMGC systems

Scheduling strategy	Yard-block layout								
	Small	Low	Narrow	Short	Medium	Long	Wide	High	Big
Resulting $\overline{\overline{\omega}}_{ws}^{hr+}$ with the SRMGC system (s)									
FIFO	2.26	5.16	64.25	54.51	178.79	844.45	638.67	2,408.70	5,333.66
EDD	2.20	5.39	95.69	68.10	244.36	1,000.01	763.55	2,802.77	5,829.00
NN	1.70	4.76	72.63	55.01	158.14	489.98	427.46	2,049.65	4,198.16
PRIO1	1.82	3.24	49.39	37.79	147.38	626.03	517.82	2,195.70	4,597.52
PRIO2	**1.69**	**2.86**	**40.46**	**28.71**	**102.93**	**410.23**	**350.05**	**1,597.83**	**2,837.74**
SFE-ignore	1.60	3.61	46.01	32.54	133.99	624.27	523.79	2,250.94	4,870.70
GAM-ignore	1.48	3.42	48.02	33.13	116.14	491.91	409.50	2,102.20	4,202.13
SFE-replan	1.92	2.62	24.57	17.90	47.66	123.32	104.27	869.27	1,471.58
GAM-replan	1.85	2.65	34.79	22.55	82.49	228.67	186.47	1,008.39	1,351.40
Resulting $\overline{\overline{\omega}}_{ws}^{hr+}$ with the TRMGC system (s)									
FIFO	1.69	3.41	14.71	10.68	21.99	38.96	34.91	361.59	2,087.56
EDD	1.31	2.51	15.63	12.06	24.73	57.65	45.36	499.07	2,275.53
NN	1.66	3.10	16.28	13.53	27.62	54.06	50.38	406.56	2,698.87
PRIO1	1.25	2.14	10.06	7.77	14.15	28.91	24.08	320.40	1,974.72
PRIO2	**1.19**	**2.14**	**7.79**	**6.74**	**13.31**	**25.15**	**21.79**	**247.50**	**1,586.02**
SFE-ignore	1.16	2.94	7.92	6.44	12.94	21.45	19.12	290.79	1,764.50
GAM-ignore	1.31	2.85	8.13	6.52	11.90	23.05	18.93	228.30	1,493.81
SFE-replan	1.13	2.66	7.15	5.22	9.97	16.60	12.76	180.13	1,465.72
GAM-replan	1.47	1.77	7.35	5.55	8.84	16.94	14.91	180.69	1,254.44
Resulting $\overline{\overline{\omega}}_{ws}^{hr+}$ with the DRMGC system (s)									
FIFO	1.50	3.19	13.43	12.52	26.00	55.01	44.80	528.15	2,562.00
EDD	1.22	3.56	15.55	14.08	28.03	57.81	60.61	613.91	2,650.87
NN	1.72	2.91	14.68	12.82	26.31	46.18	48.50	330.20	2,095.79
PRIO1	1.38	2.94	11.27	11.04	17.88	31.28	33.92	386.23	1,976.31
PRIO2	**1.44**	**2.76**	**10.37**	**9.57**	**15.89**	**24.57**	**23.92**	**259.60**	**1,401.64**
SFE-ignore	0.87	2.32	7.73	6.40	14.10	22.90	22.38	325.33	1,917.11
GAM-ignore	1.09	2.29	11.20	9.65	18.32	29.89	28.80	325.86	1,856.15
SFE-replan	0.84	1.89	7.50	6.81	11.30	19.49	18.71	211.46	1,501.72
GAM-replan	1.31	2.88	9.44	8.14	14.82	25.14	24.50	278.00	1,589.99
Resulting $\overline{\overline{\omega}}_{ws}^{hr+}$ with the TriRMGC system (s)									
FIFO	1.85	2.67	7.96	7.96	13.06	16.84	17.18	102.53	972.31
EDD	1.57	2.67	7.24	7.62	12.30	17.09	17.93	155.11	1,068.45
NN	1.67	2.52	7.99	7.96	13.66	18.96	22.05	107.79	858.90
PRIO1	1.29	2.92	7.33	6.88	10.07	11.00	11.42	88.18	730.05
PRIO2	**1.16**	**2.76**	**6.61**	**6.48**	**8.44**	**10.23**	**10.85**	**56.00**	**451.96**
SFE-ignore	1.00	2.08	4.64	4.46	6.56	7.86	8.43	71.17	644.99
GAM-ignore	1.04	2.95	5.83	6.92	9.49	10.90	9.99	62.49	474.82
SFE-replan	1.19	1.65	3.84	4.86	5.34	6.88	6.28	49.98	478.41
GAM-replan	1.13	1.93	5.71	5.93	8.41	8.66	9.13	56.69	408.85

Table A.78 Influence of the crane-scheduling strategy on the mean vehicle-waiting time per waterside retrieval job ($\overline{\omega}^{hr+}_{wsout}$) for selected yard-block layouts and all types of RMGC systems

Scheduling strategy	Yard-block layout								
	Small	Low	Narrow	Short	Medium	Long	Wide	High	Big
Resulting $\overline{\omega}^{hr+}_{wsout}$ with the SRMGC system (s)									
FIFO	4.32	9.96	124.14	106.14	344.94	1,622.04	1,221.36	4,836.00	9,393.54
EDD	4.20	10.38	184.92	132.90	471.18	1,926.18	1,468.92	5,585.52	10,167.30
NN	3.24	9.18	140.28	107.40	306.60	949.02	824.34	4,031.46	7,176.36
PRIO1	3.48	6.24	95.52	73.92	284.82	1,204.14	992.34	4,370.10	8,023.26
PRIO2	**3.24**	**5.52**	**78.00**	**56.04**	**198.72**	**789.12**	**671.58**	**3,180.30**	**4,959.72**
SFE-ignore	3.06	6.96	88.92	63.42	258.24	1,204.50	1,003.86	4,515.54	8,518.44
GAM-ignore	2.82	6.60	92.52	64.56	224.64	951.90	788.04	4,235.22	7,430.16
SFE-replan	3.66	5.04	47.46	34.98	92.16	240.12	202.32	1,757.40	2,604.84
GAM-replan	3.54	5.10	67.26	43.98	159.66	447.72	362.88	2,055.18	2,427.60
Resulting $\overline{\omega}^{hr+}_{wsout}$ with the TRMGC system (s)									
FIFO	3.24	6.60	28.50	20.88	42.60	75.12	67.44	711.42	4,085.10
EDD	2.52	4.86	30.24	23.58	48.06	111.18	87.72	985.74	4,426.20
NN	3.18	6.00	31.56	26.46	53.52	104.04	97.38	803.34	5,056.92
PRIO1	2.40	4.14	19.50	15.18	27.42	55.68	46.62	631.02	3,837.84
PRIO2	**2.28**	**4.14**	**15.06**	**13.20**	**25.80**	**48.48**	**42.12**	**486.30**	**3,019.80**
SFE-ignore	2.22	5.70	15.36	12.60	25.14	41.34	36.96	572.34	3,409.20
GAM-ignore	2.52	5.52	15.72	12.72	23.04	44.46	36.60	450.24	2,911.68
SFE-replan	2.16	5.16	13.86	10.20	19.32	32.04	24.66	354.60	2,842.26
GAM-replan	2.82	3.42	14.22	10.86	17.10	32.64	28.86	356.16	2,452.50
Resulting $\overline{\omega}^{hr+}_{wsout}$ with the DRMGC system (s)									
FIFO	2.88	6.18	26.04	24.48	50.28	106.02	86.58	1,047.12	5,069.76
EDD	2.34	6.90	30.00	27.60	54.42	111.60	117.30	1,219.80	5,215.14
NN	3.30	5.64	28.44	25.02	51.00	89.04	93.66	655.44	4,080.06
PRIO1	2.64	5.70	21.84	21.60	34.56	60.30	65.58	760.74	3,880.08
PRIO2	**2.76**	**5.34**	**20.10**	**18.72**	**30.78**	**47.46**	**46.26**	**510.54**	**2,758.62**
SFE-ignore	1.68	4.50	15.00	12.54	27.36	44.16	43.20	641.46	3,814.56
GAM-ignore	2.10	4.44	21.72	18.84	35.58	57.54	55.68	646.80	3,714.24
SFE-replan	1.62	3.66	14.52	13.32	21.84	37.56	36.18	416.76	3,014.52
GAM-replan	2.52	5.58	18.36	15.90	28.68	48.42	47.34	549.24	3,226.98
Resulting $\overline{\omega}^{hr+}_{wsout}$ with the TriRMGC system (s)									
FIFO	3.54	5.16	15.54	15.42	25.20	32.46	33.12	200.70	1,938.48
EDD	3.00	5.16	14.10	14.82	23.76	32.94	34.62	304.38	2,125.50
NN	3.18	4.86	15.54	15.42	26.40	36.48	42.54	212.10	1,693.80
PRIO1	2.46	5.64	14.28	13.32	19.44	21.18	22.08	173.22	1,442.88
PRIO2	**2.22**	**5.34**	**12.90**	**12.54**	**16.32**	**19.68**	**20.94**	**109.68**	**883.26**
SFE-ignore	1.92	4.02	9.06	8.64	12.66	15.12	16.26	139.50	1,273.20
GAM-ignore	1.98	5.70	11.34	13.44	18.30	21.00	19.26	122.58	939.12
SFE-replan	2.28	3.18	7.50	9.42	10.32	13.26	12.12	98.10	948.12
GAM-replan	2.16	3.72	11.16	11.46	16.26	16.68	17.64	111.00	809.10

Table A.79 Influence of the crane-scheduling strategy on the mean crane-waiting time in the handover areas ($\overline{\overline{\omega}}^{\text{hr}-}_{\text{total}}$) for selected yard-block layouts and all types of RMGC systems

Scheduling strategy	Yard-block layout								
	Small	Low	Narrow	Short	Medium	Long	Wide	High	Big
Resulting $\overline{\overline{\omega}}^{\text{hr}-}_{\text{total}}$ with the SRMGC system (s)									
FIFO	124.92	95.64	66.60	69.90	43.98	23.82	27.36	15.18	7.08
EDD	124.50	96.12	63.42	66.84	40.80	21.06	24.60	13.50	6.42
NN	125.58	96.00	67.38	69.36	46.02	28.26	31.02	20.88	14.70
PRIO1	124.50	95.58	63.54	66.66	41.64	22.20	25.56	14.10	6.66
PRIO2	**124.38**	**94.92**	**63.84**	**67.26**	**41.52**	**22.86**	**25.80**	**14.64**	**7.08**
SFE-ignore	124.14	95.22	65.58	68.16	42.30	23.34	26.70	14.82	6.84
GAM-ignore	123.60	96.36	64.86	67.86	43.44	23.64	26.94	14.70	7.08
SFE-replan	124.02	95.64	63.54	67.74	41.94	23.10	26.22	15.06	7.92
GAM-replan	124.02	95.10	64.08	67.14	42.24	23.10	26.52	14.64	7.98
Resulting $\overline{\overline{\omega}}^{\text{hr}-}_{\text{total}}$ with the TRMGC system (s)									
FIFO	136.20	113.46	89.40	92.46	71.46	53.10	56.10	43.14	11.64
EDD	136.02	112.68	88.02	90.48	68.82	49.80	52.86	38.34	10.20
NN	135.66	112.86	89.40	91.74	69.54	51.66	54.60	41.82	16.56
PRIO1	136.02	112.44	89.04	90.36	68.82	50.10	53.34	38.34	10.32
PRIO2	**135.84**	**112.32**	**87.84**	**91.26**	**67.86**	**50.28**	**53.40**	**38.58**	**10.56**
SFE-ignore	136.02	112.32	88.44	91.44	69.90	51.24	53.94	39.66	10.74
GAM-ignore	135.12	112.38	88.50	90.30	69.00	51.24	53.88	39.96	11.04
SFE-replan	136.20	111.30	89.22	91.32	69.00	51.00	53.52	39.90	10.74
GAM-replan	136.44	111.06	88.44	91.14	69.30	51.30	53.58	40.26	10.92
Resulting $\overline{\overline{\omega}}^{\text{hr}-}_{\text{total}}$ with the DRMGC system (s)									
FIFO	139.38	117.66	97.32	96.90	76.44	58.02	58.44	44.88	12.06
EDD	138.12	117.48	94.50	95.82	74.28	56.34	56.82	42.06	10.86
NN	138.30	118.20	96.84	96.06	77.58	60.30	60.30	49.14	19.62
PRIO1	139.50	116.52	95.70	95.58	74.04	57.06	57.18	44.34	11.40
PRIO2	**139.32**	**117.48**	**95.28**	**95.46**	**75.18**	**57.24**	**57.66**	**44.52**	**12.60**
SFE-ignore	130.98	110.22	88.68	89.40	70.50	54.60	54.90	43.32	12.66
GAM-ignore	130.44	110.34	90.18	90.24	72.54	56.04	56.94	44.82	13.08
SFE-replan	131.64	108.36	87.84	88.44	68.94	53.22	54.54	42.84	12.66
GAM-replan	132.36	109.86	90.30	90.12	70.50	54.90	55.32	43.74	12.72
Resulting $\overline{\overline{\omega}}^{\text{hr}-}_{\text{total}}$ with the TriRMGC system (s)									
FIFO	141.36	122.88	104.04	101.58	85.08	70.08	70.56	61.38	27.06
EDD	141.30	122.82	102.54	102.54	83.94	68.76	69.30	58.08	22.44
NN	141.54	122.46	101.88	101.34	84.18	69.36	69.84	60.78	29.46
PRIO1	141.00	121.20	102.72	100.86	83.94	68.34	68.76	57.90	23.04
PRIO2	**140.40**	**121.98**	**103.44**	**101.10**	**84.00**	**68.22**	**68.64**	**58.38**	**23.88**
SFE-ignore	128.40	108.66	91.74	90.90	74.46	60.12	60.72	51.84	22.62
GAM-ignore	130.26	111.48	94.32	94.08	77.34	63.78	64.32	55.20	24.72
SFE-replan	128.28	107.94	91.02	89.82	73.74	59.94	60.00	51.66	21.96
GAM-replan	130.92	110.28	94.14	91.86	77.40	63.24	63.36	53.88	23.88

Table A.80 Influence of the crane-scheduling strategy on the mean crane-empty-movement time per job ($\overline{\overline{m}}_{\text{total}}^{\text{xye}}$) for selected yard-block layouts and all types of RMGC systems

Scheduling strategy	Yard-block layout								
	Small	Low	Narrow	Short	Medium	Long	Wide	High	Big
Resulting $\overline{\overline{m}}_{\text{total}}^{\text{xye}}$ with the SRMGC system (s)									
FIFO	26.18	32.29	28.53	24.23	28.88	33.59	29.49	27.81	33.20
EDD	26.25	32.11	28.49	24.11	29.03	33.91	29.67	27.88	33.44
NN	26.03	31.43	25.92	22.39	25.13	27.67	24.86	21.38	24.47
PRIO1	26.14	31.92	27.48	23.52	27.46	30.84	27.56	25.80	30.11
PRIO2	**26.05**	**31.87**	**26.97**	**23.22**	**26.63**	**29.48**	**26.57**	**23.73**	**27.72**
SFE-ignore	26.19	31.81	27.62	23.56	27.35	30.85	27.36	25.11	29.38
GAM-ignore	26.19	31.72	27.55	23.52	27.32	30.28	27.08	24.45	28.77
SFE-replan	26.14	31.85	27.11	23.20	26.75	29.26	26.41	23.07	26.72
GAM-replan	26.15	31.72	27.09	23.23	26.70	29.28	26.43	23.44	26.82
Resulting $\overline{\overline{m}}_{\text{total}}^{\text{xye}}$ with the TRMGC system (s)									
FIFO	23.24	28.29	34.24	30.39	34.59	39.02	35.01	39.69	44.30
EDD	23.28	28.38	34.45	30.72	34.93	39.77	35.80	40.61	44.92
NN	23.32	28.19	33.30	29.66	33.27	37.06	33.45	33.10	33.61
PRIO1	23.30	28.27	33.92	30.33	34.23	38.42	34.71	38.45	42.48
PRIO2	**23.34**	**28.35**	**33.76**	**30.25**	**34.07**	**38.12**	**34.64**	**37.21**	**40.77**
SFE-ignore	24.56	29.14	33.93	30.25	33.90	38.04	34.41	37.45	40.84
GAM-ignore	24.52	29.22	34.08	30.49	34.31	38.06	34.45	36.57	38.77
SFE-replan	24.54	29.39	33.42	29.81	33.42	37.27	33.93	35.40	38.21
GAM-replan	24.65	29.44	33.20	29.78	33.35	37.14	33.69	34.66	35.87
Resulting $\overline{\overline{m}}_{\text{total}}^{\text{xye}}$ with the DRMGC system (s)									
FIFO	55.43	70.00	65.37	65.48	66.17	67.08	65.90	60.64	58.98
EDD	54.86	69.09	63.68	63.81	64.43	64.77	63.52	58.26	57.17
NN	55.20	67.71	62.16	62.19	61.55	60.61	59.62	50.18	43.20
PRIO1	55.30	68.36	63.53	63.71	63.23	62.59	62.03	54.91	50.26
PRIO2	**55.77**	**69.14**	**62.73**	**62.89**	**62.78**	**61.85**	**60.88**	**52.25**	**45.15**
SFE-ignore	46.40	56.61	53.73	52.12	54.16	55.12	53.41	47.28	42.74
GAM-ignore	48.66	60.80	57.22	55.94	57.54	57.66	55.88	48.52	44.07
SFE-replan	45.90	56.56	51.98	50.67	52.04	52.82	50.50	44.15	38.80
GAM-replan	46.76	60.00	54.32	53.27	53.96	54.28	52.61	45.71	40.52
Resulting $\overline{\overline{m}}_{\text{total}}^{\text{xye}}$ with the TriRMGC system (s)									
FIFO	51.33	65.23	70.02	69.77	71.67	73.17	72.24	72.28	70.40
EDD	50.58	64.28	69.01	68.78	70.39	71.64	70.75	70.47	68.44
NN	50.59	64.74	68.36	67.77	69.44	69.81	69.07	64.32	56.07
PRIO1	51.36	65.42	68.87	68.64	70.24	70.98	70.48	68.33	63.68
PRIO2	**51.55**	**65.81**	**69.11**	**68.63**	**70.12**	**70.81**	**70.15**	**66.70**	**60.22**
SFE-ignore	47.40	58.54	59.82	58.99	61.49	63.81	62.69	60.39	57.46
GAM-ignore	48.56	61.12	63.62	63.08	65.19	66.29	65.89	61.61	56.31
SFE-replan	47.15	58.10	59.16	57.37	60.19	62.02	60.62	57.36	53.99
GAM-replan	48.73	59.90	60.97	59.77	62.28	63.43	62.74	58.77	53.50

Table A.81 Influence of the crane-scheduling strategy on the mean crane-interference time per job ($\overline{\overline{m}}_{\text{total}}^{\text{cit}}$) for selected yard-block layouts and all types of RMGC systems

Scheduling strategy	Yard-block layout								
	Small	Low	Narrow	Short	Medium	Long	Wide	High	Big
Resulting $\overline{\overline{m}}_{\text{total}}^{\text{cit}}$ with the SRMGC system (s)									
FIFO	0.00	0.00	0.00	0.00	0.00	0.00	0.00	0.00	0.00
EDD	0.00	0.00	0.00	0.00	0.00	0.00	0.00	0.00	0.00
NN	0.00	0.00	0.00	0.00	0.00	0.00	0.00	0.00	0.00
PRIO1	0.00	0.00	0.00	0.00	0.00	0.00	0.00	0.00	0.00
PRIO2	**0.00**	**0.00**	**0.00**	**0.00**	**0.00**	**0.00**	**0.00**	**0.00**	**0.00**
SFE-ignore	0.00	0.00	0.00	0.00	0.00	0.00	0.00	0.00	0.00
GAM-ignore	0.00	0.00	0.00	0.00	0.00	0.00	0.00	0.00	0.00
SFE-replan	0.00	0.00	0.00	0.00	0.00	0.00	0.00	0.00	0.00
GAM-replan	0.00	0.00	0.00	0.00	0.00	0.00	0.00	0.00	0.00
Resulting $\overline{\overline{m}}_{\text{total}}^{\text{cit}}$ with the TRMGC system (s)									
FIFO	2.14	2.01	11.88	12.20	11.77	11.90	11.73	19.56	20.33
EDD	2.19	2.15	12.28	12.49	12.44	12.58	12.65	20.65	20.89
NN	2.22	2.07	11.76	12.04	11.70	11.57	11.56	17.94	17.57
PRIO1	2.22	2.04	11.86	12.42	12.06	12.07	12.16	19.97	20.41
PRIO2	**2.22**	**2.10**	**11.92**	**12.42**	**12.16**	**11.92**	**12.14**	**19.43**	**20.71**
SFE-ignore	3.44	3.04	10.70	10.94	10.63	10.58	10.75	16.98	17.37
GAM-ignore	3.42	3.10	10.82	11.25	10.94	10.65	10.73	16.27	16.02
SFE-replan	3.42	3.23	10.43	10.65	10.31	10.14	10.44	15.31	15.28
GAM-replan	3.39	3.28	10.35	10.57	10.17	10.08	10.28	15.06	14.17
Resulting $\overline{\overline{m}}_{\text{total}}^{\text{cit}}$ with the DRMGC system (s)									
FIFO	30.28	38.87	37.18	41.20	37.11	32.26	35.26	31.58	24.13
EDD	29.80	38.12	35.41	39.78	35.78	30.14	33.31	29.62	22.91
NN	30.68	37.11	35.48	39.25	35.38	30.73	33.41	29.65	23.12
PRIO1	30.63	37.62	35.89	40.22	35.57	29.98	33.27	29.08	21.16
PRIO2	**31.09**	**38.13**	**35.30**	**39.74**	**35.31**	**29.73**	**32.78**	**28.21**	**20.21**
SFE-ignore	18.88	24.49	24.57	26.58	25.20	21.72	23.93	20.65	13.20
GAM-ignore	20.41	27.84	28.69	31.00	28.83	24.29	26.46	23.51	14.25
SFE-replan	18.33	23.68	22.98	25.30	23.22	19.87	21.54	18.23	10.58
GAM-replan	19.48	27.28	26.09	28.14	25.55	21.69	23.54	19.71	11.75
Resulting $\overline{\overline{m}}_{\text{total}}^{\text{cit}}$ with the TriRMGC system (s)									
FIFO	31.58	40.08	49.28	53.30	50.81	46.41	50.05	52.39	45.32
EDD	30.47	39.20	48.28	52.09	49.55	45.09	48.42	50.65	43.32
NN	30.27	39.33	48.21	51.52	49.16	44.79	48.10	49.58	42.98
PRIO1	30.76	40.30	48.68	52.52	49.40	44.88	48.69	49.91	42.27
PRIO2	**31.02**	**40.31**	**48.66**	**52.32**	**49.18**	**44.71**	**47.95**	**49.43**	**41.62**
SFE-ignore	20.09	27.44	35.50	38.43	36.67	34.48	37.21	39.94	34.17
GAM-ignore	22.70	31.93	41.01	45.14	43.09	39.09	42.04	42.14	33.28
SFE-replan	20.32	26.88	34.21	36.70	35.05	32.77	34.39	36.91	30.93
GAM-replan	22.37	29.81	37.08	40.40	39.09	35.48	38.16	39.19	31.37

Table A.82 Influence of the crane-scheduling strategy on the crane workload during the simulation horizon in terms of performed jobs ($\overline{|J|}$) for selected yard-block layouts and all types of RMGC systems

Scheduling strategy	Yard-block layout								
	Small	Low	Narrow	Short	Medium	Long	Wide	High	Big
Resulting $\overline{\lvert J\rvert}$ with the SRMGC system (jobs)									
FIFO	1,874.2	3,214.9	6,558.9	6,733.3	8,573.8	10,320.3	10,611.9	12,978.4	13,468.8
EDD	1,867.5	3,206.5	6,592.9	6,774.8	8,635.7	10,474.9	10,750.7	13,114.9	13,446.2
NN	1,872.0	3,211.6	6,589.2	6,789.6	8,726.3	10,433.0	10,742.6	13,183.0	13,477.8
PRIO1	1,869.2	3,209.1	6,625.3	6,785.8	8,675.0	10,422.2	10,735.1	13,221.4	13,618.7
PRIO2	**1,871.8**	**3,208.8**	**6,596.5**	**6,792.8**	**8,683.4**	**10,466.3**	**10,776.3**	**13,369.4**	**13,711.1**
SFE-ignore	1,860.7	3,220.2	6,564.4	6,761.6	8,694.3	10,463.0	10,739.3	13,266.6	13,706.0
GAM-ignore	1,861.8	3,219.4	6,561.2	6,780.2	8,695.5	10,463.3	10,729.2	13,368.9	13,697.9
SFE-replan	1,867.5	3,206.8	6,580.4	6,804.7	8,664.3	10,410.1	10,691.5	13,458.3	13,367.1
GAM-replan	1,866.4	3,214.8	6,579.8	6,786.7	8,698.7	10,468.5	10,742.1	13,373.3	13,362.0
Resulting $\overline{\lvert J\rvert}$ with the TRMGC system (jobs)									
FIFO	1,903.7	3,231.7	6,617.9	6,868.2	8,767.5	10,583.0	10,864.6	15,067.5	21,168.3
EDD	1,900.4	3,232.2	6,594.1	6,842.4	8,763.6	10,612.4	10,892.5	15,181.9	21,083.0
NN	1,903.6	3,234.9	6,615.4	6,835.7	8,746.0	10,584.8	10,873.0	15,178.4	20,866.6
PRIO1	1,900.7	3,220.3	6,647.1	6,838.6	8,721.1	10,599.4	10,909.9	15,248.4	21,313.6
PRIO2	**1,903.5**	**3,224.1**	**6,592.4**	**6,857.8**	**8,784.5**	**10,615.3**	**10,900.6**	**15,170.8**	**21,104.9**
SFE-ignore	1,908.2	3,230.7	6,627.5	6,833.5	8,762.7	10,618.7	10,880.9	15,285.2	21,284.3
GAM-ignore	1,907.2	3,233.6	6,587.9	6,839.7	8,755.9	10,618.5	10,889.8	15,290.1	21,512.4
SFE-replan	1,910.0	3,233.7	6,603.9	6,826.5	8,763.4	10,591.8	10,862.9	15,221.6	21,578.9
GAM-replan	1,907.6	3,231.9	6,636.8	6,810.7	8,744.3	10,589.4	10,893.0	15,321.1	21,901.7
Resulting $\overline{\lvert J\rvert}$ with the DRMGC system (jobs)									
FIFO	1,896.5	3,223.5	6,582.7	6,834.1	8,723.6	10,558.2	10,804.7	14,862.3	20,067.3
EDD	1,898.9	3,216.4	6,607.8	6,853.7	8,681.1	10,566.8	10,911.5	15,127.5	20,173.1
NN	1,911.3	3,221.1	6,646.0	6,858.1	8,759.2	10,580.4	10,836.9	15,127.9	20,599.1
PRIO1	1,902.6	3,225.9	6,623.6	6,830.5	8,733.5	10,587.6	10,870.5	14,986.3	20,829.9
PRIO2	**1,901.9**	**3,222.4**	**6,623.5**	**6,834.0**	**8,713.7**	**10,605.3**	**10,893.6**	**15,175.5**	**21,213.5**
SFE-ignore	1,905.8	3,228.3	6,620.7	6,831.5	8,727.7	10,571.6	10,829.6	15,156.9	21,384.0
GAM-ignore	1,902.0	3,233.2	6,634.0	6,844.0	8,727.2	10,559.1	10,874.1	15,026.6	21,251.6
SFE-replan	1,904.0	3,221.2	6,602.9	6,840.8	8,724.9	10,570.4	10,866.5	15,138.9	21,960.6
GAM-replan	1,902.8	3,228.3	6,605.4	6,836.2	8,722.5	10,587.3	10,867.3	15,170.5	21,697.1
Resulting $\overline{\lvert J\rvert}$ with the TriRMGC system (jobs)									
FIFO	1,907.7	3,244.1	6,623.1	6,817.1	8,684.3	10,538.8	10,870.2	15,103.9	22,786.4
EDD	1,906.7	3,241.0	6,606.3	6,841.8	8,748.2	10,598.0	10,897.8	15,283.0	22,997.3
NN	1,912.1	3,244.9	6,619.7	6,838.7	8,737.8	10,543.3	10,876.6	15,313.0	22,806.0
PRIO1	1,911.5	3,248.8	6,609.8	6,833.9	8,738.2	10,575.6	10,909.5	15,340.3	23,055.9
PRIO2	**1,907.0**	**3,249.5**	**6,614.4**	**6,831.8**	**8,732.5**	**10,583.9**	**10,895.8**	**15,192.1**	**23,097.9**
SFE-ignore	1,907.5	3,247.6	6,574.9	6,820.2	8,715.2	10,557.3	10,889.9	15,299.6	23,091.0
GAM-ignore	1,912.2	3,247.6	6,640.1	6,878.4	8,736.0	10,572.7	10,883.2	15,330.4	23,249.5
SFE-replan	1,908.5	3,241.1	6,630.0	6,812.4	8,731.7	10,574.4	10,870.5	15,303.6	23,366.7
GAM-replan	1,907.2	3,237.9	6,635.1	6,819.5	8,695.5	10,574.1	10,900.1	15,364.2	23,445.4

Table A.83 Influence of the crane-scheduling strategy on the container accessibility ($\overline{\overline{\psi}}$), in terms of the mean number of shuffle moves per retrieval job, for selected yard-block layouts and all types of RMGC systems

Scheduling strategy	Yard-block layout								
	Small	Low	Narrow	Short	Medium	Long	Wide	High	Big
Resulting $\overline{\overline{\psi}}$ with the SRMGC system (jobs)									
FIFO	0.322	0.304	1.121	1.104	1.085	1.069	1.066	1.567	1.161
EDD	0.317	0.299	1.131	1.117	1.095	1.094	1.076	1.585	1.154
NN	0.320	0.301	1.129	1.120	1.111	1.077	1.080	1.616	1.130
PRIO1	0.320	0.300	1.141	1.112	1.096	1.077	1.074	1.598	1.150
PRIO2	**0.322**	**0.300**	**1.135**	**1.120**	**1.103**	**1.083**	**1.083**	**1.606**	**1.144**
SFE-ignore	0.312	0.308	1.117	1.112	1.112	1.088	1.082	1.622	1.181
GAM-ignore	0.313	0.307	1.121	1.126	1.112	1.087	1.078	1.645	1.180
SFE-replan	0.314	0.299	1.126	1.128	1.099	1.088	1.076	1.707	1.148
GAM-replan	0.313	0.304	1.124	1.118	1.104	1.100	1.083	1.677	1.156
Resulting $\overline{\overline{\psi}}$ with the TRMGC system (jobs)									
FIFO	0.324	0.298	1.132	1.138	1.127	1.091	1.085	1.750	1.676
EDD	0.320	0.300	1.127	1.126	1.117	1.100	1.086	1.764	1.679
NN	0.323	0.301	1.127	1.121	1.115	1.092	1.081	1.772	1.658
PRIO1	0.321	0.294	1.140	1.122	1.109	1.096	1.089	1.771	1.690
PRIO2	**0.324**	**0.296**	**1.127**	**1.130**	**1.130**	**1.097**	**1.090**	**1.762**	**1.675**
SFE-ignore	0.332	0.299	1.139	1.122	1.116	1.099	1.090	1.780	1.701
GAM-ignore	0.329	0.300	1.123	1.125	1.119	1.096	1.087	1.772	1.710
SFE-replan	0.333	0.300	1.126	1.121	1.119	1.090	1.080	1.760	1.718
GAM-replan	0.327	0.299	1.141	1.109	1.119	1.090	1.087	1.780	1.742
Resulting $\overline{\overline{\psi}}$ with the DRMGC system (jobs)									
FIFO	0.317	0.294	1.122	1.120	1.119	1.087	1.072	1.714	1.611
EDD	0.319	0.291	1.133	1.126	1.096	1.085	1.093	1.762	1.620
NN	0.334	0.293	1.146	1.133	1.123	1.090	1.076	1.759	1.636
PRIO1	0.323	0.296	1.136	1.116	1.121	1.090	1.084	1.745	1.654
PRIO2	**0.320**	**0.297**	**1.137**	**1.118**	**1.107**	**1.093**	**1.087**	**1.753**	**1.673**
SFE-ignore	0.327	0.297	1.131	1.120	1.109	1.092	1.076	1.769	1.702
GAM-ignore	0.320	0.302	1.135	1.121	1.108	1.086	1.084	1.761	1.702
SFE-replan	0.321	0.294	1.130	1.123	1.113	1.091	1.084	1.760	1.736
GAM-replan	0.323	0.298	1.121	1.127	1.114	1.094	1.083	1.765	1.737
Resulting $\overline{\overline{\psi}}$ with the TriRMGC system (jobs)									
FIFO	0.332	0.298	1.132	1.116	1.108	1.077	1.080	1.753	1.736
EDD	0.327	0.293	1.123	1.118	1.121	1.092	1.087	1.781	1.752
NN	0.334	0.294	1.137	1.114	1.114	1.082	1.083	1.782	1.744
PRIO1	0.331	0.297	1.121	1.125	1.118	1.091	1.087	1.779	1.745
PRIO2	**0.325**	**0.298**	**1.122**	**1.123**	**1.113**	**1.092**	**1.090**	**1.763**	**1.758**
SFE-ignore	0.328	0.297	1.113	1.114	1.107	1.084	1.088	1.771	1.757
GAM-ignore	0.332	0.299	1.133	1.135	1.116	1.085	1.085	1.780	1.763
SFE-replan	0.330	0.291	1.126	1.115	1.111	1.088	1.080	1.771	1.781
GAM-replan	0.329	0.292	1.133	1.119	1.109	1.086	1.084	1.783	1.774

Table A.84 Influence of the maximum number κ_{sfe}^{jobs} of plannable jobs by the SFE method on the mean XT-waiting time ($\overline{\omega}_{ls}^{hr+}$) for different types of RMGC systems and online policies

	Ignore				Replan			
κ_{sfe}^{jobs}	SRMGC	TRMGC	DRMGC	TriRMGC	SRMGC	TRMGC	DRMGC	TriRMGC
1	304.54	98.45	142.71	79.69	304.54	98.45	142.71	79.69
2	366.44	95.46	136.97	79.42	407.93	96.11	129.78	79.24
3	386.26	95.98	138.91	79.46	442.63	94.03	126.30	77.49
4	387.86	96.43	138.85	79.02	458.06	94.73	125.27	78.10
5	394.74	94.97	142.04	79.56	444.10	94.28	123.65	77.24
6	406.70	94.93	139.32	79.08	445.58	93.10	125.24	79.54
7	407.97	94.65	142.23	80.20	471.55	93.92	122.24	78.84

Table A.85 Influence of the maximum number κ_{sfe}^{jobs} of plannable jobs by the SFE method on the mean SC-waiting time ($\overline{\omega}_{ws}^{hr+}$) for different types of RMGC systems and online policies

	Ignore				Replan			
κ_{sfe}^{jobs}	SRMGC	TRMGC	DRMGC	TriRMGC	SRMGC	TRMGC	DRMGC	TriRMGC
1	244.36	24.73	28.03	12.30	244.36	25.31	28.03	12.30
2	173.61	13.90	15.83	7.71	76.54	14.24	15.57	6.71
3	155.72	12.58	15.43	6.66	64.48	10.25	12.50	6.20
4	139.39	12.35	14.69	6.09	52.82	9.47	12.51	5.66
5	133.99	12.94	14.10	6.56	47.66	9.97	11.30	5.34
6	121.26	11.29	12.98	6.90	44.03	9.28	11.59	6.05
7	118.62	10.98	13.27	6.68	39.04	8.82	12.00	5.43

Table A.86 Influence of the maximum number κ_{sfe}^{jobs} of plannable jobs by the SFE method on the mean vehicle-waiting time per waterside retrieval job ($\overline{\omega}_{wsout}^{hr+}$) for different types of RMGC systems and online policies

	Ignore				Replan			
κ_{sfe}^{jobs}	SRMGC	TRMGC	DRMGC	TriRMGC	SRMGC	TRMGC	DRMGC	TriRMGC
1	282.96	53.28	47.58	21.00	282.96	49.02	47.58	19.44
2	336.06	26.94	30.66	14.88	148.02	27.60	30.12	12.96
3	301.38	24.36	29.88	12.90	124.86	19.86	24.24	12.00
4	269.58	23.88	28.50	11.76	102.06	18.36	24.24	10.92
5	258.24	25.14	27.36	12.66	92.16	19.32	21.84	10.32
6	234.78	21.90	25.14	13.32	85.26	18.00	22.50	11.70
7	229.86	21.30	25.68	12.90	75.54	17.10	23.28	10.50

Table A.87 Influence of the maximum number $\kappa_{\text{sfe}}^{\text{jobs}}$ of plannable jobs by the SFE method on the mean crane-waiting time in the handover areas ($\overline{\overline{\omega}}_{\text{total}}^{\text{hr}-}$) for different types of RMGC systems and online policies

	Ignore				Replan			
$\kappa_{\text{sfe}}^{\text{jobs}}$	SRMGC	TRMGC	DRMGC	TriRMGC	SRMGC	TRMGC	DRMGC	TriRMGC
1	41.94	68.16	66.24	71.22	41.94	68.04	66.24	70.92
2	41.46	68.64	68.64	73.56	42.24	68.58	68.10	73.50
3	43.14	68.94	69.12	74.64	41.76	68.58	68.58	73.92
4	43.14	68.58	70.32	73.98	42.00	68.70	68.94	73.38
5	42.30	69.90	70.50	74.46	41.94	69.00	68.94	73.74
6	43.56	69.78	69.96	74.34	42.06	69.00	69.66	73.98
7	43.74	69.66	69.66	73.98	41.70	69.06	69.84	73.74

Table A.88 Influence of the maximum number $\kappa_{\text{sfe}}^{\text{jobs}}$ of plannable jobs by the SFE method on the mean crane-empty-movement time per job ($\overline{\overline{m}}_{\text{total}}^{\text{xye}}$) for different types of RMGC systems and online policies

	Ignore				Replan			
$\kappa_{\text{sfe}}^{\text{jobs}}$	SRMGC	TRMGC	DRMGC	TriRMGC	SRMGC	TRMGC	DRMGC	TriRMGC
1	27.17	30.40	53.54	58.14	27.17	30.55	53.54	58.00
2	27.96	34.04	55.42	61.95	27.08	33.90	52.05	60.37
3	27.81	34.15	54.17	62.08	27.03	33.65	52.23	60.05
4	27.57	34.01	54.38	61.80	26.86	33.62	51.81	60.26
5	27.35	33.90	54.16	61.49	26.75	33.42	52.04	60.19
6	27.37	33.90	53.90	61.58	26.63	33.58	52.07	60.23
7	27.22	33.79	53.83	62.02	26.53	33.52	51.82	59.87

Table A.89 Influence of the maximum number $\kappa_{\text{sfe}}^{\text{jobs}}$ of plannable jobs by the SFE method on the mean crane-interference time per job ($\overline{\overline{m}}_{\text{total}}^{\text{cit}}$) for different types of RMGC systems and online policies

	Ignore				Replan			
$\kappa_{\text{sfe}}^{\text{jobs}}$	SRMGC	TRMGC	DRMGC	TriRMGC	SRMGC	TRMGC	DRMGC	TriRMGC
1	0.00	7.61	24.33	33.42	0.00	7.64	24.33	33.25
2	0.00	10.79	25.83	37.37	0.00	10.77	23.25	35.40
3	0.00	10.89	24.99	37.12	0.00	10.45	23.37	34.93
4	0.00	10.82	25.27	36.99	0.00	10.51	23.01	35.16
5	0.00	10.63	25.20	36.67	0.00	10.31	23.22	35.05
6	0.00	10.47	24.72	36.73	0.00	10.44	23.26	35.34
7	0.00	10.57	24.82	37.11	0.00	10.36	23.02	34.87

Table A.90 Influence of the maximum number $\kappa_{\text{sfe}}^{\text{jobs}}$ of plannable jobs by the SFE method on the crane workload during the simulation horizon in terms of performed jobs ($\overline{|J|}$) for different types of RMGC systems and online policies

	Ignore				Replan			
$\kappa_{\text{sfe}}^{\text{jobs}}$	SRMGC	TRMGC	DRMGC	TriRMGC	SRMGC	TRMGC	DRMGC	TriRMGC
1	8,677.7	8,771.0	8,741.2	8,763.3	8,677.7	8,757.5	8,741.2	8,764.8
2	8,701.0	8,754.9	8,724.2	8,725.6	8,672.6	8,764.8	8,778.6	8,720.5
3	8,704.1	8,749.1	8,735.2	8,724.7	8,681.8	8,732.5	8,752.1	8,748.7
4	8,666.5	8,763.5	8,723.3	8,713.4	8,672.0	8,767.9	8,754.2	8,715.5
5	8,694.3	8,762.7	8,727.7	8,715.2	8,664.3	8,763.4	8,724.9	8,731.7
6	8,651.0	8,706.9	8,728.4	8,726.0	8,664.2	8,756.3	8,759.4	8,725.5
7	8,690.9	8,756.5	8,733.8	8,713.3	8,683.9	8,762.4	8,744.4	8,738.8

Table A.91 Influence of the maximum number $\kappa_{\text{sfe}}^{\text{jobs}}$ of plannable jobs by the SFE method on the container accessibility ($\overline{\overline{\psi}}$), in terms of the mean number of shuffle moves per retrieval job, for different types of RMGC systems and online policies

	Ignore				Replan			
$\kappa_{\text{sfe}}^{\text{jobs}}$	SRMGC	TRMGC	DRMGC	TriRMGC	SRMGC	TRMGC	DRMGC	TriRMGC
1	1.103	1.126	1.118	1.122	1.103	1.119	1.118	1.127
2	1.110	1.118	1.110	1.114	1.098	1.120	1.127	1.116
3	1.110	1.118	1.117	1.108	1.108	1.113	1.118	1.116
4	1.094	1.123	1.109	1.112	1.108	1.121	1.123	1.112
5	1.112	1.116	1.109	1.107	1.099	1.119	1.113	1.111
6	1.092	1.102	1.112	1.110	1.098	1.119	1.120	1.113
7	1.105	1.118	1.111	1.110	1.104	1.121	1.115	1.114

A.5.8 Influence of the Crane-Routing Strategy

Table A.92 Influence of the crane-routing strategy on the mean vehicle-waiting time ($\overline{\overline{\omega}}_{\text{total}}^{\text{hr+}}$) for selected yard-block layouts with the DRMGC and TriRMGC systems

		Yard-block layout								
CCP	HAC	Small	Low	Narrow	Short	Medium	Long	Wide	High	Big
Resulting $\overline{\overline{\omega}}_{\text{total}}^{\text{hr+}}$ with the SRMGC system (s)										
		28.26	**41.28**	**117.06**	**100.44**	**198.96**	**561.06**	**484.56**	**1,861.32**	**3,269.94**
Resulting $\overline{\overline{\omega}}_{\text{total}}^{\text{hr+}}$ with the TRMGC system (s)										
		8.82	**13.44**	**38.16**	**35.58**	**48.30**	**67.44**	**61.98**	**304.08**	**1,567.38**
Resulting $\overline{\overline{\omega}}_{\text{total}}^{\text{hr+}}$ with the DRMGC system (s)										
1	–	18.54	31.38	67.14	68.70	93.30	134.46	135.72	634.14	2,215.20
2	–	16.02	25.02	58.68	60.54	76.86	104.04	106.02	453.48	1,902.00
3	–	13.68	23.40	52.86	53.88	68.70	87.90	90.48	348.30	1,594.50
4	**–**	**13.86**	**23.58**	**53.82**	**54.36**	**69.24**	**88.86**	**88.86**	**360.18**	**1,607.82**
1	√	17.04	27.24	63.00	62.88	86.88	127.80	128.10	655.20	2,253.78
2	√	13.92	22.32	53.58	56.04	70.92	97.98	98.40	470.88	1,854.30
3	√	12.78	20.46	47.88	48.54	63.00	84.78	83.94	350.76	1,606.44
4	√	12.12	20.52	49.08	47.94	62.70	84.36	83.40	360.30	1,568.28
Resulting $\overline{\overline{\omega}}_{\text{total}}^{\text{hr+}}$ with the TriRMGC system (s)										
1	–	10.74	16.02	35.94	36.60	44.28	54.00	53.58	152.10	787.86
2	–	9.42	13.38	32.82	34.08	39.78	47.88	49.68	140.64	640.08
3	–	8.94	12.72	31.98	32.04	38.70	47.34	46.92	119.94	592.20
4	**–**	**8.82**	**12.48**	**31.26**	**31.86**	**37.98**	**46.86**	**46.86**	**117.54**	**574.98**
1	√	10.44	14.28	33.84	34.92	42.06	51.30	51.84	146.64	747.24
2	√	8.76	12.54	31.32	31.92	37.50	46.26	47.70	148.20	634.08
3	√	7.62	11.34	29.16	30.06	35.76	44.22	43.56	121.14	577.14
4	√	7.80	11.22	28.98	29.94	35.82	43.92	44.64	125.04	575.58

Table A.93 Influence of the crane-routing strategy on the mean vehicle-waiting time per waterside retrieval job ($\overline{\overline{\omega}}_{\mathrm{wsout}}^{\mathrm{hr+}}$) for selected yard-block layouts with the DRMGC and TriRMGC systems

		Yard-block layout								
CCP	HAC	Small	Low	Narrow	Short	Medium	Long	Wide	High	Big
Resulting $\overline{\overline{\omega}}_{\mathrm{wsout}}^{\mathrm{hr+}}$ with the SRMGC system (s)										
		3.24	**5.52**	**78.00**	**56.04**	**198.72**	**789.12**	**671.58**	**3,180.30**	**4,959.72**
Resulting $\overline{\overline{\omega}}_{\mathrm{wsout}}^{\mathrm{hr+}}$ with the TRMGC system (s)										
		2.28	**4.14**	**15.06**	**13.20**	**25.80**	**48.48**	**42.12**	**486.30**	**3,019.80**
Resulting $\overline{\overline{\omega}}_{\mathrm{wsout}}^{\mathrm{hr+}}$ with the DRMGC system (s)										
1	–	3.00	6.48	28.08	29.58	52.92	100.56	102.18	982.62	3,652.62
2	–	3.24	4.44	24.12	22.44	36.72	64.74	68.64	670.08	3,220.50
3	–	2.10	5.28	19.38	18.36	30.78	43.32	46.62	484.38	2,735.46
4	**–**	**2.76**	**5.34**	**20.10**	**18.72**	**30.78**	**47.46**	**46.26**	**510.54**	**2,758.62**
1	√	0.60	2.22	23.34	20.82	42.84	93.12	91.62	1,029.90	3,723.84
2	√	0.96	2.10	16.14	17.22	31.20	58.44	57.06	712.62	3,130.44
3	√	1.50	2.04	12.36	12.00	22.26	43.32	43.20	498.90	2,752.44
4	√	1.14	3.12	13.50	10.50	22.50	41.58	41.58	510.18	2,677.56
Resulting $\overline{\overline{\omega}}_{\mathrm{wsout}}^{\mathrm{hr+}}$ with the TriRMGC system (s)										
1	–	2.28	6.36	14.22	15.12	21.72	25.44	25.86	162.42	1,310.58
2	–	2.04	4.56	13.32	13.74	17.88	20.22	23.46	146.16	1,013.34
3	–	2.28	5.10	13.44	12.54	17.46	21.84	21.66	112.80	930.06
4	**–**	**2.22**	**5.34**	**12.90**	**12.54**	**16.32**	**19.68**	**20.94**	**109.68**	**883.26**
1	√	1.38	1.80	8.28	9.84	13.14	19.08	18.42	150.72	1,229.22
2	√	0.72	1.92	7.08	7.38	10.44	14.52	16.86	152.52	999.96
3	√	0.48	1.86	6.36	7.14	10.92	13.50	12.06	111.54	900.18
4	√	0.78	2.04	6.12	6.72	9.90	13.08	15.06	119.22	899.46

Table A.94 Influence of the crane-routing strategy on the mean crane-waiting time in the handover areas ($\overline{\omega}_{total}^{hr-}$) for selected yard-block layouts with the DRMGC and TriRMGC systems

CCP	HAC	Yard-block layout Small	Low	Narrow	Short	Medium	Long	Wide	High	Big
Resulting $\overline{\omega}_{total}^{hr-}$ with the SRMGC system (s)										
		124.38	**94.92**	**63.84**	**67.26**	**41.52**	**22.86**	**25.80**	**14.64**	**7.08**
Resulting $\overline{\omega}_{total}^{hr-}$ with the TRMGC system (s)										
		135.84	**112.32**	**87.84**	**91.26**	**67.86**	**50.28**	**53.40**	**38.58**	**10.56**
Resulting $\overline{\omega}_{total}^{hr-}$ with the DRMGC system (s)										
1	–	136.38	114.42	92.58	92.46	69.78	51.78	51.42	38.10	9.48
2	–	139.50	117.60	94.86	94.80	73.68	56.10	55.98	42.42	11.46
3	–	137.22	117.36	95.34	95.10	75.06	56.94	57.48	44.46	12.66
4	**–**	**139.32**	**117.48**	**95.28**	**95.46**	**75.18**	**57.24**	**57.66**	**44.52**	**12.60**
1	✓	20.58	15.12	11.58	12.60	9.42	6.84	6.78	4.56	1.50
2	✓	20.70	15.48	12.48	13.26	10.14	7.38	7.68	5.04	1.86
3	✓	21.72	16.02	12.48	12.96	10.44	7.56	7.68	5.46	1.92
4	✓	22.38	16.74	12.66	13.50	10.08	7.68	7.80	5.34	2.10
Resulting $\overline{\omega}_{total}^{hr-}$ with the TriRMGC system (s)										
1	–	139.32	120.36	101.28	98.88	81.54	66.06	66.48	55.68	20.22
2	–	141.18	121.50	102.00	100.56	83.64	67.86	68.10	57.00	23.28
3	–	141.36	121.62	103.68	100.86	84.12	68.70	68.58	57.84	23.22
4	**–**	**140.40**	**121.98**	**103.44**	**101.10**	**84.00**	**68.22**	**68.64**	**58.38**	**23.88**
1	✓	31.74	26.04	21.42	24.24	19.92	15.72	17.04	13.56	5.64
2	✓	31.26	25.62	20.22	21.54	17.64	14.10	14.88	13.62	4.98
3	✓	31.86	26.04	20.40	22.20	17.94	14.28	14.88	11.22	5.16
4	✓	32.34	26.28	20.46	22.02	18.48	13.80	15.06	11.70	5.40

Table A.95 Influence of the crane-routing strategy on the mean crane-empty-movement time per job ($\overline{\overline{m}}^{xye}_{total}$) for selected yard-block layouts with the DRMGC and TriRMGC systems

CCP	HAC	Yard-block layout Small	Low	Narrow	Short	Medium	Long	Wide	High	Big
Resulting $\overline{\overline{m}}^{xye}_{total}$ with the SRMGC system (s)										
		26.05	**31.87**	**26.97**	**23.22**	**26.63**	**29.48**	**26.57**	**23.73**	**27.72**
Resulting $\overline{\overline{m}}^{xye}_{total}$ with the TRMGC system (s)										
		23.34	**28.35**	**33.76**	**30.25**	**34.07**	**38.12**	**34.64**	**37.21**	**40.77**
Resulting $\overline{\overline{m}}^{xye}_{total}$ with the DRMGC system (s)										
1	–	60.25	73.97	67.36	67.32	68.11	67.97	67.23	58.40	56.19
2	–	56.37	69.67	62.91	63.06	63.54	62.89	62.14	53.78	48.80
3	–	55.33	68.60	61.87	61.51	61.79	61.26	59.65	50.53	43.91
4	**–**	**55.77**	**69.14**	**62.73**	**62.89**	**62.78**	**61.85**	**60.88**	**52.25**	**45.15**
1	✓	155.80	157.44	117.31	116.41	105.95	96.95	95.68	75.65	60.51
2	✓	152.77	153.44	113.87	113.58	103.51	93.12	92.84	73.58	54.07
3	✓	152.58	154.70	113.61	112.80	101.93	91.84	90.81	70.79	49.32
4	✓	153.17	153.34	114.65	113.53	103.46	93.55	91.82	72.38	50.57
Resulting $\overline{\overline{m}}^{xye}_{total}$ with the TriRMGC system (s)										
1	–	53.22	68.00	69.98	70.25	71.93	72.98	71.68	68.19	62.75
2	–	51.24	65.73	68.89	67.51	70.50	70.94	70.19	66.48	60.81
3	–	51.69	65.68	68.88	68.32	69.89	70.57	69.83	66.24	59.63
4	**–**	**51.55**	**65.81**	**69.11**	**68.63**	**70.12**	**70.81**	**70.15**	**66.70**	**60.22**
1	✓	143.01	147.81	119.52	115.57	110.29	104.30	102.79	90.21	70.06
2	✓	142.97	145.14	119.33	117.25	111.22	104.97	103.90	90.04	69.97
3	✓	143.43	145.36	119.92	116.89	111.04	104.31	103.60	89.93	69.41
4	✓	142.33	145.05	120.41	117.10	110.70	105.04	103.54	90.36	69.80

Table A.96 Influence of the crane-routing strategy on the mean crane-interference time per job ($\overline{\overline{m}}^{cit}_{total}$) for selected yard-block layouts with the DRMGC and TriRMGC systems

		Yard-block layout								
CCP	HAC	Small	Low	Narrow	Short	Medium	Long	Wide	High	Big
Resulting $\overline{\overline{m}}^{cit}_{total}$ with the SRMGC system (s)										
		0.00	**0.00**	**0.00**	**0.00**	**0.00**	**0.00**	**0.00**	**0.00**	**0.00**
Resulting $\overline{\overline{m}}^{cit}_{total}$ with the TRMGC system (s)										
		2.22	**2.10**	**11.92**	**12.42**	**12.16**	**11.92**	**12.14**	**19.43**	**20.71**
Resulting $\overline{\overline{m}}^{cit}_{total}$ with the DRMGC system (s)										
1	–	31.80	38.92	36.31	40.26	35.68	30.42	33.45	28.82	23.60
2	–	31.63	38.54	35.28	39.50	35.48	30.03	33.04	28.50	21.46
3	–	30.46	38.12	35.00	39.12	34.81	29.62	32.24	27.29	19.64
4	**–**	**31.09**	**38.13**	**35.30**	**39.74**	**35.31**	**29.73**	**32.78**	**28.21**	**20.21**
1	✓	72.86	66.53	51.38	53.45	44.84	37.14	39.53	32.93	24.64
2	✓	72.60	67.87	50.79	54.43	45.62	37.06	40.35	33.21	22.83
3	✓	71.88	68.74	51.09	53.23	44.86	36.91	39.28	32.21	20.99
4	✓	74.15	68.74	51.57	53.65	45.68	37.63	39.78	32.93	21.50
Resulting $\overline{\overline{m}}^{cit}_{total}$ with the TriRMGC system (s)										
1	–	30.60	40.53	48.66	53.40	49.72	45.01	48.33	50.57	42.90
2	–	30.78	40.67	48.57	52.13	50.19	45.02	48.77	50.32	42.63
3	–	31.24	40.64	49.04	52.43	49.14	44.80	48.37	49.80	41.37
4	**–**	**31.02**	**40.31**	**48.66**	**52.32**	**49.18**	**44.71**	**47.95**	**49.43**	**41.62**
1	✓	62.37	63.08	59.99	62.40	56.85	49.58	52.51	53.47	43.59
2	✓	64.18	62.82	59.53	63.00	56.89	50.08	53.48	53.46	43.54
3	✓	65.14	62.45	59.67	62.70	56.31	49.61	52.42	52.77	42.57
4	✓	64.11	62.37	60.20	61.72	55.87	49.40	52.61	52.68	42.68

Table A.97 Influence of the crane-routing strategy on the crane workload during the simulation horizon in terms of performed jobs ($\overline{|J|}$) for selected yard-block layouts with the DRMGC and TriRMGC systems

		Yard-block layout								
CCP	HAC	Small	Low	Narrow	Short	Medium	Long	Wide	High	Big
Resulting $\overline{|J|}$ with the SRMGC system (jobs)										
		1,871.8	**3,208.8**	**6,596.5**	**6,792.8**	**8,683.4**	**10,466.3**	**10,776.3**	**13,369.4**	**13,711.1**
Resulting $\overline{|J|}$ with the TRMGC system (jobs)										
		1,903.5	**3,224.1**	**6,592.4**	**6,857.8**	**8,784.5**	**10,615.3**	**10,900.6**	**15,170.8**	**21,104.9**
Resulting $\overline{|J|}$ with the DRMGC system (jobs)										
1	–	1,905.7	3,231.8	6,602.4	6,834.9	8,756.2	10,611.8	10,843.9	14,871.9	19,156.4
2	–	1,909.5	3,227.5	6,655.4	6,829.6	8,678.7	10,603.2	10,840.3	15,063.0	20,552.6
3	–	1,905.2	3,218.9	6,596.0	6,853.6	8,705.8	10,551.4	10,907.8	15,141.2	21,150.8
4	**–**	**1,901.9**	**3,222.4**	**6,623.5**	**6,834.0**	**8,713.7**	**10,605.3**	**10,893.6**	**15,175.5**	**21,213.5**
1	✓	1,897.6	3,230.1	6,589.1	6,798.6	8,747.8	10,560.1	10,869.8	15,083.1	19,148.1
2	✓	1,905.8	3,240.0	6,618.1	6,834.0	8,709.2	10,597.2	10,858.7	15,076.0	20,452.8
3	✓	1,903.2	3,218.4	6,580.9	6,844.7	8,731.8	10,610.3	10,896.3	15,176.0	21,226.8
4	✓	1,896.6	3,237.2	6,590.4	6,832.8	8,741.4	10,553.8	10,873.8	15,234.1	21,176.6
Resulting $\overline{|J|}$ with the TriRMGC system (jobs)										
1	–	1,901.4	3,245.3	6,626.3	6,855.1	8,724.3	10,617.3	10,897.9	15,218.2	22,989.0
2	–	1,910.9	3,243.7	6,620.6	6,826.3	8,718.8	10,571.1	10,883.9	15,434.1	22,996.1
3	–	1,908.6	3,240.5	6,641.2	6,806.2	8,728.6	10,604.8	10,921.3	15,251.1	23,187.8
4	**–**	**1,907.0**	**3,249.5**	**6,614.4**	**6,831.8**	**8,732.5**	**10,583.9**	**10,895.8**	**15,192.1**	**23,097.9**
1	✓	1,906.2	3,243.9	6,652.9	6,809.5	8,746.9	10,585.1	10,848.2	15,185.6	22,904.4
2	✓	1,899.6	3,246.3	6,632.7	6,813.3	8,677.4	10,554.1	10,884.4	15,263.2	22,995.2
3	✓	1,901.3	3,248.9	6,611.3	6,830.3	8,712.3	10,566.8	10,881.3	15,394.1	23,034.7
4	✓	1,894.9	3,247.1	6,612.3	6,818.8	8,709.9	10,583.2	10,887.6	15,415.3	23,105.7

Table A.98 Influence of the crane-routing strategy on the container accessibility ($\overline{\overline{\psi}}$), in terms of the mean number of shuffle moves per retrieval job, for selected yard-block layouts with the DRMGC and TriRMGC systems

		Yard-block layout								
CCP	HAC	Small	Low	Narrow	Short	Medium	Long	Wide	High	Big
Resulting $\overline{\overline{\psi}}$ with the SRMGC system (jobs)										
		0.322	**0.300**	**1.135**	**1.120**	**1.103**	**1.083**	**1.083**	**1.606**	**1.144**
Resulting $\overline{\overline{\psi}}$ with the TRMGC system (jobs)										
		0.324	**0.296**	**1.127**	**1.130**	**1.130**	**1.097**	**1.090**	**1.762**	**1.675**
Resulting $\overline{\overline{\psi}}$ with the DRMGC system (jobs)										
1	–	0.328	0.300	1.132	1.127	1.122	1.101	1.077	1.724	1.543
2	–	0.331	0.299	1.146	1.120	1.100	1.095	1.078	1.742	1.642
3	–	0.328	0.292	1.125	1.130	1.104	1.085	1.091	1.751	1.664
4	**–**	**0.320**	**0.297**	**1.137**	**1.118**	**1.107**	**1.093**	**1.087**	**1.753**	**1.673**
1	✓	0.316	0.296	1.133	1.109	1.120	1.084	1.084	1.748	1.545
2	✓	0.328	0.303	1.133	1.118	1.108	1.095	1.078	1.747	1.621
3	✓	0.325	0.291	1.121	1.118	1.116	1.098	1.090	1.761	1.673
4	✓	0.318	0.304	1.125	1.118	1.113	1.082	1.087	1.760	1.665
Resulting $\overline{\overline{\psi}}$ with the TriRMGC system (jobs)										
1	–	0.323	0.295	1.141	1.129	1.111	1.097	1.088	1.773	1.761
2	–	0.333	0.296	1.129	1.115	1.108	1.091	1.085	1.786	1.752
3	–	0.329	0.293	1.135	1.111	1.116	1.097	1.092	1.769	1.766
4	**–**	**0.325**	**0.298**	**1.122**	**1.123**	**1.113**	**1.092**	**1.090**	**1.763**	**1.758**
1	✓	0.327	0.293	1.141	1.113	1.123	1.090	1.077	1.759	1.746
2	✓	0.322	0.297	1.133	1.114	1.105	1.083	1.086	1.770	1.754
3	✓	0.323	0.299	1.131	1.117	1.108	1.083	1.082	1.785	1.761
4	✓	0.317	0.295	1.123	1.117	1.107	1.091	1.088	1.791	1.752

References

Ahrholdt, D. (2010). *Erfolgsfaktoren einer E-Commerce-Website – Empirische Identifikation vertrauensfördernder Signale im Internet-Einzelhandel*, Vol. 23 of *Betriebswirtschaftliche Aspekte lose gekoppelter Systeme und Electronic Business*. Wiesbaden: Gabler.

Alessandri, A., Sacone, S., & Siri, S. (2007). Modelling and optimal receding-horizon control of maritime container terminals. *Journal of Mathematical Modelling and Algorithms*, *6*(1), 109–133.

Alvarez, J. F. (2006). A heuristic for vessel planning in a reach stacker terminal. *Journal of Maritime Research*, *3*(1), 3–16.

Ambrosino, D., Sciomachen, A., & Tanfani, E. (2006). A decomposition heuristics for the container ship stowage problem. *Journal of Heuristics*, *12*(3), 211–233.

Ascheuer, N., Grötschel, M., Kamin, N., & Rambau, J. (1998). Combinatorial online optimization in practice. *OPTIMA*, *57*, 1–6.

Atkins, W. H. (1983). *Modern marine terminal operations and management*. Oakland, CA: Port of Oakland.

Aydin, C. (2007). Improved Rehandling Strategies for Container Retrieval Process. Master Thesis, Graduate School of Engineering and Natural Sciences, Sabanci University, Istanbul.

Backhaus, K., Erichson, B., Plinke, W., & Weiber, R. (2008). *Multivariate Analysemethoden: Eine anwendungsorientierte Einführung* (12th ed.). Berlin: Springer.

Ballestero, E., & Romero, C. (1998). *Multiple criteria decision making and its applications to economic problems*. Dordrecht: Kluwer.

Bangsow, S. (2008). *Fertigungssimulation mit Plant Simulation und SimTalk*. Munich: Carl Hansner Verlag.

Banks, J., Carson, J., Nelson, B. L., & Nicol, D. (2004). *Discrete-event system simulation* (4th ed.). Saddle River, NJ: Prentice Hall.

Bellmore, M., & Hong, S. (1974). Transformation of multisalesmen problem to the standard traveling salesman problem. *Journal of the Association of Computing Machinery*, *21*(3), 500–504.

Biebig, P., Althof, W., & Wagner, N. (2008). *Seeverkehrswirtschaft* (4th ed.). Munich: Oldenburg Verlag.

Bohrer, P. (2010). *Crane scheduling in container terminals: mathematical models, heuristics and algorithms*. Saarbrücken: VDM Verlag Dr. Müller.

Borgman, B., van Asperen, E., & Dekker, R. (2010). Online rules for container stacking. *OR Spectrum*, *32*(3), 687–716.

Böse, J. W. (2011). General considerations on container terminal planning. In J. W. Böse, R. Sharda, & S. Voß (Eds.), *Handbook of terminal planning*, Vol. 49 of *Operations research/computer science interfaces series* (pp. 3–22). Berlin: Springer.

N. Kemme, *Design and Operation of Automated Container Storage Systems*, Contributions to Management Science, DOI 10.1007/978-3-7908-2885-6,

Böse, J. W., Reiners, T., Steenken, D., & Voß, S. (2000). Vehicle dispatching at seaport container terminals using evolutionary algorithms. In *Proceedings of the 33rd Hawaii international conference on system sciences* (pp. 1–10).

Boysen, N., & Fliedner, M. (2010). Determining crane areas in intermodal transshipment yards: the yard partition problem. *European Journal of Operational Research*, *204*(2), 336–342.

Bozer, A. Y., & White, J. A. (1990). Design and performance models for end-of-aisle order picking systems. *Management Science*, *36*(7), 852–866.

Brandt, A., & Jung, H.-U. (2007). Strategische Ansätze für ein regionales standortmanagement Jade-Weser-Raum. Report, Norddeutsche Landesbank and Niedersächsisches Institut für Wirtschaftsforschung.

Brinkmann, B. (2011). Operations systems of container terminals: a compendious overview. In J. W. Böse, R. Sharda, & S. Voß (Eds.), *Handbook of terminal planning*, Vol. 49 of *Operations research/computer science interfaces series* (pp. 25–39). Berlin: Springer.

Briskorn, D., Drexl, A., & Hartmann, S. (2006). Inventory-based dispatching of automated guided vehicles on container terminals. *OR Spectrum*, *28*(4), 611–630.

Brosius, F. (1998). *SPSS 8 Professionelle Statistik unter windows*. Heidelberg: MITP.

Bruns, R., Günthner, W., Hompel, M., Kessler, F., Krause, F., Kunze, G., Marquardt, H., Poppy, W., Scholten, J., Severin, D., & Wagner, G. (2007). Fördertechnik. In K.-H. Grote & J. Feldhusen (Eds.), *Dubbel* (pp. U1–U113). Berlin: Springer.

Bruzzone, A. G., Giribone, P., & Revetria, R. (1999). Operative requirements and advances for the new generation simulators in multimodal container terminals. In P. A. Farrington, H. B. Nembhard, D. T. Sturrock, & G. W. Evans (Eds.), *Proceedings of the 1999 winter simulation conference* (pp. 1234–1252). New York: IEEE Conference Publications.

Cao, Z., Lee, D.-H., & Meng, Q. (2008). Deployment strategies of double-rail-mounted gantry crane systems for loading outbound containers in container terminals. *International Journal of Production Economics*, *115*(1), 221–228.

Carlo, H. J., & Vis, I. F. A. (2008). Routing new types of stacking crane configurations at container terminals. In K. Ellis, R. Meller, M. K. Ogle, B. A. Peter, G. D. Taylor, & J. S. Usher (Eds.), *Progress in material handling reserach* (pp. 55–70). Charlotte: Material Handling Institute.

Carrol, J. K., Thomas, J. C., & Malhotra, A. (1980). Presentation and representation in design problem solving. *British Journal of Psychology*, *71*(1), 143–153.

Caserta, M., Voß, S., & Sniedovich, M. (2011). Applying the corridor method to a blocks relocation problem. *OR Spectrum*, *33*(4), 885–914.

Caserta, M., Schwarze, S., & Voß, S. (2011). Container rehandling at maritime container terminals. In J. W. Böse, R. Sharda, & S. Voß (Eds.), *Handbook of terminal planning*, Vol. 49 of *Operations research/computer science interfaces series* (pp. 247–269). Berlin: Springer.

Chen, T. (1999). Yard Operations in the Container Terminal –A Study in the 'Unproductive Moves'. *Maritime Policy & Management*, *26*(1), 27–38.

Chen, T., Lin, K., & Juang, Y.-C. (2000). Empirical studies on yard operations part 2: quantifying unproductive moves undertaken in quay transfer operations. *Maritime Policy & Management*, *27*(2), 191–207.

Cheng, T. C. E., & Sin, C. C. S. (1990). A state-of-the-art review of parallel-machine scheduling research. *European Journal of Operational Research*, *47*(3), 271–292.

Choe, R., Park, T., Seung, M. O., & Kwang, R. R. (2007). Real-time scheduling for non-crossing stacking cranes in an automated container terminal. In M. A. Orgun & J. Thornton (Eds.), *AI 2007: Advances in artificial intelligence*, Vol. 4830 of *Lecture notes in computer science* (pp. 625–631). Berlin: Springer.

Chu, C.-Y., & Huang, W.-C. (2005). Determining container terminal capacity on the basis of an adopted yard handling system. *Transport Reviews*, *25*(2), 181–199.

Cohen, J. (1992). A power primer. *Psychological Bulletin*, *112*(1), 155–159.

Copeland, T. E., Weston, J. F., & Shastri, K. (2003). *Financial theory and corporate policy* (4th ed.). Amsterdam: Addison-Wesley Longman.

Cordeau, J.-F., Laporte, G., Legato, P., & Moccia, L. (2005). Models and tabu search heuristics for the berth-allocation problem. *Transportation Science*, *39*(4), 526–538.

Croce, F. D., Tadei, R., & Volta, G. (1995). A genetic algorithm for the job shop problem. *Computers & Operations Research, 22*(1), 15–24.

Daganzo, C. F. (1989). The crane scheduling problem. *Transportation Research Part B: Methodological, 23*(3), 159–175.

Dai, J., Lin, W., Moorthy, R., & Teo, C.-P. (2008). Berth allocation planning optimization in container terminals. In C. S. Tang, C.-P. Teo, K.-K. Wei, & F. S. Hillier (Eds.), *Supply chain analysis*, Vol. 119 of *International series in operations research & management science* (pp. 69–104). Berlin: Springer.

Das, S. K., & Spasovic, L. (2003). Scheduling material handling vehicles in a container terminal. *Production Planning & Control: The Management of Operations, 14*(7), 623–633.

De Castilho, B., & Daganzo, C. F. (1993). Handling strategies for import containers at marine terminals. *Transportation Research Part B: Methodological, 27*(2), 151–166.

Dekker, R., Voogd, P., & van Asperen, E. (2006). Advanced methods for container stacking. *OR Spectrum, 28*(4), 563–586.

Domschke, W., & Drexl, A. (2011). *Einführung in das Operations Research* (8th ed.). Berlin: Springer.

Dorndorf, U., & Schneider, F. (2010). Scheduling automated triple cross-over stacking cranes in a container yard. *OR Spectrum, 32*(3), 617–632.

Drira, A., Pierreval, H., & Hajri-Gabouj, S. (2007). Facility layout problems: a survey. *Annual Reviews in Control, 31*(2), 255–267.

Duinkerken, M., Dekker, R., Kurstjens, S., Ottjes, J., & Dellaert, N. (2006). Comparing transportation systems for inter-terminal transport at the maasvlakte container terminals. *OR Spectrum, 28*(4), 469–493.

Duinkerken, M. B., & Ottjes, J. A. (2000). A simulation model for automated container terminals. In *Proceedings of advanced simulation technology conference*, Washington, D.C.

Duinkerken, M. B., Evers, J. J. M., & Ottjes, J. A. (2001). A simulation model for integrating quay transport and stacking policies on automated container terminals. In *Proceedings of the 15th european simulation multiconference*, Prague (pp. 909–916).

Eben-Chaime, M. (1992). Operations sequencing in automated warehousing systems. *International Journal of Production Research, 30*(10), 2401–2409.

Edmonson, R. G. (2007). Calling a new tune. *The Journal of Commerce, 8*(37), 1–5.

Egbelu, P. J., & Tanchoco, J. M. A. (1984). Characterization of automated guided vehicle dispatching rules. *International Journal of Production Research, 22*(3), 359–374.

Evers, J. J. M., & Koppers, S. A. J. (1996). Automated guided vehicle traffic control at a container terminal. *Transportation Research Part A: Policy and Practice, 30*(1), 21–34.

Fiat, A., & Woeginger, A. J. (Eds.) (1998). *Online algorithms: the state of the art*, Vol. 1442 of *Lecture notes in computer science*. Berlin: Springer.

Fink, A., Voß, S., & Schneidereit, G. (2005). *Grundlagen der Wirtschaftsinformatik* (2nd ed.). Heidelberg: Physica.

Froyland, G., Koch, T., Megow, N., Duane, E., & Wren, H. (2008). Optimizing the landside operation of a container terminal. *OR Spectrum, 30*(1), 53–75.

Garey, M. R., & Johnson, D. S. (1979). *Computers and intractability – a guide to the theory of NP-completeness*. San Francisco, CA: Freeman.

Goldberg, D. E. (1989). *Genetic algorithms in search, optimization and machine learning*. Boston, MA: Addison-Wesley Longman.

Goldberg, D. E., & Deb, K. (1991). A comparative analysis of selection schemes used in genetic algorithms. In G. J. E. Rawlins (Ed.), *Foundations of genetic algorithms* (pp. 69–93). Waltham, MA: Morgan Kaufmann.

Goussiatiner, A. (2009). Systematic approach to quayside container crane productivity improvement. *Container Management, 2009*(2, 3), 54–57, 42–45.

Grötschel, M., Krumke, S. O., Rambau, J., Winter, T., & Zimmermann, U. (2001). Combinatorial online optimization in real time. In M. Grötschel, S. O. Krumke, & J. Rambau (Eds.), *Online optimization of large scale systems* (pp. 679–704). Berlin: Springer.

Grunow, M., Günther, H.-O., & Lehmann, M. (2004a). Dispatching multi-load agvs in highly automated seaport container terminals. *OR Spectrum*, *26*(2), 211–235.

Grunow, M., Günther, H.-O., & Lehmann, M. (2004b). Online- versus Offline-Einsatzplanung von fahrerlosen Transportsystemen in Containerhäfen. In T. Sprengler, S. Voß, & H. Kopfer (Eds.), *Logistikmanagement: Prozesse, Systeme, Ausbildung* (pp. 399–410). Berlin: Springer.

Grunow, M., Günther, H.-O., & Lehmann, M. (2006). Strategies for dispatching agvs at automated seaport container terminals. *OR Spectrum*, *28*(4), 587–610.

Günther, H.-O., & Kim, K. H. (Eds.) (2005). *Container terminals and automated transport systems*. Berlin: Springer.

Günther, H.-O., & Kim, K. H. (2006). Container terminals and terminal operations. *OR Spectrum*, *28*(4), 437–445.

Gutin, G., & Punnen, A. P. (Eds.) (2002). *The traveling salesman problem and its variations*. Berlin: Springer.

Hall, N. G., & Posner, M. E. (2001). Generating experimental data for computational testing with machine scheduling applications. *Operations Research*, *49*(6), 854–865.

Han, Y., Lee, L., Chew, E., & Tan, K. (2008). A yard storage strategy for minimizing traffic congestion in a marine container transshipment hub. *OR Spectrum*, *30*(4), 697–720.

Hartmann, S. (2004). Generating scenarios for simulation and optimization of container terminal logistics. *OR Spectrum*, *26*(2), 171–192.

Hartmann, S., Briskorn, D., & Kemme, N. (2007). Simulation und optimierung fahrerloser transportsysteme. *Industrie Management*, *23*(4), 37–40.

Hartmann, S., Pohlmann, J., & Schönknecht, A. (2011). Simulation of container ship arrivals and quay occupation. In J. W. Böse, R. Sharda, & S. Voß (Eds.), *Handbook of terminal planning*, Vol. 49 of *Operations research/computer science interfaces series* (pp. 135–154). Berlin: Springer.

Hecht, H., & Pawlik, T. (2007). *Containerseeschifffahrt*. Bremen: Hanseatic Lloyd Reederei.

Henesey, L., Davidsson, P., & Persson, J. A. (2004). Using simulation in evaluating berth allocation at a container terminal. http://www.ide.bth.se/~pdv/Papers/COMPIT2004.pdf, Accessed 09 September 2011.

Hering, E., Martin, R., & Stohrer, M. (2009). *Taschenbuch der Mathematik und Physik* (5th ed.). Berlin: Springer.

HHLA (2009). *Geschäftsbericht 2008*. Hamburg: Hamburger Hafen und Logistik AG.

Hirashima, Y. (2008). A Q-learning system for container transfer scheduling based on shipping order at container terminals. *International Journal of Innovative Computing, Information and Control*, *4*(3), 547–558.

Hirashima, Y. (2009). A Q-learning system for container marshalling with group-based learning model at container yard terminals. In *Proceedings of the international multi-conference of engineers and computer scientist* (pp. 18–20).

Hirashima, Y., Takeda, K., Harada, S., Deng, M., & Inoue, A. (2006). A Q-learning for group-based plan of container transfer scheduling. *JSME International Journal Series C*, *49*(2), 473–479.

Holland, J. H. (1992). *Adaptation in natural and artificial systems: an introductory analysis with applications to biology, control, and artificial intelligence*. Cambridge, MA: MIT.

Homburg, C. (2007). Betriebswirtschaftslehre als empirische Wissenschaft – Bestandsaufnahme und Empfehlungen. *Zeitschrift für betriebswirtschaftliche Forschung*, *56*(7), 27–60.

HPA (2010). *Prognose des Umschlagpotenzials des Hamburger Hafens für die Jahre 2015, 2020 und 2025*. Bremen: Institute of Shipping Economics and Logistics, IHS Global Insight, Deutschland, Raven Trading.

Johansen, R. S. (2006). Container terminal planning: improving system productivity to service larger container vessels. *Port Technology International*, *31*, 104–106.

Jung, S. H., & Kim, K. H. (2006). Load scheduling for multiple quay cranes in port container terminals. *Journal of Intelligent Manufacturing*, *17*(4), 479–492.

Kalmar (2011a). Kalmar Container Handling Systems – Complete Range of Products and Knowhow. http://www.rrtobe.com, Accessed 09 September 2011.

Kalmar (2011b). Straddle Carriers. http://www.kalmarind.com, Accessed 09 September 2011.

Kang, J., Oh, M.-S., Ahn, E. Y., Ryu, K. R., & Kim, K. H. (2006). Planning for intra-block remarshalling in a container terminal. In M. Ali & R. Dapoigny (Eds.), *Advances in applied artificial intelligence*, Volume 4031 of *Lecture notes in computer science* (pp. 1211–1220). Berlin: Springer.

Kang, J., Ryu, K. R., & Kim, K. H. (2006a). Deriving stacking strategies for export containers with uncertain weight information. *Journal of Intelligent Manufacturing*, *17*(4), 399–410.

Kang, J., Ryu, K. R., & Kim, K. H. (2006b). Determination of storage locations for incoming containers of uncertain weight. In M. Ali & R. Dapoigny (Eds.), *Advances in applied artificial intelligence*, Vol. 4031 of *Lecture notes in computer science* (pp. 1159–1168). Berlin: Springer.

Kemme, N. (2012). Effects of storage block layout and automated yard crane systems on the performance of seaport container terminals. *OR Spectrum*, *34*(3), 563–591.

Kemme, N. (2011b). RMG crane scheduling and stacking: overview and implications on terminal planning. In J. W. Böse, R. Sharda, & S. Voß (Eds.), *Handbook of terminal planning*, Vol. 49 of *Operations research/computer science interfaces series* (pp. 271–301). Berlin: Springer.

Kemme, N. (2011c). *RMGC simulation model – documentation of a simulation model for automated rail-mounted-gantry-crane systems at seaport container terminals*. Institute for Operations Research, University of Hamburg. www.uni-hamburg.de/OR/RMGC-Simulation, Accessed 09 September 2011.

Kendall, M. G. (1938). A new measure of rank correlation. *Biometrika*, *30*(1/2), 81–93.

Kim, K. H. (1997). Evaluating the number of rehandles in container yards. *Computer and Industrial Engineering*, *32*(4), 701–711.

Kim, K. H., & Bae, J. W. (1998). Re-marshalling export containers in port container terminals. *Computer and Industrial Engineering*, *35*(3/4), 655–658.

Kim, K. H., & Hong, G.-P. (2006). A heuristic rule for relocating blocks. *Computers and Operations Research*, *33*(4), 940–954.

Kim, K. H., & Kim, B. H. (1998). The optimal determination of the space requirement and the number of transfer cranes for import containers. *Computer and Industrial Engineering*, *35*(3/4), 427–430.

Kim, K. H., & Kim, H. B. (1999a). Segregating space allocation models for container inventories in port container terminals. *International Journal of Production Economics*, *59*(1–3), 415–423.

Kim, K. H., & Kim, K. Y. (1999b). An optimal routing algorithm for a transfer crane in port container terminals. *Transportation Science*, *33*(1), 17–33.

Kim, K. H., & Park, Y.-M. (2004). A crane scheduling method for port container terminals. *European Journal of Operational Research*, *156*(3), 752–768.

Kim, K. H., Park, Y. M., & Ryu, K. R. (2000). Deriving decision rules to locate export containers in container yards. *European Journal of Operational Research*, *124*(1), 89–100.

Kim, K. H., Wang, S. J., Park, Y.-M., Yang, C.-H., & Bae, J. W. (2002). A simulation study on operation rules for automated container yards. In *Proceedings of the 7th annual international conference on industrial engineering*, Busan (pp. 250–253).

Kim, K. H., Kang, J. S., & Ryu, K. R. (2004). A beam search algorithm for the load sequencing of outbound containers in port container terminals. In H.-O. Günther & K. H. Kim (Eds.), *Container terminals and automated transport systems* (pp. 183–206). Berlin: Springer.

Kim, K. H., Park, Y. M., & Jin, M.-J. (2008). An optimal layout of container yards. *OR Spectrum*, *30*(4), 675–695.

Kim, K. Y., & Kim, K. H. (1997). A routing algorithm for a single transfer crane to load export containers onto a containership. *Computer and Industrial Engineering*, *33*(3/4), 673–676.

Kim, K. Y., & Kim, K. H. (2003). Heuristic algorithms for routing yard-side equipment for minimizing loading times in container terminals. *Naval Research Logistics*, *50*(5), 498–514.

Kleijnen, J. P. C. (1999). Validation of models: statistical techniques and data availability. In P. A. Farrington, H. B. Nembhard, D. T. Sturrock, & G. W. Evans (Eds.), *Proceedings of the 1999 winter simulation conference*, Phoenix, AZ (pp. 647–654).

Koch, T. (2004). Automatik-portalkrane im CTA-containerlager. *Hebezeuge und Fördermittel*, *44*(11), 632–636.

Kolisch, R., & Sprecher, A. (1995). Characterization and generation of a general class of resource-constrained project scheduling problems. *Management Science*, *41*(10), 1693–1704.

Konecranes (2011). Rail Mounted Gantry Crane with Active Load Control system. http://www.konecranes.com/attachments/brochures/rmg_lowres.pdf, Accessed 09 September 2011.

Kozan, E., & Preston, P. (1999). Genetic algorithms to schedule container transfers at multi-modal terminals. *International Transactions in Operational Research*, *6*(3), 311–329.

Krieger, W. (2005a). Container. In *Gabler Wirtschaftslexikon* (16th ed.). (pp. 617). Wiesbaden: Gabler. Author Information in http://wirtschaftslexikon.gabler.de, Accessed 09 September 2011.

Krieger, W. (2005b). Lager. In *Gabler Wirtschaftslexikon* (16th ed.). (pp. 1847). Wiesbaden: Gabler. Author Information in http://wirtschaftslexikon.gabler.de.

Krieger, W. (2005c). Logistik. In *Gabler Wirtschaftslexikon* (16th ed.). (pp. 1918). Wiesbaden: Gabler. Author Information in http://wirtschaftslexikon.gabler.de.

Law, A. M. (2009). How to build valid and credible simulation models. In M. D. Rossetti, R. R. Hill, B. Johansson, A. Dunkin, & R. G. Ingalls (Eds.), *Proceedings of the 2009 winter simulation conference*, Austin, TX (pp. 24–32).

Law, A. M., & Kelton, W. D. (2000). *Simulation modeling and analysis* (3rd ed.). Boston, MA: McGraw Hill.

Lawler, E. L., Lenstra, J. K., Rinnoy Kan, A. H. G., & Shmoys, D. B. (Eds.) (1985). *The traveling salesman problem – a guided tour of combinatorial optimization*. New York: Wiley.

Lee, B. K., & Kim, K. H. (2010). Optimizing the block size in container yards. *Transportation Research Part E: Logistics and Transportation Review*, *46*(1), 120–135.

Lee, D.-H., Meng, Q., & Cao, Z. (2006). Scheduling of multiple-yard crane system with container loading sequence consideration. In *TRB 85th annual meeting compendium of papers CD-ROM* (pp. 1–16).

Lee, D.-H., Cao, Z., & Meng, Q. (2007). Scheduling of two-transtainer systems for loading out-bound containers in port container terminals with simulated annealing algorithm. *International Journal of Production Economics*, *107*(1), 115–124.

Lee, D.-H., Wang, H. Q., & Miao, L. (2008). Quay crane scheduling with non-interference constraints in port container terminals. *Transportation Research Part E: Logistics and Transportation Review*, *44*(1), 124–135.

Lee, L. H., Chew, E. P. Tan, K. C., & Han, Y. (2006). An optimization model for storage yard management in transshipment hubs. *OR Spectrum*, *28*(4), 539–561.

Lee, Y., & Hsu, N.-Y. (2007). An optimization model for the container pre-marshalling problem. *Computers and Operations Research*, *34*(11), 3295–3313.

Legato, P., & R. M. Mazza (2001). Berth Planning and Resources Optimisation at a Container Terminal via Discrete Event Simulation. *European Journal of Operational Research*, *133*(3), 537–547.

Li, W., Wu, Y., Petering, M. E. H., Goh, M., & de Souza, R. (2009). Discrete time model and algorithms for container yard crane scheduling. *European Journal of Operational Research*, *198*(1), 165–172.

Linn, R. J., & Zhang, C.-Q. (2003). A heuristic for dynamic yard crane deployment in a container terminal. *IIE Transactions*, *35*(2), 161–174.

Liu, C.-I., Jula, H., & Ioannou, P. A. (2002). Design, simulation and evaluation of automated container terminals. *IEEE Transactions on Intelligent Transportation Systems*, *3*(1), 12–26.

Liu, C.-I., Jula, H., Vukadinovic, K., & Ioannou, P. (2004). Automated guided vehicle system for two container yard layouts. *Transportation Research Part C: Emerging Technologies*, *12*(5), 349–368.

MacCarthy, B. L., & Liu, J. (1993). Addressing the gap in scheduling research: a review of optimization and heuristic methods in production scheduling. *International Journal of Production Research*, *31*(1), 59–79.

Meersmans, P. J. M. (2002). *Optimization of container handling systems*. Ph.D. Thesis, Tinbergen Institute, Rotterdam.

Meersmans, P. J. M., & Dekker, R. (2001). Operations Research Supports Container Handling. Working Paper EI 2001–22, Econmetric Institute, Erasmus University Rotterdam.

Meisel, F., & Bierwirth, C. (2011). A technique to determine the right crane capacity for a continuous quay. In J. W. Böse, R. Sharda, & S. Voß (Eds.), *Handbook of terminal planning*, Vol. 49 of *Operations research/computer science interfaces series* (pp. 155–178). Berlin: Springer.

Mietschnig, W. (2005). Telelader, insbesondere Reachstacker. European Patent: EP 1 586 529 A2.

Min, D., Wang, F., & Zhan, S. (2009). Impact analysis of the global financial crisis on global container fleet. In *Proceedings of 6th international conference on services systems and services management* (pp. 161–166). Los Alamitos: IEEE Computer Society.

Mizunuma, W., Tsuji, H., & Shinosaki, A. (2005). Efficient container handling by Reachstacker. *Mitsubishi Heavy Industries Technical Review*, *42*(1), 1–2.

Mühlenbein, H. (1997). Genetic algorithms. In E. H. L. Aarts & J. K. Lenstra (Eds.), *Local search in combinatorial optimization* (pp. 137–171). Princeton, NJ: Princeton University Press.

Mühlenbein, H., & Schlierkamp-Voosen, D. (1995). Analysis of selection, mutation and recombination in genetic algorithms. In W. Banzhaf & F. Eeckman (Eds.), *Evolution and biocomputation*, Vol. 899 of *Lecture notes in computer science* (pp. 142–168). Berlin: Springer.

Mumm, M. (2008). *Kosten- und Leistungsrechnung: Internes Rechnungswesen für Industrie- und Handelsbetriebe*. Heidelberg: Physica.

Murty, K. G., Liu, J., Wan, Y.-W., & Linn, R. (2005). a decision support system for operations in a container terminal. *Decision Support Systems*, *39*(3), 309–332.

Musselman, K. J. (1994). Guidelines for simulation project success. In M. S. Manivannan & J. D. Tew (Eds.), *Proceedings of the 26th conference on winter simulation* (pp. 88–95). San Diego, CA: Society for Computer Simulation International.

Nam, K.-C., & Ha, W.-I. (2001). Evaluation of handling systems for container terminals. *Journal of Waterway, Port, Coastal, and Ocean Engineering*, *127*(3), 171–175.

Narasimhan, A., & Palekar, U. S. (2002). Analysis and algorithms for the transtainer routing problem in container port operations. *Transportation Science*, *36*(1), 63–78.

Nazari, D. (2005). Evaluating Container Yard Layout – A Simulation Approach. Master Thesis, Erasmus University Rotterdam.

Ng, W. C. (2005). Crane scheduling in container yards with inter-crane interference. *European Journal of Operational Research*, *164*(1), 64–78.

Ng, W. C., & Mak, K. L. (2005a). An effective heuristic for scheduling a yard crane to handle jobs with different ready times. *Engineering Optimization*, *37*(8), 867–877.

Ng, W. C., & Mak, K. L. (2005b). Yard crane scheduling in port container terminals. *Applied Mathematical Modelling*, *29*(3), 263–276.

Noell (2011). The Sprinter. http://www.noellmobilesystems.com/en/sprinter-carrier-range.121.html, Accessed 09 September 2011.

Oakshott, L. (1996). *Business modelling and simulation*. Upper Saddle River, NJ: Prentice Hall.

Ottjes, J. A., Veeke, H. P. M., & Duinkerken, M. B. (2002). Simulation studies of robotized multi terminal systems. In *Proceedings of the international congress on freight transport automation and multimodality*, Delft (pp. 1–24).

Ottjes, J. A., Veeke, H. P. M., Duinkerken, M. B., Rijsenbrij, J. C., & Lodewijks, G. (2007). Simulation of a multiterminal system for container handling. In K. H. Kim & H.-O. Günther (Eds.), *Container terminals and cargo systems* (pp. 15–36). Berlin: Springer.

Park, B., Choi, H., Kwon, H., & Kang, M. (2006). Simulation analysis on effective operation of handling equipments in automated container terminal. In A. Sattar & B.-H. Kang (Eds.), *AI 2006: Advances in artificial intelligence*, Vol. 4304 of *Lecture notes in computer science* (pp. 1231–1238). Berlin: Springer.

Park, S. K., & Miller, K. W. (1988). Random number generators: good ones are hard to find. *Communications of the ACM*, *31*(10), 1192–1201.

Park, T., Choe, R., Ok, S., & Ryu, K. R. (2010). Real-time scheduling for twin RMGs in an automated container yard. *OR Spectrum*, *32*(3), 593–615.

Park, T., Choe, R., Kim, Y. H., & Ryu, K. R. (2011). Dynamic adjustment of container stacking policy in an automated container terminal. *International Journal of Production Economics*, *133*(1), 385–392.

Parola, F., & Sciomachen, A. (2005). Intermodal container flows in a port system network: analysis of possible growths via simulation models. *International Journal of Production Economics*, *97*(1), 75–88.

Petering, M. E. H. (2009). Effect of block width and storage yard layout on marine container terminal performance. *Transportation Research Part E: Logistics and Transportation Review*, *45*(4), 591–610.

Petering, M. E. H., & Murty, K. G. (2009). Effect of block length and yard crane deployment systems on overall performance at a seaport container transshipment terminal. *Computers & Operations Research*, *36*(5), 1711–1725.

Petering, M. E. H., Wu, Y., Li, W., Goh, M., & de Souza, R. (2009). Development and simulation analysis of real-time yard crane control systems for seaport container transshipment terminals. *OR Spectrum*, *31*(4), 801–835.

Pirhonen, J. (2011). Automated shuttle carrier concept. In J. W. Böse, R. Sharda, & S. Voß (Eds.), *Handbook of terminal planning*, Vol. 49 of *Operations research/computer science interfaces series* (pp. 41–59). Berlin: Springer.

Pirkul, H., Gupta, R., & Rolland, E. (1999). VisOpt: a visual interactive optimization tool for P-Median problems. *Decision Support Systems*, *26*(3), 209–223.

PNC (1999). The Enforcement Plan for Pusan New Port. Final Report, Pusan New Port Company Ltd.

Port of Hamburg (2011a). Container Port Handling in a Global Comparison. http://www.hafen-hamburg.de/en/top20, Accessed 09 September 2011.

Port of Hamburg (2011b). Jahrespressekonferenz 2011. http://www.hafen-hamburg.de/news/jahrespressekonferenz-2011, Accessed 09 September 2011.

Ranau, M. (2011). Planning approach for dimensioning of automated traffic areas at seaport container terminals. In J. W. Böse, R. Sharda, & S. Voß (Eds.), *Handbook of terminal planning*, Vol. 49 of *Operations research/computer science interfaces series* (pp. 179–193). Berlin: Springer.

Randhawa, S. U., McDowell, E. D., & Wang, W. T. (1991). Evaluation of scheduling rules for single- and dual-dock automated storage/retrieval systems. *Computer and Industrial Engineering*, *28*(1), 71–79.

Rijsenbrij, J. C., & Wieschemann, A. (2011). Sustainable container terminals: a design approach. In J. W. Böse, R. Sharda, & S. Voß (Eds.), *Handbook of terminal planning*, Volume 49 of *Operations research/computer science interfaces series* (pp. 61–82). Berlin: Springer.

Rouwenhorst, B., Reuter, B., Stockrahm, V., Van Houtm, G. J., Mantel, R. J., & Zijm, W. H. M. (2000). Warehouse design and control: framework and literature overview. *European Journal of Operational Research*, *122*(3), 515–533.

Saanen, Y. A. (2004). *An approach for designing robotized maritime container terminals*. Ph.D. Thesis, Technical University of Delft, Rotterdam.

Saanen, Y. A. (2006). High density terminals: RTG or RMG? In *Proceedings of TOC Americas 2006*, Acapulco (pp. 1–21).

Saanen, Y. A. (2007). State-of-the-Art Technology in automation: comparing the key technologies on cost and performance. In *Proceedings of TOC Europe 2007*, Istanbul.

Saanen, Y. A. (2008). Automated container handling. *Freight international*. http://www.freight-int.com/categories/automated-container-handling/automated-container-handling.asp, Accessed 09 September 2011.

Saanen, Y. A. (2011). Modeling techniques in planning of terminals: the quantitative approach. In J. W. Böse, R. Sharda, & S. Voß (Eds.), *Handbook of terminal planning*, Vol. 49 of *Operations research/computer science interfaces series* (pp. 83–102). Berlin: Springer.

Saanen, Y. A., & Dekker, R. (2006a). Intelligent stacking as way out of congested yards? Part1. *Port Technology International*, *31* (pp. 87–92).

Saanen, Y. A., & Dekker, R. (2006b). Intelligent stacking as way out of congested yards? Part2. *Port Technology International*, *32* (pp. 80–86).

Saanen, Y. A., & Rijsenbrij, J. (2007). Which system fits your Hub? *Cargo Systems*, *2007*(6), 47–51.

Saanen, Y. A., & Valkengoed, M. V. (2005). Comparison of three automated stacking alternatives by means of simulation. In M. E. Kuhl, N. M. Steiger, F. B. Armstrong, & J. A. Joines (Eds.), *Proceedings of the 2005 winter simulation conference*, Orlando, FL (pp. 1567–1576).

Saanen, Y. A., Verbraeck, A., & Rijsenbrij, J. (2000). The application of advanced simulations for the engineering of logistic control systems. In K. Mertins & M. Rabe (Eds.), *The new simulation in production and logistics - prospects, views and attitudes*. (pp. 217–231). Berlin: IPK.

Saanen, Y. A., van Meel, J., & Verbraeck, A. (2003). The design and assessement of next generation automated container terminals. In A. Verbraeck & V. Hlupic (Eds.), *Proceedings 15th European simulation symposium*, Delft (pp. 1–8).

Sarker, B. R., & Babu, P. S. (1995). Travel time models in automated storage/retrieval systems: a critical review. *International Journal of Production Economics*, *40*(2/3), 173–184.

Schlittgen, R. (2008). *Einführung in die Statistik - Analyse und Modellierung von Daten* (11th ed.). Munich: Oldenburg Verlag.

Schmidt, J. W., & Taylor, R. E. (1970). *Simulation analysis of industrial systems* (3rd ed.). Burr Ridge, IL: Richard D. Irwin.

Schneider, M. (2008). Lager- und Materialflussprozesse. In D. Arnold, H. Isermann, A. Kuhn, H. Tempelmeier, & K. Fuhrmans (Eds.), *Handbuch Logistik* (pp. 371–404). Berlin: Springer.

Scholtens, M., Wijnolst, N., & Waals, F. (1999). *Malacca-max: the ultimate container carrier*. Delft, NL: Delft University Press.

Schroeder, L. D., Sjoquist, D. L., & Stephan, P. E. (1986). *Understanding regression analysis*, Vol. 57 of *Quantitative applications in the social sciences*. London: Sage.

Schütt, H. (2011). Simulation technology in planning, implementation and operation of container terminals. In J. W. Böse, R. Sharda, & S. Voß (Eds.), *Handbook of terminal planning*, Vol. 49 of *Operations research/computer science interfaces series* (pp. 103–116). Berlin: Springer.

Sciomachen, A., & Tanfani, E. (2003). The master bay plan problem: a solution method based on its connection to the three-dimensional Bin Packing Problem. *IMA Journal of Management Mathematics*, *14*(3), 251–269.

Sciomachen, A., & Tanfani, E. (2007). A 3D-BPP approach for optimising stowage plans and technical productivity. *European Journal of Operational Research*, *183*(3), 1433–1446.

Shields, J. J. (1984). Containership stowage: a computer aided pre-planning system. *Marine Technology*, *21*(4), 370–383.

Siepermann, M., & Krieger, W. (2005). Just in time (JIT). In *Gabler Wirtschaftslexikon* (16th ed.). Wiesbaden: Gabler. Author Information in http://wirtschaftslexikon.gabler.de.

Singh, S., & Sharma, R. (2006). A review of different approaches to the facility layout problems. *The International Journal of Advanced Manufacturing Technology*, *30*(5/6), 425–433.

Smith, A. (1776). *An inquiry into the nature and causes of the wealth of nations*. London: W. Strahan and T. Cadell.

Sniedovich, M., & Voß, S. (2006). The corridor method: a dynamic programming inspired metaheuristic. *Control and Cybernetics*, *35*(2), 551–578.

Speer, U., John, G., & Fischer, K. (2011). Scheduling yard cranes considering crane interference. In J. Böse, H. Hu, C. Jahn, X. Shi, R. Stahlbock, & S. Voß (Eds.), *Computational logistics*, Vol. 6971 of *Lecture notes in computer science* (pp. 321–340). Berlin: Springer.

Stahlbock, R., & Voß, S. (2008). Operations research at container terminals: a literature update. *OR Spectrum*, *30*(1), 1–52.

Stahlbock, R., & Voß, S. (2010). Efficiency considerations for sequencing and scheduling of double-rail-mounted gantry cranes at maritime container terminals. *International Journal of Shipping and Transport Logistics*, *2*(1), 95–123.

Steenken, D. (1992). Fahrwegoptimierung am containerterminal unter echtzeitbedingungen. *OR Spectrum*, *14*(3), 161–168.

Steenken, D., Voß, S., & Stahlbock, R. (2004). Container terminal operation and operations research - a classification and literature review. *OR Spectrum*, *26*(1), 3–49.

Stenzel, B. (2008). *Online disjoint vehicle routing with application to AGV routing*. Ph.D. Thesis, Faculty of Maths and Natural Sciences, Technical University of Berlin.

Stigler, S. M. (1989). Francis Galton's account of the invention of correlation. *Statistical Science*, *4*(2), 73–79.

Taleb-Ibrahimi, M., de Castilho, B., & Daganzo, C. F. (1993). Storage space vs handling work in container terminals. *Transportation Research Part B: Methodological*, *27*(1), 13–32.

Toth, P., & Vigo, D. (Eds.) (2002). *The vehicle routing problem*. Philadelphia, PA: SIAM.

UNCTAD (1985). *Port development – a handbook for planners in developing countries*. New York: United Nations Conference on Trade and Development.

UNCTAD (2007). *Review of maritime transport 2007*. New York: United Nations Conference on Trade and Development.

UNCTAD (2008). *Review of maritime transport 2008*. New York: United Nations Conference on Trade and Development.

Urlings, T., Ruiz, R., & Serifoglu, F. S. (2010). Genetic algorithms with different representation schemes for complex hybrid flexible flow line problems. *International Journal Metaheuristics*, *1*(1), 30–54.

Valkengoed, M. P. J. v. (2004). How passing cranes influence stack operations in a container terminal: a simulation study. Diploma Thesis, University of Amsterdam.

van den Honert, R. (1999). Intermediate statistical methods for business and economics. Cape Town: JUTA Academics.

VDI (Ed.) (2005). *Basic organisational functions in warehousing — VDI 3629*. Düsseldorf: VDI.

Vis, I. F. A. (2002). *Planning and control concepts for material handling systems*. Ph.D. Thesis, Erasmus University of Rotterdam.

Vis, I. F. A. (2006a). A comparative analysis of storage and retrieval equipment at a container terminal. *International Journal of Production Economics*, *103*(2), 680–693.

Vis, I. F. A. (2006b). Survey of research in the design and control of automated guided vehicle systems. *European Journal of Operational Research*, *170*(3), 677–709.

Vis, I. F. A., & Carlo, H. J. (2010). Sequencing two cooperating automated stacking cranes in a container terminal. *Transportation Science*, *44*(2), 169–182.

Vis, I. F. A., & de Koster, R. (2003). Transshipment of containers at a container terminal. *European Journal of Operational Research*, *147*(1), 1–16.

Vis, I. F. A., & Harika, I. (2004). Comparison of vehicle types at an automated container terminal. *OR Spectrum*, *26*(1), 117–143.

Vis, I. F. A., & Roodbergen, K. J. (2009). Scheduling of container storage and retrieval. *Operations Research*, *57*(2), 456–467.

Vis, I. F. A., de Koster, R., Roodbergen, K. J., & Peeters, L. W. P. (2001). Determination of the number of automated guided vehicles required at a semi-automated container terminal. *The Journal of the Operational Research Society*, *52*(4), 409–417.

Voß, S. (2001). Meta-heuristics: The state of the art. In A. Nareyek (Ed.), *Local search for planning and scheduling*, Vol. 2148 of *Lecture notes in computer science* (pp. 1–23). Berlin: Springer.

Voß, S., & Gutenschwager, K. (2001). *Infomationsmanagement*. Berlin: Springer.

Voogd, P., R. Dekker, & Meersmans, P. J. M. (1999). FAMAS-Newcon: A Generator Program for Stacking in the Reference Case. Econometric Institute Report EI 9943-/A, Erasmus University of Rotterdam.

Wang, F., & Lim, A. (2007). A stochastic beam search for the berth allocation problem. *Decision Support Systems*, *42*(4), 2186–2196.

Watanabe, I. (2001). *Container terminal planning: a theoretical approach*. Surrey, GB: World Cargo News Publishing.

Welch, P. (1981). On the Problem of the Initial Transient in Steady-State Simulation. Yorktown Heights, New York: IBM Watson Research Center.

Wiese, J., Kliewer, N., & Suhl, L. (2009a). A Survey of Container Terminal Characteristics and Equipment Types. Working Paper 0901, Decision Support & Operations Research Lab, University of Paderborn.

Wiese, J., Suhl, L., & Kliewer, N. (2009b). Mathematical programming and simulation based layout planning of container terminals. *International Journal of Simulation and Process Modelling*, *5*(4), 313–323.

Wiese, J., Suhl, L., & Kliewer, N. (2010). Mathematical models and solution methods for optimal container terminal yard layouts. *OR Spectrum*, *32*(3), 427–452.

Wiese, J., Suhl, L., & Kliewer, N. (2011). Planning container terminal layouts considering equipment types and storage block design. In J. W. Böse, R. Sharda, & S. Voß (Eds.), *Handbook of terminal planning*, Vol. 49 of *Operations research/computer science interfaces series* (pp. 219–245). Berlin: Springer.

Wilson, I. D., & Roach, P. A. (1999). Principles of combinatorial optimization applied to container-ship stowage planning. *Journal of Heuristics*, *5*(4), 403–418.

Wilson, I. D., Roach, P. A., & Ware, J. A. (2001). Container stowage pre-planning: using search to generate solutions: a case study. *Knowledge-Based Systems*, *14*(3/4), 137–145.

Winston, W. L. (2004). *Operations research – applications and algorithms* (4th ed.). Belmont, CA: Thomson Learning.

Yang, C. H., Choi, Y. S., & Ha, T. Y. (2004). Simulation-based performance evaluation of transport vehicles at automated container terminals. *OR Spectrum*, *26*(2), 149–170.

Zauner, T. (2005). *Implementierung eines Multiagentensystems zur Simulation von Containerterminalprozessen*. Ph.D. Thesis, Georg-August-Universität Göttingen Zentrum für Informatik, Göttingen.

Zhang, C., Wan, Y.-W., Liu, J., & Linn, R. J. (2002). Dynamic crane deployment in container storage yards. *Transportation Research Part B: Methodological*, *36*(6), 537–555.

Zhang, C., Chen, W., Shi, L., & Zheng, L. (2010). A note on deriving decision rules to locate export containers in container yards. *European Journal of Operational Research*, *205*(2), 483–485.

Zijderveld, E. J. A. v. (1995). *A structured terminal design method, with a focus on rail terminals*. Ph.D. Thesis, Faculty of Mechanical Engineering, Delft University of Technology.

ZPMC (2009). Twin 40' quayside container crane. http://www.zpmc.com, Accessed 17 February 2010.

Zyngiridis, I. (2005). Optimizing Container Movements Using one and two Automated Stacking Cranes. Master Thesis, Naval Postgraduate School Monterry, Monterey, CA.

Index

N. Kemme, *Design and Operation of Automated Container Storage Systems*, Contributions to Management Science, DOI 10.1007/978-3-7908-2885-6,

FSC
www.fsc.org
MIX
Papier | Fördert
gute Waldnutzung
FSC® C083411

Kolibri 360 GmbH
Ferdinand-Jühlke-Straße 7
99095 Erfurt, Deutschland
produktsicherheit@kolibri360.de